We're here
for you in
Scotland
With over 150 years' experience,
you can count on Co-op Funeralcare
for a caring and personal
service every step of the way
Visit your local funeral home today
or visit us at coop.co.uk/funeralcare
co
op
Co-op Funeralcare is a trading name for Funeral Services Limited (FSL) and Co op Funeral Plans Limited (CFPL).
Co-op funerals are provided and sold by FSL and Co-op funeral plans are provided and sold by CFPL.
CFPL is authorised and regulated by the Financial Conduct Authority. Firm Reference Number 962119.

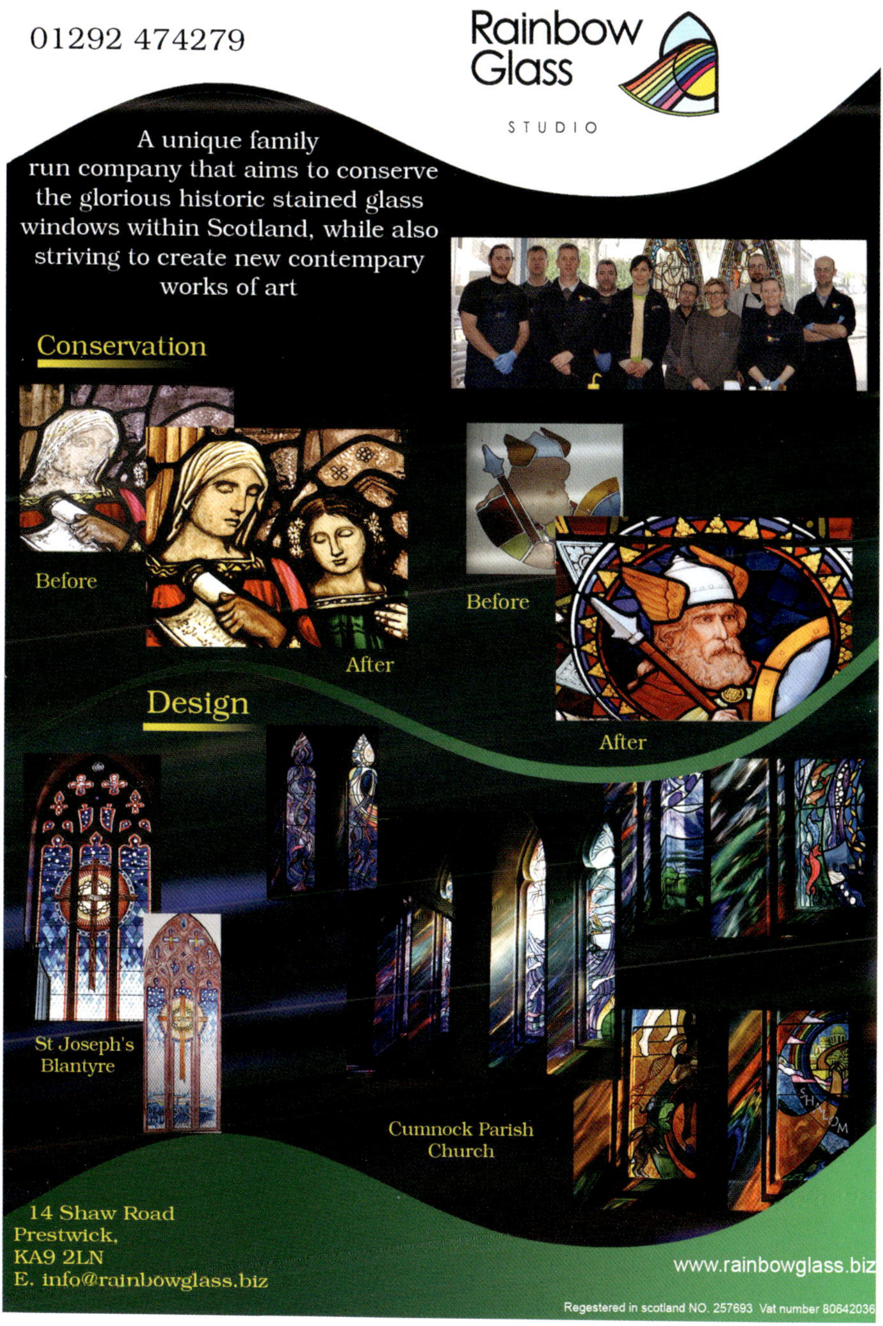
01292 474279
Rainbow Glass
STUDIO
A unique family run company that aims to conserve the glorious historic stained glass windows within Scotland, while also striving to create new contempary works of art
Conservation
Before
After
Before
After
Design
St Joseph's Blantyre
Cumnock Parish Church
14 Shaw Road
Prestwick,
KA9 2LN
E. info@rainbowglass.biz
www.rainbowglass.biz
Regestered in scotland NO. 257693 Vat number 80642036

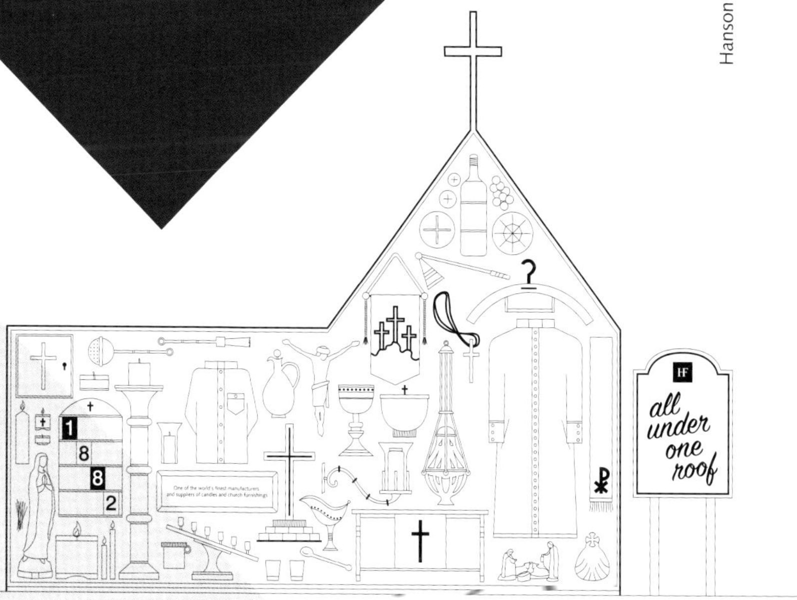
1
8
8
2
all under one roof

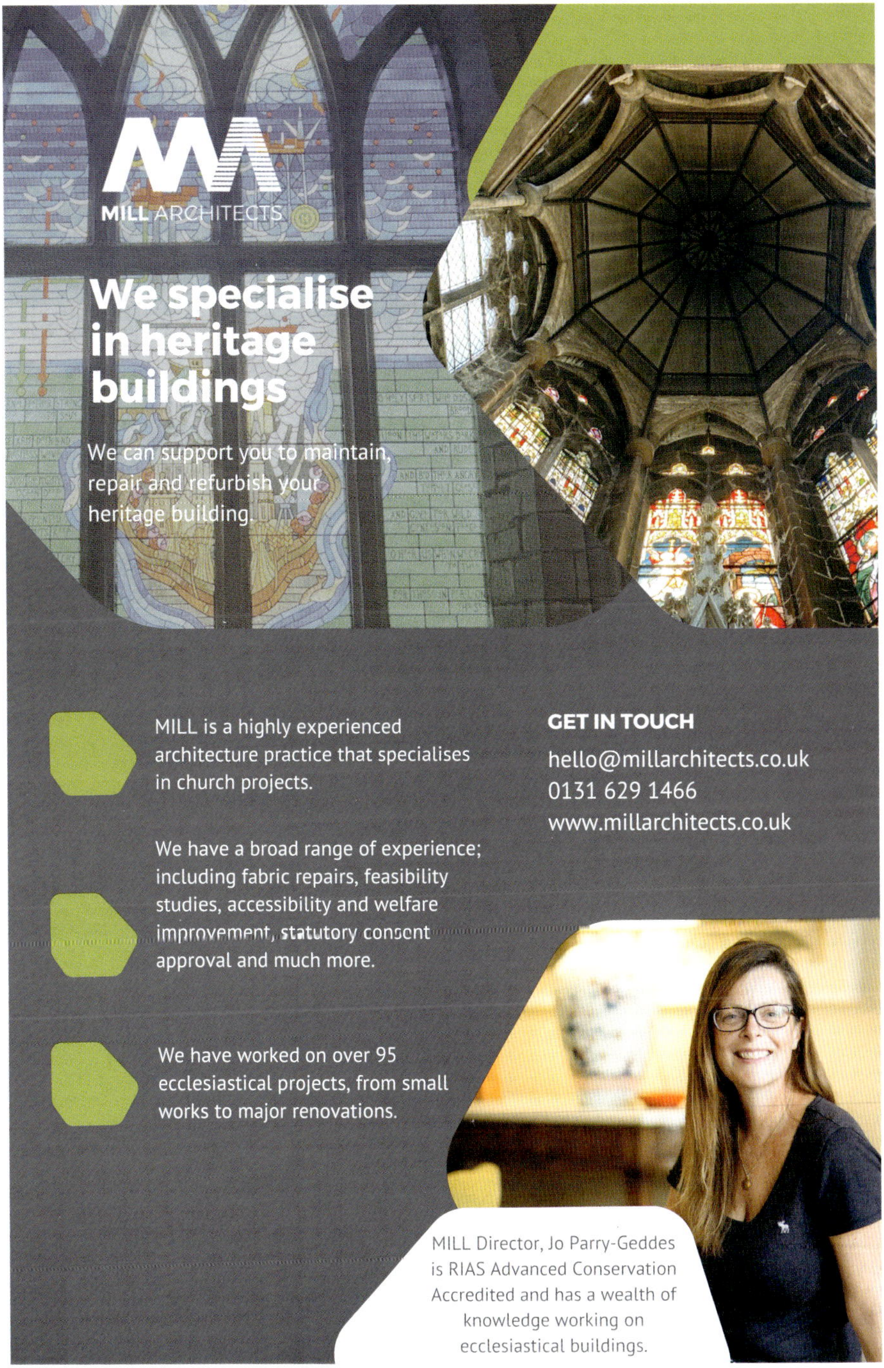
MILL ARCHITECTS
We specialise in heritage buildings
We can support you to maintain, repair and refurbish your heritage building.
MILL is a highly experienced architecture practice that specialises in church projects.
We have a broad range of experience; including fabric repairs, feasibility studies, accessibility and welfare improvement, statutory consent approval and much more.
We have worked on over 95 ecclesiastical projects, from small works to major renovations.
GET IN TOUCH
hello@millarchitects.co.uk
0131 629 1466
www.millarchitects.co.uk
MILL Director, Jo Parry-Geddes is RIAS Advanced Conservation Accredited and has a wealth of knowledge working on ecclesiastical buildings.

Pushing your vision ...
CRGP have provided architectural and surveying services to The Church of Scotland from our Glasgow and Inverness offices for over 60 years. We have a talented team of people ready to assist any sized building issue or project.
Don't hesitate to contact us for a free first consultation.
... beyond imagination.
CRGP
Contact us | 0141 337 2255 | crgp.co.uk
CRGP ARCHITECTS

greenbarnes
VISIT OUR WEBSITE WWW.GREENBARNES.CO.UK
FOR A FAST NO OBLIGATION QUOTE, CALL 01280 701093
WELCOME TO ST SWITHUNS CHURCH
Priest in Charge
Revd Jane Burgess
FELSHAM PARISH COUNCIL
PARISH CHURCH OF ST MICHAEL & ALL ANGELS
Kensington Unitarians
ST JOHN THE EVANGELIST
SPECIALISTS IN THE MANUFACTURE OF
• OUTDOOR NOTICEBOARDS
• SIGN PANELS
• INFORMATION LECTERNS
• INDOOR NOTICEBOARDS
• HONOURS BOARDS
PARISH CHURCH OF ST. GEORGE EVENLEY
GREENBARNES LTD. UNIT 7 BARRINGTON COURT | WARD ROAD
BUCKINGHAM ROAD INDUSTRIAL ESTATE | BRACKLEY | NORTHAMPTONSHIRE | NN13 7LE
SALES: 01280 701093 EMAIL: SALES@GREENBARNES.CO.UK

CRIEFF HYDRO
FAMILY OF HOTELS
WHERE
MEMORIES
ARE MADE
CRIEFF HYDRO
MURRAYPARK HOTEL
Peebles Hydro
THE PARK
THE ISLES OF GLENCOE
BALLACHULISH HOTEL
KINGSHOUSE HOTEL
1881
CRIEFFHYDROFAMILY.COM

Ships of **Hope**

Mercy Ships is a world-leading health charity. We bring life-changing surgeries to women, men and children across sub-Saharan Africa.

We're looking for more servant-hearted people like you to come and volunteer on our hospital ships.

Could you, or someone in your church, come and serve with Mercy Ships?

You'll join a compassionate crew of people from around the world. We follow the model of Jesus to bring hope and healing to people who need it most.

From chaplains to cooks, seafarers to surgeons, teachers to engineers, it takes all skills and talents to run our hospital ships.

Could you come and share your time and talents on board? Register your interest today: mercyships.org.uk/volunteer

Caring for persecuted Christians

Aster was imprisoned in Eritrea for her faith. She chose following Christ Jesus over her worldly freedom. What would you choose?

Release International's ministry is to love and serve persecuted Christians around the world. Will you join us in caring for those who suffer for Christ and the gospel?

To receive Release International's free quarterly magazine, *Voice*, and to find out how you can help, contact us, or use the QR Code, below.

www.releaseinternational.org
info@releaseinternational.org
01689 823491

RELEASE INTERNATIONAL
voice
of Persecuted Christians

Registered with FUNDRAISING REGULATOR

Registered Charity 280577 (SC040456)

ScotsCare
The charity for Scots in London
Please scan our QR Code to become a valued supporter to our Saltire Donor Club
THE POWER OF KINDNESS
THE SALTIRE DONORS CLUB
ScotsCare's Monthly Giving Programme
"Homelessness is a prevalent issue in London. The numbers continue to rise, and this represents a real issue for Scots in London who have fallen on harder times."
Shona Fleming
Chief Executive
PLEASE SUPPORT US!
Every pound you donate goes exclusively to fund our client services, with overhead costs funded separately.
The charity for Scots in London
ScotsCare
scotscareldn
ScotsCare
ScotsCare
Registered charity number: 207326 (England and Wales), SC052739 (Scotland).

GOD WELCOMES ALL

God Welcomes All is a supplement to the Church of Scotland's popular hymn book, the Church Hymnary Fourth Edition.

This exciting new collection features over 200 hymns and songs in a wide range of styles by writers from Scotland and around the world. The majority have been written in the last 20 years and the book has a strong focus on hospitality and welcome.

Includes:

- Scripture Songs from the Psalms, Old Testament and New Testament
- Music for use throughout services, including Gathering, Confession, Approach, Prayer, Communion, Baptism, Sending and Blessing
- Music for all parts of the Church Year
- Hymns and songs covering a range of themes, including The Living God, Creation, Christian Life, Hurt and Healing, Church and Community, and Justice and Peace.

Full music edition out now. Words only to follow in autumn 2024.

For more information see canterburypress.co.uk or saintandrewpress.co.uk

Emma Butler-Cole Aiken
BA (Hons) AMGP
Stained Glass Artist

Bespoke window design, construction, and installation

www.ebcaglass.com
ebcaglass@yahoo.co.uk
07948 744725

Detail from *The Well* 2024

The Right Reverend Dr Shaw J. Paterson
MODERATOR

The Church of Scotland
YEAR BOOK
2024–2025

139th year of issue

Editor
David A. Stewart

Published on behalf of
THE CHURCH OF SCOTLAND
by SAINT ANDREW PRESS
121 George Street, Edinburgh EH2 4YN

THE OFFICES OF THE CHURCH

121 George Street, Edinburgh, EH2 4YN
0131 225 5722
Fax: 0131 220 3113
www.churchofscotland.org.uk

Office Hours: Monday–Friday 9:00am–5:00pm

CrossReach operates from Charis House, 47 Milton Road East, Edinburgh, EH15 2SR
0131 657 2000
Fax: 0131 657 5000
info@crossreach.org.uk
www.crossreach.org.uk

Scottish Charity Numbers

The Church of Scotland: unincorporated Councils and Committees	SC011353
The Church of Scotland General Trustees	SC014574
The Church of Scotland Investors Trust	SC022884
The Church of Scotland Trust	SC020269

For the Scottish Charity Numbers of presbyteries and congregations, see Section 7

Corrections and alterations to the Year Book
Contact the Editor, David A. Stewart:
yearbookeditor@churchofscotland.org.uk
0131 441 3362

The General Assembly of 2025 will convene on
Saturday 17 May

First published in 2024 by SAINT ANDREW PRESS, 121 George Street, Edinburgh EH2 4YN on behalf of THE CHURCH of SCOTLAND

ISBN 978-1-80083-055-4

It is the Publisher's policy only to use papers that are natural and recyclable and that have been manufactured from timber grown in renewable, properly managed forests. All of the manufacturing processes of the papers are expected to conform to the environmental regulations of the country of origin.

Acceptance of advertisements for inclusion in *The Church of Scotland Year Book* does not imply endorsement of the goods or services or of any views expressed within the advertisements.

British Library Cataloguing in Publication Data
A catalogue record for this book is available from the British Library.

Printed and bound by Bell and Bain Ltd, Glasgow

CONTENTS

Page

From the Moderator 5
Editorial 6

1 **Assembly Trustees, Agencies, Committees and Departments 7**

2 **General Information 25**

1. Gaelic development in the Church of Scotland 26
2. Other Churches in the United Kingdom 28
3. Overseas Churches 29
4. His Majesty's Household in Scotland Ecclesiastical 29
5. Lord High Commissioners to the General Assembly 30
6. Moderators of the General Assembly 31
7. Scottish Divinity Faculties 32
8. Societies and Associations 33
9. Trusts and Funds 39
10. Long Service Certificates 47
11. Records of the Church of Scotland 47
12. Fasti Ecclesiae Scoticanae 47

3 **Church Procedure 49**

A The Minister and Baptism 50
B The Minister and Marriage 50
C Marriage Services: Code of Good Practice 50
D Marriage and Civil Partnership (Scotland) Act 2014 50
E Funeral Services: Fees 50
F Pulpit Supply Fees and Expenses 51
G Vacancy Procedure 52

4 **General Assembly 2024 . . . . . 53**

Office-bearers of the General Assembly 53
The Moderator 54
Report from the General Assembly 55

5 **Presbytery Lists 59**

Explanation and abbreviations 59
(1) Edinburgh and West Lothian 61
(2) Lothian and Borders 80
(3) South West 94
(4) Clyde 115
(5) Glasgow 127
(6) Forth Valley and Clydesdale 149
(7) Fife 167
(8) Perth 181

(9) North East and Northern Isles 204
(10) Clèir Eilean Ì: Highlands and Hebrides. 224
(11) Lewis. 244
(12) England and Channel Islands 247
(13) International Charges 250
(14) Jerusalem. 253

6 Additional Lists of Personnel 255

A Ordained Local Ministers and Auxiliary Ministers 256
B Diaconate. 259
C Healthcare Chaplains. 261
D HM Forces Chaplains 265
E Mission Partners serving internationally. 268
F Prison Chaplains 270
G University Chaplains 272
H Council Education Committees: Church Representatives 273
I Ministers Ordained for Sixty Years and Upwards 274
J Deceased Ministers and Deacons 276

7 Legal Names and Scottish Charity Numbers: Presbyteries and Congregations . . 279

8 Church Buildings: Ordnance Survey National Grid References 279

9 Parish and Congregational Changes 281

10 Congregational Statistics – 2023 289

Index of MINISTERS 315

Index of PARISHES AND PLACES 324

Index of SUBJECTS 330

FROM THE MODERATOR

As parish minister, former presbytery clerk and in my role as Moderator, the Year Book has never been far out of reach. Even in the age of 'everything can be found on the Internet', the Year Book provides a very speedy source of information about who's where together with statistics for every church and parish, as well as providing a concise summary of church law. In addition, it's a ready compendium of information about such things as divinity faculties, societies and trusts.

The Year Book also serves as a reminder that we all belong to a national church, the Church of Scotland, and that's important. At a time of great change within the church, the temptation is to see ourselves in isolation. As we flick through the pages and see the lists it is heart-warming to know that we are not alone, and in doing so the lists become more than just names and places on a page. The book gives us a very tangible reminder that we are part of the community of faith in our own locality and beyond.

In commending the Year Book I would also like to acknowledge the dedication and commitment of the Editor and all involved in its production for their attention to detail. Thank you for giving us this valuable resource.

Shaw J. Paterson

BHON MHODARÀTAIR

Mar mhinistear paraiste, chlàrc clèire aig aon àm is a-nis mar Mhodaràtair, chan eil an Leabhar Bliadhnail riamh air a bhith fada bhom làimh. Fiù 's aig àm far am faighear gach nì air an eadar-lìon, tha an Leabhar Bliadhnail a' toirt dhut tobar fiosrachaidh glè dheiseil mu dheidhinn cò tha càite cuide ri àireamhan mu gach eaglais is paraiste cho math ri geàrr-chunntas sgiobalta air lagh na h-eaglais. A bharrachd air sin, tha e na thobar fiosrachaidh mu rudan mar dhàmhan diadhachd, chomainn is urrasan.

Tha an Leabhar Bliadhnail cuideachd a' cur nur cuimhne gum buin sinn uile do dh' eaglais nàiseanta, Eaglais na h-Alba, agus tha sin cudromach. Aig àm far a bheil uimhir ag atharrachadh anns an eaglais, tha sinn buailteach sinn fhìn fhaicinn air leth o chàch. Mar a ruitheas sinn tro na duilleagan agus a chì sinn na liostaichean, tha e na thogail fhaicinn nach eil sinn leinn fhìn agus tha na liostaichean a' riochdachadh barrachd na dìreach ainmean is àiteachan air duilleig. Tha an leabhar a' cur nur cuimhne gu susbainteach gu bheil sinn nur pàirt de choimhearsnachd creideimh nur sgìre fhèin agus nas fharsainne.

Ann a bhith a' moladh an Leabhair Bhliadhnail dhuibh, bu mhath leam cuideachd dìcheall is dealas an Neach Deasachaidh aithneachadh cho math ri gach neach a bha an lùib a bhith ga chur ri chèile airson an eagnaidheachd. Taing dhuibh airson a' ghoireis luachmhoir seo a thoirt dhuinn.

Shaw J. Paterson
Translation by Professor Boyd Robertson

EDITORIAL

In addition to the usual extensive updating across most pages:

- Presbytery (10) Clèir Eilean Ì: Highlands and Hebrides, was formed by the union in January 2024 of the Presbyteries of Argyll, Abernethy, Inverness, Lochaber, Ross, Sutherland, Caithness, Lochcarron-Skye and Uist. That new presbytery is shown in Section 5;
- There have been a substantial number of unions within most of the large presbyteries, as shown in each presbytery list, and summarised in Section 9B. Indeed, more congregations have been united in one twelve-month period than in any year in the history of the church, including the year after 1929 union of the Church of Scotland and the United Free Church of Scotland. More will follow in the next few years as the Presbytery Mission Plans continue to be implemented;
- Sections 7, 8, 9, 10 and the Indexes have been further revised to reflect the continuing reorgansation of the Church; and
- The Congregational Statistics in Section 10 include the first set of financial figures under the first year of implementation of the *Giving to Grow* scheme.

Many people contribute to the Year Book. My thanks to the Presbytery Clerks and their administrators, the staff in the Church offices (in particular Angus Mathieson, Ruth Wilson, Karen Keil and Fiona Wyllie of Faith Action), and those who compile some sections or subsections: Boyd Robertson and Duncan Sneddon (Gaelic), Sheena Orr (Prison Chaplains), Madelaine Sproule (legal names and Scottish charity numbers), Roy Pinkerton (church grid references, parishes and congregations: names no longer in use, index of parishes and places, and editorial advice), and Fiona Tweedie, Laura Bryce and Sandy Gemmill (statistics). Thanks also to Claire Ruben of FairCopy for again tackling the significant amount of copy editing required for this edition and to our contacts at Hymns Ancient and Modern who publish the book via the St Andrew Press.

I am grateful to those readers who sent corrections and updates. Corrections, amendments and suggestions are always welcome.

David Stewart
yearbookeditor@churchofscotland.org.uk

SECTION 1

Assembly Trustees, Agencies, Committees and Departments

		Page
1.	Office of the General Assembly	8
2.	Office of the Assembly Trustees	8
3.	Faith Action Programme	9
4.	CrossReach	11
5.	Assembly Business Committee	11
6.	Audit Committee	12
7.	Church of Scotland Trust	12
8.	Committee to Nominate the Moderator	12
9.	Communications Department	13
10.	Ecumenical Relations Committee	13
11.	Estates and Procurement Department	13
12.	Forces Chaplains Committee	14
13.	General Trustees	14
14.	The Guild	15
15.	Housing and Loan Fund	15
16.	Human Resources Department	16
17.	Information Technology Department	16
18.	Investors Trust	16
19.	Investors Trust Ethical Oversight Committee	17
20.	Iona Community Board	17
21.	Law Department	17
22.	Legal Questions Committee	18
23.	Life and Work	19
24.	Nomination Committee	19
25.	Pension Trustees	19
26.	Presbytery Review Committee	20
27.	Registration of Ministries Committee	20
28.	Safeguarding Service	21
29.	Saint Andrew Press	21
30.	Scottish Churches Parliamentary Office	21
31.	Scottish Storytelling Centre (The Netherbow)	22
32.	Stewardship and Finance Department	22
33.	Theological Forum	23

The symbol > used in website information indicates the headings to be selected as they appear

---

1. OFFICE OF THE GENERAL ASSEMBLY

The Office supports the General Assembly, Presbyteries and Kirk Sessions, the Moderator and the process of Presbytery reform. In addition, the staff service the following: Assembly Business Committee, Legal Questions Committee, Nomination Committee, Judicial Commission, Judicial Panel, Appeals Committee of the Commission of Assembly, Ministries Appeal Panel, Mission Plan Review Group, the Committee to Nominate the Moderator, the Chalmers Lectureship Trust, the Committee on Overtures and Cases, the Delegation of Assembly, the Committee on Classifying Returns to Overtures, the Ecumenical Relations Committee and the Theological Forum. The Clerks of Assembly are responsible for consultation on matters of Church Law, Practice and Procedure.

Secretaries:

Principal Clerk of the General Assembly:	Rev. Fiona E. Smith LLB BD
Depute Clerk:	Ms Christine Paterson LLB DipLP
Presbytery Resource Adviser:	Rev. Victoria J. Linford LLB BD DMin
Senior Public Sector Policy Adviser:	Mr Robert Marshall BMus LLB WS
Executive Assistant to the Principal Clerk:	Mrs Nicola Nicholls, 0131 376 1137
Senior Administration Officer (Assembly Arrangements and Moderatorial Support):	Miss Catherine McIntosh MA, 0131 376 1594
Secretary, Ecumenical Relations Committee:	Rev. Dr John L. McPake
Secretary, Theological Forum:	Ms Nathalie A. Mareš MacCallum MA MTh

Personnel in this department are also listed with the bodies and Committees that they serve.
Contact: pcoffice@churchofscotland.org.uk 0131 225 5722

---

2. OFFICE OF THE ASSEMBLY TRUSTEES

The Trustees have responsibility for governance, finance and stewardship, budgeting and general oversight of the agencies of the Church. They assist the General Assembly to determine the strategy and priorities of the Church, and seek to ensure the implementation of the policies, priorities and strategic objectives of the General Assembly through working with the agencies of the Church to achieve a collaborative approach to the nurturing of the people of the Church in their witness, worship and service. They are the Charity Trustees of the Church of Scotland (the Unincorporated Entities) Scottish Charity No. SC011353.

Assembly Trustees:

Convener:	Rev. David S. Cameron
Vice-Convener:	Geoff Miller
Administrative Trustee:	Rev. Barry J. Hughes

Other Trustees: Jean Couper CBE
Ian Forrester
Crawford Gillies
David Harrison
Miranda Heggie
Jennifer MacDonald
Rev. Norman A. Smith
Michael Yuille
Rev. Prof. Philip G. Ziegler

Chief Officer:	Dave Kendall
Head of Analysis and Programme Development:	Catherine Skinner
Head of Estates and Procurement: *(see 11. below)*	Liam Fennell 0131 376 1131
Health and Safety Manager:	Jacqueline Collins
Business Support Analyst:	Karen Bass
Statistician:	Rev. Dr Fiona J. Tweedie
Research Officer:	Laura Bryce
Grants Manager:	David Williams 0131 376 5846 grants@churchofscotland.org.uk
Grants Administrator:	Lynne Hood 0131 376 3682
Programme and Innovation Manager:	Hannah Sanderson
Executive PA to the Chief Officer:	Carron Lunt
Programme Support Officer:	Kirsty Hunt

Contact: OATadmin@churchofscotland.org.uk 0131 225 5722

Further information:
www.churchofscotland.org.uk > About us > Our structure > The Assembly Trustees
www.churchofscotland.org.uk > Connect > Seeds for Growth
www.churchofscotland.org.uk > Resources > Statistics for Mission

---

3. FAITH ACTION PROGRAMME

The Faith Action Programme Leadership Team seek to shape and implement the instructions, policies, priorities and strategic objectives of the General Assembly. FAPLT works with the Assembly Trustees, Presbyteries and other parts of the Church to achieve a collaborative approach with the purpose of nurturing the people of the Church of Scotland in their witness, worship and service. FAPLT has begun to:

- Build and launch an integrated training programme for members of local churches, which carries resources for faith, life and mission;
- Create pathways that attract and allow us to recruit the required number of resilient and emotionally intelligent leaders for the recognised ministries for which they are suited and called;
- Develop and support churches to grow in Christian faith and deliver missional activity and establish new worshipping communities;

- Equip all those responsible for evolving fresh forms of worship including digitized ministry alongside continued support for developing best practice in existing worship;
- Contribute to public life and social justice on behalf of the church;
- Deliver the Presbytery Mission Plan Act – with a configuration of ministries and congregational estates which is sustainable and affordable; and
- Decrease annually the operating costs of national programmes while seeking to devolve or end tasks which would best be served by the local and generate income to fulfil the Programme and further the wider work of the Church.

The Faith Action Programme works through five Programme Groups: Mission Support, People and Training, Presbytery and Partnership Support, Public Life and Social Justice, and Resource and Presence.

FAITH ACTION PROGRAMME LEADERSHIP TEAM

Convener:	Rev. Tommy MacNeil
Deputy Convener and Resource and Presence Programme Group Leader:	Rev. Alistair Cumming
Vice-Convener and Mission Support Programme Group Leader:	Rev. Jonathan C. Fleming
Vice-Convener and People and Training Programme Group Leader:	Rev. Bill M. Wishart
Vice-Convener and Public Life and Social Justice Programme Group Leader:	Emma Jackson
Vice-Convener and Presbytery Mission Plan Implementation Group Leader:	Rev. Dr Karen K. Campbell

FAITH ACTION PROGRAMME STAFF

Head of Ministries and Mission:	Kay Cathcart
Mission Support Senior Manager:	Sarah Johnson
Presbytery and Partnership Support Senior Manager:	Rev Angus R. Mathieson
People and Training Senior Manager:	Vacant
Public Life and Social Justice Senior Manager:	David Bradwell
Resource and Presence Senior Manager (including centres in Israel & Palestine):	Kenny Roger

Contact: FaithAction@churchofscotland.org.uk 0131 225 5722

Further information:
www.churchofscotland.org.uk > About us > Faith Action programme, committees and departments
www.churchofscotland.org.uk > Connect > Interfaith; Global Partnerships; Priority Areas; Campaigns; Scottish Faiths Action for Refugees
www.churchofscotland.org.uk > Resources > Net Zero Pathway; Presbytery Planning; Children and Young People; Church of Scotland Learning; Ministries handbooks
Church of Scotland Learning: The Church of Scotland > Learning@churchofscotland.org.uk
www.churchofscotland.org.uk > Serve > Towards Ministry
www.ascend.churchofscotland.org.uk

4. CROSSREACH

Charis House, 47 Milton Road East, Edinburgh EH15 2SR
0131 657 2000 Fax: 0131 657 5000
info@crossreach.org.uk www.crossreach.org.uk

CrossReach, overseen by the CrossReach Board (formally recognised as the Social Care Council), provides social care services as part of the Christian mission and ministry of the Church to the people of Scotland, and engages with other bodies in responding to emerging areas of need. CrossReach provides social care services throughout Scotland: www.crossreach.org.uk/our-locations

Convener:	Dr Mike Cantlay OBE
Vice-Convener:	Rev. Douglas Hamilton
Chief Executive Officer:	Viv Dickenson (viv.dickenson@crossreach.org.uk)
Director of Services to Older People:	Allan Logan (allan.logan@crossreach.org.uk)
Director of Adult Care Services:	Vic Walker (vic.walker@crossreach.org.uk)
Director of Children and Families:	Sheila Gordon (sheila.gordon@crossreach.org.uk)
Director of Finance and Resources:	Eoin McDunphy (eoin.mcdunphy@crossreach.org.uk)
Director of Human Resources and Organisational Development:	Claire Hay (claire.hay@crossreach.org.uk)

Further information: www.crossreach.org.uk

5. ASSEMBLY BUSINESS COMMITTEE

The Committee makes the arrangements and ordering of business for the General Assembly and Commissions of Assembly. It keeps under review the functions, membership, processes and procedures of the Assembly, and monitors the implementation of Assembly decisions. It has responsibility for the Assembly Hall and the Moderator's residence and oversight of presbytery restructuring

Convener:	Rev. Michael J. Mair MStJ BD MTh
Vice-Convener:	Rev. Sheila M. Kirk BA LLB BD
Secretary:	Principal Clerk
	cmcintosh@churchofscotland.org.uk 0131 376 1594

Further information:
www.churchofscotland.org.uk > About us > General Assembly
www.churchofscotland.org.uk > About us > Faith Action Programme, committees and departments > Committees > Assembly Business

6. AUDIT COMMITTEE

Remit: to oversee the financial and other relevant reporting processes implemented by management; to work with the Assembly Trustees in setting appropriate standards of financial management and in overseeing compliance; and to keep under review the effectiveness of the systems for internal financial control, financial reporting and risk management, including compliance with the legal and regulatory environment.

Convener: Kenneth Baldwin

Contact: OATadmin@churchofscotland.org.uk 0131 225 5722

Further information:
www.churchofscotland.org.uk > About us > Faith Action Programme, committees and departments > Committees > Audit

---

7. CHURCH OF SCOTLAND TRUST

The Trust's function is to hold properties outwith Scotland and to act as trustee in a number of third-party trusts.

Chairman: Mr Leon M. Marshall CA
Vice-Chairman: Mrs Morag Angus MA DipLS FRICS
Treasurer: Mrs Jenny Simpson BSc FCA DChA
Secretary and Clerk: Mrs Madelaine Sproule LLB MSc DipLP NP
msproule@churchofscotland.org.uk 0131 376 1307; 0131 225 5722

Further information:
www.churchofscotland.org.uk > About us > Stewardship, finance and trusts > Church of Scotland Trust

---

8. COMMITTEE TO NOMINATE THE MODERATOR

Convener: The immediate past Moderator
Secretary: Principal Clerk
Contact: pcoffice@churchofscotland.org.uk
0131 225 5722

9. COMMUNICATIONS DEPARTMENT

Head of Communications:	Ruth MacLeod Ruth.Macleod@churchofscotland.org.uk
Communications Manager:	Helen Silvis HSilvis@churchofscotland.org.uk
Senior Communications Officer:	Cameron Brooks CBrooks@churchofscotland.org.uk
Communications Officer:	Jane Bristow JBristow@churchofscotland.org.uk
Communications Officer:	Calum Macleod CMacleod@churchofscotland.org.uk
Communications Officer:	Corrie Douglas-Young CDouglas-Young@churchofscotland.org.uk
Web Editor:	Marta Negro Puig MNegroPuig@churchofscotland.org.uk
Web Developer:	Alan Murray
Design Team Leader:	Chris Flexen
Senior Designer:	Steve Walker

Contact the Media Team after hours: 07854 783539
Contact department: 0131 225 5722
Further information:
www.churchofscotland.org.uk > About us > Faith Action Programme, committees and departments > Departments > Communications

10. ECUMENICAL RELATIONS COMMITTEE

The Committee is composed of Convener, Vice Convener and eight members appointed by the General Assembly, plus representatives of other denominations in Scotland and Church of Scotland members elected to British and international ecumenical bodies.

Convener:	Rev. I. Ross Blackman BSc MBA BD CertTh
Vice-Convener:	Pauline E.D. Weibye MA FCIPD
Secretary and Ecumenical Officer:	Rev. Dr John L. McPake

Contact: ecumenical@churchofscotland.org.uk 0131 225 5722

Further information:
www.churchofscotland.org.uk > Connect > Ecumenical relations
World Council of Churches: www.oikumene.org
Churches Together in Britain and Ireland: www.ctbi.org.uk
For other international ecumenical bodies see Committee's web pages as above
See also 'Other Churches in the United Kingdom' at Section 2.2.

11. ESTATES AND PROCUREMENT DEPARTMENT

Remit: to provide property, facilities, and procurement services to the Agencies and Departments of the central administration of the Church, and to manage the church offices.

Head of Estates and Procurement: Liam Fennell
Facilities Manager, Church Offices: Eunice Smith 0131 380 3054
eunice.smith@churchofscotland.org.uk

Contact: cpd@churchofscotland.org.uk 0131 225 5722

Further information:
www.churchofscotland.org.uk > About us > Faith Action Programme, committees and departments > Departments > Estates and Procurement

---

12. FORCES CHAPLAINS COMMITTEE

The Committee has responsibility for the recruitment of chaplains and takes an interest in their welfare and that of their families. It makes a contribution to the formulation of Ministry of Defence policy as it concerns the spiritual well-being of the women and men of the Armed Forces.

Convener: Rev. Scott J. Brown CBE BD
Vice-Convener: Group Captain Andrew G. Tait CEng FRAeS RAF(Ret'd)
Secretary: Daran Golby, Faith Action Staff
DGolby@churchofscotland.org.uk 0131 225 5722

Further information:
www.churchofscotland.org.uk > About us > Faith Action Programme, committees and departments > Forces Chaplains Committee
A list of Chaplains is found at Section 6 D

---

13. GENERAL TRUSTEES

The General Trustees hold properties and investments for the Church as a whole. They are charged with ensuring church buildings and funds are managed in the best interest of the Church as a whole and in support of parish ministry. The Trustees offer practical advice and guidance on maintaining and improving Church properties, manses and glebes. They also offer a limited amount of financial aid to congregations facing expenditure on their buildings.

Chair: Mr Alan F.K. Kennedy BSc FFA
Vice-Chair: Rev. Scott M. Rennie MA BD STM FRSA
Chief Executive: Mr Brian D. Waller LLB DipLP
Depute Chief Executive & Head of Land & Estates: Mrs Morag J. Menneer BSc MRICS
PA to Chief Executive & Head of Business Support: Mrs Eva Elder
Head of Land & Estates: Ms Claire L. Cowell LLB

Head of Buildings & Projects: Ms Katharine Isherwood BSc MRICS
Finance Manager: Ms Jennifer Law BSc CA

Buildings insurance, all enquiries to: Church of Scotland Insurance Services Ltd.
121 George Street, Edinburgh EH2 4YN
enquiries@cosic.co.uk 0131 220 4119
Chief Executive (COSIS): Mr Barry Clarkson

Contact: gentrustees@churchofscotland.org.uk 0131 225 5722
Further information:
www.churchofscotland.org.uk > About us > Faith Action Programme, committees and departments > Departments > General Trustees
www.churchofscotland.org.uk > Resources > General Trustees building and property resources

14. THE GUILD

The Church of Scotland Guild is a movement within the Church of Scotland whose aim is 'to invite and encourage both women and men to commit their lives to Jesus Christ and to enable them to express their faith in worship, prayer, action and fellowship'.

Convener: Christina Paterson, Stirling and Clackmannshire Guilds Together
Vice-Conveners: Kay Coull, Edinburgh Guilds Together
Morag Duncan, Lewis Guilds Together
Margaret Dundas, Glasgow North Guilds Together
Renee Riddell, Perth and Kinross Guilds Together
General Secretary: Karen Gillon
Administrator: Mandy Moir

Contact: guild@churchofscotland.org.uk 0131 380 6306

Further information:
www.churchofscotland.org.uk > Serve > The Guild

15. HOUSING AND LOAN FUND

Chair: Rev. Dorothy U. Anderson LLB DipLP BD
Deputy Chair: Rev. Bruce H. Sinclair BA BD
Secretary: Hazel Bett
HBett@churchofscotland.org.uk
0131 225 5722; 07929 418762
Property Manager: Hilary J. Hardy
Project Manager: Mark Learmonth
Property Assistant: Selena MacArthur

Further information:
www.churchofscotland.org.uk > About us > Faith Action Programme, committees and departments > Departments > Housing and Loan Fund

---

16. HUMAN RESOURCES DEPARTMENT

Head of Human Resources: Elaine McCloghry
Human Resources Managers: Karen Smith
Angela Ocak
Human Resources Advisers: Sarah-Jayne McVeigh
Stephanie Thomson

Contact: hr@churchofscotland.org.uk 0131 225 5722

Further information:
www.churchofscotland.org.uk > About us > Faith Action Programme, committees and departments > Departments > Human Resources

---

17. INFORMATION TECHNOLOGY DEPARTMENT

Head of IT: Richard MacLennan
0131 376 1597

Contact: itdept@churchofscotland.org.uk 0131 376 1597

Further information:
www.churchofscotland.org.uk > About us > Faith Action Programme, committees and departments > Departments > IT

---

18. INVESTORS TRUST

The Trust provides the Church's agencies, committees and congregations with a simple and economical facility for the investment of their funds.

Chair: Robert D. Burgon
Vice-Chair: Elaine Crichton
Treasurer: Jenny Simpson BSc FCA DChA
Executive Officer: June Lee
investorstrust@churchofscotland.org.uk 0131 376 3678

Further information:
www.churchofscotland.org.uk > About us > Stewardship, finance and trusts > Departments > Investors Trust

19. INVESTORS TRUST ETHICAL OVERSIGHT COMMITTEE

An advisory group to help the Church of Scotland think about the theological and ethical background of investments made through the Church of Scotland Investors Trust, consider the complexities of the investment options, and be a space for intelligent conversations that can support the Investors Trust to provide the investment managers with very specific briefs, in line with the Church's values.

Convener: Val Brown vbrown@christian-aid.org
Secretary: Rev. Ian W. Alexander
IAlexander@churchofscotland.org.uk 0131 225 5722

20. IONA COMMUNITY BOARD

To report to the General Assembly, and, through the Assembly to the wider Church, on the activities, concerns and current aspects of the life and work of the Iona Community. Includes members appointed of other denominations (at present the Baptist Union of Scotland, Religious Society of Friends, Roman Catholic Church and Scottish Episcopal Church).

Convener: Rev. Anikó Schütz Bradwell BA MA BD
anikosb@churchofscotland.org.uk 07936 042191

Further information: www.iona.org.uk

21. LAW DEPARTMENT

The Law Department gives advice and acts in legal matters for the Church and its courts, agencies, committees, congregations, the General Trustees, the Church of Scotland Trust and the Investors Trust. It is responsible for buying and selling churches, manses and other buildings/land on behalf of the Church's agencies, committees and congregations. The Department also provides advice and assistance to congregations and other Church bodies on a diverse range of issues including employment law, contract matters, trusts, charity law, data protection and litigation of various sorts and prepares circulars on legal topics affecting congregations such as health and safety, employment and discrimination law and data protection.

Solicitor of the Church
and of the General Trustees: Mary Macleod LLB DipLP NP
Depute Solicitor: Elspeth Annan LLB DipLP NP
Solicitors: Anne Steele LLB DipLP NP
Jennifer Campbell LLB LLM DipLP NP
Gregor Buick LLB DipLP WS NP
Madelaine Sproule LLB MSc DipLP NP
David di Paola LLB DipLP NP
Shirley Davidson LLB DipLP
John Wilson LLB DipLP NP
Rachel Davies LLB DipLP NP
Cecilia Miller LLB Dip LP NP
Data Protection Officer: Alice Wilson BA PCDP

Contact: lawdept@churchofscotland.org.uk 0131 225 5722 ext. 2230

Further information:
www.churchofscotland.org.uk > About us > Faith Action Programme, committees and departments > Departments > Law

22. LEGAL QUESTIONS COMMITTEE

Remit: to advise on legal questions of Church and civil law, assist in formulating responses to consultations by the Scottish and UK governments, provide the legislative drafting service for Agencies of the General Assembly, advise on reform to Church law in terms of practice and procedure, report on proposed amendments to Standing Orders, and inspect annually the records of Agencies of the General Assembly.

Convener: Rev. Dr Marjory A. MacLean
Vice-Convener: Rev. Katherine A. Taylor LLB MDiv
Secretary: Principal Clerk
Depute Clerk: Ms Christine Paterson LLB DipLP

Contact: NNicholls@churchofscotland.org.uk 0131 376 1137

Further information:
www.churchofscotland.org.uk > About us > Faith Action Programme, committees and departments > Committees > Legal Questions

23. LIFE AND WORK
the Church of Scotland's monthly magazine

The magazine's purpose is to keep the Church informed about events in church life at home and abroad and to provide a forum for Christian opinion and debate on a variety of topics. It has an independent editorial policy. Contributions which are relevant to any aspect of the Christian faith are welcome. The website, www.lifeandwork.org, includes up-to-date news, extracts from the magazine and additional features. To subscribe to the magazine through your church, speak to your Life and Work co-ordinator, or subscribe to a print or digital copy or buy a one-off issue via the Life and Work website. Subscriptions are also available by telephone on the number below.

Editor: Lynne McNeil magazine@lifeandwork.org 0131 225 5722

Further information:
www.lifeandwork.org
www.churchofscotland.org.uk > News and Events > Life and Work

---

24. NOMINATION COMMITTEE

Remit: to bring before the General Assembly names of persons to serve on the Standing Committees of the General Assembly; to work with the Standing Committees to ensure an open, fair and robust process for identifying suitable persons to serve as Conveners; and to comment on recommendations for the appointment of Assembly Trustees.

Convener: Rev. Dr Andrew Gardner
Vice-Convener: Rev. Bryan Kerr BA BD
Secretary: Rev. Dr Victoria J. Linford

Contact: Nominations@churchofscotland.org.uk 0131 225 5722

Further information:
www.churchofscotland.org.uk > About us > Faith Action Programme, committees and departments > Committees > Nomination Committee

---

25. PENSION TRUSTEES

The Trustees are responsible for the Church's three defined benefit pension schemes, now closed to future accrual and new members. The schemes are for: Ministers and Overseas Missionaries (including sections for Ministers Main Pension Fund, Widows and Orphans and the Contributors Fund); Staff (including sections for staff of the Social Care Council and of the Central Services Committee); and Ministries Development Staff (previously Presbytery and Parish Workers).

Chair:	Mr Stuart Stephen BSc
Vice-Chair:	Miss Lin J. Macmillan MA
Scheme Secretary and Pensions Manager:	Miss Jane McLeod BSc FPMI
Senior Pensions Administrator:	Mrs Fiona McCulloch-Stevenson
Pensions Administrators:	Ms Birgit Mosemann
	Mrs Lesley Elder
	Mrs Ruth Farquharson

Contact: pensions@churchofscotland.org.uk 0131 240 2255

Further information:
www.churchofscotland.org.uk > About us > Stewardship, finance and trusts > Pension Trustees

---

26. PRESBYTERY REVIEW COMMITTEE

Remit: to exercise on behalf of the General Assembly powers of oversight of Presbyteries, and in doing so to be satisfied that each Presbytery Review is thorough and forward-looking, key points of Review Reports are shared with the General Assembly, good practice is highlighted and shared across the Church, non-compliance is addressed and rectified, and to inspect annually records of Presbyteries.

Convener:	Rev. Moria McDonald MA BD
Vice-Convener:	Miss Catherine Coull
Secretary:	Principal Clerk

Contact: pcoffice@churchofscotland.org.uk 0131 225 5722

---

27. REGISTRATION OF MINISTRIES COMMITTEE

The Committee considers applications from ministers who wish to have the status of Category O, which entitles them to be inducted to a charge.

Convener:	Rev. Robert A. Hamilton BA BD
Vice-Convener:	Rev. Hilary N. McDougall MA PGCE BD
Registrar:	Rev. Angus R. Mathieson MA BD

Contact: RegistrationofMinistries@churchofscotland.org.uk 0131 376 6388

Further information:
www.churchofscotland.org.uk > Faith Action Programme, committees and departments > Committees > Registration of Ministries Committee

28. SAFEGUARDING SERVICE

The service ensures that the Church has robust structures and policies in place for the prevention of harm and abuse of children and adults at risk; and to ensure a timely and appropriate response when harm or abuse is witnessed, suspected or reported.

Convener: Rev. Dr A. Sonia Blakesley
Vice-Convener: Judy Wilson
Service Manager: Deborah Blackhurst

Contact: safeguarding@churchofscotland.org.uk 0131 225 5722

Further information:
www.churchofscotland.org.uk > About us > Departments > Safeguarding Service

---

29. SAINT ANDREW PRESS

Saint Andrew Press is managed on behalf of the Church of Scotland by Hymns Ancient and Modern Ltd and publishes a broad range of titles, focussing principally on resources for the mission and ministry of the contemporary church but also including backlist favourites such as William Barclay's much-loved *Daily Study Bible* commentaries. The full list of publications can be viewed on the Saint Andrew Press website (see below).

Contact: Christine Smith, Publishing Director christine@hymnsam.co.uk 0207 776 7546

Further information: www.standrewpress.com

---

30. SCOTTISH CHURCHES PARLIAMENTARY OFFICE

121 George Street, Edinburgh EH2 4YN

The purpose of the Scottish Churches Parliamentary Office is to build good relations between Scottish Churches, the Scottish and UK Parliaments and the Scottish and UK Governments. It aims to do this by: creating space for ecumenical fellowship and encounter on parliamentary and political affairs in Scotland; facilitating and enabling Scottish Churches to speak on legislation and political developments; and sharing news of parliamentary and political developments timeously and to the right people in the Churches.

Scottish Churches Parliamentary Officer: David Bradwell

Contact: DBradwell@churchofscotland.org.uk 0131 376 9104

Further information: www.scpo.scot

31. SCOTTISH STORYTELLING CENTRE (THE NETHERBOW)

43–45 High Street, Edinburgh EH1 1SR

The integrated facilities of the **Netherbow Theatre** and the **John Knox House**, together with the outstanding conference and reception areas, form an important cultural venue on the Royal Mile in Edinburgh. The Centre captures both the historical roots of storytelling and the forward-looking mission to preserve it: providing an extensive year-round cultural and literary programme. Faith Action Programme is pleased to partner with TRACS (Traditional Arts and Culture Scotland), a grant-funded body which provides advice and assistance nationally in the use of traditional arts in a diversity of settings.

Contact: reception@scottishstorytellingcentre.com 0131 556 9579

Further information: www.scottishstorytellingcentre.com

---

32. STEWARDSHIP AND FINANCE DEPARTMENT

The Department provides financial, governance and accounting advice to congregations and accounting, banking, payroll and budgeting services to the Church's agencies, committees and its statutory corporations - General Trustees, Investors Trust, Church of Scotland Trust – and to the Pension Trustees. It promotes Christian stewardship throughout the Church.

Head of Finance & General Treasurer:	Jenny Simpson BSc FCA DChA
Deputy Treasurer (Unincorporated Entities):	Gillian E. Coghlan MA CA
Deputy Treasurer (Wider Church and Statutory Corporations):	Leanne Thompson BSc CA
Finance Managers:	Lisa Erskine BA FCCA
	Jennifer Law BSc CA
	Elaine Macadie BA CA
	Suzanne Nolte BCom PA(SA)
Stewardship Team Leader:	Pauline Wilson MA

Contact: sfadmin@churchofscotland.org.uk
Further information and details of consultants:
www.churchofscotland.org.uk > About us > Faith Action Programme, committees and departments > Stewardship and Finance
www.churchofscotland.org.uk > Resources > Finance resources
www.churchofscotland.org.uk > Resources > Stewardship
www.churchofscotland.org.uk > About us > Stewardship Finance and Trusts

33. THEOLOGICAL FORUM

The purpose of the Forum is to continue to develop and bring to expression doctrinal understanding of the Church with reference to Scripture and to the confessional standards of the Church of Scotland, and the implications of this for worship and witness in and beyond contemporary Scotland. It responds to requests to undertake enquiries as they arise, draws the Church's attention to particular matters requiring theological work, and promotes theological reflection throughout the Church.

Convener:	Rev. Liam J. Fraser LLB BD MTh PhD
Vice-Convener:	Professor Paul T. Nimmo MA DipIA BD MTh PhD FHEA
Secretary:	Nathalie A. Mareš MacCallum MA MTh

Contact: NMaresMacCallum@churchofscotland.org.uk
Further information:
www.churchofscotland.org.uk > About us > Faith Action Programme, committees and departments > Committees > Theological Forum

SECTION 2

General Information

		Page
1.	Gaelic development in the Church of Scotland	26
2.	Other Churches in the United Kingdom	28
3.	Overseas Churches	29
4.	His Majesty's Household in Scotland Ecclesiastical	29
5.	Lord High Commissioners to the General Assembly	30
6.	Moderators of the General Assembly	31
7.	Scottish Divinity Faculties	32
8.	Societies and Associations	33
9.	Trusts and Funds	39
10.	Long Service Certificates	47
11.	Records of the Church of Scotland	47
12.	Fasti Ecclesiae Scoticanae	47

1. GAELIC DEVELOPMENT IN THE CHURCH OF SCOTLAND

Leasachadh na Gàidhlig ann an Eaglais na h-Alba

Tha Comataidh na Gàidhlig air a bhith a' coinneachadh gu cunbhalach tron bhliadha, agus an sàs ann an caochadh phròiseactan.

Nam measg, dh'obraich sinn còmhla ri Go Chatter gus tionndaidhean Gàidhlig air bhide-othan Lego a dhèanamh, stèidhichte air sgeulachdan às a' Bhìoball. Tha còig dhiubh ann thuige seo: Sgeulachd na Nollaige, Sgeulachd na Càisge, Slànachadh an fhir air an robh a' pahairilis, An Samaratanach Math, agus Daibhidh agus Goliat.

A bharrachd air a sin, dh'obraich sinn còmhla ri Comann Bhìobaill na h-Alba gus an leabhar *Innis Stòiridh às a' Bhìoball* fhoillseachadh (eadar-theangachadh Gàidhlig air *The Lion Share A Story Bible*). Chaidh na ceudan dhen leabhair seo a thoirt saor an asgaidh do chlann air feadh na dùthcha agus fiù 's do theaghlaichean ann an Canada. An luib an leabhair tha tionndadh claisneachd ann, ach am b' urrainn do chlann èisteachd ris an sgeulachd fhad 's a tha iad ga leughadh – rud a bhios na bhuannachd gu sònraiachte airson na feadhna a tha ann am foghlam Gàidhlig, ach aig nach Gàidhlig san taigh.

Tha an dà phròiseact seo an luib Pròiseact Pentecostes, iomairt aig a' Chomataidh ag amas air goireasan Bìoballach, eadar-ghinealach sa Ghàidhlig a chruthachadh.

Tha sinn cuideachd air a bhith obair còmhla ri Comann Bhìobaill na h-Alba ann an dearbhadh deasaichean ùra dhen Bhìoball Gàidhlig (1992) agus an eadar-theangachadh ùr dhen Tiomnaidh Nuaidh (2017). Tha an dà chuid a-nis a-mach à clò, agus tha CBA a' ceartachadh an teacsa san dà chuid mus tèid iad fhoillseachadh a-rithist. Tha buill a' Chomataidh a bhith a' toirt comhairle agus air a bhith an sàs san obair cheartachaidh.

San aon dòigh, bha sinn an sàs le leughadh-dearbhaidh airson tionndaidhean Gàidhlig air na goireasan aig Bibleworld a dh'fhoillsich CBA.

Tha *Na Duilleagan Gàidhlig* fhathast air fhoillseachadh gu ràitheil.

Tha dà bhuidheann leughaidh air loidhne, a' dol tron Tiomnadh Nuadh airson luchd-ionnsa-chaidh, a chaidh a stèidheachadh ri linn glasadh-sluaigh Covid, fhathast a' coinneachadh gach seachdain.

An t-Oll. Donnchadh Sneddon

Gaelic Development in the Church of Scotland

The Gaelic Committee has continued to meet regularly and to be involved in different projects.

These have included working with Go Chatter to produce Gaelic versions of Lego animated Bible stories for children. To date five videos have been produced: The Nativity, The Easter Story, The Healing of the Paralysed Man, The Good Samaritan and David and Goliath.

We have also worked with the Scottish Bible Society to produce a Gaelic version of *The Lion Share A Story Bible*, hundreds of free copies of which have been distributed to families across Scotland and also to Gaelic speakers in Canada. These come with a free audio version, enabling children to listen to and read along with the stories, something that will be especially useful for children in Gaelic education whose parents may not be able to speak or read Gaelic.

These are both part of the Gaelic Committee's Pròiseact Pentecostes (Project Pentecost) initiative, aimed at creating intergenerational Biblically-based resources in Gaelic.

We have also been working with the Scottish Bible Society in the proofing of the new edition of the Revised Gaelic Bible and the new translation of the New Testament. Both of these are currently out of print, and the SBS is undertaking a process of corrections before reprinting them. Members of the Committee have been helping by providing expertise in the proofing process.

We have also helped with proofing the preparation of the Gaelic versions of the Bibleworld resources published by the SBS.

Na Duilleagan Gàidhlig, the Gaelic supplement to *Life and Work*, continues to be published on a quarterly basis.

The two online New Testament reading groups, established during the first Covid lockdown, continue to run on a weekly basis.

Dr Duncan Sneddon

2. OTHER CHURCHES IN THE UNITED KINGDOM

ASSOCIATED PRESBYTERIAN CHURCHES: Assistant Clerk of Scottish Presbytery: Rev. J.R. Ross Macaskill (077110 648665; jrrm@gmail.com; www.apchurches.org).

BAPTIST UNION OF SCOTLAND: General Director: Rev. Martin Hodson, 48 Speirs Wharf, Glasgow G4 9TH (0141 423 6169; martin@scottishbaptist.org.uk; www.scottishbaptist.com).

CHURCH OF ENGLAND: Secretary General of General Synod: Mr William Nye, Church House, Great Smith Street, London SW1P 3AZ (020 7898 1000; enquiry@churchofengland.org).

CONGREGATIONAL FEDERATION IN SCOTLAND: Secretary: Miss Margaret McGuiness, Coatdyke Congregational Church, Kippen Street, Airdrie ML6 9AX (www.congregational.org.uk).

FREE CHURCH OF SCOTLAND: Principal Clerk: Rev. Callum Macleod, 15 North Bank Street, Edinburgh EH1 2LS (0131 226 5286; offices@freechurch.org; www.freechurch.org).

FREE CHURCH OF SCOTLAND (CONTINUING): Principal Clerk: Rev. Graeme Craig, Free Church Manse, 46A Craigie Road, Ayr KA8 0HA (01292 737447; principalclerk@fccontinuing.org; www.freechurchcontinuing.org).

FREE PRESBYTERIAN CHURCH OF SCOTLAND: Clerk of Synod: Rev. Keith M. Watkins, Free Presbyterian Manse, Ferry Road, Leverburgh, Isle of Harris HS5 3UA (kmwatkins@fpchurch.org.uk; www.fpchurch.org.uk).

METHODIST CHURCH IN SCOTLAND: District Administrator: Sue Marshall-Jennings, Methodist Church in Scotland, 25 Nicolson Square, Edinburgh EH8 9BX (07884 236761; districtadmin@methodistchurchinscotland.net; methodistchurchinscotland.net).

PRESBYTERIAN CHURCH IN IRELAND: Clerk of the General Assembly and General Secretary: Rev. Trevor D. Gribben, Assembly Buildings, 2–10 Fisherwick Place, Belfast BT1 6DW (028 9041 7208; clerk@presbyterianireland.org; www.presbyterianireland.org).

PRESBYTERIAN CHURCH OF WALES: General Secretary: Rev. Nan Wyn Powell-Davies, Tabernacle Chapel, 81 Merthyr Road, Whitchurch, Cardiff CF14 1DD (02920 627465; swyddfa.office@ebcpcw.org.uk; www.ebcpcw.cymru).

REFORMED PRESBYTERIAN CHURCH OF SCOTLAND: Clerk of Presbytery: Rev. Peter Loughridge, 7 West Pilton Road, Edinburgh EH4 4GX (07791 369626; peterloughridge@hotmail.com; www.rpcscotland.org).

RELIGIOUS SOCIETY OF FRIENDS (QUAKERS): Clerk to the General Meeting for Scotland: Michael Hutchinson (scotfriends@gmail.com; www.quakerscotland.org).

ROMAN CATHOLIC CHURCH: Fr. Gerard Maguiness, General Secretary, Bishops' Conference of Scotland, 64 Aitken Street, Airdrie ML6 6LT (01236 764061; gensec@bcos.org.uk; www.bcos.org.uk).

SALVATION ARMY: Colonel Sylvia Hinton, Secretary for Scotland, Scotland Office, 12A Dryden Road, Loanhead EH20 9LZ (0131 440 9109; sylvia.hinton@salvationarmy.org.uk; www.salvationarmy.org.uk).

SCOTTISH EPISCOPAL CHURCH: Secretary General: Dr Dee Bird, 21 Grosvenor Crescent, Edinburgh EH12 5EE (0131 225 6357; secgen@scotland.anglican.org; www.scotland.anglican.org).

UNITED FREE CHURCH OF SCOTLAND: Principal Clerks: Rev. Martin C. Keane and Rev. Colin C. Brown, United Free Church Offices, 11 Newton Place, Glasgow G3 7PR (0141 332 3435; office@ufcos.org.uk; www.ufcos.org.uk).

UNITED REFORMED CHURCH: General Secretary: Rev. Dr John Bradbury, Church House, 86 Tavistock Place, London WC1H 9RT (020 7916 2020; john.bradbury@urc.org.uk; www.urc.org.uk).

UNITED REFORMED CHURCH SYNOD OF SCOTLAND: Synod Clerk: Rev. Jan Adamson, United Reformed Church, 3/2 Atlantic Chambers, 45 Hope Street, Glasgow G2 6AE (0141 248 5382; clerk@urcscotland.org.uk; www.urcscotland.org.uk).

---

3. OVERSEAS CHURCHES

See www.churchofscotland.org.uk > Connect > Global Partnerships > Partner Churches

---

4. HIS MAJESTY'S HOUSEHOLD IN SCOTLAND ECCLESIASTICAL

Dean of the Order of the Thistle and Dean of the Chapel Royal:	Very Rev. Prof. David A.S. Fergusson OBE MA BD DPhil DD FRSE FBA
Domestic Chaplains:	Rev. Kenneth I. Mackenzie LVO DL BD CPS Rev. Neil N. Gardner DL CStJ MA BD
Chaplains in Ordinary:	Very Rev. Susan M. Brown BD DipMin DUniv Rev. Elizabeth M. Henderson OBE MA BD MTh Rev. George J. Whyte OBE BSc BD DMin KSG Rev. Marjory A. MacLean LLB BD PhD Rev. S. Grant Barclay LLB DipLP BD MSc PhD Rev. Prof. John Swinton BD PhD RMN RNMD FRSE FBA Rev. Moira McDonald MA BD
Extra Chaplains:	Very Rev. James Harkness KCVO CB OBE MA DD Rev. John L. Paterson MA BD STM

Rev. Charles Robertson LVO MA
Very Rev. John B. Cairns KCVO LTh LLB LLD DD
Very Rev. Finlay A.J. Macdonald MA BD PhD DD
Rev. Alastair H. Symington MA BD
Rev. James M. Gibson TD LTh LRAM
Very Rev. Prof. Iain R. Torrance KCVO Kt DD FRSE
Rev. Norman W. Drummond CBE MA BD DUniv FRSE
Rev. Alistair G. Bennett BSc BD
Very Rev. John P. Chalmers BD CPS DD
Very Rev. Angus Morrison MA BD PhD DD
Very Rev. E. Lorna Hood OBE MA BD DD

5. LORD HIGH COMMISSIONERS TO THE GENERAL ASSEMBLY

** deceased*

1980/81	The Earl of Elgin and Kincardine KT DL JP
1982/83	*Colonel Sir John Edward Gilmour Bt DSO TD
1984/85	*Charles Hector Fitzroy Maclean, Baron Maclean of Duart and Morvern KT GCVO KBE
1986/87	*John Campbell Arbuthnott, Viscount of Arbuthnott KT CBE DSC FRSE FRSA
1988/89	*Sir Iain Mark Tennant KT FRSA
1990/91	The Rt Hon. Donald MacArthur Ross FRSE
1992/93	The Rt Hon. Lord Macfarlane of Bearsden KT FRSE
1994/95	*Lady Marion Fraser KT
1996	Her Royal Highness the Princess Royal KG KT GCVO GCStJ
1997	The Rt Hon. Lord Macfarlane of Bearsden KT FRSE
1998/99	*The Rt Hon. Lord Hogg of Cumbernauld CBE DL JP
2000	His Royal Highness Prince Charles, Duke of Rothesay KG KT GCB OM
2001/02	*The Rt Hon. Viscount Younger of Leckie KT KCVO TD PC
	*Her Majesty Queen Elizabeth II attended the opening session in 2002
2003/04	The Rt Hon. Lord Steel of Aikwood KT KBE
2005/06	The Rt Hon. Lord Mackay of Clashfern KT
2007	His Royal Highness Prince Andrew, Duke of York KG KCVO
2008/09	The Rt Hon. George Reid PC MA
2010/11	Lord Wilson of Tillyorn KT GCMG PRSE
2012/13	*The Rt Hon. Lord Selkirk of Douglas KC MA LLB
2014	His Royal Highness Prince Edward, Earl of Wessex KG GCVO
2015/16	The Rt Hon. Lord Hope of Craighead KT PC FRSE
2017	Her Royal Highness the Princess Royal KG KT GCVO GCStJ QSO
2018/19	The Duke of Buccleuch and Queensberry KT KBE DL FSA FRSE
2020	*The General Assembly in May was cancelled due to the pandemic*
2021	His Royal Highness Prince William, Earl of Strathearn KG KT MA
2022/23	The Rt Hon. Lord Hodge PC KC MA LLB
2024	His Royal Highness Prince Edward, Duke of Edinburgh KG KT GCVO

6. MODERATORS OF THE GENERAL ASSEMBLY

** deceased*

1995 James Harkness KCVO CB OBE MA DD, Chaplain General (Emeritus)
1996 *John H. McIndoe MA BD STM DD, London: St Columba's linked with Newcastle: St Andrew's
1997 *Alexander McDonald BA DUniv CMIWSc, General Secretary, Department of Ministry
1998 *Alan Main TD MA BD STM PhD DD, University of Aberdeen
1999 John B. Cairns KCVO LTh LLB LLD DD, Dumbarton: Riverside
2000 Andrew R.C. McLellan CBE MA BD STM DD, Edinburgh: St Andrew's and St George's
2001 John D. Miller BA BD STM DD, Glasgow: Castlemilk East
2002 Finlay A.J. Macdonald MA BD PhD DD, Principal Clerk of Assembly
2003 Iain R. Torrance KCVO Kt DD FRSE, University of Aberdeen
2004 Alison Elliot CBE MA MSc PhD LLD DD FRSE, Associate Director, Centre for Theology and Public Issues, University of Edinburgh
2005 David W. Lacy DL BA BD DLitt, Kilmarnock: Henderson
2006 Alan D. McDonald LLB BD MTh DLitt DD, Cameron linked with St Andrews: St Leonard's
2007 Sheilagh M. Kesting BA BD DD DSG, Secretary of Ecumenical Relations Committee
2008 David W. Lunan MA BD DLitt DD, Clerk to the Presbytery of Glasgow
2009 William C. Hewitt BD DipPS, Greenock: Westburn
2010 John C. Christie BSc BD CBiol MRSB, Interim Minister
2011 A. David K. Arnott MA BD, St Andrews: Hope Park linked with Strathkinness
2012 Albert O. Bogle BD MTh, Bo'ness: St Andrew's
2013 E. Lorna Hood OBE MA BD DD, Renfrew: North
2014 John P. Chalmers BD CPS DD, Principal Clerk of Assembly
2015 Angus Morrison MA BD PhD DD, Orwell and Portmoak
2016 G. Russell Barr BA BD MTh DMin, Edinburgh: Cramond
2017 Derek Browning MA BD DMin, Edinburgh: Morningside
2018 Susan M. Brown BD DipMin DUniv, Dornoch Cathedral
2019 Colin A.M. Sinclair BA BD, Edinburgh: Palmerston Place
2020 W. Martin Fair BA BD DMin, Arbroath: St Andrew's
2021 James R. Wallace, The Rt Hon. Lord Wallace of Tankerness PC KC FRSE MA LLB DUniv
2022 Iain M. Greenshields BD CertMin DipRS ACMA MSc MTh DD, Dunfermline: St Margaret's
2023 Sally Foster-Fulton BA BD, Head of Christian Aid Scotland
2024 Shaw J. Paterson BSc BD MSc DPT, Strathaven: Trinity

MATTER OF PRECEDENCE

The Lord High Commissioner (while the Assembly is sitting) ranks next to the Sovereign and before the rest of the Royal Family. The Moderator ranks next to the Lord Chancellor of Great Britain and before the Keeper of the Great Seal of Scotland (the First Minister) and the Dukes.

7. SCOTTISH DIVINITY FACULTIES

* denotes a Minister of the Church of Scotland

ABERDEEN

School of Divinity, History and Philosophy
50–52 College Bounds, Old Aberdeen AB24 3DS
01224 272366; divinity@abdn.ac.uk

Master of Christ's College: Rev. Professor John Swinton* BD PhD RMN RNMD FRSE FBA
christs-college@abdn.ac.uk
Head of School: Professor Beth Lord MA PhD
Head of Divinity: Rev. Professor John Behr DPhil DD
Co-ordinator, Centre for Ministry Studies Rev. Emma Percy BA MA PhD
Senior Lecturer: Rev. Kenneth S. Jeffrey* BA BD PhD DMin
ksjeffrey@abdn.ac.uk

For other teaching staff and further information see www.abdn.ac.uk/sdhp/

ST ANDREWS

University College of St Mary
The School of Divinity, South Street, St Andrews, Fife KY16 9JU
01334 462850; divinity@st-andrews.ac.uk

Principal and Head of School: Professor Oliver Crisp BD MTh LLM PhD DLitt
Professor of World Christianity: Professor Sabine Hyland BA MPhil PhD

For other teaching staff and further information see www.st-andrews.ac.uk/divinity/people

---

EDINBURGH

School of Divinity and New College
New College, Mound Place, Edinburgh EH1 2LX
0131 650 8959; divinity@ed.ac.uk

Head of School: Professor Jeremy R. Carette BA MPhil PhD
Principal of New College: Rev. Professor Alison M. Jack* MA BD PhD SFHEA
Vice Principal of New College: Rev. Alexander C. Forsyth* LLB DipLP BD MTh PhD

For other teaching staff and further information see www.ed.ac.uk/divinity/our-people

GLASGOW

School of Critical Studies
Theology and Religious Studies
4 Professors' Square, University of Glasgow, Glasgow G12 8QQ
0141 330 6526; trinitycollegeglasgow@gmail.com

Head of Subject:	Dr Mia Spiro
Professor of Theology and Creative Practice:	Professor Heather Walton
Principal of Trinity College:	Rev. Doug C. Gay* MA BD PhD

For other teaching staff and further information see www.gla.ac.uk/subjects/theology and www.trinitycollegeglasgow.co.uk

---

HIGHLAND THEOLOGICAL COLLEGE UHI

High Street, Dingwall IV15 9HA
01349 780000; htc@uhi.ac.uk

Principal of HTC:	Rev. Hector Morrison* BSc BD MTh Cert ITL
Vice-Principal (Academic):	Jamie Grant LLB MA PhD
Vice Principal (Finance and Operations):	Blair Gardner BSc PGDip
Access Course Leader, Lecturer in Youth, Church and Culture:	Rev. Jonathan Fraser* MA(Div) MTh ThM PhD
Lecturer in Evangelism:	Rev. Thomas MacNeil* MA BD

For other teaching staff and further information see www.htc.uhi.ac.uk

---

8. SOCIETIES AND ASSOCIATIONS

** Church of Scotland Societies*

*** ASSEMBLY AND PRESBYTERY CLERKS FORUM:** Secretary: Rev. Dr John A. Ferguson, Presbytery of Perth, Suite F3, Riverside House, Friarton Road, Perth PH2 8DF (07596 868064; clerksforum@churchofscotland.org.uk).

BOYS' BRIGADE: A volunteer-led Christian youth organisation which was founded in Scotland in 1883 and now operates in many different countries around the world. Our vision is that children and young people experience life to the full (John 10:10). We provide opportunities for young people to learn, grow and discover in a safe, caring and fun environment. Contact: John Sharp, Carronvale House, Carronvale Road, Larbert FK5 3LH (01324 562008; support@boys-brigade.org.uk; www.boys-brigade.org.uk). Scottish Chaplain: Rev Derek Gunn (scottishchaplain@boys-brigade.org.uk).

BROKEN RITES: Support group for divorced and separated clergy spouses. Scottish representative: Janet Forbes (07398 222118; janetruth018@gmail.com; www.brokenrites.org).

CHRISTIAN AID SCOTLAND: Sally Foster-Fulton, Head of Nations and Church Relations; Val Brown, Head of Christian Aid Scotland, 41 George IV Bridge, Edinburgh EH1 1EL (0131 220 1254; edinburgh@christian-aid.org; www.christianaid.org.uk/get-involved-locally/scotland).

*** CHURCH OF SCOTLAND MILITARY CHAPLAINS' ASSOCIATION:** The Association consists of serving and retired chaplains to HM Forces. It holds an annual meeting and lunch on Shrove Tuesday, and organises the annual Service of Remembrance in St Giles' Cathedral. Hon. Secretary: Rev. Stephen A. Blakey BSc BD CStJ, Balduff House, Kilry, Blairgowrie PH11 8HS (01575 560226; SBlakey@churchofscotland.org.uk).

*** CHURCH OF SCOTLAND RETIRED MINISTERS' ASSOCIATION:** The Association meets in The New Town Church, 13 George St., Edinburgh, normally on the first Monday of the month, from October to April. The group includes members of other denominations. Meetings include a talk, which can be on a wide variety of topics, which is followed by afternoon tea. Details of the programme from Hon. Secretary: Rev. Matthew S. Bicket, 9/2 Connaught Place, Edinburgh EH6 4RQ (0131 552 8781; matthew.bicket1952@gmail.com).

*** CHURCH SERVICE SOCIETY:** Founded in 1865 to study the development of Christian worship through the ages and in the Reformed tradition, and to work towards renewal in contemporary worship. It has published since 1928, and continues to publish, a liturgical journal, archived on its website. Secretary: Rev. Elspeth M. McKay (07789 993535; EMcKay@churchofscotland.org.uk; www.churchservicesociety.org).

*** COVENANT FELLOWSHIP SCOTLAND (formerly FORWARD TOGETHER):** An organisation for evangelicals within the Church of Scotland. Contact the Chairman, Rev. Mark Malcolm (07731 737377; MMalcolm@churchofscotland.org.uk; https://www.facebook.com/covenantfellowshipscotland).

DAY ONE CHRISTIAN MINISTRIES: Day One has produced Christian literature for over 40 years. A variety of books are published for both adults and young people, as well as cards, bookmarks and stationery items. Ryelands Road, Leominster, Herefordshire HR6 8NZ. Contact Mark Roberts for further information (01568 613740; sales@dayone.co.uk; www.dayone.co.uk).

ECO-CONGREGATION SCOTLAND: An ecumenical environmental charity supporting the largest movement of community-based environment groups across Scotland to care and act for God's creation. Eco-Congregation Scotland offers a programme to help local congregations reduce their impact on climate change and live sustainably. 121 George Street, Edinburgh EH2 4YN (0131 240 2274; manager@ecocongregationscotland.org; www.ecocongregationscotland.org).

FELLOWSHIP OF ST ANDREW: The fellowship promotes dialogue between Churches of the east and the west in Scotland. Further information available from the Secretary, Rev. Dr Robert Pickles, 10 Houliston Avenue, Dumfries DG2 7BF (07448 858818; RPickles@churchofscotland.org.uk).

* **FRIENDS OF ST ANDREW'S JERUSALEM & TIBERIAS:** The Friends support the work of the ministers and congregation of St Andrew's Jerusalem and Tiberias. This includes support of partner organisations. In this The Friends are very much helped by staff members of the Faith Action Programme. Hon. Secretary: Carol Miller, secretary@friendsofstandrews.com

* **FRIENDS OF TABEETHA SCHOOL, JAFFA:** The Friends seek to support the only school run by the Church of Scotland in the world. Based in Jaffa, Israel, it seeks to promote tolerance and understanding amongst pupils and staff alike. President: Irene Anderson. Hon. Secretary: Rev. David J. Smith, 16 Allan Street, Leslie, Glenrothes KY6 3LA (David.Smith@churchofscotland.org.uk).

FRONTIER YOUTH TRUST: A movement journeying with young people on the margins of church and society. We host a community of practice for those working with young people in the community. We are resourcing the church to take pioneering risks in their work with young people. And we are calling others to join the pioneer movement to reach young people on the margins. Contact us for training and coaching, or find practical resources on our website at www.fyt.org.uk. Contact us at info@fyt.org.uk, 0121 771 2328 or find us on social media.

GIRLGUIDING SCOTLAND: 16 Coates Crescent, Edinburgh EH3 7AH (Tel: 0131 226 4511; administrator@girlguiding-scot.org.uk; www.girlguidingscotland.org.uk).

GIRLS' BRIGADE SCOTLAND: 11A Woodside Crescent, Glasgow G3 7UL (0141 332 1765; caroline.goodfellow@girls-brigade-scotland.org.uk; www.girls-brigade-scotland.org.uk).

INTERSERVE GREAT BRITIAN AND IRELAND: An international, evangelical and interdenominational organisation with 170 years of Christian service. The purpose of Interserve is 'to make Jesus Christ known through *wholistic* ministry in partnership with the global church, among the neediest peoples of Asia and the Arab world', and our vision is 'Lives and communities transformed through encounter with Jesus Christ'. Interserve supports over 800 people in cross-cultural ministry in a wide range of work including children and youth, the environment, discipleship, Bible training, education, engineering, agriculture, business development and health care. We look to support churches and individuals as they seek to serve the Lord cross-culturally both locally and throughout Asia and the Arab world. (03333 601600; janef@isgbi.org (Jane Fucella); www.interserve.org.uk).

IONA COMMUNITY: We are an ecumenical Christian community with a dispersed worldwide membership, and an international network of supporters and volunteers. Inspired by our faith, we pursue justice and peace in and through community. Our Glasgow centre is the base for Wild Goose Publications and the Wild Goose Resource Group. The Iona Community welcomes thousands of visitors each year to its daily worship in Iona Abbey, and to its Welcome Centre and Community shop. It also welcomes guests to share in the common life on Iona and at Camas outdoor centre on Mull, which mainly hosts youth groups. Leader: Rev. Ruth Harvey, Suite 9, Fairfield, 1048 Govan Road, Glasgow, G51 4XS (0141 429 7281, admin@iona.org.uk; www.iona.org.uk; Facebook: Iona Community; Twitter: @ionacommunity). Iona Warden: Caro Penney, Iona Abbey, Isle of Iona, Argyll, PA76 6SN (01681 700404; enquiries@iona.org.uk).

* **KIRK ABSTAINERS:** Recognising that alcohol is a major – indeed a growing – problem within Scotland, the aim of the Church of Scotland Abstainers' Association, with its motto 'Abstinence makes sense', is to encourage more people to choose a healthy alcohol-free lifestyle.

Further details are available from 'Blochairn', 17A Culduthel Road, Inverness IV24 4AG (jamwall@talktalk.net).

LEPROSY MISSION: The Leprosy Mission is a global fellowship united by our Christian faith and commitment to ending leprosy and transforming lives in the name of Jesus. To book your Leprosy Sunday, contact us at The Leprosy Mission, Goldhay Way, Orton Goldhay, Peterborough PE2 5GZ (01733 370505; hello@lm.org.uk; www.leprosymission.org.uk).

PLACE FOR HOPE: exists to accompany and equip people and faith communities so that all may reach their potential as peacemakers, able to navigate change and conflict well. For 15 years, Place for Hope has provided high quality mediation and training services in faith-based peace and reconciliation, supporting faith communities to notice brokenness and division, nurture relationships and community, navigate conflict with graciousness and nourish wholeness in themselves and their communities. In times of change and challenge, we know that practical support can help. Place for Hope supports the Church of Scotland through the Living Peace Programme which offers:

- support for groups and individuals experiencing conflict
- facilitation of sensitive or difficult group conversations, such as preparing for change or transition
- individual or team coaching
- community dialogues on difficult, potentially divisive issues
- training, workshops and resources for understanding and working with conflict and change.

Please get in touch for information, or a confidential conversation: 07884 580359; info@placeforhope.org.uk; www.placeforhope.org.uk.

PRISON FELLOWSHIP SCOTLAND is a Christian charity working with those in Scotland's 15 prisons from Dumfries in the south to Inverness in the north. We run weekly Bible study groups for men and women in prison to explore faith and the Bible. We deliver a 6-week Restorative Justice/Victim awareness course that helps offenders look at the consequences of their offending. We run a letter-writing programme helping alleviate loneliness and isolation felt especially by older prisoners. Through our Angel Tree programme, we provide Christmas presents for the children of those in prison and we partner with SU and Circle to help Children affected by imprisonment to attend an adventure holiday. We would be happy to come to speak or provide information about work in prisons close to you. Contact Executive Director: John Nonhebel, Connect House, 42 Hollowglen Road, Glasgow G32 0DP (0141 266 0136; office@pfscotland.org; www.pfscotland.org).

RELATIONSHIPS SCOTLAND: Scotland's largest provider of relationship counselling, family mediation and child contact centre services. Chief Executive: Mr Stuart Valentine, 18 York Place, Edinburgh EH1 3EP (Tel: 0345 119 2020; Fax: 0845 119 6089; enquiries@relationships-scotland.org.uk; www.relationships-scotland.org).

ST COLM'S FELLOWSHIP: An association for all from any denomination who have trained, studied or been resident at St Colm's, either when it was a college or later as International House. There is an annual retreat and a meeting for Commemoration; and some local groups meet on a regular basis. Hon. Secretary: Rev. Margaret Nutter, 'Kilmorich', 14 Balloch Road, Balloch G83 8SR (01389 754505; maenutter@gmail.com).

SCOTTISH BIBLE SOCIETY: Chief Executive: Elaine Duncan, 7 Hampton Terrace, Edinburgh EH12 5XU (0131 337 9701; info@scottishbiblesociety.org; https://scottishbiblesociety.org).

SCOTTISH CHURCH HISTORY SOCIETY: Promoting interest in the history of Christianity in Scotland. Journal: *Scottish Church History*. Secretary: Dr Ben Rogers (schssec@outlook.com; www.scottishchurchhistory.org.uk).

*** SCOTTISH CHURCH SOCIETY:** Founded in 1892 to 'defend and advance Catholic doctrine as set forth in the Ancient Creeds and embodied in the Standards of the Church of Scotland', the Society meets for worship and discussion at All Saints' Tide, holds a Lenten Quiet Day, an AGM, and other meetings by arrangement; all are open to non-members. The Society wishes to encourage a younger membership and invites those in training for the ministry to consider its aims and objectives. The Society works closely with the Church Service Society and is arranging meetings which are of joint interest. Secretary: Rev. W. Gerald Jones MA BD MTh, The Manse, Patna Road, Kirkmichael, Maybole KA19 7PJ (01655 750286; WJones@churchofscotland.org.uk).

*** SCOTTISH CHURCH THEOLOGY SOCIETY:** The Society encourages theological exploration and discussion of the main issues confronting the Church in the twenty-first century. Rev. Alec Shuttleworth (07845 290486; AShuttleworth@churchofscotland.org.uk).

SCOTTISH CHURCHES ORGANIST TRAINING SCHEME (SCOTS): Established in 1995, SCOTS is run by the Royal College of Organists in partnership with the Scottish Federation of Organists, the Royal School of Church Music and the Scottish Churches. It is a self-propelled ecumenical scheme by which organists and those called upon to play the organ in churches follow a three-stage syllabus, receiving a certificate at each stage. Participants each have an Adviser whom they meet occasionally for help and assessment, and also take part in one of the Local Organ Workshops which are held in different parts of Scotland each year. Syllabus information at www.rco.org.uk/scots; information from Andrew Macintosh (01382 521210); andrew.macintosh@rco.org.uk.

SCOTTISH REFORMATION SOCIETY: Exists to defend and promote the work of the Protestant Reformation in Scotland by organising meetings, publishing literature and running an essay competition. Chairman: Rev. John Keddie. Vice-Chairman: Mr Allan McCulloch. Secretary: Rev. Dr Douglas Somerset. Treasurer: Mr Hugh Morrison. The Magdalen Chapel, 41 Cowgate, Edinburgh EH1 1JR (0131 220 1450; info@scottishreformationsociety.org; www.scottishreformationsociety.org).

SCOUTS SCOTLAND: Scottish Headquarters, Fordell Firs, Hillend, Dunfermline KY11 7HQ (01383 419073; hello@scouts.scot; www.scouts.scot).

SCRIPTURE UNION SCOTLAND: Scripture Union Scotland's vision is to see every child and young person in Scotland exploring the Bible and responding to the significance of Jesus. SU Scotland works in schools running SU groups and supporting Curriculum for Excellence. Its three activity centres, Lendrick Muir, Alltnacriche and Gowanbank, accommodate school groups and weekends away during term-time. During the school holidays it runs an extensive programme of events for school-age children – including residential holidays (some focused on disadvantaged children and young people), missions and church-based holiday clubs. In addition, it runs discipleship and training programmes for young people and is committed to promoting prayer for, and by, the young people of Scotland through a range of national prayer events and the *Pray for Schools Scotland* initiative. Scripture Union Scotland, New Olympia House, 13 Olympia Street, Glasgow G40 3TA (0141 332 1162; info@suscotland.org.uk; www.suscotland.org.uk).

STUDENT CHRISTIAN MOVEMENT: SCM is a student-led movement inspired by Jesus to act for justice and show God's love in the world. As a community we come together to pray, worship and explore faith in an open and non-judgemental environment. The movement is made up of a network of groups and individual members across Britain, as well as link churches and chaplaincies. As a national movement we come together at regional and national events to learn more about our faith and spend time as a community, and we take action on issues of social justice chosen by our members. SCM provides resources and training to student groups, churches and chaplaincies on student outreach and engagement, leadership and social action. Chief Executive: Rev. Naomi Nixon, SCM, Grays Court, 3 Nursery Road, Edgbaston, Birmingham B15 3JX (0121 426 4918; scm@movement.org.uk; www.movement.org.uk).

TEARFUND: A Christian charity which partners with local churches and organisations in more than 50 of the world's poorest countries. It tackles poverty and injustice by responding to disasters, through sustainable community development, and by challenging unjust policies and practices at a local, national and global level. Head of Tearfund Scotland: Bee Roy (0141 332 3621; scotland@tearfund.org; www.tearfund.org).

WALDENSIAN MISSIONS AID SOCIETY FOR WORK IN ITALY: Supporting the outreach of the Waldensian Churches, including important work with immigrant communities in the *Mediterranean Hope* project. Scottish Charity No. SC001346. David A. Lamb SSC, 36 Liberton Drive, Edinburgh EH16 6NN (0131 664 3059; david@dlamb.co.uk; www.scottishwaldensian.org.uk).

WORLD DAY OF PRAYER: SCOTTISH COMMITTEE: Convener: Mary Welsh, 4 Tweedsmuir, Bishopbriggs, Glasgow G64 1EE (07516 310394; marypwelsh@icloud.com). Secretary: Marjorie Paton, Muldoanich, Stirling Street, Blackford, Auchterarder PH4 1QG (01764 682234; marjoriepaton.wdp@btinternet.com; www.wdpscotland.org.uk).

YMCA SCOTLAND: Offers support, training and guidance to churches seeking to reach out to love and serve young people's needs. Chief Executive – National General Secretary: Mrs Kerry Reilly, YMCA Scotland, 1 Chesser Avenue, Edinburgh EH14 1TB (0131 228 1464; kerry@ymca.scot; www.ymca.scot).

YOUTH FOR CHRIST: Youth for Christ is a national Christian Youth Work charity who are about seeing young people's lives change by Jesus. In Scotland there are 4 locally governed, staffed and financed centres, communicating and demonstrating the Christian faith. We are passionate about equipping, resourcing and encouraging the church in reaching unchurched young people and produce a wide variety of resources to serve the local church across Scotland as they seek to support and share the gospel with the young people in their communities. Scotland Relational Pioneer: Sandra Blair (0121 502 9620; sandra.blair@yfc.co.uk; www.yfc.co.uk).

YOUTH SCOTLAND: Balfour House, 19 Bonnington Grove, Edinburgh EH6 4BL (0131 554 2561; office@youthscotland.org.uk; www.youthscotland.org.uk).

9. TRUSTS AND FUNDS

ABERNETHY ADVENTURE CENTRES: Full board residential accommodation and adventure activities available for all Church groups, plus a range of Christian retreats, summer camps, gap year programmes and adventure leadership training courses at our three centres in Scotland. 01479 821279; info@abernethy.org.uk; www.abernethy.org.uk).

BAIRD TRUST: Assists in the building and repair of churches and halls, and generally assists the work of the Church of Scotland. Apply to Iain A.T. Mowat CA, 182 Bath Street, Glasgow G2 4HG (0141 332 0476; info@bairdtrust.org.uk; www.bairdtrust.org.uk).

Rev. Alexander BARCLAY BEQUEST: Assists a family member of a deceased minister of the Church of Scotland who at the time of his/her death was acting as his/her housekeeper and who is in needy circumstances, and in certain circumstances assists Ministers, Deacons, Ministries Development Staff and their spouses facing financial hardship. Applications can only be submitted to the trustees by the Faith Action Ministries Support Team, 121 George Street, Edinburgh EH2 4YN (pastoralsupport@churchofscotland.org.uk).

BELLAHOUSTON BEQUEST FUND: Gives grants to Protestant denominations in the City of Glasgow and certain areas within five miles of the city boundary for building and repairing churches and halls and the promotion of religion. Apply to Mitchells Roberton, 36 North Hanover Street, Glasgow G1 2AD (0141 552 3422; info@mitchells-roberton.co.uk).

BEQUEST FUND FOR MINISTERS OF CHURCH OF SCOTLAND: Provides financial assistance to ministers in need including towards the cost of manse furnishings, pastoral efficiency aids, and personal and family dental, medical or educational costs. Apply to A. Linda Parkhill CA, 60 Wellington Street, Glasgow G2 6HJ (0141 226 4994; mail@parkhillmackie.co.uk).

CARNEGIE TRUST FOR THE UNIVERSITIES OF SCOTLAND: The Carnegie Trust invites applications by students who have had at least two years education at a secondary school in Scotland (or can demonstrate evidence of a substantial link to Scotland), for Tuition Fee Grants towards tuition fee costs for a first undergraduate degree at a Scottish university. For more information and a link to the online application form visit the Trust's website (https://www.carnegie-trust.org/award-schemes/undergraduate-tuition-fee-grants/) or contact the Carnegie Trust for the Universities of Scotland, Andrew Carnegie House, Pittencrieff Street, Dunfermline KY12 8AW (01383 724990; admin@carnegie-trust.org; www.carnegie-trust.org).

CHURCH HYMNARY TRUST: The trust is 'formed for the advancement of the Christian Faith through the promotion and development of hymnody in Scotland with particular reference to the Church of Scotland by assisting in the development, promotion, provision and understanding of hymns, psalms and paraphrases suitable for use in public worship, and in the distribution and making available of the same in books, discs, electronically and in other media for use by the Church of Scotland ….' The trust wishes to encourage applications for projects or schemes which are consistent with its purposes. These can include training courses, provision of music and guides to music, but the trust is not limited to those activities. Applications should be made to the Secretary and Treasurer Anne Steele, 121 George Street, Edinburgh EH2 4YN (0131 380 1970; asteele@churchofscotland.org.uk).

CHURCH OF SCOTLAND INSURANCE SERVICES LTD: Insurance intermediary, authorised and regulated by the Financial Conduct Authority, which arranges and manages the facility providing insurance protection for Church of Scotland congregations, including their activities and assets. Cover can also be arranged for other religious groups, charities, and non-profitmaking organisations. All profits are distributed to the General Trustees of the Church of Scotland through Gift Aid. Contact 121 George Street, Edinburgh EH2 4YN (0131 220 4119; b.clarkson@cosic.co.uk; www.cosic.co.uk).

CHURCH OF SCOTLAND MINISTRIES BENEVOLENT FUND: Makes grants to the following beneficiaries who are in need:
(a) any retired person who has been ordained or commissioned for the Ministry of the Church of Scotland;
(b) Ministers inducted or introduced to a charge or appointment, Probationer Ministers, Admissions Candidates during Familiarisation Placement or Ordained National Ministers appointed to posts under approval of Presbytery;
(c) Ministries Development Staff appointed to a Presbytery planned post (including Deacons);
(d) Ordained Local Minsters, Auxiliary Ministers or Deacons serving under the appointment of Presbytery;
(e) Readers set apart by Presbytery to carry out the work of the Church;
(f) any widow, widower and/or orphan of any person categorised in (a) to (e) above;
(g) any spouse or former spouse and/or child (natural or otherwise) of any person categorised by (a) to (e) above.
Contact pastoralsupport@churchofscotland.org.uk for an application form. Enquiries to Alison Stewart, Senior Administrator, Faith Action Ministries Support Team, 121 George Street, Edinburgh EH2 4YN (0131 376 3685).

CHURCH OF SCOTLAND SEEDS FOR GROWTH FUNDING: Provides grants at four levels from a one-off £1000 to £100,000 per year for three years possibly extendable to five. The purposes of Seeds for Growth funding are to support the numerical and spiritual growth of the Church of Scotland through: (i) developing mission through new worshipping communities, (ii) developing and nurturing faith in those under the age of 40, and (iii) fostering discipleship and revitalisation within established congregations, with the aim of growing an existing congregation or developing a new worshipping community. Working with ecumenical partners is encouraged though applications must come from Church of Scotland congregations or groups of congregations, presbyteries or groups of presbyteries. Guidance at: www.churchofscotland.org.uk/connect/seeds-for-growth Contact: David Williams, Grants Manager, grants@churchofscotland.org.uk

CHURCH OF SCOTLAND SMALL GRANTS FUND: Provides grants of up to £1000 for short-term project funding of between 3 and 12 months for developing mission through new worshipping communities, engaging and attracting those aged under 40, addressing pressing issues in the church, and innovation in church practices. Individual Church of Scotland churches and presbyteries and groups of churches or presbyteries may apply. Churches and presbyteries are also able to work with ecumenical partners, though the application will need to come from the Church of Scotland church or presbytery. Guidance on applications at: www.churchofscotland.org.uk/connect/small-grants-fund Contact: David Williams, Grants Manager, SGF@churchofscotland.org.uk

CINTRA BEQUEST: See 'Tod Endowment Trust …' entry below.

CLAREMONT TRUST: aims to assist small, innovative projects of Christian witness, renewal and social action in their very early stages of development. Typically grants are of £500–£600 and not more than £1000. Completed application forms must be received by the last working day of April for consideration in May. Application forms available on www.claremonttrust.org.uk – further information from the Secretary, Sylvia Marchant (smarchant1944@gmail.com)

CLARK BURSARY: Awarded to accepted candidate(s) for the ministry of the Church of Scotland whose studies for the ministry are pursued at the University of Aberdeen. Applications or recommendations for the Bursary to the Clerk to the Presbytery of the North East and the Northern Isles, Suite 2, Ocean Spirit House West, 31 Waterloo Quay, Aberdeen AB11 5BS.

CRAIGCROOK MORTIFICATION: The Trust has power to award a pension to men and women of 60 years of age or over born in Scotland or who have resided in Scotland for not less than 10 years who appear to be in poor circumstances. The Trust awards pensions of £1,230 payable per annum in half-yearly instalments. Ministers are invited to notify the Clerk and Factor, Sophie Mills, The WS Society, The Signet Library, Parliament Square, Edinburgh EH1 1RF (0131 220 3249; smills@wssociety.co.uk) of deserving persons and should be prepared to act as a referee on the application form.

DRUMMOND TRUST: Makes grants towards the cost of publication of books of 'sound Christian doctrine and outreach'. The Trustees are also willing to receive grant requests towards the cost of audio-visual programme material, but not equipment, software but not hardware. Requests for application forms should be made to the Secretaries, Hill and Robb Limited, 3 Pitt Terrace, Stirling FK8 2EY (01786 450985; catherineberrill@hillandrobb.co.uk). Manuscripts should *not* be sent.

DUNCAN McCLEMENTS TRUST FOR ECUMENICAL TRAINING: Makes grants towards the cost of attendance at ecumenical assemblies and conferences; gatherings of young people; short courses or conferences promoting ecumenical understanding. Also to enable schools to organise one-off events to promote better understanding among differing communities and cultures with different religious backgrounds. The Trust also helps towards the cost of resources and study materials. Enquiries to: Committee on Ecumenical Relations, Church of Scotland, 121 George Street, Edinburgh EH2 4YN (ecumenicalofficer@churchofscotland.org.uk).

David DUNCAN TRUST: Makes grants annually (December) to students for the ministry and students in training to become deacons in the Church of Scotland in the Faculties of Arts and Divinity. All applications are considered with slight preference given to those born or educated within the bounds of the former Presbytery of Arbroath. Applications to be received no later than 21 October to Thorntons Law LLP, Brothockbank House, Arbroath DD11 1NE (reference: Glyn Roberts (Trust Manager); 01382 346299; groberts@thorntons-law.co.uk).

ERSKINE CUNNINGHAM HILL TRUST: Donates its annual income to charities and to CrossReach. Individual donations are in the region of £1,000. Priority is given to charities registered and operating in Scotland (with an annual income of less than £500,000) and relating to the elderly, young people, ex-service personnel or seafarers. Application forms from the Secretary, Alan Ritchie, 121 George Street, Edinburgh EH2 4YN (0131 225 5722; aritchie@churchofscotland.org.uk).

ESDAILE TRUST: Assists the education and advancement of daughters of ministers, missionaries and widowed deaconesses of the Church of Scotland between 12 and 25 years of age. Applications are to be lodged by 31 May in each year with Kirsty Ashworth, Charity Administration Service, Exchange Place 3, Semple Street, Edinburgh EH3 8BL (0131 473 3500; SM-Charity@azets.co.uk).

FERGUSON BEQUEST FUND: Assists with the building and repair of churches and halls and, more generally, with the work of the Church of Scotland. Priority is given to the Counties of Ayr, Kirkcudbright, Wigtown, Lanark, Dunbarton and Renfrew, and to Greenock, Glasgow, Falkirk and Ardrossan; applications are, however, accepted from across Scotland. Apply to Iain A.T. Mowat CA, 182 Bath Street, Glasgow G2 4HG (0141 332 0476; info@fergusonbequestfund.org.uk; www.fergusonbequestfund.org.uk).

James GILLAN'S BURSARY FUND: Bursaries are available for male or female Candidates for the Ministry in the Church of Scotland who are currently resident in, or were born and had their home for not less than three years continually in the Parishes of Dyke, Edinkillie, Forres St Leonard's and Rafford. In certain circumstances the Trustees may be able to make a grant to Church Candidates resident in the old counties of Moray or Nairn, but only while resident. Apply to Roy Anderson, royand@btinternet.com.

GLASGOW SOCIETY OF THE SONS AND DAUGHTERS OF MINISTERS OF THE CHURCH OF SCOTLAND: The Society's primary purpose is to grant financial assistance to children (no matter what age) of deceased ministers of the Church of Scotland. Applications for first grants can be lodged at any time. Thereafter annual applications must be lodged by 31 December for consideration by Council in February. To the extent that funds are available, grants are also given for the children of ministers or retired ministers, although such grants are normally restricted to university and college students. These latter grants are considered in conjunction with the Edinburgh-based Societies. Limited funds are also available for individual application for special needs or projects. Applications are to be submitted by 31 May in each year. Emergency applications can be dealt with at any time when need arises. More information can be found at www.mansebairnsnetwork.org. Application forms may be obtained from Kirsty Ashworth, Charity Administration Service, Exchange Place 3, Semple Street, Edinburgh EH3 8BL (0131 473 3500; SM-Charity@azets.co.uk).

GUNTRIP TRUST: SC051488 www.guntriptrust.com For the advancement of education and training in the field of human relations and to provide bursary assistance for people who may be ordained or non-ordained, and are fulfilling a designated ministerial role. Applications are welcomed from those wishing to undertake individual psychodynamic counselling or psychoanalytic psychotherapy, or to undergo training in these fields, or to participate in work-related reflective practice groups led by experienced practitioners. Recipients of bursaries choose their own therapist/training course accredited by appropriate bodies as approved by the Trustees. Applications are assessed confidentially by the Bursar and one other trustee. Enquiries to the Secretary, Mrs Joyce Watkinson, 20 Stirling Street, Tillycoultry FK13 6EA; joyce.watkinson@gmail.com

HAMILTON BURSARY: Awarded, subject to the intention on graduation to serve overseas under the Church of Scotland Faith Action Programme or to serve with some other Overseas Mission Agency approved by the Church, to a student at the University of Aberdeen (failing whom to Accepted Candidate(s) for the Ministry of the Church of Scotland whose studies for the Ministry are pursued at Aberdeen University). Applications or recommendations for the Bursary to the Clerk to the Presbytery of the North East and the Northern Isles, Suite 2, Ocean Spirit House West, 31 Waterloo Quay, Aberdeen AB11 5BS.

Martin HARCUS BEQUEST: Makes annual grants to candidates for the ministry resident within the Presbytery of Edinburgh and West Lothian and currently under the jurisdiction of the Presbytery. Applications by 20 October each year to the Principal's Secretary, New College, Mound Place, Edinburgh EH1 2LX (NewCollege@ed.ac.uk).

HOPE TRUST: Gives support to organisations that (1) advance the cause of temperance through the promotion of temperance work and the combatting of all forms of substance abuse and (2) promote Reformed theology and Reformed church life especially in Scotland and the social mission of charities with historical or contemporary links to the Reformed tradition, and includes a scholarship programme for ministers undertaking post-graduate study, the appointment of a part-time post-doctoral fellowship and support for students in full time training. Apply to the Secretary, Lyn Sutherland, Glenorchy House, 20 Union Street, Edinburgh, EH1 3LR (Tel: 0131 226 5151; Fax: 0131 556 5354 or e-mail: hopetrust@drummondmiller.co.uk). Application forms can be found online at www.thehopetrust.net.

KEAY THOM TRUST: The purposes of the Trust are:

1. To benefit impoverished widows, widowers, surviving civil partners or relatives of deceased ministers, or of spouses or civil partners who have been deserted by ministers or have grounds for divorce or separation, who have been wholly dependent upon and assisted the minister in the fulfilment of his or her duties and who, by reason of death, divorce or separation, have been required to leave the manse. The Trust can assist in the purchase of a house or by providing financial or material assistance.
2. To assist financially in the education or training of the above relatives or children of deceased ministers.

Further information and application forms are available from Lindsays, Solicitors, 10 Blackfriars Street, Perth PH1 5NS (01738 637311; JohnThom@lindsays.co.uk).

LADIES' GAELIC SCHOOLS AND HIGHLAND BURSARY ASSOCIATION: Distributes small grants to students, preferably with a Highland/Gaelic background, who are training to be ministers in the Church of Scotland. Apply by 15 October in each year to the Secretary, Mrs Marion McGill, 61 Ladysmith Road, Edinburgh EH9 3EY (0131 667 4243; marionmcgill61@gmail.com).

LYALL BEQUEST: Offers grants to ministers:

1. Grants to individual ministers, couples and families, for a holiday where the purpose is recuperation or relaxation for a minimum of seven nights. No reapplication within a three-year period; and thereafter a 50 per cent grant to those reapplying.
2. Grants towards sickness and convalescence costs so far as not covered by the National Health Service.

Applications should be made to the Secretary and Clerk, The Church of Scotland Trust, 121 George Street, Edinburgh EH2 4YN (0131 376 1307; msproule@churchofscotland.org.uk).

Gillian MACLAINE BURSARY FUND: Open to candidates for the ministry of the Church of Scotland of Scottish or Canadian nationality. Preference is given to Gaelic-speakers. Application forms available from Rev Dr Roderick A.R. MacLeod, Presbytery Clerk, Clèir Eilean Ì: Highlands and Hebrides, 7 Goathill Crescent, Stornoway, Isle of Lewis HS1 2TA (07841 654281, CleirEileanI@churchofscotland.org.uk). Closing date for receipt of applications is 31 October.

Alexander J. MacLEOD GAELIC FUND: This historic bequeathed fund is able to support Ministers who wish to study Gaelic for preaching purposes or to enable Gaelic learning projects within a parish. Church of Scotland Ministers of full-time word and sacrament can apply for funding. The fund is administered by Faith Action Programme. Applications must be received by the end of the first week in January to be considered for the annual allocation of grants. Decisions will be made in late January and grants will be paid upon the submission of receipts. A 300 word report on the impact of the work should be submitted along with receipts. Contact via ascend@churchofscotland.org.uk

E. McLAREN FUND: The persons intended to be benefited are widows and unmarried ladies, preference being given to ladies above 40 years of age in the following order:
(a) Widows and daughters of Officers in the Highland Regiment, and
(b) Widows and daughters of Scotsmen.
Further details from the Secretary, The E. McLaren Fund, Messrs Wright, Johnston & Mackenzie LLP, Solicitors, St Vincent Plaza, 319 St Vincent Street, Glasgow G2 5RZ (Tel: 0141 248 3434; Fax: 0141 221 1226; rmd@wjm.co.uk).

MEIKLE AND PATON TRUST: Grants are available to Ministers and Missionaries for rest and recuperation at the following hotels: Crieff Hydro; Murraypark Hotel, Crieff; Peebles Hydro; Park Hotel, Peebles; Ballachulish Hotel and Isle of Glencoe Hotel. Grants are in addition to any regular discount offered by the hotels, but not seasonal offers; and give a subsidy for overnight residence, such subsidy being decreed by the Trustees at any given time, subject to a limit of seven nights in any one calendar year. Booking should be made online, by the minister (not the spouse) via the respective hotel's website, quoting the promotion code MEIKLEBB and should be made no more than six months in advance in order to obtain Meikle Paton benefit. Chairman: Rev. Iain F. Paton (iain.f.paton@btinternet.com).

MORGAN BURSARY FUND: Makes grants to candidates for the Church of Scotland ministry studying at the University of Glasgow. Apply to the Clerk to the Presbytery of Glasgow, 260 Bath Street, Glasgow G2 4JP (0141 332 6606; glasgow@churchofscotland.org.uk). Closing date October 31.

NEW MINISTERS' FURNISHING LOAN FUND: Makes loans (of £1,000) to ministers in their first charge to assist with furnishing the manse. Apply to ministriesfinance@churchofscotland.org.uk. Enquiries to Faith Action Finance Team, 121 George Street, Edinburgh EH2 4YN (0131 225 5722).

NOVUM TRUST: Provides small short-term grants – typically between £300 and £2,500 – to initiate projects in Christian action and research which cannot readily be financed from other sources. Trustees welcome applications from projects that are essentially Scottish, are distinctively new, and are focused on the welfare of young people, on the training of lay people or on new ways of communicating the Christian faith. The Trust cannot support large building projects, staff salaries or individuals applying for maintenance during courses or training. Application forms and guidance notes from contact@novumtrust.org.uk or Mrs Susan Masterton, Blair Cadell LLP, The Bond House, 5 Breadalbane Street, Edinburgh EH6 5JH (0131 555 5800; www.novumtrust.org.uk).

PARK MEMORIAL BURSARY FUND: Provides grants for the benefit of candidates for the ministry of the Church of Scotland from the Presbytery of Glasgow under full-time training. Apply to the Clerk to the Presbytery of Glasgow, 260 Bath Street, Glasgow G2 4JP (0141 332 6606; glasgow@churchofscotland.org.uk). Closing date November 15.

PRESBYTERY OF ARGYLL BURSARY FUND: Open to students who have been accepted as candidates for the ministry and the readership of the Church of Scotland. Preference is given to applicants who are natives of the bounds of the Presbytery, or are resident within the bounds of the Presbytery, or who have a strong connection with the bounds of the Presbytery. Application forms available from Rev Dr Roderick A.R. MacLeod, Presbytery Clerk, Clèir Eilean Ì: Highlands and Hebrides, 7 Goathill Crescent, Stornoway, Isle of Lewis HS1 2TA (07841 654281, CleirEileanI@churchofscotland.org.uk). Closing date for receipt of applications is 31 October.

Margaret and John ROSS TRAVELLING FUND: Offers grants to ministers and their spouses for travelling and other expenses for trips to the Holy Land where the purpose is recuperation or relaxation. Applications should be made to the Secretary and Clerk, The Church of Scotland Trust, 121 George Street, Edinburgh EH2 4YN (0131 376 1307; msproule@churchofscotland.org.uk).

SCOTLAND'S CHURCHES TRUST: Strives to preserve, promote and protect Scotland's rich ecclesiastical built heritage. In addition to providing an advocacy and advice service for the owners and users of Scotland's religious built heritage, the Trust focusses much of its efforts on improving the long-term sustainability of Scotland's places of worship. It is currently involved in a collaboration with Historic Environment Scotland in the recording of church buildings facing closure, and continues to develop new and existing initiatives that strengthen the ties between the country's ecclesiastical built heritage, the communities that surround these buildings and the wider tourist economy. Scotland's Churches Trust, 15 North Bank Street, Edinburgh EH1 2LP (office@scotlandschurchestrust.org.uk; www.scotlandschurchestrust.org.uk).

SMIETON FUND: To assist ministers who would benefit from a holiday because of a recent pastoral need. Contact pastoralsupport@churchofscotland.org.uk for an application form. Enquiries to Alison Stewart, Senior Administrator, Faith Action Ministries Support Team, 121 George Street, Edinburgh EH2 4YN (0131 376 3685).

Mary Davidson SMITH CLERICAL AND EDUCATIONAL FUND FOR ABERDEENSHIRE: Assists ministers who have been ordained for five years or over and are in full charge of a congregation in Aberdeen, Aberdeenshire and the north, to purchase books, or to travel for educational purposes, and assists their children with scholarships for further education or vocational training. Apply to Messrs Peterkins, 100 Union Street, Aberdeen AB10 1QR (01224 428000; maildesk@peterkins.com).

SOCIETY FOR THE BENEFIT OF THE SONS AND DAUGHTERS OF THE CLERGY OF THE CHURCH OF SCOTLAND: Annual grants are made to assist in the education of the children (normally between the ages of 12 and 25 years) of ministers of the Church of Scotland. The Society also gives grants to aged and infirm daughters of ministers and ministers' unmarried daughters and sisters who are in need. Applications are to be lodged by 31 May in each year with Kirsty Ashworth, Charity Administration Service, Exchange Place 3, Semple Street, Edinburgh EH3 8BL (0131 473 3500; SM-Charity@azets.co.uk).

SOCIETY IN SCOTLAND FOR PROPAGATING CHRISTIAN KNOWLEDGE: The SSPCK gives grants to: 1. Resourcing mission within Scotland; 2. The training and education of Christians in Commonwealth countries overseas, aimed to equip them for service in the mission and outreach of the Church; 3.The training of British young people volunteering for periods of service in Christian mission and education overseas; 4. The resourcing of new initiatives in worldwide Christian mission. Chairman: Rev. Michael W. Frew; Secretary: Rev. Ian W. Alexander, SSPCK, c/o 121 George Street, Edinburgh EH2 4YN (SSPCK@churchofscotland.org.uk).

Nan STEVENSON CHARITABLE TRUST FOR RETIRED MINISTERS: Provides loans and grants at or after retirement to ministers and others in a recognised ministry for the purchase, maintenance, repair or alteration of a property, primarily for those with a North Ayrshire connection. Secretary and Treasurer: Mrs Christine Thomas, 18 Brisbane Street, Largs KA30 8QN (01475 338564; 07891 838778; cathomas54@gmail.com).

SYNOD OF GRAMPIAN CHILDREN OF THE CLERGY FUND: Makes annual grants to children of deceased ministers. Apply to Rev. G. Euan D. Glen, Secretary and Treasurer, The Manse, 26 St Ninians, Monymusk, Inverurie AB51 7HF (01467 651470; GGlen@churchofscotland.org.uk).

SYNOD OF GRAMPIAN WIDOWS' FUND: Makes annual grants (currently £450 p.a.) to widows or widowers of deceased ministers who have served in a charge in the former Synod. Apply to Rev. G. Euan D. Glen, Secretary and Treasurer, The Manse, 26 St Ninians, Monymusk, Inverurie AB51 7HF (01467 651470; GGlen@churchofscotland.org.uk).

TOD ENDOWMENT TRUST; CINTRA BEQUEST; TOD ENDOWMENT SCOTLAND HOLIDAY FUND: The Trustees of the Cintra Bequest and of the Tod Endowment Scotland Holiday Fund can consider an application for a grant from the Tod Endowment funds from any ordained or commissioned minister or deacon in Scotland of at least two years' standing before the date of application, to assist with the cost of the beneficiary and his or her spouse or partner and dependants obtaining rest and recuperation in Scotland. The Trustees of the Tod Endowment Scotland Holiday Fund can also consider an application from an ordained or commissioned minister or deacon who has retired. Application forms are available from Madelaine Sproule, Law Department at msproule@churchofscotland.org.uk (for the Cintra Bequest), and from Alison Stewart, Senior Administrator, Faith Action Ministries Support Team at pastoralsupport@churchofscotland.org.uk (for the Tod Endowment Scotland Holiday Fund). The address in both cases is 121 George Street, Edinburgh EH2 4YN (0131 225 5722).

Stephen WILLIAMSON & ALEX BALFOUR FUND: Offers grants to Ministers in Scotland, with first priority being given to Ministers in the boundaries of the former Presbyteries of Angus and Dundee, followed by the Presbytery of Fife, to assist with the cost of educational school/ college/university trips for sons and daughters of the Manse who are under 25 years and in full time education. Application for trips in any year will be considered by the Trustees in the January of that year, when the income of the previous financial year will be awarded in grants. The applications for trips in that calendar year must be submitted by 31 December of the preceding year. For applications from outwith the 3 priority Presbyteries the total cost of the trip must be in excess of £500, with the maximum grant which can be awarded being £200. The trustees will always give priority to new applicants. If funds still remain for distribution after the allocation of grants in January further applications for that year will be considered. Applications from the Presbyteries of Angus, Dundee and Fife will be considered at any time of year as the Trustees have retained income for these grants. Applications should be made to the Secretary and Clerk, The Church of Scotland Trust, 121 George Street, Edinburgh EH2 4YN (0131 376 1307; msproule@churchofscotland.org.uk).

10. LONG SERVICE CERTIFICATES

Long Service Certificates, signed by the Moderator, are available for presentation to elders and voluntary office bearers in respect of not less than thirty years of service. At the General Assembly of 2015, it was agreed that further certificates could be issued at intervals of ten years thereafter. It should be noted that the period is years of *service*, not (for example) years of ordination in the case of an elder. In the case of those volunteers engaged in children's and youth work, the qualifying period is twenty-one years of service. Certificates are not issued posthumously, nor is it possible to make exceptions to the rules, for example by recognising quality of service in order to reduce the qualifying period, or by reducing the qualifying period on compassionate grounds, such as serious illness. Applications for Long Service Certificates should be made in writing to the Principal Clerk at 121 George Street, Edinburgh EH2 4YN by the parish minister, or by the session clerk on behalf of the Kirk Session. Certificates are not issued from this office to the individual recipients, nor should individuals make application themselves. If a note of the award of the Certificate is to be inserted in *Life and Work* contact should be made with that publication direct.

---

11. RECORDS OF THE CHURCH OF SCOTLAND

Church records more than fifty years old, unless still in use, should be sent or delivered to the Principal Clerk for onward transmission to the National Records of Scotland. Where ministers or session clerks are approached by a local repository seeking a transfer of their records, they should inform the Principal Clerk, who will take the matter up with the National Records of Scotland.

---

12. FASTI ECCLESIAE SCOTICANAE

The *Fasti Ecclesiae Scoticanae* ('The Register of Officials of the Church of Scotland') is an ongoing series of volumes which documents the succession of the ordained ministry in the Church of Scotland. The initial volumes, published in the second half of the nineteenth century, offered a comprehensive account of the ministers of the church throughout the previous three hundred years. Since then there have been several updates, and the whole series now presents a complete record from the Reformation in the mid-sixteenth century to the present day of those who have served in parishes, as chaplains, as missionaries, and in academic, administrative and other appointments, including auxiliary and ordained local ministers. Since the bulk of the work is arranged by parishes, the *Fasti* also forms the only permanent record of unions, linkages and other forms of parish readjustment within the church.

The latest volume, volume XII, edited by Roy M. Pinkerton, covering the period from 1 October 1999 to 30 September 2020, was published in June 2021, and gives information about those who served as ordained ministers during the previous twenty years. The cost of this volume is £30 plus p&p: to obtain a copy, please e-mail fasti@churchofscotland.org.uk confirming that you wish to purchase a copy and giving your full postal address. The book will then be despatched to you together with instructions about payment.

SECTION 3

Church Procedure

Besides the items in this section, there is a wide range of material on the church website at:

Acts of Assembly
www.churchofscotland.org.uk/about-us/church-law/acts

Regulations
www.churchofscotland.org.uk/about-us/church-law/regulations

Law Department circulars
www.churchofscotland.org.uk/resources/law-circulars

General Trustees resources
www.churchofscotland.org.uk/resources/building-and-property-resources

and information on many aspects of ministry and mission at:
www.churchofscotland.org.uk/resources

A. THE MINISTER AND BAPTISM

See www.churchofscotland.org.uk > Resources > Yearbook > Section 3A

B. THE MINISTER AND MARRIAGE

See www.churchofscotland.org.uk > Resources > Yearbook > Section 3B

C. MARRIAGE SERVICES: CODE OF GOOD PRACTICE

See www.churchofscotland.org.uk > Resources > Yearbook > Section 3C

D. MARRIAGE AND CIVIL PARTNERSHIP (SCOTLAND) ACT 2014

See www.churchofscotland.org.uk > About us > Our views > Same-sex-marriage; and www.churchofscotland.org.uk > About us > Church law > Acts of the General Assembly > 2022 Act 6: Solemnisation of Same Sex Marriages Act

The Legal Questions Committee prepared a guidance document, available from Presbytery Clerks.

E. FUNERAL SERVICES: FEES

The Report of the Legal Questions Committee to the 2007 General Assembly included a statement regarding fees for funerals. That statement was engrossed in the Minutes of the General Assembly, and it was felt helpful to include it also in the Year Book.

The statement

The Committee believes that the question is two-fold, relating firstly to parish ministers (including associate and assistant ministers, deacons and the like) within their regular ministry, and secondly to ministers and others taking an occasional funeral, for instance by private invitation or in the course of pastoral cover of another parish.

Ministers in receipt of a living

The Committee believes that the position of the minister of a parish, and of other paid staff on the ministry team of a parish, is clear. The Third Declaratory Article affirms the responsibility of the Church of Scotland to provide the ordinances of religion through its territorial ministry, while the stipend system (and, for other staff members, the salary) provides a living that enables that ministry to be exercised without charging fees for services conducted. The implication of this principle is that no family in Scotland should ever be charged for the services of a Church of Scotland minister at the time of bereavement. Clearly, therefore, no minister in receipt of a living should be charging separately (effectively being paid doubly) for any such service. The Committee is conscious that the position of congregations outside Scotland may be different, and is aware that the relevant Presbyteries will offer appropriate superintendence of these matters.

A related question is raised about the highly varied culture of gift-giving in different parts of the country. The Committee believes it would be unwise to seek to regulate this. In some places, an attempt to quash a universal and long-established practice would seem ungracious, while in other places there is no such practice, and encouragement in that direction would seem indelicate.

A second related question was raised about Funeral Directors charging for the services of the minister. The Committee believes that Presbyteries should make it clear to Funeral Directors that, in the case of Church of Scotland funerals, such a charge should not be made.

Ministers conducting occasional services

Turning to the position of ministers who do not receive a living that enables them to conduct funerals without charge, the Committee's starting point is the principle articulated above that no bereaved person should have to pay for the services of a minister. The territorial ministry and the parish system of this Church mean that a bereaved family should not find itself being contingently charged because the parish minister happens to be unavailable, or because the parish is vacant.

Where a funeral is being conducted as part of the ministry of the local parish, but where for any reason another minister is taking it and not otherwise being paid, it is the responsibility of the congregation (through its financial body) to ensure that appropriate fees and expenses are met. Where that imposes a financial burden upon a congregation because of the weight of pastoral need, the need should be taken into account in calculating the resource-needs of that parish in the course of updating the Presbytery Plan.

It is beyond the remit of the Committee to make judgements about the appropriate level of payment. The Committee suggests that the [now] Faith Action Programme should give the relevant advice on this aspect of the issue.

The Committee believes that these principles could be applied to the conduct of weddings and are perfectly compatible with the Guidelines on that subject [in Section 3C of the Year Book].

In its Report to the General Assembly of 2024 the Faith Action Programme Leadership Team reiterated that:

> Where a congregation calls upon the services of a minister not already in receipt of a stipend, or other suitably qualified person, to conduct a funeral, a fee of £100 [set at GA 2023] may be paid by the congregation. On no account should such a fee be charged to the family of the deceased. For the avoidance of doubt, no fee may be offered to or received by a serving Parish Minister for the conduct of a funeral service, whether in their own or another parish.

F. PULPIT SUPPLY FEES AND EXPENSES

The Pulpit Supply Regulations (Regulations 6, 2008, as amended) are set out below, with the fee levels as approved by the 2023 and 2024 General Assemblies inserted.

1. In Charges where there is only one diet of worship, the Pulpit Supply Fee shall be a Standard Fee of £100 (or as from time to time agreed by the Faith Action Programme).

2. In Charges where there are additional diets of worship on a Sunday, the person fulfilling the Supply shall be paid £50 for each additional Service (or as from time to time agreed by the Faith Action Programme). (Where two ministers are involved, they each receive half the total fee).

3. Where the person is unwilling to conduct more than one diet of worship on a given Sunday, he or she shall receive a pro-rata payment based on the total available Fee shared on the basis of the number of Services conducted.

4. The Fee thus calculated shall be payable in the case of all persons permitted to conduct Services under section 7(1) to (9) of Act 2, 2018.

5. In all cases, Travelling Expenses shall be paid. Where there is no convenient public conveyance, the use of a private car shall be paid for at the rate of 45p per mile for Travelling Expenses. In exceptional circumstances, to be approved in advance, the cost of hiring a car may be met.

6. Where weekend board and lodging are agreed as necessary, these may be claimed for the weekend at a maximum rate of that allowed when attending the General Assembly, currently £100 per night. The Fee and Expenses should be paid to the person providing the Supply before he or she leaves on the Sunday.

G. VACANCY PROCEDURE

See www.churchofscotland.org.uk > Resources > Ministries handbooks, forms and guidance notes:
Vacancy Guidelines for Kirk Sessions and Interim Moderators (also covers appointing locums)
Guidelines for Nominating Committees
Guidelines for Advisory Committees
Guidance Notes on compiling Parish Profiles

SECTION 4

General Assembly 2024

The General Assembly of 2024 was held from 18–23 May with the majority of commissioners in the Assembly Hall, and some participating online via Zoom.

OFFICE-BEARERS OF THE GENERAL ASSEMBLY

The Lord High Commissioner:	HRH Prince Edward, Duke of Edinburgh
Moderator:	Rev. Dr Shaw J. Paterson
Chaplains to the Moderator:	Rev. Robert S. T. Allan
	Rev. Robert A. Hamilton
Principal Clerk:	Rev. Fiona E. Smith
Depute Clerk:	Ms Christine Paterson
Procurator:	Mr P. Jonathan Brodie KC
Law Agent:	Miss Mary Macleod
Convener, Procedure Committee:	Rev. Michael J. Mair
Vice-Convener, Procedure Committee:	Rev. Sheila M. Kirk
Precentor:	Rev. Colin C. Renwick
Chief Steward:	Mr Alexander F. Gemmill
Depute Steward:	Mr Simon Bolam
Assembly Officer:	Mr William Mearns
Depute Assembly Officer:	Mrs Karen W.F. McKay

THE MODERATOR

The Right Reverend Shaw J. Paterson BSc BD MSc DPT

Shaw is a Lanarkshire lad, brought up close to the building trade, and no doubt would have made a mark in that line of business had God not called him away to the ordained ministry. He is married to Christine, a rock by his side, and they have three lovely children, Euan, Ross, and Kirstie, all of whom are now making their own way in life and pursuing good careers.

Shaw is a family man and he knows the importance of family and friends to every person, hence his great pastoral nature in ministering alongside many in his community and beyond with great sensitivity and compassion through the tough times, and with great humour in the midst of the joyful times. Since his ordination in 1991, he has ministered in Strathaven all his ministerial life, well known and well loved within the village and wider area. His links with the building trade, which stem from his father, are quite apt, for Shaw has sought to build God's Kingdom amongst his people in Strathaven, and amongst his people throughout the Church of Scotland through his service within Presbytery as a former Clerk and through his work on national committees, notably the Board of Ministry. He has a heart for ministry and ministers, and he longs to see our national Church grow again, hence his strapline for the year, "Building Together". Shaw is a great builder.

Shaw has had many a student work alongside him who has benefitted from his wisdom and care as they set out on their own ministry journeys. He himself was very proud to have been a probationer minister under the guidance of the late Very Rev. Dr Hugh Wyllie at Hamilton Old Parish Church, which gave him a great grounding for his own future ministry. Shaw, as the prophet Micah would say, seeks to do justice, to love kindness, and to walk humbly with his Lord. His humility screens his exceptional mind which has gained a doctorate, remaining modest to the end for he did not study to gain more letters after his name but in order to help and support others.

Does he have any faults? Of course, we all do. He's exceptionally cheeky, especially to his friends. He works way too many hours, often way into the early hours – we know because we can see the time he sent the emails! And he laughs at all his own jokes – someone has to! But Shaw has a large heart, full of love for God and his Church, as well as his family and friends, and this is evident in all he does.

Shaw would describe himself as "just a parish minister". Is there such a thing? He has applied himself well to the many traditional tasks of ministry and has adapted well to the changing scenario that faces the Kirk. The ordained ministry is still the frontline where disciples are made, worship conducted, mission performed, and relationships cemented. Shaw is a man with his head in the clouds, with his feet firmly on the ground.

We are proud to call Shaw our friend and we know that he will become a friend to many through his year as Moderator.

Robert Allan and Robert Hamilton
Moderator's Chaplains

REPORT FROM THE GENERAL ASSEMBLY 2024

The Convener of the Faith Action Programme Leadership Team (FAPLT), the Rev Tommy MacNeil, told the Assembly that the Church needs 'a fresh vision'. The Church continues to do 'truly remarkable work' but it was 'in the midst of a deeply challenging and uncertain moment' as it struggles with shortages of money and ministers, and falling membership. "In our hurt and pain, we need to know Christ as our healer and restorer if we are to have any hope of having a different future."

The Assembly Trustees warned that, on current trends, the Church's available reserves will be exhausted by 2032. The Rev Scott Rennie urged the Trustees to bring proposals to next year's Assembly so that the Church is breaking even financially within four years, so the Unincorporated Entities (the national charity which includes the church's central services, Faith Action programme and CrossReach) have a balanced budget by the end of 2027.

Much discussion focused on the fact that 71% of charges in the Church do not contribute enough to cover their ministry costs, and are supported by the other 29%. Convener of the Assembly Trustees, the Rev David Cameron, said that the majority of the reforms instructed from 2019 had now been delivered, with new presbyteries in place and initial savings targets met at the National Office but 'we have a way to go, because the hard truth is that limited resources are becoming ever scarcer'.

The Rev Christopher Rowe, minister in a Priority Areas parish in Milton, Glasgow, feared that a review of Priority Areas (the church's mission to the most deprived 5% of areas in Scotland) was a euphemism for cuts, and called for people experiencing poverty 'to be at the root of any consultations taking place'. "Priority to the poorest feels as though it is part of our denominational DNA," he said. "I want to thank the 29% who support the 71%, because that includes the bottom 5%." However, there were also calls for the 29% who do pay for their ministries to be protected. The Very Rev Prof David Fergusson said: "Support for the poorest and most remote congregations is necessary and desirable, but it was never envisaged that this number would include 71% of our charges. The 29% are crucial to our future."

The Assembly passed an Overture from the Presbytery of Lothian and Borders which will reduce the national church's influence over presbytery mission plans. The rules agreed in recent years had stated that the review and development of mission plans must be approved annually by FAPLT and the General Trustees. Under the Overture, those bodies must be consulted but approval will only be needed every five years. Another Overture from the Presbytery of Glasgow, asking for churches to be given permission to call ministers even while the Presbytery was over its allocation (due to ministers in unrestricted tenure being reluctant to move), was defeated.

The Assembly passed an amendment to the rules of the Seeds for Growth fund to allow it to be accessed for work in existing congregations, as well as new worshipping communities.

There were calls for the reform of the General Assembly after it was revealed that the estimated cost of this year's gathering is over £800,000 (including staff costs and Commissioners' expenses). The Rev Dr Alan Hamilton said that it could be done 'twice as effectively at half the cost'. The convener of the Assembly Business Committee, the Rev Michael Mair, pledged that budgets would be looked at as part of conversations about the future of the Assembly.

There were comments on behalf of the newly-qualified ministers who have been serving as assistant ministers under special arrangements while churches have not been allowed to call during the presbytery mission planning process. Those arrangements are expected to end in 2025. The Rev Douglas Reid, said: "There is a great deal of anger within the cohort... who feel they may have to look at options for employment outside the Church of Scotland." The Rev

Angus Mathieson, Presbytery and Partnership Manager, said that with nearly all the mission plans now approved, there would be enough vacancies over the next few years to match the supply of candidates, including the assistant ministers.

Significant changes to the education of ministers were agreed which will allow new ministers to qualify through an Apprenticeship Route. The Rev Tommy MacNeil said the proposals provide more routes for people into the ministry and speed up the process from first discernment to ordination. Initial proposals had encountered resistance among the Church's academic providers, but were changed following discussions. The Rev Professor Alison Jack said that the University of Edinburgh was 'deeply committed' to working with the church to meet its needs.

As the Assembly discussed the situation in Gaza, a young Palestinian Christian, Joanne Billeh, who lives in Jordan, said her family had been forced to leave Palestine in the 1948 war: "The chances of me going to see the land that I spent my whole childhood hearing about are slim, which obviously breaks my heart." The Assembly passed the sections of the FAPLT Deliverance calling for prayers for peace in Gaza, to share the voices of Palestinian Christians and for the UK Government to recognise the State of Palestine alongside the State of Israel. It added a call on the UK Government to call for an immediate and permanent ceasefire in Gaza, and to stop granting export licences for weapons to Israel.

The Assembly Trustees are to explore how the Church conducts its external affairs work, and to consider proposals for a new committee to have responsibility for the Church's work on social justice, ecumenical and interfaith relations, and work with international partners. The Rev Peter Johnston, who moved the motion, argued: "FAPLT's remit is too big to be able to manage this vitally important work effectively."

Members of the Church were urged to lobby their MSPs about the crisis in social care. Debating the report of the Social Care Council (CrossReach), the Assembly agreed to 'express alarm about the cuts to vital care services being experienced by CrossReach and other care providers… and ask CrossReach, working with FAPLT, to raise awareness about the crisis in social care with Presbyteries and congregations and to make representations to the Scottish Parliament and Scottish Government'. Convener, the Rev Thom Riddell, said: 'If we don't do something about (social care) the whole system is going to collapse'. The Assembly also approved calls for further work on fair pay in social care. Average pay in the sector is considerably lower than equivalent NHS positions, making recruitment and retention of staff harder for organisations like CrossReach.

The Assembly approved, and speakers mostly welcomed, the Theological Forum's report on Transgender People in the Church of Scotland. The convener, the Rev Dr Liam Fraser, said: "Despite a wide range of theological and political views on the Forum, we are unanimous that… transgender people should be loved, and respected, and welcomed in our congregations. It is the foundation of Christian ethics that all people are made in the image of God, and are worthy of our respect and love, and this is true of transgender people also… Based on our exploration of gender in the Bible… transgender people should not only be welcomed into our church, but allowed to serve in our Church... Our report offers the Church a route through a debate that has, at times, become toxic, and allows us to model a better way of engaging with issues of gender." FAPLT accepted an instruction to consider the implications of the Cass Review into gender identity services for under 18s.

During discussion on the interim Joint Report of the Theological Forum and FAPLT on Assisted Dying, the Assembly heard moving testimony from Susan Pym, who saw her sister die from a rare neurological condition. Mrs Pym said that her sister had asked three times for help to end her life, but that she couldn't do it. "In her final hours I considered what I might do (to ease her suffering)... I couldn't do it. The final words I barely heard her whisper were 'please help me' but I couldn't do it." "If you have walked in my shoes I know you will support my plea for the Church to (support assisted dying). If you haven't walked in my shoes I pray you never will."

The shortage of Church of Scotland ministers serving as military chaplains was 'now a big issue'. The convener of the committee on Chaplains to HM Forces, the Rev Scott Brown, said: "The Church of Scotland could more or less disappear from the chaplaincies of the three Services. That would, in our view, be a disaster." The Assembly was also addressed by Air Vice Marshal Tim Jones, Assistant Chief of the Air Staff, who said that chaplains played a 'vital role' in the work of the services: "Let me assure you, friends, that it would simply not be possible to navigate Service life without the ability to talk, to confide, to reflect, to laugh, to cry, or to remember. And that's what our Service chaplains help us to do."

The Duke of Edinburgh, Prince Edward, this year's Lord High Commissioner, thanked the people of Scotland and the chaplains of the Chapel Royal for their support following the death of the late Queen Elizabeth II. He said: "The outpouring of emotions, the demonstrations of respect, love and grief was overwhelming, and a privilege to experience and behold. I think I can speak for my whole family when I say we will remain forever grateful for that support."

Mrs Rae Lind, national convener of the Church of Scotland Guild, revealed that over £425,000 has been raised for the Guild's partner projects over the past three years, despite losing a year to Covid-19 disruption. The Assembly was played a video by the steering group of the Young Adults Guild, rebranded Love in Fellowship and Trust (LIFT), but still working in partnership with the Guild.

The General Trustees accepted motions to give urgent consideration to artworks and to pipe organs in churches scheduled for closure, and to work with congregations where redundant buildings may be bought by local communities.

The Assembly passed a motion from the Rev Lynn Brady inviting the Safeguarding committee to 'consider its processes as relate to people who have been found not guilty in criminal proceedings but who are subject to Safeguarding procedures'. The Assembly passed a new 'support for survivors of historic abuse' policy. Safeguarding convener the Rev Adam Dillon said: "This marks the culmination of many years of work in drawing together a policy for survivors of non recent abuse, and… our commitment to ensure that survivors' voices are heard, and that we can start to become a trauma informed organisation so that no one will ever be met with indifference or silence, again."

Invited to speak on the final morning of the Assembly, the Archbishop of Canterbury celebrated the growing friendship between the Churches of Scotland and England. The Most Rev Justin Welby said that the two national churches 'must be the mortar that holds together the diverse stones that so beautifully make up the United Kingdom'.

The Assembly closed with the Moderator, the Rt Rev Dr Shaw Paterson, encouraging the Church to 'keep moving forward'. It had been 'a wonderful experience' being Moderator, and he told the Commissioners not to become despondent as they returned to their parishes. "We don't know where God's spirit will lead us. But let's step out in faith, following the example and commandment of our saviour Jesus Christ."

This is a summary of a report of proceedings which appeared in the July 2024 issue of Life and Work and online at www.lifeandwork.org

SECTION 5

Presbytery Lists

(1) Edinburgh and West Lothian
(2) Lothian and Borders
(3) South West
(4) Clyde
(5) Glasgow
(6) Forth Valley and Clydesdale
(7) Fife
(8) Perth
(9) North East and Northern Isles
(10) Clèir Eilean Ì: Highlands and Hebrides
(11) Lewis
(12) England and Channel Islands
(13) International Charges
(14) Jerusalem

In each Presbytery list, the parishes/congregations ('charges') are listed in alphabetical order. In a linked charge, the names appear under the first-named. Under the name of the charge will be found the name of the minister and, where applicable, that of an associate or assistant minister, ordained local minister, auxiliary minister and member of the Diaconate. The years indicated after a name in the congregational section of each Presbytery list are the year of ordination (column 1) and the year of current appointment (column 2). Where only one year is given, it is both the year of ordination and the year of appointment. Where no other name is listed, the name of the session clerk(s) or interim moderator is given.

The subsequent parts of each Presbytery list comprise:

B. ministers and deacons, members of Presbytery, in other appointments;

C. minsters and deacons, members of Presbytery, registered under the Registration of Ministries Act (Act 2, 2017, as amended) mainly as Category R (Retaining) and authorised to perform the functions of ministry outwith an appointment covered by Category O (a charge) or Category E (an employed appointment), though some of those listed who have ceased to hold an appointment may have chosen to retain Category O registration for a period of up to 3 years;

D. ministers and deacons, not members of Presbytery, in other appointments;

E. ministers and deacons, not members of Presbytery, registered as 'Retaining';

F. ministers and deacons, not members of presbytery, registered as 'Inactive'. Only those who have given consent under the (civil) General Data Protection Regulation to publication of their details are included;

G. Readers in active service; and

H. Ministries Development Staff.

In parts **B. to F.** the first year is the year of ordination, and the second is the year of appointment or retirement. If the person is retired, then the appointment last held is shown in brackets.

Addresses for the churches in places with multiple parishes are given after part H. Some parishes, mainly in rural areas, have more than one church – see Section 8. For a map of a particular parish boundary go to: www.churchofscotland.org.uk > Find your local church > insert name of place /parish > Church profile > Parish statistics.

Abbreviations in the list of parishes:

F	A charge with a Facebook page.
GD	A charge where it is desirable that the minister should have a knowledge of Gaelic.
GE	A charge where public worship must be regularly conducted in Gaelic.
H	A hearing aid loop system has been installed.
L	A chair lift or lift has been installed.
T	A charge with an X, formerly Twitter, account.
W	A charge with a website.

(1) EDINBURGH AND WEST LOTHIAN (F W)

Meets at Edinburgh: Palmerston Place on Tuesdays 5 November and 3 December 2024, and in 2025 on 4 February, 1 April, 17 June, 9 September, 4 November and 2 December.

Clerk:	**HAZEL HASTIE MA CQSW PhD AIWS**	**Postal Address: Morningside Parish Church, 2 Cluny Gardens, Edinburgh EH10 6BQ**	**0131 225 9137**
			07827 314374
		edinburghwestlothian@churchofscotland.org.uk	
Depute Clerk:	**REV. DANIEL J.M. CARMICHAEL MA BD**	**DCarmichael@churchofscotland.org.uk**	**07950 726139**
Mission Co-ordinator:	**REV. KENNETH BROWN BD**	**Kenneth.Brown@churchofscotland.org.uk**	**07366 622365**

1	**Abercorn, Pardovan, Kingscavil and Winchburgh (F H W)**				
	Vacant			The Manse, West End, Winchburgh, Broxburn EH52 6TT	01506 890919
	Derek R. Henderson MA DipTCP DipCS (Ordained Local Minister)	2017		45 Priory Road, Linlithgow EH49 6BP DHenderson@churchofscotland.org.uk	01506 844787 07968 491441
	New charge formed by the union of Abercorn and Kingscavil, Pardovan and Winchburgh				
2	**Armadale (F H W) linked with Blackridge (F H)**			**blackridgeparishchurch@outlook.com**	
	Julia C. Wiley (Ms) MA(CE) MDiv	1998	2010	70 Mount Pleasant, Armadale, Bathgate EH48 3HB JWiley@churchofscotland.org.uk	01501 730358
3	**Avonbridge (F H) linked with Torphichen (F H W)**			**admin@torphichenkirk.com**	
	Vacant			Manse Road, Torphichen, Bathgate EH48 4LT	01506 635957
	Interim Moderator: A. Scott Marshall			asm66015@gmail.com	07415 028678
4	**Bathgate (F H W)**			**info@bathgateparish.com**	**01506 650517**
	Vacant			19 Hunter Grove, Bathgate EH48 1NN	
	Interim Moderator: Nelu I. Balaj			NBalaj@churchofscotland .org.uk	01506 411888
	New charge formed by the union of Bathgate: High and Bathgate: St John's				
5	**Bathgate: Boghall (F H W)**				
	Vacant			1 Manse Place, Ash Grove, Bathgate EH48 1NJ	01506 652715
	Interim Moderator: Hanneke I. Janse van Vuren			HJansevanVuren@churchofscotland.org.uk	
6	**Blackridge** See Armadale				

7	**Broxburn (F H W)**				
	Vacant			2 Church Street, Broxburn EH52 5EL	01506 337560
	Interim Moderator: Derek R. Henderson			DHenderson@churchofscotland.org.uk	01506 844787 07968 491441
	Session Clerk: Anne Gunn (Mrs)			anne.gunn42@gmail.com	07833 701274
8	**Edinburgh: Balerno (F H W)**			**bpc-admin@balernochurch.org.uk**	**0131 449 7245**
	Vacant			3 Johnsburn Road, Balerno EH14 7DN	0131 449 3830
	Interim Moderator: Douglas A.O. Nicol			Douglas.Nicol@churchofscotland.org.uk	07811 437075
9	**Edinburgh: Barclay Viewforth (F W)**			**admin@barclaychurch.org.uk**	**0131 229 6810**
	David Clarkson BSc BA MTh	2010	2020	113 Meadowspot, Edinburgh EH10 5UY DClarkson@churchofscotland.org.uk	0131 478 2376
10	**Edinburgh: Blackhall St Columba's (F T W)**			**secretary@blackhallstcolumba.org.uk**	**0131 332 4431**
	Fergus M. Cook BD	2020		5 Blinkbonny Crescent, Edinburgh EH4 3NB FCook@churchofscotland.org.uk	0131 466 7503
11	**Edinburgh: Broughton St Mary's (F H L W)**			**mail@bstmchurch.org.uk**	**0131 556 4252**
	Laurene M. Lafontaine BA MDiv	1987	2021	78 March Road, Edinburgh EH4 3SY LLafontaine@churchofscotland.org.uk	0131 312 7440
12	**Edinburgh: Canongate (F H T W)**			**canongatekirk@btinternet.com**	**0131 556 3515**
	Neil N. Gardner CStJ MA BD DL	1991	2006	The Manse of Canongate, Edinburgh EH8 8BR NGardner@churchofscotland.org.uk	0131 556 3515
13	**Edinburgh: Corstorphine Craigsbank (F H T W)**			**admin@craigsbankchurch.org.uk**	**0131 334 6365**
	Alan Childs BA BD MBA	2000	2019	17 Craigs Bank, Edinburgh EH12 8HD AChilds@churchofscotland.org.uk	0131 466 5196
14	**Edinburgh: Corstorphine Old (F H W)**			**corold@aol.com**	**0131 334 7864**
	Moira McDonald MA BD	1997	2005	23 Manse Road, Edinburgh EH12 7SW MMcDonald@churchofscotland.org.uk	0131 476 5893
	William D. Watt BD MPhil LTCL (Assistant Minister)	2023		WWatt@churchofscotland.org.uk	07950 617560

15	**Edinburgh: Corstorphine St Anne's (F H L T W)**			**office@stannes.corstorphine.org.uk**	**0131 316 4740**
	James J. Griggs BD MTh ALCM PGCE	2011	2013	1/5 Morham Gait, Edinburgh EH10 5GH	0131 447 7063
				JGriggs@churchofscotland.org.uk	
16	**Edinburgh: Corstorphine St Ninian's (F H W)**			**office@st-ninians.co.uk**	**0131 539 6204**
	James D. Aitken BD	2002	2017	17 Templeland Road, Edinburgh EH12 8RZ	0131 334 2978
				JAitken@churchofscotland.org.uk	
17	**Edinburgh: Craiglockhart (F H T W)**			**office@craiglockhartchurch.org**	**0131 455 8229**
	Gordon Kennedy BSc BD MTh	1993	2012	20 Craiglockhart Quadrant, Edinburgh EH14 1HD	0131 444 1615
				GKennedy@churchofscotland.org.uk	
18	**Edinburgh: Craigmillar Park (F H W)**			**cpkirk@btinternet.com**	**0131 667 5862**
	linked with Edinburgh: Reid Memorial (F H W)			**reid_memorial@outlook.com**	**0131 662 1203**
	Alexander T. McAspurren BD MTh	2002	2019	14 Hallhead Road, Edinburgh EH16 5QJ	0131 667 1623
	CPS CertSMM			AMcAspurren@churchofscotland.org.uk	
19	**Edinburgh: Currie (F H W)**			**currie_kirk@btconnect.com**	**0131 451 5141**
	Vacant				
	Interim Moderator: Anne T. Logan			annetlogan@sky.com	0131 663 9550
20	**Edinburgh: Dalmeny and Queensferry (F H W)**			**office@qpcweb.org**	**0131 331 1100**
	Vacant			12 Whinny Row, South Queensferry EH30 9EG	
	Derek B. Munn	2022		DMunn@churchofscotland.org.uk	07592 953261
	(Ordained Local Minister)				
	Interim Moderator: Fiona M. Mathieson			FMathieson@churchofscotland.org.uk	0131 334 9774
21	**Edinburgh: Davidson's Mains (F H W)**			**life@dmainschurch.plus.com**	**0131 312 6282**
	Daniel Robertson BA BD	2009	2016	1 Hillpark Terrace, Edinburgh EH4 7SX	0131 336 3078
				Daniel.Robertson@churchofscotland.org.uk	07909 840654
22	**Edinburgh: Drylaw (F W)**			**drylawparishchurch@btinternet.com**	**0131 332 6863**
	Vacant				
	Interim Moderator: Elisabeth G.B. Spence			revspence121@gmail.com	07772 548121
23	**Edinburgh: Duddingston (F H W)**			**dodinskirk@aol.com**	**0131 661 4240**
	James A.P. Jack	1989	2001	Manse of Duddingston, Old Church Lane, Edinburgh EH15 3PX	0131 661 4240
	BSc BArch BD DMin RIBA ARIAS			JJack@churchofscotland.org.uk	

24	**Edinburgh: Fairmilehead (F H W)**			**office@fhpc.org.uk**	**0131 445 2374**
	Cheryl S. McKellar-Young (Mrs) BA BD MSc PGCertHC	2013	2018	14 Margaret Rose Drive, Edinburgh EH10 7ER CMcKellarYoung@churchofscotland.org.uk	07590 230121
25	**Edinburgh: Gorgie and Palmerston Place (F H T W)**			**contactus@gdschurch.org.uk**	**0131 337 7936**
	Vacant			**admin@palmerstonplacechurch.com** 90 Myreside Road, Edinburgh EH10 5BZ	**0131 220 1690** 0131 337 2284
	Dean L. Batchelor BCom MPysch BTh (Assistant Minister)	2004	2023	DBatchelor@churchofscotland.org.uk	0131 337 7936
	Douglas H. Reid LLB DipLP MDiv (Assistant Minister)	2022		Douglas.Reid@churchofscotland.org.uk	0131 220 1690
	Reuben Addis (Ordained Local Minister)	2023		85 Acredales, Linlithgow EH49 6JA Reuben.Addis@churchofscotland.org.uk	07867 915022
	Interim Moderator: Samuel A.R. Torrens			STorrens@churchofscotland.org.uk	0131 466 5308
	New charge formed by the union of Edinburgh: Gorgie Dalry Stenhouse and Edinburgh: Palmerston Place				
26	**Edinburgh: Granton (F H T W)**			**info@granton.org.uk**	**0131 552 3033**
	Vacant				
	Mary A. MacLeod Rivett BA MA PhD (Ordained Local Minister)	2023		MMacLeodRivett@churchofscotland.org.uk	
	Interim Moderator: Fergus M. Cook			FCook@churchofscotland.org.uk	0131 466 7503
27	**Edinburgh: Greenbank (F H W)**			**office@greenbankchurch.org**	**0131 447 9969**
	Vacant			112 Greenbank Crescent, Edinburgh EH10 5SZ	0131 447 4032
	Interim Moderator: Moira McDonald			MMcDonald@churchofscotland.org.uk	0131 476 5893
28	**Edinburgh: Greyfriars Kirk (F GE H T W)**			**enquiries@greyfriarskirk.com**	**0131 225 1900**
	Vacant			12 Tantallon Place, Edinburgh EH9 1NZ	0131 667 6610
	Interim Moderator: Karen K. Campbell			KKCampbell@churchofscotland.org.uk	0131 447 2834
29	**Edinburgh: High (St Giles') (F T W)**			**corinne.macinnes@stgilescathedral.org.uk**	**0131 225 4363**
	Vacant			St Giles' Cathedral, High Street, Edinburgh EH1 1RE	0131 225 4363
	Sigrid Marten (Associate Minister)	1997	2021	St Giles' Cathedral, High Street, Edinburgh EH1 1RE SMarten@churchofscotland.org.uk	0131 225 4363
	Interim Moderator: George J. Whyte			GWhyte@churchofscotland.org.uk	07902 645109

30	**Edinburgh: Holy Trinity (F H W)**			**admin@holytrinitywesterhailes.org.uk**	**0131 442 3304**
	Ian A. MacDonald BD MTh	2005	2017	5 Baberton Mains Terrace, Edinburgh EH14 3DG	0131 281 6153
				Ian.Angus.MacDonald@churchofscotland.org.uk	
	Rita M. Welsh BA PhD	2017		19 Muir Wood Road, Currie EH14 5JW	0131 451 5943
	(Ordained Local Minister)			RWelsh@churchofscotland.org.uk	
31	**Edinburgh: Inverleith St Serf's (F H W)**			**inverleithstserfs@gmail.com**	**0131 467 7185**
	Vacant				
	Interim Moderator: Ian W. Alexander			IAlexander@churchofscotland.org.uk	0131 225 5722
32	**Edinburgh: Kirkliston (F W)**			**kpc.officeangels@gmail.com**	
	G.F. (Erick) du Toit BTh	2016	2020	43 Main Street, Kirkliston EH29 9AF	0131 333 3298
				EduToit@churchofscotland.org.uk	
33	**Edinburgh: Leith North and South (H W)**			**slpcoffice@gmail.com**	**0131 554 2578**
	Vacant	2012		37 Claremont Road, Edinburgh EH6 7NN	0131 555 0392
	Interim Moderator: Suzie M. Stark			sstark1962@btinternet.com	0131 551 1633
	New charge formed by the union of Edinburgh: Leith North and Edinburgh: Leith South				
34	**Edinburgh: Leith St Andrew's (F H W)**			**leithstandrews@yahoo.co.uk**	**0131 553 8839**
	A. Robert A. Mackenzie LLB BD	1993	2013	30 Lochend Road, Edinburgh EH6 8BS	0131 553 2122
				AMackenzie@churchofscotlandorg.uk	
35	**Edinburgh: Marchmont St Giles' (F H T W)**			**office@marchmontstgiles.org.uk**	**0131 447 4359**
	Karen K. Campbell BD MTh DMin	1997	2002	2 Trotter Haugh, Edinburgh EH9 2GZ	0131 447 2834
				KKCampbell@churchofscotland.org.uk	
36	**Edinburgh: Mayfield Salisbury (F W)**			**churchmanager@googlemail.com**	**0131 667 1522**
	Alexander C. Forsyth	2009	2021	26 Seton Place, Edinburgh EH9 2JT	0131 667 1286
	LLB DipLP BD MTh PhD			AForsyth@churchofscotland.org.uk	07739 639037
	Pauline Robertson (Mrs)	2003	2023	6 Ashville Terrace, Edinburgh EH6 8DD	0131 554 6564
	DCS BA CertTheol BD			pastoralassistantms@gmail.com	07587 043191
37	**Edinburgh: Meadowbank and Willowbrae (F H T W)**			**willowbrae@meadowbankchurch.com**	**0131 661 8259**
	Vacant			19 Abercorn Road, Edinburgh EH8 7DP	0131 652 2938
	Interim Moderator: John S. (Iain) May			JMay@churchofscotland.org.uk	0131 555 0392

38 Edinburgh: Morningside (F H W) — **office@morningsideparishchurch.org.uk** — **0131 447 6745**
Derek Browning MA BD DMin — 1987 — 2001 — 20 Braidburn Crescent, Edinburgh EH10 6EN — 0131 447 1617
Derek.Browning@churchofscotland.org.uk

39 Edinburgh: Morningside United (F H W) — **churchoffice.muc@gmail.com** — **0131 447 3152**
Sarah Moore BA MA LLB FdA — 2005 — 2023 — 1 Midmar Avenue, Edinburgh EH10 6BS — 0131 447 7943
(Transition Minister URC) — Transition@urcscotland.org.uk

Morningside United is a Local Ecumenical Partnership with the United Reformed Church

40 Edinburgh: Murrayfield (F H W) — **mpchurch@btconnect.com** — **0131 337 1091**
Keith Edwin Graham MA PGDipADS BD MTh — 2008 — 2014 — 45 Murrayfield Gardens, Edinburgh EH12 6DH — 0131 337 1364
KEGraham@churchofscotland.org.uk

41 Edinburgh: New Town, The (F H L W) — **info@stagw.org.uk** — **0131 225 3847**
Vacant — 8 Berry Drive, Edinburgh EH12 8FE
Interim Moderator: Ann Inglis — revainglis@gmail.com — 0131 629 0233
Incorporating **Albany Deaf Church Presbytery Mission Initiative** — **0131 444 2054**

New charge formed by the union of Edinburgh: Greenside and Edinburgh: St Andrew's and St George's West

42 Edinburgh: Newhaven (F H W)
Peter B. Bluett BTh — 1996 — 2007 — 158 Granton Road, Edinburgh EH5 3RF — 0131 476 5212
PBluett@churchofscotland.org.uk

43 Edinburgh: Northwest Kirk: Cramond and Old Kirk and Muirhouse (F H T W) — **cramond.kirk@blueyonder.co.uk** — **0131 336 2036**
Julia A. Cato BA MDiv — 2022 — 2024 — 35 Silverknowes Road, Edinburgh EH4 5LL
JCato@churchofscotland.org.uk

44 Edinburgh: Pentlands (F H W) — **church.office@colinton-parish.com** — **0131 441 2232**
jgpc@supanet.com — **0131 458 5147**
Vacant
Susan G. Galloway (Ordained Local Minister) — 2023 — SGalloway@churchofscotland.org.uk — 01506 202135
Interim Moderator: Ian A. MacDonald — Ian.Angus.MacDonald@churchofscotland.org.uk — 0131 281 6153

New charge formed by the union of Edinburgh: Colinton and Edinburgh: Juniper Green

45 Edinburgh: Pilrig St Paul's (F W) — **mail@pilrigstpauls.org.uk** — **0131 553 1876**
Mark M. Foster BSc BD CertCS CertTM — 1998 — 2013 — Pilrig St Paul's, 1B Pilrig Street, Edinburgh EH6 5AS — 0131 332 5736
MFoster@churchofscotland.org.uk

46	**Edinburgh: Polwarth (F H W)**			**office@polwarth.org.uk**	**0131 346 2711**
	Vacant				
	Interim Moderator: Peter Nelson			PNelson@churchofscotland.org.uk	07500 057889
47	**Edinburgh: Portobello and Joppa (F H W)**			**office@portyjoppachurch.org**	**0131 657 3401**
	Stewart G. Weaver BA BD PhD	2003	2014	6 St Mary's Place, Edinburgh EH15 2QF SWeaver@churchofscotland.org.uk	0131 669 2410
	Lourens de Jager PgDip MDiv BTh (Associate Minister)	2013	2015	1 Brunstane Road North, Edinburgh EH15 2DL LDeJager@churchofscotland.org.uk	07521 426644
48	**Edinburgh: Priestfield (F H W)**				**0131 468 3302**
	Vacant			13 Lady Road, Edinburgh EH16 5PA	0131 468 1254
	Interim Moderator: Alexander C. Forsyth			AForsyth@churchofscotland.org.uk	0131 667 1286
49	**Edinburgh: Ratho (F W)**				
	Vacant			2 Freelands Road, Ratho, Newbridge EH28 8NP	0131 333 1346
	Interim Moderator: Julia C. Wiley			JWiley@churchofscotland.org.uk	01501 730358
50	**Edinburgh: Reid Memorial** See Edinburgh: Craigmillar Park				
51	**Edinburgh: Richmond Craigmillar (F H W)**				**0131 661 6561**
	Elizabeth M. Henderson OBE MA BD MTh	1985	1997	Manse of Duddingston, Old Church Lane, Edinburgh EH15 3PX EHenderson@churchofscotland.org.uk	0131 661 4240
	Kirsty C. Forsyth BD DCS	2022		KForsyth@churchofscotland.org.uk	0131 661 6561
52	**Edinburgh: St Andrew's Clermiston (F)**			**clermistonstandrews@gmail.com**	**0131 336 1507**
	Vacant				
	Interim Moderator: Andrea E. Price			APrice@churchofscotland.org.uk	0131 443 4355
53	**Edinburgh: St Catherine's Argyle (F H W)**				**0131 667 7220**
	Vacant			5 Palmerston Road, Edinburgh EH9 1TL	0131 667 9344
	Interim Moderator: Adrian J. Lough			revlough@btinternet.com	07795 514032
54	**Edinburgh: St Cuthbert's (F H L T W)**			**office@st-cuthberts.net**	**0131 229 1142**
	Peter R.B. Sutton BA(AKC) BD MTh DMin PGCertCouns	2017		St Cuthbert's Church, 5 Lothian Road, Edinburgh EH1 2EP PSutton@churchofscotland.org.uk	07718 311319

55 Edinburgh: St David's Carrick Knowe (F H W) — **ckchurch@talktalk.net** — **0131 334 1505**
Fiona M. Mathieson (Mrs) BEd BD PGCommEd MTh — 1988 — 2001 — 21 Traquair Park West, Edinburgh EH12 7AN — 0131 334 9774
FMathieson@churchofscotland.org.uk

New charge formed by the union of Edinburgh: Carrick Knowe and Edinburgh: St David's Broomhouse

56 Edinburgh: St John's Colinton Mains (F W)
Peter Nelson BSc BD — 2015 — 2 Caiystane Terrace, Edinburgh EH10 6SR — 07500 057889
PNelson@churchofscotland.org.uk

57 Edinburgh: St Margaret's (F H W) — **stmpc@btconnect.com** — **0131 554 7400**
John R. Wells BD PGCE DipMin — 1991 — 2020 — 43 Moira Terrace, Edinburgh EH7 6TD — 0131 322 9272
JWells@churchofscotland.org.uk

58 Edinburgh: St Martin's (F W)
William M. Wishart BD — 2017 — 68 Milton Road West, Edinburgh EH15 1QY — 0131 237 5834
BWishart@churchofscotland.org.uk

59 Edinburgh: St Michael's (F H W) — **office@stmichaels-kirk.co.uk** — **0131 478 9675**
Andrea E. Price (Mrs) — 1997 — 2018 — 13 Dovecot Park, Edinburgh EH14 2LN — 0131 443 4355
APrice@churchofscotland.org.uk

60 Edinburgh: St Nicholas' Sighthill (F T W) — **07306 100111**
Thomas M. Kisitu BD MTh PhD — 1993 — 2015 — 122 Sighthill Loan, Edinburgh EH11 4NT — 0131 442 3978
TMKisitu@churchofscotland.org.uk
Nikki J. Kirkland BSc (Ordained Local Minister) — 2021 — St Nicholas' Sighthill Church, 124 Sighthill Loan EH11 4NT
NKirkland@churchofscotland.org.uk

61 Edinburgh: St Stephen's Comely Bank (F W) — **office@comelybankchurch.com** — **07393 577074**
George Vidits BD MTh — 2000 — 2015 — 8 Blinkbonny Crescent, Edinburgh EH4 3NB — 07581 449540
GVidits@churchofscotland.org.uk

62	**Edinburgh: South East (F H T W)**			**churchsecretary@libertonkirk.net**	**0131 664 8264**
	John N. Young MA BD PhD (Moderator)	1996		7 Kirk Park, Edinburgh EH16 6HZ JYoung@churchofscotland.org.uk	0131 664 3067
	Cameron Mackenzie BSc BD (Team Minister)	1997	2010	4 Fordell Road, Edinburgh EH17 8XZ Cammy.Mackenzie@churchofscotland.org.uk	07838 912361
	Janet R. McKenzie (Mrs) BA DipHS Cert CS (Ordained Local Minister)	2016		80C Colinton Road, Edinburgh EH14 1DD JMcKenzie@churchofscotland.org.uk	0131 444 2054 07980 884653
	Kay O. N. Haggarty BEd (Ordained Local Minister)	2021		KHaggarty@churchofscotland.org.uk	
	Liz Crocker DipComEd DCS	1985	2015	77c Craigcrook Road, Edinburgh EH4 3PH ECrocker@churchofscotland.org.uk	0131 332 0227
	New charge formed by the union of Edinburgh: Gracemount, Edinburgh: Liberton, Edinburgh: Liberton Northfield and Edinburgh: Tron Kirk (Gilmerton and Moredun)				
63	**Edinburgh: Slateford Longstone (F W)**				
	Samuel A.R. Torrens BSc BD	1995	2019	50 Kingsknowe Road South, Edinburgh EH14 2JW STorrens@churchofscotland.org.uk	0131 466 5308
64	**Edinburgh: Stockbridge (F H T W)**			**stockbridgechurch@btconnect.com**	**0131 332 0122**
	Vacant			19 Eildon Street, Edinburgh EH3 5JU	0131 557 6052
	Interim Moderator: Peter B. Bluett			PBluett@churchofscotland.org.uk	0131 476 5212
65	**Edinburgh: Wardie (F H T W)**			**churchoffice@wardie.org.uk**	**0131 551 3847**
	Dolly Purnell BD	2003	2021	35 Lomond Road, Edinburgh EH5 3JN DPurnell@churchofscotland.org.uk	0131 563 6495
66	**Fauldhouse and Harthill: St Andrew's (F H)**				
	Vacant			East Main Street, Harthill, Shotts ML7 5QW	01501 751239
	Session Clerk: Anne Donaldson			andon15@btinternet.com	01501 752608 07708 293048
	New charge formed by the union of Fauldhouse: St Andrew's and Harthill: St Andrew's				
67	**Kirknewton (H) and East Calder (F H W)**				
	Vacant			8 Manse Court, East Calder, Livingston EH53 0HF	01506 357083
	Interim Moderator: Darren Philip (Mr)			DPhilip@churchofscotland.org.uk	07740 414404
68	**Kirk of Calder (F H W)**				
	Vacant			19 Maryfield Park, Mid Calder, Livingston EH53 0SB	01506 882495
	Interim Moderator: Liam J. Fraser			LFraser@churchofscotland.org.uk	01506 842195

69	**Linlithgow: St Michael's (F H W)**			**info@stmichaels-parish.org.uk**	**01506 842188**
	Liam J. Fraser LLB BD MTh PhD	2017	2019	St Michael's Manse, Kirkgate, Linlithgow EH49 7AL LFraser@churchofscotland.org.uk	01506 842195
	Thomas S. Riddell BSc CEng FIChemE (Auxiliary Minister)	1993	1994	4 The Maltings, Linlithgow EH49 6DS TRiddell@churchofscotland.org.uk	01506 843251
70	**Linlithgow: St Ninian's Craigmailen (F H W)**				
	Vacant			29 Philip Avenue, Linlithgow EH49 7BH	01506 202246
	Interim Moderator: Cameron Mackenzie			Cammy.Mackenzie@churchofscotland.org.uk	07838 912361
71	**Livingston: Old (F H W)**				
	Nelu I. Balaj BD MA ThD	2010	2017	The Manse, Charlesfield Lane, Livingston EH54 7AJ NBalaj@churchofscotland.org.uk	01506 411888
72	**Livingston United (F W)**				
	Marc B. Kenton BTh MTh	1997	2019	2 Eastcroft Court, Livingston EH54 7ET MKenton@churchofscotland.org.uk	01506 467426
	John S. Bremner BD MTh (URC Minister)	1987	2023	71 Venacher Road, Falkirk FK1 5UP ecumenical@urcscotland.org.uk	01324 306887 07927 260304
	Livingston United is a Local Ecumenical Partnership with the Scottish Episcopal, Methodist and United Reformed Churches				
73	**Polbeth Harwood (F W) linked with West Kirk of Calder (F H W)**				
	Jonanda Groenewald BA BD MTh DD	2000	2014	3 Johnsburn Road, Balerno EH14 7DN JGroenewald@churchofscotland.org.uk	0131 261 7977
	Alison I. Quilter DipCS (Ordained Local Minister)	2018		27 Northfield Meadows, Longridge, Bathgate EH47 8SA AQuilter@churchofscotland.org.uk	07741 985597
74	**Strathbrock (F H T W)**			**office@strathbrockparish.org.uk**	**01506 856433**
	Hanneke I. Janse van Vuren (Ms) BTh MDiv LTh MTh	2012	2020	1 Manse Park, Uphall, Broxburn EH52 6NX HJansevanVuren@churchofscotland.org.uk	01506 206045
75	**Torphichen** See Avonbridge				
76	**Uphall: South (F H W)**				
	Ian D. Maxwell MA BD PhD	1977	2013	8 Fernlea, Uphall, Broxburn EH52 6DF IMaxwell@churchofscotland.org.uk	01506 239840
77	**West Kirk of Calder (H)** See Polbeth Harwood				

78 Whitburn: Burnfield Valley North (F H W)			**contact@brucefieldchurch.org.uk**	**01501 748666**
Sandra Boyd (Mrs) BEd BD	2007	2019	The Manse, 5 MacDonald Gardens, Blackburn, Bathgate EH47 7RE SBoyd@churchofscotland.org.uk	07919 676242

New charge formed by the union of Blackburn and Seafield and Whitburn: Brucefield

79 Whitburn: Burnfield Valley South (F H W)			**admin@whitburnsouthparishchurch.org.uk**	
Robert Craig BA BD DipRS PGCertHC	2008	2020	5 Mansewood Crescent, Whitburn, Bathgate EH47 8HA RCraig@churchofscotland.org.uk	01501 493666

New charge formed by the union of Breich Valley and Whitburn: South

B. In other appointments: members of Presbytery

Name	Years	Appointment	Address	Telephone
Alexander, Ian W. BA BD STM DMin	1990 2020	International Partnerships Manager Faith Action Programme	121 George Street, Edinburgh EH2 4YN IAlexander@churchofscotland.org.uk	0131 225 5722
Ashley-Emery, Stephen BD DPS RN	2006 2019	Staff Chaplain, Naval Chaplaincy Service, HMS Excellent, Portsmouth	Holmhill, East Main Street, Chirnside, Duns TD11 3XR Stephen.Ashley-Emery100@mod.gov.uk	
Barclay, Iain C. MBE TD MA BD MTh MPhil PhD FRSA	1976 2020	Chaplain: The Robin Chapel	The Thistle Foundation, Edinburgh EH16 4EA chaplain@robinchapel.org.uk	(Home) 07882 885684 (Office) 07393 232736
Billes, Rolf H. BD	1996 2023	Learning Development Manager, Iona Community	Rolf@iona.org.uk	
Carmichael, Daniel J.M. MA BD	1994 2024	Depute Clerk, Presbytery of Edinburgh and West Lothian	c/o 2 Cluny Gardens, Edinburgh EH10 6BQ DCarmichael@churchofscotland.org.uk	0131 225 9137 07950 726139
Evans, Mark BSc MSc DCS	1988 2022	National Spiritual Advisor Operational Lead, Scottish Govt.	13 Easter Drylaw Drive, Edinburgh EH4 2QA mark.evans59@nhs.scot	0131 343 3089
Fergusson, David A.S. (Prof.) OBE MA BD DPhil DD FRSE FBA	1984 2021	Regius Professor of Divinity, University of Cambridge	19 The Eights Marina, Mariners Way, Cambridge CB4 1ZA daf52@cam.ac.uk	01223 666779
Foster, Joanne G. (Mrs) DipTMus BD AdvDipCouns MBACP(Acc)	1996 2021	Healthcare Chaplain	Western General Hospital, Crewe Road South, Edinburgh EH4 2XU joanne.foster2@nhslothian.scot.nhs.uk	0131 537 1401
Galbraith, Christopher G. BA LLB BD	2012 2022	Team Leader, Faith Service Team, HM Prison Addiewell	HM Prison Addiewell, Station Road, Addiewell, West Calder EH55 8QA chris.galbraith@sodexogov.co.uk	01506 874500
Glienecke, Urzula PhD	2022	Associate Chaplain, University of Edinburgh	Chaplaincy Centre, 1 Bristo Square, Edinburgh EH8 9AL urzula.glienecke@ed.ac.uk	0131 650 2595
Howitt, Jane M. MA BD	1996 2022	Chaplain, Heriot-Watt University	The Chaplaincy, Heriot-Watt University, Edinburgh EH14 4AS j.howitt@hw.ac.uk	0131 451 4508 07522 621233
Kennedy, Fiona BA DipHE	2022	Ordained Local Minister, Edinburgh: Barclay Viewforth, Craiglockhart, Polwarth, St Michael's	20 Craiglockhart Quadrant, Edinburgh EH14 1HD FKennedy@churchofscotland.org.uk	0131 444 1615
Mathieson, Angus R. MA BD	1988 2020	Presbytery and Partnership Support Senior Manager, Faith Action Programme	21 Traquair Park West, Edinburgh EH12 7AN AMathieson@churchofscotland.org.uk	0131 334 9774
McPheat, Elspeth DCS	1985 2001	Deacon: CrossReach	53 Wood Street, Grangemouth FK3 8LS elspeth176@sky.com	01324 282406

Orr, Sheena BA MSc MBA BD DPT	2011	2018	Chaplaincy Adviser, Scottish Prison Service	Calton House, 5 Redheughs Rigg, South Gyle, Edinburgh EH12 9HW sheena.orr@prisons.gov.scot	0131 330 3575 07922 649160
Pennykid, Gordon J. BD DCS	2015	2018	Chaplain, HM Prison Edinburgh	8 Glenfield, Livingston EH54 7BG GPennykid@churchofscotland.org.uk	07747 652652
Ross, Matthew Z. LLB BD MTh FSAScot	1998	2023	Researcher, University of Glasgow	Trinity College, 77 Southpark Avenue, Glasgow G12 8LE matthew.ross@glasgow.ac.uk	07711 706950
Swan, David BVMS BD DipTh CDRS	2005	2018	Chaplain, HM Prison Edinburgh	159 Redhall Drive, Edinburgh EH13 2LR davidswan97@gmail.com	07944 598988
Tweedie, Fiona J. BSc PhD	2011	2014	Ordained Local Minister: Statistician, Office of Assembly Trustees	121 George Street, Edinburgh EH2 4YN FTweedie@churchofscotland.org.uk	0131 225 5722
Wishart, Erica M. (Mrs) MA BD	2014	2021	Hospice Chaplain	St Columba's Hospice, 15 Boswall Road, Edinburgh EH5 3RW EWishart@churchofscotland.org.uk	0131 551 1381 07503 170173

C. Retaining: members of Presbytery

Aitchison, James W. BD	1993	2021	(Aberdalgie and Forteviot with Aberuthven and Dunning)	JAitchison@churchofscotland.org.uk	
Alexander, Helen J.R. BD DipSW CQSW	1981	2019	(Assistant, Edinburgh: High (St Giles'))	7 Polwarth Place, Edinburgh EH11 1LG HAlexander@churchofscotland.org.uk	0131 346 0685
Anderson, Dorothy U. LLB DipLP BD	2006	2021	(Associate, Dunblane Cathedral)	4GF Glencairn Crescent, Edinburgh EH12 5BS DAnderson@churchofscotland.org.uk	0131 226 4242 07926 090489
Baird, Kenneth S. MSc PhD BD MIMarEST	1998	2009	(Edinburgh: Leith North)	3 Maule Terrace, Gullane EH31 2DB	01620 843447
Bicket, Matthew S. BD	1989	2017	(Carnoustie: Panbride)	9/2 Connaught Place, Edinburgh EH6 4RQ matthew.bicket1952@gmail.com	0131 552 8781
Booth, Jennifer (Mrs) LTh BD	1996	2005	(Associate: Edinburgh: Leith South)	39 Lilyhill Terrace, Edinburgh EH8 7DR	0131 661 3813
Borthwick, Kenneth S. MA BD	1983	2016	(Edinburgh: Holy Trinity)	34 Rodger Crescent, Armadale EH48 3GR kennysamuel@aol.com	07735 749594
Brown, William D. BD CQSW	1987	2013	(Edinburgh: Murrayfield)	79 Carnbee Park, Edinburgh EH16 6GG wdb@talktalk.net	0131 261 7297
Cowie, John A. BSc BD DMin	1983	2021	(Edinburgh: Stockbridge)	1 Liberton Place, Edinburgh EH16 6NA JCowie@churchofscotland.org.uk	0131 672 1766
Crawford, Morag (Miss) MSc DCS	1977	2021	(Deacon, Rosyth)	8 Ashbank Court, Bathgate EH4 2BL MCrawford@churchofscotland.org.uk	01506 204672 07970 982563
Davidson, D. Hugh MA	1965	2009	(Edinburgh: Inverleith)	Flat 1/2, 22 Summerside Place, Edinburgh EH6 4NZ hdavidson35@btinternet.com	0131 554 8420
Dewar, James S. MA BD	1983	2023	(Edinburgh: Juniper Green)	29 Crosshill Drive, Bo'ness EH51 9JB jimdewar476@gmail.com	07837 420848
Douglas, Alexander B. BD	1979	2014	(Edinburgh: Blackhall St Columba's)	15 Inchview Gardens, Dalgety Bay, Dunfermline KY11 9SA alexandjill@douglas.net	01383 791080
Dunleavy, Suzanne BD DipEd	1990	2016	(Bridge of Weir: St Machar's Ranfurly)	44 Tantallon Gardens, Bellsquarry, Livingston EH54 9AT suzanne.dunleavy@btinternet.com	

Dunn, W. Iain C. DA LTh	1983	1998	(Edinburgh: Pilrig and Dalmeny Street)	10 Fox Covert Avenue, Edinburgh EH12 6UQ	0131 334 1665
Dunphy, Rhona B. (Mrs) BD DPTheol DrPhil	2005	2020	(Pastoral Support, Faith Nurture Forum)	92 The Vennel, Linlithgow EH49 7ET RDunphy@churchofscotland.org.uk	07791 007158
Embleton, Brian M. BD CPS	1976	2015	(Edinburgh: Reid Memorial)	54 Edinburgh Road, Peebles EH45 8EB bmembleton@gmail.com	01721 602157
Embleton, Sara R. (Mrs) BA BD MTh	1988	2010	(Edinburgh: Leith St Serf's)	54 Edinburgh Road, Peebles EH45 8EB srembleton@gmail.com	01721 602157
Farquharson, Gordon MA BD DipEd	1998	2007	(Stonehaven: Dunnottar)	26 Learmonth Court, Edinburgh EH4 1PB gfarqu@talktalk.net	0131 343 1047
Forrester, Margaret R. (Mrs) MA BD DD	1974	2003	(Edinburgh: St Michael's)	25 Kingsburgh Road, Edinburgh EH12 6DZ margaret@rosskeen.org.uk	0131 337 5646
Fraser, Shirley A. (Miss) MA BD DipASS	1992	2008	(Scottish Field Director: Friends International)	6/50 Roseburn Drive, Edinburgh EH12 5NS	0131 347 1400
Frazer, Richard E. BA BD DMin	1986	2023	(Edinburgh: Greyfriars Kirk)	Calamura, 208 Findhorn, Forres IV36 3YS findhornfrazer@gmail.com	07715 069041
Frew, Michael W. BSc BD	1978	2017	(Edinburgh: Slateford Longstone)	37 Swanston Terrace, Edinburgh EH10 7DN	07712 162375
Gardner, John V.	1997	2003	(Glamis, Inverarity and Kinnettles)	75/1 Lockharton Avenue, Edinburgh EH14 1BD jvgardner66@googlemail.com	0131 443 7126
Gilmour, Ian Y. BD CertMin	1985	2018	(Edinburgh: St Andrew's and St George's West)	1 Groathill Loan, Drylaw, Edinburgh EH4 2WL ianyg2@gmail.com	07794 149852
Gordon, Margaret (Mrs) DCS	1998	2012	(Deacon, Edinburgh: Currie)	92 Lanark Road West, Currie EH14 5LA	0131 449 2554
Graham, W. Peter MA BD	1967	2008	(Presbytery Clerk: Edinburgh)	23/6 East Comiston, Edinburgh EH10 6RZ	0131 445 5763
Greig, Ronald G. MA BD	1987	2018	(Livingston United)	47 Mallace Avenue, Armadale EH48 2QD rgglep@gmail.com	01501 731969 07787 887427
Groenewald, Andre J. BA BD MDiv DD CertPS DipPSRP	1995	2024	(Edinburgh: Balerno)	AGroenewald@churchofscotland.org.uk	
Halley, Ruth D. BEd BD PGCert	2012	2023	(Associate Minister, Edinburgh: Greyfriars)	9 Bellcote Lane, Bonnyrigg EH19 3SP RHalley@churchofscotland.org.uk	07530 307413
Harkness, James KVCO CB OBE KHC MA DD	1961	1995	(Chaplain General: Army)	Lang Glen, Durisdeer, nr Thornhill DG3 5BJ	01848 500225
Harley, Elspeth S. BA MTh	1991	2020	(Caddonfoot with Galashiels: Trinity)	EHarley@churchofscotland.org.uk	07950 076528
Hay, Jared W. BA MTh DipMin DMin	1987	2017	(Edinburgh: Priestfield)	39 Netherbank, Edinburgh EH16 6YR jaredhay3110@gmail.com	07906 662515
Herbold Ross, Kristina M.	2008	2018	(Work Place Chaplain, Edinburgh)	kristinaherboldross@gmail.com	
Holt, Jack BSc BD MTh	1985	2023	(Edinburgh: Polwarth)	3/8 Perdrixknowe, 82 Colinton Road, Edinburgh EH14 1AF JHolt@churchofscotland.org.uk	07762 359781
Houston, W. Richard BSc BD MTh	1998	2023	(Linlithgow: St Ninian's Craigmailen)	WHouston@churchofscotland.org.uk	
Inglis, Ann (Mrs) LLB BD	1986	2015	(Langton and Lammermuir Kirk)	34 Echline View, South Queensferry EH30 9XL revainglis@gmail.com	0131 629 0233
Irving, William D. LTh	1985	2005	(Golspie)	122 Swanston Muir, Edinburgh EH10 7HY	0131 441 3384
Keil, Alistair H. BD DipMin	1989	2021	(Edinburgh: St Andrew's Clermiston)	14 Comiston Terrace, Edinburgh EH10 6AH AKeil@churchofscotland.org.uk	07758 009250
Logan, Anne T. (Mrs) MA BD MTh DMin PhD	1981	2012	(Edinburgh: Stockbridge)	Sunnyside Cottage, 18 Upper Broomieknowe, Lasswade EH18 1LP annetlogan@sky.com	0131 663 9550

Name	Ord.	Ret.	Former charge	Address	Phone
Lough, Adrian J. BD AFSERT MIERE DipSW	2012	2020	(Auchtergaven and Moneydie with Redgorton and Stanley)	12 Dundrennan Cottages, Edinburgh EH16 5RG revlough@btinternet.com	07795 514032
Mackay, Kenneth J. MA BD	1971	2007	(Edinburgh: St Nicholas' Sighthill)	46 Chuckethall Road, Livingston EH54 8FB knnth_mackay@yahoo.co.uk	01506 410884
Mackenzie, James G. BA BD	1980	2005	(Jersey: St Columba's)	26 Drylaw Crescent, Edinburgh EH4 2AU jgmackenzie@jerseymail.co.uk	0131 332 3720
Maclean, Ailsa G. (Mrs) BD DipCE	1979	2017	(Chaplain: George Heriot's School)	28 Swan Spring Avenue, Edinburgh EH10 6NJ	
MacLeod, Calum I. BA BD	1996	2023	(Edinburgh: High (St Giles'))	Calum.MacLeod@churchofscotland.org.uk	
Manners, Stephen MA BD	1989	2022	(Kelso Country Churches)	SManners@churchofscotland.org.uk	
Marshall, A. Scott DipComm BD	1984	2021	(Abercorn with Pardovan, Kingscavil and Winchburgh)	13 Leyland Road, Bathgate EH48 2SG asm66015@gmail.com	07415 028678
May, John S. (Iain) BSc MBA BD DMin	2012	2024	(Edinburgh: Leith North and South)	3 Lyne View, West Linton EH6 7EQ JMay@churchofscotland.org.uk	
McPake, John M. LTh	2000	2013	(Edinburgh: Liberton Northfield)	3 Kilburn Wood Drive, Roslin EH25 9AA john_mcpake9@yahoo.co.uk	0131 285 8386
Moir, Ian A. MA BD	1962	2000	(Adviser for Urban Priority Areas)	28/6 Comely Bank Avenue, Edinburgh EH4 1EL	0131 332 2748
Morrison, Angus MA BD PhD DD	1979	2021	(Orwell and Portmoak)	170 The Murrays, Edinburgh EH17 8UP AMorrison@churchofscotland.org.uk	
Mulligan, Anne MA DCS	1974	2013	(Deacon: Hospital Chaplain)	27A Craigour Avenue, Edinburgh EH17 1NH mulliganne@aol.com	0131 664 3426
Munro, John R. BD	1976	2017	(Edinburgh: Fairmilehead)	23 Braid Farm Road, Edinburgh EH10 6LE revjohnmunro@hotmail.com	0131 446 9363
Nelson, Georgina MA BD PhD DipEd	1990	2022	(Hospital Chaplain, NHS Lothian)	63 Hawthorn Bank, Seafield, Bathgate EH47 7EB	
Nicol, Douglas A.O. MA BD	1974	2018	(Hobkirk and Southdean with Ruberslaw)	1/2 North Werber Park, Edinburgh EH4 1SY Douglas.Nicol@churchofscotland.org.uk	07811 437075
Paterson, Douglas S. MA BD DipTP	1976	2010	(Edinburgh: St Colm's)	4 Ards Place, High Street, Aberlady EH32 0DB	01875 870192
Povey, John M. DL BD PhD	1981	2021	(Kirk of Calder)	5 Ainslie Road, East Calder, Livingston EH53 0PU RevJPovey@aol.com	07549 525498
Raby, Scott LTh CertMin	1991	2023	(Fauldhouse: St Andrew's)	11 Balcarres Street, Tillicoultry FK13 6NP SRaby@churchofscotland.org.uk	07986 901578
Ramsay, A. Malcolm BA LLB DipMin	1986	2022	(Transition Minister, Edinburgh: Willowbrae)	Ford Cottage, Ford, Pathhead EH37 5RE amalcolmramsay@gmail.com	
Rennie, Agnes M. (Miss) DCS	1974	2012	(Deacon, Edinburgh: Bristo Memorial Craigmillar)	3/1 Craigmillar Court, Edinburgh EH16 4AD	0131 661 8475
Reynolds, Fiona J. LLB BD FdSc	2018	2023	(Monifieth)	7 Ruthven Place, Edinburgh EH16 5TU FReynolds@churchofscotland.org.uk	
Ribbons, Frank MA BD DipEd	1985	2023	(Aboyne-Dinnet with Cromar)	54 Traquair Park West, Edinburgh EH12 7AL FRibbons@churchofscotland.org.uk	
Ridland, Alistair K. MStJ MA BD PGDip MRAeS MInstLM RAFAC	1982	2022	(Chaplain: Western General Hospital)	13 Stewart Place, Kirkliston EH29 0BQ a.ridland@btinternet.com	0131 333 2711

Name	Ord.	Ret.	Former charge / appointment	Address	Phone
Robertson, Charles LVO MA	1965	2005	(Edinburgh: Canongate)	3 Ross Gardens, Edinburgh EH9 3BS canongate1@aol.com	0131 662 9025
Roger, Alexander M. BD PhD	1982	2020	(Whitburn: Brucefield)	4 Lugton Circle, South Gilmerton Brae, Edinburgh EH17 8GT amroger1951@outlook.com	0131 664 8109
Scott, J. Martin C. DipMusEd RSAM BD PhD	1986	2019	(Secretary, Council of Assembly)	52 Ravenscroft Gardens, Edinburgh EH17 8RP martin.scott14@sky.com	0131 431 4195 07856 165820
Shaw, Duncan BD MTh	1975	2020	(Bathgate: St John's)	30 Meadowpark Crescent, Bathgate EH48 2SX duncan.shaw11@btinternet.com	01506 654563
Smith, Angus MA LTh	1965	2006	(Chaplain to the Oil Industry)	3/7 West Powburn, West Savile Gait, Edinburgh EH9 3EW	0131 667 1761
Stark, Suzie M. BD CertMin	2013	2021	(Chaplain, St Columba's Hospice, Edinburgh	The Lodge, 40 Warriston Gardens, Edinburgh EH3 5NE sstark1962@btinternet.com	0131 551 1633
Stevenson, John MA BD PhD HonFEIS	1963	2001	(General Secretary, Department of Education)	12 Swanston Gardens, Edinburgh EH10 7DL	0131 445 3960
Tait, John M. BSc BD	1985	2012	(Edinburgh: Pilrig St Paul's)	82 Greenend Gardens, Edinburgh EH17 7QH johnmtait@me.com	0131 258 9105
Taylor, William R. MA BD MTh	1983	2018	(Chaplaincy Adviser, Scottish Prison Service)	33 Kingsknowe Drive EH14 2JY wlretl@outlook.com	0131 443 5590 07447 258525
Teague, Yvonne (Mrs) DCS	1965	2002	(Education and Development Officer, Board of Ministry)	46 Craigcrook Avenue, Edinburgh EH4 3PX y.teague.1@blueyonder.co.uk	0131 336 3113
Watson, Nigel G. MA	1998	2012	(Associate: East Kilbride: Old/Stewartfield/West)	7 St Catherine's Place, Edinburgh EH9 1NU nigel.g.watson@gmail.com	0131 662 4191
Wells, Ian J. BD	1999	2023	(Edinburgh: Ratho)	11 Catelbock Close, Kirkliston EH29 9FF IWells@churchofscotland.org.uk	
Whyte, George J. OBE BSc BD DMin KSG	1981	2022	(Principal Clerk)	4 Baberton Mains Lea, Edinburgh EH14 3HB GWhyte@churchofscotland.org.uk	07902 645109
Williams, Jenny M. BSc CQSW BD MTh	1996	2022	(Transition Minister, Edinburgh: Drylaw)	5 Kilmundy Drive, Burntisland KY3 0JN jennywilliams@gmx.co.uk	
Wynne, Alistair T.E. BA BD	1982	2009	(Nicosia Community Church, Cyprus)	Flat 6, 14 Burnbrae Drive, Edinburgh EH12 8AS awynne2@googlemail.com	0131 339 6462

D. In other appointments: not members of Presbytery

Name	Ord.	Appt	Appointment	Address	Phone
Aitken, Ewan R. BA BD	1992	2014	CEO, Edinburgh Cyrenians	159 Restalrig Avenue, Edinburgh EH7 6PJ	0131 467 1660
Storrar, William F. (Prof.) MA BD PhD	1984	2005	Director, Center of Theologica Inquiry	50 Stockton Street, Princeton, NJ 08540, USA cti@ctinquiry.org	

E. Retaining: not members of Presbytery

Name	Ord.	Ret.	Former charge / appointment	Address	Phone
Boyd, Kenneth M. (Prof.) MA BD PhD FRCPE	1970	2011	(University of Edinburgh: Medical Ethics)	1 Doune Terrace, Edinburgh EH3 6DY k.boyd@ed.ac.uk	0131 225 6485
Crossan, William	2014	2022	(Ordained Local Minister, Campbeltown: Lorne and Lowland)	57 Caldercruix Crescent, Eliburn, Livingston EH54 7FS w.crossan@btinternet.com	07833 152345

Douglas, Colin R. MA BD STM	1969	2007	(Livingston Ecumenical)	34 West Pilton Gardens, Edinburgh EH4 4EQ colin.r.douglas@gmail.com	0131 551 3808
Drake, Wendy F. (Mrs) BD	1978	2007	(Cockpen and Carrington with Lasswade and Rosewell)	21 William Black Place, South Queensferry EH30 9QR revwdrake@hotmail.co.uk	0131 331 1520
Duncanson, Mary B. (Ms) BTh	2013	2023	(Ordained Local Minister, Cromdale and Advie with Grantown-on-Spey and Dulnain Bridge)	11a/4 Milton Road East, Edinburgh EH15 2ND	07807 322120
Espie, Howard	2011	2014	(Mission Facilitator/Enabler, Edinburgh: Barclay Viewforth)	1 Sprucebank Avenue, Langbank, Port Glasgow PA14 6YX howardespie.me.com	01475 540391
Hardman Moore, Susan (Prof.) MA MAR PhD	2013	2023	(Ordained Local Minister, Vice Principal, New College, University of Edinburgh)	Professor Emerita of Early Modern Religion, New College, Mound Place, Edinburgh EH1 2LX s.hardmanmoore@ed.ac.uk	07811 345699
Lockerbie, Caroline R. BA MDiv DMin	1978	2017	(Lerwick and Bressay: Transition Minister)	102 3300 Centenial Drive, Vernon, BC, Canada V1T 9Md5 lockerbie21@gmail.com	001 519 429 5563
MacGregor, Margaret S. (Miss) MA BD DipEd	1985	1994	(Bishop's College, Calcutta)	16 Learmonth Court, Edinburgh EH4 1PB	0131 332 1089
MacMurchie, F. Lynne LLB BD	1998	2023	(Chaplain, St John's Hospital, Livingston)	101/5 Easter Warriston, Edinburgh EH7 4QZ l.macmurchie01@btinternet.com	0131 554 2714
Merrilees, Ann (Miss) DCS	1994	2006	(Deacon, Glasgow: St James' (Pollok))	7/1 Slaeside, Balerno EH14 7HL amerrilees@gmail.com	0131 449 3325
Morrison, Mary B. (Mrs) MA BD DipEd	1978	2000	(Edinburgh: Stenhouse St Aidan's)	174 Craigcrook Road, Edinburgh EH4 3PP	0131 336 4706
Newell, Alison M. (Mrs) BD 1986	1986	2021	(Associate Chaplain, University of Edinburgh)	1A Inverleith Terrace, Edinburgh EH3 5NS alinewell@aol.com	0131 556 3505
Penman, Iain D. BD DipMS	1977	2008	(Edinburgh: Kaimes Lockhart Memorial)	33/5 Carnbee Avenue, Edinburgh EH16 6GA iainpenmanklm@aol.com	0131 664 0673 07931 993427
Provan, Iain W. (Prof.) MA BA PhD	1991	2022	(Professor of Biblical Studies, Regent College, Vancouver)		
Robson, Brenda PhD	2005	2019	(Auxiliary Minister, Kirknewton and East Calder)	22 Ratho Park Road, Ratho, Newbridge EH28 8NY BRobson@churchofscotland.org.uk	0131 281 9511
Smart, V. Easter BA MDiv DMin	1996	2023	(Edinburgh: Currie)	Centre Presbyterian Church, 83 New Park Road, Pennslyvania 17352, USA	001 717 993 2345
Smith, Ronald W. BA BEd BD	1979	2011	(Falkirk: St James')	4 Lambs Court, Newhaven, Edinburgh EH6 4LS	07900 896954
Stewart, Lezley J. BD ThM MTh DMin	2000	2023	(Ministries Support Manager, Faith Action Programme)	68 St Davids, Newtongrange EH22 4LF ljstewart@btinternet.com	
Thomson, Donald M. BD	1975	2013	(Tullibody: St Serf's)	50 Sighthill Road, Edinburgh EH11 4NY donniethomson@tiscali.co.uk	
Torrance, Iain R. (Prof.) KCVO Kt DD FRSE	1982	2012	(President: Princeton Theological Seminary)	25 The Causeway, Duddingston Village, Edinburgh EH15 3QA irt@ptsem.edu	0131 661 3092

F. Inactive: not members of Presbytery

Name	Ord.	Ret.	Former charge	Address	Phone
Beckett, David M. BA BD	1964	2002	(Edinburgh: Greyfriars, Tolbooth and Highland Kirk)	31/1 Sciennes Road, Edinburgh EH9 1NT davidbeckett3@aol.com	0131 667 2672
Black, David W. BSc BD	1968	2008	(Strathbrock)	66 Bridge Street, Newbridge EH28 8SH dw.black666@yahoo.co.uk	0131 333 2609
Blakey, Ronald S. MA BD MTh	1962	2000	(Secretary, Assembly Council)	24 Kimmerghame Place, Edinburgh EH4 2GE kathleen.blakey@gmail.com	0131 343 6352
Brook, Stanley A. BD MTh CPS	1977	2016	(Newport-on-Tay)	4 Scotstoun Green, South Queensferry EH30 9YA stan_brook@btinternet.com	0131 331 4237
Buchanan, Neil BD	1991	2019	(East Kilbride: Moncrieff)	40 Links View, Port Seton, Prestonpans EH32 0EZ neil.buchanan@talk21.com	07993 720497
Chalmers, Murray MA	1965	2006	(Chaplain, Royal Edinburgh Hospital)	8 Easter Warriston, Edinburgh EH7 4QX murray.chalmers8448@gmail.com	0131 552 4211
Corrie, Margaret (Miss) DCS	1989	2023	(Deacon, Armadale)	deakcorr@virginmedia.com	07955 633969
Cuthell, Tom C. MA BD	1965	2007	(Edinburgh: St Cuthbert's)	Flat 10, 2 Kingsburgh Crescent, Waterfront, Edinburgh EH5 1JS tcuthell@gmail.com	0131 476 3864
Darroch, Richard J.G. BD MTh MA	1993	2010	(Whitburn: Brucefield)	23 Barnes Green, Livingston EH54 8PP richdarr@aol.com	01506 436648
Davidson, Ian M.P. MBE MA BD	1954	1994	(Stirling: Allan Park South with Church of the Holy Rude)	13/8 Craigend Park, Edinburgh EH16 5XX ian.m.p.davidson@btinternet.com	0131 664 0074
Dickson, Graham T. MA BD	1985	2005	(Edinburgh: St Stephen's Comely Bank)	43 Hope Park Gardens, Bathgate EH48 2QT gtd194@googlemail.com	01506 237597
Lamont, Stewart J. BSc BD	1972	2015	(Arbirlot with Carmyllie)	Mas des Pins, 23 Rue du 19 mars 1962, 11500 Quillan, France lamonts@lamonts.eu	0033 9 86 56 16 78
Lithgow, Anne R. (Mrs) MA BD	1992	2009	(Dunglass)	13 Cameron Park, Edinburgh EH16 5JY anne.lithgow@btinternet.com	
McGillivray, A. Gordon MA BD STM	1951	1993	(Presbytery Clerk, Edinburgh)	Thorburn Manor, 2 Thorburn Road, Edinburgh EH13 0BQ	0131 441 6984
Millar, Peter W. MA BD ThM PhD	1971	1998	(Warden, Iona Abbey)	6/5 Ettrickdale, Edinburgh EH3 5JN ionacottage@hotmail.com	0131 557 0517
Monteith, W. Graham MA BD BPhil PhD	1974	1994	(Flotta and Fara with Hoy and Walls)	20/3 Grandfield, Edinburgh EH6 4TL	0131 552 2564
Petrie, Ian D. MA BD	1970	2008	(Dundee: St Andrew's)	27/111 West Savile Terrace, Edinburgh EH9 3DR idp-77@hotmail.com	0131 237 2857
Plate, Maria A.G. (Miss) BA LTh CQSW DSW	1983	2000	(South Ronaldsay and Burray)	Flat 29, 77 Barnton Park View, Edinburgh EH4 6EL riaplate@gmail.com	0131 339 8539
Scott, Jayne E. BA MEd MBA	1988	2019	(Secretary, Ministries Council)	52 Ravenscroft Gardens, Edinburgh EH17 8RP jayne.scott5@btinternet.com	07740 151542
Stephen, Donald M. TD MA BD ThM	1962	2001	(Edinburgh: Marchmont St Giles')	10 Hawkhead Crescent, Edinburgh EH16 6LR donaldmstephen@gmail.com	0131 658 1216
Wilson, John M. (Ian) MA	1964	1995	(Adviser, Religious Education, Highland Region)	27 Bellfield Street, Edinburgh EH15 2BR ianandshirley@talktalk.net	0131 669 5257

G. Readers (active)

Devoy, Fiona (Mrs)	196 The Murrays Brae, Edinburgh EH17 8UH	fiona.devoy@yahoo.co.uk	
Drummond, Brian		BDrummond@churchofscotland.org.uk	0131 441 9201
Elliott, Sarah (Miss)	105 Seafield Rows, Seafield, Bathgate EH47 7AW	sarah.elliott6@btopenworld.com	01506 654950
Farrow, Edmund	14 Brunswick Terrace, Edinburgh EH7 5PG	edmundfarrow@blueyonder.co.uk	0131 558 8210
Kerrigan, Herbert A. (Prof.) MA LLB KC DipPTh	Airdene, 20 Edinburgh Road, Dalkeith EH22 1JY	kerrigan@kerriganqc.com	0131 660 3007 07725 953772
McFadzean, John	121 South Street, Armadale, Bathgate EH48 3JT	jmcfadzean2@gmail.com	01501 730260
Middleton, Alex	19 Cramond Place, Dalgety Bay KY11 9LS	alex.middleton@btinternet.com	01383 820800
Orr, Elizabeth (Mrs)	64a Marjoribanks Street, Bathgate EH48 1AL	liz-orr@hotmail.co.uk	01596 653116
Paxton, James	5 Main Street, Longridge, Bathgate EH47 8AE	jimpaxton1950@gmail.com	01501 772192
Pearce, Martin J.	4 Corbiehill Avenue, Edinburgh EH4 5DR	martin.j.pearce@blueyonder.co.uk	0131 336 4864 07801 717222
Tew, Helen (Mrs)	5/5 Moat Drive, Edinburgh EH14 1NU	helentew9@gmail.com	07986 170802
Wilkie, David	55 Goschen Place, Broxburn EH52 5JH	david-fmu_09@tiscali.co.uk	01506 238644

H. Ministries Development Staff

Crocker, Liz DipComEd DCS	Edinburgh: South East – Parish Assistant	ECrocker@churchofscotland.org.uk
de Jager, Lourens (Rev) PgDip MDiv BTh	Edinburgh: Portobello and Joppa – Associate Minister	LDeJager@churchofscotland.org.uk
Fejszes, Violetta (Dr)	Edinburgh: Northwest (Cramond & Old Kirk & Muirhouse) – Parish Development Worker	VFejszes@churchofscotland.org.uk
Forsyth, Kirsty BD DCS	Edinburgh: Richmond Craigmillar – Parish Deacon	KForsyth@churchofscotland.org.uk
Laoshe, Fadeke	Edinburgh: St Margaret's – Children, Youth and Family Worker	FLaoshe@churchofscotland.org.uk
Lawrie, Lesley	Livingston: Old – Community Outreach Worker	LLawrie@churchofscotland.org.uk
Linde, Jessica	Edinburgh: Gorgie and Palmerston Place – Families and Children's Worker	JLinde@churchofscotland.org.uk
Richardson, Ian (Dr)	Edinburgh: Holy Trinity – Discipleship Team Leader	IRichardson@churchofscotland.org.uk
Robertson, Douglas S. BEng BA MTh	Edinburgh: South East – Church Leader and Project Worker	Douglas.Robertson@churchofscotland.org.uk
Rous, Daniel J.	Linlithgow: St Michael's - Community Audit Worker	DRous@churchofscotland.org.uk
Young, Yvonne	Edinburgh: Granton – Outreach Parish Assistant	YYoung@churchofscotland.org.uk

EDINBURGH ADDRESSES

Balerno	Johnsburn Road, Balerno
Barclay Viewforth	Barclay Place
Blackhall St Columba's	Queensferry Road
Broughton St Mary's	Bellevue Crescent
Canongate	Canongate
Corstorphine	
Craigsbank	Craigs Crescent
Old	Kirk Loan
St Anne's	Kaimes Road
St Ninian's	St John's Road
Craiglockhart	Craiglockhart Avenue
Craigmillar Park	Craigmillar Park
Currie	Kirkgate, Currie
Dalmeny and Queensferry	Main Street, Dalmeny; The Loan, S. Queensferry
Davidson's Mains	Quality Street
Drylaw	Groathill Road North
Duddingston	Old Church Lane, Duddingston
Fairmilehead	Frogston Road West
Gorgie and Palmerston Place	Gorgie Road; Palmerston Place
Granton	Boswall Parkway
Greenbank	Braidburn Terrace
Greyfriars Kirk	Greyfriars Place
High (St Giles')	High Street
Holy Trinity	Hailesland Place, Wester Hailes
Inverleith St Serf's	Ferry Road
Kirkliston	The Square, Kirkliston
Leith	
North and South	Kirkgate, Leith
St Andrew's	Easter Road
Marchmont St Giles'	Kilgraston Road
Mayfield Salisbury	Mayfield Road x West Mayfield
Meadowbank and Willowbrae	Dalziel Place x London Road; Willowbrae Road
Morningside	Cluny Gardens
Morningside United	Bruntsfield Place x Chamberlain Rd
Murrayfield	Abinger Gardens
New Town, The	George Street
Newhaven	Craighall Road
Northwest Kirk	Cramond Glebe Road; Pennywell Gardens
Pentlands	Dell Road, Colinton; Lanark Road, Juniper Green
Pilrig St Paul's	Pilrig Street
Polwarth	Polwarth Terrace x Harrison Road
Portobello and Joppa	Abercorn Terrace
Priestfield	Dalkeith Road x Marchhall Place
Ratho	Baird Road, Ratho
Reid Memorial	West Savile Terrace
Richmond Craigmillar	Niddrie Mains Road
St Andrew's Clermiston	Clermiston View
St Catherine's Argyle	Grange Road x Chalmers Crescent
St Cuthbert's	Lothian Road
St David's Carrick Knowe	North Saughton Road
St John's Colinton Mains	Oxgangs Road North
St Margaret's	Restalrig Road South
St Martin's	Magdalene Drive
St Michael's	Slateford Road
St Nicholas' Sighthill	Calder Road
St Stephen's Comely Bank	Comely Bank
Slateford Longstone	Kingsknowe Road North
South East	Ravenscroft Street; Kirkgate, Liberton; Gilmerton Road, Liberton; Craigour Gardens
Stockbridge	Saxe Coburg Street
Wardie	Primrosebank Road

(2) LOTHIAN AND BORDERS (W)

Meets at different venues throughout the Presbytery, in 2024 on the first Saturday in November and in 2025 on the first Saturday of February, third Saturday of June, and the first Saturdays of September and November.

Clerk:	**REV. NORMAN A. SMITH MA BD**	**21 St Margarets Avenue, Loanhead EH20 9FH** **lothianandborders@churchofscotland.org.uk**	**07787 421234**
Mission Officer:	**REV. PETER J. WOOD MA BD**	**PWood@churchofscotland.org.uk**	**07776 119901**

1	**Aberlady and Gullane (F H W)** Elisabeth M. Stenhouse BD	2006	2023	The Manse, 9 Fenton Road, Gullane EH31 2EU EStenhouse@churchofscotland.org.uk	**01875 870777** 0131 324 3134
2	**Ale and Teviot United (F H W)** Vacant Interim Moderator: Derek G. Brown			**info@aleandteviot.org.uk** kerednodrog@outlook.com	07939 691908
3	**Ayton (H) and District Churches (F)** Vacant Interim Moderator: Jeliase Mutimbairi			The Manse, Beanburn, Ayton, Eyemouth TD14 5QY jmutimbairi@churchofscotland.org.uk	01890 781333 07546 953843
4	**Belhaven and Spott (F H T W)** Vacant Interim Moderator: Brian C. Hilsley			**secretarybelhavenchurch@outlook.com** BHilsley@churchofscotland.org.uk	07791 557350
	New charge formed by the union of Belhaven and Spott				
5	**Berwick-upon-Tweed: St Andrew's Wallace Green (H) and Lowick (F W)** Adam J.J. Hood MA BD DPhil	1989	2012	3 Meadow Grange, Berwick-upon-Tweed TD15 1NW AHood@churchofscotland.org.uk	01289 332787
6	**Bonnyrigg (F H W)** Louise I. Purden BD	2020		**officebonnyriggparishchurch@gmail.com** 9 Viewbank View, Bonnyrigg EH19 2HU LPurden@churchofscotland.org.uk	**0131 654 0140** 0131 258 6219
7	**Bowden (H) and Melrose (F H W)** Rosemary Frew (Mrs) MA BD	1988	2017	**bowden.melrosepc@btinternet.com** The Manse, Tweedmount Road, Melrose TD6 9ST RFrew@churchofscotland.org.uk	**01896 823339** 01896 822217

8 Caddonfoot (H W) linked with Stow: St Mary of Wedale and Heriot (W)
Vacant — 20 Wedale View, Stow, Galashiels TD1 2SJ — 01578 730237
Session Clerk, Caddonfoot: Anne Grieve (Mrs) — anneblakehope@hotmail.com — 07968 433547
Session Clerk, Stow and Heriot: Dianne Wilson (Mrs) — wilsond31@live.co.uk — 01896 668381

9 Carlops (W) linked with Kirkurd and Newlands (F H) linked with Upper Tweeddale (F H W) linked with West Linton: St Andrew's (F H W)
(West Tweeddale Parishes) — **info@uppertweeddale.org.uk**
T.A. (Tony) Foley PhD — 1992 — 2021 — Old Joiners Croft, Skirling, Biggar ML12 6HD — 07793 294000
TFoley@churchofscotland.org.uk

10 Cavers and Kirkton (W) linked with Hawick: Trinity (H W) — **trinityhawick@outlook.com**
Vacant — Trinity Manse, Howdenburn, Hawick TD9 8PH — 01450 378248
Session Clerk, Cavers and Kirkton: Jane Cox (Mrs) — jane.cox2401@btinternet.com — 01450 379171
Session Clerk, Hawick: Trinity: Muriel S. Bowie (Mrs) — murielbowie80@outlook.com — 01450 372195
07790 689997

11 Channelkirk and Lauder (F W)
Vacant — The Manse, Brownsmuir Park, Lauder TD2 6QD — 01578 718996
Session Clerk: Billy Anderson — wdanderson0709@hotmail.com — 07384 720245

12 Cheviot Churches (H W)
Colin D. Johnston MA BD — 1986 — 2019 — Cheviot Manse, Main Street, Morebattle, Kelso TD5 8QG — 01573 440539
CDJohnston@churchofscotland.org.uk

13 Cockenzie and Port Seton — **contact@chalmerschurch.co.uk**
Robin N. Allison BD DipMin — 1994 — 2018 — 2 Links Road, Port Seton, Prestonpans EH32 0HA — 01875 812225
RAllison@churchofscotland.org.uk

New charge formed by the union of Cockenzie and Port Seton: Chalmers Memorial and Cockenzie and Port Seton: Old

14 Cockpen and Carrington (F H W) linked with Lasswade (H) and Rosewell (H W)
Lorna M. Souter MA BD MSc — 2016 — 11 Pendreich Terrace, Bonnyrigg EH19 2DT — 0131 663 6392
LSouter@churchofscotland.org.uk — 07889 566418

15 Coldingham and St Abbs (F W) linked with Eyemouth (F W)
Andrew N. Haddow BEng BD — 2012 — The Manse, Victoria Road, Eyemouth TD14 5JD — 01890 750327
AHaddow@churchofscotland.org.uk

16	**Coldstream and District Parishes (F H W) linked with Eccles and Leitholm**			**coldstreampc@gmail.com**	
	Vacant			36 Bennecourt Drive, Coldstream TD12 4BY	01890 883887
	Session Clerk, Coldstream: Richard Fawkes			richard@fawkes.me.uk	
	Session Clerk, Eccles and Leitholm: Rob Cockburn			rob.cockburn@icloud.com	
17	**Dalkeith: St John's and Newton (F H W)**			**sjkpdalkeith@gmail.com**	**0131 660 5871**
	Keith L. Mack BD MTh DPS	2002		13 Weir Crescent, Dalkeith EH22 3JN KMack@churchofscotland.org.uk	0131 454 0206
	Andrew Don MBA (Ordained Local Minister)	2006	2013	5 Eskvale Court, Penicuik EH26 8HT ADon@churchofscotland.org.uk	01968 675766
18	**Dalkeith: St Nicholas Buccleuch (F H T W)**				
	Alexander G. Horsburgh MA BD	1995	2004	1 Nungate Gardens, Haddington EH41 4EE AHorsburgh@churchofscotland.org.uk	01620 824728
19	**Dirleton (F H) linked with North Berwick: Abbey (F H W)**			**abbeychurch@abbeychurch.co.uk**	**01620 892800**
	David J. Graham BSc BD PhD	1982	1998	Sydserff, Old Abbey Road, North Berwick EH39 4BP DGraham@churchofscotland.org.uk	01620 890800
20	**Dryburgh District Churches (F W)**			**web4churches@gmail.com**	
	Sheila W. Moir (Ms) MTheol	2008		7 Strae Brigs, St Boswells, Melrose TD6 0DH SMoir@churchofscotland.org.uk	01835 822255
21	**Dunbar (H W)**				
	Gordon Stevenson BSc BD	2010		The Manse, 10 Bayswell Road, Dunbar EH42 1AB revgstev@gmail.com	01368 865482
22	**Dunglass (W)**				
	Suzanne G. Fletcher BA MDiv MA DMin	2001	2011	The Manse, Cockburnspath TD13 5XZ SFletcher@churchofscotland.org.uk	01368 830713 07973 960544
23	**Duns and District Parishes (F W)**			**admin@dunsanddistrict.org.uk**	**01361 884502**
	Vacant			The Manse, Castle Street, Duns TD11 3DG	01361 883496
	Session Clerk: Kenneth McLean			admin@dunsanddistrict.org.uk	01361 882744
24	**Earlston (F W)**				
	Vacant				
	Session Clerk: Robert Turnbull			rgtapoth@btinternet.com	01896 848515

25 Eccles and Leitholm See Coldstream

26 Eddleston (F H) linked with Peebles: Old (F H W) linked with Stobo and Drumelzier (F W)

			admin@topcop.org.uk	**01721 723986**
Aftab Gohar MA MDiv PgDip	1996	2021	7 Clement Gunn Square, Peebles EH45 8LW	07528 143784
			AGohar@churchofscotland.org.uk	

27 Ettrick and Yarrow (F W) linked with Selkirk and Ashkirk (F H W)

			office@selkirkparish.church	**01750 22078**
Vacant			1 Loanside, Selkirk TD7 4DJ	01750 23308
Session Clerk, Ettrick and Yarrow: Nora Hunter			norabirks@btinternet.com	01750 52349
				07776 343952
Session Clerk, Selkirk and Ashkirk: Fiona Corbett			fiona.m.corbett@live.co.uk	01750 22687
				07780 078085

Selkirk and Ashkirk was formed by the union of Ashkirk and Selkirk

28 Eyemouth See Coldingham and St Abbs

29 Fogo (F W)
Vacant

30 Galashiels (H W)

			office@galashielschurchofscotland.org.uk	**01896 752967**
Graeme M. Glover MA MBA MSc DMin	2017	2022	Woodlea, Abbotsview Drive, Galashiels TD1 3SL	01896 209455
			GGlover@churchofscotland.org.uk	

31 Garvald and Morham (W) linked with Haddington: West (F H W)

			hwcofs@hotmail.com	
John D. Vischer	1993	2011	15 West Road, Haddington EH41 3RD	01620 822213
			JVischer@churchofscotland.org.uk	

32 Gladsmuir linked with Longniddry (F H W)

Robin E. Hill LLB BD PhD	2004		The Manse, 8a Elcho Road, Longniddry EH32 0LB	01875 853195
			RHill@churchofscotland.org.uk	

33 Gordon: St Michael's (F)
Guardianship of the Presbytery

Session Clerk: Janice Cossigny (Mrs)			gordonkirktd3@gmail.com	01573 410518

34	**Gorebridge (F H W)**			**office@gorepc.com**	**01875 820387**
	Mark S. Nicholas MA BD	1999		100 Hunterfield Road, Gorebridge EH23 4TT	01875 820387
				MNicholas@churchofscotland.org.uk	07816 047493
	Timothy N.C. Linford HND BD PGDip	2024		Woodlea, Victoria Road, Haddington EH41 4DJ	01629 823747
	(Assistant Minister)			TLinford@churchofscotland.org.uk	07739 477791
35	**Greenlaw (F H)**				
	Susan M. Brown BD DipMin DUniv	1985	2021	The Manse, Todholes, Greenlaw, Duns TD10 6XD	01361 810553
				Susan.Brown@churchofscotland.org.uk	07747 825755
36	**Haddington: St Mary's (F H T W)**				**01620 829354**
	Alison P. McDonald MA BD	1991	2019	1 Nungate Gardens, Haddington EH41 4EE	01620 823109
				Alison.McDonald@churchofscotland.org.uk	
37	**Haddington: West See Garvald and Morham**				
38	**Hawick: Burnfoot (F T W)**				
	Vacant			29 Wilton Hill, Hawick TD9 8BA	01450 373181
	Session Clerk: Marlynn Kerr (Miss)			marlynn.kerr231@btinternet.com	01450 375724
39	**Hawick: St Mary's and Old (F H W) linked with Hawick: Teviot (H) and Roberton (F W)**			**info@smop-tero.org**	
	Alistair W. Cook BSc CA BD	2008	2017	4 Heronhill Close, Hawick TD9 9RA	01450 378175
				ACook@churchofscotland.org.uk	07802 616352
40	**Hawick: Teviot and Roberton** See Hawick: St Mary's and Old				
41	**Hawick: Trinity** See Cavers and Kirkton				
42	**Hawick: Wilton linked with Teviothead**				
	Lisa-Jane Rankin BD CPS	2003		4 Wilton Hill Terrace, Hawick TD9 8BE	01450 370744
				LRankin@churchofscotland.org.uk	
43	**Hobkirk and Southdean (F W) linked with Ruberslaw (F W)**				
	Rachel Wilson BA MTh	2018		The Manse, Leydens Road, Denholm, Hawick TD9 8NB	01450 870874
				RWilson@churchofscotland.org.uk	

44	**Innerleithen (H), Traquair and Walkerburn (F W)**				
	Fraser Edwards BSc BA	2021		The Manse, 1 Millwell Park, Innerleithen, Peebles EH44 6JF FEdwards@churchofscotland.org.uk	01896 490742
45	**Jedburgh and Oxnam (F W)**				
	Vacant Session Clerk: Richard Gordon			The Manse, Honeyfield Drive, Jedburgh TD8 6LQ r.j.gordon@talk21.com	01835 863417 01835 864365 07971 298541
	New charge formed by the union of Jedburgh: Old and Trinity and Oxnam				
46	**Kelso: North (H) and Country Churches (F H W)**			**office@kelsonorthandednam.org.uk**	**01573 224154**
	Anna S. Rodwell BD DipMin	1998	20[illegible]6	The Manse, 20 Forestfield, Kelso TD5 7BX ARodwell@churchofscotland.org.uk	01573 224248 07508 810237
	New charge formed by the union of Kelso: North and Ednam and Kelso Country Churches				
47	**Kelso: Old and Sprouston (F)**				
	Vacant Session Clerk: Frances Gordon			The Manse, Glebe Lane, Kelso TD5 7AU francesgordon38@btinternet.com	01573 348749 07966 435484
48	**Kirkurd and Newlands** See Carlops				
49	**Lammermuir (F W)**				
	Anikó Schütz Bradwell BA MA BD	2015		The Manse, Tweeddale Avenue, Gifford, Haddington EH41 4QN ASchuetzBradwell@churchofscotland.org.uk	01620 811193
	New charge formed by the union of Humbie and Yester, Bolton and Saltoun				
50	**Lasswade and Rosewell** See Cockpen and Carrington				
51	**Legerwood (F)**				
	Guardianship of the Presbytery Interim Moderator: Susan M. Brown			Susan.Brown@churchofscotland.org.uk	01361 810553 07747 825755
52	**Loanhead and Bilston (F T W)**				
	Graham L. Duffin BSc BD DipEd	1989	2001	120 The Loan, Loanhead EH20 9AJ GDuffin@churchofscotland.org.uk	0131 448 2459
53	**Longniddry** See Gladsmuir				

54 Lyne and Manor (W) linked with Peebles: St Andrew's Leckie (F H W)
office@standrewsleckie.co.uk **01721 723121**
Malcolm S. Jefferson 2012 Mansefield, Innerleithen Road, Peebles EH45 8BE 01721 725148
MJefferson@churchofscotland.org.uk

55 Musselburgh: Northesk (F H W)
Hayley L. Cohen BA MDiv 2020 34 Battlefield Drive, Musselburgh EH21 7DF 0131 665 8688
HCohen@churchofscotland.org.uk

56 Musselburgh: St Andrew's High (H W) **0131 665 7239**
A. Leslie Milton MA BD PhD 1996 2019 8 Ferguson Drive, Musselburgh EH21 6XA 0131 665 1124
AMilton@churchofscotland.org.uk

57 Musselburgh: St Clement's and St Ninian's
Guardianship of the Presbytery
Michael D. Watson CertCS 2013 2023 2/1 Stanton Marches, Haddington EH41 3FB 01620 614009
(Ordained Local Minister; MWatson@churchofscotland.org.uk
Interim Moderator)

58 Musselburgh: St Michael's Inveresk (F W)
Malcolm M. Lyon BD 2007 2017 5 Crookston Ct., Crookston Rd., Inveresk, Musselburgh EH21 7TR 0131 653 2411
MLyon@churchofscotland.org.uk

59 Newbattle (F H W) **0131 663 3245**
Vacant

60 North Berwick: Abbey See Dirleton

61 North Berwick: St Andrew Blackadder (F H W) **admin@standrewblackadder.org.uk** **01620 895233**
Neil J. Dougall BD DipMin DMin 1991 2003 7 Marine Parade, North Berwick EH39 4LD 01620 892132
NDougall@churchofscotland.org.uk

62 Ormiston (F W) linked with Pencaitland (F W)
Vacant The Manse, Pencaitland, Tranent EH34 5DL 01875 340963
Session Clerk, Ormiston: Lesley McConnachie lesleymcconnachie@btinternet.com
Session Clerk, Pencaitland: Eileen Henderson henders2@sky.com 07986 241116

63 Peebles: Old See Eddleston				
64 Peebles: St Andrew's Leckie See Lyne and Manor				
65 Pencaitland See Ormiston				
66 Penicuik: North (F H W)				
Graham D. Astles BD MSc	2007	2019	35 Esk Bridge, Penicuik EH26 8QR GAstles@churchofscotland.org.uk	07906 290568
67 Penicuik: Trinity (F H W)				
John C.C. Urquhart MA MA BD	2010	2017	10 Fletcher Grove, Penicuik EH26 0JT JCUrquhart@churchofscotland.org.uk	01968 382116 07821 402901
68 Prestonpans: Prestongrange (F W)				
Vacant				
Session Clerk: Jane Hepburn			hpbrnfmly@aol.com	07599 193544
69 Roslin (H)				
Guardianship of the Presbytery				
Session Clerk: Kathleen Taylor (Mrs)			kathtaylor1212@gmail.com	
70 Ruberslaw See Hobkirk and Southdean				
71 Selkirk and Ashkirk See Ettrick and Yarrow				
72 Stobo and Drumelzier See Eddleston				
73 Stow: St Mary of Wedale and Heriot See Caddonfoot				
74 Teviothead See Hawick: Wilton				
75 Tranent (F W)				
Katherine A. Taylor LLB MDiv	2021		1 Toll House Gardens, Tranent EH33 2QQ KTaylor@churchofscotland.org.uk	01875 880011
76 Traprain (F W)			**admin@parishoftraprain.org.uk**	
Douglas Hamilton LLB MSc MDiv	2022		5 The Glebe, East Linton EH40 3EF dhamilton@churchofscotland.org.uk	07831 657854
77 Tyne Valley (F H W)				
Dale K. London BTh FSAScot	2011	2018	Cranstoun Cottage, Ford, Pathhead EH37 5RE DLondon@churchofscotland.org.uk	01875 321329
78 Upper Tweeddale See Carlops				

79 West Linton: St Andrew's See Carlops

80 Whiteadder (F)

Michael A. Taylor DipTh MPhil	2006	2018	The New Manse, The Glebe, Chirnside, Duns TD11 3XE MTaylor@churchofscotland.org.uk	01890 819947 07479 985075

New charge formed by the union of Chirnside, and Hutton and Fishwick and Paxton

B. In other appointments: members of Presbytery

Berry, Geoff T. BSc BD	2009	2011	Army Chaplain	3 SCOTS, Fort George, Ardersier, Inverness IV2 7TE revgeoffberry@gmail.com	
Cobain, Alan R. BD	2000	2017	Army Chaplain	HQ SW, Building 56, Jellabad Barracks, Tidworth SP9 7BQ Alan.Cobain100@mod.gov.uk	
Kellock, Chris N. MA BD	1998	2012	Army Chaplain	Permanent Joint Headquarters, Sandy Lane, Northwood HA6 3HP nicandchris@hotmail.co.uk	
Linford, Victoria J. LLB BD DMin	2010	2023	Presbytery Resource Adviser, Office of the General Assembly	121 George Street, Edinburgh EH2 4YN VLinford@churchofscotland.org.uk	0131 225 5722
Magee, Rosemary E. BSc MSc MDiv DMin	2009	2023	Healthcare Chaplain	Royal Infirmary of Edinburgh, 51 Little France Crescent, Edinburgh EH16 4SA rosie.magee@nhslothian.scot.nhs.uk	0131 242 1997
Smith, Norman A. MA BD	1997	2022	Presbytery Clerk: Lothian and Borders	21 St Margarets Avenue, Loanhead EH20 9FH NSmith@churchofscotland.org.uk	07787 421234
Wood, Peter J. MA BD	1993	2023	Presbytery Mission Officer, Lothian and Borders	49 Oxgangs Farm Drive, Edinburgh EH13 9PT PWood@churchofscotland.org.uk	07776 119901

C. Retaining: members of Presbytery

Allison, Ann BSc PhD BD	2000	2017	(Crail with Kingsbarns)	99 Coalgate Avenue, Tranent EH33 1JW revann@sky.com	01875 571778 07857 525439
Arnott, A. David K. MA BD	1971	2010	(St Andrews: Hope Park with Strathkinness)	53 Whitehaugh Park, Peebles EH45 9DB adka53@btinternet.com	01721 725979 07759 709205
Atkins, Yvonne E.S. (Mrs) BD	1997	2018	(Musselburgh: St Andrew's High)	6 Robert de Quincy Place, Prestonpans EH32 9NS yveatkins@yahoo.com	01875 819858
Brown, Derek G. BD DipMin DMin	1989	2021	(Lead Chaplain: NHS Highland)	The Manse, Todholes, Greenlaw, Duns TD10 6XD kerednodrog@outlook.com	01361 810553 07939 691908
Burt, Thomas W. BD	1982	2013	(Carlops with Kirkurd and Newlands with West Linton: St Andrew's)	7 Arkwright Court, North Berwick EH39 4RT tomburt@westlinton.com	01620 895494
Campbell, Thomas R.	1986	1993	(Paisley: St James)	The White House, Nairns Mains, Haddington EH41 4HF tom@trcampbell.co.uk	07778 183830
Cartwright, Alan C.D. BSc BD	1976	2016	(Fogo and Swinton with Ladykirk and Whitsome with Leithholm)	Drumgray, Edrom, Duns TD11 3PX alan@cartwright-family.org.uk	01890 819191

Name	Ord.	Ret.	Former charge	Address	Phone
Coltart, Ian O. CA BD	1988	2010	(Arbirlot with Carmyllie)	25 Bothwell Gardens, Dunbar EH42 1PZ	01368 860064
Dick, Andrew B. BD DipMin	1986	2015	(Musselburgh: St Michael's Inveresk)	4 Kirkhill Court, Gorebridge EH23 4TW dixbit@aol.com	07540 099480
Dodd, Marion E. (Miss) MA BD LRAM	1988	2010	(Kelso: Old and Sprouston)	Esdaile, Tweedmount Road, Melrose TD6 9ST mariondodd@btinternet.com	01896 822446
Donaldson, David MA BD DMin	1969	2018	(Manish-Scarista)	13 Rose Park, Peebles EH45 8HP davidandjeandonaldson@gmail.com	07817 479866
Duncan, Maureen M. (Mrs) BD	1996	2018	(Lochend and New Abbey)	2 Chalybeate, Haddington EH41 4NX revmo43@gmail.com	01620 248559 07443 501738
Duncan, Rosslyn P. BD MTh	2007	2018	(Stonehaven: Dunnottar with Stonehaven: South)	Four Oaks, Broomdykes, Duns TD1 3LZ rosslynpduncan@gmail.com	07899 878427
Glover, Robert L. BMus BD MTh ARCO	1971	2010	(Cockenzie and Port Seton: Chalmers Memorial)	12 Seton Wynd, Port Seton, Prestonpans EH32 0TY rlglover@btinternet.com	07790 844474
Gordon, Thomas J. MA BD	1974	2009	(Chaplain, Marie Curie Hospice, Edinburgh)	22 Gosford Road, Port Seton, Prestonpans EH32 0HF tom.swallowsnest@gmail.com	01875 812262
Guy, Scott C. BD	1989	2020	(Aberdeen: Northfield)	41 Jenny Moore's Road, St Boswells TD6 0AN scguy55@gmail.com	07805 711148
Harrison, Frederick CertCT	2013	2023	(Ordained Local Minister, Aberlady and Gullane)	50 Dundas Gardens, Gorebridge EH23 4BB revfred@hotmail.co.uk	07703 527240
Hilsley, Brian C. LLB BD	1990	2020	(Aberlady with Gullane)	15 Letham Place, Dunbar EH42 1AJ BHilsley@churchofscotland.org.uk	07791 557350
Hogg, Thomas M. BD	1986	2007	(Tranent)	22 Douglas Place, Galashiels TD1 3BT	01896 759381
Hope, Geraldine H. (Mrs) MA BD	1986	2007	(Foulden and Mordington with Hutton and Fishwick and Paxton)	4 Well Court, Chirnside, Duns TD11 3UD geraldine.hope@virgin.net	01890 818134
Johnston, June E. BSc MEd BD	2013	2023	(Ordained Local Minister, Bilston with Roslin)	21 Caberston Road, Walkerburn EH43 6AT June.Johnston@churchofscotland.org.uk	01896 870754 07754 448889
Landale, William S.	2005	2016	(Auxiliary Minister, Chirnside with Hutton and Fishwick and Paxton)	Green Hope Guest House, Ellemford, Duns TD11 3SG WLandale@churchofscotland.org.uk	01361 890242
Levison, Chris L. MA BD	1972	2010	(Health Care Chaplaincy Training and Development Officer)	Gardenfield, Nine Mile Burn, Penicuik EH26 9LT chrislevison@hotmail.com	01968 674566
Macdougall, Malcolm M. BD MTh DipCE	1981	2019	(Eddleston with Peebles: Old)	2 Woodilee, Broughton, Biggar ML12 6GB calum.macdougall@btopenworld.com	01899 830615
McHaffie, Robin D. BD	1979	2016	(Cheviot Churches)	55 Lennel Mount, Coldstream TD12 4NS robinmchaffie@btinternet.com	01890 882472 07772 072327
McLarty, R. Russell MA BD DipArch	1985	2022	(Transition Minister, Edinburgh: Meadowbank)	9 Sanderson's Wynd, Tranent EH33 1DA rrussellmclarty@yahoo.com	01875 614496 07751 755986
McNab, Douglas G. BA BD	1999	2021	(New Machar)	17 Wester Kippielaw Park, Dalkeith EH22 2GE dougie.mcnab@btinternet.com	0131 563 8034 07766 042033
Mitchell, John LTh CertMin	1991	2018	(Bonnyrigg)	28 Shiel Hall Crescent, Rosewell EH24 9DD JMitchell@churchofscotland.org.uk	0131 448 2676
Neill, Bruce F. MA BD	1966	2007	(Maxton and Mertoun with Newtown with St Boswells)	18 Brierydean, St Abbs, Eyemouth TD14 5PQ bneill@phonecoop.coop	01890 771569
Norman, Nancy M. (Miss) BA MDiv MTh	1988	2012	(Lyne and Manor)	25 March Street, Peebles EH45 8EP nancy.norman1@googlemail.com	01721 721699

Riddell, John A. MA BD	1967 2006	(Jedburgh: Trinity)	Orchid Cottage, Gingham Row, Earlston TD4 6ET	01896 848784
Scott, Donald H. BA BD	1983 2024	(Edinburgh: Priestfield)	5 Marion Crescent, Selkirk TD7 4LY Donald.Scott@churchofscotland.org.uk	07720 040081
Scott, Ian G. BSc BD STM	1965 2006	(Edinburgh: Greenbank)	50 Forthview Walk, Tranent EH33 1FE igscott50@btinternet.com	01875 612907
Shand, George C. MA BD	1981 2021	(Cairngryffe with Libberton and Quothquan with Symington)	15 Kittlegairy Place, Peebles EH45 9LW George.Shand@churchofscotland.org.uk	07765 987163
Simpson, Robert R. BA BD	1994 2014	(Callander)	19 Cadwell Walk, Gorebridge EH23 4LF robert@pansmanse.co.uk	01875 823180
Sinclair, Colin A.M. BA BD	1981 2022	(Edinburgh: Palmerston Place)	18 Dukehaugh, Peebles EH45 9DN camsinclair90@gmail.com	07752 538954
Spence, Elisabeth G.B. BD DipEd	1995 2021	(Pioneer Minister, Hopefield Connections)	18 Castell Maynes Avenue, Bonnyrigg EH19 3RW revspence121@gmail.com	07772 548121
Steele, Leslie M. MA BD	1973 2013	(Galashiels: Old Parish and St Paul's)	23 Mayburn Avenue, Loanhead EH20 9EY lmslms@hotmail.co.uk	
Steele, Margaret D.J. (Miss) BSc BD	2000 2022	(Ashkirk with Ettrick and Yarrow with Selkirk)	33 Anderson Drive, Perth PH1 1JX MSteele@churchofscotland.org.uk	07801 365068
Steele, Marilynn J. (Mrs) BD DCS	1999 2012	(Deacon, Edinburgh: Granton)	2 Northfield Gardens, Prestonpans EH32 9LQ marilynnsteele@aol.com	01875 811497
Stein, Jock MA BD PhD	1973 2008	(Tulliallan and Kincardine)	35 Dunbar Road, Haddington EH41 3PJ jstein@handselpress.org.uk	01620 824896
Stein, Margaret E. (Mrs) DA BD DipRE	1984 2008	(Tulliallan and Kincardine)	35 Dunbar Road, Haddington EH41 3PJ margaretestein@hotmail.com	01620 824896
Strachan, Pamela D. (Lady)	2015 2021	(Ordained Local Minister, Broughton, Glenholm and Kilbucho with Carlops with Kirkurd and Newlands with Skirling with Tweedsmuir with West Linton: St Andrew's)	Glenhighton, Broughton, Biggar ML12 6JF PStrachan@churchofscotland.org.uk	01899 830423 07837 873688
Taverner, David J. MCIBS ACIS BD	1996 2023	(Coldstream and District Parishes with Eccles and Leitholm)	Woodcot, Waverley Road, Innerleithen, Peebles TD12 4BY DTaverner@churchofscotland.org.uk	01896 829289
Watson, James B. BSc	1969 2009	(Coldstream with Eccles)	20 Randolph Crescent, Dunbar EH42 1GL jimwatson007@hotmail.com	01368 865045 07419 759451
Willoughby, Muriel F. (Mrs) MA BD	2006 2023	(Dunfermline: St Andrew's Erskine)	42 Yosemite Park, Dunbar EH42 1FL MWilloughby@churchofscotland.org.uk	07841 473323

D. In other appointments: not members of Presbytery

Scouler, Michael D. MBE BSc BD	1988 2018	Head of Spiritual Care, NHS Borders	Chaplaincy Centre, Borders General Hospital, Melrose TD6 9BS michael.scouler@borders.scot.nhs.uk	01896 826565

E. Retaining: not members of Presbytery

Black, James S.	1976	1978	(Associate. Paisley: St Ninian's Ferguslie)	7 Breck Terrace, Penicuik EH26 0RJ jsb.black@btopenworld.com	01968 677559
Cairns, John B. KCVO LTh LLB LLD DD	1974	2009	(Aberlady with Gullane)	Bell House, Roxburghe Park, Dunbar EH42 1LR johncairns@mail.com	01368 862501
Haslett, Howard J. BA BD	1972	2010	(Traprain)	26 The Maltings, Haddington EH41 4EF howard.haslett@btinternet.com	01620 481208
Macaulay, Glendon D. BD ALCM	1999	2012	(Falkirk: Erskine)	43 Gavin's Lee, Tranent EH33 2AP gd.macaulay@btinternet.com	01875 615851
Milloy, A. Miller DipPE LTh DipTrMan LHD	1979	2011	(General Secretary: United Bible Societies)	18 Kittlegairy Crescent, Peebles EH45 9NJ ammilloy@aol.com	01721 723380
Paterson, William BD	1977	2001	(Bonkyl and Preston with Chirnside with Edrom Allanton)	Benachie, Gavinton, Duns TD11 3QT billdm.paterson@btinternet.com	01361 882727
Stewart, Una B. (Ms) BD DipEd	1995	2014	(Law)	10 Inch Park, Kelso TD5 7BQ rev.ubs@virgin.net	01573 219231
Thornthwaite, Anthony P. MTh	1995	2019	(Dundee: Coldside)	19 Dovecote Way, Haddington EH41 4HY tony.thornthwaite@sky.com	07706 761841
Turnbull, Julian S. BSc BD MSc CEng MBCS	1980	1986	(Dumfries: Lochside with Terregles)	39 Suthren Yett, Prestonpans EH32 9GL jules@turnbull25.plus.com	01875 818305

F. Inactive: not members of Presbytery

Auld, A. Graeme (Prof.) MA BD PhD DLitt FSAScot FRSE	1973	2008	(Principal, New College, University of Edinburgh)	Nether Swanshiel, Hobkirk, Bonchester Bridge, Hawick TD9 8JU a.g.auld@ed.ac.uk	01450 860636
Buchanan, Marion (Mrs) MA DCS	1983	2019	(Deacon, Glasgow: Garthamlock and Craigend East; Glasgow: Ruchazie)	40 Links View, Port Seton, Prestonpans EH32 0EZ	01875 814632
Cowie, James M. BD CCE	1977	2016	(Paris: The Scots Kirk)	24 Cowdrait, Burnmouth, Eyemouth TD14 5SW jimcowie@europe.com	01890 781394
Dick, J. Ronald BD	1973	2012	(Spiritual Care Manager, NHS Borders)	1 Viewfield Terrace, Leet Street, Coldstream TD12 4BL ron.dick180@yahoo.co.uk	01890 882206
Dobie, Rachel J.W. (Mrs) LTh	1991	2008	(Broughton, Glenholm and Kilbucho with Skirling with Stobo and Drumelzier with Tweedsmuir)	20 Moss Side Crescent, Biggar ML12 6GE revracheldobie@gmail.com	01899 229244
Dutton, David W. BA MTh MPhil	1973	2008	(Stranraer: High Kirk)	13 Acredales, Haddington, East Lothian, EH41 4NT duttondw@gmail.com	01620 825999
Finlay, Quintin BA BD	1975	1996	(North Bute)	Ivy Cottage, Greenlees Farm, Kelso TD5 8BT	07901 981171
Fraser, John W. MA BD	1974	2011	(Penicuik: North)	66 Camus Avenue, Edinburgh EH10 6QX jjjjj2005@hotmail.co.uk	07469 704091
Jones, Anne M. (Mrs) BD	1998	2011	(Hospital Chaplain, NHS Lothian)	7 North Elphinstone Farm, Tranent EH33 2ND revamjones@aol.com	01875 614442
Kenny, Celia G. BA MTh MPhil LLM PhD	1994	2004	(Bonkyl and Preston with Chirnside with Edrom Allanton)	37 Grosvenor Road, Dublin, Ireland cgkenny@tcd.ie	
Kingston, David V.F. BD DipPTh	1993	2015	(Chaplain: Army)	2 Cleuch Avenue, North Middleton, Gorebridge EH23 4RP	01875 822026

Lawrie, Bruce B. BD DPSS	1974	2012	(Duffus, Spynie and Hopeman)	5 Thorncroft House, Scotts Place, Selkirk TD7 4LN thorncroft54@gmail.com	01750 725427
Ledgard, J. Christopher BA CertTh	1969	1998	(Upper Donside)	Streonshalh, 8 David Hume View, Chirnside, Duns TD11 3SX	01890 817124
Lyall, David BSc BD STM PhD	1965	2002	(Lecturer and Principal, New College, University of Edinburgh)	Flat 2, 9 Bayswell Road, Dunbar EH42 1AB lyall3@gmail.com	01368 864079
Macdonald, Finlay A.J. MA BD PhD DD	1971	2010	(Principal Clerk)	8 St Ronan's Way, Innerleithen EH44 6RG finlaymacdonald5@gmail.com	01896 831631
Shields, John M. MBE LTh	1972	2007	(Channelkirk and Lauder)	12 Eden Park, Ednam, Kelso TD5 7RG john.shields118@btinternet.com	01573 229015
Spowart, Mary G. (Mrs) BD	1978	1991	(Papa Westray with Westray)	Aldersyde, St Abbs Road, Coldingham, Eyemouth TD14 5NR	01890 771697
Steven, Gordon R. BD DCS	2000	2012	(Deacon, Newbattle)	51 Nantwich Drive, Edinburgh EH7 6RB grsteven@btinternet.com	0131 669 2054 07904 385256
Torrance, David W. MA BD	1955	1991	(Earlston)	38 Forth Street, North Berwick EH39 4JQ torrance103@btinternet.com	01620 895109
Wallace, James H. MA BD	1973	2011	(Peebles: St Andrew's Leckie)	52 Waverley Mills, Innerleithen EH44 6RH jimwallace121@btinternet.com	01896 831637

G. Readers (active)

Findlay, Elizabeth (Mrs)	7e Rose Lane, Kelso TD5 7AP	findlay290@gmail.com	01573 226641
Hogg, David MA	82 Eskhill, Penicuik EH26 8DQ	hogg-d2@sky.com	01968 676350 07821 693946
Johnston, Alan C.	36 Foster Road, Penicuik EH26 0FL	alanacj2@gmail.com	01968 664860 07901 501819
Knox, Dagmar (Mrs)	3 Stichill Road, Ednam, Kelso TD5 7QQ	dagmar.knox.riding@btinternet.com	01573 224883
Landale, Alison (Mrs)	Green Hope Guest House, Ellemford, Duns TD11 3SG	alison@greenhope.co.uk	01361 890242
Millan, Mary (Mrs)	33 Polton Vale, Loanhead EH20 9DF	maryrmillan@gmail.com	0131 440 1624 07814 466104
Selkirk, Frances (Mrs)	21 Park Crescent, Newtown St Boswells, Melrose TD6 0QR	f.selkirk@hillview2selkirk.plus.com	01835 823669
Waugh, Jacqueline (Mrs)	15 Garleton Drive, Haddington EH41 3BL	jacqueline.waugh@yahoo.com	01620 825007
Yeoman, Edward T.N. FSAScot	75 Newhailes Crescent, Musselburgh EH21 6EF	edwardyeoman6@aol.com	0131 653 2291 07896 517666

H. Ministries Development Staff

McKenzie, Susan	Newton – Mission and Discipleship Outreach Worker	SMcKenzie@churchofscotland.org.uk
Pryde, Erika	Newton – Mission and Outreach Co-ordinator	EPryde@churchofscotland.org
Stark, Jennifer MA MATheol	Newbattle – Congregational Support Worker	JStark@churchofscotland.org.uk

HAWICK ADDRESSES

Burnfoot	Fraser Avenue	St Mary's and Old	Kirk Wynd	Wilton	Princes Street
		Teviot	St George's Lane		
		Trinity	Central Square		

(3) SOUTH WEST (F)

Meets at 10.30am on the second Saturday in June and September and the first Tuesday in March and December.

Clerk:	**MRS CHRISTINE M. MURRAY LLB**	**southwestscotland@churchofscotland.org.uk**	**07526 892228**
Depute Clerk:	**REV. H. TAYLOR BROWN BD CertMin FRAI**	**HBrown@churchofscotland.org.uk**	**07596 111310**
Presbytery Office:		**Room 1008, Airline Corridor, Aviation House, Glasgow Prestwick Airport, Prestwick KA9 2PL** **SCaldwell@churchofscotland.org.uk**	**07955 943773**

1	**Alloway and Fisherton (F H W)**			**secretary.allowaypc@gmail.com**	**01292 442083**
	Neil A. McNaught BD MA	1987	1999	1A Parkview, Alloway, Ayr KA7 4QG NMcNaught@churchofscotland.org.uk	01292 441252
	David A. Hume MSc PhD CertHE (Ordained Local Minister)	2020		8 Finlaggan Place, Kilmarnock KA3 1UY DHume@churchofscotland.org.uk	07858 966367
	New charge formed by the union of Alloway and Fisherton				
2	**Annan: Old and Dornock (F H W)**				
	David Whiteman BD	1998	2018	12 Plumdon Park Avenue, Annan DG12 6EY DWhiteman@churchofscotland.org.uk	01461 392048
	New charge formed by the union of Annan: Old and Dornock				
3	**Annan: St Andrew's and St Bryde's (H W)**			**admin@stabc.online**	
	John G. Pickles BD MTh MSc	2011		1 Annerley Road, Annan DG12 6HE JPickles@churchofscotland.org.uk	01461 202626
	New charge formed by the union of Annan: St Andrew's, Brydekirk and Dalton and Hightae				
4	**Annbank (F H W) linked with Tarbolton (F W)**				
	Mandy R. H. Ralph RGN CertCS BTh	2013	2019	The Manse, Tarbolton, Mauchline KA5 5QJ MRalph@churchofscotland.org.uk	01292 541452
5	**Ardrossan (W)**				**01294 463711**
	Vacant				
	New charge formed by the union of Ardrossan: Park, Saltcoats: North and Saltcoats: St Cuthbert's				

6	**Ardrossan and Saltcoats: Kirkgate (F H W)**				**01294 472001**
	T. Nigel Chikanya BTh BA MTh	2014	2020	10 Seafield Drive, Ardrossan KA22 8NU NChikanya@churchofscotland.org.uk	07566 278132
7	**Arnsheen Barrhill and Colmonell: St Colmon (W) linked with Ballantrae (H W)**				
	Theodore L. Corney BA MTh GDipTh	2006	2019	The Manse, 1 The Vennel, Ballantrae, Girvan KA26 0NH TCorney@churchofscotland.org.uk	01465 831252
8	**Arran, Isle of (F W)**				
	Vacant				
	Session Clerk: Sharon R. MacLeod			arransessionclerk@gmail.com	01770 700353
	New charge formed by the union of Brodick, Corrie, Kilmory, Lamlash, Lochranza and Pirnmill, Shiskine, and Whiting Bay and Kildonan				
9	**Auchinleck (F H) linked with Catrine (F)**				
	Stephen F. Clipston MA BD	1982	2006	28 Mauchline Road, Auchinleck KA18 2BN SClipston@churchofscotland.org.uk	01290 424776
10	**Ayr: Auld Kirk of Ayr (St John the Baptist) (H L W)**			**auldkirkayr@hotmail.co.uk**	**01292 262938**
	David R. Gemmell MA BD	1991	1999	20 Seafield Drive, Ayr KA7 4BQ DGemmell@churchofscotland.org.uk	01292 864140
11	**Ayr: Castlehill (F H W)**			**castlehillchurch44@gmail.com**	**01292 267520**
	Paul R. Russell MA BD	1984	2019	3 Old Hillfoot Road, Ayr KA7 3LW PRussell@churchofscotland.org.uk	01292 261464
12	**Ayr: Newton Wallacetown (F H W)**				**01292 611371**
	Vacant			9 Nursery Grove, Ayr KA7 3PH	01292 264251
	Session Clerk: John Bell			johnbell31@gmail.com	07777 496095
13	**Ayr: St Andrew's (F H W)**			**ayrstandrews@gmail.com**	
	Stanley Okeke BA BD MSc	2012	2020	17 Whiteford View, Ayr KA7 3LL SOkeke@churchofscotland.org.uk	01292 268164
14	**Ayr: St Columba (F H W)**			**irene@ayrstcolumba.co.uk**	**01292 265794**
	Scott S. McKenna BA BD MTh MPhil PhD	1994	2019	3 Upper Crofts, Alloway, Ayr KA7 4QX SMcKenna@churchofscotland.org.uk	01292 226075

15	**Ayr: St James' (F H W)**			**admin@stjamesayr.plus.com**	**01292 266993**
	Barbara V. Suchanek-Seitz CertMin DTh	2016		1 Prestwick Road, Ayr KA8 8LD	01292 262420
				BSuchanek-Seitz@churchofscotland.org.uk	
16	**Ayr: St Leonard's (F H W) linked with Dalrymple (F)**			**st_leonards@btinternet.com**	**01292 611117**
	Brian R. Hendrie BD CertMin	1992	2015	35 Roman Road, Ayr KA7 3SZ	01292 283825
				BHendrie@churchofscotland.org.uk	
17	**Ayr: St Quivox (F H W)**				
	John McCutcheon BA BD(Min)	2014	2019	11 Springfield Avenue, Prestwick KA9 2HA	01292 861641
				JMcCutcheon@churchofscotland.org.uk	
18	**Ballantrae** See Arnsheen Barrhill and Colmonell: St Colmon				
19	**Balmaclellan, Kells (H) and Dalry (H) linked with Carsphairn (H)**				
	Vacant				
	Pamela A. Bellis BA DipTheol	2004	2022	12 Woodlands Avenue, Kirkcudbright DG6 4BP	07751 379249
	(Ordained Local Minister)			PBellis@churchofscotland.org.uk	
	Interim Moderator: Mark R.S. Smith			Mark.Smith@churchofscotland.org.uk	01387 820475
20	**Beith (F H W)**			**beithchurch@btinternet.com**	**01505 502686**
	Adri la Grange BTh MDiv MTh	2010	2023	2 Glebe Court, Beith KA15 1ET	01505 341876
				AlaGrange@churchofscotland.org.uk	
21	**Bengairn Parishes (W) linked with Castle Douglas (F H W)**				
	Alison H. Burnside (Mrs) MA BD	1990	2018	1 Castle View, Castle Douglas DG7 1BG	01556 505983
				ABurnside@churchofscotland.org.uk	
22	**Border Kirk (F W)**			**Chapel Street, Carlisle CA1 1JA**	**01228 591757**
	Wesley C. Brandon BA MDiv	2003	2022	95 Pinecroft, Carlisle CA3 0DB	01228 599572
				WBrandon@churchofscotland.org.uk	
23	**Caerlaverock (F) linked with Dumfries: St Mary's-Greyfriars' (F H W)**				
	Vacant			4 Georgetown Crescent, Dumfries DG1 4EQ	01387 270128
	Interim Moderator: Fiona A. Wilson			FWilson@churchofscotland.org.uk	01556 610708

24	**Caldwell and Dunlop (F W)**				
	Alison J.S. McBrier MA BD	2011	2017	4 Dampark, Dunlop, Kilmarnock KA3 4BZ AMcBrier@churchofscotland.org.uk	01560 673686
	New charge formed by the union of Caldwell and Dunlop				
25	**Canonbie United (F H W) linked with Liddesdale (F H W)**			**churchoffice@liddesdalechurch.org.uk**	**Liddesdale: 01387 375488**
	Morag Crossan BA	2016	2020	23 Langholm Street, Newcastleton TD9 0QX MCrossan@churchofscotland.org.uk	01387 375603 07861 736071
	Canonbie United is a Local Ecumenical Partnership with the United Free Church				
26	**Carsphairn** See Balmaclellan, Kells and Dalry				
27	**Castle Douglas** See Bengairn Parishes				
28	**Catrine** See Auchinleck				
29	**Closeburn (W) linked with Kirkmahoe (W)**				
	Vacant			The Manse, Kirkmahoe, Dumfries DG1 1ST	01387 710572
	Session Clerk, Closeburn: Jack Tait			jacktait1941@gmail.com	01848 331700
	Session Clerk, Kirkmahoe: Bob McBride			rjmcbride91@hotmail.com	07717 247092
30	**Colvend, Southwick and Kirkbean (W)**				
	John A.H. Murdoch BA BD DPSS	1979	2022	The Manse, Colvend, Dalbeattie DG5 4QN JMurdoch@churchofscotland.org.uk	01556 630255 07578 558978
31	**Corsock and Kirkpatrick Durham (W) linked with Crossmichael, Parton and Balmaghie (W)**				
	Vacant				
	Session Clerk, Corsock and Kirkpatrick Durham: Mary Burney			maryburney1@btinternet.com	01556 650503
	Session Clerk, Crossmichael, Parton and Balmaghie: Anne Carstairs			annegcarstairs@gmail.com	01556 670279
32	**Coylton (F W) linked with Drongan: The Schaw Kirk (F W)**				
	Alwyn Landman BTh MDiv MTh DMin	2005	2019	4 Hamilton Place, Coylton, Ayr KA6 6JQ ALandman@churchofscotland.org.uk	01292 571287
33	**Craigie Symington (W) linked with Prestwick: South (H W)**			**office.pwksouth@gmail.com**	**01292 678556**
	Vacant			68 St Quivox Road, Prestwick KA9 1JF	01292 478788
	Tom McLeod (Ordained Local Minister)	2014	2015	3 Martnaham Drive, Coylton KA6 6JE TMcLeod@churchofscotland.org.uk	01292 570100
	Session Clerk, Craigie Symington: Doreen Tait			tait_doreen@yahoo.co.uk	01563 830050

34	**Crosshouse (F H W)**			**crosshouseparishchurch@cpcteam.org.uk**	
	Vacant				
	Interim Moderator: John A. Urquhart			John.Urquhart@churchofscotland.org.uk	01563 538289
35	**Crossmichael, Parton and Balmaghie** See Corsock and Kirkpatrick Durham				
36	**Cumbrae, Fairlie and Largs (F H W)**				**Cumbrae: 01475 531198; Largs: 01475 675186**
	T. David Watson BSc BD (Moderator)	1988	2014	31 Douglas Street, Largs KA30 8PT DWatson@churchofscotland.org.uk	01475 672370
	Graham McWilliams BSc BD DMin (Team Minister)	2005	2019	14 Fairlieburne Gardens, Fairlie, Largs KA29 0ER GMcWilliams@churchofscotland.org.uk	01475 568515
	New charge formed by the union of Cumbrae, Fairlie, Largs: Clark Memorial, Largs: St Columba's and Largs: St John's				
37	**Cummertrees, Mouswald and Ruthwell (H W)**				
	Vacant			The Manse, Ruthwell, Dumfries DG1 4NP	01387 870217
	Interim Moderator: Gary J. Peacock			GPeacock@churchofscotland.org.uk	01387 730759
38	**Dalbeattie and Kirkgunzeon (F H W) linked with Urr (H W)**				
	Fiona A. Wilson (Mrs) BD	2008	2014	36 Mill Street, Dalbeattie DG5 4HE FWilson@churchofscotland.org.uk	01556 610708
39	**Dalmellington (F) linked with Patna Waterside (F)**				
	Vacant			4 Carsphairn Road, Dalmellington, Ayr KA6 7RE	01292 551503
	Interim Moderator: Allan S. Vint			AVint@churchofscotland.org.uk	01290 518528
40	**Dalry: St Margaret's (F W)**			**stmargaret@talktalk.net**	**01294 832264**
	Vacant				
	Interim Moderator: Norman R. Whyte			burraman@msn.com	07387 229806
41	**Dalry: Trinity (F H W)**				
	Vacant			Trinity Manse, 3 West Kilbride Road, Dalry KA24 5DX	01294 832363
42	**Dalrymple** See Ayr: St Leonard's				
43	**Drongan: The Schaw Kirk** See Coylton				

44	**Dumfries: Maxwelltown West (F H W)**				**01387 255900**
	Johannes Wildner MTh	2006	2021	Maxwelltown West Manse, 11 Laurieknowe, Dumfries DG2 7AH JWildner@churchofscotland.org.uk	01387 257238
45	**Dumfries: Northwest (F T)**				
	Vacant			c/o Church Office, Dumfries Northwest Church, Lochside Road, Dumfries DG2 0DZ	01387 249964
	Session Clerk: Clara Jackson			sessionclerk.dumfriesnorthwest@gmail.com	01387 249964
46	**Dumfries: St George's (F H W)**			**office@saint-georges.org.uk**	**01387 267072**
	Donald Campbell BD	1997		9 Nunholm Park, Dumfries DG1 1JP DCampbell@churchofscotland.org.uk	01387 252965
47	**Dumfries: St Mary's-Greyfriars'** See Caerlaverock				
48	**Dumfries: St Michael's and South (F W)**				
	Vacant			39 Cardoness Street, Dumfries DG1 3AL	01387 253849
	Session Clerk: Esther Preston			prestoncraigavon@supanet.com	01387 263402
49	**Dumfries: Troqueer (F H W)**			**secretary@troqueerparishchurch.com**	
	Vacant			Troqueer Manse, Troqueer Road, Dumfries DG2 7DF	01387 253043
	Interim Moderator: Pamela A. Bellis			PBellis@churchofscotland.org.uk	07751 379249
50	**Dundonald (F H W)**				
	Lynsey J. Brennan BSc MSc BA	2019		64 Main Street, Dundonald, Kilmarnock KA2 9HG LBrennan@churchofscotland.org.uk	01563 850243
51	**Dunscore (F W) linked with Glencairn and Moniaive (F W)**				
	Mark R.S. Smith BSc CertMin	1990	202[illegible]	The Manse, Wallaceton, Auldgirth, Dumfries DG2 0TJ Mark.Smith@churchofscotland.org.uk	01387 820475
52	**Durisdeer linked with Penpont, Keir and Tynron linked with Thornhill (H)**				
	Vacant			The Manse, Manse Park, Thornhill DG3 5ER	01848 331191
	Interim Moderator: David Gibson (Mr)			gibson186@btinternet.com	01387 250318
53	**Ervie Kirkcolm (H W) linked with Leswalt (W)**				
	Guardianship of the Presbytery				
	Interim Moderator: Gillian Lynn (Mrs)			randglynn@btinternet.com	01776 860665

54 Fenwick (F H W)				
Vacant				
Interim Moderator: Kim Watt			KWatt@churchofscotland.org.uk	07881 680982
55 Gatehouse and Borgue (W) linked with Tarff and Twynholm				
Valerie J. Ott (Mrs) BA BD DipARSM	2002		The Manse, Planetree Park, Gatehouse of Fleet, Castle Douglas DG7 2EQ VOtt@churchofscotland.org.uk	01557 814233
56 Girvan: Valley (F H W)			**churchoffice12@btconnect.com**	**01465 712672**
Vacant			38 The Avenue, Girvan KA26 9DS	01465 713203
New charge formed by the union of Barr, Dailly, Girvan: North and Girvan: South				
57 Glasserton, Isle of Whithorn and Whithorn: St Ninian's Priory (F W)				
Alexander I. Currie BD CPS	1990		The Manse, St Ninian's Grove, Whithorn, Newton Stewart DG8 8PT ACurrie@churchofscotland.org.uk	01988 500267
New charge formed by the union of Glasserton and Isle of Whithorn and Whithorn: St Ninian's Priory				
58 Glencairn and Moniaive See Dunscore				
59 Gretna: Old, Gretna: St Andrew's, Half Morton and Kirkpatrick Fleming (F H) linked with Hoddom, Kirtle-Eaglesfield and Middlebie (F W)				
Lynn Brady BD DipMin (Transition Minister)	1996	2024	The Manse, Main Road, Ecclefechan, Lockerbie DG11 3BU LBrady@churchofscotland.org.uk	01576 300108 07815 922889
60 Hoddom, Kirtle-Eaglesfield and Middlebie (F W) See Gretna: Old, Gretna: St Andrew's, Half Morton and Kirkpatrick Fleming				
61 Hurlford (F H W)				
Vacant			12 Main Road, Crookedholm, Kilmarnock KA3 6JT	01563 539739
Session Clerk: Elizabeth F.G. Lauchlan			elizabeth.lauchlan@btinternet.com	01563 537381
Interim Moderator: Colin G.F. Brockie			revcolin@uwclub.net	01563 559960
62 Irongray, Lochrutton and Terregles				
Gary J. Peacock MA BD MTh	2015		The Manse, Shawhead, Dumfries DG2 9SJ GPeacock@churchofscotland.org.uk	01387 730759
63 Irvine: Old (F H)				**01294 273503**
Vacant			22 Kirk Vennel, Irvine KA12 0DQ	01294 279265
Interim Moderator: Alexander C. Wark			alecwark@yahoo.co.uk	01563 559581

64	**Irvine: United (F H T W)**			**secretary@fullartonchurch.co.uk**	**01294 273741**
	Neil Urquhart BD DipMin DipSC (Moderator)	1989		48 Waterside, Irvine KA12 8QJ NUrquhart@churchofscotland.org.uk	01294 279909
	Jamie W. Milliken BD DMin PGCertADS (Team Minister)	2005	2020	7 Sycamore Wynd, Perceton, Irvine KA11 2FA JMilliken@churchofscotland.org.uk	01294 211893

New charge formed by the union of Dreghorn and Springside, Irvine: Fullarton, Irvine: Girdle Toll, Irvine: Mure Relief and Irvine: St Andrew's

65	**Irvine Valley (F H W)**				**Darvel: 01560 322924; Galston: 01563 820136**
	Vacant			19 Manse Gardens, Galston KA4 8DJ	01563 257172

New charge formed by the union of Darvel, Galston, and Newmilns: Loudoun

66	**Kilbirnie: New (F H W)**				
	Fiona C. Ross (Miss) BD DipMin	1996	2004	Manse of St Columba's, Dipple Road, Kilbirnie KA25 7JU FRoss@churchofscotland.org.uk	01505 683342

New charge formed by the union of Kilbirnie: Auld Kirk and Kilbirnie: St Columba's

67	**Kilmarnock: Kay Park (F H W)**			**kppcchurchoffice@gmail.com**	**01563 318052**
	Fiona E. Maxwell BA BD	2004	2013	1 Glebe Court, Kilmarnock KA1 3BD FMaxwell@churchofscotland.org.uk	01563 521762
68	**Kilmarnock: New Laigh Kirk (F H W)**			**newlaighkirkchurch@hotmail.com**	**01563 573307**
	David S. Cameron BD	2001		1 Holmes Farm Road, Kilmarnock KA1 1TP David.Cameron@churchofscotland.org.uk	01563 525416

New charge formed by the union of Kilmarnock: New Laigh Kirk and Kilmarnock: St John's Onthank

69	**Kilmarnock: St Kentigern's (F W)**			**hub@stkentigern.org.uk**	
	Vacant				
	Interim Moderator: George K. Lind			gklind@talktalk.net	01560 428732
70	**Kilmarnock: St Marnock's (F W)**				
	James McNaughtan BD DipMin	1983	1989	35 South Gargieston Drive, Kilmarnock KA1 1TB JMcNaughtan@churchofscotland.org.uk	01563 521665

Ayrshire Mission to the Deaf meets here

71	**Kilmaurs: St Maur's Glencairn (F H)**				
	John A. Urquhart BD	1993		9 Standalane, Kilmaurs, Kilmarnock KA3 2NB John.Urquhart@churchofscotland.org.uk	01563 538289

72	**Kilwinning: Abbey (F W)**				**01294 552606**
	Vacant			54 Dalry Road, Kilwinning KA13 7HE	01294 552606
	Isobel Beck BD DCS	2014	2016	16 Patrick Avenue, Stevenston KA20 4AW IBeck@churchofscotland.org.uk	07919 193425
	Interim Moderator: James J. McNay			JMcNay@churchofscotland.org.uk	07486 882099
73	**Kilwinning: Mansefield Trinity (F W)**				**01294 550746**
	Hilary J. Beresford BD PGCertCS	2000	2018	Mansefield Trinity Church, West Doura Way, Kilwinning KA13 6DY HBeresford@churchofscotland.org.uk	01294 550746
74	**Kirkconnel (H) linked with Sanquhar: St Bride's (F H W)**				
	Vacant				
	Session Clerk, Kirkconnel: Fay Rafferty			fayrafferty1957@gmail.com	01659 67650
	Session Clerk, Sanquhar: Robert Hughes			mackiehughes@hotmail.com	01659 50553
75	**Kirkcowan (H) linked with Wigtown (F H W)**				
	Eric Boyle BA MTh	2006		Seaview Manse, Church Lane, Wigtown, Newton Stewart DG8 9HT EBoyle@churchofscotland.org.uk	01988 402314
76	**Kirkcudbright (H W)**			**church@kirkcudbrightparishchurch.org.uk**	
	James F. Gatherer BD	1984	2020	6 Bourtree Avenue, Kirkcudbright DG6 4AU JGatherer@churchofscotland.org.uk	01557 339108
77	**Kirkmabreck (W) linked with Monigaff (H W)**				
	Vacant				
	Session Clerk, Kirkmabreck: Robert McQuistan			mcquistan@mcquistan.plus.com	01671 820327
	Session Clerk, Monigaff: Margaret McDowall (Mrs)			monigaffsessionclerk@gmail.com	01671 403847
78	**Kirkmahoe** See Closeburn				
79	**Kirkmaiden (H)**				
	Guardianship of the Presbytery				
	Session Clerk: Maureen Graham (Mrs)			maureen.grahamm@btinternet.com	01776 840209
80	**Kirkmichael linked with Straiton: St Cuthbert's (W)**			**straitonchurchayr@gmail.com**	
	W. Gerald Jones MA BD ThM	1984	1985	The Manse, Patna Road, Kirkmichael, Maybole KA19 7PJ WJones@churchofscotland.org.uk	01655 750286

81	**Kirkmichael, Tinwald and Torthorwald (W)**				
	Vacant			Manse of Tinwald, 6 Sundew Lane, Dumfries DG1 3TW	
	Mhairi Wallace (Ordained Local Minister)	2013	2017	5 Dee Road, Kirkcudbright DG 4HQ MWallace@churchofscotland.org.uk	07701 375064
82	**Langholm, Eskdalemuir, Ewes and Westerkirk (F)**			**leewparishchurch@outlook.com**	
	Vacant			The Manse, Thomas Telford Road, Langholm DG13 0BL	01387 380252
	Interim Moderator: Morag Crossan			MCrossan@churchofscotland.org.uk	01387 375603 07861 736071
83	**Leswalt** See Ervie Kirkcolm				
84	**Liddesdale** See Canonbie United				
85	**Lochend and New Abbey (W)**			**lochendnachurch@gmail.com**	
	Vacant			New Abbey Manse, 32 Main Street, New Abbey, Dumfries DG2 8BY	01387 850490
	Elizabeth A. Mack (Miss) DipPE (Auxiliary Minster)	1994	2018	24 Roberts Crescent, Dumfries DG2 7RS mackliz@btinternet.com	01387 264847
	Interim Moderator: Johannes Wildner			JWildner@churchofscotland.org.uk	01387 257238
86	**Lochmaben (H W)**				
	Vacant			The Manse, Barrashead, Lochmaben, Lockerbie DG11 1QF	01387 810640
	Session Clerk, Lochmaben: Winifred B. Dickie (Mrs)			michael.dickie44@btinternet.com	01387 810713
	New charge formed by the union of Lochmaben and St Mungo				
87	**Lockerbie: Dryfesdale, Hutton, Corrie and Applegarth (F W)**				
	Frances M. Henderson BA BD PhD (Transition Minister)	2006	2024	Dryfesdale Manse, 5 Carlisle Road, Lockerbie DG11 2DW FHenderson@churchofscotland.org.uk	01576 204188
	New charge formed by the union of Applegarth, Sibbaldbie and Johnstone, and Lockerbie: Dryfesdale, Hutton and Corrie				
88	**Luce Valley and Inch (F W) linked with Portpatrick (F) linked with Stoneykirk (F)**				
	Stephen Ogston MPhys MSc BD	2009	2017	Ladyburn Manse, Main Street, Glenluce, Newton Stewart DG8 0PU SOgston@churchofscotland.org.uk	01581 300316
	Luce Valley and Inch was formed by the union of Inch and Luce Valley				
89	**Lugar (W) linked with Old Cumnock: Old (H)**				
	Vacant			33 Barrhill Road, Cumnock KA18 1PJ	01290 420769

90 Mauchline (F H W) linked with Sorn (F) — **mauchlineparish@yahoo.com**
Allan S. Vint BSc BD MTh PhD 1989 2021 — 4 Westside Gardens, Mauchline KA5 5DJ — 01290 518528
AVint@churchofscotland.org.uk — 07795 483070

91 Millisle (H) linked with Mochrum
Guardianship of the Presbytery
Session Clerk, Mochrum: Jenni Gray (Mrs) — j.saunders201@btinternet.com — 01988 700948

Millisle was formed by the union of Kirkinner and Sorbie

92 Mochrum See Millisle
93 Monigaff See Kirkmabreck

94 Monkton and Prestwick: North (F H T W) — **office@mpnchurch.org.uk** — **01292 678810**
Vacant — 40 Monkton Road, Prestwick KA9 1AR — 01292 471379
Interim Moderator: Brian R. Hendrie — BHendrie@churchofscotland.org.uk — 01292 283825

95 Muirkirk (H W) linked with Old Cumnock: Trinity (F W)
Vacant — 46 Ayr Road, Cumnock KA18 1DW — 01290 422145
Interim Moderator: Alwyn Landman — ALandman@churchofscotland.org.uk — 01292 571287

96 New Cumnock (F H W)
Vacant — 37 Castle, New Cumnock, Cumnock KA18 4AG — 01290 338296
Interim Moderator: Kenneth B. Yorke — kenyorke@yahoo.com — 01292 670476

97 North Carrick (F H W)
Vacant

New charge formed by the union of Crosshill, Kirkoswald and Maybole

98 Ochiltree (F W) linked with Stair (F W)
Vacant — 10 Mauchline Road, Ochiltree KA18 2PZ — 01290 700365
Interim Moderator: George R. Fiddes — grfiddes@outlook.com — 01292 737512

99 Old Cumnock: Old See Lugar
100 Old Cumnock: Trinity See Muirkirk
101 Patna Waterside See Dalmellington

102 Penninghame (F H W)				
Edward D. Lyons BD MTh	2007		The Manse, 1A Corvisel Road, Newton Stewart DG8 6LW ELyons@churchofscotland.org.uk	01671 404425
103 Penpont, Keir and Tynron See Durisdeer				
104 Portpatrick See Luce Valley and Inch				
105 Prestwick: Kingcase (F H W)			**office@kingcase.co.uk**	**01292 470755**
Ian Wiseman BTh DipHSW	1993	2015	15 Bellrock Avenue, Prestwick KA9 1SQ IWiseman@churchofscotland.org.uk	01292 479571
106 Prestwick: St Nicholas' (H W)			**office@stnicholasprestwick.org.uk**	**01292 671547**
Vacant			3 Bellevue Road, Prestwick KA9 1NW	
Interim Moderator: David R. Gemmell			DGemmell@churchofscotland.org.uk	01292 864140
107 Prestwick: South See Craigie Symington				
108 Sanquhar: St Bride's See Kirkconnel				
109 Sorn See Mauchline				
110 Stair See Ochiltree				
111 Stevenston (F H W)				
Vacant			27 Cuninghame Drive, Stevenston KA20 4AB	01294 608993
New charge formed by the union of Stevenston: Ardeer, Stevenston: High and Stevenston: Livingstone				
112 Stewarton: John Knox (F T W)			**getconnected@johnknox.org.uk**	**01560 484560**
Gavin A. Niven BSc MSc BD	2010		27 Avenue Street, Stewarton, Kilmarnock KA3 5AP GNiven@churchofscotland.org.uk	01560 482418
113 Stewarton: St Columba's (H W)			**stewartonstcolumbas@gmail.com**	
Vacant			1 Kirk Glebe, Stewarton, Kilmarnock KA3 5BJ	01560 485113
Interim Moderator: William C. Hewitt			WHewitt@churchofscotland.org.uk	01563 533312
114 Stoneykirk See Luce Valley and Inch				
115 Straiton: St Cuthbert's See Kirkmichael				
116 Stranraer (F H W)				
Andy Muir BA	2022		Birchgrove, Whitehouse Road, Stranraer DG9 0JB AMuir@churchofscotland.org.uk	01776 700867

117 Tarbolton See Annbank
118 Tarff and Twynholm See Gatehouse and Borgue
119 Thornhill See Durisdeer

120 Troon (F H W)		**office@troonportlandchurch.org.uk** **stmeddanschurch@gmail.com**	**01292 317929** **01292 317750**
Vacant (Moderator)			
Vacant (Team Minister)			
Gillean S.M. Richmond BDS BA (Assistant Minister)	2022	GRichmond@churchofscotland.org.uk	07811 835197

New charge formed by the union of Troon: Old, Troon: Portland and Troon: St Meddan's

121 Tundergarth			
Guardianship of the Presbytery			
Session Clerk: David Paterson		jilljoe@tiscali.co.uk	07982 037029

122 Upper Annandale (F H W)			
Elsie Macrae BA	2020	The Manse, 1 Meadow Bank, Moffat DG10 9LR Elsie.Macrae@churchofscotland.org.uk	01683 225146

New charge formed by the union of Kirkpatrick Juxta, Moffat: St Andrew's and Wamphray

123 Urr See Dalbeattie and Kirkgunzeon

124 West Kilbride (F H T W)		**office@wkpc.church**	**01294 829902**
James J. McNay MA BD	2008	The Manse, Goldenberry Avenue, West Kilbride KA23 9LJ JMcNay@churchofscotland.org.uk	07486 882099

125 Wigtown See Kirkcowan

B. In other appointments: members of Presbytery

Blackshaw, Christopher J. BA(Theol) *Chris Blackshaw is a Methodist Minister*	2015 2017	Pioneer Minister, Farming Community	Ellwood Croft, Gamblesby, Penrith CA10 1HY CBlackshaw@churchofscotland.org.uk	07980 975062
Campbell, Duncan	2023	Ordained Local Minister	Duncan.Campbell@churchofscotland.org.uk	
Campbell, Neil G. BA BD	1988 2018	Chaplain, HM Prison Dumfries	12 Charles Street, Annan DG12 5AJ neil.campbell2@prisons.gov.scot	

Clancy, P. Jill (Mrs) BD DipMin	2000	2017	Chaplain, HM Prison Barlinnie	27 Cross Street, Galston KA4 8AA JClancy@churchofscotland.org.uk	07956 557087
Frail, Nicola R. BLE MBA MDiv	2000	2012	Army Chaplain	Chaplains Office, DM (SW), Whittington Barracks, Lichfield WS14 9PY Nicola.Frail188@mod.gov.uk	
Harvey, P. Ruth (Ms) MA BD	2007	2020	Leader, Iona Community	Croslands, Beacon Street, Penrith CA11 7TZ ruth@iona.org.uk	01768 840749 07403 638339
Hogg, James	2018		Ordained Local Minister	JHogg@churchofscotland.org.uk	07974 576295
Kelly, Ewan R. BSc MB ChB BD PhD	1994	2020	Lecturer in Healthcare Chaplaincy, University of Glasgow	ewan.kelly@glasgow.ac.uk	
Steenbergen, Pauline (Ms) MA BD	1996	2022	Cumbria Fresh Expression Team Leader, Diocese of Carlisle	p.steenbergen1@gmail.com	07743 927182
Watt, Kim CertThS	2015		Ordained Local Minister, Presbytery	Reddans Park Gate, The Crescent, Stewarton, Kilmarnock KA3 5AY KWatt@churchofscotland.org.uk	01560 482267

C. Retaining: members of Presbytery

Adamson, R. Angus BD	2006	2020	(Brodick with Corrie with Lochranza and Pirnmill with Shiskine)	Otterburn, Corriecravie, Isle of Arran KA27 8PD	01770 870228
Aitken, Fraser R. GCSJ MA BD	1978	2019	(Ayr: St Columba)	Sandringham, 38 Coylebank, Prestwick KA9 2DH sandringham381@outlook.com	01292 225087
Anderson, Robert A. MA BD DPhil	1984	2017	(Blackburn and Seafield)	Aiona, 8 Old Auchans View, Dundonald KA2 9EX robertanderson307@btinternet.com	01563 850554 07484 206190
Baker, Carolyn M. (Mrs) BD	1997	2008	(Ochiltree with Stair)	Clanary, 1 Maxwell Drive, Newton Stewart DG8 6EL cncbaker@btinternet.com	01671 404292
Becker, Allison E. BA MDiv	2015	2022	(Kilmarnock: St John's Onthank)	ABecker@churchofscotland.org.uk	
Black, Andrew R. BD CertMin	1987	2018	(Irvine: Relief Bourtreehill)	4 Nursery Wynd, Kilwinning KA13 6ER andrewblack@tiscali.co.uk	01294 673090
Bogle, Thomas C. BD CPS HDipRE	1983	2003	(Fisherton with Maybole: West)	38 McEwan Crescent, Mossblown, Ayr KA6 5DR	01292 521215
Bond, Maurice S. BA DipEd MTh PhD	1983	2019	(Dumfries: St Michael's and South)	15 Pleasance Avenue, Dumfries DG2 7JJ	
Brockie, Colin G.F. BSc(Eng) BD SOSc	1967	2007	(Kilmarnock: Grange)	36 Braehead Court, Kilmarnock KA3 7AB colin@brockie.org.uk	01563 559960
Brown, H. Taylor BD CertMin FRAI	1997	2022	(Kilmarnock: St Marnock's)	HBrown@churchofscotland.org.uk	07596 111310
Brown, Jack M. BSc BD	1977	2012	(Applegarth, Sibbaldbie and Johnstone with Lochmaben)	69 Berelands Road, Prestwick KA9 1ER jackmbrown47@gmail.com	01292 477151
Buck, Maxine SRN ONC CertMgS	2007	2023	(Auxiliary Minister, Presbytery of Forth Valley and Clydesdale)	Kirkgate, 92 Main Street, Dunlop, Kilmarnock KA3 4AG MBuck@churchofscotland.org.uk	07812 712197
Burgess, Paul C.J. MA	1970	2003	(World Mission Partner, Gujranwala Theological Seminary, Pakistan)	Springvale, Halket Road, Lugton, Kilmarnock KA4 3EE paulandcathie@gmail.com	01505 850254
Burns, John H. BSc BD	1985	2019	(Inch with Portpatrick with Stranraer: Trinity)	The Cabin, Dundeugh, Dalry DG7 3SY	01644 460553
Cairns, Alexander B. MA	1957	2009	(Turin)	Beechwood, Main Street, Sandhead, Stranraer DG9 9JG dorothycairns@aol.com	01776 830389
Cant, Thomas M. MA BD	1964	2004	(Paisley: Laigh Kirk)	3 Meikle Cutstraw, Stewarton, Kilmarnock KA3 5HU revtmcant@aol.com	01560 480566

Name	Ord.	Ret.	Charge	Address	Phone
Crichton, James MA BD MTh	1969	2010	(Crosshill with Dalrymple)	60 Kyle Court, Ayr KA7 3AW crichton.james@btinternet.com	07549 988643
Cruickshank, Norman BA BD	1983	2006	(West Kilbride: Overton)	24D Faulds Wynd, Seamill, West Kilbride KA23 9FA	01294 822239
Cuthbert, Helen E. MA MSc BD	2009	2021	(New Cumnock)	63 Haining Avenue, Bellfield, Kilmarnock KA1 3QN helenncuthbertk21@hotmail.co.uk	07941 027480
Dee, Oonagh	2014	2019	(Ordained Local Minister, Bengairn Parishes with Castle Douglas)	Kendoon, Merse Way, Kippford, Dalbeattie DG5 4LL ODee@churchofscotland.org.uk	01556 620001
Dempster, Eric T. MBA	2016	2021	(Ordained Local Minister, Lockerbie: Dryfesdale, Hutton and Corrie)	Annanside, Wamphray, Moffat DG10 9LZ	01576 470496
Dickie, Michael M. BSc	1955	1993	(Ayr: Castlehill)	8 Noltmire Road, Ayr KA8 9ES	01292 618512
Dobby, D. Brian BA MA	1999	2023	(Rosyth)	51 Darg Road, Stevenston KA20 3AZ	
Elliott, Kenneth C. BD BA Cert Min	1989	2024	(Craigie Symington with Prestwick: South)	KElliott@churchofscotland.org.uk	
Falconer, Alan D. MA BD DLitt DD	1972	2011	(Aberdeen: St Machar's Cathedral)	18 North Crescent Road, Ardrossan KA22 8NA alanfalconer@gmx.com	07491 484800
Faris, Janice M. (Mrs) BSc BD	1991	2018	(Innerleithen, Traquair and Walkerburn)	Overdale Cottage, Grange Park Road, Orton Grange, Carlisle CA5 6LT revjfaris@gmail.com	07427 371239
Fiddes, George R. BD	1979	2019	(Prestwick: St Nicholas')	4 St Cuthbert's Crescent, Prestwick KA9 2EG grfiddes@outlook.com	01292 737512 07925 004062
Finch, Graham S. MA BD	1977	2015	(Cadder)	32a St Mary Street, Kirkcudbright DG6 4DN gsf231@gmail.com	01557 620123
Garrity, T. Alan W. BSc BD MTh	1969	2008	(Bermuda: Christ Church, Warwick)	17 Solomon's View, Dunlop, Kilmarnock KA3 4ES alangarrity@btinternet.com	01560 486879
Glencross, William M. LTh	1968	1999	(Bellshill: Macdonald Memorial)	1 Lochay Place, Troon KA10 7HH	01292 317097
Godfrey, Linda BSc BD	2012	2014	(Ayr: St Leonard's with Dalrymple)	9 Taybank Drive, Ayr KA7 4RL godfreykayak@aol.com	07825 663866
Guthrie, James A.	1969	2005	(Corsock and Kirkpatrick Durham with Crossmichael and Parton)	2 Barrhill Road, Pinwherry, Girvan KA26 0QE p.h.m.guthrie@btinternet.com	01465 841236
Hall, William M. BD	1972	2010	(Kilmarnock: Old High Kirk)	33 Cairns Terrace, Kilmarnock KA1 2JG revwillie@talktalk.net	01563 525080
Hammond, Richard J. BA BD	1993	2007	(Kirkmahoe)	3 Marchfield Mount, Marchfield, Dumfries DG1 1SE libby.hammond@virgin.net	07764 465783
Harper, David L. BSc BD	1972	2012	(Troon: St Meddan's)	19 Calder Avenue, Troon KA10 7JT d.l.harper@btinternet.com	01292 312626
Hewitt, William C. BD DipPS	1977	2017	(Presbytery Clerk: Glasgow)	60 Woodlands Grove, Kilmarnock KA3 1TZ WHewitt@churchofscotland.org.uk	01563 533312
Hine, Kristina I. BS MDiv	2011	2024	(Galston)	KHine@churchofscotland.org.uk	
Hogg, William T. MA BD	1979	2018	(Kirkconnel with Sanquhar: St Bride's)	30 Castle Street, Kirkcudbright DG6 4JD	07515 102776
Horsburgh, Gary E. BA	1977	2015	(Dreghorn and Springside)	1 Woodlands Grove, Kilmarnock KA3 1TY garyhorsburgh@hotmail.co.uk	01563 624508
Howie, Marion L.K. (Mrs) MA ARCS	1992	2019	(Auxiliary Minister, Dalry: St Margaret's)	51 High Road, Stevenston KA20 3DY MHowie@churchofscotland.org.uk	01294 466571

Huggett, Judith A. (Miss) BA BD	1990	2020	(Lead Chaplain, NHS Ayrshire and Arran)	3 Black Morrow Close, Kirkcudbright DG6 4DF	01557 330931
Hutcheson, Norman M. MA BD	1973	2013	(Dalbeattie with Urr)	66 Maxwell Park, Dalbeattie DG5 4LS norman.hutcheson@gmail.com	01556 610102
Irving, Douglas R. LLB BD WS	1984	2016	(Kirkcudbright)	17 Galla Crescent, Dalbeattie DG5 4JY douglas.irving@outlook.com	01556 610156
Jackson, Nancy M. CertThRS CertChS	2009	2015	(Auxiliary Minister, Crosshill with Maybole)	35 Auchentrae Crescent, Ayr KA7 4BD nancyjaxon@btinternet.com	01292 262034
Keating, Glenda K. (Mrs) MTheol	1996	2015	(Craigie Symington)	8 Wardlaw Gardens, Irvine KA11 2EW kirkglen@btinternet.com	01294 218820
Kelly, William W. BSc BD	1994	2014	(Dumfries: Troqueer)	8 Talia Drive, Stirling, WA 6021 Australia wwkelly@yahoo.com	04 11 104890
Kyle, Caryl A.E. BD DipEd	2008	2021	(Holytown with New Stevenston: Wrangholm Kirk)	58 Kelvin Walk, Netherhall, Largs KA30 8SJ caryl_kyle@hotmail.com	01475 310390
Lacy, David W. DL BA BD DLitt	1976	2017	(Kilmarnock: Kay Park)	4 Cairns Terrace, Kilmarnock KA1 2JG DLacy@churchofscotland.org.uk	01563 624034 07974 760272
Lamarti, Samuel H. BD MTh PhD	1979	2006	(Stewarton: John Knox)	7 Dalwhinnie Crescent, Kilmarnock KA3 1QS samlamar@pobroadband.co.uk	01563 529632
Lennox, Lawrie I. MA BD DipEd	1991	2006	(Cromar)	7 Carwinshoch View, Ayr KA7 4AY lennox127@btinternet.com	01292 288658
Lind, George K. BD MCIBS	1998	2017	(Stewarton: St Columba's)	Endrig, 98 Loudoun Road, Newmilns KA16 9HQ gklind@talktalk.net	01560 428732
Lines, Charles M.D. BA	2010	2022	(Carnock and Oakley)	CLines@churchofscotland.org.uk	07909 762257
Lochrie, John S. BSc BD MTh PhD	1967	2008	(Arnsheen Barrhill and Colmonell: St Colmon)	Cosyglen, Kilkerran, Maybole KA19 8LS revjslochrie@btinternet.com	01465 811262
MacDonald, Roderick I.T. BD CertMin	1992	2022	(Beith)	27 Holmston Crescent, Ayr KA7 3JJ RMacDonald@churchofscotland.org.uk	
Macintyre, Thomas MA BD	1972	2011	(Sandsting and Aithsting with Walls and Sandness)	lappideks46@gmail.com	
Mackay, Marjory H. (Mrs) BD DipEd CCE	1998	2008	(Cumbrae)	4 Golf Road, Millport, Isle of Cumbrae KA28 0HB marjory.mackay@gmail.com	01475 530388
MacLeod, Ian LTh BA MTh PhD	1969	2006	(Brodick with Corrie)	Cromla Cottage, Corrie, Isle of Arran KA27 8JB i.macleod829@btinternet.com	01770 810237
MacPherson, Gordon C. MA BD MTh	1963	1988	(Associate, Kilmarnock: Henderson)	6 Crosbie Place, Troon KA10 6EY ggmacpherson@btinternet.com	01292 679146
Matthews, John C. OBE MA BD MTh	1992	2010	(Glasgow: Ruchill Kelvinside)	12 Arrol Drive, Ayr KA7 4AF mejohnmatthews@gmail.com	01292 264382
Mayes, Robert BD CertMin	1982	2017	(Dundonald)	Garfield Cottage, Sorn Road, Mauchline KA5 6HQ bobmayes3@gmail.com	01290 519869
McAllister, Anne C. BSc DipEd CCS	2013	2021	(Ordained Local Minister, Kilmarnock: St Kentigern's)	39 Bowes Rigg, Stewarton, Kilmarnock KA3 5EN AMcAllister@churchofscotland.org.uk	01560 483191
McCallum, Alexander D. BD	1987	2005	(Saltcoats: New Trinity)	59 Woodcroft Avenue, Largs KA30 9EW sandyandjose@madasafish.com	01475 670133
McCulloch, James D. BD MIOP MIP3 FSAScot	1996	2016	(Hurlford)	18 Edradour Place, Dunsmuir Park, Kilmarnock KA3 1US mccullochmanse1@btinternet.com	01563 535833

McGurk, Andrew F. BD	1983	2011	(Largs: St John's)	15 Fraser Avenue, Troon KA10 6XF afmcg.largs@talk21.com	01292 676008
McKay, David M. MA BD	1979	2007	(Kirkpatrick Juxta with Moffat: St Andrew's with Wamphray)	20 Auld Brig View, Auldgirth, Dumfries DG2 0XE davidmckay20@tiscali.co.uk	01387 740013
McKenzie, William M. DA	1958	1993	(Dumfries: Troqueer)	41 Kingholm Road, Dumfries DG1 4SR mckenzie.dumfries@btinternet.com	01387 253688
McKinnon, Lily F. H. (Mrs) MA BD PGCE	1993	2021	(Kilmory with Lamlash)	Rowan Cottage, 6 Sheean Drive, Brodick, Isle of Arran KA27 8DH lily.mackinnon@yahoo.co.uk	07917 548357
McLauchlan, Mary C. (Mrs) LTh	1997	2013	(Mochrum)	3 Ayr Street, Moniaive, Thornhill DG3 4HP mary@revmother.co.uk	01848 200786
McLeod, David C. BSc MEng BD	1969	2001	(Dundee: Fairmuir)	76 Ayr Road, Prestwick KA9 1RR	
McNidder, Roderick H. BD DipCE	1987	2007	(Chaplain: NHS Ayrshire and Arran Trust)	6 Hollow Park, Alloway, Ayr KA7 4SR roddymcnidder@sky.com	01292 442554
Mitchell, D. Ross BA BD	1972	2007	(West Kilbride: St Andrew's)	11 Dunbar Gardens, Saltcoats KA21 6GJ ross.mitchell@virgin.net	01294 474375
Moore, Douglas T.	2003	2019	(Auxiliary Minister, Coylton with Drongan: The Schaw Kirk)	9 Midton Avenue, Prestwick KA9 1PU douglastmoore@hotmail.com	01292 671352
Morrison, Alistair H. BTh DipYCS	1985	2004	(Paisley: St Mark's Oldhall)	92 St Leonard's Road, Ayr KA7 2PU alistairhmorrison@gmail.com	01292 266021
Ness, David T. LTh	1972	2008	(Ayr: St Quivox)	17 Winston Avenue, Prestwick KA9 2EZ davidtness@gmail.com	01292 471625
Ogston, Edgar J. BSc BD	1976	2017	(North West Lochaber)	14 North Park Avenue, Girvan KA26 9DH edgar.ogston@macfish.com	01465 713081
Owen, John J.C. LTh	1967	2001	(Applegarth and Sibbaldbie with Lochmaben)	5 Galla Avenue, Dalbeattie DG5 4JZ jj.owen@onetel.net	01556 612125
Paterson, John L. MA BD STM	1964	2003	(Linlithgow: St Michael's)	9 The Pines, Murdoch's Lane, Alloway, Ayr KA7 4WD lip38rev@gmail.com	01292 443615
Paterson, John W. BSc BD DipEd	1994	2024	(Lugar with Old Cumnock: Old)	paterson-j6@sky.com	
Pickles, Robert G. D. W. BD MPhil PhD	1984	2023	(Langholm, Eskdalemuir, Ewes and Westerkirk)	10 Houliston Avenue, Dumfries DG2 7BF RPickles@churchofscotland.org.uk	07448 858818
Rae, Scott M. MBE BD CPS	1976	2016	(Muirkirk with Old Cumnock: Trinity)	2 Primrose Place, Kilmarnock KA1 2RR scottrae1@btopenworld.com	01563 532711
Roy, Iain M. MA BD	1960	1997	(Stevenston: Livingstone)	2 The Fieldings, Dunlop, Kilmarnock KA3 4AU	01560 483072
Sanderson, Alastair M. LTh BA	1971	2007	(Craigie with Symington)	26 Main Street, Monkton, Prestwick KA9 2QL aesanderson2@gmail.com	01292 475819
Shaw, Catherine A.M. MA DipCE BA	1998	2005	(Auxiliary Minister, Kilmarnock: St. John's Onthank)	40 Merrygreen Place, Stewarton, Kilmarnock KA3 5EP catherine.shaw@tesco.net	01560 483352
Sheppard, Michael J. BD	1997	2016	(Ervie Kirkcolm with Leswalt)	4 Mill Street, Drummore, Stranraer DG9 9PS michaelsheppard00@gmail.com	01776 840369
Simpson, Edward V. BSc BD	1972	2009	(Glasgow: Giffnock South)	7 Whitehill Grove, Newton Mearns, Glasgow G77 5DH eddie.simpson3@talktalk.net	0141 237 4048 07896 013605

Sorensen, Alan K. DL BD MTh DipMin FSAScot	1983	2022	(Greenock: Wellpark Mid Kirk)	51A Castlepark Drive, Fairlie KA29 0DG ASorensen@churchofscotland.org.uk	01475 568314
Steele, Hugh D. LTh DipMin	1994	2020	(Kelty)	23 Mossgiel Avenue, Troon KA10 7DQ hugdebra@btinternet.com	07449 974940
Stewart, David MA DipEd BD MTh	1977	2013	(Howwood)	72 Glen Avenue, Largs KA30 8QQ revdavidst@aol.com	01475 675159
Stirling, Ian R. BSc BD MTh MSc DPT	1990	2021	(Fisherton with Kirkoswald)		
Sutherland, Colin A. LTh	1995	2007	(Blantyre: Livingstone Memorial)	71 Caulstran Road, Dumfries DG2 9FJ colin.csutherland@btinternet.com	01387 279954
Taylor, Andrew S. BTh FPhS	1959	1992	(Greenock: The Union)	9 Raillies Avenue, Largs KA30 8QY andrew.taylor_123@btinternet.com	01294 674709
Telfer, Alan B. BA CQSW BD	1983	2021	(Strathaven: Avendale Old and Drumclog)	22 Crawford Avenue, Prestwick KA9 2BN ATelfer@churchofscotland.org.uk	01292 474041
Thomson, Martin BSc DipEd BD	1988	2024	(Dalry: Trinity)	MThomson@churchofscotland.org.uk	
Urquhart, Barbara (Mrs) DCS	1986	2017	(Deacon, Kilmarnock: New Laigh Kirk)	9 Standalane, Kilmaurs, Kilmarnock KA3 2NB barbaraurquhart1@gmail.com	01563 538289
Ward, Alan H. MA BD	1978	2015	(Interim Minister, Kilwinning: Mansfield Trinity)	47 Meadowfoot Road, West Kilbride KA23 9BU alanhward@hotmail.co.uk	01294 822244 07709 906130
Wark, Alexander C. MA BD STM	1982	2017	(Mid Deeside)	43 Mure Avenue, Kilmarnock KA 3 1TT alecwark@yahoo.co.uk	01563 559581
Watson, Elizabeth R.L. (Miss) BA BD	1981	2021	(Whiting Bay and Kildonan)	3 Fernside, Brisbane Street, Largs KA30 8QG revewatson@btinternet.com	01475 673548
Welsh, Alex M. MA BD	1979	2019	(Hospital Chaplain, NHS Ayrshire and Arran)	8 Greenside Avenue, Prestwick KA9 2HB alexandevelyn@hotmail.com	01292 475341
Whitecross, Jeanette BD	2002	2019	(Kilwinning: Old)	4 Fir Bank, Ayr KA7 3SX jeanettewx@yahoo.com	07803 181150
Whyte, Norman R. BD MTh DipMin	1982	2022	(Ayton and District Churches)	34 Hollywood, Largs KA 30 8SP burraman@msn.com	07387 229806
Wilson, Muriel (Miss) MA BD DCS	1997	2011	(Deacon, Dalmellington with Patna Waterside)	28 Bellevue Crescent, Ayr KA7 2DR me.wilson28@btinternet.com	01292 264039
Yorke, Kenneth B. BD DipEd	1982	2009	(Dalmellington with Patna Waterside)	13 Annfield Terrace, Prestwick KA9 1PS kenyorke@yahoo.com	01292 670476
Young, Rona M. (Mrs) BD DipEd	1991	2015	(Ayr: St Quivox)	16 Macintyre Road, Prestwick KA9 1BE revronyoung@hotmail.com	01292 471982

D. In other appointments: not members of Presbytery

Nil

E. Retaining: not members of Presbytery

Name	Ord.	Ret.	Charge	Address	Phone
Bartholomew, David S. BSc MSc PhD BD	1994	2022	(Balmaclellan, Kells and Dalry with Carsphairn)	Craigend Cottage, Broughton, Biggar ML12 6HH dhbart99@gmail.com	
Christie, Robert S. MA BD ThM	1964	2000	(Kilmarnock: West High)	24 Homeroyal House, 2 Chalmers Crescent, Edinburgh EH9 1TP	
Cox, Lesley Paton BD	1994	2013	(Saline and Blairingone)		07468 852376
Davidson, Amelia (Mrs) BD	2004	2011	(Coatbridge: Calder)	11 St Mary's Place, Saltcoats KA21 5NY	
Finlay, William P. MA BD	1969	2000	(Glasgow: Townhead Blochairn)	High Corrie, Brodick, Isle of Arran KA27 8JB	01770 810689
Jackson, William BD CertMin	1994	2020	(Airdrie: New Monkland with Greengairs)	15 Dalwhinnie Crescent, Kilmarnock KA3 1QS	
Travers, Robert BA BD	1993	2015	(Irvine: Old)	74 Caledonian Road, Stevenston KA20 3LF roberttravers@live.co.uk	01294 279265
Webster, John G. BSc	1964	1998	(Glasgow: St John's Renfield)	Plane Tree, King's Cross, Brodick, Isle of Arran KA27 8RG	01770 700747

F. Inactive: not members of Presbytery

Name	Ord.	Ret.	Charge	Address	Phone
Gillon, D. Ritchie M. BD DipMin	1994	2017	(Paisley: St Luke's)	12 Fellhill Street, Ayr KA7 3JF revgillon@hotmail.com	01292 270018
Harris, Samuel McC. OStJ BA BD	1974	2010	(Rothesay: Trinity)	56 Rowland Street, Skipton, North Yorkshire BD23 2DU mhar10@hotmail.com	01756 794505
Logan, Thomas M. LTh	1971	1995	(Clydebank: Abbotsford)	3 Duncan Court, Kilmarnock KA3 7TF thomasmlogan8@gmail.com	01563 524398
MacKinnon, Ronald M. DCS	1996	2012	(Deacon, Cumbernauld: St Mungo's)	32 Strathclyde House, Shore Road, Skelmorlie PA17 5AN ronnie@ronniemac.plus.com	01475 521333 07594 427960
McIntyre, Allan G. BD	1985	2017	(Greenock: St Ninian's)	9a Templehill, Troon KA10 6BQ agmcintyre@lineone.net	07876 445626

G. Readers (active)

Anderson, James PhD DVM FRCPath	67 Henrietta Street, Girvan KA26 9AN	jc.anderson2@talktalk.net	01465 710059 07952 512720
Brown, S. Jeffrey BA	Skara Brae, Holm Park, 8 Ballplay Road, Moffat DG10 9JU	sjbrown@btinternet.com	01683 220475
Bruce, Andrew J.	57 Dockers Gardens, Ardrossan KA22 8GB	andrew_bruce2@sky.com	01294 605113
Cash, Marlane (Mrs)	5 Maxwell Drive, Newton Stewart DG8 6EL	marlaneg690@btinternet.com	01671 401375
Clarke, Elizabeth (Mrs)	Swallowbrae, Torbeg, Isle of Arran KA27 8HE	lizahclarke@gmail.com	01770 860219 07780 574367
Corson, Gwen (Mrs)	7 Sunnybrae, Borgue, Kirkcudbright DG46 4SJ	gwendolyn@hotmail.com	01557 870328
Currie, Archie BD	55 Central Avenue, Kilbirnie KA25 6JP	Archie.Currie@churchofscotland.org.uk	01505 681474 07881 452115
Dodds, Alan	Trinco, Battlehill, Annan DG12 6SN	alanandjen46@talktalk.net	01461 201235
Graham, Barbara (Miss) MA MLitt MPhil CertChSt	42 Annanhill Avenue, Kilmarnock KA1 2LQ	barbara.graham74@btinternet.com	01563 522108
Hunter, Jean C.Q. (Mrs) BD	Leucheram, Corrie, Isle of Arran KA27 8JB	j.hunter744@btinternet.com	01770 810218
Jackson, Susan (Mrs)	2 Northfield Park Gardens, Annan DG12 5FB	peter-jackson24@sky.com	07498 714675

Jamieson, Ian A.	2 Whinfield Avenue, Prestwick KA9 2BH	ian4189.jamieson@gmail.com	01242 476898
MacLeod, Sharon (Mrs)	Creag Dhubh, Golf Course Road, Whiting Bay, Isle of Arran KA27 8QT	macleodsharon@hotmail.com	01770 700353
Matheson, David	44 Auchenkeld Avenue, Heathhall, Dumfries DG1 3QY	davidb.matheson44@btinternet.com	01387 252042
McCool, Robert	17 McGregor Avenue, Stevenston KA20 4BA		01294 466548
McGeever, Gerard	23 Kinloch Avenue, Stewarton, Kilmarnock KA3 3HQ	mcgeege1@gmail.com	01560 484331
Mills, Catherine (Mrs)	59 Crossdene Road, Crosshouse, Kilmarnock KA2 0JU	cfmills5lib@hotmail.com	01563 535305
Monk, Geoffrey	Hilbre Cottage, Laurieston, Castle Douglas DG7 2PW		01644 450679
Morrison, James	27 Monkton Road, Prestwick KA9 1AP	jamessmorrisonprestwick@gmail.com	01292 479313 07773 287852
Morton, Andrew A. BSc	19 Sherwood Park, Lockerbie DG11 2DX	andrew_morton@mac.com	01576 203164
Murphy, Ian	56 Lamont Crescent, Netherthird, Cumnock KA18 3DU	ianm_cumnock@yahoo.co.uk	01290 423675
Murray, Brian	19 Snowdon Terrace, Seamill KA23 9HN	brian.murray100@btinternet.com	01294 822272
Ogston, Jean (Mrs)	14 North Park Avenue, Girvan KA26 9DH	jeanogston@gmail.com	01465 713081
Robertson, William	1 Archers Avenue, Irvine KA11 2GB	willie.robert@yahoo.co.uk	01294 203577
Ronald, Glenn	188 Prestwick Road, Ayr KA8 8NP	glennronald@btinternet.com	01292 286861
Ross, Magnus M.B. BA MEd	39 Beachway, Largs KA30 8QH	m.b.ross@btinternet.com	01475 689572
Savill, Hilda		qjhnic@gmail.com	01683 222854
Stewart, Christine (Mrs)	52 Kilnford Drive, Dundonald KA2 9ET	christistewart@btinternet.com	01563 850486
Whitelaw, David	9 Kirkhill, Kilwinning KA13 5NB	whitelawfam@talktalk.net	01294 551695

H. Ministries Development Staff

Algeo, Paul	North Ayr Parish Grouping – Family/Development Worker	PAlgeo@churchofscotland.org.uk
Anderson, Peter	Stewarton 20s-40s Initiative – Mission Pioneer	PAnderson@churchofscotland.org.uk
Beck, Isobel BD DCS	Kilwinning Abbey – Deacon	IBeck@churchofscotland.org.uk
Blackshaw, Christopher J. (Rev) BA(Theol)	Pioneer Minister, Farming Community	CBlackshaw@churchofscotland.org.uk
Devlin, Brian	Stevenston: Ardeer linked with Livingstone – Community Mission Worker	BDevlin@churchofscotland.org.uk
Forsyth, Stuart	Irvine Virtual Church Initiative – Mission Pioneer	SForsyth@churchofscotland.org.uk
Hendry, Jill	Kilmarnock South Area – Growing Together with God – Mission Pioneer	JHendry@churchofscotland.org.uk
Jenkinson, Barbara (Dr)	Dalmellington linked with Patna Waterside – Parish Assistant	BJenkinson@churchofscotland.org.uk
MacDonald, John	Irvine: United – Pastoral Assistant	John.MacDonald@churchofscotland.org.uk
Muir, Alison	Irvine Towerlands Church Plant Initiative – Mission Pioneer	Alison.Muir@churchofscotland.org.uk
Templeton, Katrona	Irvine Open Door (Disability Inclusion) Initiative – Mission Pioneer	KTempleton@churchofscotland.org.uk
Wardrop, Elaine	Kilmarnock: St Marnock's: Mission Development Worker	EWardrop@churchofscotland.org.uk

TOWN ADDRESSES

Ayr

Auld Kirk	Kirkport (116 High Street)
Castlehill	Castlehill Road x Hillfoot Road
Newton Wallacetown	Main Street
St Andrew's	Park Circus
St Columba	Midton Road x Carrick Park
St James'	Prestwick Road x Falkland Park Road
St Leonard's	St Leonard's Road x Monument Road

Dumfries

Maxwelltown West	Laurieknowe

Northwest	Lochside Road
St George's	George Street
St Mary's-Greyfriars	St Mary's Street
St Michael's and South	St Michael's Street
Troqueer	Troqueer Road
Girvan Valley	Montgomerie Street
Irvine	
Old	Kirkgate
United	
Dreghorn	Townfoot, Dreghorn
Fullarton	Marress Road x Church Street
Girdle Toll	Bryce Knox Court
Mure	West Road
Kilmarnock	
Kay Park	London Road
New Laigh Kirk	John Dickie Street
St Marnock's	St Marnock Street
St Kentigern's	Dunbar Drive
Prestwick	
Kingcase	Waterloo Road
Monkton and Prestwick North	Monkton Road
St Nicholas	Main Street
South	Main Street
Troon	St Meddan's Street

(4) CLYDE (W)

Meets for ordinary business on 10 September 2024, and 11 February and 17 June 2025.

Clerk: REV. ROBERT A. HAMILTON BA BD			**The Presbytery Office (see below)** **clyde@churchofscotland.org.uk**	**01505 801166**
Presbytery Office:			**'Homelea', Faith Avenue, Quarrier's Village, Bridge of Weir PA11 3TF**	**01505 615033**
1 Arrochar (F W) linked with Luss (F W)				
Vacant				
Ian J. Millar BA (Ordained Local Minister)	2020	2023	Lochfada House, Succoth, Arrochar G83 7AL IMillar@churchofscotland.org.uk	01301 702133
Interim Moderator: David Nicolson			DNicolson@churchofscotland.org.uk	0141 570 8103
2 Baldernock (H) linked with Milngavie: St Paul's (F H W)			**stpauls@btconnect.com**	**0141 956 4405**
Vacant				
Interim Moderator: Barbara A. O'Donnell			revbarb1@gmail.com	01389 752356
3 Barrhead: Bourock (F H W)				**0141 881 9813**
Pamela Gordon BD	2006	2014	14 Maxton Avenue, Barrhead, Glasgow G78 1DY PGordon@churchofscotland.org.uk	0141 881 8736
4 Barrhead: St Andrew's (F H W)				**0141 881 8442**
Timothy Mineard BA BD	2020		10 Arthurlie Avenue, Barrhead, Glasgow G78 2BU TMineard@churchofscotland.org.uk	0141 587 7913
5 Bearsden: Baljaffray (F H W)				**0141 942 5304**
Vacant			5 Fintry Gardens, Bearsden, Glasgow G61 4RJ	0141 942 0366
Interim Moderator: Alan J. Hamilton			AHamilton@churchofscotland.org.uk	0141 942 0021
6 Bearsden: Boclair (F H W)				
Alan J. Hamilton LLB BD PhD	2003		8 Clathic Avenue, Bearsden, Glasgow G61 2HF AHamilton@churchofscotland.org.uk	0141 942 0021
New charge formed by the union of Bearsden: Killermont and Bearsden: Westerton Fairlie Memorial				
7 Bearsden: Cross (F H W)			**secretary@bearsdencross.org**	**0141 942 0507**
Graeme R. Wilson MCIBS BD ThM DMin	2006	2013	61 Drymen Road, Bearsden, Glasgow G61 2SU GWilson@churchofscotland.org.uk	0141 942 0507

Charge / Minister	Ord.	Ind.	Address	Telephone
8 Bearsden: New Kilpatrick (F H W)			**mail@nkchurch.org.uk**	**0141 942 8827**
Roderick G. Hamilton MA BD	1992	2011	51 Manse Road, Bearsden, Glasgow G61 3PN	0141 942 0035
			Roddy.Hamilton@churchofscotland.org.uk	
9 Bishopton (F H W)			**office@bishoptonkirk.org.uk**	**01505 862583**
Yvonne Smith BSc BD	2017		The Manse, Newton Road, Bishopton PA7 5JP	01505 862161
			YSmith@churchofscotland.org.uk	
10 Bonhill (F H W) linked with Renton: Trinity (F H)			**bonhillchurchoffice@gmail.com**	**Bonhill: 01389 756516**
Vacant			1 Glebe Gardens, Bonhill G83 9NZ	01389 609329
Interim Moderator: Graeme R. Wilson			GWilson@churchofscotland.org.uk	0141 942 0507
11 Bridge of Weir: Freeland (F H W)				**01505 612610**
Kenneth N. Gray BA BD	1988		15 Lawmarnock Crescent, Bridge of Weir PA11 3AS	01505 690918
			aandkgray@btinternet.com	
12 Bridge of Weir: St Machar's Ranfurly (F W)				**01505 612975**
Hanneke A.S. Marshall (Mrs) MTh MA PGCE CertMin	2017		9 St Andrew's Drive, Bridge of Weir PA11 3HS	01505 612975
			Hanneke.Marshall@churchofscotland.org.uk	
13 Cardross (F H W)				**01389 841322**
Margaret McArthur BD DipMin	1995	2015	16 Bainfield Road, Cardross G82 5JQ	01389 849329
			MMcArthur@churchofscotland.org.uk	07799 556367
14 Clydebank: Faifley and Duntocher (F W)				
Gregor McIntyre BSc BD	1991		Kirklea, Cochno Road, Hardgate, Clydebank G81 6PT	01389 876836
			Gregor.McIntyre@churchofscotland.org.uk	
New charge formed by the union of Clydebank: Faifley and Duntocher: Trinity				
15 Clydebank: Kilbowie St Andrew's (F) linked with Clydebank: Radnor Park (H)				
Vacant			11 Tiree Gardens, Old Kilpatrick, Glasgow G60 5AT	01389 875599
Interim Moderator: Robert Kinloch (Mr)			rkinloch@blueyonder.co.uk	01389 750544
16 Clydebank: Radnor Park See Clydebank: Kilbowie St Andrew's				

17 Clydebank: Waterfront (F W) linked with Dalmuir: Barclay (F W)
lifeatwaterfront@virginmedia.com — **Dalmuir Barclay: 0141 941 3988**

Vacant — 16 Parkhall Road, Dalmuir, Clydebank G81 3RJ — 0141 941 3317
Steven Henderson BA DipHE RN BSc MPH CertCS (Ordained Local Minister) — 2023 — 22 Campbell Avenue, Bishopton PA7 5DA, SHenderson@churchofscotland.org.uk — 07734 994898
Interim Moderator: Gregor McIntyre — Gregor.McIntyre@churchofscotland.org.uk — 01389 876836

18 Craigrownie (F W) linked with Garelochhead (F W) linked with Rosneath: St Modan's (F H W) — **Garelochhead: 01436 810589**

Christine M. Murdoch BD — 1999 2015 — The Manse, Argyll Road, Kilcreggan, Helensburgh G84 0JW — 01436 842274
CMurdoch@churchofscotland.org.uk — 07973 331890

19 Dalmuir: Barclay See Clydebank: Waterfront

20 Dumbarton: Riverside (F H W) linked with Dumbarton: St Andrew's (H W) linked with Dumbarton: West Kirk (F H W)
office@dumbartonriverside.org.uk — **Riverside: 01389 742551**
administration@standrewsdumbarton.co.uk

Vacant — 18 Castle Road, Dumbarton G82 1JF — 01389 726685
Mark Boshoff AB BTh (Assistant Minister) — 2006 2022 — mboshoff@churchofscotland.org.uk — 07541 604255
Interim Moderator: Ian J. Millar — IMillar@churchofscotland.org.uk — 01301 702133

21 Dumbarton: St Andrew's See Dumbarton: Riverside
22 Dumbarton: West Kirk See Dumbarton: Riverside

23 Elderslie Kirk (F H W) — **01505 323348**

G. Gray Fletcher BSc BD — 1989 2019 — 282 Main Road, Elderslie, Johnstone PA5 9EF — 01505 321767
GFletcher@churchofscotland.org.uk

24 Erskine (F T W) — **erskineparishchurch@hotmail.com** — **0141 586 0559**

David Nicolson BA — 2019 — The Manse, 7 Leven Place, Linburn, Erskine PA8 6AS — 0141 570 8103
DNicolson@churchofscotland.org.uk

25 Garelochhead See Craigrownie

26 Gourock: Old Gourock and Ashton (H W) linked wth Greenock: St Ninian's **secretary@ogachurch.org.uk**

David W.G. Burt BD DipMin MTh — 1989 2014 — 331 Eldon Street, Greenock PA16 7QN — 01475 633914
DBurt@churchofscotland.org.uk

27 Gourock: St John's (F H T W)			**office@stjohns-gourock.org.uk**	
Teri C. Peterson BMus MDiv	2006	2018	6 Barrhill Road, Greenrock PA19 1JX	01475 632143
			TPeterson@churchofscotland.org.uk	
28 Greenock: East End (F) linked with Greenock: Mount Kirk (F W)			**info@themountkirk.org.uk**	
Francis E. Murphy BEng DipDSE BD	2006		76 Finnart Street, Greenock PA16 8HJ	01475 722338
			FMurphy@churchofscotland.org.uk	
29 Greenock: Lyle Kirk (F T W)			**office@lylekirk.org**	**01475 722694**
Jonathan C. Fleming MA BD	2012	2021	333 Eldon Street, Greenock PA16 7QN	07393 995397
			JFleming@churchofscotland.org.uk	
30 Greenock: Mount Kirk See Greenock: East End				
31 Greenock: St Margaret's (F W)				**01475 781953**
Guardianship of the Presbytery				
Interim Moderator: Teri C. Peterson			TPeterson@churchofscotland.org.uk	01475 632143
32 Greenock: St Ninian's See Gourock: Old Gourock and Ashton				
33 Greenock: Wellpark Mid Kirk (F)				
Vacant			101 Brisbane Street, Greenock PA16 8PA	01475 721741
Interim Moderator: Jonathan C. Fleming			JFleming@churchofscotland.org.uk	07393 995397
34 Greenock: Westburn (F W)				**01475 720257**
Karen E. Harbison (Mrs) MA BD	1991	2014	50 Ardgowan Street, Greenock PA16 8EP	01475 721048
			KHarbison@churchofscotland.org.uk	
35 Helensburgh (F W)			**office@helensburghcos.org**	**01436 676880**
Vacant				
Interim Moderator: Ann J. Cameron			anncameron2@googlemail.com	01436 831800
36 Houston and Killellan (F H W)				
Vacant			The Manse of Houston, Main Street, Houston, Johnstone PA6 7EL	01505 612569
Interim Moderator: Barbara Ann Sweetin			BSweetin@churchofscotland.org.uk	07988 938476

37 Howwood (W) linked with Johnstone: St Paul's (F H W) — **St Paul's: 01505 321632**
Vacant — 9 Stanley Drive, Brookfield, Johnstone PA5 8UF — 01505 320060
Interim Moderator: Philip D.Wallace — PWallace@churchofscotland.org.uk — 0141 570 3502

38 Inchinnan (F H W) — **0141 812 1263**
Ann Knox BD Cert.Healthc.Chap — 2017 — 51 Old Greenock Road, Inchinnan, Renfrew PA4 9PH — 0141 389 1724
AKnox@churchofscotland.org.uk — 07534 900065

39 Inverkip Skelmorlie and Wemyss Bay (H W) — **admin@inverkip.org.uk**
Vacant — 3a Montgomerie Terrace, Skelmorlie PA17 5DT — 01475 529320
Interim Moderator: Karen E. Harbison — KHarbison@churchofscotland.org.uk — 01475 721048

40 Johnstone: High (F H W) — **jhpchurch@yahoo.co.uk** — **01505 336303**
Vacant — 76 North Road, Johnstone PA5 8NF — 01505 320006
Interim Moderator: William A. Boyle — WBoyle@churchofscotland.org.uk — 01475 745407

41 Johnstone: St Andrew's Trinity — **01505 337827**
Vacant
Interim Moderator: Stephen J. Smith — SSmith@churchofscotland.org.uk — 01505 702621

42 Johnstone: St Paul's See Howwood

43 Kilbarchan (F T W)
Stephen J. Smith BSc BD — 1993 — 2015 — 41 Shuttle Street, Kilbarchan PA10 2JR — 01505 702621
SSmith@churchofscotland.org.uk

44 Kilmacolm: Old (F H W) — **01505 873911**
Vacant
Interim Moderator: A. Sonia Blakesley — SBlakesley@churchofscotland.org.uk — 0141 258 1161

45 Kilmacolm: St Columba (F H)
Vacant — 6 Churchill Road, Kilmacolm PA13 4LH — 01505 873271
Interim Moderator: Ann Knox — AKnox@churchofscotland.org.uk — 0141 389 1724

46 Langbank (F T W) — **info@langbankparishchurch.co.uk**
Guardianship of the Presbytery
Interim Moderator: Stuart C. Steell — SSteell@churchofscotland.org.uk — 0141 387 2464

47 Linwood (F H)				
Vacant				
Interim Moderator: Stuart Stevenson			SStevenson@churchofscotland.org.uk	0141 886 2131
48 Lomond (F H)			**lomondparishchurch@gmail.com**	
Vacant			1 Inchbruin, Balloch, Alexandria G83 8SG	
Session Clerk: Robert M. Kinloch			rkinloch@blueyonder.co.uk	07760 276505
New charge formed by the union of Kilmaronock Gartocharn and Lomond				
49 Luss See Arrochar				
50 Milngavie: Cairns (H W)			**office@cairnschurch.org.uk**	**0141 956 4868**
Andrew Frater BA BD MTh	1987	1994	4 Cairns Drive, Milngavie, Glasgow G62 8AJ	0141 956 1717
			AFrater@churchofscotland.org.uk	
51 Milngavie: St Luke's (W)				**0141 956 4226**
Ramsay B. Shields BA BD	1990	1997	70 Hunter Road, Milngavie, Glasgow G62 7BY	0141 577 9171
			RShields@churchofscotland.org.uk	Fax 0141 577 9181
52 Milngavie: St Paul's See Baldernock				
53 Neilston (F W)				**0141 881 9445**
Matthew D. Ritchie BA	2020		The Church Hall, 45 High Street, Neilston, Glasgow G78 3HJ	07548 342672
			Matthew.Ritchie@churchofscotland.org.uk	
54 Old Kilpatrick Bowling (F W)				
Vacant			The Manse, 175 Dumbarton Road, Old Kilpatrick, Glasgow G60 5JQ	08005 668242
Interim Moderator: Yvonne Smith			YSmith@churchofscotland.org.uk	01505 862161
55 Paisley: Abbey (F H W)			**info@paisleyabbey.org.uk**	**0141 889 7654; Fax 0141 887 3929**
Vacant			1 Carriagehall Drive, Paisley PA2 6JG	
Interim Moderator: James M. Gibson			jamesmgibson@msn.com	01698 854907
56 Paisley: North (F W)			**wallneuknorthchurch@gmail.com**	**0141 889 9265**
Vacant			5 Glenvilla Crescent, Paisley PA2 8TL	0141 884 4429
Stuart Davidson BD	2008	2017	25H Cross Road, Paisley PA2 9QJ	07717 503059
(Pioneer Minister)			SDavidson@churchofscotland.org.uk	

57 Paisley: Oakshaw Trinity (F H W)				**0141 887 4647; Fax 0141 848 5139**
Gordon B. Armstrong BD FIAB BRC CertCS	1998	2012	The Manse, 52 Balgonie Drive, Paisley PA2 9LP GArmstrong@churchofscotland.org.uk	0141 587 3124

Oakshaw Trinity is a Local Ecumenical Partnership with the United Reformed Church

58 Paisley: St George's (F W T)				
Hazel M. Shaw BA	2024		10 Hawick Avenue, Paisley PA2 9LD HShaw@churchofscotland.org.uk	07988 503723
Mhairi M. Breingan BSc CertCS (Ordained Local Minister)	2011	2019	6 Park Road, Inchinnan, Renfrew PA4 4QJ mhairi.b@btinternet.com	0141 812 1425
59 Paisley: St Mark's Oldhall (F H L W)			**office@stmarksoldhall.org.uk**	**0141 882 2755**
A. Sonia Blakesley MB ChB BD	2020		36 Newtyle Road, Paisley PA1 3JX SBlakesley@churchofscotland.org.uk	0141 258 1161
60 Paisley: Sherwood Greenlaw (F H W)				**0141 889 7060**
Vacant Interim Moderator: Gordon B. Armstrong			5 Greenlaw Drive, Paisley PA1 3RX GArmstrong@churchofscotland.org.uk	0141 316 2678 0141 587 3124
61 Paisley: South (F H W)				**0141 561 7139**
David P. Hood BD CertMin IOB(Scot)	1997	2020	6 Southfield Avenue, Paisley PA2 8BY DHood@churchofscotland.org.uk	0141 587 9374
62 Paisley: West (F W)				
Sandra Black BSc BD (Interim Minister)	1988	2024	36 Glencairn Drive, Glasgow G41 4PW SBlack@churchofscotland.org.uk	07703 827057
63 Port Glasgow: Hamilton Bardrainney (F)				
Guardianship of the Presbytery Interim Moderator: Francis E. Murphy			FMurphy@churchofscotland.org.uk	01475 722338
64 Port Glasgow: New (F H W)				
William A. Boyle BA	2020		New Parish Church Manse, 15 Whitelees Road, Greenock PA15 2RG WBoyle@churchofscotland.org.uk	01475 745407
65 Renfrew: North (F T W)			**contact@renfrewnorth.org.uk**	**0141 530 1308**
Philip D. Wallace BSc BTh DTS	1998	2018	1 Alexandra Drive, Renfrew PA4 8UB PWallace@churchofscotland.org.uk	0141 570 3502
G. Douglas Adam BD BA (Assistant Minister)	2023		132 Castle Gardens, Paisley PA2 9RD DAdam@churchofscotland.org.uk	07895 593660

66 Renfrew: Trinity (F H W)

Stuart C. Steell BD CertMin 1992 2015 25 Paisley Road, Renfrew PA4 8JH **0141 885 2129**
SSteell@churchofscotland.org.uk 0141 387 2464

67 Renton: Trinity See Bonhill

68 Rhu and Shandon (F W) **01436 820605**

Vacant
Interim Moderator: Ann J. Cameron anncameron2@googlemail.com 01436 831800

69 Roseneath: St Modan's See Craigrownie

B. In other appointments: members of Presbytery

Dalton, Mark F. BD DipMin RN	2002	Chaplain: Royal Navy	The Chaplaincy, HMS Neptune, HM Naval Base Clyde, Faslane, Helensburgh G84 8HL Mark.Dalton242@mod.gov.uk	
Hamilton, Robert A. BA BD	1995 2023	Presbytery Clerk: Clyde	Homelea, Faith Avenue, Quarriers Village, Bridge of Weir PA11 3TF RHamilton@churchofscotland.org.uk	01505 801166
McMahon, Eleanor J. BEd BD	1994 2023	Ministries Recruitment and Training Manager, Faith Action Programme	81 Moorpark Square, Renfrew PA4 8DB EMcMahon@churchofscotland.org.uk	07974 116539
Peel, Jeanette L. BA BD MTh	2020	Healthcare Chaplain	Inverclyde Royal Hospital, Larkfield Road, Greenock PA16 0XN Jeanette.Peel@churchofscotland.org.uk	01475 504759 07903 681003
Stevenson, Stuart CertCE	2011	Ordained Local Minister	143 Springfield Park, Johnstone PA5 8JT SStevenson@churchofscotland.org.uk	0141 886 2131

C. Retaining: members of Presbytery

Bell, Ian W. LTh	1990 2011	(Erskine)	40 Brueacre Drive, Wemyss Bay PA18 6HA revianbell@gmail.com	01475 529312
Bell, May (Mrs) LTh	1998 2012	(Johnstone: St Andrew's Trinity)	40 Brueacre Drive, Wemyss Bay PA18 6HA revmaybell22@gmail.com	01475 529312
Buchanan, Fergus C. MA BD MTh	1982 2022	(Baldernock with Milngavie: St Paul's)	114 Moorpark Square, Renfrew PA4 8JF Fergus.Buchanan@churchofscotland.org.uk	07760 138960
Cameron, Ann J. (Mrs) CertCS	2005 2019	(Auxiliary Minister, Craigrownie with Garelochhead with Rosneath: St Modan's)	Water's Edge, Ferry Road, Rosneath, Helensburgh G84 0RS anncameron2@googlemail.com	01436 831800
Coull, Morris C. BD	1974 2018	(Greenock St Margaret's)	14 Kelvin Gardens, Largs KA30 8SY	01475 338674
Cowie, Marian (Mrs) MA BD MTh	1990 2012	(Aberdeen: Midstocket)	2 Glenmore Avenue, Alexandria, Glasgow G83 0QA mcowieou@aol.com	07740 174969
Geddes, Elizabeth (Mrs)	2013 2021	(Ordained Local Minister, Langbank)	9 Shillingworth Place, Bridge of Weir PA11 3DY geddes_liz@hotmail.com	01505 612639

Name	Ord.	Ret.	Former charge	Address / Email	Phone
Goldie, Christine M. LLB BD MTh DMin	1984	2024	(Bearsden: Westerton Fairlie Memorial)	Flat 1/3, 28 Castlegate Avenue, Dumbarton G82 1AL CGoldie@churchofscotland.org.uk	
Gray, Greta (Miss) DCS	1992	2014	(Deacon, Paisley: Lylesland)	67 Crags Avenue, Paisley PA3 6SG greta.gray@ntlworld.com	0141 884 6178
Hamilton, David G. MA BD	1971	2004	(Braes of Rannoch with Foss and Rannoch)	79 Finlay Rise, Milngavie, Glasgow G62 6QL davidhamilton40@googlemail.com	0141 956 4202
Hood, E. Lorna OBE MA BD DD	1978	2016	(Renfrew: North)	4 Thornly Park Drive, Paisley PA2 7RR revlornahood@gmail.com	0141 384 9516
Houston, Elizabeth W. MA BD DipEd	1985	2018	(Alexandria)	Croftengea, 25 Honeysuckle Lane, Jamestown, Alexandria G83 8PL Cleric2@hotmail.com	01389 721165
Kemp, Tina MA	2005	2021	(Auxiliary Minister, Helensburgh with Rhu and Shandon)	12 Oaktree Gardens, Dumbarton G82 1EU tinakemp@blueyonder.co.uk	01389 730477
Leitch, Maureen (Mrs) BA BD DipPhysEd	1995	2011	(Barrhead: Bourock)	Rockfield, 92 Paisley Road, Barrhead G78 1NW maureen.leitch@ntlworld.com	0141 580 2927
Macdonald, Alexander MA BD	1966	2006	(Neilston)	35 Lochore Avenue, Paisley PA3 4BY alexsmacdonald42@aol.com	0141 889 0066
Manson, Eileen (Mrs) DipCE	1994	2021	(Auxiliary Minister, Greenock: St Ninian's)	1 Cambridge Avenue, Gourock PA19 1XT EManson@churchofscotland.org.uk	01475 632401
Marshall, T. Edward BD CertMin	1987	2020	(Crosshouse)	20 Alloway Drive, Paisley PA2 7DS	
McCool, Ann C. (Mrs) BD DSD IPA ALCM	1989	2024	(Johnstone: High)	76 North Road, Johnstone PA5 8NF ann.mccool38@gmail.com	01505 320006
McFarlane, Robert G. BD	2001	2018	(Paisley St Mark's Oldhall)	990 Crookston Road, Glasgow G53 7DY	
Miller, Ian H. BD BA	1975	2012	(Bonhill)	Derand, Queen Street, Alexandria G83 0AS revianmiller@btinternet.com	01389 753039
Moore, Norma MA BD	1995	2017	(Jamestown)	25 Miller Street, Dumbarton G82 2JA norma-moore@sky.com	
Murning, John BD CPS	1988	2024	(Paisley: Sherwood Greenlaw)	9 Tait Circle, Paisley PA2 7EQ JMurning@churchofscotland.org.uk	07772 865027
Nutter, Margaret A.E. BA BD MFPh	2014	2021	(Ordained Local Minister, Presbytery-wide)	Kilmorich, 14 Balloch Road, Balloch, Alexandria G83 8SR MNutter@churchofscotland.org.uk	01389 754505
O'Donnell, Barbara A. BD PGSE	2007	2022	(Bonhill with Renton: Trinity)	Ashbank, 258 Main Street, Alexandria G83 0NU revbarb1@gmail.com	07787 433903
Read, Paul R. BSc DipEd MA(Th)	2000	2021	(Applegarth, Sibbaldbie and Johnstone with Lochmaben)	21 Brechanshaw, Erskine PA8 7EZ prr747@icloud.com	0141 560 0561 07791 724162
Robertson, Ishbel A. R. MA BD	2013	2018	(Ordained Local Minister, Dumbarton: St Andrew's with Old Kilpatrick Bowling)	Oakdene, 81 Bonhill Road, Dumbarton G82 2DU	01389 763436
Shaw, Alistair N. MA BD MTh PhD	1982	2023	(Howwood with Johnstone: St Paul's)	2 Burnside Avenue, Brookfield, Johnstone PA5 8UT ans2006@talktalk.net	07748 821777
Sweetin, Barbara Ann BD	2011	2024	(Forfar: East Old and Inverarity)	3/1 Highgrove Court, Renfrew PA4 8PX BSweetin@churchofscotland.org.uk	07988 938476
Whyte, Margaret A. (Mrs) BA BD	1988	2011	(Glasgow: Pollokshaws)	4 Springhill Road, Barrhead G78 2AA mawhyte@hotmail.co.uk	0141 881 4942
Wilson, John BD CPS	1985	2010	(Glasgow: Temple Anniesland)	4 Carron Crescent, Bearsden, Glasgow G61 1HJ revjwilson@btinternet.com	07848 635967

D. In other appointments: not members of Presbytery

Nil

E. Retaining: not members of Presbytery

Christie, John C. BSc BD CBiol MRSB	1990	2012	(Interim Minister, Paisley: Oakshaw Trinity)	10 Cumberland Avenue, Helensburgh G84 8QG JChristie@churchofscotland.org.uk	01436 674078 07711 336392
Clark, David W. MA BD	1975	2014	(Helensburgh: St Andrew's Kirk with Rhu and Shandon)	3 Ritchie Avenue, Cardross, Dumbarton G82 5LL clarkdw@talktalk.net	01389 849319
McCrum, Scott BD	2015	2022	(Old Kilpatrick Bowling)	SMcCrum@churchofscotland.org.uk	
McEwan, Ian K. BSc PhD BD FRSE FRAE	2008	2022	(Bearsden: Baljaffray)	IMcEwan@churchofscotland.org.uk	
Reid, A. Gordon BSc BD	1982	2008	(Dunfermline: Gillespie Memorial)	7 Arkleston Crescent, Paisley PA3 4TG reid501@fsmail.com	0141 842 1542 07773 300989
Speirs, Archibald BD	1995	2021	(Inverkip with Skelmorlie and Wemyss Bay)	27 Amochrie Road, Paisley PA2 0LB archiespeirs1@aol.com	01505 815327
Stewart, Charles E. BSc BD MTh PhD	1976	2010	(Chaplain, Royal Hospital School, Holbrook)	105 Sinclair Street, Helensburgh G84 9HY c.e.stewart@btinternet.com	01436 678113

F. Inactive: not members of Presbytery

Alexander, Douglas N. MA BD	1961	1999	(Bishopton)	West Morningside, Main Road, Langbank, Port Glasgow PA4 6XP	01475 540249
Black, Janette M.K. (Mrs) BD	1993	2006	(Assistant: Paisley: Oakshaw Trinity)	5 Craigiehall Avenue, Erskine PA8 7DB	0141 812 0794
Booth, Frederick M. LTh	1970	2005	(Helensburgh: St Columba)	Achnashie Coach House, Clynder, Helensburgh G84 0QU boothef@btinternet.com	01436 831858
Fraser, Ian C. BA BD	1982	2008	(Glasgow: St Luke's and St Andrew's)	62 Kingston Avenue, Neilston, Glasgow G78 3JG ianandlindafraser@gmail.com	0141 563 6794
Harris, John W.F. MA	1967	2012	(Bearsden: Cross)	21 Strathmore Court, 20 Abbey Drive, Jordanhill, Glasgow G14 9JX jwfh@sky.com	0141 463 1046 07740 982079
Johnston, Mary (Miss) DCS	1988	2003	(Deacon, Paisley: St Columba Foxbar)	19 Lounsdale Drive, Paisley PA2 9ED	0141 849 1615
Kay, David BA BD MTh	1974	2008	(Paisley: Sandyford: Thread Street)	36 Donaldswood Park, Paisley PA2 8RS david.kay500@o2.co.uk	0141 884 2080
Lawrie, Robert M. BD MSc DipMin LLCM(TD) MCMI FCMI	1994	1998	(Fyvie with Rothienorman)	West Benview, Main Road, Langbank PA14 6XP revrmlawrie@gmail.com	01475 540240 07789 824479
Lees, Andrew P. BD	1984	2017	(Baldernock)	58 Lindores Drive, Stepps G33 6PD andrew.lees@yahoo.co.uk	0141 389 5840
McCully, M. Isobel (Miss) DCS	1974	1999	(Deacon, Greenock: Old West Kirk)	10 Broadstone Avenue, Port Glasgow PA14 5BB mi.mccully@btinternet.com	01475 742240
McIntyre, J. Ainslie MA BD	1963	1984	(Lecturer, New Testament, University of Glasgow)	60 Bonnaughton Road, Bearsden, Glasgow G61 4DB jamcintyre@hotmail.com	0141 942 5143

Nicol, Joyce (Mrs) BA DCS	1974	2001	(Deacon, Greenock: St Ninian's)	93 Brisbane Street, Greenock PA16 8NY joycenicol@hotmail.co.uk	01475 723235 07957 642709
Prentice, George BA BTh	1964	1997	(Paisley: Martyrs')	46 Victoria Gardens, Corsebar Road, Paisley PA2 9AQ g.prentice04@talktalk.net	0141 842 1585
Steven, Harold A.M. OStJ LTh FSAScot	1970	2001	(Baldernock)	9 Cairnhill Road, Bearsden, Glasgow G61 1AT harold.allison.steven@gmail.com	0141 942 1598
Taylor, Jane C. BD DipMin	1990	2013	(Insch-Leslie-Premnay-Oyne)	Timbers, Argyll Road, Kilcreggan G84 0JW jane.c.taylor@btinternet.com	01436 842336
Watson, Valerie G.C. MA BD STM	1987	2018	(North and West Islay)	11 Roxburgh Street, Greenock PA5 4PU vgcwatson@btinternet.com	01475 787116
Webster, Brian G. BD BSc CEng MIEE	1988	2011	(Cambusbarron: The Bruce Memorial)	3/1 Cloch Court, 57 Albert Road, Gourock PA19 1NJ revwebby@aol.com	

G. Readers (active)

Bird, Mary Jane (Miss)	Greenhill Farm, Barochan Road, Houston PA6 7HS	mjbird55@gmail.com	
Boag, Jennifer (Miss)	11 Madeira Street, Greenock PA16 7UJ	jenniferboag@hotmail.com	01475 720125
Davey, Charles L.	16 Divert Road, Gourock PA19 1DT	charlesdavey16@hotmail.co.uk	01475 631544
Hood, Eleanor (Mrs)	12 Clochoderick Avenue, Kilbarchan, Johnstone PA10 2AY	eleanor.hood.kilbarchan@ntlworld.com	01505 704208
MacDonald, Christine (Ms)	33 Collier Street, Johnstone PA5 8AG	christine.macdonald10@ntlworld.com	01505 355779
Marshall, Leon M.	Glenisla, Gryffe Road, Kilmacolm PA13 4BA	lm@stevenson-kyles.co.uk	01505 872417
Maxwell, Margaret A. (Sandra) (Mrs) BD	2 Grants Avenue, Paisley PA2 6AZ	sandra@maxwellmail.co.uk	0141 884 3710
McFarlan, Elizabeth (Miss)	20 Fauldswood Crescent, Paisley PA2 9PA	elizabeth.mcfarlan@ntlworld.com	01505 358411
McHugh, Jack	Earlshaugh, Earl Place, Bridge of Weir PA11 3HA	jackmchugh1@btinternet.com	01505 612789
Morgan, Richard	Annandale, School Road, Rhu, Helensburgh G84 8RS	themorgans@hotmail.co.uk	01436 821269
Rankin, Kenneth	20 Bruntsfield Gardens, Glasgow G53 7QJ	krankin@hotmail.co.uk	0141 880 7474
Spooner, John R. BSc PGC(Mgt)	Onslow, Uplawmoor Road, Neilston, Glasgow G78 3LB	jrspooner@btopenworld.com	0141 881 5182 07481 008033

H. Ministries Development Staff

Davidson, Stuart (Rev) BD	Pioneer Minister, Paisley: North	SDavidson@churchofscotland.org.uk
Graham, Gillian	Clydebank: Waterfront linked with Dalmuir: Barclay – Children, Young People and Family Worker	GGraham@churchofscotland.org.uk
Wilson, Lorraine	Clydebank: Waterfront linked with Dalmuir: Barclay – Pastoral Assistant	LWilson@churchofscotland.org.uk

TOWN ADDRESSES

Bearsden	
Baljaffray	Grampian Way
Boclair	Rannoch Drive; and Crarae Avenue
Cross	Drymen Road
Killermont	Rannoch Drive
New Kilpatrick	Manse Road
Clydebank	
Faifley and Duntocher	Faifley Road
Kilbowie St Andrew's	Kilbowie Road
Radnor Park	Radnor Street
Waterfront	Town Centre
Dumbarton	
Riverside	High Street
St Andrew's	Aitkenbar Circle
West Kirk	West Bridgend
Gourock	
Old Gourock and Ashton	41 Royal Street
St John's	Bath Street x St John's Road
Greenock	
East End	49–51 Belleville Street
Lyle Kirk	31 Union Street
Mount Kirk	Dempster Street at Murdieston Park
St Margaret's	Finch Road x Kestrel Crescent
St Ninian's	Warwick Road, Larkfield
Wellpark Mid Kirk	Cathcart Square
Westburn	9 Nelson Street
Helensburgh	Colquhoun Square
Milngavie	
Cairns	Buchanan Street
St Luke's	Kirk Street
St Paul's	Strathblane Road
Paisley	
Abbey	Cotton Street
North	off Renfrew Road
Oakshaw Trinity	Churchill
St George's	Causeyside Street, and Nethercraigs Drive
St Mark's Oldhall	Glasgow Road, Ralston
Sherwood Greenlaw	Glasgow Road
South	Rowan Street off Neilston Road
West	King Street
Port Glasgow	
Hamilton Bardrainney	Bardrainney Avenue x Auchenbothie Road
New	Princes Street

(5) GLASGOW (F W)

Meets at 7pm on the second Tuesday of every month apart from June when it is the third Tuesday and July, August and January when it does not meet. Details of the venue are displayed on the Presbytery website.

Clerk:	**REV. S. GRANT BARCLAY LLB DipLP BD MSc PhD**	**260 Bath Street, Glasgow G2 4JP** **glasgow@churchofscotland.org.uk**	**0141 332 6606** **07743 779929**
Depute Clerk:	**REV. HILARY N. McDOUGALL MA PGCE BD**	**HMcDougall@churchofscotland.org.uk**	
Treasurer:	**MRS ALISON WHITELAW**	**treasurer@presbyteryofglasgow.org.uk**	

1	**Bishopbriggs: Kenmure (F W)** Vacant Session Clerk: Aniela Allan			kenmure.sc@gmail.com	**0141 762 4242** 0141 563 1551
2	**Bishopbriggs: Springfield Cambridge (F W)** Ian Taylor ACIBS BD ThM DipPSRP	1995	2006	**office@springfieldcambridge.org.uk** 64 Miller Drive, Bishopbriggs, Glasgow G64 1FB ITaylor@churchofscotland.org.uk	**0141 772 1596** 0141 772 1540
3	**Broom (F W)** James A.S. Boag BD CertMin	1992	2007	**office@broomchurch.org.uk** 3 Laigh Road, Newton Mearns, Glasgow G77 5EX JBoag@churchofscotland.org.uk	**0141 639 3528** Tel 0141 639 2916 Fax 0141 639 3528
4	**Burnside Blairbeth (F W)** William T.S. Wilson BSc BD	1999	2006	**theoffice@burnsideblairbeth.church** 59 Blairbeth Road, Burnside, Glasgow G73 4JD WWilson@churchofscotland.org.uk	**0141 634 7383** 0141 583 6470
5	**Busby (F W)** Jeremy C. Eve BSc BD	1995	1998	17A Carmunnock Road, Busby, Glasgow G76 8SZ JEve@churchofscotland.org.uk	**0141 644 2073** 0141 644 3670
6	**Cadder (F W)** John B. MacGregor BD	1999	2017	231 Kirkintilloch Road, Bishopbriggs, Glasgow G64 2JB JMacGregor@churchofscotland.org.uk	**0141 772 7436** 0141 576 7127

7	**Cambuslang (F W)**			**office@churchofscotland.org.uk**	**0141 642 9271**
	Vacant			74 Stewarton Drive, Cambuslang, Glasgow G72 8DG	0141 586 2126
	Karen M. Hamilton (Mrs) DCS	1995	2014	6 Beckfield Gate, Glasgow G33 1SW	0141 558 3195
				KHamilton@churchofscotland.org.uk	07514 402612
	Interim Moderator: Derek W. Hughes			DHughes@churchofscotland.org.uk	07723 578573
8	**Cambuslang: Flemington Hallside (F W)**				
	Ian A. Cathcart BSc BD	1994	2018	59 Hay Crescent, Cambuslang, Glasgow G72 6QA	0141 641 1049
				ICathcart@churchofscotland.org.uk	07588 441895
9	**Campsie (F W)**			**campsieparishchurch@gmail.com**	**01360 310939**
	Vacant				
	Session Clerk: George Kelly			geojkelly@btinternet.com	01360 311739
10	**Chryston (H T W)**			**chrystonchurch@hotmail.com**	**0141 779 4188**
	Mark Malcolm MA BD	1999	2008	The Manse, 109 Main Street, Chryston, Glasgow G69 9LA	0141 779 1436
				MMalcolm@churchofscotland.org.uk	07731 737377
11	**Cumbernauld: Abronhill (H W)**				
	Vacant			26 Ash Road, Cumbernauld, Glasgow G67 3ED	01236 723833
	Session Clerk: Linda Gray			sessionclerk.apc@outlook.com	07950 207427
12	**Cumbernauld: Condorrat (H W)**				
	Vacant			11 Rosehill Drive, Cumbernauld, Glasgow G67 4EQ	01236 452090
	Session Clerk: Kenneth Mackenzie			kirksessionclerk@outlook.com	07771 884074
13	**Cumbernauld: Trinity (H W)**				
	Vacant				
	James R. Gemmell MA BD (Assistant Minister)	2022		James.Gemmell@churchofscotland.org.uk	07577 907824
	New charge formed by the union of Cumbernauld: Kildrum and St Mungo's and Cumbernauld: Old				
14	**Eaglesham (F W)**			**office@eagleshamparishchurch.co.uk**	**01355 302087**
	Jade M. Ableitner BA	2021		2 West Glebe, Cheapside Street, Eaglesham, Glasgow G76 0NS	07470 046982
				Jade.Ableitner@churchofscotland.org.uk	

15	**Fernhill and Cathkin (F W)**				
	Aquila R. Singh BA PGCE BD	2017		20 Glenlyon Place, Rutherglen, Glasgow G73 5PL ASingh@churchofscotland.org.uk	0141 389 3599
16	**Gartcosh (F H T W) linked with Glenboig (F T W)**				**Gartcosh: 01236 872274**
	David G. Slater BSc BA DipThRS	2011		26 Inchnock Avenue, Gartcosh, Glasgow G69 8EA DSlater@churchofscotland.org.uk	07722 876616
17	**Giffnock: Orchardhill (F W)**				**0141 638 3604**
	Gillian Rooney BA	2021		23 Huntly Avenue, Giffnock, Glasgow G46 6LW GRooney@churchofscotland.org.uk	0141 387 8254
18	**Giffnock: South (F W)**			**giffnocksouth@gmail.com**	**0141 638 2599**
	Catherine J. Beattie (Mrs) BD	2008	2011	164 Ayr Road, Newton Mearns, Glasgow G77 6EE CBeattie@churchofscotland.org.uk	0141 258 7804
19	**Giffnock: The Park (F W)**			**contact@parkchurch.org.uk**	**0141 620 2204**
	Calum D. Macdonald BD CertMin	1993	2001	41 Rouken Glen Road, Thornliebank, Glasgow G46 7JD CMacdonald@churchofscotland.org.uk	0141 638 3023
20	**Glenboig** See Gartcosh				
21	**Greenbank (F H W)**			**greenbankoffice@tiscali.co.uk**	**0141 644 1841**
	Vacant				
	Session Clerk: Helen Howard			helen.howard360@gmail.com	0141 585 7909
22	**Kilsyth: Anderson (F T W)**				
	Vacant				
	Session Clerk: Christine Johnston			johnstonchristine@hotmail.co.uk	01236 821060
23	**Kilsyth: Burns and Old (F W)**			**boldchurch@hotmail.com**	
	Vacant			The Grange, 17 Glasgow Road, Kilsyth G65 9AE	07810 377582
	Session Clerk: John Comrie			jsc1950@live.co.uk	01236 823290
24	**Kirkintilloch: St Columba's Hillhead (H W)**			**stcolumbassecretary@outlook.com**	**0141 578 0016**
	Philip A. Wright BSc MSc PhD BTh	2017		14 Crossdykes, Kirkintilloch G66 3EU PWright@churchofscotland.org.uk	07427 623393

25	**Kirkintilloch: St David's Memorial Park (F H W)**			**sdmp2@outlook.com**	**0141 776 4989**
	Vacant				
	Session Clerk: David S. Forsyth			forsyth12@btinternet.com	07715 971397
26	**Kirkintilloch: St Mary's (W)**			**office@stmarysnursery.uk**	**0141 775 1166**
	Ruth H.B. Morrison MA BD PhD	2009	2021	23 Braes o' Yetts, Kirkintilloch, Glasgow G66 3FF	07557 657079
				RMorrison@churchofscotland.org.uk	
27	**Lenzie: Old (H W)**				
	Vacant				
	Julie Hearty (Assistant Minister)	2024		JHearty@churchofscotland.org.uk	
	Contact: Eleanor Yates			eyates321@aol.com	07893 985263
28	**Lenzie: Union (F H W)**			**office@lenzieunion.org**	**0141 776 1046**
	Vacant			1 Larch Avenue, Lenzie, Glasgow G66 4HX	0141 776 3831
	Session Clerk: Fiona Menzies			fee_menzies@yahoo.co.uk	0141 572 6803
29	**Maxwell Mearns Castle (F W)**			**maxwellmearns@hotmail.com**	**0141 639 5169**
	Vacant				
	Session Clerk: Chris Dunn			dchrisdunn@hotmail.co.uk	07935 832984
30	**Mearns (F H W)**			**office@mearnskirk.church**	**0141 639 6555**
	Vacant				
	Session Clerk: Marje Gillies			marje.gillies@gmail.com	0141 639 1043
31	**Milton of Campsie (F H W)**				
	Julie H.C. Moody BA BD PGCE	2006		16 Cannerton Park, Milton of Campsie, Glasgow G66 8HR	01360 310548
				JMoody@churchofscotland.org.uk	
32	**Moodiesburn (F W)**			**info@moodiesburn.church**	**01236 870515**
	Mark W.J. McKeown MEng MDiv DipMin	2013	2020	6 Glenapp Place, Moodiesburn, Glasgow G69 0HS	01236 263406
				MMcKeown@churchofscotland.org.uk	07761 097633
33	**Netherlee and Stamperland (F H W)**			**nethandstamchurch@gmail.com**	**0141 637 2503**
	Scott Blythe BSc BD MBA	1997	2017	25 Ormonde Avenue, Netherlee, Glasgow G44 3QY	0141 533 7147
				SBlythe@churchofscotland.org.uk	07504 692046

34	**Newton Mearns (F H W)**			**office@churchatthecross.org.uk**	**0141 639 7373**
	Vacant			28 Waterside Avenue, Newton Mearns, Glasgow G77 6TJ	07305 239128
	Session Clerk: Irene Munro			irenemunro1@aol.com	07970 246738
35	**Rutherglen: Old (F H T W)**				
	Jean J. de Villiers BATheol BTh HonPsych	2003	2021	31 Highburgh Drive, Rutherglen, Glasgow G73 3RR	07960 312218
				JdeVilliers@churchofscotland.org.uk	
36	**Rutherglen: Stonelaw (F T W)**			**info@stonelawchurch.org**	**0141 647 5113**
	Neil H. Watson BD	2017	2021	12 Hawthorn Way, Cambuslang, Glasgow G72 7AF	07871 615840
				NWatson@churchofscotland.org.uk	
37	**Rutherglen: West and Wardlawhill (F W)**			**info@westandwardlawhill.org**	
	Vacant				
	Session Clerk: Alistair K. McInnes			session.clerk@westandwardlawhill.org	07971 079660
38	**Stepps (F H W)**				
	Vacant				
	Session Clerk: Lorraine Robertson			sessionclerkspc2020@gmail.com	07952 490036
39	**Thornliebank (F H W)**				
	Vacant				
	Session Clerk: Margaret O'Neil (Mrs)			margareton54@yahoo.co.uk	0141 638 4937
40	**Torrance (F T W)**			**office@tpc.org.uk**	**01360 620970**
	Stuart D. Irvin BD	2013	2021	1 Atholl Avenue, Torrance, Glasgow G64 4JA	07421 352 893
				SIrvin@churchofscotland.org.uk	
41	**Williamwood (F W)**				**0141 638 2091**
	Vacant				
	Interim Moderator: Aquila R. Singh			ASingh@churchofscotland.org.uk	0141 389 3599
42	**Glasgow: Baillieston Mure Memorial (F W) linked with Glasgow: Baillieston St Andrew's (F W)**			**Mure Memorial:**	**0141 773 1216**
	Fiona S. Morrison BA	2019	2024	FMorrison@churchofscotland.org.uk	07710 331746

43	**Glasgow: Baillieston St Andrew's** See Glasgow: Baillieston Mure Memorial				
44	**Glasgow: Barlanark Greyfriars (F W)**			**enquiries@barlanark-greyfriars.co.uk**	**0141 771 6477**
	Vacant				
	Fiona M.E. Crawford BA BD (Assistant Minister)	2022	2024	FCrawford@churchofscotland.org.uk	07801 855314
	Session Clerk: Janette McMaster			janettemcmaster@yahoo.co.uk	07956 579799
45	**Glasgow: Blawarthill (F T W) linked with Glasgow: St Columba (F GE W)**				
	Vacant				
	Interim Moderator: David G. Slater			DSlater@churchofscotland.org.uk	07722 876616
46	**Glasgow: Bridgeton St Francis in the East (F H L W)**			**bridgetonstfrancis@gmail.com**	**0141 556 2830** **Church House: 0141 554 8045**
	Vacant				
	Session Clerk: Barbara Jennings (Mrs)			barbara.jennings1@ntlworld.com	07856 912267
47	**Glasgow: Broomhill Hyndland (F W)**			**info@broomhillhyndlandchurch.org**	**0141 334 2540**
	George C. Mackay BD CertMin CertEd DipPC	1994	2014	27 St Kilda Drive, Glasgow G14 9LN GMackay@churchofscotland.org.uk	0141 959 8697 07711 569127
48	**Glasgow: Calton Parkhead**				**0141 554 3866**
	Vacant			98 Drumover Drive, Glasgow G31 5RP	
49	**Glasgow: Cardonald (F W)**				**0141 882 6264**
	Vacant				
50	**Glasgow: Carmunnock (F)**				**0141 644 0655**
	Vacant				
	Session Clerk: George Dow			george.dow2019@outlook.com	0141 644 0689 07801 613 127
51	**Glasgow: Carmyle and Kenmuir Cornerstone**				
	Murdo MacLean BD CertMin	1997	1999	3 Meryon Road, Glasgow G32 9NW Murdo.MacLean@churchofscotland.org.uk	0141 778 2625

New charge formed by the union of Glasgow: Carmyle and Glasgow: Kenmuir Mount Vernon

52	**Glasgow: Carntyne and Cranhill (W)**			**contact@carntynechurch.org**	**0141 778 4186**
	Rhona E. McDonald BA BD	2015	2024	163 Lethamhill Road, Glasgow G33 2SQ	0141 770 9247
				RMcDonald@churchofscotland.org.uk	07812 560372
53	**Glasgow: Carnwadric (F L W)**				
	James Gemmell BD MTh	1999	2020	62 Loganswell Road, Thornliebank, Glasgow G46 8AX	0141 638 9575
				JGemmell@churchofscotland.org.uk	07577 907824
54	**Glasgow: Castlemilk (F H W)**				**0141 634 7113**
	Vacant				
	Session Clerk: David Fraser			david.fraser1959@gmail.com	07803 825116
55	**Glasgow: Cathcart Old (F)**				**0141 637 4168**
	Vacant				
	Session Clerk: Anne Neilson			aneilson@btinternet.com	07307 865530
56	**Glasgow: Cathcart Trinity (F H W)**			**office@cathcarttrinity.org.uk**	**0141 637 6658**
	Alasdair R. MacMillan LLB BD	2015		21 Muirhill Avenue, Glasgow G44 3HP	0141 391 9102
				Alasdair.MacMillan@churchofscotland.org.uk	
57	**Glasgow: Cathedral (High or St Mungo's) (F W)**				**0141 552 8198**
	Mark E. Johnstone DL MA BD	1993	2019	41 Springfield Road, Bishopbriggs, Glasgow G64 1PL	07515 285374
				Mark.Johnstone@churchofscotland.org.uk	
58	**Glasgow: Causeway (Tollcross) (F)**				
	Monica Michelin-Salomon BD	1999	2007	228 Hamilton Road, Glasgow G32 9QU	0141 778 2413
				MMichelin-Salomon@churchofscotland.org.uk	
59	**Glasgow: Clincarthill (F H W)**				**0141 632 4206**
	Stuart Love BA MTh	2016		90 Mount Annan Drive, Glasgow G44 4RZ	0141 632 2985
				SLove@churchofscotland.org.uk	
60	**Glasgow: Colston Milton (F)**				**0141 772 1922**
	Christopher J. Rowe BA BD	2008		118 Birsay Road, Milton, Glasgow G22 7QP	0141 564 1138
				CRowe@churchofscotland.org.uk	

61	**Glasgow: Colston Wellpark (F H W)**				**0141 772 8672**
	Guardianship of the Presbytery				
	Leslie E.T. Grieve BSc BA (Ordained Local Minister)	2014		23 Hertford Avenue, Kelvindale, Glasgow G12 0LG LGrieve@churchofscotland.org.uk	07813 255052
62	**Glasgow: Croftfoot (F H W)**				**0141 637 3913**
	Robert M. Silver BA BD	1995	2011	4 Inchmurrin Gardens, High Burnside, Rutherglen, Glasgow G73 5RU RSilver@churchofscotland.org.uk	0141 258 7268
63	**Glasgow: Dennistoun New (F H W)**				**0141 554 1350**
	Ian M.S. McInnes BD DipMin	1995	2008	31 Pencaitland Drive, Glasgow G32 8RL IMcInnes@churchofscotland.org.uk	0141 564 6498
64	**Glasgow: Drumchapel St Andrew's and Yoker (F W)**				**0141 944 3758**
	Karen E. Hendry BSc BD	2005		6 Firdon Crescent, Glasgow G15 5QQ KHendry@churchofscotland.org.uk	0141 944 4566 07878 555155
	New charge formed by the union of Glasgow: Drumchapel St Andrew's and Glasgow: Yoker				
65	**Glasgow: Drumchapel St Mark's (F)**				
	Audrey J. Jamieson BD MTh	2004	2007	146 Garscadden Road, Glasgow G15 6PR AJamieson@churchofscotland.org.uk	0141 944 5440
66	**Glasgow: Easterhouse (F W)**				
	Derek W. Hughes BSc BD DipEd	1990	2018	3 Barony Gardens, Springhill, Glasgow G69 6TS DHughes@churchofscotland.org.uk	07723 578573
67	**Glasgow: Eastwood (F W)**				
	James R. Teasdale BA BD	2009	2016	54 Mansewood Road, Eastwood, Glasgow G43 1TL JTeasdale@churchofscotland.org.uk	0141 571 7648
68	**Glasgow: Gairbraid (F H W)**				
	Donald Michael MacInnes BD	2002	2011	4 Blackhill Gardens, Summerston, Glasgow G23 5NE DMacInnes@churchofscotland.org.uk	0141 946 0604
69	**Glasgow: Gallowgate (F)**				
	Peter L.V. Davidge BD MTh	2003	2009	98 Drumover Drive, Glasgow G31 5RP PDavidge@churchofscotland.org.uk	07765 096599

70	**Glasgow: Garthamlock, Ruchazie and Craigend (F W)**				
	Vacant			9 Craigievar Court, Garthamlock, Glasgow G33 5DJ	07725 037394
	Session Clerk: Brian Stewart			sessionclerk@gracchurch@gmail.com	07393 550455
	New charge formed by the union of Glasgow: Garthamlock and Craigend and Glasgow: Ruchazie				
71	**Glasgow: Gorbals (W)**				
	Vacant				
	Session Clerk: Douglas Ellis			dandvellis@btinternet.com	07786 678783
72	**Glasgow: Govan and Linthouse (F T W)**			**glpcglasgow@googlemail.com**	**0141 445 2010**
	David T. Gray BArch BD	2010	2020	44 Forfar Avenue, Glasgow G52 3JQ DGray@churchofscotland.org.uk	07789 718622
73	**Glasgow: Hillington Park (F H W)**				
	David A. Sutherland BD	2001	2022	81 Raeswood Road, Glasgow G53 7HH DSutherland@churchofscotland.org.uk	0141 883 5897
74	**Glasgow: Ibrox (F H W)**			**ibroxparishchurch@gmail.com**	**07380 830030**
	Tara P. Granados (Ms) BA MDiv	2018		Ibrox Parish Church, 67 Clifford Street, Glasgow G51 1QH TGranados@churchofscotland.org.uk	07380 830030
75	**Glasgow: Jordanhill (F W)**			**jordchurch@btconnect.com**	**0141 959 2496**
	Bruce H. Sinclair BA BD	2009	2015	12 Priorwood Gardens, Academy Park, Glasgow G13 1GD BSinclair@churchofscotland.org.uk	0141 959 1310
76	**Glasgow: Kelvinbridge (F W)**				**0141 339 1750**
	Gordon Kirkwood BSc BD MTh MPhil PGCE	1987	2003	Flat 2/2, 94 Hyndland Road, Glasgow G12 9PZ GKirkwood@churchofscotland.org.uk	0141 334 5352
77	**Glasgow: Kelvinside Hillhead (F W)**				**0141 334 2788**
	Vacant				
	Roger D. Sturrock (Prof.) BD MD FCRP (Ordained Local Minister)	2014		36 Thomson Drive, Bearsden, Glasgow G61 3PA RSturrock@churchofscotland.org.uk	0141 286 8130
78	**Glasgow: King's Park (F H W)**			**office@kingspark.church.co.uk**	**0141 636 8688**
	Stuart J. Crawford BD MTh	2017	202[illegible]	1101 Aitkenhead Road, Glasgow G44 5SL SCrawford@churchofscotland.org.uk	07305 239128

79 Glasgow: Kinning Park (W)				
Vacant			168 Arbroath Avenue, Cardonald, Glasgow G52 3HH	0141 810 3782
Session Clerk: Sandra Smith			sms56@hotmail.co.uk	07778 291152
80 Glasgow: Knightswood Anniesland Trinity (F H W)			**info@tachurch.org.uk**	**0141 530 9745**
Fiona M.E. Gardner (Mrs) MA MLitt BD	1997	2011	76 Victoria Park Drive North, Glasgow G14 9PJ FGardner@churchofscotland.org.uk	0141 959 5647
Ruth Forsythe (Mrs) DipRS MCS (Ordained Local Minister)	2017	2018	28 Gardenside Avenue, Carmyle, Glasgow G32 8DY RForsythe@churchofscotland.org.uk	07824 641212
81 Glasgow: Langside (F T W)			**langsidechurch@gmail.com**	**0141 632 7520**
Vacant			36 Madison Avenue, Glasgow G44 5AQ	0141 637 0797
Session Clerk: Douglas McCulloch			d.mcculloch3@btinternet.com	07770 928130
82 Glasgow: Maryhill Ruchill (F H W)				**0141 946 3512**
Stuart C. Matthews BD MA	2006	2010	251 Milngavie Road, Bearsden, Glasgow G61 3DQ SMatthews@churchofscotland.org.uk	0141 942 0804
James Hamilton DCS	1997	2000	6 Beckfield Gate, Glasgow G33 1SW James.Hamilton@churchofscotland.org.uk	0141 558 3195 07584 137314
83 Glasgow: Merrylea (F W)				**0141 637 2009**
Vacant			4 Pilmuir Avenue, Glasgow G44 3HX	
Session Clerk: Ralph P. Boettcher			merryleasessionclerk@outlook.com	07806 453724
84 Glasgow: Newlands South (H T W)			**secretary@newlandschurch.org.uk**	**0141 632 3055**
Vacant			24 Monreith Road, Glasgow G43 2NY	0141 632 2588
Session Clerk: Catherine Taylor			catherine.taylor10@ntlworld.com	07929 292479
85 Glasgow: Partick Trinity (F H T W)			**enquiry@partricktrinity.org.uk**	
Timothy D. Sinclair MA MDiv	2018		99 Balshagray Avenue, Glasgow G11 7EQ TSinclair@churchofscotland.org.uk	0141 563 6424
86 Glasgow: Partick Victoria Park (F H W)				**0141 339 8816**
James Andrew McIntyre BD	2010		3 Branklyn Crescent, Glasgow G13 1GJ Andy.McIntyre@churchofscotland.org.uk	0141 959 3732

87 Glasgow: Pollokshaws (F) **0141 649 1879**
Roy J.M. Henderson MA BD DipMin 1987 2013 33 Mannering Road, Glasgow G41 3SW 0141 632 8768
RHenderson@churchofscotland.org.uk

88 Glasgow: Pollokshields (F H T W)
David R. Black MA BD 1986 1997 36 Glencairn Drive, Glasgow G41 4PW 0141 423 4000
DBlack@churchofscotland.org.uk

89 Glasgow: Possilpark (F) **0141 336 8028**
Vacant
Session Clerk: Edward Hyde 1262 Balmuildy Road, Glasgow G23 5HE 07493 261202
wee.eddy@ntlword.com

90 Glasgow: Queen's Park Govanhill (F W) **officeQPG@btinternet.com** **0141 423 3654**
Vacant
Interim Moderator: Roy J.M. Henderson RHenderson@churchofscotland.org.uk 0141 632 8768
Incorporating **Glasgow: John Ross Memorial Deaf Local Mission Church**

91 Glasgow: Robroyston (F W) **info@robroystonchurch.org.uk** **0141 558 8414**
Jonathan A. Keefe BSc BD 2009 7 Beckfield Drive, Glasgow G33 1SR 0141 558 2952
JKeefe@churchofscotland.org.uk

92 Glasgow: St Andrew and St Nicholas (F W) **0141 882 3601**
Vacant
M. Elizabeth (Liz) Johnson Blythe (Assistant Minister) 2005 2024 80 Tweedsmuir Road, Glasgow G52 2RX 0141 883 9873
LJohnsonBlythe@churchofscotland.org.uk
Session Clerk: Stewart Boyle stewartmboyle@gmail.com 0141 427 2666

93 Glasgow: St Andrew's East (F W) **0141 554 1485**
Vacant
Session Clerk: Elizabeth McIvor 43 Broompark Drive, Glasgow G31 2JB 0141 556 4838
emcivor@talktalk.net

94 Glasgow: St Andrew's West (F W) **info@rsscentre.org.uk** **0141 332 4293**
Kleber Machado BD MTh BTh MSc PhD 1998 2019 101 Hill Street, Glasgow G3 6TY 0141 353 6551
KMachado@churchofscotland.org.uk

95 Glasgow: St Christopher's Priesthill and Nitshill (F W) **0141 881 6541**
Vacant
Session Clerk: Douglas MacLaren douglas_maclaren@hotmail.co.uk 07948 193783

96 Glasgow: St Columba See Glasgow: Blawarthill				
97 Glasgow: St David's Knightswood (F W)				**0141 954 1081**
Graham M. Thain LLB BD	1988	1999	60 Southbrae Drive, Glasgow G13 1QD GThain@churchofscotland.org.uk	0141 959 2904
98 Glasgow: St Enoch's Hogganfield (F H W)			**church@st-enoch.org.uk**	**0141 770 5694**
Vacant				
Session Clerk: Allison Doig			aggsbaggs@sky.com	07914 573087
99 Glasgow: St George's Tron (F W)			**info@sgt.church**	**0141 229 5746**
Alastair S. Duncan MA BD	1989	2013	29 Hertford Avenue, Glasgow G12 0LG ADuncan@churchofscotland.org.uk	07968 852083
100 Glasgow: St James' (Pollok) (W)			**info@stjamespollok.com**	**0141 882 4984**
Vacant				
M. Elizabeth (Liz) Johnson Blythe (Assistant Minister)	2005	2024	LJohnsonBlythe@churchofscotland.org.uk	
Session Clerk: David T. Arbuckle			davidtarbuckle@outlook.com	07469 878303
101 Glasgow: St John's Renfield (F W)			**office@sjrchurch.com**	**0141 334 0782**
Vacant			26 Leicester Avenue, Glasgow G12 0LU	0141 339 4637
Interim Moderator: Kleber Machado			KMachado@churchofscotland.org.uk	0141 353 6551
102 Glasgow: St Paul's (F T W)				**0141 770 8559**
Vacant			38 Lochview Drive, Glasgow G33 1QF	0141 770 1561
Session Clerk: Scott Stewart			scottstewart@live.co.uk	07999 007900
103 Glasgow: St Rollox (F W)			**inbox@strollox.co.uk**	**0141 558 1809**
Vacant			42 Melville Gardens, Bishopbriggs, Glasgow G64 3DE	0141 581 0050
104 Glasgow: Sandyford Henderson Memorial (F H L T W)			**enquiries@sandyfordhenderson.net**	**0141 226 3696**
Benjamin Thorp BD	2021		66 Woodend Drive, Glasgow G13 1TG BThorp@churchofscotland.org.uk	07707 608562

105 Glasgow: Sandyhills (F W)				**0141 778 3415**
Norman A. Afrin BA MRes	2018		60 Wester Road, Glasgow G32 9JJ NAfrin@churchofscotland.org.uk	0141 778 1213
106 Glasgow: Scotstoun (W)				
Richard Cameron BD DipMin	2000		15 Northland Drive, Glasgow G14 9BE RCameron@churchofscotland.org.uk	0141 959 4637
107 Glasgow: Shawlands Trinity (F W)				**0141 649 0266**
Vacant				
Session Clerk: Scctt van den Akker			vanandtractor@gmail.com	07960 458463
108 Glasgow: Sherbrooke Mosspark (F H W)			**sherbrooke-init@btconnect.com**	**0141 427 1968**
Adam J. Dillon BD ThM	2003	202	114 Springkell Avenue, Glasgow G41 4EW ADillon@churchofscotland.org.uk	0141 737 7299
109 Glasgow: Shettleston New (F W)				**0141 778 4769**
W. Louis T. Reddick MA BD	2017		211 Sandyhills Road, Glasgow G32 9NB LReddick@churchofscotland.org.uk	0141 230 7365 07843 083548
110 Glasgow: Springburn (F H T W)			**springburnparishchurch@btconnect.com**	**0141 557 2345**
Brian M. Casey MA BD	2014		c/o Springburn Parish Church, 180 Springburn Way, Glasgow G21 1TU BCasey@churchofscotland.org.uk	07703 166772
111 Glasgow: Toryglen (F H T W)			**toryglenparish@gmail.com**	
Guardianship of the Presbytery				
Kaye Gardiner BD (Assistant Minister)	2023	2024	KGardiner@churchofscotland.org.uk	07554 442252
112 Glasgow: Trinity Possil and Henry Drummond (W)			**tphdcofs@yahoo.com**	
Richard G. Buckley BD MTh DMin	1990	1995	50 Highfield Drive, Glasgow G12 0HL RBuckley@churchofscotland.org.uk	0141 339 2870 07587 207981
113 Glasgow: Tron St Mary's (F)				**0141 558 1011**
Vacant	2015		30 Louden Hill Road, Robroyston, Glasgow G33 1GA	0141 389 8816
Session Clerk: Louise Dunn			dunnlooloo@hotmail.co.uk	07882 995292

114 Glasgow: Wallacewell (New Charge Development) (F T W) **admin@wallacewell.org** **0141 558 4466**

Vacant				
Kaye Gardiner BD (Assistant Minister)	2023		KGardiner@churchofscotland.org.uk	07554 442252
Team Member: Marysia Roberts			marysia1@hotmail.com	07572 153019

115 Glasgow: Wellington (F H T W) **wellingtonchurch@btinternet.com** **0141 339 0454**

Richard Baxter MA BD (Transition Minister)	1997	2022	31 Hughenden Gardens, Glasgow G12 9YH RBaxter@churchofscotland.org.uk	07958 541418
Roger D. Sturrock (Prof.) BD MD FCRP (Ordained Local Minister)	2014		36 Thomson Drive, Bearsden, Glasgow G61 3PA RSturrock@churchofscotland.org.uk	0141 286 8130

116 Glasgow: Whiteinch (F W) **0141 959 9317**

Laura Digan	2021		65 Victoria Park Drive South, Glasgow G14 9NX LDigan@churchofscotland.org.uk	0141 576 9020

B. In other appointments: members of Presbytery

Barclay, S. Grant LLB DipLP BD MSc PhD	1995	2021	Presbytery Clerk: Glasgow	Presbytery Office, 260 Bath Street, Glasgow G2 4JP GBarclay@churchofscotland.org.uk	0141 332 6606
Cathcart, John Paul DCS	2000	2023	Presbytery Vacant Charge Enabler	9 Glen More, East Kilbride, Glasgow G74 2AP John.Cathcart@churchofscotland.org.uk	01355 243970 07708 396074
Foster-Fulton, Sally BA BD	1999	2016	Head of Nations and Church Relations, Christian Aid Scotland	sfoster-fulton@churchofscotland.org	07850 937226
Gardner, Peter M. MA BD	1988	2016	Pioneer Minister, Glasgow Arts Community	Flat 3/2, 10 Haggswood Avenue, Glasgow G41 4RE PGardner@churchofscotland.org.uk	07743 539654
Gay, Douglas C. MA BD PhD	1998	2005	University of Glasgow: Trinity College	4 Copland Place, Glasgow G51 2RS douggay@mac.com	0141 330 2073 07971 321452
Herbert, Claire DCS	2019		Chaplain, Lodging House Mission, Glasgow	35 East Campbell Street, Glasgow G51 5DT CHerbert@churchofscotland.org.uk	0141 552 0285
Love, Joanna R. (Ms) BSc DCS	1992	2009	Iona Community: Wild Goose Resource Group	92 Everard Drive, Glasgow G21 1XQ jo@wildgoose.scot	(Office) 0141 429 7281
McDougall, Hilary N. (Mrs) MA PGCE BD	2004	2013	Depute Clerk & Congregational Facilitator: Presbytery of Glasgow	Presbytery Office, 260 Bath Street, Glasgow G2 4JP HMcdougall@churchofscotland.org.uk	0141 332 6606
McPake, John L. BA BD PhD	1987	2017	Ecumenical Officer, Church of Scotland	121 George Street, Edinburgh EH2 4YN JMcPake@churchofscotland.org.uk	0131 225 5722

C. Retaining: members of Presbytery

Beaton, Margaret S. (Miss) DCS	1989	2015	(Deacon: Leader, Church House, Bridgeton)	64 Gardenside Grove, Carmyle, Glasgow G32 8EZ margaretbeaton54@hotmail.com	0141 646 2297 07796 642382

Bell, John L. MA BD FRSCM DUniv	1978	2022	(Iona Community: Wild Goose Resource Group)	148 West Princes Street, Glasgow G4 9DA jlb31@tiscali.co.uk	0141 387 7628
Birch, James PgDip FRSA FIOC	2001	2007	(Auxiliary Minister, Cambuslang: St Andrew's)	1 Kirkhill Grove, Cambuslang, Glasgow G72 8EH	0141 583 1722
Black, Ian W. MA BD	1976	2013	(Grangemouth: Zetland)	Flat 1R, 2 Carrickvale Court, Carrickstone, Cumbernauld, Glasgow G68 0LA iwblack@hotmail.com	01236 453370
Black, William B. MA BD	1970	2011	(Stornoway: High)	33 Tankerland Road, Glasgow G44 4EN revwillieblack@gmail.com	0141 637 4717
Blount, A. Sheila (Mrs) BD BA	1978	2010	(Cupar: St John's and Dairsie United)	28 Alcaig Road, Mosspark, Glasgow G52 1NH asheilablount@gmail.com	0141 419 0746
Campbell, John LTh BA MA BSc	1973	2009	(Caldwell)	96 Boghead Road, Lenzie, Glasgow G66 4EN johncampbell.lenzie@gmail.com	0141 776 0874
Cartlidge, Graham R.G. MA BD STM	1977	2015	(Glasgow: Eastwood)	5 Briar Grove, Newlands, Glasgow G43 2TG	0141 637 3228
Christie, Helen F. (Mrs) BD	1998	2015	(Haggs)	4B Glencairn Road, Cumbernauld G67 2EN andychristie747@yahoo.com	01236 611583
Cunningham, Alexander MA BD	1961	2002	(Presbytery Clerk: Glasgow)	18 Lady Jane Gate, Bothwell, Glasgow G71 8BW	01698 811051
Cuthbertson, Malcolm BA BD	1984	2023	(Rutherglen: West and Wardlawhill)	375 New Edinburgh Road, Bellshill ML4 3HH	07864 820612
Cuthbertson, Valerie S. (Miss) DipTMus DCS	2003	2024	(Deacon, Cumbernauld: Old)	2 Muirhill Court, Hamilton ML3 6DR VCuthbertson@churchofscotland.org.uk	01698 429232
Denniston, David W. BD DipMin	1981	2022	(Interim Minister, Glasgow: Queen's Park Govanhill)	25 Callander Road, Cumbernauld, Glasgow G68 0BT denniston.david@gmail.com	07903 926727
Denniston, Jane M. MA BD MTh DPT DipPSRP	2002	2023	(Campsie)	25 Callander Road, Cumbernauld, Glasgow G68 0BT jane.denniston@gmail.com	07738 123101
Drummond, John W. MA BD	1971	2011	(Rutherglen: West and Wardlawhill)	25 Kingsburn Drive, Rutherglen, Glasgow G73 2AN	0141 571 6002
Duff, T. Malcolm F. MA BD MTh	1985	2009	(Glasgow: Queen's Park)	54 Hawkhead Road, Paisley PA1 3NB	0141 570 0614 07846 926584
Dutch, Morris M. BD BA Dip BTI	1998	2013	(Costa del Sol)	41 Baronald Drive, Glasgow G12 OHN mnmdutch@yahoo.co.uk	0141 357 2286
Easton, David J.C. MA BD	1965	2005	(Burnside Blairbeth)	6 Peveril Court, Burnside, Glasgow G73 4RE deaston@btinternet.com	0141 634 9775
Farrington, Alexandra LTh	2003	2015	(Campsie)	'Glenburn', High Banton, Kilsyth G65 0RA revsfarrington@aol.co.uk	01236 824516
Ferguson, James B. LTh	1972	2002	(Lenzie: Union)	3 Bridgeway Place, Kirkintilloch, Glasgow G66 3HW	0141 588 5868
Finnie, Bill H. BA DipSW CertCRS	2015	2022	(Ordained Local Minister, Kirkintilloch: Hillhead)	27 Hallside Crescent, Cambuslang, Glasgow G72 7DY BFinnie@churchofscotland.org.uk	07518 357138
Forrest, Martin R. BA MA BD	1988	2023	(Chaplain, HM Prison Low Moss)	4/1, 7 Blochairn Place, Glasgow G21 2EB martinrforrest@gmail.com	07938 187239
Fraser, Alexander M. BD DipMin	1985	2019	(Glasgow: Knightswood St Margaret's)		
Fulton, R. Stuart M. BA BD PGCE	1991	2022	(Glasgow: Newlands South)	SFulton@churchofscotland.org.uk	07850 066104
Galbraith, Neil W. BD CertMin	1987	2023	(Glasgow: Cathcart Old)	20 Linndale Oval, Glasgow G45 9QT	0141 579 9948
Galloway, Ian F. BA BD	1977	2021	(Glasgow: Gorbals)	39 McConnell Road, Lochwinnoch PA12 4EB IGalloway@churchofscotland.org.uk	07514 581865

Name	Ord.	Ret.	Former charge	Address	Phone
Gargrave, Mary S. (Mrs) DCS	1989	2024	(Deacon, Glasgow: Carnwadric)	0/1, 6 Cartbank Grove, Glasgow G44 3JD	07927 476915
Gargrave, Mike R. BD	2008	2023	(Thornliebank)	0/1, 6 Cartbank Grove, Glasgow G44 3JD MGargrave@churchofscotland.org.uk	07927 476915
Haley, Derek BD DPS	1960	1999	(Chaplain: Gartnavel Royal Hospital)	9 Kinnaird Crescent, Bearsden, Glasgow G61 2BN	0141 942 9281
Hope, Evelyn P. (Miss) BA BD	1990	1998	(Wishaw: Thornlie)	Flat 0/1, 48 Moss Side Road, Glasgow G41 3UA	0141 649 1522
Hudson, Howard R. MA BD	1982	2021	(Glasgow: Bridgeton St Francis in the East)	4 Larch Square, Cambuslang, Glasgow G72 7BQ	
Hunt, Roland BSc PhD CertEd	2016	2024	(Ordained Local Minister, Glasgow: Carmyle and Kenmuir Cornerstone)	4 Flora Gardens, Bishopbriggs, Glasgow G64 1DS RHunt@churchofscotland.org.uk	0141 563 3257
Hunter, Alastair G. BSc MSc BD	1976	2009	(University of Glasgow: Biblical Studies)		
Johnson, C. Ian W. MA BD	1997	2022	(Dumbarton: Riverside with Dumbarton: St Andrew's with Dumbarton: West)	6 Whittingehame Court, 1350 Great Western Road, Glasgow G12 0BG ian.ciw.johnson@btinternet.com	07484 256472
Johnston, Margaret H. BD DipPEd	1988	2023	(Glasgow: Kinning Park)	MHJohnston@churchofscotland.org.uk	
Johnston, Robert BD MSc FSAScot	2017	2024	(Kilsyth: Burns and Old)	32 Newlands Road, Uddingston, Glasgow G71 5QP RJohnston@churchofscotland.org.uk	07810 377582
Johnston, Robert W.M. MA BD STM	1964	1999	(Glasgow: Temple Anniesland)	Flat 0/2, 68 Strathblane Gardens, Glasgow G13 1BX	0141 230 7287
Johnstone, H. Martin J. MA BD MTh PhD	1989	2020	(Secretary: Church and Society Council)	3/1, 952 Pollokshaws Road, Glasgow G41 2ET MJohnstone@churchofscotland.org.uk	0141 636 5819
Kavanagh, Joseph A. BD DipPTh MTh MTh	1992	2023	(Mearns)	JKavanagh@churchofscotland.org.uk	
Keyes, Joyce A. (Mrs) BD	1996	2024	(Cumbernauld: Abronhill)	1 Castlehill, Greenfoot, Mollinsburn Road, Glenboig, Coatbridge ML5 2QE abronhillpc@outlook.com	01236 874487
Lunan, David W. MA BD DLitt DD	1970	2009	(Presbytery Clerk: Glasgow)	30 Mill Road, Banton, Glasgow G65 0RD DLunan@churchofscotland.org.uk	01236 824110
Lyall, Ann DCS	1980	2022	(Deacon, Glasgow: Baillieston Mure Memorial with St Andrew's; Glasgow: Govan and Linthouse)	117 Barlia Drive, Glasgow G45 0AY ann.lyall@btinternet.com	0141 631 3643
MacDonald, Anne (Miss) BA DCS	1980	2023	(Chaplain, Glasgow Royal Infirmary)	annie.anne502@gmail.com	07976 786174
MacDonald, Kenneth D. MA BA	2001	2006	(Auxiliary Minister, Glasgow: Sandyford Henderson Memorial; Glasgow: Yoker)	5 Henderland Road, Bearsden, Glasgow G61 1AH	0141 943 1103
MacLean, Ewen D. BA BD DipBI	1995	2022	(Gibraltar: St Andrew's)	168 Arbroath Avenue, Glasgow G52 3HH Ewen.Maclean@churchofscotland.org.uk	07780 958068
MacFadyen, Anne M. (Mrs) BSc BD FSAScot	1995	2003	(Auxiliary Minister, Glasgow: Pollokshaws)	295 Mearns Road, Glasgow G77 5LT	0141 639 3605
Mackenzie, Gordon R. BScAgr BD	1977	2014	(Chapelhall)	16 Crowhill Road, Bishopbriggs, Glasgow G64 1QY rev.g.mackenzie@btopenworld.com	0141 772 6052
Mackinnon, Campbell BSc BD	1982	2019	(Glasgow: Balshagray Victoria Park)	campbellbvp@live.com	
MacKinnon, Charles M. BD CertMin	1989	2009	(Kilsyth: Anderson)	36 Hilton Terrace, Bishopbriggs, Glasgow G64 3HB cm.ccmackinnon@gmail.com	0141 772 3811
Macleod, Donald BD LRAM DRSAM	1987	2008	(Blairgowrie)	9 Millersneuk Avenue, Lenzie G66 5HJ donmac2@sky.com	0141 776 6235

MacRae, Elaine H. (Mrs) BD	1985	2021	(Glasgow: St Enoch's Hogganfield)	21 Lakeview Grove, Stepps G33 1FU EMacRae@churchofscotland.org.uk	07834 269487
MacRae, Gordon BD MTh	1985	2023	(Stepps)	21 Lakeview Grove, Stepps G33 1FU gemacrae@icloud.com	07703 163206
Mathieson, Janet S. MA BD ALCM PGSE	2003	2024	(Williamwood)	JMathieson@churchofscotland.org.uk	
Maxwell, David	2014	2020	(Ordained Local Minister, Cambuslang)	248 Old Castle Road, Glasgow G44 5EZ DMaxwell@churchofscotland.org.uk	0141 569 6379 07561 427802
McLachlan, David N. BD	1985	2021	(Glasgow: Langside)	7A Glenlyon Place, Glasgow G73 5PL	0141 482 9704
McLachlan, Eric BD MTh CPS	1978	2005	(Glasgow: Cardonald)	16 Kinpurnie Road, Paisley PA1 3HH eric.janis@btinternet.com	0141 810 5789
McLachlan, T. Alastair BSc	1972	2009	(Craignish with Kilbrandon and Kilchattan with Kilninver and Kilmelford)	9 Alder Road, Milton of Campsie, Glasgow G66 8HH talastair@btinternet.com	01360 319861
McLaren, D. Muir BA BD MTh PhD	1971	2001	(Glasgow: Mosspark)	House 44, 145 Shawhill Road, Glasgow G43 1SX muir44@yahoo.co.uk	07931 155779
McWilliam, Alan BD MTh	1993	2019	(Glasgow: Whiteinch)	1 Springbank Gardens, Glasgow G31 4QD AMcWilliam@churchofscotland.org.uk	
Miller, John D. BA BD STM DD	1971	2007	(Glasgow: Castlemilk East)	98 Kirkcaldy Road, Glasgow G41 4LD rev.john.miller@btinternet.com	0141 423 0221
Moffat, Thomas BSc BD	1976	2008	(Culross and Torryburn)	Flat 8/1, 8 Cranston Street, Glasgow G3 8GG tom@gallus.org.uk	0141 248 1886
Nelson, Thomas BSc BD	1992	2002	(Netherlee)	11a Crosshill Drive, Rutherglen, Glasgow G73 3QU	0141 534 7834
Nicholson, David DCS	1994	2020	(Deacon, Cumbernauld: Kildrum with Cumbernauld: St Mungo's)	2D Doonside, Kildrum, Cumbernauld, Glasgow G67 2HX	01236 732260
Nicol, Douglas M. CA BD	1987	2021	(Glasgow: St Christopher's Priesthill and Nitshill)	19 Rockmount Avenue, Thornliebank, Glasgow G46 7BU DNicol@churchofscotland.org.uk	0141 569 7848
Nimmo, Peter W. BD ThM	1996	2024	(Cambuslang)	PNimmo@churchofscotland.org.uk	
Ninian, Esther J. (Miss) MA BD DipLib	1993	2015	(Newton Mearns)	21 St Ronan's Drive, Burnside, Rutherglen G73 3SR estherninian5914@btinternet.com	0141 647 9720
Pacitti, Stephen A. MA	1963	2003	(Black Mount with Culter with Libberton and Quothquan)	157 Nithsdale Road, Glasgow G41 5RD	0141 423 5792
Pearson, Wilma (Mrs) BD	2004	2018	(Associate, Glasgow: Cathcart Trinity)	90 Newlands Road, Glasgow G43 2JR WPearson@churchofscotland.org.uk	0141 632 2491
Peat, Derek A. BA BD MTh	2013	2022	(Strategy Officer: Presbytery of Glasgow)	DPeat@churchofscotland.org.uk	
Pollock, Thomas L. BA BD MTh FSAScot JP	1982	2021	(Glasgow: Sherbrooke Mosspark)	27 Dorchester Court, Monmouth Avenue, Glasgow G12 0BT	
Purves, John S. LLB BD	1983	2022	(Glasgow: Drumchapel St Andrew's)	28 Cloberhill Road, Glasgow G13 2JL johnpurves278@btinternet.com	0141 286 0917
Reid, Iain M.A. BD CQSW DipSW	1990	2017	(Paisley: Glenburn)	16 Walker Court, Glasgow G16 6QP ireid@churchofscotland.org.uk	0141 577 1200
Roddick, Jeanne N. BD	2003	2023	(Greenbank)	4 Inverlair Drive, Glasgow G43 2AY	07815 520315
Rooney, Andrew D. BSc BD	2019	2024	(Kirkmuirhill)	7 Oak Place, Bishopbriggs, Glasgow G64 1FQ adrooney1@gmail.com	07704 901345
Ross, Donald M. MA	1953	1993	(Industrial Mission Organiser)	14 Cartsbridge Road, Busby, Glasgow G76 8DH	0141 644 2220

Name	Ord.	Ret.	Charge	Address	Phone
Ross, Joan BSc BD PhD	1999	2022	(Glasgow: Carntyne)	4 Moncrieff Gardens, Lenzie G66 4NN rossjoan261@gmail.com	
Spencer, John MA BD	1962	2001	(Dumfries: Lincluden with Holywood)	10 Kinkell Gardens, Kirkintilloch, Glasgow G66 2HJ	0141 777 8935
Stewart, Norma D. (Miss) MA MEd BD MTh	1977	2000	(Glasgow: Strathbungo Queen's Park)	127 Nether Auldhouse Road, Glasgow G43 2YS	0141 637 6956
Thomson, Andrew BA	1976	2007	(Airdrie: Broomknoll)	3 Laurel Wynd, Drumsagard Village, Cambuslang, Glasgow G72 7BH	0141 641 2936 07772 502774
Tuton, Robert M. MA	1957	1995	(Glasgow: Shettleston Old)	6 Holmwood Gardens, Uddingston, Glasgow G71 7BH	01698 321108
White, C. Peter BVMS BD	1974	2011	(Glasgow: Sandyford Henderson Memorial)	2 Hawthorn Place, Torrance, Glasgow G64 4EA revcpw@gmail.com	01360 622680
White, David M. BA BD DMin	1988	2016	(Kirkintilloch: St Columba's)	9 Lapwing Avenue, Lenzie, Glasgow G66 3DJ drdavidmwhite@btinternet.com	0141 578 4357
Whyte, James BD	1981	2011	(Fairlie)	32 Torburn Avenue, Giffnock, Glasgow G46 7RB jameswhyte89@btinternet.com	0141 620 3043
Wilson, Phyllis M. (Mrs) DipCom DipRE CertMin	1985	2006	(Motherwell: South Dalziel)	Glasgow thomas.wilson38@btinternet.com	
Wood, G. Melvyn MA BD	1982	2024	(Glasgow: Blawarthill with Glasgow: St Columba)	32 Seafield Street, Portsoy, Banff AB45 2QT GMelvynWood@churchofscotland.org.uk	07896 604295
Younger, Adah (Mrs) BD LLB	1978	2004	(Glasgow: Dennistoun Central)	Flat 2/3, 53 Barloch Street, Glasgow G22 5BX	07947 580924

D. In other appointments: not members of Presbytery

Nil

E. Retaining: not members of Presbytery

Name	Ord.	Ret.	Charge	Address	Phone
Anderson, Susan M. (Mrs) BD GRSM ARMCM	1997	2014	(Kilmarnock: St John's Onthank)	32 Murrayfield, Bishopbriggs, Glasgow G64 3DS susanbbriggs32@gmail.com	0141 772 6338
Blount, Graham K. LLB BD PhD	1976	2017	(Presbytery Clerk: Glasgow)	28 Alcaig Road, Mosspark, Glasgow G52 1NH Graham.Blount@churchofscotland.org.uk	0141 419 0746
Bradley, Andrew W. BD	1975	2007	(Paisley: Lylesland)	Flat 1/1, 38 Cairnhill View, Bearsden, Glasgow G61 1RP andrewwbradley@hotmail.com	0141 931 5344
Duff, Valerie J. (Miss) DMin	1993	2021	(Glasgow: Shawlands Trinity)	Flat 25, 2 Melrose Avenue, Rutherglen, Glasgow G73 3BU	
McNaughton, Janette (Miss) DCS	1982	2007	(Deacon, Cumbernauld: Condorrat)	4 Dunellan Avenue, Moodiesburn, Glasgow G69 0GB	01236 870180
Murray, George M. LTh	1995	2011	(Glasgow: St Margaret's Tollcross Park)	6 Mayfield, Lesmahagow ML11 0FH george.murray7@gmail.com	01555 895216
Saunders, Keith BD MSc CertPS	1983	2015	(Chaplain, Glasgow Western Infirmary)	39 Market Road, Kirkintilloch G66 3EZ revchap53@hotmail.com	
Shanks, Norman J. MA BD DD	1983	2007	(Glasgow: Govan Old)	1 Marchmont Terrace, Glasgow G12 9LT rufuski@btinternet.com	0141 339 4421
Spiers, John M. LTh MTh	1972	2004	(Giffnock: Orchardhill)	58 Woodlands Road, Thornliebank, Glasgow G46 7JQ j.spiers@icloud.com	0141 638 0632

F. Inactive: not members of Presbytery

Cherry, Alastair J. BD BA FPLD	1982	2009	(Glasgow: Penilee St Andrew)	8 Coruisk Drive, Clarkston, Glasgow G76 7NG ajcherry133@gmail.com	07483 221141
Cullen, William T. BA LTh	1984	1996	(Kilmarnock: St John's Onthank)	6 Laurel Wynd, Cambuslang, Glasgow G72 7BA	0141 641 4337
Fleming, Alexander F. MA BD	1966	1995	(Strathblane)	11 Bankwood Drive, Kilsyth, Glaagow G65 0GZ alex@koror99.com	01236 820915
Galloway, Kathy J. (Mrs) BD DD DipPS	1977	2020	(Co-Leader, Iona Community)	20 Hamilton Park Avenue, Glasgow G12 8UU kathygalloway200@btinternet.com	0141 357 4079
Harvey, W. John BA BD DD	1965	2002	(Interim Minister, Edinburgh: Corstorphine Craigsbank)	501A Shields Road, Glasgow G41 2RF harveydouglas1963@gmail.com	0141 429 3774 07709 651335
Kerr, Hugh F. MA BD	1968	2006	(Aberdeen: Ruthrieston South)	33 Strathmore Court, 20 Abbey Drive, Glasgow G14 9JX	0141 959 8143
Macdonald, William J. BD CPS	1976	2002	(Board of National Mission: New Charge Development)	21 Muirfield Court, 20 Muirend Road, Glasgow G44 3QP williejohnmac@gmail.com	0141 384 3014
MacKay, Alan H. BD DipFS	1974	2010	(Glasgow: Mosspark)	Flat 1/1, 18 Newburgh Street, Glasgow G43 2XR alanhmackay@aol.com	07910 167690
McKenzie, Mary O. CPS	1976	1996	(Edinburgh: Richmond Craigmillar)	4 Dunellan Avenue, Moodiesburn, Glasgow G69 0GB maemck@btinternet.com	01236 870180
McLachlan, Fergus C. BD	1982	1988	(Dunbarney with Forgandenny)	46 Queen Square, Glasgow G41 2AZ whitegoldfm@gmail.com	07544 721032
McLellan, Margaret DCS	1986	2018	(Deacon, Glasgow: Merrylea)	18 Broom Road East, Newton Mearns, Glasgow G77 5SD margaretdmclellan@outlook.com	0141 639 6853
Raeburn, Alan C. MA BD	1971	2010	(Glasgow: Battlefield East)	3 Orchard Gardens, Strathaven ML10 6UN acraeburn@hotmail.com	01357 522924
Turner, Angus BD	1976	1998	(Industrial Chaplain)	46 Keir Street, Glasgow G41 2LA	0141 424 0493

G. Readers (active)

Allan, Phillip	34 Muirhead Way, Bishopbriggs, Glasgow G64 1YG	hampdenhorror@gmail.com	07954 497930
Fullarton, Andrew	Flat 2/2, 2263 Paisley Road West, Glasgow G52 3QA	drewf225@gmail.com	0141 883 9518
Kelly, George	25 Westerton, Lennoxtown G66 7LR	geojkelly@btinternet.com	01360 311739
Kilpatrick, Joan (Mrs)	39 Brent Road, Regent's Park, Glasgow G46 8JG	je-kilpatrick@sky.com	0141 621 1809
MacGregor, Graham	9 Sir Thomas Lipton Way, Cambuslang G72 7HW	GMacGregor@churchofscotland.org.uk	07890 178105
MacLaren, Douglas M.	25 Seaforth Crescent, Barrhead, Glasgow G78 1PL	douglas_maclaren@hotmail.co.uk	07948 193783
McFarlane, Robert	25 Avenel Road, Glasgow G13 2PB	robertmcfrln@yahoo.co.uk	0141 954 5540
McInally, Gordon	10 Melville Gardens, Bishopbriggs, Glasgow G64 3DF	gmcinally@sky.com	0141 563 2685
Millar, Kathleen (Mrs)	18 Greenwood Grove West, Stewarton Road Glasgow G77 6ZF		07793 203045
Morrison, Graham	1/1, 40 Gardner Street, Glasgow G11 5DF		0141 579 4772
Morrison, Katie (Miss)	3b Lennox Court, 16 Stockiemuir Avenue, Bearsden G61 3JL	katiemorrison2003@hotmail.co.uk	0141 942 3024 07852 373840
Nicolson, John C.	2 Lindsaybeg Court, Chryston, Glasgow G69 9DD	john.c.nicolson@btinternet.com	0141 779 2447

Robertson, Lynne M. (Mrs) MA MEd	2 Greenhill, Bishopbriggs, Glasgow G64 1LE	emrobertsonmed@btinternet.com	0141 772 1323 07720 053981
Smith, Ann	52 Robslee Road, Thornliebank, Glasgow G46 7BX		0141 621 0638
Stead, May (Mrs)	9A Carrick Drive, Mount Vernon, Glasgow G32 0RW	maystead@hotmail.co.uk	07917 785109
Struthers, Ivar	7 McVean Place, Longcroft, Bonnybridge FK4 1QZ	ivar.struthers@btinternet.com	01324 841145
Tindall, Maragret (Mrs)	23 Ashcroft Avenue, Lennoxtown, Glasgow G65 7EN	margarettindall@aol.com	01360 310911

H. Ministries Development Staff

Boland, Susan (Mrs) DipHE(Theol)	Cumbernauld: Abronhill and Cumbernauld: Condorrat – Family Development Worker	SBoland@churchofscotland.org.uk
Cameron, Lisa	Glasgow: Castlemilk – Development Worker	LCameron@churchofscotland.org.uk
Cathcart, John Paul DCS	Presbytery – Vacant Charge Enabler	John.Cathcart@churchofscotland.org.uk
Cooke, Marie (Dr)	Presbytery – MDS Ministry Support Officer	MCooke@churchofscotland.org.uk
Gardner, Peter M. (Rev) MA BD	Pioneer Minister, Glasgow Arts Community	PGardner@churchofscotland.org.uk
Graham, Susan	Glasgow: Govan and Linthouse: Families Development Worker	SGraham@churchofscotland.org.uk
Halliday-Robertson, Douglas J.	Glasgow: Shettleston New – Discipleship Facilitator	DJRobertson@churchofscotland.org.uk
Hamilton, James DCS	Glasgow: Maryhill Ruchill – Deacon	James.Hamilton@churchofscotland.org.uk
Hamilton, Karen (Mrs) DCS	Cambuslang – Deacon	KHamilton@churchofscotland.org.uk
Herbert, Claire BD DCS	Lodging House Mission, Glasgow – Chaplain	CHerbert@churchofscotland.org.uk
Hyndman, Graham	Church House, Bridgeton – Youth Worker	GHyndman@churchofscotland.org.uk
Johnstone, Susan	Glasgow: Castlemilk – Community Development Worker	SJohnstone@churchofscotland.org.uk
Keenan, Brian	Glasgow: Drumchapel St Mark's – Community Project Lead	BKeenan@churchofscotland.org.uk
Macdonald-Haak, Aileen D.	Glasgow: Carntyne and Cranhill – Development Worker, Older People	AMacdonald-Haak@churchofscotland.org.uk
Mackay, Shona BA MSc	Presbytery – Strategy Officer	Shona.Mackay@churchofscotland.org.uk
McDougall, Hilary N. (Rev) MA PGCE BD	Presbytery – Depute Clerk and Congregational Facilitator	HMcDougall@churchofscotland.org.uk
McMahon, Deborah	Glasgow: Easterhouse – Children's and Development Worker Team Leader	DMcMahon@churchofscotland.org.uk
Milligan, Catriona	Glasgow: Gorbals – Community Development Worker	CMilligan@churchofscotland.org.uk
Morrison, Iain J.	Glasgow: Colston Milton – Community Arts Worker	IMorrison@churchofscotland.org.uk
Smillie, Janet	Glasgow: Drumchapel St Andrew's and Yoker – Parish Assistant	JSmillie@churchofscotland.org.uk
Thorp, Heather	Presbytery – Pioneering and Planting Co-ordinator	HThorp@churchofscotland.org.uk
Wilson, Marie	Netherlee and Stamperland – Pastoral Assistant	Marie.Wilson@churchofscotland.org.uk
Young, Neil J.	Glasgow: St Paul's – Youth Team Leader	NYoung@churchofscotland.org.uk

ADDRESSES

Bishopbriggs	
Kenmure	Viewfield Road, Bishopbriggs
Springfield Cambridge	The Leys, off Springfield Road
Broom	Mearns Road, Newton Mearns
Burnside Blairbeth	Church Avenue, Burnside Kirkriggs Avenue, Blairbeth
Busby	Church Road, Busby
Cadder	Cadder Road, Bishopbriggs
Cambuslang	Arnott Way
Flemington Hallside	Hutchinson Place
Campsie	Main Street, Lennoxtown
Chryston	Main Street, Chryston
Cumbernauld	
Abronhill	Larch Road
Condorrat	Main Road
Trinity	Baronhill
Eaglesham	Montgomery Street, Eaglesham
Fernhill and Cathkin	Neilvaig Drive
Gartcosh	113 Lochend Road, Gartcosh
Giffnock	
Orchardhill	Church Road
South	Eastwood Toll
The Park	Ravenscliffe Drive
Glenboig	Main Street, Glenboig
Greenbank	Eaglesham Road, Clarkston
Kilsyth	
Anderson	Kingston Road, Kilsyth
Burns and Old	Church Street, Kilsyth
Kirkintilloch	
St Columba's Hillhead	Newdyke Road and Waterside Road nr Auld Aisle Road
St David's Mem Pk	Alexandra Street
St Mary's	Cowgate
Lenzie	
Old	Kirkintilloch Road x Garngaber Ave
Union	65 Kirkintilloch Road
Maxwell	
Mearns Castle	Waterfoot Road
Mearns	Mearns Road, Newton Mearns
Milton of Campsie	Locheil Drive, Milton of Campsie

Moodiesburn	20 Blackwoods Crescent, Moodiesburn
Netherlee and Stamperland	Ormonde Drive x Ormonde Avenue
Newton Mearns	Ayr Road, Newton Mearns
Rutherglen	
Old	Main Street at Queen Street
Stonelaw	Stonelaw Road x Dryburgh Avenue
West and Wardlawhill	3 Western Avenue
Stepps	Whitehill Avenue
Thornliebank	61 Spiersbridge Road
Torrance	School Road, Torrance
Williamwood	4 Vardar Avenue, Clarkston
Glasgow	
Baillieston	
Mure Memorial	Maxwell Drive, Garrowhill
St Andrew's	Bredisholm Road
Barlanark Greyfriars	Edinburgh Rd x Hallhill Rd (365)
Blawarthill	Millbrix Avenue
Bridgeton St Francis in the East	26 Queen Mary Street
Broomhill Hyndland	64–66 Randolph Rd (x Marlborough Ave)
Calton Parkhead	122 Helenvale Street
Cardonald	2155 Paisley Road West
Carmunnock	Kirk Road, Carmunnock
Carmyle and Kenmuir	2405 London Road, Mount Vernon
Cornerstone	
Carntyne and Cranhill	358 Carntynehall Road
Carnwadric	556 Boydstone Road, Thornliebank
Castlemilk	1 Dougrie Road
Cathcart	
Old	119 Carmunnock Road
Trinity	90 Clarkston Road
Cathedral	Cathedral Square, 2 Castle Street
Causeway, Tollcross	1134 Tollcross Road
Clincarthill	1216 Cathcart Road
Colston Milton	Egilsay Crescent
Colston Wellpark	1378 Springburn Road
Croftfoot	Croftpark Ave x Crofthill Road

Dennistoun New	9 Armadale Street
Drumchapel	
St Andrew's and Yoker	153 Garscadden Road
St Mark's	281 Kinfauns Drive
Easterhouse	Boyndie Street
Eastwood	Mansewood Road
Gairbraid	1517 Maryhill Road
Gallowgate	Calton Parkhead halls 122 Helenvale Street
Garthamlock, Ruchazie and Craigend	46 Porchester Street
Gorbals	1 Errol Gardens
Govan and Linthouse	Govan Cross
Hillington Park	24 Berryknowes Road
Ibrox	Carillon Road x Clifford Street
Jordanhill	28 Woodend Drive (x Munro Road)
Kelvinbridge	Belmont Street at Belmont Bridge
Kelvinside Hillhead	Observatory Road
King's Park	242 Castlemilk Road
Kinning Park	Eaglesham Place
Knightswood	2000 Great Western Road
Anniesland Trinity	869 Crow Road
Langside	167–169 Ledard Road (x Lochleven Road)
Maryhill Ruchill	1990 Maryhill Road
Merrylea	78 Merrylee Road
Newlands South	Riverside Road x Langside Drive
Partick Trinity	20 Lawrence Street x Elie Street
Partick Victoria Park	259 Dumbarton Road
Pollokshaws	223 Shawbridge Street
Pollokshields	Albert Drive x Shields Road
Possilpark	124 Saracen Street
Queen's Park Govanhill	170 Queen's Drive
Robroyston	34 Saughs Road

St Andrew and St Nicholas	224 Hartlaw Crescent	St James' (Pollok)	Lyoncross Road x Byrebush Road	Shettleston New	679 Old Shettleston Road
St Andrew's East	681 Alexandra Parade	St John's Renfield	22 Beaconsfield Road	Springburn	180 Springburn Way
St Andrew's West	260 Bath Street	St Paul's	30 Langdale St (x Greenrig St)	Toryglen	Glenmore Ave nr Prospecthill Road
St Christopher's Priesthill and Nitshill	100 Priesthill Rd (x Muirshiel Cr)	St Rollox	70 Fountainwell Road	Trinity Possil and Henry Drummond	2 Crowhill Street (x Broadholm Street)
St Columba	at Blawarthill Church	Sandyford Henderson Memorial	Kelvinhaugh Street at Argyle Street	Tron St Mary's	128 Red Road
St David's Knightswood	66 Boreland Drive (nr Lincoln Avenue)	Sandyhills	28 Baillieston Rd nr Sandyhills Rd	Wallacewell	57 Northgate Rd., Balornock
St Enoch's Hogganfield	860 Cumbernauld Road	Scotstoun	Earlbank Ave x Ormiston Ave	Wellington	University Ave x Southpark Ave
St George's Tron	163 Buchanan Street	Shawlands Trinity	Shawlands Cross (1114 Pollokshaws Road)	Whiteinch	1a Northinch Court
		Sherbrooke Mosspark	Nithsdale Rd x Sherbrooke Avenue		

(6) FORTH VALLEY AND CLYDESDALE (F W)

Meets in 2024 on the last Saturday of November at Motherwell: Dalziel St Andrew's Church and in 2025 on dates and locations to be determined.

Presbytery Office:		**Rex House, 103 Bothwell Road, Hamilton ML3 0DW** **fvandc@churchofscotland.org.uk**	**01698 285672**
Clerk:	**Vacant**		**01698 662537**
Depute Clerk:	**REV. BRYAN KERR BA BD**	**bkerr@churchofscotland.org.uk**	
Treasurer:	**MR DAVID J. WATT BAcc CA CPFA**	**david.j.watt@btinternet.com**	
Administration Officer:	**CATHERINE BARCLAY**	**cbarclay@churchofscotland.org.uk**	
Buildings Officer:	**MHAIRI MACLEOD**	**mhairi.macleod@churchofscotland.org.uk**	
Education, Training and Development Officer:	**LORNA LAUGHLAND**	**llaughland@churchofscotland.org.uk**	
Mission Officer:	**DR SCOTT PAGET**	**spaget@churchofscotland.org.uk**	

1 Airdrie: Cairnlea (F H W) linked with Calderbank (F T) — **Cairnlea: 01236 762101**

Peter H. Donald MA PhD BD	1991	2018	31 Victoria Place, Airdrie ML6 9BU PDonald@churchofscotland.org.uk	01236 753159

2 Airdrie: Clarkston (F W) — **enquiries@airdrieclarkstonparishchurch.org.uk**

Hanna I. Rankine BA BD	2018		66 Wellhall Road, Hamilton ML3 9BY HRankine@churchofscotland.org.uk	01236 756862

3 Airdrie: High (F) linked with Caldercruix and Longriggend (H) — **High: 01236 779620**

Ian R.W. McDonald BSc BD PhD	2007		17 Etive Drive, Airdrie ML6 9QL IMcDonald@churchofscotland.org.uk	01236 760023

4 Airdrie: Jackson (F H W)

Kay Gilchrist (Miss) BD CertMin DipPC	1996	2008	48 Dunrobin Road, Airdrie ML6 8LR KGilchrist@churchofscotland.org.uk	01236 597649

5 Airdrie: New Monkland (F H W) linked with Greengairs (F W)

Vacant	3 Dykehead Crescent, Airdrie ML6 6PU	01236 761723
Session Clerk, Airdrie: New Monkland: Helene Marshall	helenemarshall@blueyonder.co.uk	01236 751945
Session Clerk, Greengairs: Sheena Walker	sheena.walker4@icloud.com	01236 830347

6 Airdrie: New Wellwynd (F W) — **01236 748646**

Vacant	72 Inverlochy Road, Airdrie ML6 9DJ	01236 763022
Interim Moderator: Murdo C. MacDonald	Murdo.Macdonald@churchofscotland.org.uk	01698 769699

7	**Airdrie: St Columba's (F W)**				
	Margaret F. Currie BEd BD	1980	1987	52 Kennedy Drive, Airdrie ML6 9AW MCurrie@churchofscotland.org.uk	01236 763173
8	**Airth (F H)**				
	James F. Todd BD CPS	1984	2012	The Manse, Airth, Falkirk FK2 8LS JTodd@churchofscotland.org.uk	01324 831120
9	**Bellshill: Central (F T W)**				**01698 747144**
	Kevin M. de Beer BTh	1995	2016	32 Adamson Street, Bellshill ML4 1DT KdeBeer@churchofscotland.org.uk	01698 841176 07555 265609
10	**Bellshill: West (F H W)**				**01698 747581**
	Vacant			16 Croftpark Street, Bellshill ML4 1EY	01698 842877
	Session Clerk: Annabel Leitch			leitch.a@sky.com	01698 810143
11	**Biggar (F H W) linked with Black Mount**			**biggarkirk09@gmail.com**	**01889 229291**
	Mike D. Fucella BD MTh	1997	2013	'Candlemas', 6C Leafield Road, Biggar ML12 6AY MFucella@churchofscotland.org.uk	01899 229291
12	**Black Mount** See Biggar				
13	**Blackbraes and Shieldhill (W) linked with Muiravonside (F W)**				
	Vacant				
	Interim Moderator: Scott W. Burton			Scott.Burton@churchofscotland.org.uk	01324 341590
14	**Blantyre: Livingstone Memorial (F W) linked with Blantyre St Andrew's (F)**			**info@livingstonechurch.org.uk**	
	Murdo C. Macdonald MA BD	2002	2017	332 Glasgow Road, Blantyre, Glasgow G72 9LQ Murdo.Macdonald@churchofscotland.org.uk	01698 769699
15	**Blantyre: Old (F H T W)**				
	Vacant			The Manse, Craigmuir Road, High Blantyre, Glasgow G72 9UA	01698 769046
	Jim Murphy (Ordained Local Minister; Interim Moderator)	2014	2024	10 Hillview Crescent, Bellshill ML4 1NX JMurphy@churchofscotland.org.uk	01698 740189
	Session Clerk: Mary Gallacher			mary.gallacherclerk@yahoo.com	01698 821958
16	**Blantyre: St Andrew's** See Blantyre: Livingstone Memorial				

17	**Bo'ness: Old (F H T W)**				
	Amanda J. MacQuarrie MA PGCE MTh	2014	2016	Abbotsgrange Manse, 8 Naismith Court, Grangemouth FK3 9BQ A.MacQuarrie@churchofscotland.org.uk	01324 336979
18	**Bo'ness: St Andrew's (F W)**				**01506 825803**
	Vacant			St Andrew's Manse, 11 Erngath Road, Bo'ness EH51 9DP	01506 822195
	Interim Moderator: F. Derek Gunn			RevDerekGunn@hotmail.com	01324 610349
19	**Bonnybridge: St Helen's (F H W)**				
	Vacant			The Manse, 32 Reilly Gardens, High Bonnybridge FK4 2BB	01324 874807
	Interim Moderator: Ronald Matandakufa			RMatandakufa@churchofscotland.org.uk	01324 337885
20	**Bothkennar and Carronshore (W)**				
	Andrew J. Moore BSc BD	2007		11 Hunter Place, Greenmount Park, Carronshore, Falkirk FK2 8QS AMoore@churchofscotland.org.uk	01324 570525
21	**Bothwell (F H W)**			**office@bothwellparishchurch.org.uk**	**01698 854903**
	Iain M.T. Majcher BD	2020		Bothwell Parish Church, Main Street, Bothwell, Glasgow G71 8EX IMajcher@churchofscotland.org.uk	01698 600933
22	**Brightons (F H T W)**			**info@brightonschurch.org.uk**	**01324 713855**
	Scott W. Burton BA BA	2019		77 Wallace Brae Drive, Reddingmuirhead, Falkirk FK2 0FB Scott.Burton@churchofscotland.org.uk	01324 341590
23	**Cairngryffe (F W) linked with Libberton and Quothquan (F H W) linked with Symington (F W) (The Tinto Parishes)**			**contactus@symingtonkirk.com**	
	Vacant			16 Abington Road, Symington, Biggar ML12 6JX	01899 309400
	Session Clerk, Cairngryffe: Rosmairi J. Galloway (Dr)			pepperknowes@btinternet.com	07733 446567
	Interim Moderator: Elijah O. Obinna			EObinna@churchofscotland.org.uk	01555 752389
	Session Clerk, Symington: Robert Carson			robertdcarson@yahoo.com	01899 309061
24	**Calderbank** See Airdrie: Cairnlea				
25	**Caldercruix and Longriggend** See Airdrie: High				
26	**Carluke: Forrest Kirk (F H W)**				**01555 751730**
	Elijah O. Obinna BA MTh PhD	2002	2016	18 Old Bridgend, Carluke ML8 4HN EObinna@churchofscotland.org.uk	01555 752389

New charge formed by the union of Carluke: St Andrew's and Carluke: St John's

27	**Carluke: Kirkton (F H W)**			**office@kirktonchurch.com**	**01555 750778**
	Vacant			9 Station Road, Carluke ML8 5AA	01555 771262
	Session Clerk: Susan Forbes			sessionclerk.kirktonchurch@gmail.com	01555 772585
28	**Carnwath linked with Carstairs (F W)**				
	Sumit Harrison BA DipTh BTh	2013	2020	11 Range View, Cleghorn, Carstairs, Lanark ML11 8TF	01555 668868
				SHarrison@churchofscotland.org.uk	
29	**Carstairs** See Carnwath				
30	**Chapelhall (F H W) linked with Kirk o' Shotts (F H W)**				
	Vacant			The Manse, Russell Street, Chapelhall, Airdrie ML6 8SG	01236 763439
	Session Clerk, Chapelhall: Betty McLean			bettymcl175@btinternet.com	01236 765249
	Session Clerk, Kirk o' Shotts: Eileen Ross			rossdrumduff@gmail.com	07450 275307
31	**Coalburn and Lesmahagow (F H W)**			**candle.church2@gmail.com**	**01555 892425**
	Morag V. Garrett (Mrs) BD	2011	2021	9 Elmbank, Lesmahagow ML11 0EA	01555 890460
				MGarrett@churchofscotland.org.uk	
32	**Coatbridge: Blairhill Dundyvan (H W) linked with Coatbridge: Middle (W)**			**Blairhill Dundyvan:**	**01236 435198**
	Vacant			1 Nelson Terrace, East Kilbride, Glasgow G74 2EY	01355 520093
	Session Clerk, Blairhill Dundyvan: Myra Fraser			myrafraser@hotmail.co.uk	01236 421728
	Session Clerk, Middle: Gordon Russell			gordon-russell@hotmail.co.uk	01236 603597
33	**Coatbridge: Calder (F H W) linked with Coatbridge: Old Monkland (F W)**				
	Vacant				
	Session Clerk, Calder: Olive Coventry			olive.coventry@blueyonder.co.uk	01236 625300
	Session Clerk, Old Monkland: Alison McGowan (Mrs)			alisonrobertsonmcgowan@gmail.com	07798 644253
34	**Coatbridge: Middle** See Coatbridge: Blairhill Dundyvan				
35	**Coatbridge: New St Andrew's (W)**				
	Fiona M. Nicolson BA BD CQSW	1996	2005	77 Eglinton Street, Coatbridge ML5 3JF	01236 437271
				FNicolson@churchofscotland.org.uk	
36	**Coatbridge: Old Monkland** See Coatbridge: Calder				

37	**Coatbridge: Townhead (F H)**				
	Ecilo Selemani LTh MTh	1993	2004	The Manse, Crinan Crescent, Coatbridge ML5 2LH	01236 702914
				ESelemani@churchofscotland.org.uk	
38	**Crossford (H) linked with Kirkfieldbank**				
	Vacant			74 Lanark Road, Crossford, Carluke ML8 5RE	01555 860415
	Session Clerk, Crossford: Keith Haig			keith.haig@hotmail.com	01555 860266
	Session Clerk, Kirkfieldbank: Marie Gray			mariecgray@hotmail.com	01555 664985
39	**Dalserf (F H W)**				
	Vacant			Manse Brae, Dalserf, Larkhall ML9 3BN	01698 882195
	Fiona R. Anderson DipHE BA (Ordained Local Minister; Interim Moderator)	2020	2023	52 Cooper Crescent, Ferniegair, Hamilton ML3 7FT	07913 153608
				FAnderson@churchofscotland.org.uk	
	Session Clerk: Joan Pollok			joan.pollok@btinternet.com	07728 337212
40	**Denny: Old (W) linked with Haggs (H W)**			**haggschurch1@yahoo.co.uk**	
	Raheel Arif MSc MEd BA	2019		57 Singers Place, Dennyloanhead FK4 1FD	01324 819149
				RArif@churchofscotland.org.uk	
41	**Denny: Westpark (F H W)**				
	Kipchumba Too BTh MTh MSc	2017		13 Baxter Crescent, Denny FK6 5EZ	01324 882220
				KToo@churchofscotland.org.uk	
42	**Douglas Valley (F W)**			**office.tdvc@yahoo.co.uk**	**01555 850000**
	Guardianship of the Presbytery			The Manse, Douglas, Lanark ML11 0RB	
	Session Clerk: Andy Robinson			gavdrewandjoe@aol.com	01555 851246
43	**Dunipace (F H W)**				
	Jean W. Gallacher BD CertMin CertTheol DMin	1989		The Manse, 239 Stirling Street, Dunipace, Denny FK6 6QJ	01324 824540
				JGallacher@churchofscotland.org.uk	
44	**East Kilbride: Claremont (F H W)**			**office@claremontparishchurch.co.uk**	**01355 238088**
	Vacant			17 Deveron Road, East Kilbride, Glasgow G74 2HR	01355 248526
	Session Clerk: Moraig Drumgold			mogie.drumgold@btinternet.com	01355 231815
45	**East Kilbride: Greenhills**				**01355 221746**
	Vacant				
	Interim Moderator: Mahboob Masih			MMasih@churchofscotland.org.uk	01355 224469

46	**East Kilbride: Moncreiff (F H W)**			**theoffice@moncreiffparishchurch.co.uk**	**01355 223328**
	Sarah L. Ross BD MTh PGDipCS	2004	2020	16 Almond Drive, East Kilbride, Glasgow G74 2HX SRoss@churchofscotland.org.uk	01355 715735
47	**East Kilbride: Mossneuk (F W)**			**office@mossneuk.church**	**01355 260954**
	Vacant			30 Eden Grove, Mossneuk, East Kilbride, Glasgow G75 8XU	01355 234196
	George Sneddon BD (Assistant Minister)	2022		26 Dormiston Road, Kirkmuirhill ML11 9SL GSneddon@churchofscotland.org.uk	07496 023443
	Session Clerk: Mhairi MacLeod			sessionclerk@mossneuk.church	
48	**East Kilbride: Old (H W)**			**ekopc.office@btconnect.com**	**01355 279004**
	Anne S. Paton BA BD	2001		40 Maxwell Drive, East Kilbride, Glasgow G74 4HJ APaton@churchofscotland.org.uk	01355 220732
49	**East Kilbride: South (F H W)**				
	Vacant				
	Interim Moderator: Calum M. Stark			7 Clamps Wood, St Leonard's, East Kilbride, Glasgow G74 2HB CStark@churchofscotland.org.uk	01355 902758 01357 523031
50	**East Kilbride: Stewartfield (F)**				
	Vacant				
	Interim Moderator: Colin Russell			russellc56@gmail.com	01555 759993
51	**East Kilbride: West (F H W)**				
	Mahboob Masih BA MDiv MTh	1999	2008	4 East Milton Grove, East Kilbride, Glasgow G75 8SN MMasih@churchofscotland.org.uk	01355 224469
52	**East Kilbride: Westwood (H W)**				**01355 245657**
	Kevin Mackenzie BD DipPS	1989	1996	16 Inglewood Crescent, East Kilbride, Glasgow G75 8QD Kevin.Mackenzie@churchofscotland.org.uk	01355 223992
53	**Falkirk: Bainsford (F H T W)**				
	Vacant			1 Valleyview Place, Newcarron Village, Falkirk FK2 7JB	
	Andrew Sarle BSc BD (Ordained Local Minister)	2013		5 Hodge Street, Falkirk FK1 5AA ASarle@churchofscotland.org.uk	07743 726013
	Interim Moderator: Alastair M. Horne			AHorne@churchofscotland.org.uk	01324 623308

54	**Falkirk: Camelon (F W)**				**01324 870011**
	Vacant			30 Cotland Drive, Falkirk FK2 7GE	01324 623631
	Interim Moderator: Jean W. Gallacher			JGallacher@churchofscotland.org.uk	01324 824540
55	**Falkirk: Grahamston United (F H T W)**				
	Vacant				
	Grahamston United is a Local Ecumenical Partnership with the Methodist and United Reformed Churches				
56	**Falkirk: Laurieston (W) linked with Redding and Westquarter (W)**				
	Vacant			11 Polmont Road, Laurieston, Falkirk FK2 9QQ	01324 621196
	Interim Moderator: Deborah L. van Welie			DLVanWelie@churchofscotland.org.uk	01324 713427
57	**Falkirk: St Andrew's West (H W)**				**01324 622091**
	Alastair M. Horne BSc BD	1989	1997	1 Maggiewood's Loan, Falkirk FK1 5SJ AHorne@churchofscotland.org.uk	01324 623308
58	**Falkirk: Trinity (F H T W)**			**office@falkirktrinity.org.uk**	**01324 611017**
	Robert S.T. Allan LLB DipLP BD	1991	2003	9 Major's Loan, Falkirk FK1 5QF RAllan@churchofscotland.org.uk	07895 388644
	I. Charlene Condeco BEM BSc DipHE (Ordained Local Minister)	2023		Woodside Cottage, Brownrigg Road, Slamannan FK1 3BA CCondeco@churchofscotland.org.uk	01324 851553
59	**Forth: St Paul's (F H W)**				
	Vacant			22 Lea Rig, Forth, Lanark ML11 8EA	01555 728837
	Eckhardt Bosch BTh MTh (Assistant Minister)	2022		The Manse, 9 Kirk Road, Shotts ML7 5ET EBosch@churchofscotland.org.uk	07871 959996
	Session Clerk: Margaret Hunter			sclerkforthstpauls@outlook.com	01555 811780
60	**Grangemouth: Abbotsgrange (F T W)**				
	Vacant			8 Naismith Court, Grangemouth FK3 9BQ	01324 482109
	Interim Moderator: Andrew Sarle			ASarle@churchofscotland.org.uk	07743 726013
61	**Grangemouth: Kirk of the Holy Rood (F W)**				
	Ronald Matandakufa BTh MA	2014	2019	The Manse, Bowhouse Road, Grangemouth FK3 0EX RMatandakufa@churchofscotland.org.uk	01324 337885
62	**Grangemouth: Zetland (F H W)**				
	Alison A. Meikle (Mrs) BD	1999	2014	Ronaldshay Crescent, Grangemouth FK3 9JH AMeikle@churchofscotland.org.uk	01324 336729

63	**Greengairs** See Airdrie: New Monkland				
64	**Haggs** See Denny: Old				
65	**Hamilton: Cadzow (F H W)**			**contact@cadzowchurch.org.uk**	**01698 428695**
	W. John Carswell BS MDiv DPT	1996	2009	3 Carlisle Road, Hamilton ML3 7BZ JCarswell@churchofscotland.org.uk	01698 426682
66	**Hamilton: Gilmour and Whitehill (H W) linked with Hamilton: West (H W)**				**West: 01698 284670**
	Vacant				01698 284670
	Session Clerk, Gilmour: Ann Paul			annepaul.gandw@gmail.com	01698 421697
	Session Clerk, West: Ian Hindle			ianmarilyn.hindle@googlemail.com	01698 429080
67	**Hamilton: Hillhouse (F W)**				
	Christopher A. Rankine MA MTh PgDE	2016		66 Wellhall Road, Hamilton ML3 9BY CRankine@churchofscotland.org.uk	01698 327579
68	**Hamilton: Old (F H W)**			**office@hamiltonold.co.uk**	**01698 281905**
	I. Ross Blackman BSc MBA BD CertTh	2015		1 Chateau Grove, Hamilton ML3 7DS RBlackman@churchofscotland.org.uk	01698 640185
69	**Hamilton: St John's (H W)**				**01698 286868**
	Joanne C. Hood (Miss) MA BD	2003	2012	9 Shearer Avenue, Ferniegair, Hamilton ML3 7FX JHood@churchofscotland.org.uk	01698 425002
70	**Hamilton: South (F H) linked with Quarter (F)**				**South: 01698 281014**
	Andrew (Drew) Gebbie BTh	2021		70 Huntly Gardens, Blantyre G72 0GW DGebbie@churchofscotland.org.uk	07498 947412
71	**Hamilton: Trinity (F)**				**01698 284254**
	Vacant				
	Session Clerk: Catherine Hamilton			69 Buchan Street, Hamilton ML3 8JY cathiehamilton@hotmail.com	01698 284919
72	**Hamilton: West** See Hamilton: Gilmour and Whitehill				

73 Holytown (F W) linked with New Stevenston: Wrangholm Kirk (F W)				
			info@holytownparishchurch.org.uk	
			wrangholmkirk@gmail.com	
Vacant			The Manse, 260 Edinburgh Road, Holytown, Motherwell ML1 5RU	01698 832622
Session Clerk, Holytown: Stewart McNeil			asmcneil@aol.com	01698 831269
Session Clerk, New Stevenston: Wrangholm Kirk: Netta Lithgow			n.lithgow@btinternet.com	01698 833743
74 Kirkfieldbank See Crossford				
75 Kirkmuirhill (F H W)			**kirkmuirhillchurch@gmail.com**	**01555 895593**
Vacant			The Manse, 82 Vere Road, Kirkmuirhill, Lanark ML11 9RP	01555 892409
Session Clerk: Catherine Gold			kirkmuirhillparishchurch@gmail.com	01555 893174
76 Kirk o' Shotts (H) See Chapelhall				
77 Lanark: Greyfriars (F H T W)			**office@lanarkgreyfriars.com**	**01555 437050**
Bryan Kerr BA BD	2002	2007	Greyfriars Manse, 3 Bellefield Way, Lanark ML11 7NW	01555 663363
			BKerr@churchofscotland.org.uk	07889 841511
78 Lanark: St Nicholas' (F H W)			**lanarkstnicholas@outlook.com**	**01555 666220**
Louise E. Mackay BSc BD	2017		2 Kairnhill Court, Lanark ML11 9HU	01555 661936
79 Larbert: East (F W)				
Vacant			1 Cortachy Avenue, Carron, Falkirk FK2 8DH	01324 562402
Session Clerk: Margaret Tooth			margaret.tooth@larberteast.church	
80 Larbert: Old (F H W)				
Guardianship of the Presbytery			The Manse, 38 South Broomage Avenue, Larbert FK5 3ED	01324 872760
Session Clerk: Eric Appelbe			larbertoldcontact@gmail.com	01324 556551
81 Larbert: West (F H W)				
Vacant			29 Drysdale Avenue, Kinnaird, Larbert FK2 8RE	
Mhairi M. Gilchrist BD (Assistant Minister)	2023		MGilchrist@churchofscotland.org.uk	07519 364059
82 Larkhall: New (F H W)				
Alastair G. McKillop BD DipMin	1995	2004	2 Orchard Gate, Larkhall ML9 1HA	01698 321976
			AMcKillop@churchofscotland.org.uk	

83	**Larkhall: Trinity**				
	Vacant			13 Machan Avenue, Larkhall ML9 2HE	01698 881401
	Session Clerk: Wilma Gilmour (Miss)			gilmourgilmour@btinternet.com	01698 883002
84	**Law (F W)**			**info@lawparishchurch.org**	
	Vacant			3 Shawgill Court, Law, Carluke ML8 5SJ	01698 373180
	A. Kwame Ahaligah MA STM PhD DipTh FHEA (Assistant Minister)	2004	2023	KAhaligah@churchofscotland.org.uk	01698 591961
	Interim Moderator: Lorna I. MacDougall			LMacDougall@churchofscotland.org.uk	01698 352090
85	**Libberton and Quothquan** See Cairngryffe				
86	**Motherwell: Crosshill (F H W) linked with Motherwell: St Margaret's (F W)**			**info@crosshillparishchurch.org.uk**	
	Vacant				
	Session Clerk, Motherwell: Crosshill: Willie Talbot			talbottally@aol.com	01698 269598
87	**Motherwell: Dalziel St Andrew's (F H T W)**				**01698 264097**
	Alistair S. May LLB BD PhD	2002	2020	4 Pollock Street, Motherwell ML1 1LP AMay@churchofscotland org.uk	01698 263414
88	**Motherwell: North (F W) linked with Wishaw: Craigneuk and Belhaven (H)**				
	Derek H.N. Pope BD DipYCW	1987	1995	35 Birrens Road, Motherwell ML1 3NS DPope@churchofscotland.org.uk	01698 266716
89	**Motherwell: St Margaret's** See Motherwell: Crosshill				
90	**Motherwell: St Mary's (F H T W)**			**office@stmarysmotherwell.org.uk**	**01698 268554**
	Bryce Calder MA BD	1995	2017	19 Orchard Street, Motherwell ML1 3JE BCalder@churchofscotland.org.uk	07986 144834
91	**Motherwell: South (F H T W)**				
	Alan W. Gibson BA BD	2001	2016	62 Manse Road, Motherwell ML1 2PT Alan.Gibson@churchofscotland.org.uk	01698 239279
92	**Muiravonside** See Blackbraes and Shieldhill				

93 Newarthill and Carfin (F H T W)				
Vacant				
Session Clerk: Ann Pickering			sessionclerk@nc-church.org	01698 862503
94 Newmains: Bonkle (F H W) linked with Newmains: Coltness Memorial (F H W)				**01698 344001**
Vacant			36 Glencairn Drive, Glasgow G41 4PW	07703 827057
Session Clerk: Anice Pringle			anicepringle123@btinternet.com	01698 381614
95 Newmains: Coltness Memorial See Newmains: Bonkle				
96 New Stevenston: Wrangholm Kirk See Holytown				
97 Overtown (F W)				**01698 358727**
Lorna I. MacDougall MA DipGC BD	2003	2017	The Manse, 146 Main Street, Overtown, Wishaw ML2 0QP	01698 352090
			LMacDougall@churchofscotland.org.uk	
98 Polmont: Old (F W)			**administrator@polmontold.org.uk**	**01324 715995**
Deborah L. van Welie (Ms) MTheol	2015		3 Orchard Grove, Polmont, Falkirk FK2 0XE	01324 713427
			DLVanWelie@churchofscotland.org.uk	
99 Quarter See Hamilton: South				
100 Redding and Westquarter See Falkirk: Laurieston				
101 Shotts: Calderhead Erskine (F)				
Vacant			The Manse, 9 Kirk Road, Shotts ML7 5ET	01501 823204
Session Clerk: Liam T. Haggart SSC			a2lth@hotmail.com	07896 557687
102 Slamannan				
Vacant				
Monica J. MacDonald (Mrs) (Ordained Local Minister)	2014		60 Kennedy Way, Airth FK2 8GG	01324 832782
			Monica.MacDonald@churchofscotland.org.uk	
103 Stenhouse and Carron (F H)				
Vacant			The Manse, 21 Tipperary Place, Stenhousemuir, Larbert FK5 4SX	01324 416628
Interim Moderator: Alison A. Meikle			AMeikle@churchofscotland.org.uk	01324 336729
104 Stonehouse: St Ninian's (F H T W)			**info@st-ninians-stonehouse.org.uk**	
Stewart J. Cutler BA MSc DipHE	2017		4 Hamilton Way, Stonehouse, Larkhall ML9 3PU	01698 791508
			revstewartcutler@gmail.com	

Stonehouse: St Ninian's is a Local Ecumenical Partnership with the United Reformed Church

105 Strathaven: Avendale Old and Drumclog (F H W)			**info@avendale-drumclog.org.uk**	**01357 671557**
Calum M. Stark LLB BD	2011	2021	4 Fortrose Gardens, Strathaven ML10 6FH	01357 523031
			CStark@churchofscotland.org.uk	
106 Strathaven: Trinity (F H W)			**strathaventrinity@gmail.com**	**01357 529316**
Shaw J. Paterson BSc BD MSc DPT	1991		15 Lethame Road, Strathaven ML10 6AD	Tel 01357 520019
			SPaterson@churchofscotland.org.uk	Fax 01357 529316
107 Symington See Cairngryffe				
108 Uddingston: Burnhead (F H W)				
Vacant			90 Laburnum Road, Uddingston, Glasgow G71 5DB	01698 813716
Session Clerk: David Green			dgreen1886@yahoo.co.uk	07500 861982
109 Uddingston: Old (F H W)				**01698 814015**
Fiona L.J. McKibbin (Mrs) MA BD	2011		1 Belmont Avenue, Uddingston, Glasgow G71 7AX	01698 814757
			FMcKibbin@churchofscotland.org.uk	
110 Uddingston: Viewpark (F H W)			**enquiries@viewparkparishchurch.org.uk**	**01698 810478**
Michael G. Lyall BD CertMin	1993	2001	14 Holmbrae Road, Uddingston, Glasgow G71 6AP	01698 813113
			MLyall@churchofscotland.org.uk	
111 Upper Clyde (F W)				
Nikki M. Macdonald BD MTh PhD	2014		31 Carlisle Road, Crawford, Biggar ML12 6TP	01864 502139
			NMacdonald@churchofscotland.org.uk	
112 Wishaw: Cambusnethan North (F H W)				
Vacant			350 Kirk Road, Wishaw ML2 8LH	01698 381305
Jillian C. Storrie (Mrs) BA (Assistant Minister)	2023		67 Spinningdale, Stonehouse, Larkhall ML9 3QS	01698 791414
			JStorrie@churchofscotland.org.uk	
Session Clerk: Anne McGowan			mcgowanfamily73@gmail.com	07477 934150
113 Wishaw: Cambusnethan Old and Morningside (F)				
Vacant			22 Coronation Street, Wishaw ML2 8LF	01698 384235
Session Clerk: Graeme Vincent			gvincent@theiet.org	01555 752166
114 Wishaw: Craigneuk and Belhaven See Motherwell: North				

115 Wishaw: Old (F H)				**01698 376080**
Vacant			130 Glen Road, Wishaw ML2 7NP	01698 375134
Interim Moderator: Keith W. Ross			keithwross@minister.com	07855 163449
116 Wishaw: St Mark's (F)				
Vacant			3 Laburnum Crescent, Wishaw ML2 7EH	01698 384596
Session Clerk: Barbara Curtin			barbaracurtin47@gmail.com	07939 102784
117 Wishaw: South Wishaw (F H W)			**southwishaw@tiscali.co.uk**	**01698 375306**
Terence C. Moran BD CertMin	1995	2015	3 Conservation Place, Wishaw ML2 8EF TMoran@churchofscotland.org.uk	01698 583289

B. In other appointments: members of Presbytery

Chestnutt, Deborah A. BSc PGCE BD(Min)	2022	Chaplain, Divine Healing Fellowship (Scotland)	Braehead House Christian Healing and Retreat Centre, Braidwood Road, Crossford, Carluke ML8 5NQ DChestnutt@churchofscotland.org.uk	01555 860716
Fyfe, Lorna K. BD	2020	Ordained Local Minister	20 Kennoway Crescent, Hamilton ML3 7WQ LFyfe@churchofscotland.org.uk	01698 633304
Grant, Paul G.R. BD MTh	2003 2022	Healthcare Chaplain	Glasgow Royal Infirmary, 84 Castle Street, Glasgow G4 0SF PGrant@churchofscotland.org.uk	0141 201 6300
Macpherson, Duncan J. BSc BD	1993 2022	Deputy Assistant Chaplain General: Army	177 Station Road, Shotts ML7 4BA padredjm@btinternet.com	01501 821484
Wandrum, David C.	1993	Auxiliary Minister	5 Cawder View, Carrickstone Meadows, Cumbernauld Glasgow G68 0BN david.wandrum@btinternet.com	01236 723288
White, Anne W. BA CQSW DipHE	2018	Ordained Local Minister	94 Craigleith Road, Grangemouth FK3 0BA Anne.White@churchofscotland.org.uk	01324 880864
Wilson, Angela DCS	2015 2021	Community Outreach Worker, Southern Ministry Cluster	52 Victoria Park, Lockerbie DG11 2AY Angela.Wilson@churchofscotland.org.uk	07543 796820

C. Retaining: members of Presbytery

Albon, David A. BA MCS	1991 2023	(Dalry: St Margaret's)	9 Lorne Road, Larbert FK5 4AT davidalbon@gmail.com	07745 913811
Barrie, Arthur P. LTh	1973 2007	(Hamilton: Cadzow)	30 Airbles Crescent, Motherwell ML1 3AR	01698 261147
Brunger, Les N. BD	2010 2024	(Uddingston: Burnhead)	79 Woodfoot Road, Hamilton ML3 8LP lesbrunger@hotmail.co.uk	
Campbell, James W. BD	1995 2020	(Ceres, Kemback and Springfield)	145 Mungalhead Road, Falkirk FK2 7JH revjimashkirk@aol.com	01324 638686 07975 976024
Colvin, Sharon E.F. (Mrs) BD LRAM LTCL	1985 2008	(Airdrie: Jackson)	25 Balblair Road, Airdrie ML6 6GQ dibleycol@hotmail.com	01236 590796

Name	Ord.	Ret.	Former charge	Address	Phone
Cook, J. Stanley BD DipPSS DipPC	1974	2001	(Hamilton: West)	Mansend, 137A Old Manse Road, Netherton, Wishaw ML2 0EW stancook@blueyonder.co.uk	01698 299600
Cowan, James S.A. BD DipMin	1986	2019	(Barrhead: St Andrew's)	30 Redding Road, Falkirk FK2 9XJ jim_cowan@ntlworld.com	07966 489609
Cunningham, Iain D. MA BD	1979	2022	(Carluke: Kirkton)	6 Twister Crescent, Stonehouse, Larkhall ML9 3FU idcunningham@icloud.com	07432 400360
Currie, David E.P. BSc BD	1983	2011	(Emerging Church Development Officer, Mission and Discipleship Council)	21 Rosa Burn Avenue, East Kilbride G75 9DE davidepcurrie@gmail.com	07542 958482
Doyle, David W. MA BD	1977	2015	(Motherwell: St Mary's)	76 Kethers Street, Motherwell ML1 3HN davidwdoyle@icloud.com	01698 263472
Gilroy, Lorraine (Mrs) DCS	1988	1994	(Deacon, Uddingston: Burnhead)	68 Clement Drive, Airdrie ML16 7FB lorraine.gilroy@sky.com	07923 540602
Gunn, F. Derek BD	1986	2017	(Airdrie: Clarkston)	6 Yardley Place, Falkirk FK2 7FH RevDerekGunn@hotmail.com	01324 610349
Jamieson, Helen E. (Mrs) BD DipEd	1989	2024	(Carluke: St Andrew's)	HJamieson@churchofscotland.org.uk	
Jones, Robert BSc BD	1990	2017	(Rosskeen)	3 Grantown Avenue, Airdrie ML6 8HH rob2jones@btinternet.com	07761 782714
Macdonald, Mhorag (Ms) MA BD	1989	2021	(Wishaw: Cambusnethan: North)		
McClements, Louise J.E. RGN BD	2008	2023	(Lenzie: Old)	21 Gray Buchanan Court, Polmont, Falkirk FK2 0XR LMcClements@churchofscotland.org.uk	07846 168170
McKee, Norman B. BD	1987	2010	(Uddingston: Old)	148 Station Road, Blantyre, Glasgow G72 9BW normanmckee946@btinternet.com	01698 827358
Murdoch, Iain C. MA LLB DipEd BD	1995	2017	(Wishaw: Cambusnethan Old and Morningside)	2 Pegasus Avenue, Carluke ML8 5TN iaincmurdoch@btopenworld.com	01555 773891
Ogilvie, Colin BA DCS	1998	2015	(Deacon, Kilmarnock: New Laigh Kirk)	21 Neilsland Drive, Motherwell ML1 3DZ colinogilvie2@gmail.com	01698 321836 07837 287804
Reid, Steven BAcc CA BD	1989	2024	(Crossford with Kirkfieldbank)	61 Hawthorn Avenue, Cambuslang, Glasgow G82 7EA steven.reid@sky.com	
Rose, Margaret E.S. BD	2007	2022	(Carnbee with Pittenweem)	10a Dunlop Street, Strathaven ML10 6LA MRose@churchofscotland.org.uk	01357 671664
Ross, Keith W. MA BD MTh	1984	2015	(Congregational Development Officer, Presbytery of Hamilton)	Easter Bavelaw House, Pentland Hills Regional Park, Balerno EH14 7JS keithwross@minister.com	07855 163449
Salmond, James S. BA BD MTh ThD	1979	2003	(Holytown)	165 Torbothie Road, Shotts ML7 5NE	
Smith, G. Stewart MA BD STM	1966	2006	(Glasgow: King's Park)	33 Brent Road, Stewartfield, East Kilbride, Glasgow G74 4RA stewartandmary@googlemail.com	Tel/Fax 01355 226718
Stevenson, John LTh	1998	2006	(Cambuslang: St Andrew's)	20 Knowehead Gardens, Uddingston, Glasgow G71 7PY therev20@sky.com	01698 817582
Stewart, William T. BD DipPS	1980	2018	(Glassford with Strathaven: East)	8 Cot Castle Grove, Stonehouse ML9 3RQ	01698 793979
Taylor, Terry Ann BA MTh	2005	2023	(East Kilbride: South)	9 Fairspark Terrace, Bo'ness EH51 0NE TTaylor@churchofscotland.org.uk	07590 265924
Thomson, John M.A. TD JP BD ThM	1978	2014	(Hamilton: Old)	8 Skylands Place, Hamilton ML3 8SB jmathomson105@gmail.com	01698 422511

Waddell, Elizabeth A. (Mrs) BD	1999	2014	(Hamilton: West)	114 Branchalfield, Wishaw ML2 8QD liz.waddell@hotmail.com	01698 382909
Zambonini, James LIADip	1997	2015	(Auxiliary Minister, Coatbridge: Calder)	100 Old Manse Road, Netherton, Wishaw ML2 0EP jimzambonini@yahoo.co.uk	01698 350889

D. In other appointments: not members of Presbytery

Nil

E. Retaining: not members of Presbytery

Brown, Kathryn I. (Mrs)	2014	2019	(Ordained Local Minister, Falkirk: Trinity)	15 Glenbrae Court, Kemper Avenue, Falkirk FK1 1YT kaybrown1cpw@talktalk.net	01324 617352
Brown, T. John MA BD	1995	2006	(Tullibody: St Serf's)	15 Glenbrae Court, Kemper Avenue, Falkirk FK1 1YT johnbrown1cpw@talktalk.net	01324 617352
Buchan, William BD DipTheol	1987	2001	(Kilwinning: Abbey)	9 Leafield Road, Biggar ML12 6AY billbuchan3@btinternet.com	01899 229253
Collard, John K. MA BD	1986	2019	(Interim Minister, Kirkcudbright)	1 Nelson Terrace, East Kilbride G74 2EY jkcollard@blueyonder.co.uk	01355 520093
Crosthwaite, Melville D. BD DipEd DipMin	1984	2021	(Larbert: East)	16 Southend Drive, Strathaven ML10 6QT revcrosthwaite@gmail.com	
Cutler, James S.H. BD CEng MIStructE	1986	2011	(Black Mount with Culter with Libberton and Quothquan)	Grainstore, 11 Cuthill Towers Farm, Milnathort, Kinross KY13 9SE revjimcutler@outlook.com	01577 830798
Donaghy, Leslie G. BD DipMin PGDipPsych PhD FSAScot AVCM	1990	2004	(Dumbarton: St Andrew's)	53 Oak Avenue, East Kilbride G75 9ED les.donaghy@googlemail.com	07809 484812
Donaldson, George M. MA BD	1984	2015	(Caldercruix and Longriggend)	4 Toul Gardens, Motherwell ML1 2FE g.donaldson505@btinternet.com	01698 239477
Findlay, Henry J.W. MA BD	1965	2005	(Wishaw: St Mark's)	2 Alba Gardens, Carluke ML8 5US henryfindlay@btinternet.com	01555 759995
Gauld, Beverly G.D.D. MA BD	1972	2009	(Carnwath)	7 Rowan View, Lanark ML11 9FQ fionagauld5@gmail.com	01555 665765
Gibson, James M. TD LTh LRAM	1978	2019	(Bothwell)	22 Kirklands Crescent, Bothwell, Glasgow G71 8HU jamesmgibson@msn.com	01698 854907
Jessamine, Alistair L. MA BD	1979	2011	(Dunfermline Abbey)	11 Gallowhill Farm Cottages, Strathaven ML10 6BZ chatty.1@talktalk.net	01357 520934
Kerr, Angus BD CertMin ThM DMin	1983	2019	(Whitburn: South)	27 Pelham Court, Jackton, East Kilbride G74 5PZ docakprin@gmail.com	01355 570962
Lusk, Alastair S. BD DipPS	1974	2010	(East Kilbride: Moncrieff)	9 MacFie Place, Stewartfield, East Kilbride G74 4TY	
MacDonald, George BTh	1996	2021	(Bonnybridge: St Helen's)	60 Kennedy Way, Airth, Falkirk FK2 8GG gmd1946@gmail.com	01324 832782
Mailer, Colin M.	1996	2005	(Auxiliary Minister, Grangemouth: Zetland)	25 Saltcoats Drive, Grangemouth FK3 9JP colinmailer@blueyonder.co.uk	01324 712401

Name	Ord.	Ret.	Former charge	Address	Tel
Mathers, Alexena (Sandra)	2015	2018	(Ordained Local Minister, Denny: Old with Haggs)	10 Ercall Road, Brightons, Falkirk FK2 0RS SMathers@churchofscotland.org.uk	01324 872253
McCracken, Gordon A. BD CertMin	1988	2021	(Presbytery Clerk: Hamilton)	1 Kenilworth Road, Lanark ML11 7BL GMcCracken@churchofscotland.org.uk	07918 600720
Ross, Eileen M. (Mrs) BD MTh	2005	2022	(Linwood)	2 Millburn Way, East Kilbride, Glasgow G75 8EB revemr@yahoo.co.uk	01355 247764

F. Inactive: not members of Presbytery

Name	Ord.	Ret.	Former charge	Address	Tel
Barclay, Neil W. BSc BEd BD	1986	2006	(Falkirk: Grahamston United)	4 Gibsongray Street, Falkirk FK2 7LN neil.barclay43@gmail.com	01324 874681
Chalmers, George A. MA BD MLitt	1962	2002	(Catrine with Sorn)	3 Cricket Place, Brightons, Falkirk FK2 0HZ	01324 712030
Cowell, Susan G. (Miss) BA BD	1986	1998	(Budapest: St Columba's)	10 Waterloo Road, Lanark ML11 7QN	01555 665509
Fuller, Agnes A. (Mrs) BD	1987	2014	(Bellshill: West)	14 Croftpark Street, Bellshill ML14 1EY agnesmoore@btinternet.com	07811 340898
Grier, James BD	1991	2005	(Coatbridge: Middle)	14 Love Drive, Bellshill ML4 1BY grier2@sky.com	01698 742545
Job, Anne J. BSc BD	1993	2010	(Kirkcaldy: Viewforth with Thornton)	5 Carse View, Airth, Falkirk FK2 8NY aj@ajjob.co.uk	01324 832094
MacKenzie, Ian C. MA BD	1970	2011	(Interim Minister, Carnwath)	21 Wilson Street, Motherwell ML1 1NP iancmacken@gmail.com	01698 301230
McAlpine, John BSc PGCE	1988	2004	(Auxiliary Minister, Newmains: Bonkle with Newmains: Coltness Memorial)	Braeside, 201 Bonkle Road, Newmains, Wishaw ML2 9AA jonedmcalpine@aol.com	01698 384610
McDonald, John A. MA BD	1978	1997	(Cumbernauld: Condorrat)	17 Thomson Drive, Bellshill ML4 3ND	
McKenzie, Raymond D. DipTh BD	1978	2012	(Hamilton: Burnbank with Hamilton: South)		
Morrison, Iain C. BA BD	1990	2003	(Linlithgow: St Ninian's Craigmailen)	Whaligoe, 53 Eastcroft Drive, Polmont, Falkirk FK2 0SU iain@melness.org.uk	01324 713249
Munton, James G. BA	1969	2002	(Coatbridge: Old Monkland)	2 Moorcroft Drive, Airdrie ML6 8ES revjgm1@gmail.com	01236 754848
Robertson, John M. BSc BD	1975	1992	(Campsie)	8 North Green Drive, Airth, Falkirk FK2 8RA	01324 832244
Ross, Evan J. LTh	1986	1998	(Cowdenbeath: West with Mossgreen and Crossgates)	5 Arneil Place, Brightons, Falkirk FK2 0NJ ejhross5@gmail.com	01324 719936
Smith, Elizabeth (Mrs) BD	1996	2009	(Fauldhouse: St Andrew's)	6 Birchmount Court, Forrest Street, Airdrie ML6 7BQ smithrevb44@gmail.com	01236 752971
Spence, Sheila M. (Mrs) MA BD	1979	2010	(Kirk o' Shotts)	12 Machan Avenue, Larkhall ML9 2HE revsmspence@googlemail.com	01698 310370
Wallace, Douglas W. MA BD	1981	2019	(East Kilbride: Stewartfield)	11 Cromalt Avenue, East Kilbride, Glasgow G75 9GQ DWallace@churchofscotland.org.uk	01355 260879

G. Readers (active)

Name	Address	Email	Telephone
Allan, Angus J.	Blackburn Mill, Chapelton, Strathaven ML10 6RR	angus.allan@hotmail.com	01357 300916
Beattie, Richard	4 Bent Road, Hamilton ML3 6QB	richardbeattie1958@hotmail.com	01698 420806 07505 300328
Codona, Joy (Mrs)	55 Bellsdyke Road, Airdrie ML6 9DU	jcodona772@btinternet.com	01236 767063 07979 361760
Douglas, Ian	24 Abbotsford Crescent, Strathaven ML10 6EQ	iandouglas54.id@gmail com	01357 529476 07742 022423
Duncan, Lorna M. (Mrs) BA	28 Solway Drive, Head of Muir, Denny FK6 5NS	ell.dee@blueyonder.co.uk	01324 813020
Grant, Alan	25 Moss-side Avenue, Carluke ML8 5UG	amgrant25@aol.com	01555 771419
Hastings, William Paul	186 Glen More, East Kilbride, Glasgow G74 2AN	wphastings@hotmail.co.uk	01355 521228 07954 167158
Henderson, William D.	48 Watson Street, High Blantyre G72 9SJ	bill_henderson@icloud.com	01698 829938 07779 042621
Hislop, Eric	1 Castlegait, Strathaven ML10 6FF	eric.hislop@icloud.com	01357 520003 07921 359802
Jardine, Lynette	1 Hume Drive, Uddingston, Glasgow G71 4DW	lpjardine@blueyonder.co.uk	01698 812404 07722 415981
Love, William	30 Barmore Avenue, Carluke ML8 4PE	janbill30@tiscali.co.uk	01555 751243
McCleary, Isaac	719 Coatbridge Road, Bargeddie, Glasgow G69 7PH	isaacmccleary@gmail.com	07908 547040
McMillan, Isabelle (Mrs)	17 Castle Avenue, Airth, Falkirk FK2 8GA	treetops.mcmillan@btinternet.com	07896 433314
Preston, Steven J.	24 Glen Prosen, East Kilbride, Glasgow G74 3TA	steven.preston1@btinternet.com	01355 237359 07752 120536
Scoular, Iain W.	15 Bonnyside Road, Bonnybridge FK4 2AD	scoulariain@gmail.com	01324 812395 07717 131596
Stevenson, Thomas	34 Castle Wynd, Quarter, Hamilton ML3 7XD	weetamgtr@gmail.com	01698 282263 07860 477344
Stewart, Arthur MA	51 Bonnymuir Crescent, Bonnybridge FK4 1GD	arthur.stewart1@btinternet.com	01324 812667 07576 830970
White, Ian T.	4 Gilchrist Walk, Lesmahagow ML11 0FQ	iantwhite@aol.com	07746 857682

H. Ministries Development Staff

Robertson, Julie	Strathaven: Trinity – Children and Youth Development Worker	JRobertson@churchofscotland.org.uk
Wilson, Angela	Southern Ministry Cluster – Community Outreach Worker	Angela.Wilson@churchofscotland.org.uk

TOWN ADDRESSES

Airdrie	
Cairnlea	89 Graham Street
Clarkston	Forrest Street
High	North Bridge Street
Jackson	Glen Road
New Monkland	Glenmavis
New Wellwynd	Wellwynd
St Columba's	Thrashbush Road
Bo'ness	
Old	Panbrae Road
St Andrew's	Grahamsdyke Avenue
Carluke	
Forrest Kirk	Mount Stewart Street Hamilton Street
Kirkton	Station Road
Coatbridge	
Blairhill Dundyvan	Blairhill Street
Calder	Calder Street
Middle	Bank Street
New St Andrew's	Church Street
Old Monkland	Woodside Street
Townhead	Crinan Crescent
Denny	
Old	Denny Cross
Westpark	Duke Street
Dunipace	Stirling Street
East Kilbride	
Claremont	High Common Road, St Leonard's
Greenhills	Greenhills Centre
Moncreiff	Calderwood Road
Mossneuk	Eden Drive
Old	Montgomery Street
South	Baird Hill, Murray
Stewartfield	Stewartfield Community Centre
West	Kittoch Street
Westwood	Belmont Drive, Westwood
Falkirk	
Bainsford	Hendry Street, Bainsford
Camelon	Dorrator Road
Grahamston United	Bute Street
Laurieston	Polmont Road
St Andrew's West	Newmarket Street
Trinity	Kirk Wynd
Grangemouth	
Abbotsgrange	Abbot's Road
Kirk of the Holy Rood	Bowhouse Road
Zetland	Ronaldshay Crescent
Hamilton	
Cadzow	Woodside Walk
Gilmour and Whitehill	Glasgow Road, Burnbank
Hillhouse	Clerkwell Road
Old	Leechlee Road
St John's	Duke Street
South	Strathaven Road
Trinity	Neilsland Square off Neilsland Road
West	Burnbank Road
Lanark	
Greyfriars	Bloomgate
St Nicholas	High Street x Castlegate
Larbert	
East	Kirk Avenue
Old	Denny Road x Stirling Road
West	Main Street
Motherwell	
Crosshill	Windmillhill Street x Airbles Street
Dalziel St Andrew's	Merry Street x Muir Street
North	Chesters Crescent
St Margaret's	Shields Road
St Mary's	Avon Street
South	Gavin Street
Uddingston	
Burnhead	Laburnum Road
Old	Old Glasgow Road
Viewpark	Old Edinburgh Road
Wishaw	
Cambusnethan	
North	Kirk Road
Old	Kirk Road
Craigneuk and Belhaven	Craigneuk Street
Old	Main Street
St Mark's	Coltness Road
South Wishaw	East Academy Street

(7) FIFE (F W)

Meets in varying locations on the third Saturday in February, June, September and November.

Clerk:	**REV. ALEXANDER J. SHUTTLEWORTH MA BD**			**Presbytery Office, Wellesley Centre, Wellesley Parish Church, Wellesley Road, Methil KY8 3PD** **fife@churchofscotland.org.uk**	**01333 400191**
Mission Director:	**LORRAINE ORR**			**LOrr@churchofscotland.org.uk**	**07546 966112**

1	**Anstruther and Cellardyke: St Ayle (H W) linked with Crail (F W)**				
	Vacant			16 Taeping Close, Cellardyke, Anstruther KY10 3YL	01333 311630
	Session Clerk, St Ayle: Linda Ednie			staylesessionclerk@gmail.com	01333 310854
2	**Auchterderran Kinglassie (F W)**				
	Donald R. Lawrie MA BD DipCouns	1991	2018	7 Woodend Road, Cardenden, Lochgelly KY5 0NE DLawrie@churchofscotland.org.uk	01592 720508
3	**Auchtertool (W)**				**01592 641080**
	Vacant				
	Session Clerk: Darren Rankin			dazzy76@hotmail.com	01592 873327
4	**Balmerino and Wormit (F H W)**				
	Vacant				
	Session Clerks: Christopher Hill			christopherhill566@btinternet.com	01382 330459
	Kimberley Falconer			kimberleywatt1960@gmail.com	01334 838827
	New charge formed by the union of Balmerino and Wormit				
5	**Beath and Cowdenbeath: North (F H W)**				
	Deborah J. Dobby (Mrs) BA BD PGCE RGN RSCN	2014	2018	10 Stuart Place, Cowdenbeath KY4 9BN DDobby@churchofscotland.org.uk	01383 325520
6	**Boarhills, Dunino and St Andrews: Holy Trinity (F W)**			**holytrinitystandrews@gmail.com**	**01334 478317**
	Guardianship of the Presbytery				
	Session Clerk: Michael Carslaw (Dr)			htsessionclerk@gmail.com	07860 413848
	New charge formed by the union of Boarhills and Dunino and St Andrews: Holy Trinity				

7 Buckhaven and Wemyss (F) **01592 715577**
Vacant
Jacqueline Thomson (Mrs) MTh DCS 2004 2008 16 Aitken Place, Coaltown of Wemyss, Kirkcaldy KY1 4PA
Jacqueline.Thomson@churchofscotland.org.uk 07806 776560

8 Burntisland and Kinghorn (F H W)
James Reid BD 1985 1997 17 Myre Crescent, Kinghorn, Burntisland KY3 9UB 01592 890269
JReid@churchofscotland.org.uk
New charge formed by the union of Burntisland and Kinghorn

9 Cairneyhill (F H W) linked with Limekilns (F H W) **office@limekilnschurch.org** **Cairneyhill: 01383 882352**
Limekilns: 01383 873337
Norman M. Grant BD DipMin 1990 The Manse, 10 Church Street, Limekilns, Dunfermline KY11 3HT 01383 872341
NGrant@churchofscotland.org.uk

10 Cameron and St Andrews: St Leonard's (F H W) **stlencam@btconnect.com** **01334 478702**
Graeme W. Beebee BD 1993 2017 1 Cairnhill Gardens, St Andrews KY16 8QY 01334 472793
GBeebee@churchofscotland.org.uk
New charge formed by the union of Cameron and St Andrews: St Leonard's

11 Carnbee linked with Pittenweem
Vacant 29 Milton Road, Pittenweem, Anstruther KY10 2LN 01333 312838
Session Clerk, Carnbee: Henry Watson 01333 313796
Session Clerk, Pittenweem: contact the above

12 Carnock and Oakley (F H W)
Vacant
Session Clerk: George Watt georgej18gsw@outlook.com 07799 695953

13 Ceres, Kemback and Springfield (W) **info@ckschurch.org**
Jane L. Barron (Mrs) BA DipEd BD 1999 2021 Denhead Old Farm, St Andrews KY16 8PA 01334 850135
JBarron@churchofscotland.org.uk 07545 904541

14 Cowdenbeath: Trinity (F H W)
Vacant 2 Glenfield Road, Cowdenbeath KY4 9EL 01383 510696
Session Clerk: John Bain johnbain1@btinternet.com 01383 512779

Post Office Ltd.
www.postoffice.co.uk

29/08/2025 14:12 TP:05 BP:02 SU: AA
Dunlop FAD: 1098438
45 Main Street
Dunlop
Kilmarnock
Ayrshire
KA3 4AF

Session Id: 1-176078
Txn Id: 1

Session Id: 1-176078

Horizon Certificate of Posting

Items addressed as follows:-

Service: EVRi Customer Drop Off
Building Name or No: 1 Copplestone Road
1st Line of address: Budleigh Salterton, Devon
Post Town: Budleigh Salterton
PostCode/Zip Code: EX9 6DS
Barcode Number: H00IAA1776090191
Track at: www.evri.com/track-a-parcel
After Last Despatch: N
Carrier Contact: 0330 808 5456

Have been accepted here today.

It is important that you retain this receipt as it is your Proof Of Posting.

Please refer to Separate Terms and Conditions.

This is not a VAT receipt

No.	Charge / Name	Ord.	Ind.	Address / Email	Phone
15	**Crail** See Anstruther and Cellardyke: St Ayle				
16	**Creich, Flisk and Kilmany (W)**				
	Guardianship of the Presbytery				
	Session Clerk: Patricia Pearce			p.pearce@tiscali.co.uk	01334 655799
17	**Culross and Torryburn (H W)**				
	Vacant				
	Session Clerk: Sandy Muirhead			sandy_muirhead@hotmail.com	01383 850077 07415 922570
18	**Cupar: Old and St Michael of Tarvit (H W) linked with Monimail**				
	Jeffrey A. Martin BA MDiv	1991	2016	76 Hogarth Drive, Cupar KY15 5YU JMartin@churchofscotland.org.uk	01334 209010
19	**Cupar: St John's and Dairsie United (F W)**				
	Gavin W.G. Black BD	2006	2019	The Manse, 23 Hogarth Drive, Cupar KY15 5YH GBlack@churchofscotland.org.uk	01334 650751
20	**Dunfermline: Abbey (F H T W)**			**dunfermline.abbey.church@gmail.com**	**01383 723005**
	MaryAnn R. Rennie BD MTh CPS DMin	1998	2012	3 Perdieus Mount, Dunfermline KY12 7XE MARennie@churchofscotland.org.uk	01383 727311
	Ewan S. Ritchie MA(Div) (Assistant Minister)	2023		5 Woodlands Terrace, Dalgety Bay KY11 9SX ERitchie@churchofscotland.org.uk	
21	**Dunfermline: East (F W)**				
	Andrew A. Morrice MA BD	1999	2010	71 Swift Street, Dunfermline KY11 8SN AMorrice@churchofscotland.org.uk	01383 223144 07815 719301
22	**Dunfermline: Gillespie Memorial (F H W)**			**office@gillespiechurch.org**	**01383 621253**
	Michael A. Weaver BSc BD	2017		4 Killin Court, Dunfermline KY12 7XF MWeaver@churchofscotland.org.uk	01383 724347
23	**Dunfermline: North**				
	Guardianship of the Presbytery				
	Session Clerk: Graham Primrose			sessionclerk@dunfermlinenorthparishchurch.co.uk	07920 445669

24 Dunfermline: St Columba's (F W) — **staechurch@standrewserskine.org.uk** — **01383 841660**
Vacant — 71A Townhill Road, Dunfermline KY12 0BN — 01383 738487

New charge formed by the union of Dunfermline: St Andrew's Erskine and Dunfermline: Townhill and Kingseat

25 Dunfermline: St Leonard's (F W) — **office@slpc.org** — **01383 620106**
Gayle J.A. Taylor MA BD PGDipCouns (Transition Minister) — 1999 — 2024 — St Leonard's Church, 2 Brucefield Avenue, Dunfermline KY11 4SX — 07851 548693
GTaylor@churchofscotland.org.uk
Margaret B. Mateos (Ordained Local Minister) — 2018 — 43 South Street, Lochgelly KY5 9LJ — 01592 780073
MMateos@churchofscotland.org.uk

26 Dunfermline: St Margaret's (F W)
Iain M. Greenshields BD CertMin DipRS ACMA MSc MTh DD — 1985 — 2007 — 38 Garvock Hill, Dunfermline KY12 7UU — 01383 723955
IGreenshields@churchofscotland.org.uk — 07427 477575

27 Dunfermline: St Ninian's (F W)
Vacant
Session Clerk: John Thomson — johncthomson@btinternet.com — 01383 730074

28 Dysart: St Clair (F H W)
Vacant — 42 Craigfoot Walk, Kirkcaldy KY1 1GA — 01592 561967
Session Clerk: Raymond Domin — raymonddomin@blueyonder.co.uk — 01592 203620

29 East Neuk Trinity (F H W) — **info@eastneuktrinity.org.uk** — **01333 317096**
Vacant — 6 Reaper Lane, Anstruther KY10 3FR — 01333 311045
Session Clerk: Elizabeth Meacher — sessionclerk@eastneuktrinity.org.uk — 01333 330525

30 Edenshead (F W)
Vacant — The Manse, Kirk Wynd, Strathmiglo, Cupar KY14 7QS — 01337 860256
Session Clerk: Liz Slattery — halhill14@gmail.com — 07719 724730

31 Falkland (F W) linked with Freuchie (F H W)
Guardianship of the Presbytery — 1 Newton Road, Falkland, Cupar KY15 7AQ — 01337 858557
Session Clerk, Falkland: Marion Baldie — sessionclerk.falkland@gmail.com — 07951 824488
Session Clerk, Freuchie: Margaret Cuthbert — cuthbertmargaret@yahoo.co.uk — 01337 830940

32 **Forthview (F H W)** **office@dalgety-church.co.uk** **01383 824092**
Vacant (Moderator) 9 St Colme Drive, Dalgety Bay, Dunfermline KY11 9LQ 01383 822316
Vacant (Team Minister) 42 Woodside Avenue, Rosyth KY11 2LA
Vacant (Team Minister) 36 Bellhouse Road, Aberdour, Fife KY3 0TL 01383 861522
Andrea Fraser BSc PGCert MDiv 2023 Andrea.Fraser@churchofscotland.org.uk
(Assistant Minister)
Session Clerk: Margaret Miller magmiller119@btinternet.com 01383 414299

New charge formed by the union of Aberdour: St Fillan's, Dalgety, Inverkeithing, North Queensferry and Rosyth

33 **Freuchie** See Falkland

34 **Heart of Fife (Glenrothes, Leslie, Markinch and Thornton) (F H W)**
christskirkglenrothes@yahoo.com **01592 745938**
info@st-columbas.com **01592 752539**
office@stmargaretschurch.org.uk **01592 328162**
office@stninians.co.uk **01592 610560**
Conor Fegan MA MTh PhD 2022 7 Guthrie Crescent, Markinch, Glenrothes KY7 6AY 01592 758264
(Moderator) CFegan@churchofscotland.org.uk
Alan W.D. Kimmitt BSc BD 2013 40 Liberton Drive, Glenrothes KY6 3PB 01592 742233
(Team Minister) Alan.Kimmitt@churchofscotland.org.uk
Vacant (Team Minister)

New charge formed by the union of Glenrothes: Christ's Kirk, Glenrothes: St Columba's, Glenrothes: St Margaret's, Glenrothes: St Ninian's, Leslie: Trinity and Markinch and Thornton

35 **Howe of Fife (F W)**
Vacant The Manse, 83 Church Street, Ladybank, Cupar KY15 7ND 01337 832717
Session Clerk: Anne Jeffcoat (Mrs) annejeffcoat02@gmail.com 01337 832508

36 **Kelty (F W)** **info@keltychurch.co.uk** **01383 831219**
Vacant 15 Arlick Road, Kelty KY4 0BH 01383 831362
Session Clerk: Catherine Ann Ness familyness47@btinternet.com 01383 831737
07999 918727

37 **Kennoway, Windygates and Balgonie: St Kenneth's (F W)** **stkennethsparish@gmail.com** **01333 351372**
linked with Leven (F) **office@levenparish.co.uk** **01333 423969**
Allan P. Morton MA BD PGDip 2018 2 Fernhill Gardens, Windygates, Leven KY8 5DZ 01333 350240
AMorton@churchofscotland.org.uk

38	**Kilrenny (W)** Guardianship of the Presbytery Session Clerk: Corinne Peddie			corinne@peddies.com	01333 311408
39	**Kingsbarns (F H)** Guardianship of the Presbytery Sarah Whittle BA MA PhD PGDipPsych PGCertCBT FHEA (Ordained Local Minister) Session Clerk: Elizabeth Spittal	2023		SWhittle@churchofscotland.org.uk elibby.t21@btinternet.com	07801 492158 01334 880387
40	**Kirkcaldy: Abbotshall (F H T)** Vacant Session Clerk: Morag Michael			moragmichael@icloud.com	01592 263087
41	**Kirkcaldy: Bennochy (F W)** Vacant Session Clerk: George Drummond			25 Bennochy Avenue, Kirkcaldy KY2 5QE gdrummond@btinternet.com	**01592 201723** 01592 643518 01592 200179
42	**Kirkcaldy: Hope (F W)** Joshua Z. Milton BA BA DipCSE	2022		27 Stocks Street, Kirkcaldy KY2 6ND JMilton@churchofscotland.org.uk	07359 542544
	Kirkcaldy: Templehall and Torbain United renamed as Kirkcaldy: Hope				
43	**Kirkcaldy: Linktown (F H W)** Vacant Session Clerk: J. Stewart Milne			**enquiries@linktown.org.uk** 16 Raith Crescent, Kirkcaldy KY2 5NN jstewartmilne@blueyonder.co.uk	01592 265536 01592 266018
44	**Kirkcaldy: Pathhead (F H W)** Andrew C. Donald BD DPS	1992	2005	**pathheadchurch@btconnect.com** 73 Loughborough Road, Kirkcaldy KY1 3DB ADonald@churchofscotland.org.uk	**01592 204635** 01592 652215
45	**Kirkcaldy: St Bryce Kirk (F H T W)** Vacant Session Clerk: Anne Hunter			**office@stbrycekirk.org.uk** mannehunter@hotmail.com	**01592 640016** 01592 265927
46	**Largo (F W)** Vacant Session Clerk: Andrew Gilmour			**infolargochurches@gmail.com** 1 Castaway Lane, Lower Largo KY8 6FA andrew.gilmour@montrave.net	01333 320850 01333 350209

47	**Largoward (H W)**				
	Guardianship of the Presbytery				
	Session Clerk: Robert Scott			8obandandge@gmail.com	07480 718877
48	**Leuchars: St Athernase and Tayport (F)**				
	Jonathan W. Humphrey BSc BD PhD	2015	2024	7 David Wilson Park, Balmullo, St Andrews KY16 0NP	01334 870038
				JHumphrey@churchofscotland.org.uk	07754 258036
49	**Leven** See Kennoway, Windygates and Balgonie: St Kenneth's				
50	**Limekilns** See Cairneyhill				
51	**Lindores (F H W)**			**lindoreschurch@gmail.com**	
	Guardianship of Presbytery			2 Guthrie Court, Cupar Road, Newburgh, Cupar KY14 6HA	01337 842228
	Session Clerk: Elizabeth Lee			elee1963.el@gmail.com	07761 342131
52	**Lochgelly and Benarty: St Serf's (F W)**				
	Zoltán Sáfrány BD	2000	2020	82 Main Street, Lochgelly KY5 9AA	01592 780435
				ZSafrany@churchofscotland.org.uk	07411 444743
	Pamela Scott (Mrs) BD DCS	2017		177 Primrose Avenue, Rosyth KY11 2TZ	01383 410530
				PScott@churchofscotland.org.uk	07548 819334
53	**Methil: Wellesley (F H W)**				
	Gillian Paterson (Mrs) BD	2010		10 Vettriano Vale, Leven KY8 4GD	01333 423147
				GPaterson@churchofscotland.org.uk	
54	**Methilhill and Denbeath (F)**				
	Elisabeth F. Cranfield (Ms) MA BD	1988		9 Chemiss Road, Methilhill, Leven KY8 2BS	01592 713142
				ECranfield@churchofscotland.org.uk	
55	**Monimail** See Cupar: Old and St Michael of Tarvit				
56	**Newport-on-Tay (F H W)**				
	Amos B. Chewachong BTh MTh PhD	2005	2017	17 East Station Place, Newport-on-Tay DD6 8EG	01382 542893
				AChewachong@churchofscotland.org.uk	
57	**Pittenweem** See Carnbee				

58	**St Andrews: St Mark's (F H W)**	**admin@hpmchurch.org.uk**	**01334 478144**
	Vacant	20 Priory Gardens, St Andrews KY16 8XX	Tel/Fax 01334 478287
	Session Clerk: Kenneth Fraser	kenneth@kcfraser.plus.com	01334 476024
59	**St Monans (F H W)**	**info@stmonanschurch.org.uk**	
	Guardianship of the Presbytery		
	Session Clerk: Fiona Keay (Mrs)	fionakeay@hotmail.co.uk	01333 730009
60	**Saline and Blairingone (F W) linked with Tulliallan and Kincardine (F W)**	**tulliallanandkincardine@gmail.com**	
	Vacant	62 Toll Road, Kincardine, Alloa FK10 4QZ	01259 731002
	Session Clerk, Saline and Blairingone: Margaret Graham (Mrs)	session.clerk@salineandblairingonechurch.org.uk	01383 738429
	Session Clerk, Tulliallan and Kincardine: Ian McNicol	mcnicol.ian@btopenworld.com	01259 730842
61	**Tulliallan and Kincardine** See Saline and Blairingone		

B. In other appointments: members of Presbytery

Allardice, Michael MA MPhil DipTheol FHEA	2014	2023	Ordained Local Minister, Assistant Chaplain, University of Dundee	88 Dunrobin Road, Kirkcaldy KY2 5YT MAllardice@churchofscotland.org.uk	01592 369515 07936 203465
MacEwan, Donald G. MA BD PhD	2001	2011	Chaplain: University of St Andrews	Chaplaincy Centre, 3A St Mary's Place, St Andrews KY16 9UY dgm21@st-andrews.ac.uk	01334 462865 07713 322036
McCafferty, Allan BSc BD DMin	1993	2024	Ministries Support Operations Manager, Faith Action Programme	121 George Street, Edinburgh EH2 4YN AMcCafferty@churchofscotland.org.uk	0131 225 5722
McPherson, Marjory (Mrs) LLB BD MTh	1990	2023	Chaplain, Victoria Hospital, Kirkcaldy	41 Woodlands Bank, Dalgety Bay KY11 9SX MMcPherson@churchofscotland.org.uk	07968 670765
McPherson, Stewart M. BD CertMin	1991	2023	Interim Minister, Kirkcaldy: Abbotshall, Bennochy, Linktown, St Bryce	41 Woodlands Bank, Dalgety Bay KY11 9SX SMcPherson@churchofscotland.org.uk	07814 901429
Shuttleworth, Alexander J. MA BD	2004	2024	Presbytery Clerk:	Fife Presbytery Office, Wellesley Centre, Wellesley Parish Church, Wellesley Road, Methil KY8 3PD AShuttleworth@churchofscotland.org.uk	01333 400191
Smith, Fiona E. (Mrs) LLB BD	2010	2022	Principal Clerk	11 Bridge Street, Saline, Dunfermline KY12 9TS FSmith@churchofscotland.org.uk	07824 037271
Strang, Gordon I. BSc BD	2014	2021	Chaplain, NHS Fife	Department of Spiritual Care, Victoria Hospital, Kirkcaldy KY2 5AH GStrang@churchofscotland.org.uk	01592 648158

C. Retaining: members of Presbytery

Name	Ord.	Ret.	Charge	Address	Phone
Adams, David G. BD	1991	2011	(Cowdenbeath: Trinity)	13 Fernhill Gardens, Windygates, Leven KY8 5DZ adams.69@btinternet.com	01333 351214
Alston, Colin M. BMus BD BN RN	1975	2023	(Inverkeithing with North Queensferry)	32c Townhill Road, Dunfermline KY12 0QX CAlston@churchofscotland.org.uk	01383 621050
Barr, G. Russell BA BD MTh DMin	1979	2020	(Edinburgh: Cramond)	4 Balone Steading, St Andrews KY16 8NS GBarr@churchofscotland.org.uk	01334 781142 07941 080067
Barrett, Leslie M. BD FRICS	1991	2014	(Chaplain: University of Abertay, Dundee)	Dunelm Cottage, Logie, Cupar KY15 4SJ lesliembarrett@btinternet.com	01334 870396
Boswell, Gavin R. BTheol	1993	2023	(Largo)	51 St John's Drive, Dunfermline KY12 7TL GBoswell@churchofscotland.org.uk	01383 271548
Boyle, Robert P. LTh CPS	1990	2010	(Saline and Blairingone)	23 Farnell Way, Dunfermline KY12 0SR boab.boyle@btinternet.com	01383 729568
Bradley, Ian C. (Prof.) MA BD DPhil	1990	2018	(University of St Andrews: Cultural and Spiritual History)	4 Donaldson Gardens, St Andrews KY16 9DN icb@st-andrews.ac.uk	
Brewster, John MA BD DipEd	1988	2021	(East Kilbride: Greenhills)	82 Harcourt Road, Kirkcaldy KY2 5HF brewster.140234@gmail.com	07917 333812
Burton, Scott E. BD DipMin	1999	2021	(Gigha and Cara with Kilcalmonell with Killean and Kilchenzie)	SBurton@churchofscotland.org.uk	
Cameron, David C. BD CertMin	1993	2023	(Edinburgh: Dalmeny with Edinburgh Queensferry)	17 Morayvale, Aberdour, Burntisland KY3 0XE DavidCCameron@churchofscotland.org.uk	07737 910018
Campbell, Reginald F. BSc BD DipChEd	1979	2015	(Daviot and Dunlichity with Moy, Dalarossie and Tomatin)	12 Alloway Drive, Kirkcaldy KY2 6DX campbell578@talktalk.net	
Chalmers, John P. BD CPS DD	1979	2017	(Principal Clerk)	10 Liggars Place, Dunfermline KY12 7XZ JChalmers@churchofscotland.org.uk	07980 547645
Christie, Arthur A. BD	1997	2018	(Anstruther and Cellardyke: St Ayle with Kilrenny)	194 Foulford Road, Cowdenbeath KY4 9AX revacc@btinternet.com	01383 511326
Clark, David M. MA BD	1989	2013	(Dundee: The Steeple)	2b Rose Street, St Monans, Anstruther KY10 2BQ dmclark72@gmail.com	01333 739034
Collins, Catherine E.E. (Mrs) MA BD	1993	2021	(Dundee: Broughty Ferry New Kirk)	Eden Cottage, 16 Melville Road, Ladybank, Cupar KY15 7LU revccollins@btinternet.com	01337 830707
Collins, David A. BSc BD	1993	2016	(Auchterhouse with Monikie and Newbigging and Murroes and Tealing)	Eden Cottage, 16 Melville Road, Ladybank, Cupar KY15 7LU revdacollins@btinternet.com	01337 830707
Conkey, Hugh BSc BD	1987	2023	(Newtonhill)	15 Calender Park, Kirkcaldy KY1 2HG HConkey@churchofscotland.org.uk	07476 943330
Connolly, Daniel BD DipTh DipMin	1983	2015	(Army Chaplain)	2 Cairngreen, Cupar KY15 2SY dannyconnolly@hotmail.co.uk	07951 078478
Deans, Graham D.S. MA BD MTh MLitt DMin	1978	2017	(Aberdeen: Queen Street)	38 Sir Thomas Elder Way, Kirkcaldy KY2 6ZS graham.deans@btopenworld.com	01592 641429
Dick, John H.A. (Ian) MA MSc BD	1982	2012	(Aberdeen: Ferryhill)	18 Fairfield Road, Kelty KY4 0BY	07889 411158
Donald, Kenneth W. BA BD	1982	2023	(Prestonpans: Prestongrange)	24 Fieldfare View, Dunfermline KY11 8FY KDonald@churchofscotland.org.uk	07392 069957
Elston, Ian J. BD MTh	1999	2019	(Kirkcaldy: Torbain)	65 Longbrae Gardens, Kirkcaldy KY2 5YJ IElston@churchofscotland.org.uk	01592 592393

Name	Ord.	Ret.	Charge	Address	Phone
Fairlie, George BD BVMS MRCVS	1971	2002	(Crail with Kingsbarns)	12 Dunnydeer Place, Insch AB52 6HP	
Farquhar, William E. BA BD	1987	2006	(Dunfermline: Townhill and Kingseat)	29 Queens Drive, Middlewich, Cheshire CW10 0DG	01606 835097
Fisk, Elizabeth A. BD	1996	2022	(Culross and Torryburn)	30 Masterton Road, Dunfermline KY11 8RB elizabethfisk10@hotmail.com	01383 730039
Foggie, Janet P. MA BD PhD	2003	2021	(Pioneer Minister, University of Stirling)	Old Schoolhouse, Dunbog, Newburgh KY14 6JF	07899 349246
Forrester, Ian L. MA	1964	1996	(Friockheim Kinnell with Inverkeilor and Lunan)	8 Bennochy Avenue, Kirkcaldy KY2 5QE	01592 260251
Forsyth, Alexander R. TD BA MTh	1973	2014	(Markinch)	49 Scaraben Crescent, Glenrothes KY6 3HL arforsyth516@gmail.com	07483 232581
Fraser, Ann G. BD CertMin	1990	2007	(Auchtermuchty)	24 Irvine Crescent, St Andrews KY16 8LG	01334 461329
Froude, J. Kenneth (Ken) MA BD	1979	2020	(Kirkcaldy: St Bryce Kirk)	44 Templars Crescent, Kinghorn KY3 9XS	01592 892512 07745 669096
Galbraith, D. Douglas MA BD BMus MPhil ARSCM PhD	1965	2005	(Office for Worship, Doctrine and Artistic Matters)	34 Balbirnie Street, Markinch, Glenrothes KY7 6DA dgalbraith@churchofscotland.org.uk	01592 752403
Gerbrandy-Baird, Peter S. MA BD MSc FRSA FRGS	2004	2023	(Aberdour: St Fillan's)	Shortburn, 7 Pentland Rise, Dalgety Bay, Dunfermline KY11 9LY gerbil.1881@yahoo.co.uk	07910 885689
Gordon, Ian D. LTh	1972	2001	(Markinch)	2 Somerville Way, Glenrothes KY7 5GE	01592 742487
Graham, Andrew F. BTh DPS	2001	2023	(Bendochy with Coupar Angus: Abbey)	134 Robertson Road, Cupar KY15 5YS afgmg.83@gmail.com	07488 233427
Hamilton, Ian W.F. BD LTh ALCM AVCM	1978	2012	(Nairn: Old)	Mossneuk, 5 Windsor Gardens, St Andrews KY16 8XL reviwfh@btinternet.com	01334 477745
Harrison, Cameron BSc MEd	2006	2010	(Auxiliary Minister, St Andrews: Holy Trinity)	Woodfield House, Priormuir, St Andrews KY16 8LP cameron@harrisonleimon.co.uk	01334 478067
Henderson, J. Mary MA BD DipEd PhD	1990	2020	(Falkirk: Laurieston with Redding and Westquarter)	8 Miller Terrace, St Monans KY10 2BB jmary.henderson1@gmail.com	01333 730138
Jenkins, Gordon F.C. MA BD PhD	1968	2006	(Dunfermline: North)	2 Balrymonth Court, St Andrews KY16 8XT jenkinsgordon1@sky.com	01334 476194
Johnston, Thomas N. LTh	1972	2008	(Edinburgh: Priestfield)	71 Main Street, Newmills, Dunfermline KY12 8ST tomjohnston@blueyonder.co.uk	01383 889240
Kenny, Elizabeth S.S. BD RGN SCM	1989	2010	(Carnock and Oakley)	5 Cobden Court, Crossgates, Cowdenbeath KY4 8AU esskenny@btinternet.com	07831 763494
Kesting, Sheilagh M. BA BD DD DSG	1980	2016	(Ecumenical Officer, Church of Scotland)	Restalrig, Chance Inn, Cupar KY15 5QJ smkesting@btinternet.com	07930 870885
Laidlaw, Victor W.N. BD CertCE	1975	2008	(Edinburgh: St Catherine's Argyle)	9 Tern Road, Dunfermline KY11 8GA v9wnintern@hotmail.co.uk	01383 620134
Lane, Margaret R. (Mrs) BA BD MTh	2009	2019	(Edinburgh: Kirkliston)	6 Overhaven, Limekilns KY11 3JH margaretlane@btinternet.com	07897 525692
Leitch, D. Graham MA BD	1974	2012	(Tyne Valley)	9 St Margaret Wynd, Dunfermline KY12 0UT dgrahamleitch@gmail.com	01383 249245 07811 891841
McAlpine, Robin J. BDS BD MTh	1988	2022	(Kirkcaldy: Bennochy)	1 Branxton Wynd, Kirkcaldy KY1 1SF revrobinmcalpine@gmail.com	07786 929881
McCulloch, William B. BD	1997	2016	(Rome: St Andrew's)	81 Meldrum Court, Dunfermline KY11 4XR revwbmcculloch@hotmail.com	01383 730305

McFadyen, Gavin BEng BD	2006	2024	(Glasgow: Carronald)	GMcFadyen@churchofscotland.org.uk	07960 212106
McKay, Violet C.C. BD	1988	2017	(Rosyth)	20B Blane Crescent, Dunfermline KY11 8ZF violetcm@gmail.com	01383 727255
McKimmon, Eric G. BA BD MTh PhD	1983	2014	(Cargill Burrelton with Collace)	1 Dolan Grove, Saline KY12 9UP ericmckimmon@gmail.com	07835 069115
McLellan, Andrew R.C. CBE MA BD STM DD	1970	2009	(HM Chief Inspector of Prisons for Scotland)	4 Liggars Place, Dunfermline KY12 7XZ iamclellan4@gmail.com	01383 725959
McLeod, Alistair G.	1988	2005	(Glenrothes: St Columba's)	13 Greenmantle Way, Glenrothes KY6 3QG alistairmcleod1936@gmail.com	01592 744558
McNaught, Samuel M. MA BD MTh	1968	2002	(Kirkcaldy: St John's)	6 Munro Court, Glenrothes KY7 5GD sjmcnaught@btinternet.com	01592 742352
Meager, Peter MA BD CertMgmt(Open)	1970	1998	(Elie with Kilconquhar and Colinsburgh)	7 Lorraine Drive, Cupar KY15 5DY meager52@btinternet.com	01334 656991 07777 657414
Melville, David D. BD	1989	2008	(Kirkconnel)	28 Porterfield, Comrie, Dunfermline KY12 9HJ revddm@gmail.com	07775 766198
Miller, Eileen A. BD DipComEd AdvDipCouns MBCAP(Snr Accred.)	2014	2024	(Chaplain, Queen Margaret Hospital, Dunfermline)	9 Car Craig View, Burntisland KY3 0DS EMiller@churchofscotland.org.uk	07923 033933
Neilson, Peter MA BD MTh	1975	2016	(Mission Consultant)	1 Balcomie Green, Crail KY10 3UX neilson.peter@btinternet.com	01333 450852 07818 418608
Nicol, George G. BD DPhil	1982	2013	(Falkland with Freuchie)	48 Fidra Avenue, Burntisland KY3 0AZ ggnicol@totalise.co.uk	01592 873258
Nicol, Sarah E.C. (Mrs) BSc BD MTh	1985	2023	(Saltcoats: St Cuthbert's)	13 Hawthorn Grove, Dunfermline KY12 0DZ Sarahecn1008@gmail.com	
Nisbet, Gilbert C. CA BD	1993	2019	(Leven)	2a Temple Crescent, Crail KY10 3RS gcn@insprint.co.uk	01333 450929
Paterson, Andrew E. JP	1994	2020	(Auxiliary Minister, Presbytery-wide)	6 The Willows, Kelty KY4 0FQ	01383 830998
Paterson, Maureen (Mrs) BSc	1992	2010	(Auxiliary Minister, Kennoway, Windygates and Balgonie: St Kenneth's)	91 Dalmahoy Crescent, Kirkcaldy KY2 6TA m.e.paterson@blueyonder.co.uk	01592 262300
Paton, Marion J. (Miss) MA BMus BD	1991	2017	(Dundee: St David's High Kirk)	18 Winram Place, St Andrews KY16 8XH mjpdht@gmail.com	01334 208743 07714 749988
Porteous, Brian W. BSc DipRM DipCS CertCounsS	2018	2023	(Ordained Local Minister, Kirkcaldy Templehall and Torbain United)	Kildene, Westfield Road, Cupar KY15 5DS BPorteous@churchofscotland.org.uk	01334 653561
Redmayne, David W. BSc BD	2001	2017	(Beath and Cowdenbeath: North)	10 Hawthorn Park, Dunfermline KY12 0DY DRedmayne@churchofscotland.org.uk	01383 738137 07504 342524
Redmayne, Geoffrey BSc BD MPhil	2000	2023	(Montrose: Trinity)	5 Thomson Court, Cardenden, Lochgelly KY5 0NS GRedmayne@churchofscotland.org.uk	07766 316548
Rennick, Julie M. (Mrs) BTh	2005	2024	(Presbytery Clerk, Forth Valley and Clydesdale)	JRennick@churchofscotland.org.uk	
Robb, Nigel J. FCP MA BD ThM MTh	1981	2014	(Associate Secretary, Mission and Discipleship Council)	NRobb@churchofscotland.org.uk	
Roy, Allistair D. BD DipSW PgDip	2007	2016	(Glenrothes: St Ninian's)	39 Ravenswood Drive, Glenrothes KY6 2PA minister@revroy.co.uk	
Scott, David D. BSc BD	1981	2019	(Traprain)	259 Lamond Drive, St Andrews KY16 8RR revddd.scott@gmail.com	01334 473460 07712 252724

Sharp, Alan BSc BD	1980	2019	(Burntisland)	29 Cromwell Road, Burntisland KY3 9EH alansharp03@aol.com	01592 870198
Sinclair, David I. BSc BD PhD DipSW CQSW	1990	2020	(Ecumenical and International Officer, Evangelical Church of the Czech Brethren)	42 South Road, Cupar KY15 5JF davidsinclair@btinternet.com	01334 659171
Smith, David J. BD DipMin	1992	2024	(Glenrothes: St Ninian's)	16 Allan Street, Leslie, Glenrothes KY6 3LA David.Smith@churchofscotland.org.uk	
Symington, Alastair H. MA BD	1972	2012	(Troon: Old)	70 The Walled Garden, Abbey Park Avenue, St Andrews KY16 9JW revdahs@virginmedia.com	07703 176717
Thom, Ian G. BSc PhD BD	1990	2020	(Dunfermline: North)	4 Calaiswood Crescent, Dunfermline KY11 8ZR ianthom58@btinternet.com	01383 733471 07761 967434
Thomson, John D. BD	1985	2005	(Kirkcaldy: Pathhead)	3 Tottenham Court, Hill Street, Dysart, Kirkcaldy KY1 2XY j.thomson10@sky.com	01592 655313 07885 414979
Tomlinson, Bryan L. TD	1969	2003	(Kirkcaldy: Abbotshall)	2 Duddingston Drive, Kirkcaldy KY2 6JP abbkirk@blueyonder.co.uk	01592 564843 07957 464637
Torrance, Alan J. (Prof.) MA BD DrTheol ARCM	1984	2020	(University of St Andrews: Systematic Theology)	Kincaple House, Kincaple, St Andrews KY16 9SH	01334 850755
Unsworth, Ruth BA BD CertMHS PgDipCBP BABCP	1984	1987	(Glasgow: Pollokshaws)	5 Lindsay Gardens, St Andrews KY16 8XB RUnsworth@churchofscotland.org.uk	07894 802119
Walker, James B. MA BD DPhil	1975	2011	(Chaplain: University of St Andrews)	5 Priestden Park, St Andrews KY16 8DL	01334 472839 07707 539991
Wallace, Hugh M. MA BD	1980	2018	(Newhills)	15 West End, St Monans KY10 2BX	01333 730607
Watt, Robert J. BD	1994	2009	(Dumbarton: Riverside)	101 Birrell Drive, Dunfermline KY11 8FA robertwatt101@gmail.com	01383 735417 07753 683717
Wilson, Tilly (Miss) MTh	1990	2012	(Dysart)	6 Citron Glebe, Kirkcaldy KY1 2NF tillywilson1@sky.com	01592 263134
Wotherspoon, Ian G. BA LTh	1967	2004	(Coatbridge: St Andrew's)	12 Cherry Lane, Cupar KY15 5DA wotherspoonrig@aol.com	07711 706634
Wright, Lynda BEd DCS	1979	2021	(Community Chaplaincy Listening Co-ordinator, NHS Fife)	1 Union Street, Kirkcaldy KY1 3DN lyndawright20@gmail.com	07835 303395

D. In other appointments: not members of Presbytery

Nil

E. Retaining: not members of Presbytery

Pieterse, Ben BA BTh LTh	1968	2014	(Auchterderran Kinglassie)	15 Bakeoven Close, Seaforth Sound, Simon's Town, 7975, South Africa benhp1@gmail.com	
Thrower, Charles D. BSc	1965	2002	(Carnbee with Pittenweem)	Grange House, Wester Grangemuir, Pittenweem, Anstruther KY10 2RB charlesandsteph@btinternet.com	01333 312631

F. Inactive: not members of Presbytery

Bjarnason, Sven S. CandTheol CPS	1973	2011	(Tomintoul, Glenlivet and Inveraven)	14 Edward Street, Dunfermline KY12 0JW sven@bjarnason.org.uk	01383 724625
Donaldson, Colin V.	1982	1998	(Ormiston with Pencaitland)	3A Playfair Terrace, St Andrews KY16 9HX colinmarion80@gmail.com	01334 472889
Whyte, Iain A. BA BD STM PhD	1968	2005	(Community Mental Health Chaplain)	14 Carlingnose Point, North Queensferry, Inverkeithing KY11 1ER iainwhyte67@gmail.com	01383 410732

G. Readers (active)

Brown, Gordon	Nowell, Fossoway, Kinross KY13 0UW	brown.nowell@hotmail.com.uk	01577 840248
Cunningham, Martin	5 Livingstone Place, St Andrews KY16 3JH	martincunninghamteacher@gmail.com	
Elder, Morag Anne (Ms)	5 Provost Road, Tayport DD6 9JE	benuardin@btinternet.com	01382 552218
MacMillan, John	41 Bay Road, Newport-on-Tay DD6 8LY	JMacMillan@churchofscotland.org.uk	01382 541071
Mitchell, Ian G. KC	17 Carlingnose Point, North Queensferry, Inverkeithing KY11 1ER	igmitchell@easynet.co.uk	01383 416240
Monk, Alan	36 North Road, Saline KY12 9UQ	salinemonks@gmail.com	01383 851283
Muirhead, Sandy	7 Westpark Gate, Saline KY12 9US	sandy_muirhead@hotmail.com	01383 850077
Peacock, Graham	6 Balgove Avenue, Gauldry, Newport-on-Tay DD6 8SQ	grahampeacock6@btinternet.com	01382 330124
Sheail, Sally	20 Moray Park, Dalgety Bay, Dunfermline KY11 9UN	SSheail@churchofscotland.org.uk	01383 284801
Smith, Elspeth (Mrs)	Glentarkie Cottage, Glentarkie, Strathmiglo, Cupar KY14 7RU	elspeth.smith@btinternet.com	01337 860824

H. Ministries Development Staff

Davie, Sandra	Glenrothes: St Margaret's – Children Youth and Family Worker	SDavie@churchofscotland.org.uk
Hutchison, John BA	Rothes Trinity Parish Grouping – Families Worker and Parish Assistant	JHutchison@churchofscotland.org.uk
Jones, Lauren	Kirkcaldy: Templehall and Torbain United – Community Outreach Worker	LJones@churchofscotland.org.uk
Kerr, Fiona	Methil: Wellesley – Parish Assistant	FKerr@churchofscotland.org.uk
Scott, Pamela (Mrs) DCS	Lochgelly and Benarty: St Serf's – Parish Assistant	PScott@churchofscotland.org.uk
Thomson, Jacqueline (Mrs) MTh DCS	Buckhaven and Wemyss – Deacon	Jaqueline.Thomson@churchofscotland.org.uk
Thorburn, Susan (Rev) MTh	Eden Tay Cluster – Mission Development Worker	SThorburn@churchofscotland.org.uk
Torrance, Julie	Boarhills, Dunino and St Andrews: Holy Trinity – Children and Young Peoples Worker	JTorrance@churchofscotland.org.uk
Ure, Irene	Glenrothes Area Partnership Development Co-ordinator	IUre@churchofscotland.org.uk
Walker, Valerie (Rev)	Lindores – Pioneer Ecumenical Community Chaplain	VWalker@churchofscotland.org.uk

TOWN ADDRESSES

Cupar	
Old and St Michael of Tarvit	Kirkgate
St John's and Dairsie United	Bonnygate Main Street, Dairsie
Dunfermline	
Abbey	St Catherine's Wynd
East	Nightingale Place
Gillespie Memorial	Chapel Street
North	Golfdrum Street
St Columba's	Robertson Road
St Leonard's	Brucefield Avenue
St Margaret's	Abel Place
St Ninian's	Allan Crescent
Glenrothes (now within Heart of Fife)	
Christ's Kirk	Pitcoudie Avenue
St Columba's	Church Street
St Margaret's	Woodside Road
St Ninian's	Durris Drive
Kirkcaldy	
Abbotshall	Abbotshall Road
Bennochy	Elgin Street
Hope	Carron Place
Linktown	Nicol Street x High Street
Pathhead	Harriet Street x Church Street
St Bryce Kirk	St Brycedale Avenue x Kirk Wynd
St Andrews	
Holy Trinity	South Street
St Leonard's	Donaldson Gardens
St Mark's	St Mary's Place

(8) PERTH (F W)

Meets at Perth: St Matthew's Church on the first Saturday in November 2024 and in 2025 on the first Saturday in February, the second Tuesday in June, the second Tuesday in September and the first Saturday in November.

Clerk:	**REV. JOHN A. FERGUSON BD DipMin DMin**		**07596 868064**
Depute Clerk:	**MR EDWARD MORTON**		**07525 005028 / 01738 317712**
Presbytery Office:		**Suite F3, Riverview House, Friarton Road, Perth PH2 8DF** **perth@churchofscotland.org.uk**	**07596 868064**

1	**Aberdalgie and Forteviot (F H W) linked with Dunbarney (H) and Forgandenny (F W)**			**dfpoffice@btconnect.com**	**01738 812463**
	Allan J. Wilson BSc MEd BD	2007		Dunbarney Manse, Manse Road, Bridge of Earn, Perth PH2 9DY AWilson@churchofscotland.org.uk	01738 812211
2	**Aberfeldy (F H W) linked with Dull and Weem (H W) linked with Grantully, Logierait and Strathtay (F W)**				
	Neil M. Glover BSc BD	2005	2017	The Manse, Taybridge Terrace, Aberfeldy PH15 2BS NGlover@churchofscotland.org.uk	01887 820819 07779 280074
3	**Aberfoyle (H W)**				
	Vacant				
	Interim Moderator: Dan Gunn			degunn@hotmail.co.uk	01786 823798
4	**Abernethy and Dron and Arngask (F W)**				
	Vacant				
	Interim Moderator: Michael Benneworth			mbenneworth@hotmail.com	01738 628093
5	**Abernyte (W) linked with Inchture and Kinnaird (F W) linked with Longforgan (F H W)**				
	Catriona M. Morrison MA BD	1995	2021	2 Boniface Place, Invergowrie, Dundee DD2 5DR CMorrison@churchofscotland.org.uk	01382 561523
	Marc A. Prowe	2000	2021	2 Boniface Place, Invergowrie, Dundee DD2 5DR MProwe@churchofscotland.org.uk	01382 561523
6	**Aberuthven and Dunning (F H W)**				
	Vacant				
	Interim Moderator: Alan J.S. Murray			AJSMurray@churchofscotland.org.uk	01738 269434

7	**Alloa: Ludgate (F W)**				
	Dawn A. Laing BEd PGCertPD BD	2020		28 Alloa Park Drive, Alloa FK10 1QY DLaing@churchofscotland .org.uk	01259 213134
8	**Alloa: St Mungo's (F H T W)**			**contact@alloastmungos.org**	**01259 723004**
	Sang Y. Cha BD MTh	2011		37A Claremont, Alloa FK10 2DG SCha@churchofscotland.org.uk	01259 213872
9	**Almondbank Tibbermore (F W) linked with Methven and Logiealmond (F W)**				
	Robert J. Malloch BD	1987	2019	The Manse, Dalcrue Road, Pitcairngreen, Perth PH1 3EA RMalloch@churchofscotland.org.uk	01738 583727
10	**Alva (F W)**			**alvaparishchurch@gmail.com**	
	James N.R. McNeil BSc BD	1990	1997	34 Ochil Road, Alva FK12 5JT JMcNeil@churchofscotland.org.uk	01259 760262
	Anne F. Shearer BA DipEd CertCS (Auxiliary Minister)	2010	2018	10 Colsnaur, Menstrie FK11 7HG AShearer@churchofscotland.org.uk	01259 769176
11	**Alyth (F H W)**				
	Michael J. Erskine MA BD	1985	2012	The Manse, Cambridge Street, Alyth, Blairgowrie PH11 8AW erskinemike@gmail.com	01828 632238
12	**Arbroath and District (F H W)**			**office@arbroathstandrews.org.uk** **office.stvigeans@gmail.com** **arbroathwestkirk2019@gmail.com**	**01241 431135** **01241 879567** **01241 434721**
	Christine Hay LLB CA BD (Moderator)	2020		1 Charles Avenue, Arbroath DD11 2EY Christine.Hay@churchofscotland.org.uk	01241 554189
	Peter A. Phillips BA (Team Minister)	1995	2004	The Manse, Inverkeilor, Arbroath DD11 5SA PPhillips@churchofscotland.org.uk	01241 830464
	Vacant (Team Minister)			92 Grampian Gardens, Arbroath DD11 4AQ	
	Interim Moderator for 3rd post: Ian A. Mclean			IMcLean@churchofscotland.org.uk	01674 434672
	New charge formed by the union of Arbroath: Old and Abbey, Arbroath: St Andrew's, Arbroath: St Vigeans, Arbroath: West Kirk, Carmyllie, Colliston, Friockheim Kinnell, and Inverkeilor and Lunan, and subsequent union with Arbirlot				
13	**Ardoch (H W) linked with Blackford (F H W)**			**info@ardochparishchurch.org**	
	Mairi Perkins BA BTh	2012	2016	Manse of Ardoch, Feddal Road, Braco, Dunblane FK15 5RE MPerkins@churchofscotland.org.uk	01786 880948

14	**Auchterarder (F H T W)**			**admin@auchterarderparish.org**	**01764 660152**
	Lynn M. McChlery BA BD MLitt PhD	2005	2019	22 Kirkfield Place, Auchterarder PH3 1FP	01764 662399
				LMcChlery@churchofscotland.org.uk	
15	**Auchtergaven and Moneydie (F W) linked with Redgorton and Stanley (W)**			**auchtergavenchurch@hotmail.co.uk**	**01738 788017**
	Vacant				
	Interim Moderator: Susan Thorburn			SThorburn@churchofscotland.org.uk	01821 642681
16	**Balfron (F W) linked with Fintry (F H W)**			**admin@balfronchurch.org.uk**	
	Vacant			7 Station Road, Balfron, Glasgow G63 0SX	01360 440285
	Iain S. Armstrong BTh (Ordained Local Minister)	2023		18 Spinner Street, Balfron G63 0TP	
				IArmstrong@churchofscotland.org.uk	
	Interim Moderator: Alison E.P. Britchfield			ABritchfield@churchofscotland.org.uk	07415 683871
17	**Balquhidder linked with Killin and Ardeonaig (F H W)**				
	Vacant			The Manse, Killin FK21 8TN	01567 820247
	Interim Moderator: Jeffrey A. McCormick			JMcCormick@churchofscotland.org.uk	07880 612858
18	**Bannockburn: Allan (F H T W)**			**hiya@allanchurch.org**	
	Vacant			The Manse, Bogend Road, Bannockburn, Stirling FK7 8NP	01786 814692
	Interim Moderator: Gary J. McIntyre			GMcIntyre@churchofscotland.org.uk	01786 474421
19	**Bannockburn: Ladywell (F H W)**				
	Elizabeth M.D. Robertson (Miss) BD CertMin	1997		57 The Firs, Bannockburn FK7 0EG	01786 812467
				ERobertson@churchofscotland.org.uk	
20	**Bendochy (W) linked with Coupar Angus: Abbey (W)**				
	Vacant			Caddam Road, Coupar Angus, Blairgowrie PH13 9EF	01828 627864
	Interim Moderator: Donna M. Hays			DHays@churchofscotland.org.uk	01382 580210
21	**Blackford** See Ardoch				
22	**Blair Atholl and Struan linked with Pitlochry (H W)**			**thetryst@btconnect.com**	**01796 474010**
	Vacant			Manse Road, Moulin, Pitlochry PH16 5EP	01796 472774
	Interim Moderator: R. Fraser Penny			RPenny@churchofscotland.org.uk	01350 727249

No.	Charge / Minister	Ord.	Ind.	Address / Email	Telephone
23	**Blairgowrie (F W)**			**blairgowrieparishchurch@gmail.com**	
	Vacant			The Manse, Upper David Street, Blairgowrie PH10 6HB	01250 870986
	Interim Moderator: Brian Dingwall			briandingwall2020@gmail.com	07906 656847
24	**Braes of Rannoch linked with Foss and Rannoch (H)**				
	Vacant				
	Interim Moderator: Grace M. F. Steele			GSteele@churchofscotland.org.uk	01887 820025
25	**Brechin and Farnell (F H T W)**			**office@brechinfarnellchurch.org**	**01356 629191**
	Adriaan J. J. van Tonder BTh MDiv	2016	2024	15 Caldhame Gardens, Brechin DD9 7JJ	01356 667473
				AvanTonder@churchofscotland.org.uk	
26	**Bridge of Allan (F H W)**			**office@bridgeofallanparishchurch.org.uk**	**01786 834155**
	Daniel (Dan) J. Harper BSc BD	2016		29 Keir Street, Bridge of Allan, Stirling FK9 4QJ	01786 832753
				DHarper@churchofscotland.org.uk	
	Lesley A. Stanley (Prof) MA PhD FBTS (Ordained Local Minister)	2021	2024	Lilac Cottage, Main Street, Gartmore, Stirling FK8 3RN	01506 671532
				LStanley@churchofscotland.org.uk	
27	**Buchanan linked with Drymen (F W)**				**01360 660370**
	Vacant			Buchanan Manse, Drymen, Glasgow G63 0AQ	01360 870212
	Interim Moderator: Philip R. Hacking			PHacking@churchofscotland.org.uk	07985 625831
28	**Buchlyvie and Gartmore (H W)**			**buchlyviechurch@gmail.com gartmorechurch@gmail.com**	
	Vacant				
	New charge formed by the union of Buchlyvie and Gartmore				
29	**Callander (F H W)**				**Tel/Fax: 01877 331409**
	Jeffrey A. McCormick BD DipMin	1984	2018	The Manse, Killin FK21 8TN	01567 820247
				JMcCormick@churchofscotland.org.uk	07880 612858
30	**Cambusbarron: The Bruce Memorial (F H W)**				
	Graham P. Nash MA BD	2006	2012	14 Woodside Court, Cambusbarron, Stirling FK7 9PH	01786 442068
				GPNash@churchofscotland.org.uk	
31	**Caputh and Clunie (H) linked with Kinclaven (H)**				
	Vacant				
	Interim Moderator: Harry Mowbray			mowbrayh@outlook.com	01250 873479

32 Cargill Burrelton (F) linked with Collace (F)
Vacant
Interim Moderator: Gillian Munro munrooth@gmail.com 01738 850066

33 Carnoustie: Trinity (F W)
Annette M. Gordon BD (Moderator) 2017 8 Arbroath Road, Carnoustie DD7 6BL 01241 854478
AGordon@churchofscotland.org.uk
Michael S. Goss BD DPS (Team Minister) 1991 2003 44 Terrace Road, Carnoustie DD7 7AR 01241 410194
MGoss@churchofscotland.org.uk 07787 141567
New charge formed by the union of Barry, Carnoustie and Carnoustie: Panbride

34 Clackmannan (F H W) linked with Sauchie and Coalsnaughton (F) office@clackmannankirk.org.uk 01259 214238
Austin Wicks MDiv BA 2019 2024 19 Graygoran, Sauchie, Alloa FK10 3ET 07514 233197
AWicks@churchofscotland.org.uk

35 Cleish (H W) linked with Fossoway: St Serf's and Devonside (F W)
Vacant Station House, Station Road, Crook of Devon, Kinross KY13 0PG 01577 842128
Interim Moderator: Beverley Stevenson BStevenson@churchofscotland.org.uk 07584 902508

36 Collace See Cargill Burrelton

37 Comrie (F H W) linked with Dundurn (F H) strathearnkirks@btinternet.com 01764 679555
Craig Dobney BA BD 2020 The Manse, Strowan Road, Comrie, Crieff PH6 2ES 01764 679196
CDobney@churchofscotland.org.uk

38 Coupar Angus: Abbey See Bendochy

39 Cowie and Plean (H T) linked with Fallin (F W) info@fallinchurch.com
Alison J. Grainger BD CertEd 1995 2021 5 Fincastle Place, Cowie, Stirling FK7 7DS 01786 760512
AGrainger@churchofscotland.org.uk

40 Crieff (F H W)
Andrew J. Philip BSc BD 1996 2013 8 Strathearn Terrace, Crieff PH7 3AQ 01764 218976
APhilip@churchofscotland.org.uk

41 Dollar (F H W) linked with Muckhart (W) **info@dollarparishchurch.org.uk**
muckhartchurch@gmail.com

Vacant — 2 Princes Crescent East, Dollar FK14 7BU — 01259 740286
Philip R. Hacking (Ordained Local Minister) — 2021 2023 — PHacking@churchofscotland.org.uk — 07985 625831
Interim Moderator: Ellen M. Larson Davidson — ELarsonDavidson@churchofscotland.org.uk — 01786 871249

42 Drymen See Buchanan
43 Dull and Weem See Aberfeldy
44 Dunbarney and Forgandenny See Aberdalgie and Forteviot

45 Dunblane Cathedral, Kilmadock and Blair Drummond (F H T W) **office@dunblanecathedral.org.uk** **07380 745650**

Colin C. Renwick BMus BD — 1989 2014 — Cathedral Manse, The Cross, Dunblane FK15 0AQ — 01786 822205
CRenwick@churchofscotland.org.uk
Alastair Munro RN BSc (Ordained Local Minister) — 2022 — AMunro@churchofscotland.org.uk

New charge formed by the union of Dunblane: Cathedral, Kilmadock and Kincardine-in-Menteith

46 Dunblane: St Blane's (F H W) linked with Lecropt (F H W)

Andrew Gardner BSc BD PhD (Interim Minister) — 1997 2023 — 46 Kellie Wynd, Dunblane FK15 0NR — 01786 825324
AGardner@churchofscotland.org.uk — 07411 989344

47 Dundee: Balgay (F H W)

Nardia J. Sandison BAppSc BD MLitt — 2019 — 150 City Road, Dundee DD2 2PW — 01382 903446
NSandison@churchofscotland.org.uk

48 Dundee: Broughty Ferry (F H T W) **church.office@btconnect.com** **01382 737294**
office@broughtyferrynewkirk.org.uk **01382 738264**

Vacant (Moderator) — 2 St Margaret's Lane, Barnhill, Dundee DD5 2PQ — 01382 503012
Vacant (Team Minister) — 25 Ballinard Gardens, Broughty Ferry, Dundee DD5 1BZ — 01382 778874
Interim Moderator: John C. Duncan — JDuncan@churchofscotland.org.uk — 01382 480772

New charge formed by the union of Dundee: Barnhill St Margaret's, Dundee: Broughty Ferry New Kirk, Dundee: Broughty Ferry St James' and Dundee: Broughty Ferry St Luke's and Queen Street

49 Dundee: Broughty Ferry St Stephen's and West (H W) linked with Dundee: Dundee (St Mary's) (H W)
office@dundeestmarys.co.uk — 01382 226271

Keith F. Hall MA BD — 1981 1994 — 33 Strathern Road, West Ferry, Dundee DD5 1PP — 01382 778808
KHall@churchofscotland.org.uk

50 Dundee: Camperdown (H)
Guardianship of the Presbytery
Interim Moderator: Grant R. MacLaughlan — Camperdown Manse, Myrekirk Road, Dundee DD2 4SF — GMacLaughlan@churchofscotland.org.uk — 07790 518041

51 Dundee: Craigowl (F H W) — **info@chalmersardlerchurch.org**
Vacant — 40 St Martin Crescent, Dundee DD3 0SU

New charge formed by the union of Dundee: Chalmers-Ardler and Dundee: Strathmartine

52 Dundee: Downfield Mains (F H W) — **office@downfieldmainschurch.org** — **07979 939092**
Nathan S. McConnell BS MA ThM PhD — 2002 — 2016 — 9 Elgin Street, Dundee DD3 8NL — NMcConnell@churchofscotland.org.uk — 07979 939092

53 Dundee: Dundee (St Mary's) See Dundee: Broughty Ferry St Stephen's and West

54 Dundee: Kingsgait (F H T W) — **standrewsdundee@outlook.com** — **01382 224860**
Anita D.C. Kerr MA — 2007 — 2020 — 27 Mayfield Grove, Dundee DD4 7GZ — Anita.Kerr@churchofscotland.org.uk — 01382 456659

55 Dundee: Law (F H T W) — **office@thesteeplechurch.org.uk** — **01382 200031**
Vacant

New charge formed by the union of Dundee: Coldside and Dundee: Steeple

56 Dundee: Lochee (F H)
Roderick J. Grahame BD CPS DMin DipPSRP — 1991 — 2018 — 32 Clayhills Drive, Dundee DD2 1SX — RGrahame@churchofscotland.org.uk — 01382 561872

57 Dundee: Logie and St John's Cross (F H W) — **administrator@logies.org** — **01382 668514**
Grant R. MacLaughlan BA BD — 1998 — 2021 — 7 Hyndford Street, Dundee DD2 1HQ — GMacLaughlan@churchofscotland.org.uk — 07790 518041

58 Dundee: Menzieshill (F W)
Robert Mallinson BD — 2010 — The Manse, Charleston Drive, Dundee DD2 4BD — RMallinson@churchofscotland.org.uk — 01382 667446 — 07595 249089

59 Dundee: Northeast (F W)
Vacant
Catherine J. Brodie MA BA MPhil PGCE (Ordained Local Minister) — 2017 — 48h Cleghorn Street, Dundee DD2 2NJ — CBrodie@churchofscotland.org.uk — 07432 513375

	Brenda M.M. Elwell-Sutton BA (Ordained Local Minister; Interim Moderator)	2022		BElwell-Sutton@churchofscotland.org.uk	07811 753391

New charge formed by the union of Dundee: Craigiebank, Dundee: Douglas and Mid Craigie, Dundee: Fintry and Dundee: Whitfield

60	**Dundee: Stobswell Trinity (F H W)**			**secretary@trinitychurchdundee.org**	**01382 526071**
	Jean A. Kirkwood BSc PhD BD	2015	2021	65 Clepington Road, Dundee DD4 7BQ JKirkwood@churchofscotland.org.uk	01382 526071
61	**Dundee: West (F H L W)**			**enquiries@dundeewestchurch.org**	**07341 255354**
	James Connolly DipTh CertMin DipMin MA(Theol) DMin	1982	2020	22 Hyndford Street, Dundee DD2 1HX JConnolly@churchofscotland.org.uk	07711 177655
62	**Dundurn** See Comrie				
63	**Dunkeld (F H W)**				
	R. Fraser Penny BA BD	1984	2001	The Manse, Cathedral Street, Dunkeld PH8 0AW RPenny@churchofscotland.org.uk	01350 727249
64	**Edzell (F H W)**			**elgparish@btconnect.com**	**01356 647815**
	A.S. Wayne Pearce MA PhD	2002	2017	19 Lethnot Road, Edzell, Brechin DD9 7TG ASWaynePearce@churchofscotland.org.uk	01356 648117
65	**Errol (F H W)**				
	Vacant				
	Interim Moderator: Graham W. Crawford			GCrawford@churchofscotland.org.uk	01738 626046
66	**Fallin** See Cowie and Plean				
67	**Fintry** See Balfron				
68	**Forfar: All Souls (F H W)**			**lowsonchurch@gmail.com**	**01307 460576**
	Karen M. Fenwick BSc BD MPhil PhD (Moderator)	2006		1 Jamieson Street, Forfar DD8 2HY KFenwick@churchofscotland.org.uk	01307 468585
	Margaret J. Hunt (Mrs) MA BD (Team Minister)	2014		St Margaret's Manse, 15 Potters Park Crescent, Forfar DD8 1HH MHunt@churchofscotland.org.uk	01307 462044
	Heather Gourlay (Ordained Local Minister)	2021	2024	The Schoolhouse, Pitkennedy, Forfar DD8 2UJ HGourlay@churchofscotland.org.uk	01397 830372

New charge formed by the union of Aberlemno, Dunnichen, Letham and Kirkden, Guthrie and Rescobie, Forfar: Lowson Memorial and Forfar St Margaret's

69	**Forfar: East, Old and Inverarity (F H W)**			**eoiparish@yahoo.com**	**07897 456655**
	Vacant			The Manse, Lour Road, Forfar DD8 2BB	01307 248228
	Interim Moderator: John K. Orr			JOrr@churchofscotland.org.uk	01575 572610
	New charge formed by the union of Forfar: East and Old and Inverarity and Kinnettles				
70	**Fortingall, Glenlyon, Kenmore (H) and Lawers (W)**				
	Vacant			The Manse, Balnaskeag, Kenmore, Aberfeldy PH15 2HB	01887 830218
	Interim Moderator: Robert D. Nicol			RNicol@churchofscotland.org.uk	01887 820242
71	**Foss and Rannoch** See Braes of Rannoch				
72	**Fossoway: St Serf's and Devonside** See Cleish				
73	**Gargunnock (F) linked with Kippen and Norrieston (F H W) linked with Port of Menteith (H W)**				
	Ellen M. Larson Davidson BA MDiv	2007	2015	The Manse, Main Street, Kippen, Stirling FK8 3DN ELarsonDavidson@churchofscotland.org.uk	01786 871249
	Kippen and Norrieston formed by the union of Kippen and Norrieston				
74	**Grantully, Logierait and Strathtay** See Aberfeldy				
75	**Inchture and Kinnaird** See Abernyte				
76	**Invergowrie (F H W)**			**hello@invergowrieparishchurch.org**	
	Catriona M. Morrison MA BD	1995	2020	2 Boniface Place, Invergowrie, Dundee DD2 5DR CMorrison@churchofscotland.org.uk	01382 561523
	Marc A. Prowe	2000	2020	2 Boniface Place, Invergowrie, Dundee DD2 5DR MProwe@churchofscotland.org.uk	01382 561523
77	**Isla Parishes (F W)**				
	Stephen A. Blakey BSc BD CStJ	1977	2018	Balduff House, Kilry, Blairgowrie PH11 8HS SBlakey@churchofscotland.org.uk	01575 560226
78	**Killearn (F H W) linked with Strathblane (F H T W)**			**strathblanekirk@gmail.com**	**01360 770418**
	Stuart W. Sharp MTheol DipPA	2001	2018	Killearn Kirk, Balfron Road, Killearn G63 9NL SSharp@churchofscotland.org.uk	01360 550101
79	**Killin and Ardeonaig** See Balquhidder				
80	**Kinclaven** See Caputh and Clunie				

81	**Kinross (F H W)**			**office@kinrossparishchurch.org**	**01577 862570**
	Alan D. Reid MA BD	1989	2009	15 Green Wood, Kinross KY13 8FG AReid@churchofscotland.org.uk	01577 862952
82	**Kippen and Norrieston** See Gargunnock				
83	**Kirkmichael, Straloch and Glenshee (W) linked with Rattray (H W)**				
	Linda Stewart (Mrs) BD	1996	2012	The Manse, Alyth Road, Rattray, Blairgowrie PH10 7HF Linda.Stewart@churchofscotland.org.uk	01250 872462
84	**Lecropt** See Dunblane: St Blane's				
85	**Logie (F H W)**				
	Vacant Interim Moderator: Attie van Wyk			21 Craiglea, Causewayhead, Stirling FK9 5EE AvanWyk@churchofscotland.org.uk	01786 271809 01786 478269
86	**Longforgan** See Abernyte				
87	**Menstrie (F H T W)**				
	Michael J. Goodison BSc BD	2013	2022	7 Long Row, Menstrie FK11 7BA MGoodison@churchofscotland.org.uk	01259 611109
88	**Methven and Logiealmond** See Almondbank Tibbermore				
89	**Mid Strathearn (H W)**				
	Vacant Interim Moderator: Marjorie Clark (Miss)			Beechview, Abercairney, Crieff PH7 3NF marjorie.clark@btinternet.com	01764 652116 01738 637017
90	**Monifieth South Angus (F H W)**			**office@monifiethparishchurch.co.uk**	
	Vacant Interim Moderator: Lorna H. Tunstall			8 Church Street, Monifieth, Dundee DD5 4JP LTunstall@churchofscotland.org.uk	01382 699183 07920 773382

91	**Montrose: Trinity (F W)**				
	Vacant (Moderator)			2 Rosehill Road, Montrose DD10 8ST	01674 672447
	Vacant (Team Minister)			4 Manse Road, Hillside, Montrose DD10 9FB	01674 830288
	Ian Gray (Ordained Local Minister)	2013	2017	The Mallards, 15 Rossie Island Road, Montrose DD10 9NH IGray@churchofscotland.org.uk	01674 677126
	Interim Moderator: Gavin Drummond (Mr)			gavin.drummond08@gmail.com	01307 463011
92	**Muckhart** See Dollar				
93	**Muthill (F H W)**				
	Vacant			The Manse, Station Road, Muthill, Crieff PH5 2AR	01764 681205
	Interim Moderator: Mairi Perkins			mperkins@churchofscotland.org.uk	01786 880948
94	**Oathlaw Tannadice (F W) linked with The Glens and Kirriemuir United (F W)**				**01575 572819**
	John K. Orr BD MTh	2012		26 Quarry Park, Kirriemuir DD8 4DR JOrr@churchofscotland.org.uk	01575 572610
95	**Orwell and Portmoak (F H W)**			**orwellandportmoakchurch@gmail.com**	**01577 862100**
	Vacant				
	Interim Moderator: Alan D. Reid			areid@churchofscotland.org.uk	01577 862952
96	**Perth: Craigie and Moncreiffe (F W)**				
	Vacant			The Manse, 46 Abbot Street, Perth PH2 0EE	01738 623748
	Robert F. Wilkie CertCS (Auxiliary Minister)	2011	2012	24 Huntingtower Road, Perth PH1 2JS RWilkie@churchofscotland.org.uk	01738 628301
	Interim Moderator: Kenneth D. Stott			KStott@churchofscotland.org.uk	01738 625728
97	**Perth: Kinnoull (F H W)**				
	Graham W. Crawford BSc BD STM	1991	2016	1 Mount Tabor Avenue, Perth PH2 7BT GCrawford@churchofscotland.org.uk	01738 626046 07817 504042
98	**Perth: Letham St Mark's (F H W)**			**office@lethamstmarks.org.uk**	**01738 446377**
	James C. Stewart BD DipMin	1997		35 Rose Crescent, Perth PH1 1NT JStewart@churchofscotland.org.uk	01738 624167
99	**Perth: North (F W)**			**info@perthnorthchurch.org.uk**	**01738 622298**
	Kenneth D. Stott MA BD	1989	2017	2 Cragganmore Place, Perth PH1 3GJ KStott@churchofscotland.org.uk	01738 625728

100 Perth: Riverside (F W) — **perthriverside.bookings@gmail.com** — **01738 622341**
David R. Rankin MA BD 2009 2014 — 44 Hay Street, Perth PH1 5HS — 07810 008754
DRankin@churchofscotland.org.uk

101 Perth: St John's Kirk of Perth (F H W) — **01738 633192**
Guardianship of the Presbytery
Interim Moderator: Craig Dobney — CDobney@churchofscotland.org.uk — 01764 679196

102 Perth: St Leonard's-in-the-Fields (H W) — **office@stleonardsinthefields.co.uk** — **01738 632238**
Vacant
Interim Moderator: Craig Dobney — CDobney@churchofscotland.org.uk — 01764 679196

103 Perth: St Matthew's (F T W) — **office@perthstmatthews.org.uk** — **01738 636757**
Fiona C. Bullock (Mrs) MA LLB BD 2014 — 12 Craigieknowes Avenue, Perth PH2 0DL — 07502 335258
FBullock@churchofscotland.org.uk

104 Pitlochry See Blair Atholl and Struan
105 Port of Menteith See Gargunnock
106 Rattray See Kirkmichael, Straloch and Glenshee
107 Redgorton and Stanley See Auchtergaven and Moneydie

108 St Madoes and Kinfauns (F W)
Marc F. Bircham BD MTh 2000 — The Manse, St Madoes, Glencarse, Perth PH2 7NF — 01738 860837
MBircham@churchofscotland.org.uk

109 Sauchie and Coalsnaughton See Clackmannan

110 Scone and St Martins (F W) — **sconeandstmartinschurch@talktalk.net** — **01738 553900**
Maudeen I. MacDougall BA BD MTh 1978 2019 — The Manse, Burnside, Scone PH2 6LP — 01738 551942
rev.maudeen@gmail.com

111 Sidlaw (F H T W) — **enquiries@churches-flandlm.co.uk**
Donna M. Hays (Mrs) MTheol DipEd DipTMHA 2004 — 149 Coupar Angus Road, Muirhead of Liff, Dundee DD2 5QN — 01382 580210
DHays@churchofscotland.org.uk
New charge formed by the union of Auchterhouse, Fowlis and Liff, and Lundie and Muirhead

112 Stirling: Holy Rude Viewfield (F H W)			**holyrude@holyrude.org**	
Alan F. Miller BA MA BD	2000	2010	7 Windsor Place, Stirling FK8 2HY	01786 465166
			AMiller@churchofscotland.org.uk	
New charge formed by the union of Stirling: Church of the Holy Rude and Stirling: Viewfield				
113 Stirling: North (F H W)			**info@stirlingnorth.org**	**01786 463376**
Scott McInnes MEng BD	2016		13 Calton Crescent, Stirling FK7 0BB	01786 463376
			SMcInnes@churchofscotland.org.uk	
114 Stirling: Park (F H T W)			**parkchurchstirling@gmail.com**	**01786 462400**
Attie van Wyk BTh LMus MDiv MTh	2005	2022	24 Laurelhill Gardens, Stirling FK8 2PT	01786 478269
			AvanWyk@churchofscotland.org.uk	
115 Stirling: St Mark's (F T W)			**stmarksstirling1@gmail.com**	**01786 470733**
Barry J. Hughes MA BA	2011	2018	St Mark's Parish Church, Drip Road, Stirling FK8 1RE	07597 386762
			BHughes@churchofscotland.org.uk	
116 Stirling: St Ninians Old (F H W)				
Gary J. McIntyre BD DipMin	1993	1998	7 Randolph Road, Stirling FK8 2AJ	01786 474421
			GMcIntyre@churchofscotland.org.uk	
117 Strathblane See Killearn				
118 Strathmore (F W)				
Carleen J. Robertson (Miss) BD CertEd	1992		2 Kirkton Road, Newtyle, Blairgowrie PH12 8TS	01828 650461
			CRobertson@churchofscotland.org.uk	
New charge formed by the union of Ardler, Kettins and Meigle, Eassie, Nevay and Kettins, and Glamis				
119 Tenandry				
Guardianship of the Presbytery				
Interim Moderator: Neil M. Glover			NGlover@churchofscotland.org.uk	01887 820819 07779 280074
120 The Glens and Kirriemuir United See Oathlaw Tannadice				
121 Tillicoultry (F H W)				**01259 750340**
Alison E.P. Britchfield (Mrs) MA BD	1987	2013	2 Old Harbour Square, Stirling FK8 1RB	07415 683871
			ABritchfield@churchofscotland.org.uk	

122 Tullibody: St Serf's (F H W)

Vacant	22, The Cedars, Tullibody, Alloa FK10 2PX	01259 213326
Interim Moderator: Scott McInnes	SMcInnes@churchofscotland.org.uk	01786 463376

B. In other appointments: members of Presbytery

Name	Ord.	App.	Appointment	Address	Tel
Allen, Valerie L. BMus MDiv DMin	1990	2015	Presbytery Chaplain	16 Pine Court, Doune FK16 6JE VL2allen@btinternet.com	01786 842577 07801 291538
Begg, Richard J. MA BD	2008	2016	Army Chaplain	12 Whiteyetts Drive, Sauchie FK10 3GE rbegg711@aol.com	07525 612914
Brown, Scott J. CBE BD	1993	2023	National Chaplain, Royal British Legion	SJBrown@churchofscotland.org.uk	07824 805888
Caldwell, Gary J. BSc BD	2007	2023	Chaplain, HM Prison Greenock and HM YOI Polmont	63 Skye Road, Cumbernauld, Glasgow G67 1PB gary.caldwell@prisons.gov.scot	07983 987465
Campbell, Gordon A. MA BD CDipAF DipHSM CMgr MCMI MIHM AssocCIPD AFRIN ARSGS FRGS FSAScot	2001	2004	Auxiliary Minister: an Honorary Chaplain: University of Dundee	2 Falkland Place, Kingoodie, Invergowrie, Dundee DD2 5DY g.a.campbell@dundee.ac.uk	01382 561383
Creighton, Douglas R. BSc BTh	2020	2023	Chaplain, HM Prison Perth	Chaplaincy Centre, HM Prison Perth, 3 Edinburgh Road, Perth PH2 7JH DCreighton@churchofscotland.org.uk	01738 458216
Davidson, Mark R. MA BD STM PhD PhD RN	2005	2011	Chaplain: Royal Navy	The Manse, Main Street, Kippen FK8 3DN Mark.Davidson122@mod.gov.uk	01786 871249
Douglas, Fiona C. MBE MA BD PhD	1989	1997	Chaplain: University of Dundee	10 Springfield, Dundee DD1 4JE f.c.douglas@dundee.ac.uk	01382 384157
Fair, W. Martin BA BD DMin	1992	2023	Pathways to Ministry Manager, Faith Action Programme	121 George Street, Edinburgh EH2 4YN MFair@churchofscotland.org.uk	0131 225 5722
Ferguson, John A. BD DipMin DMin	1988	2022	Presbytery Clerk: Perth	Suite F3, Riverview House, Friarton Road, Perth PH2 8DF JFerguson@churchofscotland.org.uk	07596 868064
Hacking, Philip R.	2021	2023	Ordained Local Minister; Chaplain, HM Prisons Glenochil and Low Moss	PHacking@churchofscotland.org.uk	07985 625831
Jack, Alison M. (Prof.) MA BD PhD SFHEA	1998	2022	Principal, New College; Professor, Bible and Literature, University of Edinburgh	5 Murdoch Terrace, Dunblane FK15 9JE alisonjack809@btinternet.com	01786 826953
Kennedy, Ruth BA MA PGDipPsych	2022	2023	Sanctuary First and Digital Ministries Advisor	6 Craigmore View, Aberfoyle FK8 3SJ RKennedy@churchofscotland.org.uk	01877 389427
McDonald, Emma BD	2013	2024	Pioneer Minister, Dundee	EMcDonald@churchofscotland.org.uk	
Michie, Margaret	2013		Ordained Local Minister: Loch Leven Parish Grouping	3 Loch Leven Court, Wester Balgedie, Kinross KY13 9NE margaretmichie@btinternet.com	01592 840602
Nicol, Robert D. MA	2013	2019	Ordained Local Minister: Presbytery-wide	Rappla Lodge, Camserney, Aberfeldy PH15 2JF RNicol@churchofscotland.org.uk	01887 820242
Pandian, Ali R. BA BD PGCertHC DipPS	2017	2022	Chaplain, Rachel House Children's Hospice	Rachel House Children's Hospice, Avenue Road, Kinross KY13 8FX alipandian@chas.org.uk	01577 865777 07425 630904

Redpath, Anne	2022		Presbytery Chaplain, Discipleship and Mission	9 Beveridge Place, Kinross KY13 8QY ARedpath@churchofscotland.org.uk	
Shuttleworth, Margaret MA BD	2013	2020	Chaplain, HM Prison and YOI Stirling; HM YOI Polmont; Lilias Community Custody Unit, Glasgow	margaret.shuttleworth@prisons.gov.scot	
Spencer, Daniel H. PhD	2023		Assistant Minister, Dundee Menzieshill Parish Grouping	DSpencer@churchofscotland.org.uk	07554 392895
Steele, Grace M.F. MA BTh	2014		Ordained Local Minister: Presbytery-wide	12a Farragon Drive, Aberfeldy PH15 2BQ GSteele@churchofscotland.org.uk	01887 820025
Stevenson, Beverley	2020	2023	Ordained Local Minister: Mission Co-ordinator Stirling and surrounding area	2 Robert Dick Court, Tullibody FK10 2BP BStevenson@churchofscotland.org.uk	07584 902508
Stewart, Anne E. BD CertMin	1998	2007	Chaplain: HM Prison Castle Huntly; Bella Community Custody Unit, Dundee	35 Rose Crescent, Perth PH1 1NT anne.stewart2@prisons.gov.scot	01738 624167
Stott, Anne M.	2019		Ordained Local Minister: Presbytery Pioneer Worker, Bertha Park	2 Cragganmore Place, Perth PH1 3GJ AStott@churchofscotland.org.uk	01738 625728
Strachan, Willie D. DipYCW MBA CertCS	2013	2020	Ordained Local Minister: Presbytery-wide	Ladywell House, Lucky Slap, Monikie, Dundee DD5 3QG WStrachan@churchofscotland.org.uk	07432 513375
Thorburn, Susan MTh	2014		Ordained Local Minister; Mission Development Worker, Presbytery of Fife	3 Daleally Farm Cottages, St Madoes Road, Errol, Perth PH1 7TJ SThorburn@churchofscotland.org.uk	01821 642681
Wylie, Jonathan BSc BD MTh	2000	2016	Chaplain: Strathallan School	Strathallan School, Forgandenny, Perth PH2 9EG chaplain@strathallan.co.uk	01738 815098

C. Retaining: members of Presbytery

Abeledo, Benjamin J. A. BTh DipTh PTh	1991	2024	(Blairgowrie)	26 Strathallan Way, Auchterarder PH3 1GR BAbeledo@churchofscotland.org.uk	
Allan, Jean (Mrs) DCS	1989	2011	(Deacon, Dundee: Craigiebank with Dundee: Douglas and Mid Craigie)	12C Hindmarsh Avenue, Dundee DD3 7LW jeannieallan45@googlemail.com	01382 827299 07709 959474
Ballentine, Ann M. MA BD DipRE	1981	2007	(Kirknewton and East Calder)	17 Nellfield Road, Crieff PH7 3DU annmballentine@gmail.com	01764 652567
Barr, T. Leslie LTh	1969	1997	(Kinross)	8 Fairfield Road, Kelty KY4 0BY leslie_barr@yahoo.co.uk	07727 718076
Barrie, Drew BSc BD	1984	2024	(Tullibody: St Serf's)	40 Hodgson Crescent, Alva FK12 5FA DBarrie@churchofscotland.org.uk	07854 251866
Bogle, Albert O. BD MTh	1981	2023	(Pioneer Minister, Sanctuary First)	49a Kenilworth Road, Bridge of Allan FK9 4RS AlbertBogle@churchofscotland.org.uk	07715 374557
Brennan, Anne J. BSc BD MTh	1999	2019	(Fortingall, Glenlyon, Kenmore and Lawers)	Dunmore House, Findo Gask, Auchterarder PH3 1HS annebrennan@yahoo.co.uk	01738 730350
Brough, Colin M. BSc BD	1998	2022	(Dundee: Fintry)	Westcroft, Station Road, Longforgan DD2 5EX colinbrough73@gmail.com	
Brown, Elizabeth JP RGN	1996	2007	(Auxiliary Minister, Perth: St John the Baptist)	8 Viewlands Place, Perth PH1 1BS liz.brown@blueyonder.co.uk	01738 552391
Brown, Marina D. MA BD MTh	2000	2012	(Hawick: St Mary's and Old)	Moneydie School Cottage, Luncarty, Perth PH1 3HZ revmdb1711@btinternet.com	01738 582163

Name	Ord.	Ret.	Charge	Address / Email	Tel
Buchan, Isabel C. (Mrs) BSc BD RE(PgCE)	1975	2019	(Buckie: North with Rathven)	59 Cliffburn Road, Arbroath DD11 5BA revicbuchan@bluebucket.org	01241 878862
Buwert, Klaus O.F. LLB BD DMin	1984	2022	(Muthill with Trinity Gask and Kinkell)	55 Duncan Road, Letham, Forfar DD8 2PN	
Cairns, Evelyn BD	1987	2012	(Chaplain: Rachel House Children's Hospice, Kinross)	15 Talla Park, Kinross KY13 8AB revelyn@btinternet.com	01577 863990
Calvert, Robert A. BSc BD DMin PhD	1983	2021	(Dundee: The Steeple)	5 Cowiefaulds Cottages, Gateside, Cupar KY14 7ST robertacalvert@gmail.com	07532 029343
Campbell, Richard S. LTh	1993	2010	(Gargunnock with Kilmadock with Kincardine-in-Menteith)	3 David Farquharson Road, Blairgowrie PH10 6FD revrichards@yahoo.co.uk	01250 876386
Caskie, J. Colin BA BD	1977	2012	(Rhu and Shandon)	13 Anderson Drive, Perth PH1 1JZ jcolincaskie@gmail.com	01738 445543
Clark, Marion A. (Rae) MA BD	2014	2022	(Clackmannan)	RClark@churchofscotland.org.uk	
Cloggie, June (Mrs)	1997	2006	(Auxiliary Minister, Callander)	11A Tulipan Crescent, Callander FK17 8AR david.cloggie@hotmail.co.uk	01877 331021
Cochrane, James P.N. LTh	1994	2012	(Tillicoultry)	12 Sandpiper Meadow, Alloa Park, Alloa FK10 1QU jamescochrane@pobroadband.co.uk	01259 218883
Coleman, Sidney H. BA BD MTh	1961	2001	(Glasgow: Merrylea)	15 Richmond Terrace, Dundee DD2 1BQ sidney.h.coleman@gmail.com	01382 645824
Cook, Helen K.M. (Mrs) MA BD DipSW MComC	1974	2012	(Kingussie)	60 Pelstream Avenue, Stirling FK7 0BG revhcook@btinternet.com	01786 464128
Corbett, Richard T. BSc MSc PhD BD	1992	2019	(Kilmallie)	Flat 309, Knights Court, 1 North William Street, Perth PH1 5NB richard.t.corbett@btinternet.com	01738 626315
Cowper, Alistair J. BSc BD	2011	2023	(Kirknewton and East Calder)	1 Craigiebield Crescent, Penicuik EH26 9EQ ACowper@churchofscotland.org.uk	07791 524504
Craig, Joan H. MTheol DipCE CPS	1986	2005	(East Mainland)	7 Jedburgh Place, Perth PH1 1SJ joanhcraig@btinternet.com	01738 580180
Dempster, Colin J. BD CertMin	1990	2016	(Mearns Coastal)	35 Margaret Lindsay Place, Monifieth DD6 4RD Coldcoast@btinternet.com	01382 532368
Devenny, David J. BD	1997	2011	(Chaplain, Royal Navy)		
Dingwall, Brian BTh CQSW	1999	2020	(Arbirlot with Carmyllie)	10 New Road, Rattray, Blairgowrie PH10 7RA briandingwall2020@gmail.com	07906 656847
Duncan, John C. MBE BD MPhil	1987	2021	(Leuchars: St Athernase)	21 Ravenscraig Gardens, Broughty Ferry, Dundee DD5 1LT JDuncan@churchofscotland.org.uk	01382 480772
Dunnett, Linda (Mrs) BA DCS	1976	2016	(Deacon, Cowie and Plean with Fallin)	9 Tulipan Crescent, Callander FK17 8AR lindadunnett@sky.com	01877 339640 07838 041683
Edwards, Dougal BTh	2013	2017	(Ordained Local Minister, Barry with Carnoustie)	25 Mackenzie Street, Carnoustie DD7 6HD DEdwards@churchofscotland.org.uk	01241 852666
Ewart, William BSc BD	1972	2010	(Caputh and Clunie with Kinclaven)	22 Muirend Avenue, Perth PH1 1JL ewe1@btinternet.com	
Ewart-Roberts, Peggy BA BD	2003	2022	(Caputh and Clunie with Kinclaven)	22 Muirend Avenue, Perth PH1 1JL revpeggy.r@gmail.com	07775 712686
Fraser, Donald W. MA	1958	2010	(Monifieth)	1 Blake Avenue, Broughty Ferry, Dundee DD5 3LH fraserdonald37@yahoo.co.uk	01382 477491 07531 863316

Name	Ord.	Ret.	Charge	Address	Tel.
Gaston, A. Ray C. MA BD	1969	2002	(Leuchars: St Athernase)	'Hamewith', 13 Manse Road, Dollar FK14 7AL gaston.arthur@yahoo.co.uk	01259 743202
Gilchrist, Ewen J. BD DipMin DipComm	1982	2017	(Cults)	9 David Douglas Avenue, Scone PH2 6QQ ewengilchrist@btconnect.com	07747 746418
Gill, Peter G. BA MBA MA	2008	2023	(Bannockburn: Allan with Cowie and Plean)	The Manse, Bogend Road, Bannockburn, Stirling FK7 8NP PGill@churchofscotland.org.uk	01786 814692
Gillon, C. Blair BD	1975	2007	(Glasgow: Ibrox)	St Anne's Dowally, Ballinluig, Pitlochry PH9 0NT charlesgillon21@gmail.com	07490 495936
Goring, Iain M. BSc BD	1976	2015	(Interim Minister, Edinburgh: St John's Colinton Mains)	4 Argyle Grove, Dunblane FK15 9DU imgoring@gmail.com	01786 821688
Gough, Ian G. MA BD MTh DMin	1974	2009	(Arbroath: Knox's with Arbroath: St Vigeans)	23 Keptie Road, Arbroath DD11 3ED ianggough@btinternet.com	07891 838379
Graham, Alasdair G. BD DipMin	1981	2019	(Arbroath: West Kirk)	The Manse, Caddam Road, Coupar Angus PH13 9EF alasdairgraham704@btinternet.com	01828 627864
Graham, Sydney S. DipYL MPhil BD	1987	2009	(Iona with Kilfinichen and Kilvickeon and the Ross of Mull)	'Aspen', Milton Road, Luncarty, Perth PH1 3ES syd@sydgraham.plus.com	01738 829350
Gunn, Alexander M. MA BD	1967	2006	(Aberfeldy with Amulree and Strathbraan with Dull and Weem)	'Navarone', 12 Cornhill Road, Perth PH1 1LR sandygunn@btinternet.com	01738 443216
Haddow, Mary M. (Mrs) BD	2001	2022	(Pitlochry)	16 Hobens Drive, North Berwick EH39 5GZ mary_haddow@btconnect.com	
Halliday, Archibald R. BD MTh	1964	1999	(Duffus, Spynie and Hopeman)	8 Turretbank Drive, Crieff PH7 4LW roberthalliday343@btinternet.com	01764 656464
Izett, William A.F.	1968	2000	(Law)	1 Duke Street, Clackmannan FK10 4EF william.izett@talktalk.net	01259 724203
Kay, Elizabeth (Miss) DipYCS	1993	2007	(Auxiliary Minister, Abernyte with Inchture and Kinnaird with Longforgan)	1 Kintail Walk, Inchture, Perth PH14 9RY ekay007@btinternet.com	01828 686029
Kelly, T. Clifford	1973	1993	(Ferintosh)	20 Whinfield Drive, Kinross KY13 8UB	01577 864946
Kennon, Stanley BA BD CertEd	1992	2022	(Abernethy and Dron and Arngask)	9 The Orchard, Woodside, Burrelton, Blairgowrie PH13 9NQ stankennon@outlook.com	
Knox, John W. MTheol	1992	1997	(Lochgelly: Macainsh)	2 Darroch Gate, Blairgowrie PH10 6GT ian.knox5@btinternet.com	01250 872733
Laidlaw, John J. MA	1964	1996	(Adviser, Religious Education, Tayside Region)	14 Dalhousie Road, Barnhill, Dundee DD5 2SQ jacklaidlaw@blueyonder.co.uk	01382 477458
Lawson, James B. MA BD	1961	2002	(South Uist)	4 Cowden Way, Comrie, Crieff PH6 2NW james.lawson7@btopenworld.com	01764 679180
Lillie, Fiona L. (Mrs) BA BD MLitt	1995	2017	(Glasgow: St John's Renfield)	4 McVicars Lane, Dundee DD1 4LH fionalillie@btinternet.com	01382 229082
MacDonald, James W. BD	1976	2012	(Crieff)	'Mingulay', 29 Hebridean Gardens, Crieff PH7 3BP rev_up@btinternet.com	01764 654500
Macgregor, John BD	2001	2020	(Errol with Kilspindie and Rait)	1 Le Petit Vierzon, 16490 Hiesse, France john_macg@hotmail.com	
Mack, Lynne (Mrs)	2013	2019	(Ordained Local Minister, Gargunnock with Kilmadock with Kincardine-in-Menteith)	36 Middleton, Menstrie FK11 7HD revlynnemack@gmail.com	01259 761465

Name	Ord.	Ret.	Former charge	Address	Telephone
MacRae, Malcolm H. MA PhD	1971	2010	(Kirkmichael, Straloch and Glenshee with Rattray)	10B Victoria Place, Stirling FK8 2QU malcolm.macrae1@btopenworld.com	01786 465547
Mair, Michael V.A. MA BD	1968	2007	(Dundee: Craigiebank with Douglas and Mid Craigie)	48 Panmure Street, Monifieth DD5 4EH mvamair@gmail.com	01382 530538
Majcher, Philip L. BD	1982	2020	(London: Crown Court)	5 Strathallan Bank, Ardargie, Forgandenny, Perth PH2 9FE pmajcher@me.com	
Malcolm, Alistair BD DPS	1976	2012	(Inverness: Inshes)	11 Kinclaven Gardens, Murthly, Perth PH1 4EX amalcolm067@btinternet.com	01738 710979
Malloch, Philip R.M. LLB BD	1970	2009	(Killearn)	8 Michael McParland Drive, Torrance, Glasgow G64 4EE pmalloch@mac.com	01360 620089
Mathew, J. Gordon MA BD	1973	2011	(Buckie: North)	45 Westhaugh Road, Stirling FK9 5GF jg.mathew@btinternet.com	01786 445951
McCarthy, David J. BSc BD	1985	2020	(Fresh Expressions Development Worker, Faith Nurture Forum)	Orchard House, Croft Avenue, Dunning PH2 0SG djmcclv@gmail.com	
McCormick, Alastair F.	1962	1998	(Creich with Rosehall)	14 Balmanno Park, Bridge of Earn, Perth PH2 9RJ	01738 813588
McCrum, Robert BSc BD CertMin	1982	2014	(Ayr: St James')	28 Rose Crescent, Perth PH1 1NT robert.mccrum@virgin.net	01738 447906
McDonald, Ian J.M. MA BD	1984	2024	(Chaplain, Palliative Care, Roxburghe House, NHS Tayside)	11 James Grove, Kirkcaldy KY1 1TN IanJMMcdonald@churchofscotland.org.uk	07421 775644
McFadzean, Iain MA BD CMgr FCMI MHGI	1989	2019	(Chief Executive: Work Place Chaplaincy Scotland)	2 Lowfield Crescent, Luncarty, Perth PH1 3FG iain.mcfadzean@wpcscotland.co.uk	01738 827338 07969 227696
McIntosh, Colin G. MA BD	1976	2013	(Dunblane: Cathedral)	Drumhead Cottage, Drum, Kinross KY13 0PR colinmcintosh4@btinternet.com	01577 840012
McKenzie, Alan BSc BD	1988	2013	(Bellshill: Macdonald Memorial with Bellshill: Orbiston)	89 Drip Road, Stirling FK8 1RN rev.a.mckenzie@btopenworld.com	01786 430450
McLean, Ian A. BSc BD DMin	1981	2023	(Montrose: Trinity)	9 Lunan Avenue, Montrose DD10 9DG IMcLean@churchofscotland.org.uk	01674 434672
McMillan, Edith F. (Mrs) MA BD	1981	2018	(Dundee: Craigiebank with Douglas and Mid Craigie)	39 Castlefield Court, Stepps, Glasgow G33 6NN wee_rev_edimac@btinternet.com	
McMillan, Stewart BD	1983	2022	(Dundee: Strathmartine)	39 Castlefield Court, Stepps, Glasgow G33 6NN SMcMillan@churchofscotland.org.uk	
McNaughton, David J.H. BA CA	1976	1995	(Killin and Ardeonaig)	14 Rankine Court, Wormit, Newport-on-Tay DD6 8TA	
McNicol, Bruce BL BD	1967	2006	(Jedburgh: Old and Edgerston)	22 Beechwood Gardens, Stirling FK8 2AX mcnicol942@gmail.com	01786 358308
McPherson, William BD DipEd	1994	2023	(Chief Executive, The Vine Trust)	Winterfell, West Kinfauns, Perth PH2 7JX williewmcp@aol.com	07720 893450
Millar, Alexander M. MA BD MBA	1980	2018	(Stirling: St Columba's)	17 Mapledene Road, Scone, Perth PH2 6NX alexmillar0406@gmail.com	01738 550270
Millar, Jennifer M. (Mrs) BD DipMin	1986	2021	(Teacher: Religious and Moral Education)	17 Mapledene Road, Scone, Perth PH2 6NX ajrmillar@blueyonder.co.uk	01738 550270
Milne, Robert B. BTh	1999	2017	(Broughton, Glenholm and Kilbucho with Skirling with Stobo and Drumelzier with Tweedsmuir)	3 Mid Square, Comrie PH6 2EG rbmilne@aol.com	07803 609387

Mitchell, Alexander B. BD	1981	2014	(Dunblane: St Blane's)	24 Hebridean Gardens, Crieff PH7 3BP alex.mitchell6@btopenworld.com	01764 652241
Moffat, Russel BD CPS MTh PhD	1986	2022	(Balquidder with Killin and Ardeonaig)	21 McKerrow Drive, Heathhall, Dumfries DG1 3SP russel.moffat@churchofscotland.org.uk	
Mowbray, Harry BD CA	2003	2018	(Blairgowrie)	12 Isla Road, Blairgowrie PH10 6RR mowbrayh@gmail.com	01250 873479
Munro, Gillian BSc BD	1989	2018	(Head of Spiritual Care, NHS Tayside)	The Old Town House, 53 Main Street, Abernethy, Perth PH2 9JH munrooth@aol.com	01738 850066
Munro, Patricia M. BSc DCS	1986	2016	(Deacon, Perth: St John's Kirk of Perth with Perth: St Leonard's-in-the-Fields)	4 Hewat Place, Perth PH1 2UD patmunrodcs@gmail.com	01738 443088 07814 836314
Murray, Alan J.S. BSc BD PhD	2003	2023	(Banchory-Ternan: East)	Lade Cottage, Bleachers Way, Hunting Towerfield, Perth PH1 3NY AJSMurray@churchofscotland.org.uk	01738 269434
Murray, John W. LLB BA	2001	2022	(Anstruther and Cellardyke: St Ayle with Crail)	JMurray@churchofscotland.org.uk	
Nelson, Robert C. BA BD	1980	2010	(Kilninian and Kilmore with Salen and Ulva with Tobermory with Torosay and Kinlochspelvie)	St Colme's, Perth Road, Birnam, Dunkeld PH8 0BH rcnelson49@btinternet.com	01350 727455
Nicoll, A. Norman BD	2003	2020	(Corby: St Andrew's)	14 Victoria Street, Forfar DD8 3BA	
Norrie, Graham MA BD	1967	2007	(Forfar: East and Old)	'Novar', 14A Wyllie Street, Forfar DD8 3DN grahamnorrie@hotmail.com	01307 468152
Notman, Alison BD	2014	2020	(Ardler, Kettins and Meigle)	6 Hall Street, Kettlebridge, Cupar KY15 7QF	
Ogilvie, Catriona (Mrs) MA BD	1999	2015	(Cumbernauld: Old)	Seberham Flat, 1A Bridge Street, Dollar FK14 7DF catriona.ogilvie1@btinternet.com	01259 742155
Ormiston, Hugh C. BSc BD MPhil PhD	1969	2004	(Kirkmichael, Straloch and Glenshee with Rattray)	Cedar Lea, Main Road, Woodside, Blairgowrie PH13 9NP	01828 831062
Ovens, Samuel B. BD	1982	1992	(Slamannan)	21 Bevan Drive, Alva FK12 5PD	01259 763456
Oxburgh, Brian H. BSc BD	1980	2019	(Tayport)	50 Ravensbay Park Gardens, Carnoustie DD7 7NY	
Paton, Iain F. BD FCIS	1980	2006	(Elie with Kilconquhar and Colinsburgh)	Muldoanich, Stirling Street, Blackford, Auchterarder PH4 1QG iain.f.paton@btinternet.com	01764 682234
Philip, Elizabeth A. C. MA BA PGCSE DCS	2007	2018	(Deacon, Crieff)	8 Strathearn Terrace, Crieff PH7 3AQ ephilipstitch@gmail.com	01764 218976 07970 767851
Porter, Jean T. (Mrs) BD DCS	2006	2022	(Deacon, Stirling: St Mark's)	3 Cochrie Place, Tullibody FK10 2RR JPorter@churchofscotland.org.uk	07729 316321
Quigley, Barbara D. (Mrs) MTheol ThM DPS	1979	2019	(Glasgow: St Andrew's East)	33 Castle Drive, Auchterarder PH3 1FU bdquigley@aol.com	07926 064235
Ramsay, Brian BD DPS MLitt	1980	2022	(Aberlemno with Guthrie and Rescobie)	The Manse, Guthrie, Forfar DD8 2TP	01241 828243
Redpath, James G. BD DipPTh	1988	2016	(Auchtermuchty with Edenshead and Strathmiglo	9 Beveridge Place, Kinross KY13 8QY james.redpath@gmx.co.uk	07713 919442
Reid, R. Gordon BSc BD MIEE	1993	2010	(Carriden)	6 Bayview Place, Monifieth, Dundee DD5 4TN GordonReid@aol.com	01382 520519 07952 349884
Robertson, George R. LTh	1985	2004	(Udny and Pitmedden)	3 Slateford Gardens, Edzell, Brechin DD9 7SX geomag.robertson@btinternet.com	01356 647322

Robertson, James H. BSc BD	1975	2014	(Culloden: The Barn)	'Far End', 35 Mains Terrace, Dundee DD4 7BZ jimrob838@gmail.com	01382 522773 07595 465838
Robertson, Matthew LTh	1968	2002	(Cawdor with Croy and Dalcross)	Inver, Strathtay, Pitlochry PH9 0PG	01887 840780
Robson, George K. LTh DPS BA	1983	2011	(Dundee: Balgay)	11 Ceres Crescent, Broughty Ferry, Dundee DD5 3JN gkrobson@virginmedia.com	01382 901212
Rooney, Malcolm I.G. DipPE BEd BD	1993	2017	(The Glens and Kirriemuir: Old)	23 Mart Lane, Northmuir, Kirriemuir DD8 4TL malc.rooney@gmail.com	01575 575334 07909 993233
Rose, Dennis S. DipTh LTh	1996	2016	(Arbuthnott, Bervie and Kinneff)	69 Blackthorn Grove, Menstrie FK11 7DX dennis2327@aol.com	01259 692451
Rose, Lewis (Mr) DCS	1993	2010	(Deacon, Organiser, Industrial Chaplaincy)	6 Gauldie Crescent, Dundee DD3 0RR lewis_rose48@yahoo.co.uk	01382 816580 07899 790466
Russell, John MA	1959	2000	(Tillicoultry)	Kilblaan, Gladstone Terrace, Birnam, Dunkeld PH8 0DP jsafrussell@outlook.com	01350 727965
Russell, Kenneth G. BD CertCE CertCounsS PGCertHC DipPRSP	1986	2020	(Chaplain: HM Prison Perth)	158 Bannockburn Road, Stirling FK7 0EW kenrussell1000@hotmail.com	01786 812680
Saunders, Grace I.M. BSc BTh	2007	2022	(Cumbernauld: Condorrat)	65 Slade Gardens, Kirriemuir DD8 5AG rev.grace.saunders@btinternet.com	
Scott, James MA BD	1973	2010	(Drumoak-Durris)	3 Blake Place, Broughty Ferry, Dundee DD5 3LQ jimscott73@yahoo.co.uk	01382 739595
Searle, David C. MA DipTh FSAScot	1965	2002	(Warden: Rutherford House, Edinburgh)	Stonefall Lodge, 30 Abbey Lane, Grange, Errol PH2 7GB dcs@davidsearle.plus.com	01821 641004
Sewell, Paul M.N. MA BD	1970	2010	(Berwick-upon-Tweed: St Andrew's Wallace Green and Lowick)	7 Bohun Court, Stirling FK7 7UT paulmsewell@btinternet.com	01786 489969
Shewan, Michael R.R. MA BD CPS	1985	2022	(Aberdeen: North)	13 Hatton Road, Luncarty, Perth PH1 3UZ	
Sime, Christine M. (Miss) BSc BD	1994	2023	(Dalgety)	3 St Mary's Place, Kinross KY13 8BZ CSime@churchofscotland.org.uk	
Sloan, Robert P. MA BD	1968	2007	(Interim Minister, Armadale)	1 Broomhill Avenue, Perth PH1 1EN sloan12@virginmedia.com	01738 443904
Stenhouse, W. Duncan MA BD	1989	2006	(Dunbarney and Forgandenny)	32 Sandport Gait, Kinross KY13 8FB	01577 866992
Stewart, Alexander T. MA BD FSAScot	1975	2022	(Associate, Perth: St John's Kirk of Perth with St Leonard's-in-the-Fields)	36 Viewlands Terrace, Perth PH1 1BZ alex.t.stewart@blueyonder.co.uk	01738 566675
Stewart, Robin J. MA BD STM	1959	1995	(Orwell with Portmoak)	'Oakbrae', Perth Road, Murthly, Perth PH1 4HF	01738 710220
Taylor, Caroline (Mrs)	1995	2014	(Leuchars: St Athernase)	7 Sunart Street, Broughty Ferry, Dundee DD5 3HW caro234@btinternet.com	01382 770198
Taylor, C. Graham D. BSc BD FIAB	2001	2020	(Dundee: Broughty Ferry St Luke's and Queen Street)	The Smithy, Grange, Errol, Perth PH2 7TB cgdtaylor@btinternet.com	07804 527103
Thomas, Martyn R.H. CEng MIStructE	1987	2002	(Fowlis and Liff with Lundie and Muirhead of Liff)	14 Kirkgait, Letham, Forfar DD8 2XQ martyn317thomas@btinternet.com	01307 818084
Thomson, Raymond BD DipMin	1992	2013	(Slamannan)	8 Rhodders Grove, Alva FK12 5ER	01259 769083
Thomson, Steven BSc BD	2001	2022	(Cargill Burrelton with Collace)	Flat 02, 3 Rosebery Terrace, Glasgow G5 0AS	
Tunstall, Lorna H. MA MDiv	2020	2023	(Clyne with Kildonan and Loth Helmsdale)	The Manse, Manse Road, Woodside, Blairgowrie PH13 9NQ LTunstall@churchofscotland.org.uk	01828 670384 07920 773382

Name	Ord.	Appt.	Former charge	Address / Email	Phone
Wallace, Catherine PGDipC DCS	1987	2022	(Clinical Manager, Harbour Counselling Service, Perth)	21 Durley Dene Crescent, Bridge of Earn PH2 9RD cwallacecounselling@gmail.com	01738 621709
Wallace, James K. MA BD STM	1988	2015	(Perth: St John's Kirk of Perth with St Leonard's-in-the-Fields)	21 Durley Dene Crescent, Bridge of Earn PH2 9RD jkwministry@hotmail.com	01738 621709
Wallace, Sheila D. (Mrs) BA BD DCS	2009	2020	(Deacon, Aberfeldy with Dull and Weem with Grantully, Logierait and Strathtay)	Little Orchard, Blair Atholl, Pitlochry PH18 5SH	01796 481647 07733 243046
Watt, Alan G.N. MTh CQSW DipCommEd	1996	2009	(Edzell Lethnot Glenesk with Fern Careston Menmuir)	6 Pine Way, Friockheim, Arbroath DD11 4WF watt455@btinternet.com	01241 826018
Webster, Allan F. MA BD	1978	2013	(Workplace Chaplain, Tayside and North Fife)	42 McCulloch Drive, Forfar DD8 2EB allanfwebster@aol.com	01307 464252 07546 276725
Whyte, William B. DipArch ARIBA BD	1973	2004	(Nairn: St Ninian's)	The Old Inn, Park Hill Road, Rattray, Blairgowrie PH10 7DS	01250 874401
Wilson, Hazel MA BD DipEd DipMS	1991	2015	(Dundee: Lochee)	2 Boe Court, Springfield Terrace, Dunblane FK15 9LU hmwilson704@gmail.com	01786 825850
Wilson, James L. BD CPS	1986	2022	(Dundee: Whitfield)	Burnside Cottage, 97 Peebles Drive, Dundee DD4 0TF r3vjw@aol.com	07885 618659
Wilson, John M. MA BD	1967	2004	(Altnaharra and Farr)	Berbice, The Terrace, Blair Atholl, Pitlochry PH18 5SZ	01796 481619

D. In other appointments: not members of Presbytery

Name	Ord.	Appt.	Appointment	Email	Phone
Patterson, Philip W. BMus BD MTh	1999	2022	Programme Co-ordinator, Veterans Chaplaincy Scotland	philip.patterson@vcscotland.org	07713 625792

E. Retaining: not members of Presbytery

Name	Ord.	Appt.	Former charge	Address / Email	Phone
Dawson, Michael S. BTech BD	1979	2005	(Associate: Edinburgh: Holy Trinity)	9 The Broich, Alva FK12 5NR mikpen.dawson@btinternet.com	01259 769309
Gillies, Janet E. BD	1998	2014	(Tranent)	33 Castle Road, Stirling FK9 5JD jan.gillies@yahoo.com	01786 446222
Gordon, Elinor J. (Miss) BD	1988	2015	(Cumbernauld: Kildrum)	6 Balgibbon Drive, Callander FK17 8EU elinorgordon@btinternet.com	01877 331049
Mackay, Kenneth D. DCS	1996	2020	(Deacon, Perth: Letham St Mark's)	15 Bank Street, Blairgowrie PH10 6DE	01250 369029 07891 203403
Morrice, Alastair M. MA BD	1968	2008	(International Church of Bishkek, Kyrgyzstan)	5 Brechin Road, Kirriemuir DD8 4BX ambishkek@swissmail.org	01575 574102
Roderick, Maggie R. BA BD FRSA FTSI	2010	2018	(Menstrie)	Flat A7 Oaklands, Pitheavlis Crescent, Perth PH2 0JA MRoderick@churchofscotland.org.uk	
Stevens, Linda (Mrs) BSc BD PGDipCouns	2006	2022	(West Angus Area Team Minister)	17 North Latch Road, Brechin DD9 6LE	

F. Inactive: not members of Presbytery

Name	Ord.	Ret.	Former charge	Address / Email	Phone
Dunsmore, Barry W. MA BD	1982	2018	(Aberdeen: St Machar's Cathedral)	33 Young Road, Victoria Park, Dunblane FK15 0FT barrydunsmore@gmail.com	01786 643287
Gilmour, William M. MA BD	1969	2008	(Lecropt)	14 Pine Court, Doune FK16 6JE	01786 842928
Hamilton, David S.M. MA BD STM	1958	1996	(Lecturer, Practical Theology, University of Glasgow)	Linfield, Milton of Lawton, Arbroath DD11 4RU dandmhamilton@gmail.com	01241 238369
Hastie, George I. MA BD	1971	2009	(Mearns Coastal)	23 Borrowfield Crescent, Montrose DD10 9BR george.hastie46@btinternet.com	01674 672290
Liddiard, F.G. Bernard MA	1957	1971	(Brechin: Gardner Memorial and East)	34 Trinity Fields Crescent, Brechin DD9 6YF bernardliddiard@btinternet.com	01356 622966
Ramsay, Robert J. LLB NP BD	1986	2018	(Invergowrie)	50 Nethergray Road, Dundee DD2 5GT s3rjr@tiscali.co.uk	01382 562481
Reid, Albert B. BSc BD	1966	2001	(Ardler, Kettins and Meigle)	1 Mary Countess Way, Glamis, Forfar DD8 1RF abreid019@gmail.com	01307 840999
Sloan, Robert BD	1997	2014	(Fauldhouse: St Andrew's)	3 Gean Grove, Blairgowrie PH10 6TL	01250 875286

G. Readers (active)

Archibald, Michael	Wychwood, Culdeesland Road, Methven, Perth PH1 3QE	michael.archibald@gmail.com	01783 840995
Beedie, Alexander W. (William)	68 Bloomfield Road, Arbroath DD11 3LQ	a.wbeedie38@gmail.com	01241 875001
Benneworth, Michael	7 Hamilton Place, Perth PH1 1BB	mbenneworth@hotmail.com	01738 628093
Davidson, Andrew	95 Needless Road, Perth PH2 0LD	a.r.davidson.91@cantab.net	01738 620839
Gray, Linda (Mrs)	8 Inchgarth Street, Forfar DD8 3LY	lindamgray@sky.com	01307 464039
Grier, Hunter	17 Station Road, Bannockburn, Stirling FK7 8LG	anneandhunter@gmail.com	01786 815192
Howat, David P.	Lilybank Cottage, Newton Street, Blairgowrie PH10 6HZ	david@thehowats.net	01250 874715
McPherson, Alistair M.	Springpark, Doune Road, Dunblane FK15 9AR		01786 826850
Montgomery, Nicola	8 Beechwood Terrace, Dundee DD2 1NW		
Patterson, Rosemary (Mrs)	Rowantree, Golf Course Road, Blairgowrie PH10 6LJ	pattersonrose.c@gmail.com	01250 876607
Redwood, Keith		KRedwood@churchofscotland.org.uk	01250 878312
Stewart, Anne	Ballcraine, Murthly Road, Stanley, Perth PH1 4PN	anne.stewart13@btinternet.com	01738 828637
Walker, Eric	12 Orchard Brae, Kirriemuir DD8 4JY	eric.line15@btinternet.com	01575 572082
Walker, Pat (Mrs)	12 Orchard Brae, Kirriemuir DD8 4JY	pat.line15@btinternet.com	01575 572082
Weidner, Karl J. BD CertTh	4 Drumkelbo Road, Meigle PH12 8AD	kweidner@btinternet.com	07523 091786
Xenophontos-Hellen, Tim	23 Ancrum Drive, Dundee DD2 2JG	tim.xsf@btinternet.com	01382 630355 (Work) 01382 567756
Yellowlees, Deirdre (Mrs)	Ringmill House, Gannochy Farm, Perth PH2 7JH	d.yellowlees@btinternet.com	01738 633773 07920 805399

H. Ministries Development Staff

Allen, Valerie L (Rev) BMus MDiv DMin	Presbytery – Chaplain	VL2allen@btinternet.com
Berry, Gavin R.	Dundee: Camperdown/Dundee: Lochee – Parish Assistant	GBerry@churchofscotland.org.uk
Clark, Ross	Dundee: Northeast – Discipleship, Mission and Development Worker	Ross.Clark@churchofscotland.org.uk
Dungavell, Marie Clare	Stirling: St Mark's – Community Engagement Worker	MCDungavell@churchofscotland.org.uk
Ingram, Carla BA MLitt	Arbroath and District – Children and Families Worker	CIngram@churchofscotland.org.uk
McDonald, Emma (Rev) BD	Dundee: Pioneer Minister	EMcDonald@churchofscotland.org.uk
McKenzie, Matthew	Dundee: Lochee / Dundee: Camperdown – Youth and Families Worker	MMcKenzie@churchofscotland.org.uk
Slowman, Neil BA	Perth: Letham St Mark's – Community Development Worker	NSlowman@churchofscotland.org.uk
Smith, Jane	Perth: Riverside – Community Development Worker	JSmith@churchofscotland.org.uk
Stirling, Diane BSc DipCPC BTh	Dundee: Northeast – Parish Assistant	DStirling@churchofscotland.org.uk
Stott, Anne M. (Rev)	Presbytery Pioneer Worker – Bertha Park	AStott@churchofscotland.org.uk

CITY AND TOWN ADDRESSES

Arbroath

Arbroath	Hamilton Green; Keptie Street; and St Vigeans Brae

Dundee

Balgay	at Dundee: West
Broughty Ferry	10 Invermark Terrace and 370 Queen Street
Broughty Ferry St Stephen's and West	96 Dundee Road
Camperdown	22 Brownhill Road
Craigowl	Turnberry Avenue
Downfield Mains	Haldane Street off Strathmartine Road
Dundee (St Mary's)	Nethergate
Kingsgait	2 King Street
Law	Isla Street x Main Street; Nethergate
Lochee	191 High Street, Lochee
Logie and St John's Cross	Shaftesbury Rd x Blackness Ave
Menzieshill	Charleston Drive, Menzieshill
Northeast	Balbeggie Place; Fintry Road x Fintry Drive; Haddington Crescent
Stobswell Trinity	73 Crescent Street
West	130 Perth Road

Forfar

All Souls	Jamieson Street; Aberlemno; Letham; Rescobie
East, Old and Inverarity	East High Street; Inverarity

Perth

Craigie Moncreiffe	Abbot Street; Glenbruar Crescent
Kinnoull	Dundee Rd near Queen's Bridge
Letham St Mark's	Rannoch Road
North	Mill Street near Kinnoull Street
Riverside	Bute Drive
St John's	St John's Street
St Leonard's-in-the-Fields	Marshall Place
St Matthew's	Tay Street

Stirling

Holy Rude Viewfield	St John Street; Barnton Street
North	Springfield Road
Park	Park Terrace
St Mark's	Drip Road
St Ninians Old	Kirk Wynd, St Ninians

(9) NORTH EAST AND NORTHERN ISLES (F W)

Meets at Aberdeen Fountainhall at the Cross on Tuesdays 5 November and 3 December 2024. In 2025 meets on 4 February, 22 April, 21 June and 6 September.

Clerk:	**REV. STELLA L. CAMPBELL MA BD**		**01224 049933**
Depute Clerk:	**MISS U. RUTH MACKENZIE**	**DeputeClerk@churchofscotland.org.uk**	**01779 480680**
Mission Development Officer:	**REV. ROBERT L. SMITH BS MTh PhD**	**RSmith@churchofscotland.org.uk**	**01224 049937**
Treasurer:	**MRS ELAINE MITCHELL**		**07563 878741**
Presbytery Office:		**Suite 2, Ground Floor, Ocean Spirit House West, 31 Waterloo Quay, Aberdeen AB11 5BS** **NorthEastandNorthernIsles@churchofscotland.org.uk**	**01224 049933**

1	**Aberdeen: Bridge of Don Oldmachar (F H W)**			**secretary@oldmacharchurch.org**	**01224 709299**
	Darren M. Jalland BA	2022		60 Newburgh Circle, Aberdeen AB22 8QZ DJalland@churchofscotland.org.uk	07546 738797
2	**Aberdeen: Devana (F H W)**			**admin@devanaparishchurch.org**	**Fonthill Road: 01224 213093** **Holburn Street: 01224 961430**
	J. Peter N. Johnston BSc BD (Moderator)	2001	2013	12 Craigden, Aberdeen AB15 6YW PJohnston@churchofscotland.org.uk	01224 513662
	David J. Stewart BD MTh DipMin (Team Minister)	2000	2018	54 Woodstock Road, Aberdeen AB15 5JF DStewart@churchofscotland.org.uk	01224 317975
3	**Aberdeen: Fountainhall (F H W)**			**office@fountainhallchurch.org.uk**	**01224 002891**
	Duncan C. Eddie MA BD (Moderator)	1992	1999	31 Cranford Road, Aberdeen AB10 7NJ DEddie@churchofscotland.org.uk	01224 325873
	Tanya J. Webster BCom DipAcc BD (Team Minister)	2011	2019	182 Midstocket Road, Aberdeen AB15 5HS TWebster@churchofscotland.org.uk	01224 561358
4	**Aberdeen: Hillside (F H W)**			**info@aberdeenhillsideparish.church**	**01224 494717**
	Vacant Interim Moderator: Darren M. Jalland			DJalland@churchofscotland.org.uk	07546 738797

5	**Aberdeen: Mannofield (F H T W)**			**office@mannofieldchurch.org.uk**	**01224 310087**
	Keith T. Blackwood BD DipMin	1997	2007	21 Forest Avenue, Aberdeen AB15 4TU	01224 315748
				KBlackwood@churchofscotland.org.uk	
6	**Aberdeen: North (F H W)**			**office@aberdeennorthchurch.co.uk**	**01224 694121**
	Fiona A. Lister BSc BD	2023		8 Corse Wynd, Kingswells, Aberdeen AB15 8TP	07905 770259
				FLister@churchofscotland.org.uk	
7	**Aberdeen: St Columba's Bridge of Don (F H W)**			**administrator@stcolumbaschurch.org.uk**	**01224 825653**
	Vacant			151 Jesmond Avenue, Aberdeen AB22 8UG	01224 705337
8	**Aberdeen: St John's Church for Deaf People**				
	P. Mary Whittaker BSc BD	2011	2018	16 Corthan Place, Kincorth, Aberdeen AB12 5AS	Text only 07501 454766
				MWhittaker@churchofscotland.org.uk	
9	**Aberdeen: St Machar's Cathedral (F H T W)**			**office@stmachar.com**	**01224 485988**
	Sarah A. Brown (Ms)	2012	2021	39 Woodstock Road, Aberdeen AB15 5EX	01224 539630
	MA BD ThM DipYW/Theol PDCCE DipPS			Sarah.Brown@churchofscotland.org.uk	
10	**Aberdeen: St Mary's (F H W)**			**stmaryschurch924@btinternet.com**	**01224 487227**
	Vacant				
	Interim Moderator: Ian M. Aitken			IAitken@churchofscotland.org.uk	01224 686929
11	**Aberdeen: St Stephen's (F H W)**				**01224 624443**
	Maggie Whyte BD	2010		6 Belvidere Street, Aberdeen AB25 2QS	01224 635694
				Maggie.Whyte@churchofscotland.org.uk	
12	**Aberdeen: South (F H W)**			**st.fitticks@btconnect.com**	**01224 899183**
	Edmond Gatima BEng BD	2013		11 Devanha Gardens East, Aberdeen AB11 7UH	01224 588245
	MSc MPhil PhD			EGatima@churchofscotland.org.uk	
	Joseph K. Somevi BSc MSc PhD BTh	2015	2021	97 Ashwood Road, Aberdeen AB22 8QX	01224 826362
	MRICS MRTPI MIEMA CertCRS			JSomevi@churchofscotland.org.uk	07886 533259
	(Ordained Local Minister)				
	New charge formed by the union of Aberdeen: South of St Nicholas Kincorth and Aberdeen: Torry St Fittick's				
13	**Aberdeen: Springfield (F H W)**			**office@aberdeenspringfield.church**	**01224 315649**
	Benjamin D.W. Byun	1992	2008	53 Springfield Avenue, Aberdeen AB15 8JJ	01224 312706
	BA MDiv MTh PhD			BByun@churchofscotland.org.uk	
	New charge formed by the union of Aberdeen: Craigiebuckler and Aberdeen: Ruthrieston West				

14 Aberdeen: Stockethill (F W)				
Ian M. Aitken MA BD	1999		52 Ashgrove Road West, Aberdeen AB16 5EE IAitken@churchofscotland.org.uk	01224 686929
15 Aberdour (W)				
Vacant				
Interim Moderator: Ruth Mackenzie (Miss)			ursular@tiscali.co.uk	01779 480680
16 Aberlour (F H W)				
Andrew I. M. Kimmitt MA(Div)	2020		The Manse, Mary Avenue, Aberlour AB38 9QU AKimmitt@churchofscotland.org.uk	01340 871909 07752 306462
17 Aberluthnott (F W) linked with Laurencekirk (F H W)			**contact@parishchurchofaberluthnottandlaurencekirk.co.uk**	
Vacant			The Manse, Aberdeen Road, Laurencekirk AB30 1AJ	01561 377013
Interim Moderator: Brian D. Smith			BSmith@churchofscotland.org.uk	01561 340203
18 Aboyne-Dinnet (F H W) linked with Cromar (F W)			**aboynedinnet@gmail.com**	
Sharmann Maromo	2016	2024	49 Charlton Crescent, Aboyne AB34 5GN SMaromo@churchofscotland.org.uk	01339 887267
19 Arbuthnott, Bervie and Kinneff (F T W)				
Andrew R. Morrison MA BA	2019		5 West Park Place, Inverbervie, Montrose DD10 0XA Andrew.Morrison@churchofscotland.org.uk	01561 443325 07720 275028
20 Auchterless and Auchaber (W)				
Stephen J. Potts BA	2012		The Manse, Auchterless, Turriff AB53 8BA SPotts@churchofscotland.org.uk	01888 511058
21 Banchory-Ternan: East (F H W)			**info@banchoryeastchurch.com**	**01330 820380**
Vacant			East Manse, Station Road, Banchory AB31 5YP	01330 822481
Interim Moderator: Amy C. Pierce			ACPierce@churchofscotland.org.uk	01330 850736 07814 194997
22 Banchory-Ternan: West (F H T W)			**office@banchorywestchurch.com**	**01330 822006**
Antony A. Stephen MA BD	2001	2011	The Manse, 2 Wilson Road, Banchory AB31 5UY TStephen@churchofscotland.org.uk	01330 822006 07866 704738

23	**Banff (F W) linked with King Edward (F W)**			**info@banffparishchurchofscotland.org.uk**	**01262 818211**
	Vacant			7 Colleonard Road, Banff AB45 1DZ	01261 812107
	Interim Moderator: Colin A. Strong			CStrong@churchofscotland.org.uk	01771 637365
24	**Belhelvie (F H W)**			**belhelviecofs@btconnect.com**	
	Paul McKeown BSc PhD BD	2000	2005	Belhelvie Manse, Balmedie, Aberdeen AB23 8YR	01358 742227
				PMcKeown@churchofscotland.org.uk	
25	**Bellie and Speymouth (F W)**				
	Vacant			11 The Square, Fochabers IV32 7DG	01343 820256
	Interim Moderator: Jacobus Boonzaaier			JBoonzaaier@churchofscotland.org.uk	01542 649644
26	**Bennachie (F H W)**			**office@bennachieparish.church**	**01467 643883**
	Neil W. Meyer BD MTh (Moderator)	2000	2014	28 Oakhill Road, Kintore, Inverurie AB51 0FH NMeyer@churchofscotland.org.uk	01467 632219
	G. Euan D. Glen BSc BD (Team Minister)	1992		The Manse, 26 St Ninians, Monymusk, Inverurie AB51 7HF GGlen@churchofscotland.org.uk	01467 651470
	Sheila M. Mitchell BD MTh (Team Minister)	1995	2018	The Manse, Echt, Westhill AB32 7AB SMitchell@churchofscotland.org.uk	01330 860004
	Tose Shayamunda DipTh BTh MTh (Assistant Minister)	2016	2023	TShayamunda@churchofscotland.org.uk	
27	**Birsay, Harray and Sandwick (F W)**				
	Moira Taylor-Wintersgill BD	2022		The Manse, North Biggings Road, Dounby, Orkney KW17 2HZ MTaylor-Wintersgill@churchofscotland.org.uk	01856 771599
	D. Kerr Wintersgill BA	2022		The Manse, North Biggings Road, Dounby, Orkney KW17 2HZ KWintersgill@churchofscotland.org.uk	01856 771599
28	**Birse and Feughside (W)**				
	Amy C. Pierce BA BD	2017	2019	The Manse, Finzean, Banchory AB31 6PB	01330 850736
				ACPierce@churchofscotland.org.uk	07814 194997
29	**Braemar and Crathie (F W)**				
	Kenneth I. Mackenzie LVO DL BD CPS	1990	2005	The Manse, Crathie, Ballater AB35 5UL KMacKenzie@churchofscotland.org.uk	01339 742208
30	**Brimmond (F H W)**			**office@brimmondchurch.org.uk**	**01224 716161**
	Jonathan A. Clipston BSc MDiv	2020		Brimmond Manse, Bucksburn, Aberdeen AB21 9SS JClipston@churchofscotland.org.uk	01224 712594

31 Buckie: North and Rathven (F H W) — **info@buckienorth-rathvenchurches.org**
Jacobus Boonzaaier BA BCom(OR) BD MDiv PhD | 1996 | 2021 | 20 Netherton Terrace, Findochty, Buckie AB56 4QD | 01542 649644
JBoonzaaier@churchofscotland.org.uk
New charge formed by union of Buckie: North and Rathven

32 Buckie: South, West and Enzie (F H)
Vacant
Interim Moderator: George B. Rollo | rollos@gmail.com | 01343 835226
New charge formed by the union of Buckie: South and West and Enzie

33 Crimond (F W) linked with Lonmay (W)
Vacant | The Manse, Crimond, Fraserburgh AB43 8QJ | 01346 532431
Session Clerk, Crimond: Irene Fowlie (Mrs) | fowlie_@hotmail.com | 01771 637263
Session Clerk, Lonmay: Roy Kinghorn | strathelliefarm@btinternet.com | 01346 532436

34 Cromar See Aboyne-Dinnet

35 Cruden (F H W)
Sean Swindells BD DipMin MTh | 1996 | 2019 | The Manse, 6 Garden Place, Cruden Bay, Peterhead AB42 0WA | 01779 745301
SSwindells@churchofscotland.org.uk | 07791 755976

36 Cullen and Deskford (F T W)
Vacant | 14 Seafield Road, Cullen, Buckie AB56 4AF | 01542 841963

37 Culsalmond and Rayne (F W) linked with Daviot (F H W)
Mary M. Cranfield MA BD DMin | 1989 | The Manse, Daviot, Inverurie AB51 0HY | 01467 671241
MCranfield@churchofscotland.org.uk

38 Cults (F H T W) — **cultsparishchurch@btinternet.com** | **01224 869028**
Shuna M. Dicks BSc BD | 2010 | 2018 | 1 Cairnlee Terrace, Bieldside, Aberdeen AB15 9AE | 01224 861692
SDicks@churchofscotland.org.uk

39 Daviot See Culsalmond and Rayne

40 Deer (F H)
Sheila M. Kirk BA LLB BD | 2007 | 2010 | The Manse, Abbey Street, Old Deer, Peterhead AB42 5JB | 01771 623582
SKirk@churchofscotland.org.uk

41	**Duffus, Spynie and Hopeman (F H W)**				
	Vacant			The Manse, Duffus, Elgin IV30 5QP	01343 830276
	Christine McWhirter BA (Assistant Minister)	2022		CMcWhirter@churchofscotland.org.uk	01343 545703 07842 141164
	Anne-Marie Simpson MA PGCE CertCS (Ordained Local Minister)	2023		25 Hays Crescent, Keith AB55 5AR AMSimpson@churchofscotland.org.uk	07713 200915
42	**Dyce (F H T W) linked with New Machar (F W)**			**dyceparishchurch@outlook.com** **admin-newmacharchurch@btconnect.com**	**01224 771295**
	Manson C. Merchant BD CPS	1992	2008	100 Burnside Road, Dyce, Aberdeen AB21 7HA MMerchant@churchofscotland.org.uk	01224 722380
	Joan I. Thorne BA TQFE CertCS (Ordained Local Minister)	2019		85 Mosside Drive, Portlethen, Aberdeen AB12 4QY JThorne@churchofscotland.org.uk	07368 390832
43	**East Mainland (W)**			**eastmainlandchurch@gmail.com**	
	Christopher Wallace BD DipMin	1988	2022	The Manse, Holm, Orkney KW17 2SB Christopher.Wallace@churchofscotland.org.uk	01856 781797
44	**Eday**				
	Vacant				
	Session Clerk: Johan Robertson			essonquoy@btinternet.com	01857 622251
45	**Elgin (F W)**			**elginparishchurch@gmail.com**	**01343 551501**
	Deon F. Oelofse BA MDiv LTh MTh	2002	2017	18 Reidhaven Street, Elgin IV30 1QH DOelofse@churchofscotland.org.uk	01343 208786
	Sonia Palmer RGN (Ordained Local Minister)	2017		94 Ashgrove Park, Elgin IV30 1UT Sonia.Palmer@churchofscotland.org.uk	07748 700929
	New charge formed by the union of Birnie and Pluscarden, Elgin: High and Elgin: St Giles' and St Columba's South				
46	**Ellon (F T W)**			**info@ellonparishchurch.co.uk**	**01358 725690**
	Alastair J. Bruce BD MTh PGCE	2015		The Manse, 12 Union Street, Ellon AB41 9BA ABruce@churchofscotland.org.uk	01358 723787
47	**Evie and Rendall (F) linked with Firth (F H)**				**Firth: 01856 761117**
	Vacant				
	Session Clerk, Evie and Rendall: Eileen Fraser			eileenocot@hotmail.co.uk	01856 761409
	Session Clerk, Firth: Janis Dickey			rbdickey@hotmail.com	01856 761396
	Interim Moderator: Iain D. MacDonald			IMacDonald@churchofscotland.org.uk	01857 677357

48	**Findochty (F T W) linked with Portknockie (F T W)**				
	Vacant			20 Netherton Terrace, Findochty, Buckie AB56 4QD	01542 649644
	Interim Moderator: Louis C. Bezuidenhout			macbez@gmail.com	01542 839493
49	**Fintray Kinellar Keithhall (F W)**				**01224 790439**
	Vacant				
	Interim Moderator: Sheila A. Craggs			sacraggs@outlook.com	01358 723055
50	**Firth** See Evie and Rendall				
51	**Flotta (W) linked with Orphir and Stenness (H W)**				
	Vacant				
	Session Clerk, Orphir and Stenness: Nicol Sclater				01856 811242
	Interim Moderator: June Freeth			JFreeth@churchofscotland.org.uk	01856 721449
52	**Formartine (F W)**				
	Vacant			8 Murray Avenue, Tarves, Ellon AB41 7LZ	01651 851295
	Interim Moderator: Alastair J. Bruce			ABruce@churchofscotland.org.uk	01358 723787
	New charge formed by the union of Barthol Chapel, Tarves and Udny and Pitmedden				
53	**Foveran (F W)**				
	Vacant			The Manse, Foveran, Ellon AB41 6AP	01358 789288
	Interim Moderator: Ibidun B. Daramola				07395 006113
54	**Fraserburgh and District**				
	Vacant (Moderator)			4 Robbie's Loan, Fraserburgh AB43 7AF	01346 515332
	Vacant (Team Minister)			4 Kirkton Gardens, Fraserburgh AB43 8TU	01346 517972
	New charge formed by the union of Fraserburgh: Old, Fraserburgh: South, Fraserburgh: West, Inverallochy and Rathen: East, Pitsligo, Rathen: West and Sandhaven				
55	**Fyvie linked (F W) with Rothienorman (F)**				
	Alison Jaffrey (Mrs) MA BD FSAScot	1990	2019	The Manse, Peterwell Road, Fyvie, Turriff AB53 8RD AJaffrey@churchofscotland.org.uk	01651 891961
56	**Glenmuick (Ballater) (H W)**				
	David L.C. Barr	2014		The Manse, Craigendarroch Walk, Ballater AB35 5ZB DBarr@churchofscotland.org.uk	01339 756111

57	**Hoy and Walls (F)**				
	Vacant				
	Session Clerk: Anderson Sutherland				01856 701363
	Interim Moderator: Marjory A. MacLean			MMacLean@churchofscotland.org.uk	01856 831648
58	**Huntly Cairnie Glass (F)**				
	Thomas R. Calder LLB BD WS	1994		The Manse, Queen Street, Huntly AB54 8EB	01466 792630
				TCalder@churchofscotland.org.uk	
59	**Insch-Leslie-Premnay-Oyne (F H W)**				
	Vacant			66 Denwell Road, Insch AB52 6LH	01464 820404
	Interim Moderator: Alison Jaffrey			AJaffrey@churchofscotland.org.uk	01651 891961
60	**Inverurie: St Andrew's (F W)**			**standrews@btinternet.com**	**01467 628740**
	Carl J. Irvine BSc MEd BA	2017	2020	I Ury Dale, Inverurie AB51 3XW	01467 629163
				CIrvine@churchofscotland.org.uk	
61	**Inverurie: West (F T W)**			**admin@inveruriewestchurch.org**	**01647 620285**
	Rhona P. Cathcart BA BSc BD	2017		West Manse, 1 Westburn Place, Inverurie AB51 5QS	01467 620285
				RCathcart@churchofscotland.org.uk	
62	**Keith: North, Newmill, Boharm and Rothiemay (F H W)**			**knnbrchurch@btconnect.com**	**01542 886390**
	Amy C. Bender BA PhD DDiv	2022		North Manse, Church Road, Keith AB55 5BR	01542 780486
				ABender@churchofscotland.org.uk	
63	**Keith: St Rufus, Botriphnie and Grange (F H W)**				
	J.P.L. (Wiekus) van Straaten BA BTh	1997	2020	St Rufus Manse, Church Road, Keith AB55 5BR	01542 882799
				WvanStraaten@churchofscotland.org.uk	
64	**Kincardine Coastal (F H W)**			**portlethenpc@btconnect.com**	**01224 782883**
	Vacant			18 Rowanbank Road, Portlethen, Aberdeen AB12 4NX	01224 780211
	Interim Moderator: David Galbraith			David.Galbraith@churchofscotland.org.uk	01561 320779
				New charge formed by the union of Newtonhill and Portlethen	
65	**King Edward** See Banff				

66	**Kingshill (F H W)**			**secretary.kingshillparish@gmail.com**	**01224 742512**
	Vacant	2012		The Manse, Manse Road, Kirkton of Skene, Westhill AB32 6LX	01224 745955
	Fiona Blair DCS	1994	2023	Kirk Cottage, Kirkton of Skene, Westhill AB32 6XE FBlair@churchofscotland.org.uk	07368 696550
67	**Kirkwall: East (F H W) linked with Shapinsay (F W)**				
	Julia M. Meason MTh MA MTh	2013		East Church Manse, Thoms Street, Kirkwall, Orkney KW15 1PF JMeason@churchofscotland.org.uk	01856 874789
68	**Kirkwall: St Magnus Cathedral (F H T W) linked with Rousay**				
	Vacant			Cathedral Manse, Berstane Road, Kirkwall, Orkney KW15 1NA	01856 873312
	June Freeth BA MA (Ordained Local Minister)	2015		Cumlaquoy, Orkney KW17 2ND JFreeth@churchofscotland.org.uk	01856 721449
	Interim Moderator: Marjory A. MacLean			MMacLean@churchofscotland.org.uk	01856 831648
69	**Knockando, Elchies and Archiestown (H W) linked with Rothes (W)**			**info@moraykirk.co.uk**	**01340 831497**
	Vacant			The Manse, Rothes, Aberlour AB38 7AF	01340 831381
	Session Clerk, Knockando, Elchies and Archiestown: Patricia North			patnorth82@gmail.com	01340 810687
	Session Clerk, Rothes: Dennis Malcolm			dennis.malcolm46@icloud.com	01340 831319 07399 420695
70	**Laurencekirk** See Aberluthnott				
71	**Longside (F W)**				
	Robert A. Fowlie BD	2007		The Manse, Abbey Street, Old Deer, Peterhead AB42 5JB RFowlie@churchofscotland.org.uk	01771 622228
72	**Lonmay** See Crimond				
73	**Lossiemouth (F T W)**				
	Geoffrey D. McKee BA BA DipPS	1997	2014	The Manse, St Gerardine's Road, Lossiemouth IV31 6RA GMcKee@churchofscotland.org.uk	01343 586001
	Christine McWhirter BA (Assistant Minister)	2022		CMcWhirter@churchofscotland.org.uk	01343 545703 07842 141164

New charge formed by the union of Lossiemouth: St Gerardine's High and Lossiemouth: St James'

No.	Charge / Minister	Ord.	Ind.	Address	Tel.
74	**Macduff (F T W)**			**contactus@macduffparishchurch.org**	
	Vacant			10 Ross Street, Macduff AB44 1NS	01261 832316
	Interim Moderator: Stephen J. Potts			SPotts@churchofscotland.org.uk	01888 511058
75	**Marnoch (F W)**				
	Vacant			Marnoch Manse, 53 South Street, Aberchirder, Huntly AB54 7TS	01466 781143
	Interim Moderator: John Gow			JGow@churchofscotland.org.uk	01261 838506
76	**Maryculter: Trinity (W)**			**maryculterttrinitychurch@btinternet.com**	**01224 735983**
	Vacant			The Manse, Kirkton of Maryculter, Aberdeen AB12 5FS	01224 730150
	David Galbraith (Ordained Local Minister)	2021		Myreside Steading, Auchenblae, Laurencekirk AB30 1TX	01561 320779
				David.Galbraith@churchofscotland.org.uk	
	Interim Moderator: Antony A. Stephen			TStephen@churchofscotland.org.uk	01330 822811
77	**Maud and Savoch (F W) linked with New Deer: St Kane's (F W)**				**01771 644097**
	Aileen M. McFie (Mrs) BD	2003	2018	The Manse, Fordyce Terrace, New Deer, Turriff AB53 6TD	01771 644631
				ARobson@churchofscotland.org.uk	
78	**Meldrum and Bourtie (F W)**			**info@meldrumandbourtiechurch.com**	**07968 000610**
	Alisa L. McDonald BA MDiv	2008	2020	17 Benview Gardens, Oldmeldrum, Inverurie AB51 0FY	01651 872059
				Alisa.McDonald@churchofscotland.org.uk	
79	**Methlick (F W)**				
	Vacant			The Manse, Manse Road, Methlick, Ellon AB41 7DG	01651 806264
	Interim Moderator: Richard M.C. Reid			reidricky322@gmail.com	07474 010915
80	**Mid Deeside (F W)**				**01339 889160**
	Holly Smith BSIS MDiv MEd	2009	2019	Lochnagar, Beltie Road, Torphins, Banchory AB31 4JU	01339 882915
				Holly.Smith@churchofscotland.org.uk	
81	**Monquhitter and New Byth linked with Turriff: St Andrew's (F)**			**info@standrewsturriff.co.uk**	
	Vacant			St Andrew's Manse, Balmellie Road, Turriff AB53 4DP	01888 560304
	Interim Moderator: Aileen M. McFie			ARobson@churchofscotland.org.uk	01771 644631
82	**Mormond West (F W)**				
	Colin A. Strong BSc BD	1989	2020	Kingsville, Strichen, Fraserburgh AB43 6SQ	01771 637365
				CStrong@churchofscotland.org.uk	
	New charge formed by the union of New Pitsligo and Strichen and Tyrie				

83	**Mortlach and Cabrach (F H)**			**mortlachadmin@btinternet.com**	
	Eduard Enslin BTh MDiv MTh LLB	2010	2020	Mortlach Manse, Ardean, Church Street, Dufftown, Keith, AB55 4AR	01340 820380
				EEnslin@churchofscotland.org.uk	
84	**New Deer: St Kane's** See Maud and Savoch				
85	**New Machar** See Dyce				
86	**North Ronaldsay**				
	Guardianship of the Presbytery				
	Interim Moderator: Kenneth Meason (Mr)			kennymeason@yahoo.co.uk	01856 874789
87	**Ordiquhill and Cornhill (F H) linked with Whitehills**				
	Vacant			6 Craigneen Place, Whitehills, Banff AB45 2NE	01261 861317
	Session Clerk, Ordiquhill and Cornhill: Frances Webster (Mrs)			william.webster@btconnect.com	01466 751230
	Session Clerk, Whitehills: Jenny Abel (Mrs)			jennyabel14@hotmail.co.uk	01261 861386
88	**Orphir and Stenness** See Flotta				
89	**Papa Westray (W) linked with Westray (W)**				
	Iain D. MacDonald BD DipChEd	1993		The Manse, Hilldavale, Westray, Orkney KW17 2DW	Tel/Fax 01857 677357
				IMacDonald@churchofscotland.org.uk	07710 443780
90	**Peterculter (F H W)**			**secretary@culterkirk.co.uk**	**01224 735845**
	Vacant			7 Howie Lane, Peterculter AB14 0LJ	01224 735041
	Corné Randall BTh MDiv BA BA MTh (Assistant Minister)	2010	2023	CRandall@churchofscotland.org.uk	07775 868391
	Interim Moderator: Duncan C. Eddie			DEddie@churchofscotland.org.uk	01224 325873
	New charge formed by the union of Drumoak-Durris and Peterculter				
91	**Peterhead: New (F W)**			**contact@peterheadnew.org**	
	Julia Pizzuto-Pomaco BA MA MDiv PhD	1999	2021	15 Inchmore Gardens, Boddam, Peterhead AB42 3BG	01779 471714
				JPizzuto-Pomaco@churchofscotland.org.uk	
92	**Peterhead: St Andrew's (H W)**				
	Guardianship of the Presbytery				
	Interim Moderator: Jeffrey Tippner			JTippner@churchofscotland.org.uk	01779 838287

93 Portknockie See Findochty			
94 Portsoy (F W)		**portsoychurch@gmail.com**	**01261 843125**
John Gow BA	2021	The Manse, 4 Seafield Terrace, Portsoy, Banff AB45 2QB	01261 838506
		JGow@churchofscotland.org.uk	
95 Rothes See Knockando, Elchies and Archiestown			
96 Rothienorman See Fyvie			
97 Rousay See Kirkwall: St Magnus Cathedral			
98 St Andrew's-Lhanbryd and Urquhart (F H W)			
Vacant		39 St Andrews Road, Lhanbryde, Elgin IV30 8PU	01343 842017
Interim Moderator: J.P.L. (Wiekus) van Straaten		WvanStraaten@churchofscotland.org.uk	01542 882799
99 St Cyrus (F W)			
Guardianship of the Presbytery			
Interim Moderator: Brian D. Smith		BSmith@churchofscotland.org.uk	01561 340203
100 St Fergus (F)			
Jeffrey Tippner BA MDiv MCS PhD	1991 2012	26 Newton Road, St Fergus, Peterhead AB42 3DD	01779 838287
		JTippner@churchofscotland.org.uk	
101 Sanday			
Vacant			
Interim Moderator: June Freeth		JFreeth@churchofscotland.org.uk	01856 721449
102 Shapinsay See Kirkwall: East			
103 Shetland (F W)		**ShetlandParish@churchofscotland.org.uk**	
Vacant (Moderator/ Minister, South)		The Manse, 25 Hogalee, East Voe, Scalloway, Shetland ZE1 0UU	01585 881184
Irene A. Charlton (Mrs) BTh CPS (Team Minister, East and West)	1994 1997	The Manse, Marrister, Symbister, Whalsay, Shetland ZE2 9AE	01806 566767
		ICharlton@churchofscotland.org.uk	
Vacant (Team Minister, North)		The North Isles Manse, Gutcher, Yell, Shetland ZE2 9DF	07815 922889
Interim Moderator: Keith T. Blackwood		KBlackwood@churchofscotland.org.uk	01224 315748
104 South Ronaldsay and Burray (F)			
Marjory A. MacLean LLB BD PhD	1991 2020	St Margaret's Manse, Church Road, St Margaret's Hope, Orkney KW17 2SR	01856 831648
		MMacLean@churchofscotland.org.uk	

105 Stonehaven: Carronside (F H W)			**secretary.dunnottarchurch@outlook.com**	**01569 760930**
Sarah Smith BA MDiv MA	2017	2021	Dunnottar Manse, Stonehaven AB39 3XL	01569 762166
			Sarah.Smith@churchofscotland.org.uk	
106 Stonehaven: Fetteresso (F H W)			**office@fetteresso.org.uk**	**01569 767689**
Mark Lowey BD DipTh	2012	2021	11 South Lodge Drive, Stonehaven AB39 2PN	01569 549960
			MLowey@churchofscotland.org.uk	
107 Strathbogie Drumblade (F W)			**strathbogiedrumblade@outlook.com**	
Vacant			49 Deveron Park, Huntly AB54 8UZ	01466 792702
Interim Moderator: Carol H.M. Ford			CFord@churchofscotland.org.uk	01464 820332
108 Stromness (F H)				
Moira Taylor-Wintersgill BD	2022	2024	The Manse, North Biggings Road, Dounby, Orkney KW17 2HZ	01856 771599
			MTaylor-Wintersgill@churchofscotland.org.uk	
D. Kerr Wintersgill BA	2022	2024	The Manse, North Biggings Road, Dounby, Orkney KW17 2HZ	01856 771599
			KWintersgill@churchofscotland.org.uk	
109 Stronsay: Moncur Memorial (F W)				
David I.W. Locke MA MSc BD	2000	2021	The Manse, Wardhill, Stronsay, Orkney KW17 2AG	01857 616284
			DLocke@churchofscotland.org.uk	
110 Turriff: St Andrew's See Monquhitter and New Byth				
111 Turriff: St Ninian's and Forglen (H L W)			**info@stniniansandforglen.org.uk**	**01888 560282**
Kevin R. Gruer BSc BA	2011		4 Deveronside Drive, Turriff AB53 4SP	01888 563850
			KGruer@churchofscotland	
112 West Gordon (Alford, Strathdon, Rhynie) (F H W)			**secretary@westgordonparishchurch.org.uk**	**01975 562829**
Vacant			The Manse, 110 Main Street, Alford AB33 8AD	01975 562282
Simon A. Crouch MCIPD CertCS	2019		Delhandy, Corgarff, Strathdon AB36 8YB	01975 651779
(Ordained Local Minister)			SCrouch@churchofscotland.org.uk	07713 101358
113 West Mearns (F W)				
Brian D. Smith BD	1990	2016	The Manse, Fettercairn, Laurencekirk AB30 1UE	01561 340203
			BSmith@churchofscotland.org.uk	

114 Westray See Papa Westray
115 Whitehills See Ordiquhill and Cornhill

B. In other appointments: members of Presbytery

Adams, Jenny M. BEng BD MTh	2013	2024	Chaplain, Dr Gray's Hospital	Dr Gray's Hospital, Pluscarden Road, Elgin IV30 1SN JAdams@churchofscotland.org.uk	07858 137192
Campbell, Stella L. MA BD	2012	2024	Clerk, Presbytery of the North East and Northern Isles	Presbytery Office, Suite 2, Ground Floor, Ocean Spirit House West, 31 Waterloo Quay, Aberdeen AB11 5BS SCampbell@churchofscotland.org.uk	01224 049933
Jeffrey, Kenneth S. BA BD PhD DMin	2002	2014	Senior Lecturer, School of Divinity, University of Aberdeen	The North Steading, Dalgairn, Cupar KY15 4PH ksjeffrey@btopenworld.com	01334 653196
Lancaster, Craig MA BD	2004	2011	RAF Senior Chaplain	Chaplaincy Centre, RAF Cosford, Wolverhampton WV7 3EX craig.lancaster102@mod.gov.uk	
Mair, Michael J. MStJ BD MTh	2014	2023	Chaplain to UK Oil and Gas Industry	c/o Shell Exploration and Production, Silver Fin Building, 455 Union Street, Aberdeen AB11 6DB michael.mair@ukoilandgaschaplaincy.com	01224 883355
Murray, B. Ian BD	2002	2021	Buildings Officer, Presbytery of the North East and the Northern Isles	Kilmorie House, 6 Institution Road, Elgin IV30 1RP IMurray@churchofscotland.org.uk	0131 376 3647
Smith, Robert L. BS MTh PhD	2000	2024	Mission Development Officer, Presbytery of the North East and the Northern Isles	Presbytery Office, Suite 2, Ground Floor, Ocean Spirit House West, 31 Waterloo Quay, Aberdeen AB11 5BS RSmith@churchofscotland.org.uk	01224 049937 07563 878741
Stewart, William	2015	2016	Ordained Local Minister, Presbytery-wide	Denend, Strichen, Fraserburgh AB43 6RN billandjunes@live.co.uk	01771 637256
Swinton, John (Prof.) BD PhD RMN RNMD FRSE FBA	1999	2012	Master of Christ's College, University of Aberdeen	51 Newburgh Circle, Bridge of Don, Aberdeen AB22 8XA j.swinton@abdn.ac.uk	01224 825637
van Sittert, Paul BA BD	1997	2011	Chaplain: Army	1 LANCS, Salamanca Barracks, Episkopi, BFPO 53 padre.pvs@gmail.com	
Wood, Donald	2023		Assistant Minister, Presbytery-wide	DWood@churchofscotland.org.uk	
Young, David T. BA BD MTh	2007	2022	Chaplain: RAF	Chaplaincy Centre, RAF Honington, Suffolk IP31 ?EE david.young137@mod.gov.uk	

C. Retaining: members of Presbytery

Anderson, Robert J.M. BD FInstLM	1993	2022	(Knockando, Elchies and Archiestown with Rothes)	20 Park Street, Burghead, Elgin IV30 5UG bobjmanderson@gmail.com	01343 835401 07980 750685
Bain, Brian LTh	1980	2007	(Gask with Methven and Logiealmond)	Bayview, 13 Stewart Street, Portgordon, Buckie AB56 5QT bricoreen@gmail.com	01542 831215
Bezuidenhout, Louis C. BA MA BD DD	1978	2020	(Interim Minister, Arrochar with Luss)	76 East Church Street, Buckie AB56 1LQ macbez@gmail.com	01542 839493
Blair, Fyfe BA BD DMin	1989	2019	(Stonehaven: Fetteresso)	19 Crichie Place, Fettercairn, Laurencekirk AB30 ?EZ Fyfe.Blair@churchofscotland.org.uk	01561 340579

Boyd, Barry J. LTh DPS	1993	2020	(Forres: St Laurence)	17 Birnie Crescent, New Elgin IV30 6JG boydbarry34@gmail.com	07887 499895
Boyd, Jean A. MSc BSc BA	2016	2023	(Drumoak-Durris)	11 Hazeldene Road, Aberdeen AB15 8LB	07856 573606
Broadley, Linda J. (Mrs) LTh DipEd	1996	2013	(Dun and Hillside)	Snaefell, Lochside Road, St Cyrus, Montrose DD10 0DB lindabroadley@btinternet.com	01674 850141
Butterfield, John A. BA BD MPhil DipTCP DipCC	1990	2022	(Stromness)	Bring Deeps, Buxa Road, Orphir, Orkney KW17 2RE JButterfield@churchofscotland.org.uk	01856 811707
Cheyne, Regine U. (Mrs) MA BSc BD	1988	2022	(Noth)	38 Morven Place, Aboyne AB34 5EZ RCheyne@churchofscotland.org.uk	
Christie, Andrew C. LTh	1975	2000	(Banchory-Devenick and Maryculter/Cookney)	17 Broadstraik Close, Elrick, Aberdeen AB32 6JP	01224 746888
Cook, James M. BSc MBA MDiv	1999	2023	(Monquhitter and New Byth with Turriff: St Andrew's)	JCook@churchofscotland.org.uk	
Cook, John A. MA BD DMin	1986	2024	(West Gordon (Alford, Strathdon and Rhynie)	John.Cook@churchofscotland.org.uk	
Coutts, Fred MA BD	1973	2012	(Head of Spiritual Care, NHS Grampian)	Ladebank, 1 Manse Place, Hatton, Peterhead AB42 0UQ fred.coutts@btinternet.com	01779 841320
Craggs, Sheila A. (Mrs)	2001	2016	(Auxiliary Minister, Ellon)	7 Morar Court, Ellon AB41 9GG sacraggs@outlook.com	01358 723055
Craig, Anthony J.D. BD	1987	2009	(Glasgow: Maryhill)	4 Hightown, Collieston, Ellon AB41 8RS aacraig@btinternet.com	01358 751247
Daramola, Ibidun B. BA MA PhD	2020	2023	(Associate, Skene)		07395 006113
Duff, Stuart M. BA	1997	2019	(Birnie and Pluscarden with Elgin: High)	7 Kirkton Place, Elgin IV30 6JR stuart.duff@gmail.com	01343 200233
Falconer, James B. MBE BD CertMin	1982	2018	(Chaplain, Aberdeen Royal Hospitals)	3 Brimmond Walk, Westhill AB32 6XH	01224 744621
Ford, Carolyn (Carol) H.M. DSD RSAMD BD	2003	2018	(Edinburgh: St Margaret's)	4 Mitchell Avenue, Huntly AB54 8DW CFord@churchofscotland.org.uk	01464 820332
Fortune, Elsie J. (Mrs) BSc BD	2003	2023	(Aberdeen: St Mary's)	25 Drumthwacket Drive, Portlethen, Aberdeen AB12 4TU EFortune@churchofscotland.org.uk	01224 970345
Gauld, Kay F. BD STM PhD	1999	2023	(Insch-Leslie-Premnay-Oyne)	Camrose, 20a Reidhaven Street, Cullen AB56 4SZ KGauld@churchofscotland.org.uk	07951 059272
Graham, Jennifer D. (Mrs) BA MDiv PhD	2000	2011	(Eday with Stronsay: Moncur Memorial)	Lodge, Stronsay, Orkney KW17 2AN jdgraham67@gmail.com	01857 616487
Greig, Alan BSc BD	1977	2017	(Interim Minister, Avonbridge with Torphichen)	1 Dunnydeer Place, Insch AB52 6HP greig@kincarr.free-online.co.uk	01464 820332
Griffiths, Melvyn J. BTh DipTheol DMin	1978	2021	(Maryculter Trinity)	2 Chalmers Place, Fetterangus AB42 4ED thehayvn@btinternet.com	01771 624684
Hawthorn, Daniel MA BD DMin	1965	2004	(Belhelvie)	7 Crimond Drive, Ellon AB41 8BT donhawthorn@btinternet.com	01358 723981
Johnston, Wilma A. MTheol MTh	2006	2020	(East Mainland)	Notland, Denwick Road, Deerness KW17 2QL rev.wilmajohnston@gmail.com	01856 741318 07706 091968
King, Margaret MA DCS	2002	2012	(Deacon, Bellie with Speymouth)	56 Murrayfield, Fochabers IV32 7EZ margaretking889@gmail.com	01343 820937

Kinsey, Louis BD DipMin TD	1991	2024	(Aberdeen: St Columba's Bridge of Don)	LKinsey@churchofscotland.org.uk	
Lamb, A. Douglas MA	1964	2002	(Dalry: St Margaret's)	9 Luther Drive, Laurencekirk AB30 1FE lamb.edzell@talk21.com	01561 376816
Legge, Rosemary (Mrs) BSc BD MTh	1992	2017	(Cushnie and Tough)	57 High Street, Archiestown, Aberlour AB38 7QZ revrl192@aol.com	01340 810304
Lennox-Trewren, Norman D. CertCS	2018	2023	(Ordained Local Minister, St Cyrus)	32 Haulkerton Crescent, Laurencekirk AB30 1FB NLennoxTrewren@churchofscotland.org.uk	01561 377359 07488 388718
Lundie, Ann V. (Miss) DCS	1972	2007	(Deacon, Aberdeen: St George's Tillydrone)	20 Langdykes Drive, Cove, Aberdeen AB12 3HW ann.lundie@btopenworld.com	01224 898416
Macalister, Eleanor E. DipCEd BD	1994	2006	(Ellon)	Quarryview, Ythan Bank, Ellon AB41 7TH macal1ster@aol.com	01358 761402
Macgregor, Alan BA BD PhD	1992	2022	(Marnoch)	Culag, 139 Main Street, Aberchirder, Huntly AB54 7TB a.macgregor1947@gmail.com	
Macnaughton, G. Fraser H MA BD DipCPC	1982	2024	(Kirkwall: St Magnus Cathedral)	1 Weyland Drive, Kirkwall, Orkney KW15 1WW frasermacnaughton@gmail.com	07703 438415
Macnee, Iain LTh BD MA PhD	1975	2011	(New Pitsligo with Strichen and Tyrie)	Wardend Cottage, Alvah, Banff AB45 3TR macneeiain4@googlemail.com	01261 815647
McAdoo, Michelle RMN BD	2023	2023	(Pioneer Minister, Shetland)	galluswithgod@gmail com	
McKay, Elspeth M. LLB LLM PGCert BD	2014	2023	(Clerk, Presbytery of the North East and the Northern Isles)	Conland Schoolhouse, Forgue, Huntly AB54 6DR EMcKay@churchofscotland.org.uk	07789 993535
McKenna, Edward C. BD DPS	1989	2024	(Aberdeen: South of St Nicholas, Kincorth)	53 Austen Way, Scone, Perth PH2 6FF eddiemckenna15@live.co.uk	01783 458670
McLeish, Robert S. LTh	1970	2000	(Insch-Leslie-Premnay-Oyne)	19 Western Road, Insch AB52 6JR	01464 820749
Mitchell, Valerie A. MA FSA	2019	2022	(Ordained Local Minster: Presbytery-wide)	Brownhill of Ardo, Methlick AB41 7HS VMitchell@churchofscotland.org.uk	01651 806005
Montgomerie, Jean B. (Miss) MA BD	1973	2006	(Forfar: St Margaret's)	12 St Ronan's Place, Peterculter, Aberdeen AB14 0QX revjeanb@tiscali.co.uk	01224 732350
Morton, Alasdair J. MA BD DipEd FEIS	1960	2000	(Bowden with Newtown)	16 St Leonard's Road, Forres IV36 1DW alasgilmor@hotmail.co.uk	01309 671719
Murray, Alistair BD	1984	2018	(Inverness: Trinity)	7 Clunie Street, Banff AB45 1HY a.murray111@btinternet.com	01261 390154
Noble, Alexander B. MA BD ThM	1982	2020	(Saltcoats: North)	93 Snipe Street, Ellon AB41 9FW	01358 268705
Notman, John R. BSc BD	1990	2023	(Dumfries: Troqueer)	2 Burnett Road, Stonehaven AB39 2EZ notman@sky.com	07516 599118
O'Brien, Hugh CSS MTheol	2001	2023	(Macduff)	HOBrien@churchofscotland.org.uk	
Orr, Seòras I. MSc MTh	2018	2023	(Bellie and Speymouth)	SOrr@churchofscotland.org.uk	
Petrie, Kenneth L. MA BD	1984	2024	(Aberdeen: Springfield)	KPetrie@churchofscotland.org.uk	
Pollock, Rosalind (Linda) E. (Miss) BD ThM ThM	2001	2023	(Aberluthnott with Laurencekirk)	17A Kopanga Road, Hastings, Hawke's Bay, New Zealand 4130 RPollock@churchofscotland.org.uk	
Purves, John P. S. MBE BSc BD	1978	2013	(Colombo, Sri Lanka: St Andrew's Scots Kirk)	38 Golf Road, Ballater AB35 5RE revjohnpurves@gmail.com	07746 828930
Reid, Richard M.C. BSc BD MTh	1991	2021	(Foveran)	13 Morningside Crescent, Inverurie AB51 4FA reidricky322@gmail.com	07474 010915

Rodgers, D. Mark BA BD MTh	1987	2021	(Head of Spiritual Care, NHS Grampian)	63 Cordiner Place, Aberdeen AB24 4SB dmrodgers16@gmail.com	07738 418456
Rollo, George B. BD	1974	2010	(Elgin: St Giles' and St Columba's South)	'Struan', 13 Meadow View, Hopeman, Elgin IV30 5PL rollos@gmail.com	01343 835226
Ross, David S. BSc MSc PhD BD	1978	2013	(Chaplain: HM Prison Aberdeen and HM Prison Peterhead)	3–5 Abbey Street, Old Deer, Peterhead AB42 5LN padsross@btinternet.com	01771 623994
Ross, William B. LTh CPS	1988	2016	(Aberdour with Pitsligo)	5 Strathlene Court, Rathven AB55 3DD williamross278@btinternet.com	01542 834418
Sanders, Martyn S. BA CertEd	2013	2020	(Blairdaff and Chapel of Garioch)	140 The Homend, Ledbury, Herefordshire HR8 1BZ	07814 164373
Sheret, Brian S. MA BD DPhil	1982	2009	(Glasgow: Drumchapel Drumry St Mary's)	59 Airyhall Crescent, Aberdeen AB15 7QS	01224 323032
Smith, Morris BD CertCE	1988	2013	(Cromdale and Advie with Dulnain Bridge with Grantown-on-Spey)	1 Urquhart Grove, New Elgin IV30 8TB mosmith.themanse@btinternet.com	01343 545019
Steel, G. Hutton B. MA BD	1982	2022	(Aberdeen: High Hilton)	1 Fairview Road, Bridge of Don, Aberdeen AB22 8ZG Hutton.Steel@churchofscotland.org.uk	07917 012024
Stevenson, Douglas F. BD DipMin DipHE MScR MCOSCA MBACP	1991	2024	(Cullen and Deskford)	98 Main Street, Buckpool, Buckie AB56 1XT dfstevenson@aol.com	
Sutherland, Susan J. (Mrs) BD	2009	2022	(Aberdeen: North)	53 Westhill Grange, Westhill AB32 6QJ susan.sutherland@sky.com	
Swindells, Alison I. LLB BD DMin	1998	2024	(Formartime)	6 Garden Place, Cruden Bay, Peterhead AB42 0WA ASwindells@churchofscotland.org.uk	01779 745301
Tait, Alexander	1967	1995	(Glasgow: St Enoch's Hogganfield)	Ingermas, Evie, Orkney KW17 2PH	01856 751477
Telfer, Iain J.M. BD DPS	1978	2018	(Chaplain: Royal Infirmary of Edinburgh)	66 High Street, Inverurie AB51 3XS iain_telfer@yahoo.co.uk	07749 993070
Thomson, Iain U. MA BD	1970	2011	(Skene)	4 Keirhill Gardens, Westhill AB32 6AZ iainuthomson@googlemail.com	01224 746743
Thorburn, Robert J. BD DipPS	1978	2017	(Fyvie with Rothienorman)	12 Slackadale Gardens, Turriff AB53 4UA rjthorburn@aol.com	01888 562278
Verster, W. Myburgh BA BTh LTh MTh	1981	2019	(Ordiquhill and Cornhill with Whitehills)	32 Newtown Drive, Macduff AB44 1SR myburghverster@gmail.com	
Wallace, William F. BDS BD	1968	2008	(Wick: Pulteneytown and Thrumster)	Lachlan Cottage, 29 Station Road, Banchory AB31 5XX williamfwallace39@gmail.com	01330 822259
Watson, John M. LTh	1989	2009	(Aberdeen: St Mark's)	20 Greystone Place, Newtonhill, Stonehaven AB39 3UL johnmutchwatson2065@btinternet.com	01569 730604 07733 334380
Weir, James J.C.M. BD CertMin	1991	2018	(Aberdeen: St George's Tillydrone)	114 Hilton Heights, Woodside, Aberdeen AB24 4QF	01224 901430
Whyte, David W. LTh	1993	2011	(Boat of Garten, Duthil and Kincardine)	1 Lemanfield Crescent, Garmouth, Fochabers IV32 7LS whytedj@btinternet.com	01343 870667
Wishart, James BD	1986	2009	(Deer)	Upper Westshore, Burray, Orkney KW17 2TE jwishart06@btinternet.com	01856 731672
Youngson, Elizabeth J.B. BD	1996	2015	(Aberdeen: Mastrick)	47 Corse Drive, The Links, Dubford, Aberdeen AB23 8LN elizabeth.youngson@btinternet.com	07788 294745

D. In other appointments: not members of Presbytery

Smith, Hilary W. BD DipMin MTh PhD	1999	2016	Tutor in Theology, Vanuatu Spiritual Care Development Minister	Vaughan Park Anglican Retreat Centre, New Zealand oxfordsmith28@yahoo.co.nz	0064 21 0283 5435
Strachan, David G. BD DPS FRSA	1978	1988	Producer, Religious Television	24 Kemnay Place, Aberdeen AB15 8SG dgstrachan@btinternet.com	01224 324032

E. Retaining: not members of Presbytery

Anderson, David MA BD	1975	1999	(Fordyce)	Rowan Cottage, Aberlour Gardens, Aberlour AB38 9LD maurvid@hotmail.com	01340 871906
Brown, Robert F. MA BD ThM	1971	2008	(Aberdeen: Queen's Cross)	55 Hilton Drive, Aberdeen AB24 4NJ Bjacob546@aol.com	01224 491451
Gardner, Bruce K. MA BD PhD	1988	2011	(Aberdeen: Bridge of Don Oldmachar)	21 Hopetoun Crescent, Bucksburn, Aberdeen AB21 9QY drbrucekgardner@aol.com	07891 186724
Grieg, Charles H.M. MA BD	1976	2016	(Dunrossness and St Ninian's incl. Fair Isle with Sandwick, Cunningsburgh and Quarff)	6 Hayhoull Place, Bigton, Shetland ZE2 9GA chm.greig@btinternet.com	01950 422468
Groves, Ian B. BD CPS	1989	2016	(Inverurie: West)	28 Parkhill Circle, Dyce, Aberdeen AB21 7FN ian@thegroves.me.uk	01224 774380
Hamilton, Helen D. (Miss) BD	1991	2002	(Glasgow: St James' (Pollok))	The Cottage, West Tilbouries, Maryculter, Aberdeen AB12 5GD helenhamilton125@gmail.com	01224 739632
Hobson, Diane L. (Mrs) BA BD	2002	2017	(Aberdeen: St Mark's)	173B Blatchcombe Road, Paignton, Devon TQ3 2JP diane.hobson@me.com	07850 962007
Hutchison, Alison M. (Mrs) BD DipMin	1988	2013	(Chaplain, Aberdeen General Hopsitals)	Ashfield, Drumoak, Banchory AB31 5AG ahutch@hotmail.co.uk	01330 811309
MacLean, Elspeth J. (Mrs) BVMS BD	2011	2021	(Forth: St Paul's)	17 Mameulah Crescent, Newmachar AB21 0WG revmum55@gmail.com	
McDonald, Alan D. LLB BD MTh DLitt DD	1979	2016	(Cameron with St Andrews: St Leonard's)	13 Ashley Hall Gardens, Linlithgow EH49 7DN	
Munro, Flora J. BD DMin	1993	2015	(Portlethen)	87 Gairn Terrace, Aberdeen AB10 6AY floramunro@aol.com	07762 966393
Nicholson, Thomas S. BD DPS	1982	2020	(Gordon: St Michael's with Greenlaw with Legerwood with Westruther)	Sandy Hill, St Margaret's Hope, Orkney KW17 2RN TNicholson@churchofscotland.org.uk	
Robertson, Blair MA BD ThM DipPS	1990	2016	(Head of Chaplaincy and Spiritual Care, NHS Greater Glasgow and Clyde)	West End Guest House, 282 High Street, Elgin IV30 1AG blair.robertson@tiscali.co.uk	07952 558766
Smith, William A. LTh	1972	1978	(Blairdaff with Monymusk)	82 Ashgrove Road West, Aberdeen AB16 5EE bill2us@aol.com	01224 681866
Strachan, Ian M. MA BD	1959	1994	(Ashkirk with Selkirk)	'Cardenwell', Glen Drive, Dyce, Aberdeen AB21 7EN	01224 772028
Williamson, Magnus J.C.	1982	1999	(Fetlar with Yell)	Creekhaven, Houl Road, Scalloway, Shetland ZE1 0XA	01595 880023
Wilson, Andrew G.N. MA BD DMin	1977	2012	(Aberdeen: Rubislaw)	Auchintarph, Coull, Tarland, Aboyne AB34 4TT agn.wilson@gmail.com	01339 880918

F. Inactive: not members of Presbytery

Ferguson, Ronald MA BD ThM DLitt	1972	2001	(Kirkwall: St Magnus Cathedral)	Vinbreck, Orphir, Orkney KW17 2RE ronbluebrazil@aol.com	01856 811353
Forbes, John W.A. BD	1973	1999	(Edzell Lethnot with Fern, Careston and Menmuir with Glenesk)	Little Ennochie Steading, Finzean, Banchory AB31 4LX jr6666@icloud.com	01330 850785
Grainger, Harvey L. LTh	1975	2004	(Kingswells)	13 St Ronan's Crescent, Peterculter, Aberdeen AB14 0RL harveygrainger@btinternet.com	01224 739824
Richardson, Thomas C. LTh ThB	1971	2004	(Cults: West)	19 Kinkell Road, Aberdeen AB15 8HR tomandpatrich@gmail.com	07956 308687
Wilson, Thomas F. BD	1984	1996	(Aberdeen: North of St Andrew)	55 Allison Close, Cove, Aberdeen AB12 3WG	01224 873501
Wood, James L.K.	1967	1995	(Aberdeen: Ruthrieston West)	1 Glen Drive, Dyce, Aberdeen AB21 7EN james@jamesinez.plus.com	01224 722543

G. Readers (active)

Barker, Tim	South Silverford Croft, Longmanhill, Banff AB45 3SB	tbarker05@aol.com	01261 851839
Bell, Robert BSc FIStructE MICE	27 Mearns Drive, Stonehaven AB39 2DZ	r.bell282@btinternet.com	01569 767173 07733 014826
Bichard, Susanna (Mrs)	14 Hanover Court, New Road, Tarves AB41 7LG	smbichard@aol.com	01651 851345
Coles, Stephen B.	43 Mearns Walk, Laurencekirk AB30 1FA	steve@sbcco.com	01561 378400
Cooper, Gordon	4 Springfield Place, Aberdeen AB15 7SF	ga_cooper@hotmail.co.uk	01224 316667
Cumming, Grant P. (Prof)	Dunedin, 2 Reidhaven Street, Elgin IV30 1QG	cumminggrant@gmail.com	01343 540023
Doak, Alan B.	17 Chievres Place, Ellon AB41 9WH	alanbdoak@aol.com	01358 721819
Findlay, Patricia (Mrs)	Douglas View, Tullynessle, Alford AB33 8QR	p.a.findlay@btopenworld.com	01975 562379
Forbes, Jean (Mrs)	Greenmoss, Drybridge, Buckie AB56 5JB	dancingfeet49@tinyworld.co.uk	01542 831646 07974 760337
Forsyth, Alicia (Mrs)	Rothie Inn Farm, Forgue Road, Rothienorman, Inverurie AB51 8YH	aliciaforsyth56@gmail.com	01651 821359
Gillespie, Jean (Mrs)	16 St Colm's Quadrant, Eday, Orkney KW16 3PH	jrw2810@btinternet.com	01856 701406
Givan, James	Zimra, Longmanhill, Banff AB45 3RP	jim.givan@btinternet.com	01261 833318
Grant, Margaret (Mrs)	22 Elphin Street, New Aberlour, Fraserburgh AB43 6LH	mgrant3120@gmail.com	01346 561341
Gray, Peter M.D. (Prof.)	165 Countesswells Road, Aberdeen AB15 7RA	pmdgray@bcs.org.uk	01224 318172
Greig, Martin	85 Macaulay Drive, Aberdeen AB15 8FL	mgreig@aberdeencity.gov.uk	07920 806332
Harrison, Christine BA	16 Allt-Na-Coire, Tomnavoulin, Ballindalloch AB37 9JE	chrstnhrrsn42@googlemail.com	01897 590630
Howard, Chris	Pegal, Glaitness Road, Kirkwall KW17 1BA	2201csb@gmail.com	01856 873271
Jones, Josephine (Mrs) BA CertEd LRAM	Moorside, Firth, Orkney KW17 2JZ	yetminstermusic@googlemail.com	01856 761899
MacLeod, Ali (Ms)	11 Pitfour Crescent, Fetterangus, Peterhead AB42 4EL	macleoda2@gmail.com	01771 622992
Macnee, Anthea (Mrs)	Wardend Cottage, Alvah, Banff AB45 3TR	macneeiain4@googlemail.com	01261 815647
Mair, Dorothy L.T. (Miss)	Flat F, 15 The Quay, Newburgh, Ellon AB41 6DA	dorothymair2@aol.com	01358 788832
McCafferty, W. John	Lynwood, Cammachmore, Stonehaven AB39 3NR	wjmccafferty@yahoo.co.uk	07768 925122
McDonald, Rhoda (Miss)	16 St Andrew's Drive, Fraserburgh AB43 9AW	techmc56@gmail.com	01346 514052
McFie, David	The Manse, Fordyce Terrace, New Deer, Turriff AB53 6TD	waverley710@gmx.co.uk	01771 644631 07713 734647

Middleton, Robin B. (Capt.)	7 St Ternan's Road, Newtonhill, Stonehaven AB39 3PF	robbiemiddleton7@hotmail.com	01569 730852
Mitchell, Jean (Mrs)	6 Cowgate, Oldmeldrum, Inverurie AB51 0EN	j.g.mitchell@btinternet.com	01651 872745
Pirie, Maggie (Mrs)	Uppermill Cottage, Auchterless, Turriff AB53 8AU	maggie.pirie@btinternet.com	01888 511059
Pomfret, Valerie (Mrs)	3 Clumly Avenue, Kirkwall, Orkney KW15 1YU	vpomfret@btinternet.com	
Robertson, Johan (Mrs)	Essonquoy, Eday, Orkney KW17 2AB	essonquoy@btinternet.com	01857 622251
Simpson, Andrew C.	10 Wood Street, Banff AB45 1JX	andy.louise1@btinternet.com	01261 812538
Simpson, Elizabeth (Mrs)	Connemara, 33 Golf Road, Ballater AB35 5RS	connemara33@yahoo.com	01339 755597
Sneddon, Richard	100 West Road, Peterhead AB42 2AQ	richard.sneddon@btinternet.com	01779 480803 07985 384029

H. Ministries Development Staff

Adam, Pamela BD	Ellon – Parish Assistant	PAdam@churchofscotland.org.uk
Amalanand, John C.	Aberdeen: Devana – Mission Development Worker, Families and Students	JAmalanand@churchofscotland.org.uk
Angus, Natalie	Dyce – Youth and Family Worker	NAngus@churchofscotland.org.uk
Baker, Paula (Mrs)	Elgin – Parish Assistant	PBaker@churchofscotland.org.uk
Blair, Fiona DCS	Kingshill – Deacon	FBlair@churchofscotland.org.uk
Bruce, Nicola P.S. BA MTh	Ellon – Parish Assistant, Mission Development	NBruce@churchofscotland.org.uk
Crouch, Simon A. MCIPD CertCS	West Gordon (Alford, Strathdon, Rhynie) – Parish Assistant	SCrouch@churchofscotland.org.uk
Dick, Janet	Presbytery – Mission and Discipleship Development Worker	Janet.Dick@churchofscotland.org.uk
Griffiths Weir, K. Ellen	Shetland – Youth and Children's Worker	EWeir@churchofscotland.org.uk
Ledgerwood, Morag	Brimmond – Ministerial Assistant	MLedgerwood@churchofscotland.org.uk
Mitchell, William	Aberdeen: Hillside – Parish Assistant	WMitchell@churchofscotland.org.uk
Richardson, Frances	Shetland – Administrator and Treasurer	FRichardson@churchofscotland.org.uk
Simms, Michele MA	Shetland – Parish Development Worker	MSimms@churchofscotland.org.uk
Stigant, Victoria J.	Presbytery – Youth Work Facilitator	VStigant@churchofscotland.org.uk
Taylor, Valerie AssocCIPD PGDip	Aberdeen: South – Ministry Assistant	VTaylor@churchofscotland.org.uk
Thomas, Jay MA BA	Aberdeen: North – Church and Community Worker	JThomas@churchofscotland.org.uk

ABERDEEN ADDRESSES

Bridge of Don Oldmachar	Ashwood Park	Hillside	Hilton Drive	St Machar's Cathedral	The Chanonry
		Mannofield	Great Western Road x Craigton Road	St Mary's	King Street
Devana	Fonthill Road x Polmuir Road; and Holburn Street	North	Greenfern Road, Mastrick	St Stephen's	Powis Place
		St Columba's Bridge of Don	Braehead Way, Bridge of Don	South	Walker Road
Fountainhall	Albyn Place; and and Mid Stocket Road			Springfield	Springfield Road
		St John's for the Deaf	at Devana, Fonthill Road	Stockethill	Cairncry Community Centre

Worship in the Parish of Shetland held at:

Aith	11 Wirliegert, Aith, Bixter ZE2 9NW	Lunna St Margaret's	Methodist Chapel, Vidlin, Lunnasting ZE2 9QE
Baltasound St John's	Baltasound, Unst ZE2 9DX	Ollaberry	Ollaberry, Northmavine ZE2 9QW
Brae	Grindwell, Brae, Delting ZE2 9QW	Sandwick	Sandwick ZE2 9HW
Bridgend, Burra Isle	Freefield Road, Bridge End, Burra Isle ZE2 9LD	Scalloway	Main Street, Scalloway ZE1 0TR
Cullivoe	Cullivoe, Yell ZE2 9DD	Walls St Paul's	Pier Road, Walls ZE2 9PF
Lerwick St Columba's	Greenfield Place, Lerwick ZE1 0EQ	Whalsay	Church Hall, Symbister, Whalsay ZE2 9AD

(10) CLÈIR EILEAN Ì: HIGHLANDS AND HEBRIDES (F W)

New presbytery formed by the union of the presbyteries of Argyll, Abernethy, Inverness, Lochaber, Ross, Sutherland, Caithness, Lochcarron-Skye and Uist. Meets in hybrid form (online and within hubs located throughout the presbytery) four or five times a year, including Saturday 16 November 2024, Tuesday 11 March 2025 and Saturday 21 June 2025.

Clerk: REV. RODERICK A.R. MacLEOD MA MBA BD DMin	**CleirEileanI@churchofscotland.org.uk**	**07841 654281**
Presbytery Office:	**Mrs Amanda Anderson, Presbytery Support Officer, Birchwood, Auchterawe, Fort Augustus PH32 4BT** **AAnderson@churchofscotland.org.uk**	**07906 758720**

1	**Abernethy (F H W) linked with Boat of Garten (H), Carrbridge (H) and Kincardine (F W)**				
	Graham T. Atkinson MA BD MTh	2006	2019	The Manse, Deshar Road, Boat of Garten PH24 3BN GAtkinson@churchofscotland.org.uk	01479 831637
2	**Acharacle (H) and Ardnamurchan (F W) linked with Ardgour, Morvern and Strontian (F H T W)**				
	Donald G.B. McCorkindale BD DipMin	1992	2011	The Manse, 2 The Meadows, Strontian, Acharacle PH36 4HZ DMcCorkindale@churchofscotland.org.uk	01967 402234 07554 176580
	E. Jade Maclean BD MTh (Assistant Minister)	2024		Daldregnish, Glenelg, by Kyle IV40 8JT JMaclean@churchofscotland.org.uk	07725 703029
3	**Alness (F W)**				
	Philip Gunn BSc BA	2020		The Manse, 15 Perrins Road, Alness IV17 0SX PGunn@churchofscotland.org.uk	01349 884252
				New charge formed by the union of Alness and Rosskeen	
4	**Altnaharra and Farr (F W) linked with Melness and Tongue (F H)**				
	Vacant			The Manse, Bettyhill, Thurso KW14 7SS	01641 521208
	Interim Moderator: Mary J. Stobo			MStobo@churchofscotland.org.uk	01863 766868
5	**Alvie and Insh (F H W) linked with Rothiemurchus and Aviemore (F H W)**				
	Charles J. Finnie LTh DPS	1991	2019	The Manse, 8 Dalfaber Park, Aviemore PH22 1QF CFinnie@churchofscotland.org.uk	01479 810280

6	**Appin and Lismore (F)**				
	Dugald J. Cameron BD DipMin MTh	1990	2021	An Mansa, 11 Tynribbie Place, Appin, Argyll PA38 4DS Dugald.Cameron@churchofscotland.org.uk	01631 730280
				New charge formed by the union of Appin and Lismore	
7	**Ardchattan (F H W) linked with Coll (F W) linked with Connel (F W)**				
	Willem J. Bezuidenhout BA BD MHEd MEd	1977	2019	St Oran's Manse, Connel, Oban PA37 1PJ WBezuidenhout@churchofscotland.org.uk	01631 710214 07484 333923 Coll 01879 230366
8	**Ardgour, Morvern and Strontian** See Acharacle and Ardnamurchan				
9	**Assynt, Rosehall and Scourie (F W)**			**info@assyntcofs.org**	
	Iain A. MacLeod BA	2012	2020	The Manse, Canisp Road, Lochinver, Lairg IV27 4LH IMacleod@churchofscotland.org.uk	01571 844342 07795 014889
				New charge formed by the union of Assynt and Stoer, Eddrachillis and Rosehall	
10	**Barra (GD) linked with South Uist (GD W)**				
	Vacant			The Manse, Cuithir, Grean, Isle of Barra HS9 5XU	01871 810230
	Interim Moderators: Gavin J. Elliott			gavkondwani@gmail.com	01870 602726
	Aileen Binner			ABinner@churchofscotland.org.uk	01631 710264
11	**Benbecula (F GD H) linked with Carinish (F GD H W)**			**info@carinish-church.org.uk**	
	Vacant				
	Ishabel Macdonald (Ordained Local Minister)	2011		'Cleat Afe Ora', 18 Carinish, Isle of North Uist HS6 5HN Ishie.Macdonald@churchofscotland.org.uk	01876 580367
12	**Berneray and Lochmaddy (GD H) linked with Kilmuir and Paible (GD)**				
	Alen J.R. McCulloch MA BD	1990	2017	Church of Scotland Manse, Paible, Isle of North Uist HS6 5HD AMcCulloch@churchofscotland.org.uk	01876 510310
13	**Black Isle East (W)**				
	Warren R. Beattie BSc BD MSc PhD	1990	2019	5 Ness Way, Fortrose IV10 8SS WBeattie@churchofscotland.org.uk	01381 620111
				New charge formed by the union of Avoch, Cromarty, and Fortrose and Rosemarkie	
14	**Boat of Garten, Carrbridge and Kincardine** See Abernethy				

15 Bracadale, Duirinish and Snizort (GD)
Gary N. Wilson CertDM BD | 1996 | 2023 | 3 Stormyhill Terrace, Portree, Isle of Skye IV51 9DZ | 07777 641570
Gary.Wilson@churchofscotland.org.uk
New charge formed by the union of Bracadale and Duirinish, and Snizort

16 Bute, Isle of (F H W)
Sibyl A. Tchaikovsky BA BD MLitt | 2018 | 12 Crichton Road, Rothesay, Isle of Bute PA20 9JR | 01700 504047
STchaikovsky@churchofscotland.org.uk
New charge formed by the union of Rothesay: Trinity and the United Church of Bute

17 Campbeltown: (F H W) linked with Saddell and Carradale (H W) linked with Southend (F H W) (South Kintyre)
Steven Sass BTh MDiv LTh | 2001 | 2023 | The Manse, Southend, Campbeltown PA28 6RQ | 07838 434416
SSass@churchofscotland.org.uk

18 Carinish See Benbecula

19 Clyne (H W) linked with Kildonan and Loth Helmsdale (F H W) info@brorachurchofscotland.org
Vacant | 40 Golf Road, Brora KW9 6QS | 01408 536005
Session Clerk, Clyne: Sydney L. Barnett | sydneylb43@gmail.com | 01408 621569
07376 778270
Session Clerk, Kildonan and Loth Helmsdale: Ina MacPherson (Mrs) | inamacpherson123@btinternet.com | 01431 821378

20 Coll See Ardchattan

21 Colonsay and Oronsay (W) linked with Netherlorn (F W)
Trudi Newton MA BD | 2023 | The Manse, Kilmelford, Oban PA34 4XA | 07398 667113
TNewton@churchofscotland.org.uk

22 Connel See Ardchattan

23 Contin (H W) linked with Fodderty and Strathpeffer (F H W)
Ronald Gall BSc BD | 1985 | 2021 | The Manse, Contin, Strathpeffer IV14 9ES | 01997 421028
RGall@churchofscotland.org.uk

24	**Cowal Kirk (F H W)**			**admin@cowalkirk.org**	
	Everisto Musedza BTh	2015	2023	The Manse, 13 Dhailling Park, Hunter Street, Kirn, Dunoon, PA23 8FB	01369 702256 07748 347487
				EMusedza@churchofscotland.org.uk	
	Alexander J. (Sandy) MacPherson MA BSc FRSA (Ordained Local Minister)	2021		8 Queens View, Marine Parade, Kirn, Dunoon PA23 8LF SMacPherson@churchofscotland.org.uk	01369 707969
25	**Cromdale (H) and Advie (F W) linked with Grantown-on-Spey and Dulnain Bridge (F H W)**				
	Vacant				
	Session Clerk, Cromdale and Advie: Diane Brazier (Mrs)			dbrazier39@gmail.com	01479 872547
	Session Clerk, Grantown-on-Spey and Dulnain Bridge: William Steele (Dr)			wmsteele33@aol.com	01479 870154
26	**Culloden and Ardersier (F H W)**			**admin@barnchurch.org.uk**	**01463 798946**
	Pamela Kennedy BA PGCE MEd MSc BA	2022	2024	45 Oakdene Court, Culloden IV2 7XL PKennedy@churchofscotland.org.uk	07812 994424
	New charge formed by the union of Ardersier, Culloden: The Barn, and Petty				
27	**Dalriada Mid Argyll (F T W)**				
	David Carruthers BD	1998		The Manse, Kilduskland Road, Ardrishaig, Lochgilphead PA30 8HE DCarruthers@churchofscotland.org.uk	01546 603269
28	**Dingwall: Castle Street (F H W)**				
	Drausio P. Goncalves	1993	2019	16 Achany Road, Dingwall IV15 9JB DGoncalves@churchofscotland.org.uk	01349 888379
29	**Dingwall: St Clement's (H W)**				
	Bruce Dempsey BD	1997	2014	8 Castlehill Road, Dingwall IV15 9PB BDempsey@churchofscotland.org.uk	01349 292055
30	**Dornoch Firth (F H W)**				
	Vacant			1 Allan Gardens, Dornoch IV25 3PD	01862 810296
	Interim Moderator: Alistair J. Drummond			ADrummond@churchofscotland.org.uk	01349 852480
	New charge formed by the union of Creich, Dornoch Cathedral and Kincardine, Croick and Edderton				
31	**Durness and Kinlochbervie (F W)**				
	Andrea M. Boyes (Mrs) RMN BA(Theol)	2013	2017	Manse Road, Kinlochbervie, Lairg IV27 4RG ABoyes@churchofscotland.org.uk	01971 521287

32	**Dyke and Edinkillie (F W)**				
	Richard G. Moffat BD	1994	2019	Dyke and Edinkillie Manse,Westview, Mundole, Forres IV36 2TA RMoffat@churchofscotland.org.uk	01309 271321
33	**Easter Ross Peninsula (F W)**			**enquiries@easter-rosscofs.co.uk**	
	Vacant			14 Kingsway Avenue, Tain IV19 1NJ	01862 892296
	Interim Moderator: Philip Gunn			PGunn@churchofscotland.org.uk	01349 884252
	New charge formed by the union of Fearn Abbey and Nigg, Tain and Tarbat				
34	**Ferintosh (F W)**				
	Stephen Macdonald BD MTh	2008	2018	Ferintosh Manse, Leanaig Road, Conon Bridge, Dingwall IV7 8BE SMacdonald@churchofscotland.org.uk	01349 861275 07570 804193
35	**Fodderty and Strathpeffer** See Contin				
36	**Fort Augustus (F W) linked with Glengarry (W)**				
	Anthony M. Jones BD DPS DipTheol CertMin FRSA	1994	2018	The Manse, Fort Augustus PH32 4BH AJones@churchofscotland.org.uk	01320 366210
37	**Fort William Kilmallie (F H W) linked with Kilmonivaig (F W)**				
	David R. Sim MA BA	2023		The Manse, The Parade, Fort William PH33 6BA DSim@churchofscotland.org.uk	01397 702297
	Rory N. MacLeod BA BD (Associate Minister)	1986	2021	Kilmallie Manse, Corpach, Fort William PH33 7JS RNMacLeod@churchofscotland.org.uk	01397 772736
38	**Glengarry** See Fort Augustus				
39	**Glenorchy and Strathfillan (W)**				
	Vacant				
	Session Clerk: Janet Buchanan (Mrs)			janetbuchanan567@btinternet.com	01866 833308
40	**Golspie (W)**			**pray@standrewgolspie.org**	
	John B. Sterrett BA BD PhD	2007		The Manse, Fountain Road, Golspie KW10 6TH JSterret@churchofscotland.org.uk	Tel/Fax 01408 633295
41	**Grantown-on-Spey and Dulnain Bridge** See Cromdale and Advie				

42	**Halkirk Westerdale (F) linked with Watten**				
	Vacant				
	Interim Moderator: Sheila Cormack (Mrs)			Wester Cottage, Dunnet, by Thurso KW14 8XP	01847 851274
43	**Invergordon (F W)**			**invergordonparishchurch@live.co.uk**	
	Brian Macleod BA MDiv	2021	2022	The Manse, Cromlet Drive, Invergordon IV18 0BA BMacleod@churchofscotland.org.uk	
44	**Inverness: Crown (F H W)**			**office@crown-church.co.uk**	**01463 231140**
	Douglas R. Robertson BSc BD	1991	2020	39 Southside Road, Inverness IV2 4XA DRRobertson@churchofscotland.org.uk	01463 230537
45	**Inverness: Hilton (F W)**			**office@hiltonchurch.org.uk**	**01463 233310**
	Duncan MacPherson LLB DipLP BD	1994		66 Culduthel Mains Crescent, Inverness IV2 6RG DMacPherson@churchofscotland.org.uk	01463 231417
46	**Inverness: Inshes East (F H W)**			**office@insheschurch.org**	**01463 226727**
	David S. Scott MA BD	1987	2013	48 Redwood Crescent, Milton of Leys, Inverness IV2 6HB David.Scott@churchofscotland.org.uk	01463 772402
47	**Inverness: Kinmylies (F H W)**				**01463 714035**
	Scott Polworth LLB BD	2009	2018	2 Balnafettack Place, Inverness IV3 8TQ SPolworth@churchofscotland.org.uk	01463 559137
48	**Inverness: Ness Bank (F H T W)**			**nessbankchurch@gmail.com**	**01463 221812**
	Stuart J. Smith BEng BD MTh	1994	2024	15 Ballifeary Road, Inverness IV3 5PJ Stuart.Smith@churchofscotland.org.uk	01463 220332 07800 510150
49	**Inverness: Old High St Stephen's (F T W)**			**invernesschurch@gmail.com**	**07934 285924**
	Vacant			24 Damfield Road, Inverness IV2 3HU	01463 250802
	Interim Moderator: Duncan MacPherson			DMacPherson@churchofscotland.org.uk	01463 231417
50	**Inverness: St Columba (F H T W)**			**info@stcolumbainverness.org**	
	Scott A. McRoberts BD MTh	2012		25 Moriston Road, Inverness IV2 6HN SMcRoberts@churchofscotland.org.uk	01463 832601

New charge formed by the union of Dores and Boleskine and Inverness: St Columba

51 Inverness: Trinity Dalneigh (F GD H W)
Vacant 9 St Mungo Road, Inverness IV3 5AS 01463 232339
Interim Moderator: Len Cazaly len_cazaly@btinternet.com 01463 794469
New charge formed by the union of Inverness: Dalneigh and Bona and Inverness: Trinity

52 Iona and the Ross of Mull (W) linked with North Mull (F GD H W)
Vacant
Session Clerk, Iona and RoM: Linda Dawson (Mrs) Maolbhuide, Fionnphort, Isle of Mull PA66 6BP 01681 700718
Interim Moderator: Alison Hay AHay@churchofscotland.org.uk 01546 886213
Iona and the Ross of Mull was formed by the union of Iona and Kilfinichen and Kilvickeon and the Ross of Mull

53 Jura (F GD) linked with North and West Islay (F GD) linked with South Islay (F GD H W) (Islay and Jura)
William F. Hunter MA BD 1986 2023 The Manse, Bowmore, Isle of Islay PA43 7LH 01496 810271
WHunter@churchofscotland.org.uk

54 Kilchrenan and Dalavich (W) linked with Muckairn (W)
Thomas W. Telfer BA MDiv 1986 2018 Muckairn Manse, Taynuilt PA35 1HW 01866 822204
TTelfer@churchofscotland.org.uk

55 Kildonan and Loth Helmsdale See Clyne

56 Killearnan (F H W)
Vacant

57 Kilmonivaig See Fort William Kilmallie

58 Kilmorack and Erchless (F W)
Ian A. Manson BA BD 1989 2016 'Roselynn', Croyard Road, Beauly IV4 7DJ 01463 783824
IManson@churchofscotland.org.uk

59 Kilmore and Oban (F GD W) linked with Tiree (F GD W) **obancofs@btinternet.com** **01631 562405**
Alexander MacCallum 2023 Kilmore and Oban Manse, Ganavan Road, Oban PA34 5TU 01631 566253
AMacCallum@churchofscotland.org.uk

60 Kilmuir and Logie Easter (F)
Alistair J. Drummond BSc BD ThM 1986 2020 Ellandonan, 9 Saltburn, Invergordon IV18 0JX 01349 852480
ADrummond@churchofscotland.org.uk

61 Kilmuir and Paible See Berneray and Lochmaddy

62 Kilmuir and Stenscholl (F GD)

Vacant			1 Totescore, Kilmuir, Isle of Skye IV51 9YN	01470 542297
Interim Moderator: John H. Lamont			jhlamont@btinternet.com	01445 731888 07714 720753

63 Kilmun, Strone and Ardentinny: The Shore Kirk (H W) linked with West Cowal (F H W) (Rural Cowal)
information@westcowalchurches.org.uk

Andrew J. Robertson BD	2008	2024	West Cowal Manse, Kames, Tighnabruaich PA21 2AD ARobertson@churchofscotland.org.uk	01700 811045
Janet K. MacKellar BSc ProfCertMgmt FCMI (Ordained Local Minister)	2019		Laurel Bank, 23 George Street, Dunoon PA23 8TE JMackellar@churchofscotland.org.uk	01369 705549

64 Kiltarlity and Kirkhill (F W)

Andrew (Drew) P. Kuzma DipTheol BA	2007	2021	Wardlaw Manse, Wardlaw Road, Kirkhill IV5 7NZ AKuzma@churchofscotland.org.uk	01463 831132

65 Kiltearn (H)

Donald A. MacSween BD	1991	1993	The Manse, Swordale Road, Evanton, Dingwall IV16 9UZ DMacSween@churchofscotland.org.uk	01349 830472

66 Kingussie (F H W) linked with Laggan (H) and Newtonmore (H W)

Vacant			The Manse, Fort William Road, Newtonmore PH20 1DG	01540 673238
Session Clerk, Kingussie: Sandy Peebles (Mr)			sandy@ats.me.uk	01540 661965
Session Clerk, Laggan and Newtonmore: Alison Armstrong (Mrs)			alisonmabel@hotmail.com	07841 502991

67 Knockbain (F H W)
Vacant

68 Laggan and Newtonmore See Kingussie

69 Lairg (F H W) linked with Rogart (H W)

Vacant				
Hilary M. Gardner (Miss) (Auxiliary Minister)	2010	2018	Cayman Lodge, Kincardine Hill, Ardgay IV24 3DJ HGardner@churchofscotland.org.uk	01863 766107
Interim Moderator: Sydney L. Barnett			sydneylb43@gmail.com	01408 621569

70 Latheron (W) — **parish-of-latheron@btconnect.com**
Vacant — Central Manse, Main Street, Lybster KW3 6BN — 01593 721706
Heather Stewart (Mrs) (Ordained Local Minister) — 2013 2017 — Burnthill, Thrumster, Wick KW1 5TR — 01955 651717
Heather.Stewart@churchofscotland.org.uk

71 Lochbroom and Ullapool (F GD W) — **info@ullapoolkirk.co.uk** — **01854 612360**
Heidi J. Hercus BA — 2018 — The Manse, 11 Royal Park, Mill Street, Ullapool IV26 2XT — 01854 613146
HHercus@churchofscotland.org.uk

72 Lochgoilhead (H) and Kilmorich linked with Strachur and Strathlachlan (Upper Cowal)
Robert K. Mackenzie MA BD PhD — 1976 1998 — The Manse, Strachur, Cairndow PA27 8DG — 01369 860246
RKMackenzie@churchofscotland.org.uk

73 Manish-Scarista (GD H)
Vacant — Church of Scotland Manse, Scarista, Isle of Harris HS3 3HX — 01859 550200
Session Clerk: Paul Alldred — paul.alldred@outlook.com — 01859 520494

74 Melness and Tongue See Altnaharra and Farr

75 Mid Kintyre and Gigha (H W) linked with Tarbert, Loch Fyne and Kilberry (F H W) (North Kintyre)
Lyn M. Peden (Mrs) BD — 2010 2020 — The Manse, Campbeltown Road, Tarbert, Argyll PA29 6SX — 01880 820158
LPeden@churchofscotland.org.uk

76 Muckairn See Kilchrenan and Dalavich

77 Nairn: Old (H W) — **secretary.nairnold@btconnect.com** — **01667 452382**
Alison C. Mehigan BD DPS — 2003 2015 — 15 Chattan Gardens, Nairn IV12 4QP — 01667 453777
AMehigan@churchofscotland.org.uk

78 Nairn: St Ninian's (H) and Auldearn and Dalmore (F W)
Vacant — The Manse, Auldearn, Nairn IV12 5SX — 01667 451675

79 Netherlorn See Colonsay and Oronsay
80 North and West Islay See Jura

81	**North Coast (F W)**			**northcoastparish@gmail.com**	
	Vacant				
	Session Clerk: Graham Cameron			cameroncroik@gmail.com	01641 571246
82	**North Mull** See Iona and Ross of Mull				
83	**North West Lochaber (F H W)**				
	Vacant			Church of Scotland Manse, Annie's Brae, Mallaig PH41 4RG	01687 462514
	Session Clerk: John Arnold			JohnArnold_129502@churchofscotland,org.uk	01687 460008
84	**Pentland**				
	Janet A. Easton-Berry BA BA	2016	2021	The Manse, Canisbay, Wick KW1 4YH JEaston-Berry@churchofscotland.org.uk	01955 611551
85	**Portree (GD W)**				
	Sandor Fazakas BD MTh	1977	2007	Viewfield Road, Portree, Isle of Skye IV51 9ES SFazakas@churchofscotland.org.uk	01478 611868
86	**Resolis and Urquhart (W)**				
	Terrance T. Burns BA MA	2004	2017	The Manse, Culbokie, Dingwall IV7 8JN TBurns@churchofscotland.org.uk	01349 877452
	Carol Rattenbury BA (Ordained Local Minister)	2017	2022	Balloan Farm House, Alcaig, Conon Bridge, Dingwall IV7 8HU CRattenbury@churchofscotland.org.uk	01349 877323
87	**Rogart** See Lairg				
88	**Rothiemurchus and Aviemore** See Alvie and Insh				
89	**Saddell and Carradale** See Campbeltown				
90	**South Islay** See Jura				
91	**South Lochaber (H W)**				
	Malcolm A. Kinnear MA BD PhD	2010		The Manse, 9 Cameron Brae, Kentallen, Appin PA38 4BF MKinnear@churchofscotland.org.uk	01631 561815 07710 474433
	Marion Kinnear (Mrs) BD (Auxiliary Minister)	2009	2021	The Manse, 9 Cameron Brae, Kentallen, Appin PA38 4BF Marion.Kinnear@churchofscotland.org.uk	01631 561815 07519 635976
				New charge formed by the union of Kinlochleven and South Lochaber	
92	**South Uist** See Barra				

93 South-West Ross (F GD W)

Frederick W. Vincent BA BD MPhil	1990	2021	**admin@swrossparish.com** The Manse, Glebe Road, Inverinate, Kyle of Lochalsh IV40 8HE FVincent@churchofscotland.org.uk	07971 507952

New charge formed by the union of Applecross, Lochcarron and Torridon and Glenelg, Kintail and Lochalsh

94 Southend See Campbeltown
95 Strachur and Strathlachlan See Lochgoilhead and Kilmorich

96 Strath and Sleat (F GD W)

Vacant				
Session Clerk: Nicola Thomson			The Manse, 6 Upper Breakish, Isle of Skye IV42 8PY strathandsleat@gmail.com	01471 822416 07825 302548

97 Strathnairn and Strathdearn

Robert E. Brookes BD	2009	2016	Hillswick, Regoul, Geddes, Nairn IV12 5SB RBrookes@churchofscotland.org.uk	01667 404686

New charge formed by the union of Cawdor, Croy and Dalcross, Daviot and Dunlichity, and Moy, Dalarossie and Tomatin

98 Tarbert (F GD H T W)

Ian Murdo M. MacDonald DPA BD	2001	2015	The Manse, Manse Road, Tarbert, Isle of Harris HS3 3DF Ian.MacDonald@churchofscotland.org.uk	01859 502231

99 Tarbert, Loch Fyne and Kilberry See Mid Kintyre and Gigha

100 Thurso: St Peter's and St Andrew's (F H W)

David S.M. Malcolm BD	2011	2014	11 Castle Gardens, Barrock Street, Thurso KW14 7GZ David.Malcolm@churchofscotland.org.uk	01847 895186

101 Thurso: West (H W)

Vacant				
Interim Moderator: Lyall Rennie			LRennie@churchofscotland.org.uk	01955 611756

102 Tiree See Kilmore and Oban

103 Tomintoul (H), Glenlivet and Inveraven

Guardianship of the Presbytery				
Session Clerk: Margo Stuart (Mrs)			margoandedward@hotmail.co.uk	01807 580239

104 Urquhart and Glenmoriston (F H W)			**info@lochnesschurch.org**	
Vacant			Blairbeg, Drumnadrochit, Inverness IV3 6UG	01456 450231
Interim Moderator: Adrian P.J. Varwell			adrian.varwell@btinternet.com	01456 459352
105 Urray and Kilchrist (F W)			**urraychurch@gmail.com**	
Monika R.W. Redman BA BD	2003	2021	Woodville, Ord Road, Muir of Ord IV6 7XL MRedman@churchofscotland.org.uk	01463 871625
106 Watten See Halkirk Westerdale				
107 West Cowal See Kilmun, Strone and Ardentinny: The Shore Kirk				
108 West Lochfyneside: Cumlodden, Inveraray and Lochgair (F W)				
Dorothy M. Wallace BA	2021		The Manse, Inveraray PA32 8XT Dorothy.Wallace@churchofscotland.org.uk	01499 302480
109 West Moray (F W)				
Vacant (Moderator)			St Leonard's Manse, Nelson Road, Forres IV36 1DR	01309 672380
Dewald Louw BTh MDiv (Team Minister)	2007	2021	The Manse, 4 Manse Road, Kinloss, Forres IV36 3GH DLouw@churchofscotland.org.uk	01309 690474 07464 847803
Stuart A. Finlayson BA (Community Pioneer Minister)	2022		SFinlayson@churchofscotland.org.uk	07557 472745
John A. Morrison BSc BA PGCE (Ordained Local Minister)	2013		35 Kirkton Place, Elgin IV30 6JR JMorrison@churchofscotland.org.uk	01343 550199
New charge formed by the union of Alves and Burghead, Dallas, Forres: St Leonard's, Forres: St Laurence, Kinloss and Findhorn and Rafford				
110 West Ross (F)			**ganddcofs@gmail.com**	
Vacant			Church of Scotland Manse, The Glebe, Gairloch IV21 2BT	01445 712645
Session Clerk: Donald E. MacRae			demacrae@btinternet.com	01455 712235
Gairloch and Dundonnell has been renamed West Rosss				
111 Wick: Pulteneytown and Thrumster (H W)				
Vacant			The Manse, Coronation Street, Wick KW1 5LS	01955 606192
Interim Moderator: Janet A. Easton-Berry			JEaston-Berry@churchofscotland.org.uk	01955 611551
112 Wick: St Fergus (F W)			**contact@wickstferguschurch.org.uk**	
Vacant			Mansefield, Miller Avenue, Wick KW1 4DF	01955 602167
Interim Moderator: Linda J. Broadley			lindabroadley@btinternet.com	01674 850141

B. In other appointments: members of Presbytery

Anderson, David P. BSc BD	2002	2007	Senior Army Chaplain	51 Infantry Brigade and HQ Scotland, Forthside, Stirling FK7 7RR David.Anderson646@mod.gov.uk	
Archer, Morven (Mrs)	2013	2020	Ordained Local Minister: Presbytery Assistant Minister, Inverness area	42 Firthview Drive, Inverness IV3 8QE MArcher@churchofscotland.org.uk	01463 237840
Cord, Susan	2016	2023	Chaplain, Raigmore Hospital, Inverness	Raigmore Hospital, Old Perth Road, Inverness IV2 3UJ susan.cord@nhs.scot	01463 731930
Fraser, Jonathan MA(Div) MTh ThM PhD	2012	2019	Lecturer: Highland Theological College	9 Broom Drive, Inverness IV2 4EG Jonathan.Fraser@uhi.ac.uk	07749 539981
MacLeod, Roderick A.R. MA MBA BD DMin	1994	2023	Presbytery Clerk, Clèir Eilean Ì: Highlands and Islands	7 Goathill Crescent, Stornoway, Isle of Lewis HS1 2TA RMacLeod@churchofscotland.org.uk	07841 654281
Morrison, Hector BSc BD MTh CertITL	1981	2009	Principal: Highland Theological College	24 Oak Avenue, Inverness IV2 4NX	01463 238561
Munro, Irene BA	2019		Ordained Local Minister: Presbytery Chaplain to vulnerable groups in residential care	1 Wyvis Crescent, Conan Bridge, Dingwall IV7 8BZ IMunro@churchofscotland.org.uk	01349 865752
Robertson, Michael A. BA	2014	2022	Lead Staff Support Chaplain	Raigmore Hospital, Old Perth Road, Inverness IV2 3UJ mike.robertson@nhs.scot	07740 984395
Ross, Kenneth R. OBE BA BD PhD	1982	2019	Theological Educator, Africa	Zomba Theological College, PO Box 130, Zomba, Malawi kross@thinkingmission.org	
Stobo, Mary J. (Mrs) BA	2013		Ordained Local Minister; Community Healthcare Chaplain	Druim-an-Sgairnich, Ardgay IV24 3BG MStobo@churchofscotland.org.uk	01863 766868
Thomson, Mary Ellen (Mrs)	2014		Ordained Local Minister: Presbytery Chaplain to Care Homes	Elm Cottage, Main Street, Newtonmore PH20 1DR Mary.Thomson@churchofscotland.org.uk	01479 667226
Whillis, David (Dr) DipHE	2020		Ordained Local Minister: Presbytery-wide minister to over 60s community	Helen's Lodge, Inshes, Inverness IV2 5BG DWhillis@churchofscotland.org.uk	01463 232304

C. Retaining: members of Presbytery

Anderson, David M. MSc FCOptom	1984	2017	(Ordained Local Minister, Cawdor with Croy and Dalcross)	'Mirlos', 1 Dumfries Place, Fort William PH33 6UQ David.Anderson@churchofscotland.org.uk	01397 702091
Andrews, J. Edward MA BD DipCG FSAScot	1985	2005	(Armadale)	Dunnichen, 1B Cameron Road, Nairn IV12 5NS edward.andrews@btinternet.com	01667 459466 07808 720708
Archer, Nicholas D.C. BA BD	1971	1992	(Dores and Boleskine)	3 Ferntower Place, Culloden, Inverness IV2 7TL na.overcome7@gmail.com	01463 793538
Attenburrow, A. Anne BSc MB ChB	2006	2018	(Auxiliary Minister, Dallas with Forres: St Leonard's with Rafford)	71 Osprey Crescent, Nairn IV12 5LG AAttenburrow@churchofscotland.org.uk	01667 457582 07860 934727
Barge, Nigel L. BSc BD	1991	2021	(Torrance)	2 Lephinmore Cottage, Strathlachlan, Cairndow PA27 8BU NBarge@churchofscotland.org.uk	
Barrie, Andrew A. BD	2013	2024	(Wick: Pulteneytown and Thrumster)	11 Park Avenue, Thurso KW14 8JP Andrew.Barrie@churchofscotland.org.uk	07791 663439
Bell, Graeme K. BA BD CertMS	1983	2017	(Glasgow: Carnwadric)	4 Munro Terrace, Rosemarkie, Fortrose IV10 8UR graemekbell@googlemail.com	07591 180101

Buell, F. Bart BA MDiv	1980	1995	(Urquhart and Glenmoriston)	6 Towerhill Place, Cradlehall, Inverness IV2 5FN bartbuell@talktalk.net	01463 794634
Campbell, Roderick D.M. TD MStJ BD DMin FSAScot	1975	2019	(Cumlodden, Lochfyneside and Lochgair with Glenaray and Inveraray)	Windy Ridge, Glen Loanan, Taynuilt PA35 1EY Roderick.Campbell@churchofscotland.org.uk	01866 822623
Chambers, S. John OBE BSc	1972	2009	(Inverness: Ness Bank)	Bannlagan Lodge, 4 Earls Cross Gardens, Dornoch IV25 3NR chambersdornoch@btinternet.com	01862 811520
Cleland, Robert	1997	2022	(Ardersier with Petty)	35 High Street, Ardersier, Inverness IV2 7QE	
Cringles, George G. BD CertMin	1981	2017	(Coll with Connel)	The Moorings, Ganavan Road, Oban PA34 5TU george.cringles@gmail.com	01631 564215
Cushman, Beverly W. BA MDiv MA PhD	1977	2023	(Altnaharra and Farr with Melness and Tongue)	Royston, Stemster, Halkirk KW12 6UX BCushman@churchofscotland.org.uk	01955 661265
Duncan, Esme (Miss)	2013	2017	(Ordained Local Minister, Caithness)	Avalon, Upper Warse, Canisbay, Wick KW1 4YD EDuncan@churchofscotland.org.uk	01955 611455
Earl, Jenny MA BD	2007	2023	(Iona with Kilfinichen and Kilvickeon and the Ross of Mull)	Kenilworth Cottage, Victoria Park, Minard, Inveraray PA 32 8YN	
Elliott, Gavin J. MA BD	1976	2015	(Ministries Council)	5a Aird, Isle of Benbecula HS7 5LT gavkondwani@gmail.com	01870 602726
Forbes, Farquhar A.M. MA BA	2016	2022	(Associate, Inverness: Inshes)	The Heights, Inverarnie, Inverness IV2 6XA FForbes@churchofscotland.org.uk	01808 521450
Fothergill, Andrew P. BA	2012	2023	(Tain)	12 Bruce Court, Dingwall IV15 9LG andy.fothergill@outlook.com	01349 867180 07827 575957
Fulcher, Christine P. BEd CertCS	2012	2022	(Ordained Local Minister, Team Minister, South Argyll)	Jura, The Steading, Kilmelford PA34 4XA CFulcher@churchofscotland.org.uk	01852 200538
Fulcher, Stephen BA MA	1993	2022	(Campbeltown: Highland with Saddell and Carradale with Southend)	Jura, The Steading, Kilmelford PA34 4XA steve.f2000@btinternet.com	01852 200538
Getliffe, Dot L.J. (Mrs) BA BD DipEd DCS	2006	2021	(Deacon, Inverness Old High St Stephen's)	136 Ardness Place, Lochardil, Inverness IV2 4QY DGetliffe@churchofscotland.org.uk	01463 716051
Gibson, Elizabeth A. (Mrs) MA MLitt BD	2003	2024	(North Mull)	Mo Dhachaidh, Lochdon, Isle of Mull PA64 6AP EGibson@churchofscotland.org.uk	01680 812541
Goudie, Stewart BSc BD	2010	2024	(North West Lochaber)	32/6 Forbes Road, Edinburgh EH10 4ED SGoudie@churchofscotland.org.uk	07957 237757
Griffiths, Ruth I. (Mrs)	2004	2020	(Auxiliary Minister, Dunoon: The High Kirk with Innellan with Toward)	Kirkwood, Mathieson Lane, Innellan, Dunoon PA23 7TA	01369 830145
Hood, H. Stanley C. MA BD	1966	2000	(London: Crown Court)	10 Dalriada Place, Kilmichael Glassary, Lochgilphead PA31 8QA	01546 606168
Horne, Douglas A. BD	1977	2009	(Tain)	151 Holm Farm Road, Culduthel, Inverness IV2 6BF douglas.horne@talktalk.net	01463 712677
Hunt, Trevor G. BA BD	1986	2011	(Evie with Firth with Rendall)	7 Woodville Court, Culduthel Avenue, Inverness IV2 6BX trevorghunt@gmail.com	07753 423333
Jones, John Owain MA BD FSAScot	1981	2023	(United Church of Bute)	28 Ardgowan Square, Greenock PA16 8NJ johnowainjones1@gmail.com	07806 623677
Lincoln, John BA BD MPhil	1986	2014	(Balquhidder with Killin and Ardeonaig)	59 Obsdale Park, Alness IV17 0TR johnlincoln@minister.com	01349 882791
Lind, Michael J. LLB BD	1984	2012	(Campbeltown: Highland)	Maybank, Station Road, Conon Bridge, Dingwall IV7 8BJ mijylind@gmail.com	01349 865932

Macartney, Deanne J.B. BA	2017	2023	(North Coast)	DMacartney@churchofscotland.org.uk	
Macdonald, Michael J.	2004	2024	(Auxiliary Minister, Alness)	73 Firrhill, Alness IV17 0RT Michael.Macdonald@churchofscotland.org.uk	01349 884268
MacEwan, James A.I. MA BD	1973	2012	(Abernethy with Cromdale and Advie)	Rapness, Station Road, Nethy Bridge PH25 3DN wurrus@hotmail.co.uk	01479 821116
Macfarlane, James MTh PhD	1991	2011	(Lochgoilhead and Kilmorich)	'Lindores', 11 Bullwood Road, Dunoon PA23 7QJ mac.farlane@btinternet.com	01369 710626
MacGregor, Neil I.M. BD	1995	2019	(Strathbogie Drumblade)	1 Abban Place, Inverness IV3 8GZ NMacGregor@churchofscotland.org.uk	07989 902722
MacIver, Norman BD	1976	2011	(Tarbert)	57 Boswell Road, Wester Inshes, Inverness IV2 3EW norman@n-cmaciver.freeserve.co.uk	01463 236586
MacLean, Gillean P. (Ms) BA BD PGDipCouns CertPS	1994	2023	(Lausanne: The Scots Kirk)	GMacLean@churchofscotland.org.uk	
MacLeod, Kenneth Donald BD CPS	1989	2019	(Invergordon)	10 Scott Crescent, Greenfaulds, Cumbernauld, Glasgow G67 4LG kd-macleod@tiscali.co.uk	07808 416767
MacLeod-Mair, Alisdair T. MEd DipTheol	2001	2022	(Snizort)	Flat 2/2, 44 Leven Street, Glasgow G41 2JE revalisdair@hotmail.com	
MacPherson, Alexander J. BD	1986	2021	(Buchanan with Drymen)	8 Little Cullernie Park, Balloch, Inverness IV2 7FQ revalexj1@gmail.com	
MacPherson, John BSc BD	1993	2021	(Eddrachillis)	23 Drumfield Road, Inverness IV2 4XH	01463 230038
Marshall, Freda (Mrs) BD FCII	1993	2005	(Colonsay and Oronsay with Kilbrandon and Kilchattan)	Allt Mhaluidh, Glenview, Dalmally PA33 1BE mail@freda.org.uk	01838 200693
Martin, George M. MA BD	1987	2005	(Applecross, Lochcarron and Torridon)	8(1) Buckingham Terrace, Edinburgh EH4 3AA	0131 343 3937
McCree, Ian W. BD	1971	2011	(Clyne with Kildonan and Loth Helmsdale)	Tigh Ardachu, Mosshill, Brora KW9 6NG ianmccree@live.co.uk	01408 621185
McGowan, Andrew T. B. (Prof) BD STM PhD	1979	2024	(Director, Rutherford Centre for Reformed Theology)	18 Davis Drive, Alness IV17 0ZD AMcGowan@churchofscotland.org.uk	01340 880762
McIvor, Anne (Miss) SRD BD	1996	2013	(Gigha and Cara)	20 Albyn Avenue, Campbeltown PA28 6LY annemcivor@btinternet.com	07901 964825
McKay, Margaret M. (Mrs) MA BD MTh	1991	2003	(Auchaber United with Auchterless)	2 Mackenzie Gardens, Dornoch IV25 3RU megsie38@gmail.com	01862 811859
McLaren, Glenda M. (Ms) DCS	1990	2020	(Deacon, Dunoon: St John's with Kirn and Sandbank)	Kiona, 1 Trinity Lane, Innellan PA23 7TS gmmclaren1330@gmail.com	07743 763054
McRoberts, T. Douglas BD CPS FRSA	1975	2014	(Malta: St Andrew's Scots Church)	24 Redwood Avenue, Inverness IV2 6HA DMcRoberts@churchofscotland.org.uk	01463 772594
Mill, David GCSJ MA BD	1978	2018	(Kilmun, Strone and Ardentinny: The Shore Kirk)	The Hebrides, 107 Bullwood Road, Dunoon PA23 7QN revandevmill@aol.com	01369 707544
Millar, Margaret R.M. (Miss) DipChE BTh	1977	2008	(Kilchrenan and Dalavich with Muckairn)	Fearnoch Cottage, Fearnoch, Taynuilt PA35 1JB macoje@btinternet.com	01866 822416
Mitchell, David BD DipPTheol MSc	1988	2023	(West Cowal)	DMitchell@churchofscotland.org.uk	
Mitchell, Joyce (Mrs) DCS	1994	2010	(Deacon, Edinburgh: Holy Trinity)	Sunnybank, Farr, Inverness IV2 6XG stanleymitchell121@btinternet.com	01808 521285

Morrison, Derek	1995	2013	(Gairloch and Dundonnell)	2 Cliffton Place, Poolewe, Achnasheen IV22 2JU derekmorrison1@aol.com	01445 781333
Morrison, Donald John	2001	2019	(Auxiliary Minister, Tarbert)	22 Kyles, Tarbert, Isle of Harris HS3 3BS donaldjmorrison22@outlook.com	01859 502341
Morton, Gillian M. (Mrs) MA BD PGCE	1983	1996	(Chaplain, Borders General Hospital)	16 St Leonard's Road, Forres IV36 1DW gillianmorton@hotmail.co.uk	01309 671719
Muirhead, Morag Y. (Mrs)	2013	2022	(Ordained Local Minister, Fort William Kilmallie with Kilmonivaig)	6 Dumbarton Road, Fort William PH33 6UU MMuirhead@churchofscotland.org.uk	01397 703643
Munro, James A. BD DMS	1979	2013	(Port Glasgow: Hamilton Bardrainney)	1 Wyvis Crescent, Conon Bridge, Dingwall IV7 8BZ james781munro@btinternet.com	01349 865752
Nugent, John BD	1999	2020	(Wick: St Fergus)	39 Argyle Square, Wick KW1 5AJ	07493 857689
Park, Peter B. BD MCIBS	1997	2014	(Fraserburgh: Old)	Hillview, 24 McKelvie Road, Oban PA34 4GB peterpark9@btinternet.com	01631 565849
Petrie, Jackie G.	1989	2011	(South Uist)	7B Malaclete, Isle of North Uist HS6 5BX jackiegpetrie@yahoo.com	01876 560804
Prentice, Donald K. BSc BD DipPsych MSc MLitt	1989	2023	(Dallas with Forres: St Leonard's with Rafford)	DPrentice@churchofscotland.org.uk	
Rennie, Lyall	2014	2019	(Ordained Local Minister, Pentland)	Ruachmarra, Lower Warse, Canisbay, Wick KW1 4YB LRennie@churchofscotland.org.uk	01955 611756
Ritchie, Bruce BSc BD PhD	1977	2013	(Dingwall: Castle Street)	16 Brinckman Terrace, Westhill, Inverness IV2 5BL brucezomba@hotmail.com	01463 791389
Ritchie, Christine A.Y. (Mrs) BD DipMin	2002	2012	(Braes of Rannoch with Foss and Rannoch)	25 Beachen Court, Grantown-on-Spey PH26 3JD gandcritchie70@gmail.com	01479 873419
Ritchie, Walter M.	1973	1999	(Uphall: South)	Hazel Cottage, Barr Mor View, Kilmartin, Lochgilphead PA31 8UN	01546 510343
Robertson, Peter BSc BD	1988	1998	(Dallas with Forres: St Leonard's with Rafford)	17 Ferryhill Road, Forres IV36 2GY peterrobertsonforres@talktalk.net	01309 676769
Scott, David V. BTh	1994	2014	(Fearn Abbey and Nigg with Tarbat)	29 Sunnyside, Culloden Moor, Inverness IV2 5ES	01463 795802
Scott, Randolph MA BD	1991	2013	(Jersey: St Columba's)	18 Lochan Avenue, Kirn, Dunoon PA23 8HT rev.rs@hotmail.com	01369 703175
Smith, Hilda C. (Miss) MA BD MSc	1992	2021	(Lochgilphead)	Ardmore, Kilmory Road, Lochgilphead PA31 8SZ hilda.smith2@btinternet.com	01546 603191
Smith, Murdo MA BD	1988	2011	(Manish-Scarista)	Aisgeir, 15A Upper Shader, Isle of Lewis HS3 3MX	
Smith, Russel BD	1994	2013	(Dingwall: St Clement's)	1 School Road, Conon Bridge, Dingwall IV7 8AE russanntwo@btinternet.com	01349 861011
Stewart, Joseph LTh	1979	2011	(Dunoon: St John's with Sandbank)	7 Glenmorag Avenue, Dunoon PA23 7LG	01369 703438
Stoddart, Alexander C. BD	2001	2022	(Duror with Glencoe: St Munda's)	33 Sandilands Grove, Newburgh Road, Abernethy PH2 9LH sandystoddart1@outlook.com	07593 598741
Stutter, Anita Drs (MA)	2008	2020	(Applecross Lochcarron and Torridon)	Aros, Slumbay, Lochcarron IV54 8YQ vanderwal@btinternet.com	01520 722139
Turner, Fraser K. LTh	1994	2007	(Kiltarlity with Kirkhill)	20 Caulfield Avenue, Inverness IV2 5GA fraseratq@yahoo.co.uk	01463 794004
Varwell, Adrian P.J. BA BD PhD	1983	2011	(Fort Augustus with Glengarry)	19 Enrick Crescent, Kilmore, Drumnadrochit, Inverness IV63 6TP adrian.varwell@btinternet.com	01456 459352

Walker, Donald K. BD	1979	2018	(Abernethy with Boat of Garten, Carrbridge and Kincardine)	Jabulani, Seafield Avenue, Grantown-on-Spey PH26 3JQ dwalkerjabulani@gmail.com	01479 870104
Walker, Linda A.W. BA CertCS	2008	2022	(Auxiliary Minister, Presbytery of Glasgow)	39 Elmgrove, Achareidh, Nairn IV12 4SL LWalker@churchofscotland.org.uk	01667 456082 07842 311057
Warwick, Ivan C. TD BD DipPS DipEcum	1980	2014	(Paisley: St James')	Ardcruidh Croft, Heights of Dochcarty, Dingwall IV15 9UF L70rev@btinternet.com	01349 861464 07787 535083
Watt, Hugh F. BD DPS DMin	1986	2023	(Urquhart and Glenmoriston)	7 The Cairns, Muir of Ord IV6 7AT HWatt@churchofscotland.org.uk	
Wilkinson, W. Brian MA BD	1968	2007	(Glenaray and Inveraray)	3 Achlonan, Taynuilt PA35 1JJ williambrian35@btinternet.com	01866 822036
Winning, A. Ann MA DipEd BD	1984	2006	(Morvern)	'Westering', 13C Carnoch, Glencoe, Ballachulish PH49 4HQ awinning009@btinternet.com	01855 811929
Younger, Alastair S. BScEcon ASCC	1969	2008	(Inverness: St Columba High)	33 Duke's View, Slackbuie, Inverness IV2 6BB younger873@btinternet.com	01463 242873

D. In other appointments: not members of Presbytery

Drummond, Norman W. (Prof.) CBE MA BD DUniv FRSE	1976	1997	President, Columba 1400	c/o Columba 1400 Ltd., Staffin, Isle of Skye IV51 9JY	01478 611400

E. Retaining: not members of Presbytery

Bardgett, Frank D. MA BD PhD	1987	2001	(Department of National Mission)	Tigh an Iasgair, Street of Kincardine, Boat of Garten PH24 3BY iasgair1@icloud.com	01479 831751
Bell, Sandra L.N. (Mrs) DCS	2001	2013	(Deacon: Chaplain, Glasgow Royal Infirmary)	4 Munro Terrace, Rosemarkie, Fortrose IV10 8UR	
McKean, Alan T. BD CertMin	1982	2018	(Avoch with Fortrose and Rosemarkie)	15 Park Road, Kirn, Dunoon PA23 8JL	01369 700016
McLean, Gordon LTh CertMS	1972	1992	(Edinburgh: Currie)	Beinn Dhorain, Kinnettas Square, Strathpeffer IV14 9BD gmaclean@hotmail.co.uk	01997 421380
McWilliam, Thomas M. MA BD	1964	2003	(Contin)	Flat 3, 13 Culduthel Road, Inverness IV2 4AG tommcw@tommcwl.plus.com	01463 718981
Muckart, Graeme W.M. MTh MSc FSAScot	1983	2009	(Kincardine, Croick and Edderton)	Torr Gorm, Davochfin, Dornoch IV25 3RW gw2m.kildale@gmail.com	01862 810428 07737 424565
Porter, Carol Anne B. (Mrs) BEd BD	2009	2017	(Alloa: Ludgate)	The Cottages, Dornoch Firth Caravan Park, Meikle Ferry South, Tain IV19 1JX ca.porter@icloud.com	01862 892292
Stewart, Fraser M.C. BSc BD	1980	2017	(Kilmuir and Logie Easter)	44 Great Glen Place, Inverness IV3 8FA fraserstewart1955@hotmail.com	01463 832589
Tallach, John M. MA MLitt DipPhil	1970	2010	(Cromarty)	29 Firthview Drive, Inverness IV3 8NS johntallach@talktalk.net	01463 418721
Thomson, Alexander BSc BD MPhil PhD	1973	2012	(Rutherglen: Old)	4 Munro Street, Dornoch IV25 3RA alexander.thomson6@btinternet.com	01862 811650

Webster, Peter BD DipPS	1977	2014	(Edinburgh: Portobello St James')	6 Newton Park, Dunoon PA23 7ST peterwebster101@hotmail.com	
Whyte, Ron C. BD CPS	1990	2013	(Alvie and Insh with Rothiemurchus and Aviemore)	13 Hillside Avenue, Kingussie PH21 1PA ron4xst@btinternet.com	01540 661101 07979 026973

F. Inactive: not members of Presbytery

Beautyman, Paul H. MA BD PGCCE	1993	2019	(Youth Adviser, Presbytery of Argyll)	59 Alexander Street, Dunoon PA23 7BB paulbeautyman67@gmail.com	07572 813695
Bryson, Thomas M. BD	1997	2024	(Nairn: St Ninian's and Auldearn and Dalmore)	The Manse, Manse Road, Auldearn, Nairn IV12 5SX TBryson@churchofscotland.org.uk	01667 451675
Chisholm, Archibald F. MA	1957	1997	(Braes of Rannoch with Foss and Rannoch)	32 Seabank Road, Nairn IV12 4EU arch32@btinternet.com	01667 452001
Dunlop, Alistair J. MA	1965	2004	(Saddell and Carradale)	8 Pipers Road, Cairnbaan, Lochgilphead PA31 8UF dunrevn@btinternet.com	01546 600316
Gray, William LTh	1971	2006	(Kilberry with Tarbert)	Lochnagar, Longsdale Road, Oban PA34 5DZ gray98@hotmail.com	01631 567471
MacLeod, Roderick MBE MA BD PhD(Edin) PhD(open)	1966	2011	(Cumlodden, Lochfyneside and Lochgair)	Creag-nam-Barnach, Furnace, Inveraray PA32 8XU mail@revroddy.co.uk	01499 500629
Millar, John L. MA BD	1981	1990	(Fort William: Duncansburgh with Kilmonivaig)	Flat 0/1, 12 Chesterfield Gardens, Glasgow G12 0BF johnmillar123@btinternet.com	0141 339 4090 07919 524415
Minto, Joan E. (Mrs) MA BD	1993	1997	(Wemyss)	1 Lochaber Cottages, Forres IV36 2RL joanminto.123@gmail.com	07800 669074
Muir, Eleanor D. MTheol DipPTheol	1986	2015	(Fowlis Wester, Madderty and Monzie with Gask)	Heatherdale, 6 Lochcarnan, South Uist HS8 5NU eleanordmuir@gmail.com	01870 610320
Munro, Sheila BD DipPsych	1995	2021	(RAF Chaplain)		07468 339330
Ramsay, Alan MA	1967	2007	(Fort William: MacIntosh Memorial)	12 Riverside Grove, Lochyside, Fort William PH33 7RD	01397 702054
Stirling, G. Alan S. MA	1960	1999	(Leochel Cushnie and Lynturk with Tough)	97 Lochlann Road, Culloden, Inverness IV2 7HJ	01463 798313
Bryson, Thomas M. BD	1997	2024	(Nairn: St Ninian's and Auldearn and Dalmore)	The Manse, Manse Road, Auldearn, Nairn IV12 5SX TBryson@churchofscotland.org.uk	01667 451675
Waugh, John L. LTh	1973	2002	(Ardclach with Auldearn and Dalmore)	58 Wyvis Drive, Nairn IV12 4TP jswaugh31@gmail.com	01667 456397

G. Readers (active)

Allan, Douglas	1 Camplen Court, Rothesay, Isle of Bute PA20 0NL	douglas.allan423@gmail.com	01700 502331
Appleby, Jonathan	91 Cradlehall Park, Inverness IV2 5DB	jon.wyvis@gmail.com	01463 791470
Bardgett, Alison (Mrs)	Tigh an Iasgair, Street of Kincardine, Boat of Garten PH24 3BY	iasgair10@icloud.com	01479 831751
Baxter, A. Rosie (Dr)	Daylesford, Invershin, Lairg IV27 4ET	drrosiereid@yahoo.co.uk	01549 421326 07748 761694
Binner, Aileen (Mrs)	Ailand, North Connel, Oban PA37 1QX	binners@ailand.plus.com	01631 710264
Black, Barbara J. (Mrs)	Carn Eilrig, Nethy Bridge PH25 3EE	bjcarneilrig54@gmail.com	01479 821641

Cazaly, Leonard	9 Moray Park Gardens, Culloden, Inverness IV2 7FY	len_cazaly@btinternet.com	01463 794469
Cook, Arnett D.	66 Millerton Avenue, Inverness IV3 8RY	arnett.cook@btinternet.com	01463 224795
Dennis, Barry	5 Loch Ness View, Dores, Inverness IV2 6TW	barrydennis@live.co.uk	01463 751393
Finlayson, Michael R.	Amberlea, Glenskiach, Evanton, Dingwall IV16 9UU	finlayson935@btinternet.com	01349 830598
Gill, Ella (Mrs)	5 Camus Inas, Acharacle PH36 4JQ	ellagill768@gmail.com	01967 431834
Greer, Kathleen (Mrs) MEd	17 Duthac Wynd, Tain IV19 1LP	greer2@talktalk.net	01862 892065
Jackson, Simon	Broomton Farm, Balintore IV20 1XN	simonjackson@procam.co.uk	01862 832831
Jamieson, Patricia A. (Mrs)	9 Craig Avenue, Tain IV19 1JP	hapijam179@yahoo.co.uk	01862 893154
King, Fiona	23 Torr Gardens, Dores, Inverness IV2 6TS	kingdores@btinternet.com	01463 751293
Lamont, John H. BD	6 Tigh na Filine, Aultbea, Achnasheen IV22 2JE	jhlamont@btinternet.com	07714 720753
Logue, David	3 Braeface, Tayvallich, Lochgilphead PA31 89N	david@loguenet.co.uk	01546 870647
MacDonald, Morag (Dr)	Orkney View, Portskerra, Melvich KW14 7YL	liliasmacdonald@btinternet.com	01641 531281
MacInnes, Ailsa (Mrs)	Kilmartin, 17 Southside Road, Inverness IV2 3BG	ailsa.macinnes@btopenworld.com	01463 230321 07704 485055
MacNab, Ann (Mrs)	Druim Skilivat, Scolpaig, Lochmaddy, Isle of North Uist HS6 5DH	annabhan@hotmail.com	01876 510701
MacRae, Donald E.	Nethania, 52 Strath, Gairloch IV21 2DB	dmgair@aol.com	01445 712235
Malcolm, James	Courtyard Cottage, Barrmor View, Kilmartin PA31 8UN	jgmalcolm@btinternet.com	01546 510540
McAlpine, James	5 Cromlet Park, Invergordon IV18 0RN	jmca2@tiscali.co.uk	01349 852801
McHugh, Douglas	Tigh Na Criche, Cairndow, Argyll PA27 8BY	dmchugh6@gmail.com	01369 860147
McLellan, James A.	West Drimvore, Lochgilphead PA31 8SU	james.mclellan8@btinternet.com	01546 606403
Mills, Peter A.	Northton, Ganavan, Oban PA34 5TU	peter@peteramills.com	
Morrison, John L.	Tigh na Barnashaig, Tayvallich, Lochgilphead PA31 8PN	jolomo@thejolomostudio.com	01546 870637
O'Neill, Leslie	Holytree Cottage, Parkside, Lybster KW3 6AS	leslie_oneill@hotmail.co.uk	01593 721738
O'Neill, Maureen (Mrs)	Holytree Cottage, Parkside, Lybster KW3 6AS	oneill.maureen@yahoo.com	01593 721738
Ramsay, Matthew M.	Portnastorm, Carradale, Campbeltown PA28 6SB	kintyre@fishermensmission.org.uk	01583 431381
Roberts, Irene (Miss)	Flat 4, Harbour Buildings, Main Street, Portmahomack, Tain IV20 1YG	ireneroberts43@hotmail.com	01862 871166 07854 436854
Robertson, Hendry	Park House, 51 Glenurquhart Road, Inverness IV3 5PB	hendryrobertson046@btinternet.com	01463 231858 07929 766102
Robertson, Stewart J.H.	6 Raasay Road, Inverness IV2 3LR	sjhro@tiscali.co.uk	01463 417937
Roden, Vivian (Mrs)	15 Old Mill Road, Tomatin, Inverness IV13 7YW	vroden@btinternet.com	01808 511355 07887 704915
Scouller, Alastair	15 Allanwater Apartments, Bridge of Allan, Stirling FK9 4DZ	scouller@globalnet.co.uk	01786 832496
Sinclair, Margaret (Ms)	2 Quarry Place, Furnace, Inveraray PA32 8XW	margaret_sinclair@btinternet.com	01499 500633
Skene, William	Tiree, Gairlochy, Spean Bridge PH34 4EQ	bill.skene@lochaber.presbytery.org.uk	01397 712594
Stather, Angela (Ms)	1 Dunlossit Cottages, Port Askaig, Isle of Islay PA46 7RB	angstat@btinternet.com	01496 840726
Thornhill, Christopher R.	4 Ardfern Cottages, Ardfern, Lochgilphead PA31 8QN	c.thornhill@btinternet.com	01852 300011
Zielinski, Jeneffer C. (Mrs)	7 Wallace Court, Ferguslie Street, Sandbank, Dunoon PA23 8QA	jenefferzielinski@gmail.com	01369 706136

H. Ministries Development Staff

Binner, Aileen	Presbytery – Ministries Co-ordinator, South Argyll	ABinner@churchofscotland.org.uk
Black, Barbara J. (Mrs)	Tomintoul, Glenlivet and Inveraven – Parish Assistant	BBlack@churchofscotland.org.uk
Bowker, Thomas	Presbytery – Fresh Expressions Worker, South Badenoch	TBowker@churchofscotland.org.uk
Brayshaw, Elizabeth	Presbytery – Advisor, under 40s focus, Argyll	EBrayshaw@churchofscotland.org.uk
D'Silva, Emily	Kilmore and Oban – Parish Assistant	EDSilva@churchofscotland.org.uk
Hall, Meghann	Campbeltown linked with Saddell and Carradale linked with Southend – Parish Assistant	MHall@churchofscotland.org.uk
Hay, Alison	Presbytery – Ministries Co-ordinator, North and East Argyll	AHay@churchofscotland.org.uk
MacLeod, Rory N. (Rev) BA BD	Fort William Kilmallie linked with Kilmonivaig – Associate Minister	RNMacLeod@churchofscotland.org.uk
Petersen, Robert	Pentland – Parish Assistant	RPetersen@churchofscotland.org.uk
Sikorski, Anne	Presbytery – Mission and Ministry Development Worker, Lochcarron-Skye	ASikorski@churchofscotland.org.uk
Whyte, Susan	Presbytery – Youth Worker – Team Leader, Argyll	SWhyte@churchofscotland.org.uk
Wilson, John K. (Kenny)	Presbytery – Youth and Children's Worker, Argyll	KWilson@churchofscotland.org.uk

INVERNESS ADDRESSES

Crown	Kingsmills Road x Midmills Road	Old High St Stephen's	Old Edinburgh Road x Southside Road	**Nairn**	
				Old	Academy Street x Seabank Road
Hilton	Druid Road x Tomatin Road	St Columba	Drummond School, Drummond Road; and Boleskine	St Ninian's	High Street x Queen Street
Inshes East	Inshes Retail Park				
Kinmylies	Kinmylies Way	Trinity Dalneigh	St Mary's Avenue		
Ness Bank	Ness Bank x Castle Road				

(11) LEWIS

Meets at Stornoway, in St Columba's Church Hall, on the second Tuesday of March, June, September and November and at other times as required.

Clerk:	**REV. BEN JOHNSTONE MA BD DMin**			**Loch Alain, 5 Breaclete, Bernera, Isle of Lewis HS2 9LT** **lewis@churchofscotland.org.uk**	**01851 612445** **07444 125719**
1	**Barvas (F GD H W)** Vacant Interim Moderator: Duncan M. Macaskill			**contact@barvaschurchofscotland.org** Church of Scotland Manse, Lower Barvas, Isle of Lewis HS2 0QY DMacaskill@churchofscotland.org.uk	 01851 840218 01851 643761
2	**Carloway (F GD H)** Duncan M. Macaskill BA BD MPhil DMin	 1992	 2019	 Church of Scotland Manse, Knock, Carloway, Isle of Lewis HS2 9AU DMacaskill@churchofscotland.org.uk	**01851 643211** 01851 643761
3	**Cross Ness (F GD H T W)** John M. Nicolson BD DipMin	 1997	 2019	**crossnesschurch@gmail.com** Church of Scotland Manse, Cross Skigersta Road, Ness, Isle of Lewis HS2 0TB JNicolson@churchofscotland.org.uk	 07899 235355
4	**Kinloch (F GD H)** Iain M. Campbell BD	 2004	 2008	 Laxay, Lochs, Isle of Lewis HS2 9LA Iain.Campbell@churchofscotland.org.uk	 01851 830218
5	**Knock (GD H)** Guardianship of the Presbytery Interim Moderator: Gordon M. Macleod			 GMacleod@churchofscotland.org.uk	 07717 065739
6	**Lochs-Crossbost (GD H)** Guardianship of the Presbytery Interim Moderator: Donald Macleod			 donaldmacleod25@btinternet.com	 01851 704516
7	**Lochs-in-Bernera (F GD H) linked with Uig (F GD H)** Hugh Maurice Stewart DPA BD	 2008		 Church of Scotland Manse, Uigen, Miavaig, Isle of Lewis HS2 9HX HStewart@churchofscotland.org.uk	 01851 672388

8 Stornoway: High (F GD H W)				
Gordon M. Macleod BA	2017	2019	Woodside, Laxdale Lane, Stornoway, Isle of Lewis HS1 0DR GMacleod@churchofscotland.org.uk	07717 065739
9 Stornoway: Martin's Memorial (F H W)			**enquiries@martinsmemorial.org.uk**	**01851 700820**
Thomas MacNeil MA BD	2002	2006	Martin's Memorial Manse, Matheson Road, Stornoway, Isle of Lewis HS1 2LR TMacNeil@churchofscotland.org.uk	01851 704238
10 Stornoway: St Columba (F GD H)				**01851 701546**
William J. Heenan BA MTh	2012		St Columba's Manse, Lewis Street, Stornoway, Isle of Lewis HS1 2JF WHeenan@churchofscotland.org.uk	01851 705933 07837 770589

11 Uig See Lochs-in-Bernera

B. In other appointments: members of Presbytery

Shadakshari, T.K. BTh BD MTh	1998	2006	Head of Spiritual Care, Western Isles Health Board	23D Benside, Newmarket, Stornoway, Isle of Lewis HS2 0DZ tk.shadakshari@nhs.scot	Home 01851 701727 Office 01851 704704 07403 697138

C. Retaining: members of Presbytery

Amed, Paul LTh DPS	1992	2015	(Barvas)	6 Scotland Street, Stornoway, Isle of Lewis H51 2JQ paul.amed@outlook.com	01851 706450
Campbell, Murdo M. BD DipMin	1997	2023	(Strathblane)	20 Allotments, Garrabost, Isle of Lewis HS2 0PJ MCampbell@churchofscotland.org.uk	07342 981139
Jamieson, Esther M.M. (Mrs) BD	1984	2002	(Glasgow: Penilee St Andrew)	1 Redburn, Bayview, Stornoway, Isle of Lewis HS1 2UU iandejamieson@btinternet.com	01851 704789
Johnstone, Ben MA BD DMin	1973	2013	(Strath and Sleat)	Loch Alain, 5 Breaclete, Bernera, Isle of Lewis HS2 9LT benonbernera@gmail.com	01851 612445 07444 125719
Maclean, Donald A. DCS	1988	1990	(Deacon, Tarbert)	8 Upper Barvas, Isle of Lewis HS2 0QX	01851 840454
Macleod, William	1957	2006	(Uig)	54 Lower Barvas, Isle of Lewis HS2 0QY	01851 840217
Wolf, Dougie BA(Theol)	2017	2024	(Barvas)	Stornoway View, 111 Newmarket, Isle of Lewis HS2 0ED DWolf@churchofscotland.org.uk	

D. In other appointments: not members of Presbytery

Nil

E. Retaining: not members of Presbytery

Nil

F. Inactive: not members of Presbytery

Nil

G. Readers (active)

Macleod, Donald	14 Balmerino Drive, Stornoway, Isle of Lewis HS1 2TD	donaldmacleod25@btinternet.com	01851 704516
Macmillan, Iain	34 Scotland Street, Stornoway, Isle of Lewis HS1 2JR	iainmacmillan.alba34@gmail.com	01851 704826 07943 420817

H. Ministries Development Staff

Nil

LEWIS Communion Sundays

Barvas	3rd Mar, Sep	Lochs-Crossbost	4th Mar, Sep	Stornoway: St Columba	3rd Feb, last Aug
Carloway	1st Mar, last Sep	Lochs-in-Bernera	1st Apr, 2nd Sep	Uig	3rd Jun, 4th Oct
Cross Ness	2nd Mar, Oct	Stornoway: High	3rd Feb, last Aug		
Kinloch	3rd Mar, 2nd Jun, 2nd Sep	Stornoway: Martin's Memorial	3rd Feb, last Aug, 1st Dec, Easter		
Knock	3rd Apr, 1st Nov				

(12) ENGLAND AND CHANNEL ISLANDS (F)

Meets at London, in Crown Court Church, on the second Tuesday of February and the second Saturday of October, and at St Columba's, Pont Street, on the second Tuesday of June.

Clerk:	**REV. ALISTAIR CUMMING MSc CCS FInstLM FLPI**		**50 Burgh Heath Road, Epsom KT17 4LX** **england@churchofscotland.org.uk**	**07534 943986**

1	**Corby (F H W)**				**01536 265245**
	Vacant			The Manse, 46 Glyndebourne Gardens, Corby, Northants NN18 0PZ	01536 66947
	I. Scott McCarthy BD (Associate Minister)	2010	2024	The Manse, 46 Glyndebourne Gardens, Corby, Northants NN18 0PZ ISMcCarthy@churchofscotland.org.uk	01536 66947
	Interim Moderator: Scott M. Rennie			SRennie@churchofscotland.org.uk	020 7278 5022
2	**Guernsey: St Andrew's in the Grange (F H W)**				
	Justin W. Taylor BTh MTh MTh	2018	2022	The Manse, Le Villocq, Castel, Guernsey GY5 7SB JTaylor@churchofscotland.org.uk	01481 257345
3	**Jersey: St Columba's (F H T W)**				
	Carolann Birnie BD DipPDSRP	2009	2023	18 Claremont Avenue, St Saviour, Jersey JE2 7SF CBirnie@churchofscotland.org.uk	01534 730659
4	**London: Crown Court (F H T W)**				**020 7836 5643**
	Scott M. Rennie MA BD STM FRSA	1999	2022	53 Sidmouth Street, London WC1H 8JX SRennie@churchofscotland.org.uk	020 7278 5022
5	**London: St Columba's (F H T W) linked with Newcastle: St Andrew's (H T W)**			**office@stcolumbas.org.uk**	**St Columba's: 020 7584 2321**
	C. Angus MacLeod MA BD	1996	2012	29 Hollywood Road, Chelsea, London SW10 9HT Angus.MacLeod@churchofscotland.org.uk	Office 020 7584 2321
	William McLaren MA BD (Associate Minister)	1990	2021	St Columba's, Pont Street, London SW1X 0BD WMcLaren@churchofscotland.org.uk	Office 020 7584 2321
6	**Newcastle: St Andrew's** See London: St Columba's				

B. In other appointments: members of Presbytery

Binks, Mike	2007	2015	Auxiliary Minister – Churches Together in Corby	Hollybank, 10 Kingsbrook, Corby NN18 9HY MBinks@churchofscotland.org.uk	07590 507917
Cumming, Alistair MSc CCS FInstLM FLPI	2010	2013	Presbytery Clerk: Auxiliary Minister	50 Burgh Heath Road, Epsom KT17 4LX ACumming@churchofscotland.org.uk	07534 943986
Francis, James MBE BD PhD	2002	2009	Army Chaplain	37 Millburn Road, Coleraine BT52 1QT JFrancis@churchofscotland.org.uk	02870 353869
Lovett, Mairi F. BSc BA DipPS MTh	2005	2013	Hospital Chaplain	Royal Brompton Hospital, Sydney Street, London SW3 6NP m.lovett@rbht.nhs.uk	020 7351 8060
MacKay, Stewart A. BA	2009	2020	Army Chaplain	ATR (P) 3ATR, Alexander Barracks, Pirbright, Woking GU24 0QQ Stewart.Mackay762@mod.gov.uk	
MacKenzie, Hector M.	2008		Army Chaplain	ITC (C) 2ITB, Helles Barracks, Catterick Garrison DL9 4HH Hector.MacKenzie657@mod.gov.uk	
Mather, James BA DipArch MA MBA	2010	2019	Auxiliary Minister: Woodley Airfield Church, Woodley, Reading	24 Ellison Road, Barnes, London SW13 0AD JMather@churchofscotland.org.uk	020 8876 6540 07836 715655
McLay, Neil BA BD MTh	2006	2012	Army Chaplain	HQ Regional Point of Control for Central England, Kendrew Barracks, Cottesmore, Oakham LE15 7BL Neil.McLay100@mod.gov.uk	
McMahon, John K.S. MA BD	1998	2012	Head of Spiritual and Pastoral Care, West London NHS Trust	Broadmoor Hospital, Joshua Webb Way, Crowthorne, Berkshire RG45 7EG JohnKSMcMahon@churchofscotland.org.uk	01344 754098
Middleton, Paul (Prof) BMus BD ThM PhD FRSA FHEA	2000	2018	New Testament and Early Christianity, University of Chester	10 Raymond Street, Chester CH1 4EL p.middleton@chester.ac.uk	01244 378766
Shackleton, Scott J.S. KCVS BA BD PhD	1993	2023	Strategic Lead Officer, Transforming Plymouth Together	4 Meadow View Close, Woodbury, Exeter EX5 1FW shackletonscott@hotmail.com	
Thom, David J. BD DipMin	1999	2015	Army Chaplain	HQ SHAPE, EJSU, SHAPE, BFPO 26 revdjt@gmail.com	
Wright, Allan BVMS MRCVS	2021		Ordained Local Minister: Pioneer Minister to Veterinary Community in NE England	27 Prospect Terrace, Burnopfield, Newcastle NE16 6EL AWright@churchofscotland.org.uk	07984 541587

C. Retaining: members of Presbytery

Anderson, Andrew F. MA BD	1981	2011	(Edinburgh: Greenside)	58 Reliance Way, Oxford OX4 2FG andrew.relianceway@gmail.com	01865 778397
Cairns, W. Alexander BD	1978	2006	(Corby: St Andrew's)	Kirkton House, Kirkton of Craig, Montrose DD10 9TB sandy.cairns@btinternet.com	07808 588045
Cameron, R. Neil	1976	2005	(Chaplain: Army)	neilandminacameron@yahoo.co.uk	
Clark, Christine M. BA BD MTh DMin	2006	2019	(Chaplain, Royal Hospital for Sick Children, Edinburgh)	CClark@churchofscotland.org.uk	07444 819237
Coulter, David G. CB OStJ KHC BA BD MDA PhD	1989	2024	(Presbytery Clerk: Fife)	62B Buchanan Gardens, St Andrews KY16 9LX DCoulter@churchofscotland.org.uk	01334 473836

Lunn, Dorothy I.M.	2002	2016	(Auxiliary Minister, Newcastle: St Andrew's)	14 Bellerby Drive, Ouston, Co.Durham DH2 1TW dorothylunn@hotmail.com	0191 492 0647
Macfarlane, Peter T. BA LTh	1970	1994	(Chaplain: Army)	4 rue de Rives, 37160 Abilly, France	
McEnhill, Peter BD PhD	1992	2023	(Presbytery Clerk: Clyde)	59a College Street, Bury St Edmunds, Suffolk IP33 1NL PMcEnhill@churchofscotland.org.uk	07837 729333
Mills, Peter W. CB BD DD CPD	1984	2018	(East Neuk Trinity with St Monans)	16 Pearce Drive, Lawley, Telford TF3 5JQ	
Ogg, M. Fiona (Mrs) BA BD	2012	2021	(Acharacle with Ardnamurchan)	6a Stamford Road, Essendine, Stamford PE9 4LQ Fiona.Ogg@churchofscotland.org.uk	
Pitkeathly, David G. LLB DipLP BD	1996	2021	(Border Kirk)	11 Butlers Road, Horsham, Sussex RH13 6AJ david.pitkeathly@btinternet.com	07546 064607
Stone, Lance B. BD MTh PhD	1978	2021	(Amsterdam: English Reformed Church)	Flat C Branksome Court, 2 Sudbourne Road, London SW2 5AQ LStone@churchofscotland.org.uk	07443 321184
Walker, R. Forbes BSc BD ThM	1987	2023	(School Chaplain, Emmanuel School, London)	15 Selhurst New Court, Selhurst New Road, London SE25 5PT revrfw@gmail.com	

D. In other appointments: not members of Presbytery

Nil

E. Retaining: not members of Presbytery

Hutchison, David S. BSc BD ThM	1991	2022	(Chaplain: University of Aberdeen)	40 The Lane, Alwoodley, Leeds LS17 7BS

F. Inactive: not members of Presbytery

Nil

G. Readers (active)

Menzies, Rena (Mrs)	40 Elizabeth Avenue, St Brelade's, Jersey JE3 8GR	menzfamily@jerseymail.co.uk	01534 741095
Milligan, Elaine (Mrs)	16 Surrey Close, Corby, Northants NN17 2TG	emill523@outlook.com	01536 205259

H. Ministries Development Staff

McCarthy, I. Scott (Rev) BD	Corby – Associate Minister	ISMcCarthy@churchofscotland.org.uk
McLaren, William (Rev) MA BD	London: St Columba's with Newcastle: St Andrew's – Associate Minister	WMcLaren@churchofscotland.org.uk

ADDRESSES

Corby	Beanfield Avenue	**Jersey**	Midvale Road, St Helier	**London:** St Columba's	Pont Street SW1
Guernsey	The Grange, St Peter Port	**London:** Crown Court	Crown Court WC2	**Newcastle**	Sandyford Road

(13) INTERNATIONAL CHARGES (F W)

Meets over the weekend of the second Sunday of March and October, hosted by congregations in mainland Europe.

Clerk: REV. DEREK G. LAWSON LLB BD	**16 Rue de la Madeleine, 22210 La Chèze, France** **international@churchofscotland.org.uk** **clerk@internationalpresbytery.org** **www.internationalpresbytery.org**	**0033 6 09 57 66 71**

1	**Amsterdam: English Reformed Church (F T W)**			**info@erc.amsterdam**	
	Marius Louw BTh MDiv NGDT	2017	2024	Jan Willem Brouwersstraat 9, NL-1071 LH Amsterdam, The Netherlands MLouw@churchofscotland.org.uk Church address: Begijnhof 48, 1012WV Amsterdam	0031 20 672 2288
2	**Bermuda: Christ Church, Warwick (F H W)**			**christchurch@logic.bm**	**001 441 236 1882**
	Alistair G. Bennett BSc BD	1978	2016	1 Steele's Drive, Paget PG03, Bermuda ABennett@churchofscotland.org.uk	001 441 236 0400
	Cindy F. Campbell (Ordained Local Minister)	2023		9 Cavello Heights, Sandys MA 05, Bermuda CCampbell@churchofscotland.org.uk Church address: Christ Church, Middle Road, Warwick, Bermuda Mailing address: PO Box WK 130, Warwick WK BX, Bermuda	001 441 234 3797
3	**Bochum: English-Speaking Christian Congregation (Associated congregation) (W)**				
	Anja Nicole Stuckenberger (*not a minister of the CofS*)			Ev. Stadtakademie Bochum, Westring 26a, 44787 Bochum astuckenberger@ekvw.de Church address: Pauluskircke, Grabenstrasse 9, 44787 Bochum	0049 234 962904 ext 661 0049 175 2518757
4	**Brussels: St Andrew's (F H W)**			**secretary@churchofscotland.be**	**0032 2 649 02 19**
	Eric W. Foggitt MA BSc BD	1991	2020	23 Square des Nations, B-1000 Brussels, Belgium EFoggitt@churchofscotland.org.uk Church address: Chaussée de Vieurgat 181, 1050 Brussels	0032 2 672 40 56
5	**Budapest: St Columba's (F W)**				**0036 30 567 6356**
	Aaron C. Stevens BA MDiv MACE	2004	2006	Locsei ut 14, 4e, 21a, 1147, Budapest, Hungary AStevens@churchofscotland.org.uk	0036 70 615 5394
	Szabina Sztojka (*Associate Minister, Reformed Church of Hungary*)	2021		sztojka.szabina@reformatus.hu Church address: Vörösmarty utca 51, 1064 Budapest	

6	**Colombo, Sri Lanka: St Andrew's Scots Kirk (F W)**			**churchofficer@scotskirk.lk**	**0094 112 323 765**
	Guardianship of the Presbytery			73 Galle Road, Colpetty, Colombo 3, Sri Lanka	0094 112 386 774
				minister@standrewsscotskirk.org	
				Church address: 73 Galle Road, Colpetty, Colombo	
	Interim Moderator: Paraic Reamonn			paraic.reamonn@gmail.com	0041 79 151 91 43
7	**Geneva (F W)**				**0041 22 788 08 31**
	Laurence H. Twaddle MA BD MTh	1977	2017	6 chemin Taverney, 1218 Geneva, Switzerland	0041 22 788 08 31
				LTwaddle@churchofscotland.org.uk	
				Church address: Auditoire de Calvin, 1 Place de la Taconnerie, Geneva	
8	**Lausanne: The Scots Kirk (F H W)**				
	Vacant			26 Avenue de Rumine, CH-1005 Lausanne, Switzerland	0041 21 323 98 28
	Interim Moderator: Graham Austin			Church address: 26 Avenue de Rumine, Lausanne	
				GAustin@churchofscotland.org.uk	0031 10 412 5709
9	**Lisbon: St Andrew's (F W)**			**lisbonstandrewschurch@gmail.com**	
	Guardianship of the Presbytery			Rua Coelho da Rocha, N°75 - 1°	00351 213 951 165
				Campa de Ourique, 1350-073 Lisbon, Portugal	
				cofslx@netcabo.pt	
				Church address: Rua da Arriaga, Lisbon	
	Session Clerk: Nina O'Donnell			sessionclerklisbon@gmail.com	00351 21 483 8750
	Interim Moderator: Alexander B. Douglas			alexandjill@douglas.net	01383 791080
10	**Malta: St Andrew's Scots Church (F H W)**				
	Beata (Betsi) Thane MA BD	2020		2 Casa Cappella, Triq L-Infanterija, KKP 1270 Hal-Kirkop, Malta	00356 993 53246
				minister@saintandrewsmalta.com	
				Church address: 210 Old Bakery Street, Valletta, Malta	

Malta is a Local Ecumenical partnership with the Methodist Church

11	**Paris: The Scots Kirk (F T W)**			**scotskirkparis@orange.fr**	**0033 9 82 46 09 59**
	Vacant			10 Rue Thimmonier, F-75009 Paris, France	0033 1 48 78 47 94
	Interim Moderator: Lawrence H. Twaddle			LTwaddle@churchofscotland.org.uk	0041 22 788 08 31
				Church address: 17 Rue Bayard, 75009 Paris	
12	**Rome: St Andrew's (F W)**			**scotskirkrome@gmail.com**	
	Tara Curlewis	1994	2023	Via XX Settembre 7, 00187 Rome, Italy	Tel 0039 06 482 7627
				TCurlewis@churchofscotland.org.uk	Fax 0039 06 487 4370
				Church address: Via XX Settembre 7, 00187 Rome	

13 Rotterdam: Scots International Church (F W) **info@scotsintchurch.com** **0031 10 412 4779**

Graham Austin BD	1997	2020	Schiedamse Vest 121, 3012BH Rotterdam, The Netherlands GAustin@churchofscotland.org.uk Church address: Schiedamsesingel 2, Rotterdam, The Netherlands	0031 10 412 5709

14 Trinidad: Greyfriars St Ann's, Port of Spain (W) linked with Arouca and Sangre Grande **greyfriarscos@yahoo.com**

Vacant			50 Frederick Street, Port of Spain, Trinidad	001 868 623 6684
Interim Moderator: Alistair G. Bennett			ABennett@churchofscotland.org.uk	001 441 236 0400

B. In other appointments: members of Presbytery

Bom, Irene M.E. BA DipCS	2008		Ordained Local Minister-Worship and Prayer Promoter	Bergpolderstraat 53A, NL-3038 KB Rotterdam, The Netherlands ibsalem@xs4all.nl	0031 10 265 1703
Evans-Boiten, Joanne H.G. BD	2004	2018	Retreat Centre Director	Colomba le Roc, 510 Chemin du Faurat, Belmontet, 46800 Montcuq en Quercy, France Joanne.evansboiten@gmail.com	0033 5 65 22 13 11
McGeoch, Graham G. MA BD MTh PhD	2009	2017	Theology Lecturer	Faculdade Unida de Vitoria, R.Eng. Fabio Ruschi, 161 Bento Ferreira, Vitoria ES 29050-670, Brazil graham@fuv.edu.br	

C. Retaining: members of Presbytery

Brown, James M. MA BD	1982	2022	(Bochum: English-Speaking Christian Congregation)	Verkehrsstrasse 37, 44809 Bochum, Germany JBrown@churchofscotland.org.uk	0049 234 133363
Homewood, I. Maxwell MSc BD	1997	2003	(Edinburgh: Drylaw)	Ander Fließwiese 26, D-14052 Berlin, Germany maxhomewood@me.com	0049 151 2758 6921
Lawson, Derek G. LLB BD	1998	2020	(Rotterdam: Scots International Church) DLawson@churchofscotland.org.uk	16 Rue de la Madeleine, 22210 La Chèze, France	0036 09 57 66 71
Reamonn, Paraic BA BD	1982	2018	(Jerusalem: St Andrew's)	395B Route de Mandement, 1281 Ruissin, Switzerland paraic.reamonn@gmail.com	0041 79 151 91 43

D. In other appointments: not members of Presbytery

Nil

E. Retaining: not members of Presbytery

Pitkeathly, Thomas C. MA CA BD	1984	2004	(Brussels: St Andrew's)	77 St Thomas Road, Lytham St. Anne's FY8 1JP tpitkeathly@yahoo.co.uk	01253 789634

F. Inactive: not members of Presbytery
Nil

G. Readers (active)

Goodman, Alice (Mrs)	Route de Sallaz 23. Rivaz 1071, Switzerland	alice.goodman@epfl.ch	0041 21 946 1727
van den Bremt, Sia	85 Boulevard Louis Mettewie, Bte 36, Molenbeek-Saint-John, 1080 Belgium	SVandenBremt@churchofscotland.org.uk	0032 475 752 384

H. Ministries Development Staff
Nil

(14) JERUSALEM

Clerk: JOANNA OAKLEY-LEVSTEIN BA — **St Andrew's, Galilee, PO Box 104, Tiberias 14100, Israel** **j.oak.lev@gmail.com** — **00972 50 5842517**

Jerusalem and Tiberias: St Andrew's (F W) — **jerusalem@churchofscotland.org.uk**

D. Stewart Gillan BSc MDiv PhD	1985	2022	St Andrew's Scots Memorial Church, 1 David Remez Street, PO Box 8619, Jerusalem 91086, Israel SGillan@churchofscotland.org.uk **tiberias@churchofscotland.org.uk**	00972 2 673 2401
Muriel B. Pearson (Ms) MA BD PGCE (Associate Minister)	2004	2021	St Andrew's, Galilee, 1 Gdud Barak Street, PO Box 104, Tiberias 14100, Israel MPearson@churchofscotland.org.uk	+447951 888860

G. Reader (active)

Oakley-Levstein, Joanna (Mrs) BA	Mevo Hamma, 12934, Israel	j.oak.lev@gmail.com	00972 50 584 2517

SECTION 6

Additional Lists of Personnel

		Page
A	Ordained Local Ministers and Auxiliary Ministers	256
B	Diaconate	259
C	Healthcare Chaplains	261
D	HM Forces Chaplains	265
E	Mission Partners serving internationally	268
F	Prison Chaplains	270
G	University Chaplains	272
H	Council Education Committees: Church representatives	273
I	Ministers Ordained for Sixty Years and Upwards	274
J	Deceased Ministers and Deacons	276

Ministers not members of Presbytery are listed in Section 5 under each Presbytery: Employed part D, Retaining part E, Inactive part F.

Readers and Ministries Development Staff are listed in Section 5 under each Presbytery: parts G and H respectively.

LIST A – ORDAINED LOCAL MINISTERS AND AUXILIARY MINISTERS

Those in active service only. Where only one date is given it is the year of ordination and appointment. Contact details are under the relevant Presbytery in Section 5.

NAME	ORD	APP	APPOINTMENT	OLM / Aux
1. EDINBURGH AND WEST LOTHIAN				
Addis, Reuben	2023		Edinburgh: Gorgie and Palmerston Place	OLM
Galloway, Susan G.	2023		Edinburgh: Pentlands	OLM
Haggarty, Kay O.N. BEd	2021		Edinburgh: South East	OLM
Henderson, Derek R. MA DipTCP DipCS	2017		Abercorn, Pardovan, Kingscavil and Winchburgh	OLM
Kennedy, Fiona	2022		Edinburgh: Barclay Viewforth, Craiglockhart, Polwarth, St Michael's	OLM
Kirkland, Nikki J. BSc	2021		Edinburgh: St Nicholas' Sighthill	OLM
MacLeod Rivett, Mary A. BA MA PhD	2023		Edinburgh: Granton	OLM
McKenzie, Janet R. (Mrs) BA DipHS CertCS	2016		Edinburgh: South East	OLM
Munn, Derek B.	2022		Edinburgh: Dalmeny and Queensferry	OLM
Quilter, Alison I. DipCS	2018		Polbeth Harwood linked with West Kirk of Calder	OLM
Riddell, Thomas S. BSc CEng FIChemE	1993	1994	Linlithgow: St Michael's	Aux
Tweedie, Fiona J. BSc PhD	2011	2014	Statistician, Church Offices	OLM
Welsh, Rita M. BA PhD	2017		Edinburgh: Holy Trinity	OLM
2. LOTHIAN AND BORDERS				
Don, Andrew MBA	2006	2013	Dalkeith: St John's and Newton	OLM
Watson, Michael D. CertCS	2013	2023	Musselburgh: St Clement's and St Ninian's	OLM
3. SOUTH WEST				
Bellis, Pamela A. BA DipTheol	2014	2022	Balmaclellan, Kells and Dalry linked with Carsphairn	OLM
Campbell, Duncan	2023			
Hogg, James	2018	— —	— —	OLM
Hume, David MSc PhD CertHE	2020		Alloway and Fisherton	OLM
Mack, Elizabeth A. (Miss) DipPE	1994	2018	Lochend and New Abbey	Aux
McLeod, Tom	2014	2015	Craigie Symington linked with Prestwick: South	OLM
Wallace, Mhairi	2013	2017	Kirkmichael, Tinwald and Torthorwald	OLM
Watt, Kim CertThS	2015		Presbytery-wide	OLM
4. CLYDE				
Breingan, Mhairi M. BSc CertCS	2011	2019	Paisley: St George's	OLM
Henderson, Steven BA DipHE RN BSc MPH CertCS	2023		Clydebank: Waterfront linked with Dalmuir: Barclay	OLM
Millar, Ian J. BA	2020	2022	Arrochar linked with Luss	OLM
Stevenson, Stuart CertCE	2011	— —	— —	OLM

5. GLASGOW

Forsythe, Ruth (Mrs) DipRS MCS	2017	2018	Glasgow: Knightswood Anniesland Trinity	OLM
Grieve, Leslie E.T. BSc BA	2014		Glasgow: Colston Wellpark	OLM
Sturrock, Roger D. (Prof.) BD MD FCRP	2014		Glasgow: Kelvinside Hillhead and Glasgow: Wellington	OLM

6. FORTH VALLEY AND CLYDESDALE

Anderson, Fiona DipHE	2020	2023	Dalserf	OLM
Condeco, I. Charlene BEM BSc DipHE	2023		Falkirk: Trinity	OLM
Fyfe, Lorna K. BD	2020	— —	— —	OLM
MacDonald, Monica J. (Mrs)	2014		Slamannan	OLM
Murphy, Jim	2014	2024	Blantyre: Old	OLM
Sarle, Andrew BSc BD	2013		Falkirk: Bainsford	OLM
Wandrum, David C.	1993	— —	— —	Aux
White, Anne W. BA CQSW DipHE	2018	— —	— —	OLM

7. FIFE

Allardice, Michael MA MPhil DipTheol FHEA	2014	2023	Assistant Chaplain, University of Dundee	OLM
Mateos, Margaret B.	2018		Dunfermline: St Leonard's	OLM
Whittle, Sarah BA MA PhD	2022		Kingsbarns	OLM

8. PERTH

Armstrong, Iain S. BTh	2023		Balfron linked with Fintry	OLM
Brodie, Catherine J. MA BA MPhil PGCE	2017		Dundee: Northeast	OLM
Campbell, Gordon A. MA BD CDipAF DipHSM CMgr MCMI MIHM AssocCIPD AFRIN ARSGS FRGS FSAScot	2001	2004	An Honorary Chaplain, University of Dundee	Aux
Elwell-Sutton, Brenda M.M. BA	2022		Dundee: Northeast	OLM
Gourlay, Heather	2021	2024	Forfar: All Souls	OLM
Gray, Ian	2013	2017	Montrose: Trinity	OLM
Hacking, Philip R.	2021	2023	Dollar linked with Muckhart	OLM
Michie, Margaret (Mrs)	2013		Loch Leven Parish Grouping	OLM
Munro, Alastair RN BSc	2022		Dunblane Cathedral, Kilmadock and Blair Drummond	OLM
Nicol, Robert D. MA	2013	2019	Fortingall, Glenlyon, Kenmore and Lawers	OLM
Shearer, Anne F. BA DipEd CertCS	2010	2018	Alva	Aux
Stanley, Lesley (Prof) MA PhD FBTS	2021	2024	Bridge of Allan	OLM
Steele, Grace M.F. MA BTh	2014		Presbytery-wide	OLM
Stevenson, Beverley	2020	2023	Mission Co-ordinator, Stirling and surrounding area	OLM
Stott, Anne M.	2019		Presbytery Pioneer Worker, Bertha Park	OLM
Strachan, Willie D. DipYCW MBA CertCS	2013	2020	Presbytery-wide	OLM
Thorburn, Susan (Mrs) MTh	2014	2019	Mission Development Worker, Presbytery of Fife	OLM
Wilkie, Robert F. CertCS	2011	2012	Perth: Craigie and Moncrieffe	Aux

9. NORTH EAST AND NORTHERN ISLES

Crouch, Simon A. MCIPD CertCS	2019		West Gordon (Alford, Strathdon, Rhynie)	OLM
Freeth, June BA MA	2015		Kirkwall: St Magnus Cathedral linked with Rousay	OLM
Galbraith, David	2021		Maryculter Trinity	OLM
Palmer, Sonia RGN	2017		Elgin	OLM
Simpson, Anne-Marie MA PGCE CertCS	2023		Duffus, Spynie and Hopeman	OLM
Somevi, Joseph K. BSc MSc PhD MRICS MRTPI MIEMA CertCRS	2015	2021	Aberdeen: South	OLM
Stewart, William	2015	2016	Presbytery-wide	OLM
Thorne, Joan I. BA TQFE CertCS	2019		Dyce linked with New Machar	OLM

10. CLÈIR EILEAN Ì: HIGHLANDS AND HEBRIDES

Archer, Morven (Mrs)	2013	2020	Presbytery Assistant Minister, Inverness area	OLM
Gardner, Hilary M. (Miss)	2010	2018	Lairg linked with Rogart	Aux
Kinnear, Marion (Mrs) BD	2009	2021	South Lochaber	Aux
Macdonald, Ishabel	2011		Benbecula linked with Carinish	OLM
MacKellar, Janet K. BSc ProfCertMgmt FCMI	2019		Kilmun, Strone and Ardentinny: The Shore Kirk linked with West Cowal	OLM
MacPherson, Alexander J. MA BSc FRSA	2021		Cowal Kirk	OLM
Morrison, John A. BSc BA PGCE	2013		West Moray	OLM
Munro, Irene BA	2019		Presbytery Chaplain to vulnerable groups in residential care	OLM
Rattenbury, Carol BA	2017	2022	Resolis and Urquhart	OLM
Stewart, Heather (Mrs)	2013	2017	Latheron	OLM
Stobo, Mary J. (Mrs) BA	2013		Community Healthcare Chaplain	OLM
Thomson, Mary Ellen (Mrs)	2014		Presbytery Chaplain to Care Homes	OLM
Whillis, David (Dr) DipHE	2020		Presbytery-wide minister to over 60s community	OLM

11. LEWIS

Nil

12. ENGLAND AND CHANNEL ISLANDS

Binks, Mike	2007	2015	Churches Together in Corby	Aux
Cumming, Alistair MSc CCS FInstLM FLPI	2010	2013	Presbytery Clerk, England and Channel Islands	Aux
Mather, James BA DipArch MA MBA	2010	2019	Woodley Airfield Church, Woodley, Reading	Aux
Wright, Allan BVMS MRCVS	2021		Pioneer Minister to Veterinary Community in NE England	OLM

13. INTERNATIONAL CHARGES

Bom, Irene M.E. BA DipCS	2008		Worship Resourcing	OLM
Campbell, Cindy	2023		Bermuda: Christ Church, Warwick	OLM

LIST B – DIACONATE

Those in active service. Contact details are under the relevant Presbytery in Section 5.

Prior to the General Assembly of 2002, Deacons were commissioned. In 2002 existing Deacons were ordained, as have been those subsequently.

NAME	ORD	APP	APPOINTMENT	PRESBYTERY
Beck, Isobel BD DCS	2014	2016	Kilwinning: Abbey	3 South West
Blair, Fiona (Miss) DCS	1994	2023	Kingshill	9 North East and Northern Isles
Cathcart, John Paul (Mr) DCS	2000	2023	Presbytery Vacant Charge Enabler	5 Glasgow
Crocker, Liz (Mrs) DipComEd DCS	1985	2015	Edinburgh: South East	1 Edinburgh and West Lothian
Evans, Mark (Mr) BSc MSc DCS	1988	2023	National Spiritual Care Strategic Advisor Operational Lead, Scottish Government	1 Edinburgh and West Lothian
Forsyth, Kirsty C. BD DCS	2022		Edinburgh: Richmond Craigmillar	1 Edinburgh and West Lothian
Hamilton, James (Mr) DCS	1997	2000	Glasgow: Maryhill Ruchill	5 Glasgow
Hamilton, Karen M. (Mrs) DCS	1995	2014	Glasgow: Cambuslang	5 Glasgow
Herbert, Claire BD DCS	2019		Chaplain, Lodging House Mission, Glasgow	5 Glasgow
Love, Joanna R. (Ms) BSc DCS	1992	2009	Iona Community: Wild Goose Resource Group	5 Glasgow
McPheat, Elspeth (Miss) DCS	1985	2001	CrossReach: Manager, St Margaret's House, Polmont	1 Edinburgh and West Lothian
Pennykid, Gordon J. BD DCS	2015	2018	Chaplain, HM Prison Edinburgh	1 Edinburgh and West Lothian
Robertson, Pauline (Mrs) BA CertTheol BD DCS	2003	2023	Edinburgh: Mayfield Salisbury	1 Edinburgh and West Lothian
Scott, Pamela (Mrs) BD DCS	2017		Lochgelly and Benarty: St Serf's	7 Fife
Thomson, Jacqueline (Mrs) MTh DCS	2004	2008	Buckhaven and Wemyss	7 Fife
Wilson, Angela DCS	2015	2021	Community Outreach Worker, Southern Ministry Cluster	6 Forth Valley and Clydesdale

Registered as Retaining or Inactive

Those who are retired and registered under the Registration of Ministries Act (Act 2, 2017, as amended) as 'Retaining' or 'Inactive.' Only those 'Inactive' Deacons who have given consent under the GDPR to publication of their details are included. Contact details are under the relevant Presbytery in Section 5.

NAME	COM/ORD	RET	PRESBYTERY	
Allan, Jean (Mrs) DCS	1989	2011	8C	Perth
Beaton, Margaret S. (Miss) DCS	1989	2015	5C	Glasgow
Bell, Sandra L.N. (Mrs) DCS	2001	2013	10E	Clèir Eilean Ì: Highlands and Hebrides
Buchanan, Marion (Mrs) MA DCS	1983	2019	2F	Lothian and Borders
Corrie, Margaret (Miss) DCS	1989	2023	1F	Edinburgh and West Lothian
Crawford, Morag (Miss) MSc DCS	1977	2021	1C	Edinburgh and West Lothian
Cuthbertson, Valerie (Miss) DipTMus DCS	2003	2024	5C	Glasgow
Dunnett, Linda (Mrs) BA DCS	1976	2016	8C	Perth
Gargrave, Mary S. (Mrs) DCS	1989	2024	5C	Glasgow
Getliffe, Dot L.J. (Mrs) BA BD DipEd DCS	2006	2021	10E	Clèir Eilean Ì: Highlands and Hebrides
Gilroy, Lorraine (Mrs) DCS	1988	1994	6C	Forth Valley and Clydesdale
Gordon, Margaret (Mrs) DCS	1998	2012	1C	Edinburgh and West Lothian
Gray, Greta (Miss) DCS	1992	2014	4C	Clyde
Johnston, Mary (Miss) DCS	1988	2003	4F	Clyde
King, Margaret MA DCS	2002	2012	9C	North East and Northern Isles
Lundie, Ann V. (Miss) DCS	1972	2007	9C	North East and Northern Isles
Lyall, Ann (Miss) DCS	1980	2022	5C	Glasgow
MacDonald, Anne (Miss) BA DCS	1980	2023	5C	Glasgow
Mackay, Kenneth D. DCS	1996	2020	8E	Perth
MacKinnon, Ronald M. (Mr) DCS	1996	2012	3F	South West
Maclean, Donald A. (Mr) DCS	1988	1990	11C	Lewis
McCully, M. Isobel (Miss) DCS	1974	1999	4F	Clyde
McLaren, Glenda M. (Ms) DCS	1990	2020	10C	Clèir Eilean Ì: Highlands and Hebrides
McNaughton, Janette (Miss) DCS	1982	2007	5E	Glasgow
Merrilees, Ann (Miss) DCS	1994	2006	1E	Edinburgh and West Lothian
Mitchell, Joyce (Mrs) DCS	1994	2010	10C	Clèir Eilean Ì: Highlands and Hebrides
Mulligan, Anne MA DCS	1974	2013	1C	Edinburgh and West Lothian
Munro, Patricia M. BSc DCS	1986	2016	8C	Perth
Nicholson, David (Mr) DCS	1994	2020	5C	Glasgow
Nicol, Joyce (Mrs) BA DCS	1974	2001	4F	Clyde
Ogilvie, Colin (Mr) BA DCS	1998	2015	6C	Forth Valley and Clydesdale
Philip, Elizabeth A. C. (Mrs) MA BA PGCSE DCS	2007	2018	8C	Perth
Porter, Jean T. (Mrs) BD DCS	2006	2022	8C	Perth

Rennie, Agnes M. (Miss) DCS	1974	2012	1C	Edinburgh and West Lothian
Rose, Lewis (Mr) DCS	1993	2010	8C	Perth
Steele, Marilynn J. (Mrs) BD DCS	1999	2012	2C	Lothian and Borders
Steven, Gordon R. BD DCS	2000	2012	2F	Lothian and Borders
Teague, Yvonne (Mrs) DCS	1965	2002	1C	Edinburgh and West Lothian
Urquhart, Barbara (Mrs) DCS	1986	2017	3C	South West
Wallace, Catherine (Mrs) PGDipC DCS	1987	2022	8C	Perth
Wallace, Sheila D. (Mrs) BA BD DCS	2009	2020	8C	Perth
Wilson, Muriel (Miss) MA BD DCS	1997	2011	3C	South West
Wright, Lynda (Miss) BEd DCS	1979	2021	7C	Fife

LIST C – HEALTHCARE CHAPLAINS

SCOTTISH GOVERNMENT

National Spiritual Care Strategic Advisor Operational Lead
Mr Mark Evans DCS, Healthcare Quality and Improvement, Directorate of the Chief Operating Officer, Scottish Government, St Andrew's House, Edinburgh EH1 3DG; mark.evans2@gov.scot

LOTHIAN

Head of Spiritual Care and Bereavement
Vacant
Spiritual Care Office: The Royal Infirmary of Edinburgh, 51 Little France Crescent, Edinburgh EH16 4SA; 0131 242 1990
Full details of chaplains and contacts in all hospitals: www.nhslothian.scot > Our Services > Spiritual Care

Chaplaincy team includes from the Church of Scotland:
Rev. Joanne G. Foster, Western General Hospital, Edinburgh; joanne.foster2@nhslothian.scot.nhs.uk; 0131 537 1401
Rev. Dr Rosie Magee, Royal Infirmary of Edinburgh; rosie.magee@nhslothian.scot.nhs.uk; 0131 242 1997

Outwith NHS
Rev. Erica M. Wishart, St Columba's Hospice, 15 Boswall Road, Edinburgh EH5 3RW; EWishart@churchofscotland.org.uk; 0131 551 1381

BORDERS

Head of Spiritual Care
Rev. Michael D. Scouler; michael.scouler@borders.scot.nhs.uk; 01896 826565
Spiritual Care Department: Chaplaincy Centre, Borders General Hospital, Melrose TD6 9BS; 01896 826564
Further information: www.nhsborders.scot.nhs.uk > Patients and Visitors > Our services > Chaplaincy Centre

DUMFRIES AND GALLOWAY

Spiritual Care Lead
Rev. Nathan Mesnikoff, Dumfries and Galloway Royal Infirmary; 01387 246246 Ext 31544
DGRI Sanctuary Office, Cargenbridge, Dumfries DG2 8RX dg.spiritual-care@nhs.scot
Further information: https://dghscp.co.uk/spiritual-care-support

AYRSHIRE AND ARRAN

Head of Spiritual Care, Staff Care and Person-Centred Care
Andy Gillies, University Hospital Crosshouse, Kilmarnock Road KA2 0BE; 07866 984823
Point of contact for all chaplains: Susan Robertson, 01583 825988; aa.chaplaincy@aapct.scot.nhs.uk
University Hospital Crosshouse Healthcare Chaplains: Karen Crosbie and Lee Given
University Hospital Ayr Healthcare Chaplains: Elaine Hough and Suzanne Algeo
Woodland View Spiritual Care and Person-Centred Care Lead: Colin Scott
Woodland View and UHC Healthcare Chaplain: Pauline Brown
Further information: www.nhsaaa.net > Services A-Z > Chaplaincy service

GREATER GLASGOW AND CLYDE

Spiritual Care Service Manager: Dawn Allan, dawn.allan3@ggc.scot.nhs.uk
Chaplains Office, Inverclyde Royal Hospital, Larkfield Road, Greenock PA16 0XN; 07814 313249
Spiritual Care Administrator: chaplains@ggc.scot.nhs.uk
Further information: www.nhsggc.org.uk > Services Directory > Spiritual Care

Healthcare chaplains from Church of Scotland:
Rev. Paul G.R. Grant, Glasgow Royal Infirmary; 07890 966965; 0141 201 6300
Rev. Jeanette L. Peel, Chaplains Office, Inverclyde Royal Hospital; 07903 681003; 01475 504759

FORTH VALLEY

Head of Spiritual Care: Eilidh Gallagher, Person Centred Manager
Spiritual Care Centre: Forth Valley Royal Hospital, Larbert FK5 4WR; fv.spiritualcare@nhs.scot; 01324 566071; 07824 460882
Chaplain Team: Mary Anne Burgoyne, David Harper, Sharon McPhee
Further information: www.nhsforthvalley.com > Services A–Z > Spiritual Care Centre

LANARKSHIRE

Head of Spiritual Care and Wellbeing
Paul Graham, paul.graham@lanarkshire.scot.nhs.uk; 07717 815581
Spiritual Care and Wellbeing Office: University Hospital Hairmyres, 218 Eaglesham Road, East Kilbride G75 8RG; spiritualcare@lanarkshire.scot.nhs.uk; 01698 754251
Further information: www.nhslanarkshire.org.uk > Our services A-Z > Spiritual care

FIFE

Head of Spiritual Care and Bereavement Lead
Mr Ian Campbell, Department of Spiritual Care, Victoria Hospital, Hayfield Road, Kirkcaldy KY2 5AH; ian.campbell3@nhs.scot; 01592 648158
Victoria Hospital, Kirkcaldy and NHS Fife Community Hospitals: Chaplain's Office: 01592 648158 or 01592 729675
Queen Margaret Hospital, Dunfermline: Chaplains Office: 01383 674136
Mental Health and Community Chaplain, Adamson and Stratheden Hospitals: 07976 918909
Further information: www.nhsfife.org > Spiritual Care

Chaplaincy team includes from the Church of Scotland:
Rev. Gordon I. Strang, Victoria Hospital, Kirkcaldy; 01592 648158
Rev. Marjory McPherson, Victoria Hospital, Kirkcaldy; 01592 728158

TAYSIDE

Head of Spiritual Care: Vacant
The Wellbeing Centre, Royal Victoria Hospital, Dundee DD2 1SP; lynne.downie@nhs.scot; 01382 423110
Further information: www.nhstayside.scot.nhs.uk > Our Services A-Z > Spiritual Care and Wellbeing

Outwith NHS
Rev. Ali R. Pandian, CHAS, Rachel House Children's Hospice, Avenue Road, Kinross KY13 8FX; APandian@churchofscotland.org.uk; 01577 865777

GRAMPIAN

Spiritual Care
Chaplains' Office, Aberdeen Royal Infirmary, Foresterhill, Aberdeen AB25 2ZN; gram.chaplaincy@nhs.scot; 01224 553166
Further information: www.nhsgrampian.co.uk > Home > Our services > A-Z > Spiritual Care

Chaplaincy team includes from Church of Scotland:
Rev. Jenny M. Adams, Dr Gray's Hospital, Elgin, Pluscarden Road, Elgin IV30 1SN; 0345 456 6000

ORKNEY

Spiritual Care Team
ork.chaplaincy@nhs.scot; 01856 888184
Further information: www.ohb.scot.nhs.uk/service/chaplaincy-and-spiritual-care

SHETLAND

Spiritual Care Lead
Rev Canon Neil Brice, neil.brice@nhs.scot; 01595 743662; 07771 380989
Further information: www.shb.scot.nhs.uk/hospital/spiritualcare.asp

HIGHLAND

Head of Spiritual Care and Staff Support
Janet Davidson, Raigmore Hospital, Old Perth Road, Inverness IV2 3UJ; janet.davidson2@nhs.scot; 01463 704463
Further information: www.nhshighland.scot.nhs.uk/your-services/related-services-and-accessibility/spiritual-care

Chaplaincy team includes from the Church of Scotland:
Lead Staff Support Chaplain: Rev. Mike Robertson, Raigmore Hospital; mike.robertson@nhs.scot; 01463 704463
Rev. Susan Cord, Raigmore Hospital; susan.cord@nhs.scot; 01463 704463

WESTERN ISLES HEALTH BOARD

Lead Chaplain
Rev. T. K. Shadakshari, 23D Benside, Newmarket, Stornoway, Isle of Lewis HS2 0DZ; tk.shadakshari@nhs.scot;
(Office) 01851 704704; (Home) 01851 701727; (Mbl) 07403 697138

NHS EDUCATION FOR SCOTLAND

Spiritual Care
nes.spiritualcare.nhs.scot

Church of Scotland Chaplains in NHS ENGLAND
Rev. Mairi F. Lovett, Chaplain, Royal Brompton Hospital, Sydney Street, London SW3 6NP; m.lovett@rbht.nhs.uk; 020 7351 8060
Rev. John K.S. McMahon, Head of Spiritual and Pastoral Care, West London NHS Trust, Broadmoor Hospital, Crowthorne, Berkshire RG45 7EG; john.mcmahonrev@westlondon.nhs.uk; 01344 754098

LIST D – HM FORCES CHAPLAINS

The columns give years of ordination and commissioning.

NAME	ORD	COM	ADDRESS
ROYAL NAVY			
Ashley-Emery, Stephen BD DPS RN	2006	2019	Staff Chaplain Naval Chaplaincy Service, Naval Chaplaincy Service Headquarters, Tanner Building, HMS Excellent, Portsmouth PO2 8BY Stephen.Ashley-Emery100@mod.gov.uk
Dalton, Mark F. BD DipMin RN	2002	2002	The Chaplaincy, HMS Neptune, HM Naval Base Clyde, Faslane, Helensburgh G84 8HL Mark.Dalton242@mod.gov.uk
Davidson, Mark R. MA BD STM PhD PhD RN	2005	2011	Principal AFCC, Armed Forces Chaplaincy Centre, Beckett House, Defence Academy of the United Kingdom, Shrivenham SN6 8LA Mark.Davidson122@mod.gov.uk
Royal Naval Reserve			
Nil			
ARMY			
Anderson, David P. BSc BD	2002	2007	51 Infantry Brigade and HQ Scotland, Forthside, Stirling FK7 7RR David.Anderson646@mod.gov.uk
Begg, Richard J. MA BD	2008	2016	3 RSME Regiment, Gibraltar Barracks, Blackwater, Camberley GU17 9LP Richard.Begg100@mod.gov.uk
Berry, Geoff T. BSc BD	2009	2012	3 SCOTS, Fort George, Ardersier, Inverness IV2 7TE Geoff.Berry102@mod.gov.uk
Cobain, Alan R. BD	2000	2017	HQ SW, Building 56, Jellabad Barracks, Tidworth SP9 7BQ Alan.Cobain100@mod.gov.uk

Frail, Nicola R. BLE MBA MDiv	2000	2012	Chaplains Office, DM(SW), Whittington Barracks, Lichfield WS14 9PY Nicola.Frail188@mod.gov.uk
Francis, James MBE BD PhD	2002	2009	HQ Regional Command, Montgomery House, Queen's Avenue, Aldershot GU11 2JN James.Francis369@mod.gov.uk
Kellock, Chris N. MA BD	1998	2012	Permanent Joint Headquarters, Sandy Lane, Northwood HA6 3HP Christopher.Kellock935@mod.gov.uk
MacKay, Stewart A. BA	2009	2009	ATR (P) 3ATR, Alexander Barracks, Pirbright, Woking GU24 0QQ Stewart.Mackay762@mod.gov.uk
MacKenzie, Hector M.	2008	2008	ITC (C) 2ITB, Helles Baracks, Catterick Garrison DL9 4HH Hector.MacKenzie657@mod.gov.uk
Macpherson, Duncan J. BSc BD	1993	2002	HQ 1 Deep Recce Strike Brigade Combat Team, Building 57, Delhi Barracks, Tidworth SP9 7DX Duncan.Macpherson183@mod.gov.uk
McLay, Neil BD MTh	2006	2012	HQ Regional Point of Control for Central England, Kendrew Barracks, Cottesmore, Oakham LE15 7BL Neil.McLay100@mod.gov.uk
Thom, David J. BD DipMin DipPS DipLM	1999	2015	HQ SHAPE, EJSU, BFPO 26 David.Thom410@mod.gov.uk
van Sittert, Paul BA BD	1997	2011	1 LANCS, Salamanca Barracks, Episkopi, BFPO 53 Paul.VanSittert218@mod.gov.uk
Army Reserve			
Goodison, Michael J. BSc BD	2013	2013	105 Regiment Royal Artillery, Army Reserve Centre, Crawfordsburn Road, Newtonards Michael.Goodison100@mod.gov.uk
Jeffrey, Kenneth S. BA BD PhD DMin	2002	2021	7 SCOTS, Queens Barracks, 131 Dunkeld Road, Perth PH1 5BT 8472jeffre@armymail.mod uk
Mair, Michael J. MStJ BD MTh	2014	2019	32 (Scottish) Signal Regiment, 21 Jardine Street, Glasgow G20 6JU 5558mai@armymail.mod.uk
Rowe, Christopher J. BA BD	2008	2008	5 Military Intelligence Battalion, Edinburgh Castle, Edinburgh EH1 2NG 9607row@armymail.mod.uk
Officiating Chaplains to the Military			
Blakey, Stephen A. BSc BD	1977	1977	Staff Chaplain, HQ Scotland, Forthside, Stirling FK7 7RR
Duncan, John C. MBE BD MPhil	1987	2001	Waterloo Lines, Leuchars Station, St Andrews KY1 0JX
Gardner, Neil N. DL CStJ MA BD	1991	1991	Edinburgh Universities Officers' Training Corps, 301 Colinton Road, Edinburgh EH13 0LA
Rankin, Lisa-Jane BD CPS	2003		2 Bn Royal Regiment of Scotland, Glencorse Barracks, Penicuik EH26 0QH
Selemani, Ecilo LTh MTh	1993		51 Infantry Brigade and HQ Scotland, Forthside, Stirling FK7 7RR
ROYAL AIR FORCE			
Lancaster, Craig MA BD	2004	2011	Chaplaincy Centre, RAF Cosford, Wolverhampton WV7 3EX craig.lancaster102@mod.gov.uk
Young, David T. BA BD MTh	2007	2020	Chaplaincy Centre, RAF Honington, Suffolk IP31 1EE david.young137@mod.gov.uk

Royal Air Force Reserve
Nil

Sea Cadets

Campbell, Gordon MA BD	Sea Cadets Dundee, East Camperdown Street, Dundee DD1 3LG
Fletcher, Suzanne G. BA MDiv MA DMin	Sea Cadets Dunbar, ACF Building, Castle Park Barracks, 33 North Road, Dunbar EH42 1EU
MacKay, Colin (Mr)	Sea Cadets Wick, The Scout Hall, Kirkhill, Wick KW1 4PN
May, John S. (Iain) BSc MBA BD DMin	Sea Cadets Leith, Prince of Wales Dock, Leith, Edinburgh EH6 7DX
Robertson, Pauline DCS BA CertTheol	Sea Cadets Musselburgh, 9-11 South Street, Musselburgh EH21 6AT
Ross, Sarah L. BD MTh PGDipCS	Sea Cadets East Kilbride, Army Reserve Centre, Whitemoss, East Kilbride G74 2HP

Army Cadet Force

Blackwood, Keith T. BD DipMin	2 Bn The Highlanders, ACF, Cadet Training Centre, Rocksley Drive, Boddam, Peterhead AB42 3BA
Dicks, Shuna M. BSc BD	2 Bn The Highlanders, ACF, Cadet Training Centre, Rocksley Drive, Boddam, Peterhead AB42 3BA
Mackenzie, Cameron BD	Lothian and Borders Bn, ACF, Drumshoreland House, Broxburn EH52 5PF
McCulloch, Alen J.R. MA BD	1 Highlanders Bn, ACF, Gordonville Road, Inverness IV2 4SU
Selemani, Ecilo LTh MTh	Glasgow and Lanarkshire Bn, ACF, Gilbertfield Road, Cambuslang, Glasgow G72 8YP
Stewart, Fraser M.C. BSc BD	1 Highlanders Bn, ACF, Gordonville Road, Inverness IV2 4SU
Swindells, Sean BD DipMin MTh	Angus and Dundee Bn, ACF, Barry Buddon Cadet Training Centre, by Carnoustie DD7 7RY
Wilson, Fiona A. BD	West Lowland Battalion, ACF, Fusilier House, Seaforth Road, Ayr KA8 9HX

Air Training Corps

Regional Chaplain, Scotland & N. Ireland	Alistair K. Ridland MStJ MA BD PGDip MRAeS MInstLM RAFAC	chaplain.sni@rafac.mod.gov.uk	01334 857136 07891 501859
North Scotland Wing			
Wing Chaplain & 2405 Sqn	Russel Smith BD	russanntwo@yahoo.co.uk	01349 861011
107 (Aberdeen) Sqn	James L.K. Wood	james@jamesinez.plus.com	01224 722543
379 (County of Ross) Sqn	Michael J. Macdonald	Michael.Macdonald@churchofscotland.org.uk	01349 884268
423DF (Speyside) Sqn	Robert J.M. Anderson BD FInstLM	bobjmanderson@gmail.com	01343 835401 07980 750685
1298 (Huntly) Sqn	Kay F. Gauld BD STM PhD	KGauld@churchofscotland.org.uk	07951 059272
Central Scotland Wing			
Wing Chaplain & 2450 (Dudhope) Sqn	C. Graham D. Taylor BSc BD FIAB	AT Corps, MOD Leuchars KY16 0JX	
775 (Burntisland) Sqn	Alan Sharp BSc BD	Unity Hall, Links Place, Burntisland KY3 9DY	
1370 (Leven) Sqn	Jacqueline Thomson MTh DCS	Jacqueline.Thomson@churchofscotland.org.uk	07806 776560
1743 (Crieff) Sqn	Robert D. Nicol MA	RNicol@churchofscotland.org.uk	01887 820242
2288 (Montrose) Sqn	Ian A. McLean BSc BD DMin	IMcLean@churchofscotland.org.uk	01674 434672
South East Scotland Wing			
Wing Chaplain	Regional Chaplain at present		
132 (North Berwick) Sqn	Neil J. Dougall BD DipMin DMin	NDougall@churchofscotland.org.uk	01620 892132

867 (Denny) Sqn	F. Derek Gunn BD	RevDerekGunn@hotmail.com	01324 624938
870 (Dreghorn) Sqn, Edinburgh	Peter Nelson BSc BD	PNelson@churchofscotland.org.uk	07500 057889
1716 (Roxburgh) Sqn	Sheila W. Moir MTheol	SMoir@churchofscotland.org.uk	01835 822255
2535 (Livingston) Sqn	Nelu I. Balaj BD MA ThD	NBalaj@churchofscotland.org.uk	01506 411888
West Scotland Wing			
Wing Chaplain & 2166 (Hamilton) Sqn	I. Ross Blackman BSc MBA BD CertTh	RBlackman@churchofscotland.org.uk	01698 640185
327 (Kilmarnock) Sqn	Kristina I. Hine BS MDiv	KHine@churchofscotland.org.uk	
498 (Wishaw) Sqn	Ian Douglas (Mr) (Reader)	IDouglas@churchofscotland.org.uk	07742 022423
1001 (Monklands) Sqn	Robert A. Hamilton BA BD	RHamilton@churchofscotland.org.uk	01236 763022

VETERANS CHAPLAINCY SCOTLAND

VCS provides pastoral care for military veterans and their families across Scotland. Working alongside local churches, and with a wide range of veteran charities, we provide individual veterans with a proactive listening ear, supporting them through the challenges of life. We seek to provide an approachable, confidential, experienced chaplaincy which mirrors the quality of ministry delivered by our serving chaplains. Our twenty chaplains, deployed across Scotland, are professionally qualified and recognised for their pastoral gifts. Our support is only a phone call or text away on 07521 638848, the first step to hope, healing and acceptance. www.vcscotland.org

Programme Coordinator:	Rev. Philip W. Patterson BMus BD MTh	philip.patterson@vcscotland.org	07713 625792
Administrator:	Rev. Stephen A. Blakey BSc BD CStJ	stephen.blakey@vcscotland.org	07712 542518

LIST E – MISSION PARTNERS SERVING INTERNATIONALLY

AFRICA

Malawi: Church of Central Africa Presbyterian **www.ccapsolinia.org**

Mr Gary Brough (2019) Capacity Development Facilitator, CCAP General Assembly Office, PO Box 30398, Lilongwe, Malawi
ccapgeneral@africa-online.net; GBrough@churchofscotland.org.uk
office + 265 79 6064
mobile +265 883 626 500

Malawi: Church of Central Africa Presbyterian, Synods of Livingstonia, Nkhoma and Blantyre
Mozambique: Evangelical Church of Christ
South Sudan: Presbyterian Church of South Sudan

Rev Dr Kenneth R Ross (2019) Theological Educator: Africa, based at: Zomba Theological College, PO Box 130, Zomba
KRoss@churchofscotland.org.uk
+265 1 524 419

Zambia: United Church of Zambia **http://uczsynod.org**

Mr Keith and Mrs Ida Waddell (2016) Special Needs Support and Health Support, UCZ, Mwandi Mission, Box 60693, Livingstone, Zambia
keithida2014@gmail.com
mobile (Keith) +260 977 143 692
mobile (Ida) +260 964 761 039

EUROPE

Budapest

Rev Aaron C. Stevens (2023) Regional Liaison (Central Europe) & Minister, St Columba's, Budapest **www.scottishmission.org**
Scottish Mission, Vörösmarty utca 51, 1064 Budapest +36 (70) 615 5394
AStevens@churchofscotland.org.uk

Rome **www.mediterraneanhope.com**

Ms Fiona Kendall (2018) (Ecumenical appointment: Global Ministries USA) Mediterranean Hope, Federation of Protestant Churches in Italy, Via Firenze 38, 00138 Roma, Italy +39 (0)6 4825 120
FKendall@churchofscotland.org.uk

Rev Tara Curlewis (2023) Regional Ecumenical Liaison Officer & Minister, St Andrew's Rome **www.presbyterianchurchrome.org**
Reformed Ecumenical Office, Via Firenze 38, 00138 Roma, Italy mobile: +39 351 3030 368
St Andrew's Church, Via Venti Settembre 7, 00187 Roma, Italy church office: +39 06 482 7627
TCurlewis@churchofscotland.org.uk; tara.curlewis@wcrc.eu

MIDDLE EAST: ISRAEL & PALESTINE

Jerusalem **www.standrewsjerusalem.org**

Rev Dr D. Stewart Gillan (2022) St Andrew's Jerusalem, PO Box 8619, Jerusalem 91086, Israel guesthouse: +972 2 673 2401
SGillan@churchofscotland.org.uk mobile: +972 (0)50 762 4463

Tiberias **https://standrewsgalilee.com**

Rev Muriel C. Pearson (2021) St Andrew's Galilee, PO Box 104, Tiberias 14100, Israel +972 53 244 4314; +447951 888860
MPearson@churchofscotland.org.uk

The Church of Scotland also operates:

St Andrew's House Hotel, Jerusalem
Originally 'Hospice' and opened in 1930 beside St Andrew's Church in central Jerusalem. 23 bedrooms, meeting rooms, Fairtrade handcrafts sales.
General Manager: Mrs Lilian Lepejian, PO Box 8619, 1 David Remez Street, Jerusalem 910986, Israel. www.scotsguesthouse.com info@scotsguesthouse.com
+972 2 673 2401

The Scots Hotel, Tiberias
Hotel & Wellness Centre, opened in 2004 in the historic compound of the Scottish Hospital. 69 bedrooms, restaurant, wine bar, swimming pool, spa, historical visitors centre. General Manager: Mr Shaul Hadas, 1 Gdud Barak Street, Tiberias, Israel. www.scotshotels.com info@scotshotels.co.il
+972 4 671 0710

Tabeetha School, Jaffa
An English speaking school founded in 1863, where girls and boys of different languages, faiths and cultures are educated together through an English curriculum leading to IGCSE, GCSE and A level qualifications accepted by universities in Israel and elsewhere. Executive Director: Mrs Mona Ashkar PO Box 8170, 21 Jeffet Street, Jaffa 61081, Israel. www.tabeethaschool.org +972 3 682 1581

See also the Presbyteries of International Charges and Jerusalem (Section 5: 13 and 14)

LIST F – PRISON CHAPLAINS

SCOTTISH PRISON SERVICE CHAPLAINCY ADVISER (Church of Scotland)

Rev. Dr Sheena Orr	SPS HQ, One Lochside, 1 Lochside Avenue, Edinburgh EH12 9DJ sheena.orr@prisons.gov.scot	0131 330 3575; 07922 649160
ADDIEWELL Rev. Chris Galbraith	HM Prison Addiewell, Station Road, Addiewell, West Calder EH55 8QA chris.galbraith@sodexogov.co.uk	01506 874500
CASTLE HUNTLY Rev. Anne E. Stewart	HM Prison Castle Huntly, Longforgan, Dundee DD2 5HL anne.stewart2@prisons.gov.scot	01382 319388
DUMFRIES Rev. Neil Campbell	HM Prison Dumfries, Terregles Street, Dumfries DG2 9AX neil.campbell2@prisons.gov.scot	01387 294214
DUNDEE: BELLA Rev. Anne E. Stewart	Bella Community Custody Unit, 81 Ann Street, Dundee DD3 7TF anne.stewart2@prisons.gov.scot	01382 319388
EDINBURGH Mr Gordon Pennykid DCS Rev. Keith Graham Rev. David Swan Rev. Bob Akroyd (Free Church)	HM Prison Edinburgh, 33 Stenhouse Road, Edinburgh EH11 3LN gordon.pennykid@prisons.gov.scot KEGraham@churchofscotland.org.uk david.swan@prisons.gov.scot robert.akroyd@prisons.gov.scot	0131 444 3115
GLASGOW: BARLINNIE Rev. Jill Clancy Rev. Beki Wakeling (Episcopal) Rev. Jonathan Keefe Rev. John Murfin (Elim)	HM Prison Barlinnie, 81 Lee Avenue, Riddrie, Glasgow G33 2QX jill.clancy@prisons.gov.scot; JClancy@churchofscotland.org.uk rebekah.wakeling@prisons.gov.scot jonathan.keefe@prisons.gov.scot john.murfin@prisons.gov.scot	0141 770 2059
GLASGOW LILIAS Rev. Margaret Shuttleworth	Lilias Community Custody Unit, 41 Shawpark Street, Wyndford, Glasgow G20 9BT margaret.shuttleworth@prisons.gov.scot	01736 835300

GLENOCHIL	HM Prison Glenochil, King o' Muir Road, Tullibody FK10 3AD	01259 767211
Rev. Graham Bell (Baptist)	graham.bell@prisons.gov.scot	
Rev. Philip Hacking	philip.hacking@prisons.gov.scot	
GRAMPIAN	HM Prison and Young Offender Institution, South Road, Peterhead AB42 2YY	01779 485744
Rev. Paul Innes (Assemblies of God)	paul.innes@prisons.gov.scot	
Mrs Julie Innes (Assemblies of God)	julie.innes@prisons.gov.scot	
GREENOCK	HM Prison Greenock, Old Inverkip Road, Greenock PA16 9AH	01475 787801
Rev. Gary Caldwell	gary.caldwell@prisons.gov.scot	
INVERNESS	HM Prison Inverness, Duffy Drive, Inverness IV2 3HN	01463 229020
Rev. Dr Hugh Watt	hugh.watt@prisons.gov.scot	
Rev. John Beadle (Methodist)	john.beadle@methodist.org.uk	
KILMARNOCK	HM Prison Kilmarnock, Mauchline Road, Kilmarnock KA1 5AA	01563 548928
Rev. John Murfin (Elim)	john.murfin@prisons.gov.scot	
LOW MOSS	HM Prison Low Moss, 190 Crosshill Road, Bishopbriggs, Glasgow G64 2QB	0141 762 9727
Rev. Fiona Morrison	fiona.morrison@prisons.gov.scot	
Rev. James Faddes	james.faddes@prisons.gov.scot	
Rev. Philip Hacking	philip.hacking@prisons.gov.scot	
PERTH	Chaplaincy Centre, HM Prison Perth, 3 Edinburgh Road, Perth PH2 7JH	01738 458216
Rev. Douglas Creighton	douglas.creighton@prisons.gov.scot	
Mrs Deirdre Yellowlees	deirdre.yellowlees@prisons.gov.scot	
POLMONT	Chaplaincy Centre, HM Young Offender Institution Polmont, Brightons, Falkirk FK2 0AB	01324 722241
Rev. Hillary Nyika (Baptist)	hillary.nyika@prisons.gov.scot	
Rev. Margaret Shuttleworth	margaret.shuttleworth@prisons.gov.scot	
Rev. Gary Caldwell	gary.caldwell@prisons.gov.scot	
SHOTTS	HM Prison Shotts, Canthill Road, Shotts ML7 4LE	01501 824071
Rev. John Caldwell (Apostolic Church UK)	john.caldwell@prisons.gov.scot	
Rev. Murdo MacLean	murdo.maclean@prisons.gov.scot	
STIRLING	HM Prison and Young Offender Institution, Cornton Road, Stirling FK9 5NU	01786 835300
Rev. Margaret Shuttleworth	margaret.shuttleworth@prisons.gov.scot	
Mrs Deirdre Yellowlees	deirdre.yellowlees@prisons.gov.scot	

LIST G – UNIVERSITY CHAPLAINS

Name	Email	Telephone
ABERDEEN		
Rev. Marylee Anderson MA BD	m.anderson@abdn.ac.uk	01224 272137
Rev. Sarah A. Brown MA BD ThM DipYP/Theol PDCCE DipPS (Honorary)	Sarah.Brown@churchofscotland.org.uk	
ABERTAY, DUNDEE		
Vacant		
CAMBRIDGE		
Rev. Nigel Uden (U.R.C. and C. of S.)	nigel.uden@downingplaceurc.org	01223 314586
DUNDEE		
Rev. Fiona C. Douglas MBE MA BD PhD	f.c.douglas@dundee.ac.uk	01382 384156
Rev. Michael Allardice MA MPhil DipTheol FHEA (Assistant Chaplain)	m.allardice@dundee.ac.uk	01382 384127
Rev. Gordon A. Campbell MA BD (Honorary)	g.a.campbell@dundee.ac.uk	01382 384045
EDINBURGH		
Rev. Harriet A. Harris MBE BA DPhil	chaplain@ed.ac.uk	0131 650 2595; 07896 244792
Rev. Dr Urzula Glienecke (Associate Chaplain)	urzula.glienecke@ed.ac.uk	
Rev. F. Lynne MacMurchie LLB BD (Listener)	fmacmurc@ed.ac.uk	0131 650 9502
EDINBURGH NAPIER (Honorary Chaplain)	chaplaincy@napier.ac.uk	
Rev. Karen K. Campbell BD MTh DMin	KKCampbell@churchofscotland.org.uk	0131 447 4359
GLASGOW		
Vacant	chaplain@glasgow.ac.uk	0141 330 4160
Rev. Roz Lawson MA MA BD (Assistant Chaplain)	roz.lawson@glasgow.ac.uk	0141 330 1888
Rev. Roger D. Sturrock BD MD FCRP (Hononary)	RSturrock@churchofscotland.org.uk	0141 339 0454
Rev. Richard Baxter MA BD (Honorary)	RBaxter@churchofscotland.org.uk	07958 541418
GLASGOW CALEDONIAN		
Rev. Alastair S. Duncan MA BD	ADuncan@churchofscotland.org.uk	07968 852083
HERIOT-WATT, EDINBURGH		
Rev. Jane M. Howitt MA BD	j.howitt@hw.ac.uk	0131 451 4508; 07522 621233
Rev. Graeme M. Glover MA MBA MSc (Honorary, Scottish Borders Campus)	GGlover@churchofscotland.org.uk	01896 209455
OXFORD		
Vacant		

ROBERT GORDON, ABERDEEN
Rev. Canon Isaac. M. Poobalan BD MTh DMin — chaplaincy@rgu.ac.uk — 01224 640119

ST ANDREWS
Rev. Donald G. MacEwan MA BD PhD — dgm21@st-andrews.ac.uk — 01334 462865
Rev. Samantha J. Ferguson MTheol (Assistant) — sjf6@st-andrews.ac.uk — 01334 461766
Rev. Giles W. Dove MA MPhil BD FSAScot (Assistant)

STIRLING (Honorary Chaplain)
Rev. Lesley Stanley (Prof) MA PhD FBTS — lesley.stanley@stir.ac.uk — 01786 467164

STRATHCLYDE, GLASGOW
Meg Masson BA PGDipEdRes PGDipHRM FCIPD FHEA — meg.masson@strath.ac.uk — 0141 548 2212

LIST H – COUNCIL EDUCATION COMMITTEES: CHURCH REPRESENTATIVES

Aberdeen City	Ms Hilda Smith	smithh09@hotmail.com	01224 311309
Aberdeenshire	Rev. Carl J. Irvine	CIrvine@churchofscotland.org.uk	01467 629163
Angus	Rev. Christine Hay	Christine.Hay@churchofscotland.org.uk	01241 554189
Argyll and Bute	Vacant		
City of Edinburgh	Mrs Fiona E. Beveridge	fbeveridge1@gmail.com	0131 661 8831
Clackmannanshire	Rev. Sang Y. Cha	SCha@churchofscotland.org.uk	01259 213872
Comhairle nan Eilean Siar	Rev. Hugh M. Stewart	berneralwuig@btinternet.com	01851 672388
Dumfries and Galloway	Mr Robert McQuistan	mcquistan@mcquistan.plus.com	01671 820327
Dundee City	Ms Margaret McVean	margaret.mcvean@btinternet.com	01382 860894
East Ayrshire	Dr David F. Lewis	iadl@btinternet.com	01292 570663
East Dunbartonshire	Mrs Barbara Jarvie	jarviebj@gmail.com	01360 319729
East Lothian	Mr Ray Lesso	ray.lesso@gmail.com	07884 448224
East Renfrewshire	Mrs Fiona M. Gilchrist	fionagilchrist0@gmail.com	0141 391 9551
Falkirk	Mrs Agnes Mullen	mullenagnescc@gmail.com	07447 393343
Fife	Mr Ian Macaulay	ianinsudan@hotmail.com	01337 828477
Glasgow City	Mr James Hamilton DCS	James.Hamilton@churchofscotland.org.uk	0141 558 3195; 07584 137314
Highland	Mr William Skene	bill.skene@lochaber.presbytery.org.uk	01397 712594
Inverclyde	Rev. David W.G. Burt	dwgburt@btinternet.com	07971 431185
Midlothian	Mrs Elizabeth Morton	elizabethmorton180@gmail.com	0131 663 8916
Moray	Ms. Sheila A. Brumby	sheilabrumby50@btinternet.com	01340 831588
North Ayrshire	Mr Andrew J. Bruce	andrew_bruce2@sky.com	07484 150461

North Lanarkshire	Margaret S. Clarkson	clarkson492@btinternet.com	01698 261723
Orkney Islands	Rev. G. Fraser H. Macnaughton	FMacnaughton@churchofscotland.org.uk	01856 873312
Perth and Kinross	Mrs Margaret B. Conroy	margaretbconroy@hotmail.com	07817 627725
Renfrewshire	Miss Mary Jane Bird	mjbird55@gmail.com	
Scottish Borders	Rev. Dr Adam J.J. Hood	AHood@churchofscotland.org.uk	01289 332787
Shetland Islands	Ms K. Ellen Griffiths Weir	EWeir@churchofscotland.org.uk	
South Ayrshire	Rev. David R. Gemmell	DGemmell@churchofscotland.org.uk	01292 864140
South Lanarkshire	Rev. Jillian Storrie	JStorrie@churchofscotland.org.uk	01698 791414
Stirling	Mr Colin O'Brien	cobrien20@btinternet.com	01360 660616
West Dunbartonshire	Rev. Ian H. Miller	revianmiller@btinternet.com	01389 753039
West Lothian	Mrs Lynne McEwen	lynnemcewen@hotmail.co.uk	07933 352935

LIST I – MINISTERS ORDAINED FOR SIXTY YEARS AND UPWARDS

1951	6 November	Alexander Gordon McGillivray MA BD STM	(Edinburgh: Presbytery Clerk)
1953	21 October	Donald Maciver Ross MA	(Industrial Mission Organiser)
	6 December	Mark Wilson	(Church of North India)
1954	17 January	Arthur William Alexander Main MA BD	(Kirkintilloch: St David's Memorial)
	6 June	Ian Murray Pollock Davidson MBE MA BD	(Stirling: Allan Park South with Stirling: Church of the Holy Rude)
1955	10 August	Michael Muir Dickie BSc	(Ayr: Castlehill)
	14 November	David Wishart Torrance MA BD	(Earlston)
1957	11 January	William Macleod	(Uig)
	15 July	Alexander Brown Cairns MA	(Turin)
	3 November	George Gordon Cameron MA BD STM	(Edinburgh: Juniper Green)
	7 November	Robert Milne Tuton MA	(Glasgow: Shettleston Old)
	24 November	Archibald Freeland Chisholm MA	(Braes of Rannoch with Foss and Rannoch)
	24 November	Francis George Bernard Liddiard MA	(Brechin: Gardner Memorial and East)
1958	11 June	William Moncur McKenzie DA	(Dumfries: Troqueer)
	13 July	Donald William Fraser MA	(Monifieth)
	23 October	David Sage Millen Hamilton MA BD STM	(Lecturer, Practical Theology, University of Glasgow)
	14 December	Francis Campbell Tollick BSc DipEd	(Port Glasgow: St Martin's)
	23 December	John McLeod MA	(Resolis and Urquhart)
1959	16 March	Robert James Stewart MA BD STM	(Orwell with Portmoak)
	12 April	Ian Morrison Strachan MA BD	(Ashkirk with Selkirk)
	31 May	John Russell MA	(Tillicoultry)
	28 October	Andrew Stark Taylor BTh FPhS	(Greenock: The Union)
1960	6 January	Alasdair James Morton MA BD DipEd FEIS	(Bowden with Newtown)
	5 July	Derek Haley BD DPS	(Chaplain: Gartnavel Royal Hospital, Glasgow)

	15 July	Iain McDougall Roy MA BD	(Stevenston: Livingstone)
	14 September	George Alan Simpson Stirling MA	(Leochel Cushnie and Lynturk with Tough)
	17 November	Alistair Andrew Benvie Davidson MA BD	(Grange with Rothiemay)
1961	8 April	Douglas Niven Alexander MA BD	(Bishopton)
	26 April	John Pattison Cubie MA BD	(Caldwell)
	21 May	James Harkness KVCO CB OBE KHC MA DD	(Chaplain General, Army)
	June	Sidney Hall Coleman BA BD MTh	(Glasgow: Merrylea)
	24 October	James Barbour Lawson MA BD	(South Uist)
	17 November	Alexander Cunningham MA BD	(Glasgow: Presbytery Clerk)
		Robin Graeme Brown BA BD	(Birsay with Rousay)
1962	11 January	John Mackenzie Kellet MA	(Edinburgh: Leith South)
	4 March	Ian Andrew Moir MA BD	(Adviser for Urban Priority Areas)
	6 April	Alastair Fleming McCormick	(Creich with Rosehall)
	12 June	David Ferguson Huie MA BD	(Rome: St Andrew's)
	26 August	Ronald Stanton Blakey MA BD MTh	(Assembly Council)
	25 September	John Diamond Rennie MA	(Broughton, Glenholm and Kilbucho with Skirling with Stobo and Drumelzier with Tweedsmuir)
	10 October	John Spencer MA BD	(Dumfries: Lincluden with Holywood)
	11 November	Donald Murray Stephen TD MA BD ThM	(Edinburgh: Marchmont St Giles')
	14 December	George Angus Chalmers MA BD MLitt	(Catrine with Sorn)
1963	11 January	William Johnstone MA BD DLitt	(Professor of Hebrew and Semitic Languages, University of Aberdeen)
	13 September	Stephen Anton Pacitti MA	(Black Mount with Culter with Libberton and Quothquan)
	25 October	John Stevenson MA BD PhD HonFEIS	(General Secretary, Department of Education)
	4 December	James Ainslie McIntyre MA BD	(Lecturer, New Testament , University of Glasgow)
		Gordon Calderwood MacPherson MA BD MTh	(Associate, Kilmarnock: Henderson)
1964	23 February	Alexander Douglas Lamb MA	(Dalry: St Margaret's)
	26 February	George Prentice BA BTh	(Paisley: Martyrs')
	27 February	John Macfarlane (Ian) Wilson MA	(Adviser, Religious Education, Highland Region)
	10 March	Robert Smillie Christie MA BD ThM	(Kilmarnock: West High)
	8 April	David Mackay Beckett BA BD	(Edinburgh: Greyfriars, Tolbooth and Highland Kirk)
	17 May	Archibald Tearlach Black BSc	(Inverness: Ness Bank)
	5 June	John Love Paterson MA BD STM	(Linlithgow: St Michael's)
	20 June	Thomas Mathieson McWilliam MA BD	(Contin)
	30 June	John Gordon Webster BSc	(Glasgow: St John's Renfield)
	25 September	Archibald Robert Halliday BD MTh	(Duffus, Spynie and Hopeman)
	5 October	Thomas Millar Cant MA BD	(Paisley: Laigh Kirk)
	16 October	John Johnston Laidlaw MA	(Adviser, Religious Education, Tayside Region)
	1 November	William Howie MA BD CASS STM	(Director, Voluntary Service Aberdeen)
	8 November	James Hamilton Simpson BD LLB	(Greenock: Mount Kirk)
	17 December	Robert William Moffatt Johnston MA BD STM	(Glasgow: Temple Anniesland)
		Ian Lawrie Forrester MA	(Friockheim Kinnell with Inverkeilor and Lunan)

LIST J – DECEASED MINISTERS AND DEACONS

The following ministers and deacons have died since the list in the previous volume of the Year Book was compiled.

NAME	ORD	RET	CHARGE
2023			
Brady, John (Ian) Darroch BSc ARCST BD	1967	2001	(Edinburgh: Corstoprhine Old)
Buchan, Alexander MA BD PGCE	1975	1992	(North Ronaldsay with Sanday)
Clark, Douglas William LTh	1993	2015	(Lenzie Old)
Collins, Mitchell BD CPS	1996	2005	(Creich, Flisk and Kilmany with Monimail)
Dryden, Ian MA DipEd	1988	2001	(New Machar)
Firth, James Stanley MA DipEd BD	1970	1976	(Carluke: St John's)
Ford, Alan Andrew BD	1977	2013	(Glasgow: Springburn)
Haddow, Angus Halley BSc	1963	1999	(Methlick)
Hetherington, Robert Macarthur MA BD	1966	2002	(Barrhead: South and Levern)
Hughes, Helen (Miss) DCS	1977	2008	(Deacon, Glasgow: Springburn)
Lindsay, William Douglas BD CPS	1978	2004	(Eaglesham)
Ludik, Cornelius Breda BA BTh DipTheol MTh PhD	1979		St Andrew's-Lhanbryd and Urquhart
Macmillan, Gilleasbuig Iain KCVO MA BD Drhc DD FRSE HRSA FRCSEd	1969	2013	(Edinburgh: High (St Giles'))
MacQuarrie, Stuart Dougall JP BD BSc MBA MPhil	1984	2020	(Chaplain, University of Glasgow)
Main, Alan TD MA BD STM PhD DD	1963	2001	(Professor of Practical Theology, University of Aberdeen)
McDowall, Ronald John BD	1980	2001	(Falkirk: Laurieston with Redding and Westquarter)
McLeod, John MA	1958	1993	(Resolis and Urquhart)
McPhail, Andrew Montgomery BA	1968	2002	(Ayr: Wallacetown)
Rae, Robert (Robin) LTh	1968	2000	(Chaplain, Dundee Acute Hospitals)
Ryrie, Alexander Crawford MA BD STM	1956	1972	(Industrial Chaplain, North Lanarkshire)
Stewart, James Charles MA BD STM FSAScot	1960	2000	(Aberdeen: Kirk of St Nicholas)
Templeton, James Lindsay BSc BD	1975	2012	(Innerleven: East)
Torrance, David John BD DipMin	1993		Ormiston with Pencaitland
Wotherspoon, Robert Colquhoun LTh	1976	1998	(Corsock and Kirkpatrick Durham with Crossmichael and Parton)
Wyllie, Hugh Rutherford MA DD FCIBS	1962	2000	(Hamilton: Old)
2024			
Armitage, William Lister BSc BD	1976	2006	(Edinburgh: London Road)
Baxendale, Georgina Martha DipEd BD DMin	1981	2014	(Motherwell: South)
Brown, Ronald Hunt	1974	1998	(Musselburgh: Northesk)
Campbell, Archibald Iain MA DipEd	1961	1997	(Busby)
Campbell, James Ewen Ross MA BD	1967	2005	(Auchterderran: St Fothad's with Kinglassie)
Clinkenbeard, William Ward BSc BD STM	1966	2000	(Edinburgh: Carrick Knowe)

Cunningham, James Steele Allison MA BD BLitt PhD	1992	2000	(Glasgow: Barlanark Greyfriars)
Davidge, Alison Elizabeth Shaw MA BD	1990		Glasgow: Calton Parkhead
Donald, Robert Mair LTh BA	1969	2005	(Kilmodan and Colintraive)
Henderson, Grahame McLaren BD CPS	1974	2008	(Kirn)
Holland, William MA	1967	2009	(Lochend and New Abbey)
Jamieson, Gordon David MA BD	1974	2012	(Head of Stewardship)
Kent, Robert Milree MA BD	1973	2011	(Hamilton: St John's)
Langlands, Cameron Hunter BD MTh PhD MInstLM	1995		Head of Spiritual and Pastoral Care, South London and Maudsley NHS Foundation Trust
Lawson, Kenneth Charles MA BD	1963	1999	(Director, Ecumenical Spirituality Programme, Scottish Churches Open College)
MacMillan, Riada Marion BD	1991	1998	(Perth: Craigend Moncreiffe with Rynd)
Main, Douglas MacPherson BD	1986	2014	(Errol with Kilspindie and Rait)
Manson, James Allison LTh	1981	2003	(Glencorse with Roslin)
McDonald, Thomas DipCom PGCE BD	1994	2015	(Kelso: North and Ednam)
McGregor, Thomas Stewart MBE MA BD	1957	1998	(Chaplain, Edinburgh Royal Infirmary)
McIntosh, Hamish Norman Mackenzie MA	1949	1987	(Fintry)
McKay, Girvan Christie	1969	1977	(Strath)
More, William Sinclair BSc BD MEd	1966	1969	(Bishopton: Old Erskine)
Morrison, Jean C. (Dr) DCS	1964	2004	(Director, The Pastoral Foundation)
Munro, Andrew MA BD PhD	1972	2000	(Glencaple with Lowther)
Murray, Douglas Ramsay MA BD	1965	2004	(Lausanne: The Scots Kirk)
Phillippo, Michael MTh BSc BVetMed MRCVS	2003	2011	(Auxiliary Minister, Aberdeen: Middlefield)
Prentice, Martin William Moore BVMS MRCVS DipCS	2013		Ordained Local Minister, Flotta with Orphir and Stenness
Price, Peter Owen CBE KHC BA FPhS	1957	1996	(Blantyre: Old)
Rae, Peter Crighton BSc BD	1968	2000	(Beath and Cowdenbeath: North)
Rentoul, Robert Wylie MA BSc AFBPsS	1956	1969	(Missionary service in Eastern Himalayas)
Rodger, Matthew Anderson BD	1978	1999	(Ellon)
Shannon, William Gault MA BD	1955	1998	(Pitlochry)
Shaw, Duncan LTh CPS	1984	2011	(Alves and Burghead with Kinloss and Findhorn)
Sherrard, Henry Dane BD DMin	1971	2013	(Arrochar with Luss)
Simpson, James Alexander BSc BD STM DD	1960	1999	(Interim Minister, Brechin Cathedral)
Smith, Graham Walton BA BD FSAScot	1995	2016	(Livingston: Old)
Smith, Ralph Colley Philip MA STM	1960	1991	(Director, Audio-Visual Production, Department of Communications)
Smith, Richard BD	1976	2002	(Denny: Old)
Whitson, William Simpson MA	1959	1999	(Cumbernauld: St Mungo's)
Wilkie, George Davidson OBE BL	1948	1986	(Kirkcaldy: Viewforth)
Wilkie, James Lindsay MA BD	1959	1998	(Executive Secretary, Board of World Mission)
Williamson, James BA BD DipCE	1986	2009	(Cummertrees with Mouswald with Ruthwell)

SECTION 7

Legal Names and Scottish Charity Numbers: Presbyteries and Congregations

Those presbyteries, all congregations in Scotland, and those congregations furth of Scotland which are registered with OSCR, the Office of the Scottish Charity Regulator

For a complete list of legal names see:
www.churchofscotland.org.uk > Resources > Yearbook > Section 7

All documents, as defined in the Charities References in Documents (Scotland) Regulations 2007, must specify the Charity Number, Legal Name of the congregation, any other name by which the congregation is commonly known and the fact that it is a Charity. For more information, see the Law Department circular on the Regulations at:

www.churchofscotland.org.uk > Resources > Law Department Circulars > Charity Law

SECTION 8

Church Buildings: Ordnance Survey National Grid References

See: www.churchofscotland.org.uk > Resources > Yearbook > Section 8

A significant number of parishes, mainly in rural areas, have more than one church: all are listed in Section 8.

SECTION 9

Parish and Congregational Changes

The parish structure of the Church of Scotland is constantly being reshaped as the result of unions, linkages and the dissolutions.

Section 9A, 'Parishes and Congregations: names no longer in use', records one of the inevitable consequences of these changes, the disappearance of the names of many former parishes and congregations. There are, however, occasions when for legal and other reasons it is important to be able to identify the present-day successors of those parishes and congregations whose names are no longer in use and which can therefore no longer be easily traced. A list of all such parishes and congregations, with full explanatory notes, may be found at:

www.churchofscotland.org.uk/Resources/Yearbook > Section 9A

Section 9B, 'Recent Readjustment and other Congregational Changes', below, lists all instances of union, linkage and dissolution, since the compilation of the 2023-24 Year Book.

1. Edinburgh and West Lothian

Abercorn and **Pardovan, Kingscavil and Winchburgh** united as **Abercorn, Pardovan, Kingscavil and Winchburgh**

Armadale linked with **Blackridge**

Bathgate: High and **Bathgate: St John's** united as **Bathgate**

Blackburn and Seafield and **Whitburn: Brucefield** united as **Whitburn Burnfield Valley North**

Breich Valley and **Whitburn: South** united as **Whitburn Burnfield Valley South**

Edinburgh: Carrick Knowe and **Edinburgh: St David's Broomhouse** united as **Edinburgh: St David's Carrick Knowe**

Edinburgh: Colinton and **Edinburgh: Juniper Green** united as **Edinburgh: Pentlands**

Edinburgh: Gorgie Dalry Stenhouse and **Edinburgh: Palmerston Place** united as **Edinburgh: Gorgie and Palmerston Place**

Edinburgh: Gracemount, **Edinburgh: Liberton**, **Edinburgh: Liberton Northfield** and **Edinburgh: Tron Kirk (Gilmerton and Moredun)** united as **Edinburgh: South East**

Edinburgh: Greenside and **Edinburgh: St Andrew's and St George's West** united as **Edinburgh: The New Town**

Edinburgh: Leith North and **Edinburgh: Leith South** united as **Edinburgh: Leith North and South**

Fauldhouse: St Andrew's and **Harthill: St Andrew's** united as **Fauldhouse and Harthill: St Andrew's**

2. Lothian and Borders

Ashkirk linked with **Ettrick and Yarrow** linked with **Selkirk**: linkages severed

Ashkirk and **Selkirk** united as **Selkirk and Ashkirk**

Ettrick and Yarrow linked with **Selkirk and Ashkirk**

Belhaven and **Spott** united as **Belhaven and Spott**

Chirnside and **Hutton and Fishwick and Paxton** united as **Whiteadder**

Cockenzie and Port Seton: Chalmers Memorial and **Cockenzie and Port Seton: Old** united as **Cockenzie and Port Seton**

Humbie and **Yester, Bolton and Saltoun** united as **Lammermuir**

Jedburgh: Old and Trinity and **Oxnam** united as **Jedburgh and Oxnam**

Kelso: North and Ednam and **Kelso Country Churches** united as **Kelso: North and Country Churches**

3. South West

Alloway and **Fisherton** united as **Alloway and Fisherton**

Fisherton linked with **Kirkoswald**: linkage severed

Annan: Old and **Dornock** united as **Annan: Old and Dornock**

Annan: St Andrew's, **Brydekirk** and **Dalton and Hightae** united as **Annan: St Andrew's and St Bryde's**

Applegarth, Sibbaldbie and Johnstone linked with **Lochmaben:** linkage severed

Applegarth, Sibbaldbie and Johnstone and **Lockerbie: Dryfesdale, Hutton and Corrie** united as **Lockerbie: Dryfesdale, Hutton, Corrie and Applegarth**

Ardrossan: Park, **Saltcoats: North** and **Saltcoats: St Cuthbert's** united as **Ardrossan**

Barr, **Dailly**, **Girvan: North** and **Girvan: South** united as **Girvan Valley**

Brodick, **Corrie**, **Kilmory**, **Lamlash**, **Lochranza and Pirnmill**, **Shiskine**, and **Whiting Bay and Kildonan** united as **Isle of Arran**

Caldwell and **Dunlop** united as **Caldwell and Dunlop**

Crosshill, Kirkoswald and **Maybole** united as **North Carrick**

Cumbrae, **Fairlie**, **Largs: Clark Memorial**, **Largs: St Columba's** and **Largs: St John's** united as **Cumbrae, Fairlie and Largs**

Dalton and Hightae linked with **St Mungo:** linkage severed

Darvel, Galston and **Newmilns: Loudoun** united as **Irvine Valley**

Lochmaben and **St Mungo** united as **Lochmaben**

Dreghorn and Springside, **Irvine: Fullarton**, **Irvine: Girdle Toll**, **Irvine: Mure Relief** and **Irvine: St Andrew's** united as **Irvine: United**

Glasserton and Isle of Whithorn and **Whithorn: St Ninian's Priory** united as **Glasserton, Isle of Whithorn and Whithorn: St Ninian's Priory**

Gretna: Old, Gretna: St Andrew's, Halfmorton and Kirkpatrick Fleming linked with **Hoddom, Kirtle-Eagesfield and Middlebie**

Inch and **Luce Valley** united as **Luce Valley and Inch**

Luce Valley and Inch linked with **Portpatrick** linked with **Stoneykirk**

Kilbirnie: Auld Kirk and **Kilbirnie: St Columba's** united as **Kilbirnie: New**

Kilmarnock: New Laigh Kirk and **Kilmarnock: St John's Onthank** united as **Kilmarnock: New Laigh Kirk**

Kirkinner linked with **Mochrum** linked with **Sorbie:** linkages severed

Kirkinner and **Sorbie** united as **Millisle**

Millisle linked with **Mochrum**

Kirkpatrick Juxta, **Moffat: St Andrew's** and **Wamphray** united as **Upper Annandale**

Stevenston: Ardeer, Stevenston: High and **Stevenston: Livingstone** united as **Stevenston**

Troon: Old, Troon: Portland and **Troon: St Meddan's** united as **Troon**

4. Clyde

Bearsden: Killermont and **Bearsden: Westerton Fairlie Memorial** united as **Bearsden: Boclair**

Clydebank: Faifley and **Duntocher: Trinity** united as **Clydebank: Faifley and Duntocher**

Helensburgh linked with **Rhu and Shandon**: linkage severed

Inverkip and **Skelmorlie and Wemyss Bay** united as **Inverkip, Skelmorlie and Wemyss Bay**

Kilmaronock Gartocharn and **Lomond** united as **Lomond**

5. Glasgow

Cumbernauld: Kildrum and St Mungo's and **Cumbernauld: Old** united as **Cumbernauld: Trinity**

Glasgow: Carmyle and **Glasgow: Kenmuir Mount Vernon** united as **Glasgow: Carmyle and Kenmuir Cornerstone**

Glasgow: Drumchapel St Andrew's and **Glasgow: Yoker** united as **Glasgow: Drumchapel St Andrew's and Yoker**

Glasgow: Garthamlock and Craigend and **Glasgow: Ruchazie** united as **Glasgow: Garthamlock, Ruchazie and Craigend**

6. Forth Valley and Clydesdale

Carluke: St Andrew's and **Carluke: St John's** united as **Carluke: Forrest Kirk**

Carriden dissolved

Cleland dissolved

7. Fife

Aberdour: St Fillan's, **Dalgety**, **Inverkeithing**, **North Queensferry** and **Rosyth** united as **Forthview**

Auchtertool linked with **Kirkcaldy: Linktown**: linkage severed

Balmerino and **Wormit** united as **Balmerino and Wormit**

Boarhills and Dunino and **St Andrews: Holy Trinity** united as **Boarhills, Dunino and St Andrews: Holy Trinity**

Burntisland and **Kinghorn** united as **Burntisland and Kinghorn**

Cameron and **St Andrews: St Leonard's** united as **Cameron and St Andrews: St Leonard's**

Dunfermline: St Andrew's Erskine and **Dunfermline: Townhill and Kingseat** united as **Dunfermline: St Columba's**

Glenrothes: Christ's Kirk, **Glenrothes: St Columba's**, **Glenrothes: St Margaret's**, **Glenrothes: St Ninian's**, **Leslie: Trinity** and **Markinch and Thornton** united as **Heart of Fife (Glenrothes, Leslie, Markinch and Thornton)**

Kennoway, Windygates and Balgonie: St Kenneth's linked with **Leven**

Kirkcaldy: Templehall and Torbain United renamed as **Kirkcaldy: Hope**

8. Perth

Aberdalgie and Forteviot linked with **Aberuthven and Dunning**: linkage severed

Aberdalgie and Forteviot linked with **Dunbarney and Forgandenny**

Aberfoyle linked with **Port of Menteith:** linkage severed

Aberlemno, **Dunnichen, Letham and Kirkden**, **Guthrie and Rescobie**, **Forfar: Lowson Memorial** and **Forfar: St Margaret's** united as **Forfar: All Souls**

Arbirlot linked with **Carmyllie**: linkage severed

Arbroath: Old and Abbey, **Arbroath: St Andrew's**, **Arbroath: St Vigeans**, **Arbroath: West Kirk**, **Carmyllie**, **Colliston**, **Friockheim Kinnell** and **Inverkeilor and Lunan** united as **Arbroath and District**

Arbirlot and **Arbroath and District** united as **Arbroath and District**

Ardler, Kettins and Meigle, Eassie, Nevay and Newtyle and **Glamis** united as **Strathmore**

Auchterhouse, **Fowlis and Liff** and **Lundie and Muirhead** united as **Sidlaw**

Bannockburn: Allan linked with **Cowie and Plean:** linkage severed

Cowie and Plean linked with **Fallin**

Barry, **Carnoustie** and **Carnoustie: Panbride** united as **Carnoustie: Trinity**

Blair Atholl and Struan linked with **Braes of Rannoch** linked with **Foss and Rannoch**: linkage with Blair Atholl and Struan severed

Blair Atholl and Struan linked with **Pitlochry**

Buchlyvie and **Gartmore** united as **Buchlyvie and Gartmore**

Dunblane: Cathedral, **Kilmadock** and **Kincardine-in-Menteith** united as **Dunblane Cathedral, Kilmadock and Blair Drummond**

Gargunnock linked with **Kilmadock** linked with **Kincardine-in-Menteith**: linkages severed

Dundee: Barnhill St Margaret's, Dundee: Broughty Ferry New Kirk, Dundee: Broughty Ferry St James' and **Dundee: Broughty Ferry St Luke's and Queen Street** united as **Dundee: Broughty Ferry**

Dundee: Chalmers-Ardler and **Dundee: Strathmartine** united as **Dundee: Craigowl**

Dundee: Coldside and **Dundee: Steeple** united as **Dundee: Law**

Dundee: Craigiebank, **Dundee: Douglas and Mid Craigie**, **Dundee: Fintry** and **Dundee: Whitfield** united as **Dundee: Northeast**

Dundee: St David's High Kirk dissolved

Gargunnock linked with **Kippen and Norrieston** linked with **Port of Menteith**

Glamis, Inverarity and Kinnettles: union of **Glamis** and **Inverarity and Kinnettles** dissolved

Forfar: East and Old and **Inverarity and Kinnettles** united as **Forfar: East, Old and Inverarity**

Glendevon dissolved

Killearn linked with **Strathblane**

Kippen and **Norrieston** united as **Kippen and Norrieston**

Perth: St John's Kirk of Perth linked with **Perth: St Leonard's-in-the-Fields**: linkage severed

Stirling: Church of the Holy Rude and **Stirling: Viewfield Erskine** united as **Stirling: Holy Rude Viewfield**

Trinity Gask and Kinkell dissolved

9. North East and Northern Isles

Aberdeen: Craigiebuckler and **Aberdeen: Ruthrieston West** united as **Aberdeen: Springfield**

Aberdeen: South of St Nicholas Kincorth and **Aberdeen: Torry St Fittick's** united as **Aberdeen: South**

Aberdour linked with **Pitsligo**: linkage severed

Barthol Chapel, **Tarves** and **Udny and Pitmedden** united as **Formartine**

Birnie and Pluscarden, **Elgin: High** and **Elgin: St Giles' and St Columba's South** united as **Elgin**

Buckie: North and **Rathven** united as **Buckie: North and Rathven**

Buckie: South and West and **Enzie** united as **Buckie: South, West and Enzie**

Drumoak-Durris and **Peterculter** united as **Peterculter**

Fraserburgh: Old, **Fraserburgh: South**, **Fraserburgh: West**, **Inverallochy and Rathen: East**, **Pitsligo**, **Rathen: West** and **Sandhaven** united as **Fraserburgh and District**

Lossiemouth: St Gerardine's High and **Lossiemouth: St James'** united as **Lossiemouth**

New Pitsligo and **Strichen and Tyrie** united as **Mormond West**

Newtonhill and **Portlethen** united as **Kincardine Coastal**

10. Clèir Eilean Ì: Highlands and Hebrides

Alness and **Rosskeen** united as **Alness**

Alves and Burghead, **Dallas**, **Forres: St Laurence**, **Forres: St Leonard's**, **Kinloss and Findhorn** and **Rafford** united as **West Moray**

Appin and **Lismore** united as **Appin and Lismore**

Applecross, Lochcarron and Torridon and **Glenelg, Kintail and Lochalsh** united as **South-West Ross**

Ardersier, **Culloden: The Barn** and **Petty** united as **Culloden and Ardersier**

Assynt and Stoer, **Eddrachillis** and **Rosehall** united as **Assynt, Rosehall and Scourie**

Avoch linked with **Fortrose and Rosemarkie**: linkage severed

Cromarty linked with **Resolis and Urquhart**: linkage severed

Avoch, **Cromarty** and **Fortrose and Rosemarkie** united as **Black Isle East**

Bracadale and Duirinish and **Snizort** united as **Bracadale, Duirinish and Snizort**

Cawdor, **Croy and Dalcross**, **Daviot and Dunlichity** and **Moy, Dalarossie and Tomatin** united as **Strathnairn and Strathdearn**

Colonsay and Oronsay linked with **Netherlorn**

Creich linked with **Kincardine, Croick and Edderton** linked with **Rosehall**: linkages severed

Creich, **Dornoch Cathedral** and **Kincardine, Croick and Edderton** united as **Dornoch Firth**

Dores and Boleskine and **Inverness: St Columba** united as **Inverness: St Columba**

Fearn Abbey and Nigg, **Tain** and **Tarbat** united as **Easter Ross Peninsula**

Gairloch and Dundonnell renamed as **West Ross**

Iona and **Kilfinichen and Kilvickeon and the Ross of Mull** united as **Iona and the Ross of Mull**

Iona and the Ross of Mull linked with **North Mull**

Inverness: Dalneigh and Bona and **Inverness: Trinity** united as **Inverness: Trinity Dalneigh**

Killearnan linked with Knockbain: linkage severed

Kilmore and Oban linked with **Tiree**

Kinlochleven and **South Lochaber** united as **South Lochaber**

Rothesay: Trinity and the **United Church of Bute** united as **Isle of Bute**

11. Lewis - nil
12. England and Channel Islands - nil
13. International Charges - nil

Presbyteries of **Argyll, Abernethy, Inverness, Lochaber, Ross, Sutherland, Caithness, Lochcarron-Skye and Uist** united as **Clèir Eilean Ì: Highlands and Hebrides** *(see note below)*

Historical Note on *Clèir Eilean Ì: Highlands and Hebrides and the Presbytery of Lewis*

In the area which now comprises Clèir Eilean Ì and the Presbytery of Lewis, the earliest Presbyteries to be established at the end of the 16th and the beginning of the 17th centuries were the Presbyteries of Argyll, Inveraven, Forres, Inverness, Ardmannach (later renamed Chanonry) and Dornoch, followed by Skye in 1642 and the **Presbytery of Caithness** in 1697.

The Presbytery of Inveraven was divided in 1632 into the Presbyteries of Aberlour and Abernethy; these were reunited and again separated on several occasions between 1645 and 1727, continuing thereafter as two distinct entities, the Presbytery of Aberlour and the **Presbytery of Abernethy**.

The Presbytery of Argyll was divided in 1638 into the Presbyteries of Inveraray, Cowal (later renamed Dunoon), Kinloch (later renamed Kintyre) and Kilmore (later renamed Lorn). In 1724 a new Presbytery of Abertarff was disjoined from Lorn (renamed the **Presbytery of Lochaber** in 1924). In 1726 a new Presbytery of Mull was disjoined from Lorn. In 1836 a new Presbytery of Islay and Jura (later renamed the Presbytery of Islay) was disjoined from Kintyre. In 1963 Lorn and Mull were united as the Presbytery of Lorn and Mull. In 1976 Inveraray, Kintyre and Islay were united as the Presbytery of South Argyll. In 2004 Dunoon, Lorn and Mull and South Argyll were united as the **Presbytery of Argyll.**

From the Presbytery of Chanonry a new Presbytery of Dingwall was disjoined in 1638 and a new Presbytery of Tain in 1706. A new Presbytery of Gairloch was disjoined from Dingwall in 1724 (renamed the Presbytery of Lochcarron in 1775). Following the 1929 union Chanonry and Dingwall were united as the Presbytery of Chanonry and Dingwall. In 1976 Chanonry and Dingwall and Lochcarron were united as the Presbytery of Chanonry, Dingwall and Lochcarron. In 1979 the former Presbytery of Lochcarron was disjoined from Chanonry, Dingwall and Lochcarron (which then became again the Presbytery of Chanonry and Dingwall) and united with the Presbytery of Skye as the **Presbytery of Lochcarron-Skye.** In 1981 Chanonry and Dingwall and Tain were united as the **Presbytery of Ross**.

From the Presbytery of Skye a new Presbytery of the Long Island (or *Clèir Innis Fada*) was disjoined in 1724. In 1742 the Presbytery of the Long Island was divided into the **Presbytery of Lewis** and the **Presbytery of Uist.**

From the Presbyteries of Dornoch and Caithness a new Presbytery of Tongue was disjoined in 1726. In 1961 Dornoch and Tongue were united as the **Presbytery of Sutherland**.

From the Presbyteries of Forres, Inverness and Chanonry a new Presbytery of Nairn was disjoined in 1773. Following the 1929 union Inverness and Nairn were united as the **Presbytery of Inverness**, and the remainder of the Presbytery of Forres was united with Aberlour and with Elgin (both now part of the Presbytery of the North East and Northern Isles) as the Presbytery of Elgin (renamed Moray in 1976). In 2021 the parishes in the former Presbytery of Forres were transferred from the Presbytery of Moray to the Presbytery of Inverness.

SECTION 10

Congregational Statistics 2023

Comparative Statistics: 1983–2023

	2023	*2013*	*2003*	*1993*	*1983*
Communicants	259,200	398,389	553,248	732,936	902,714
Elders	20,745	32,834	42,071	46,268	47,441

NOTES ON CONGREGATIONAL STATISTICS

Com Number of communicants at 31 December 2023.

Eld Number of elders at 31 December 2023.

G Membership of the Guild including Young Woman's Groups and others as recorded on the 2023 annual return submitted to the Guild Office.

In23 Ordinary General Income for 2023. Ordinary General Income consists of members' offerings, contributions from congregational organisations, regular fund-raising events, income from investments, deposits and so on. This figure does not include extraordinary or special income, or income from special collections and fund-raising for other charities.

GtoG Final amount allocated to congregations to contribute for Giving to Grow after allowing for Presbytery-approved amendments up to 31 December 2023, but before deducting stipend endowments and normal allowances given for locum purposes in a vacancy or guardianship.

–18 This figure shows 'the number of children and young people aged 17 years and under who are involved in the life of the congregation'.

Congregations are listed as in the Section 5 Presbytery Lists, with the entries for linked congregations listed together below the first-named so that the statistics for the whole charge may be seen at a glance.

The statistics for the congregations now in the united Presbytery of Clèir Eilean Ì: Highlands and Hebrides are shown under that new presbytery.

Some congregations were united or dissolved after 31 December 2023. Their statistics are shown as the entities they were at that date, but their names are shown in italics – details of the readjustment are given in Section 9B.

Figures may also not be available for congregations which failed to submit the appropriate schedule. Where the figure for the number of elders is missing, then in nearly every case the number of communicants relates to the previous year.

Congregation .... Com		Eld	G	In23	GtoG	–18
1. Edinburgh and West Lothian						
Abercorn	64	—	—	12,912	6,949	—
Pardovan, Kingscavil and Winchburgh	204	18	—	55,313	25,439	1
Armadale	399	35	19	—	43,909	56
Blackridge	59	10	—	21,399	13,873	1
Avonbridge	39	6	—	5,680	4,333	17
Torphichen	98	12	—	59,354	17,556	1
Bathgate	609	38	18	100,890	84,897	—
Bathgate: Boghall	178	21	—	87,060	56,692	56
Blackburn and Seafield	196	22	—	—	40,421	69
Breich Valley	92	9	19	33,395	13,002	7
Broxburn	256	18	—	73,485	36,084	5
Edinburgh: Balerno	422	40	25	139,264	67,892	10
Edinburgh: Barclay Viewforth	258	29	—	203,764	99,279	38
Edinburgh: Blackhall St Columba's	537	45	—	213,336	100,658	9
Edinburgh: Broughton St Mary's	139	20	—	115,203	36,403	7
Edinburgh: Canongate	321	22	—	165,537	83,631	4
Edinburgh: Carrick Knowe	286	37	44	82,628	36,734	150
Edinburgh: Colinton	677	36	—	—	112,200	89
Edinburgh: Corstorphine Craigsbank	312	23	—	114,116	49,443	28
Edinburgh: Corstorphine Old	332	21	—	90,982	21,059	18
Edinburgh: Corstorphine St Anne's	324	45	57	132,420	65,640	48
Edinburgh: Corstorphine St Ninian's	487	66	29	185,000	86,292	16
Edinburgh: Craiglockhart	314	34	21	146,838	70,111	92
Edinburgh: Craigmillar Park	125	8	19	—	25,033	1
Edinburgh: Reid Memorial	162	7	—	125,705	57,187	3
Edinburgh: Currie	385	20	41	129,833	75,588	17
Edinburgh: Dalmeny and Queensferry	499	43	44	—	71,973	74
Edinburgh: Davidson's Mains	366	45	—	233,930	113,824	60
Edinburgh: Drylaw	68	7	—	42,928	12,357	—
Edinburgh: Duddingston	353	33	—	132,600	71,908	118
Edinburgh: Fairmilehead	451	40	38	174,446	74,244	59
Edinburgh: Gorgie and Palmerston Place	395	—	—	—	137,340	—
Edinburgh: Gracemount	18	5	—	22,531	6,090	9
Edinburgh: Granton	141	19	—	69,315	27,795	15
Edinburgh: Greenbank	589	66	27	—	136,441	202
Edinburgh: Greenside	65	13	—	59,949	19,454	3
Edinburgh: Greyfriars Kirk	291	35	—	165,270	75,400	10
Edinburgh: High (St Giles')	423	31	—	—	127,358	—
Edinburgh: Holy Trinity	231	27	—	—	81,550	64
Edinburgh: Inverleith St Serf's	257	28	28	128,324	56,758	172
Edinburgh: Juniper Green	234	16	—	118,231	57,266	8
Edinburgh: Kirkliston	202	23	45	128,142	53,351	84
Edinburgh: Leith North	88	15	—	62,242	42,406	2
Edinburgh: Leith St Andrew's	121	13	—	87,064	42,379	—
Edinburgh: Leith South	219	35	—	156,408	53,599	123
Edinburgh: Liberton	646	58	40	269,965	121,158	40
Edinburgh: Liberton Northfield	111	7	—	—	27,099	330
Edinburgh: Marchmont St Giles'	192	24	—	291,617	70,584	74

Congregation	Com	Eld	G	In23	GtoG	–18
Edinburgh: Mayfield Salisbury	389	51	—	306,909	124,919	29
Edinburgh: Meadowbank and Willowbrae	92	13	—	50,251	57,438	2
Edinburgh: Morningside	342	55	—	239,158	92,395	28
Edinburgh: Morningside United	70	9	—	102,852	890	—
Edinburgh: Murrayfield	385	23	—	—	83,543	25
Edinburgh: Newhaven	124	13	—	92,032	43,097	145
Edinburgh: Northwest Kirk: Cramond and Old Kirk and Muirhouse	841	66	—	327,057	165,012	31
Edinburgh: Pilrig St Paul's	172	13	—	80,442	28,229	—
Edinburgh: Polwarth	126	16	—	106,724	48,043	1
Edinburgh: Portobello and Joppa	584	53	59	241,438	111,310	159
Edinburgh: Priestfield	95	10	—	84,428	51,159	62
Edinburgh: Ratho	164	8	—	38,081	14,437	—
Edinburgh: Richmond Craigmillar	69	7	—	—	29,913	20
Edinburgh: St Andrew's and St George's West	242	35	—	221,435	109,614	4
Edinburgh: St Andrew's Clermiston	125	7	—	—	21,270	—
Edinburgh: St Catherine's Argyle	40	3	—	78,159	26,242	21
Edinburgh: St Cuthbert's	214	23	—	—	52,951	—
Edinburgh: St David's Broomhouse	102	14	—	31,774	14,344	7
Edinburgh: St John's Colinton Mains	168	18	—	68,633	33,519	75
Edinburgh: St Margaret's	168	21	24	—	27,072	4
Edinburgh: St Martin's	71	12	—	—	8,090	5
Edinburgh: St Michael's	322	24	30	84,063	42,169	10
Edinburgh: St Nicholas' Sighthill	285	15	—	—	16,224	18
Edinburgh: St Stephen's Comely Bank	111	8	—	111,979	59,722	20
Edinburgh: Slateford Longstone	163	11	25	51,582	18,793	26
Edinburgh: Stockbridge	171	9	—	—	44,909	21
Edinburgh: Tron Kirk (Gilmerton and Moredun)	72	10	—	90,229	10,823	24
Edinburgh: Wardie	404	32	48	—	73,626	108
Fauldhouse and Harthill: St Andrew's	304	—	21	92,073	50,010	—
Kirknewton and East Calder	269	21	26	87,670	48,093	66
Kirk of Calder	366	28	21	94,259	41,376	6
Linlithgow: St Michael's	1,203	85	47	—	149,219	75
Linlithgow: St Ninian's Craigmailen	313	25	48	—	35,851	13
Livingston: Old	257	31	14	94,805	50,395	74
Livingston: United	233	25	—	74,546	45,815	989
Polbeth Harwood	129	9	—	48,159	12,805	16
West Kirk of Calder	194	16	—	77,297	32,483	30
Strathbrock	227	17	18	65,061	52,923	32
Uphall: South	133	22	—	42,532	21,246	6
Whitburn: Brucefield	127	10	24	—	46,657	1
Whitburn: South	189	26	—	66,594	37,425	75
2. Lothian and Borders						
Aberlady and Gullane	413	33	—	96,122	40,269	40
Ale and Teviot United	299	23	—	25,025	17,979	—
Ayton and District Churches	234	16	12	25,505	8,501	1
Belhaven and Spott	492	28	50	103,146	53,686	60
Berwick-upon-Tweed: St Andrew's Wallace Green and Lowick	256	13	—	—	34,819	2

Congregation	Com	Eld	G	In23	GtoG	–18
Bonnyrigg	478	44	40	120,561	54,554	26
Bowden and Melrose	568	30	—	—	51,691	30
Caddonfoot	131	11	—	20,603	9,615	1
Stow: St Mary of Wedale and Heriot	120	—	—	18,509	11,223	—
Carlops	45	11	—	28,102	13,114	5
Kirkurd and Newlands	64	11	—	14,587	7,945	2
Upper Tweeddale	202	—	22	—	17,300	—
West Linton: St Andrew's	151	—	—	—	17,650	—
Cavers and Kirkton	82	—	—	12,059	4,778	—
Hawick: Trinity	426	—	24	—	22,446	—
Channelkirk and Lauder	335	13	9	—	29,540	10
Cheviot Churches	242	18	35	—	32,437	—
Chirnside	67	5	—	16,662	6,596	—
Cockenzie and Port Seton: Chalmers Memorial	137	26	19	82,499	43,572	30
Cockenzie and Port Seton: Old	178	19	20	—	21,995	—
Cockpen and Carrington	125	18	33	33,305	19,429	—
Lasswade and Rosewell	195	13	—	32,304	19,798	4
Coldingham and St Abbs	45	11	—	44,800	21,047	6
Eyemouth	81	15	—	44,135	21,957	10
Coldstream and District Parishes	320	25	—	36,080	7,043	—
Eccles and Leitholm	124	5	—	15,546	11,071	4
Dalkeith: St John's and Newton	448	30	31	170,826	75,894	97
Dalkeith: St Nicholas Buccleuch	294	13	—	52,838	22,975	1
Dirleton	155	10	—	—	14,746	5
North Berwick: Abbey	223	24	27	106,261	45,426	10
Dryburgh District Churches	277	21	—	43,777	24,138	25
Dunbar	267	13	14	111,613	59,110	8
Dunglass	234	8	—	18,043	12,124	15
Duns and District Parishes	473	27	30	81,683	47,024	45
Earlston	293	17	10	40,329	16,116	18
Eddleston	90	—	—	18,575	6,919	—
Peebles: Old	333	21	—	—	47,590	—
Stobo and Drumelzier	74	7	—	—	—	—
Ettrick and Yarrow	132	10	—	23,355	12,267	—
Selkirk and Ashkirk	286	22	—	66,229	35,614	—
Fogo	89	10	—	—	3,764	—
Galashiels	133	37	27	123,226	46,029	47
Garvald and Morham	31	—	—	—	3,073	—
Haddington: West	154	10	—	—	31,372	1
Gladsmuir	145	12	—	19,788	10,787	—
Longniddry	248	34	26	88,395	44,838	3
Gordon: St Michael's	56	6	—	13,166	4,595	4
Gorebridge	143	9	—	143,908	61,811	79
Greenlaw	64	3	11	—	5,832	2
Haddington: St Mary's	416	30	—	125,792	50,883	19
Hawick: Burnfoot	51	7	—	11,076	8,391	36
Hawick: St Mary's and Old	276	15	17	—	21,341	45
Hawick: Teviot and Roberton	166	11	12	65,864	27,711	30
Hawick: Wilton	212	16	—	51,288	20,112	48
Teviothead	47	3	—	—	1,167	—

Congregation	Com	Eld	G	In23	GtoG	–18
Hobkirk and Southdean	121	—	10	14,894	6,294	—
Ruberslaw	148	14	12	30,469	16,908	12
Humbie	75	6	—	—	13,833	12
Hutton and Fishwick and Paxton	54	2	—	—	7,745	—
Innerleithen, Traquair and Walkerburn	273	19	18	84,952	28,421	10
Jedburgh: Old and Trinity	515	—	23	—	32,953	—
Kelso Country Churches	157	13	—	15,306	2,767	—
Kelso: North and Ednam	784	54	—	134,680	66,130	9
Kelso: Old and Sprouston	357	20	—	52,044	26,930	2
Legerwood	51	7	—	6,363	2,363	—
Loanhead and Bilston	326	25	34	160,741	47,648	40
Lyne and Manor	89	—	—	39,102	13,476	—
Peebles: St Andrew's Leckie	416	22	—	202,307	61,664	143
Musselburgh: Northesk	263	11	28	79,271	28,545	33
Musselburgh: St Andrew's High	222	20	15	66,530	38,999	—
Musselburgh: St Clement's and St Ninian's	50	—	—	8,850	11,382	—
Musselburgh: St Michael's Inveresk	296	31	—	80,059	43,308	2
Newbattle	251	22	—	58,376	33,311	70
North Berwick: St Andrew Blackadder	542	23	27	211,213	84,919	70
Ormiston	115	6	29	45,210	20,499	3
Pencaitland	120	4	—	—	19,758	—
Oxnam	115	11	—	—	3,402	6
Penicuik: North	298	25	—	70,537	33,179	9
Penicuik: Trinity	187	17	28	—	50,366	10
Prestonpans: Prestongrange	206	—	14	55,413	33,660	—
Roslin	176	6	—	21,100	10,525	—
Tranent	180	13	35	69,327	31,592	11
Traprain	633	29	30	84,547	34,102	51
Tyne Valley	243	24	—	64,703	36,900	15
Yester, Bolton and Saltoun	239	25	—	59,623	28,951	25
3. South West						
Alloway	815	86	—	—	111,619	130
Annan: Old and Dornock	379	—	—	—	30,756	—
Annan: St Andrew's	386	33	—	60,154	32,844	45
Annbank	198	15	14	43,236	17,697	—
Tarbolton	212	19	18	50,038	25,007	40
Ardrossan: Park	321	—	28	75,308	42,319	18
Ardrossan and Saltcoats: Kirkgate	155	25	24	82,456	42,179	10
Arnsheen Barrhill and Colmonell: St Colmon	90	6	—	8,794	12,242	—
Ballantrae	199	12	10	34,450	24,128	—
Arran, Isle of	349	—	17	91,259	92,516	
Auchinleck	273	13	23	—	14,092	2
Catrine	83	7	—	13,380	8,416	—
Ayr: Auld Kirk of Ayr	347	29	—	70,287	36,990	—
Ayr: Castlehill	412	39	38	123,790	50,512	62
Ayr: Newton Wallacetown	158	29	35	—	60,991	61
Ayr: St Andrew's	173	17	—	—	28,169	81
Ayr: St Columba	815	88	48	—	121,322	10
Ayr: St James'	259	17	—	—	26,735	86

Congregation	Com	Eld	G	In23	GtoG	–18
Ayr: St Leonard's	315	41	—	63,252	59,232	—
Dalrymple	106	8	—	—	13,587	—
Ayr: St Quivox	83	10	—	41,010	19,522	10
Balmaclellan, Kells and Dalry	99	14	14	18,247	14,583	2
Carsphairn	71	—	—	5,124	3,974	—
Barr	27	—	—	5,256	621	—
Beith	539	42	19	89,147	47,656	41
Bengairn Parishes	65	11	—	18,226	16,450	—
Castle Douglas	283	20	16	—	33,580	3
Border Kirk	273	31	—	49,920	30,996	10
Brydekirk	41	4	—	14,484	4,656	5
Caerlaverock	95	7	—	10,696	5,113	—
Dumfries: St Mary's-Greyfriars'	242	22	—	—	37,739	—
Caldwell and Dunlop	489	—	—	136,599	71,094	—
Canonbie United	66	7	—	29,020	13,116	5
Liddesdale	72	7	—	27,996	14,675	25
Closeburn	141	10	—	28,291	17,291	3
Kirkmahoe	134	10	—	—	18,376	—
Colvend, Southwick and Kirkbean	145	8	—	37,142	27,821	—
Corsock and Kirkpatrick Durham	42	8	—	18,911	8,769	—
Crossmichael, Parton and Balmaghie	59	8	—	—	8,365	—
Coylton	282	—	—	35,618	16,254	—
Drongan: The Schaw Kirk	129	15	9	25,935	15,718	—
Craigie and Symington	230	20	18	40,803	22,928	—
Prestwick: South	185	29	—	80,197	45,171	70
Crosshill	*104*	—	*20*	—	*7,380*	—
Crosshouse	192	28	16	33,216	26,691	6
Cumbrae, Fairlie and Largs	1,635	—	129	212,887	214,776	—
Cummertrees, Mouswald and Ruthwell	150	9	—	—	3,679	—
Dailly	89	6	—	—	5,447	—
Dalbeattie and Kirkgunzeon	283	19	—	—	22,820	—
Urr	147	8	—	—	6,153	—
Dalmellington	104	12	—	—	6,244	15
Patna: Waterside	105	6	—	—	10,733	—
Dalry: St Margaret's	414	44	—	—	65,385	30
Dalry: Trinity	127	12	—	87,330	51,223	57
Dalton and Hightae	158	3	—	3,113	7,721	—
Darvel	224	16	27	36,768	22,869	7
Dumfries: Maxwelltown West	283	27	28	66,272	41,517	—
Dumfries: Northwest	193	9	—	—	12,174	—
Dumfries: St George's	411	37	24	110,379	61,520	10
Dumfries: St Michael's and South	542	34	21	91,444	40,504	4
Dumfries: Troqueer	145	14	19	84,000	47,789	19
Dundonald	392	32	34	—	40,229	14
Dunscore	152	15	—	30,227	15,123	13
Glencairn and Moniaive	120	5	—	25,469	13,279	1
Durisdeer	120	—	—	7,767	7,327	—
Penpont, Keir and Tynron	130	10	—	18,004	6,876	4
Thornhill	95	6	—	30,797	11,414	—
Ervie Kirkcolm	149	8	—	14,983	8,916	2

Congregation	Com	Eld	G	In23	GtoG	–18
Leswalt	239	17	—	32,788	10,281	2
Fenwick	252	18	27	—	33,368	2
Fisherton	97	14	—	13,287	8,733	3
Galston	404	37	58	74,689	41,293	9
Gatehouse and Borgue	209	15	—	—	25,878	12
Tarff and Twynholm	112	11	23	21,058	9,976	4
Girvan: South	192	17	14	24,591	14,473	1
Girvan: North	439	35	—	70,084	38,083	29
Glasserton and Isle of Whithorn	65	3	—	—	3,274	—
Whithorn: St Ninian's Priory	284	7	16	44,405	18,398	24
Gretna: Old, Gretna: St Andrew's, Half Morton and Kirkpatrick Fleming	258	13	—	36,080	10,568	16
Hoddom, Kirtle-Eaglesfield and Middlebie	154	17	—	27,428	13,944	—
Hurlford	213	16	20	47,998	29,113	—
Irongray, Lochrutton and Terregles	146	20	—	30,179	17,269	—
Irvine: Old	257	17	—	49,619	38,513	5
Irvine: United	1,245	—	122	—	178,436	
Kilbirnie: Auld Kirk	241	19	—	—	23,415	—
Kilbirnie: St Columba's	427	—	—	—	29,020	—
Kilmarnock: Kay Park	362	34	18	131,906	62,921	15
Kilmarnock: New Laigh Kirk	741	51	37	219,628	118,337	70
Kilmarnock: St Kentigern's	176	19	—	47,086	28,142	70
Kilmarnock: St Marnock's	908	42	41	206,897	93,919	300
Kilmaurs: St Maur's Glencairn	242	10	21	—	33,593	35
Kilwinning: Abbey	403	43	23	105,819	60,138	9
Kilwinning: Mansefield Trinity	164	—	25	38,539	30,076	—
Kirkconnel	168	10	—	11,538	12,261	—
Sanquhar: St Bride's	297	15	11	—	17,486	9
Kirkcowan	83	9	—	29,663	15,955	2
Wigtown	133	10	9	34,175	17,281	30
Kirkcudbright	399	24	—	97,422	49,288	30
Kirkmabreck	102	—	14	17,158	6,120	—
Monigaff	222	—	—	2,611	2,574	—
Kirkmaiden	135	6	—	14,817	4,301	8
Kirkmichael	173	16	18	28,400	11,702	2
Straiton: St Cuthbert's	140	11	18	—	8,357	7
Kirkmichael, Tinwald and Torthorwald	300	23	16	24,862	7,721	—
Kirkoswald	154	16	8	41,521	20,101	10
Langholm, Eskdalemuir, Ewes and Westerkirk	414	15	—	36,922	18,744	15
Lochend and New Abbey	158	15	10	38,291	22,117	—
Lochmaben	217	18	24	66,900	36,486	1
Lockerbie: Dryfesdale, Hutton, Corrie and Applegarth	436	36	28	—	26,744	—
Luce Valley and Inch	346	—	24	33,436	28,091	—
Portpatrick	187	10	18	20,151	7,586	—
Stoneykirk	201	15	16	—	18,846	—
Lugar	156	10	17	25,897	13,103	12
Old Cumnock: Old	276	17	25	68,153	30,164	—
Mauchline	282	20	29	—	37,550	—
Sorn	116	9	12	18,638	8,575	—

Congregation	Com	Eld	G	In23	GtoG	–18
Maybole	*172*	*21*	—	*50,132*	*36,753*	—
Millisle	173	—	—	—	7,966	—
Mochrum	192	8	15	—	6,785	3
Monkton and Prestwick: North	206	24	32	—	44,281	3
Muirkirk	137	—	—	26,050	9,748	—
Old Cumnock: Trinity	244	17	14	34,553	24,118	12
New Cumnock	402	16	15	55,892	29,530	10
Newmilns: Loudoun	143	5	15	35,953	21,564	—
Ochiltree	195	17	12	27,354	10,434	—
Stair	189	17	12	43,479	23,271	26
Penninghame	339	14	19	104,471	46,437	30
Prestwick: Kingcase	451	54	25	82,707	50,758	34
Prestwick: St Nicholas'	420	50	34	116,489	65,529	21
Saltcoats: North	195	21	7	62,453	19,306	—
Saltcoats: St Cuthbert's	185	19	12	51,560	41,126	5
Stevenston: Ardeer	83	14	—	10,483	10,067	40
Stevenston: High	179	13	23	53,568	43,830	26
Stevenston: Livingstone	162	16	12	43,889	25,269	18
Stewarton: John Knox	237	27	30	151,888	56,871	80
Stewarton: St Columba's	333	34	47	84,730	44,216	119
Stranraer	735	38	26	130,073	64,326	82
Troon: Old	*635*	*30*	—	—	*66,248*	*10*
Troon: Portland	*374*	*39*	—	—	*53,190*	*13*
Troon: St Meddan's	*515*	*53*	*23*	—	*76,977*	*82*
Tundergarth	25	4	—	—	3,090	—
Upper Annandale	401	29	—	69,106	39,114	14
West Kilbride	328	39	—	126,947	69,874	199

4. Clyde

Congregation	Com	Eld	G	In23	GtoG	–18
Arrochar	51	14	—	—	9,674	2
Luss	74	11	6	—	21,959	3
Baldernock	125	13	—	28,250	13,139	2
Milngavie: St Paul's	580	77	90	195,157	100,957	35
Barrhead: Bourock	370	26	23	80,860	44,701	61
Barrhead: St Andrew's	282	32	22	—	73,794	60
Bearsden: Baljaffray	339	6	36	96,780	50,294	90
Bearsden: Cross	421	57	17	—	80,141	35
Bearsden: Killermont	476	53	36	193,424	89,268	120
Bearsden: New Kilpatrick	1,017	90	53	320,191	118,671	30
Bearsden: Westerton Fairlie Memorial	233	19	37	94,097	52,121	—
Bishopton	539	49	—	110,182	58,338	65
Bonhill	324	40	—	—	28,711	—
Renton: Trinity	127	59	—	32,922	18,188	—
Bridge of Weir: Freeland	340	—	—	140,712	78,923	79
Bridge of Weir: St Machar's Ranfurly	221	21	23	91,524	55,966	14
Cardross	314	36	23	88,940	42,459	5
Clydebank: Faifley	165	—	31	53,184	25,451	—
Clydebank: Kilbowie St Andrew's	193	19	16	32,832	20,769	92
Clydebank: Radnor Park	54	12	—	24,807	21,449	—
Clydebank: Waterfront	112	21	—	40,513	20,169	3

Congregation	Com	Eld	G	In23	GtoG	–18
Dalmuir: Barclay	132	19	—	35,074	21,304	105
Craigrownie	63	14	—	31,072	18,242	1
Garelochhead	96	12	—	—	24,365	6
Rosneath: St Modan's	71	7	18	32,620	11,750	2
Dumbarton: Riverside	376	54	36	133,096	50,605	182
Dumbarton: St Andrew's	81	14	—	25,803	14,783	—
Dumbarton: West Kirk	119	23	—	—	22,671	80
Duntocher: Trinity	136	14	48	—	26,002	—
Elderslie Kirk	357	24	24	93,041	48,843	89
Erskine	235	23	53	—	57,559	105
Gourock: Old Gourock and Ashton	478	47	27	142,964	65,888	130
Greenock: St Ninian's	178	13	—	22,748	7,465	18
Gourock: St John's	320	41	—	—	61,427	90
Greenock: East End	41	4	—	—	3,914	7
Greenock: Mount Kirk	256	28	—	37,251	29,484	110
Greenock: Lyle Kirk	596	38	—	—	58,227	119
Greenock: St Margaret's	129	21	—	29,671	15,803	3
Greenock: Wellpark Mid Kirk	377	34	—	—	52,581	35
Greenock: Westburn	406	40	20	128,689	58,119	15
Helensburgh	689	46	15	268,853	99,753	83
Houston and Killellan	624	65	56	—	87,340	260
Howwood	100	14	21	—	25,028	—
Johnstone: St Paul's	262	47	—	73,646	39,360	58
Inchinnan	199	21	27	76,075	33,285	10
Inverkip	263	26	13	71,407	23,148	12
Johnstone: High	166	—	18	82,949	48,883	—
Johnstone: St Andrew's Trinity	156	18	—	23,935	17,166	35
Kilbarchan	349	47	23	108,694	48,301	35
Kilmacolm: Old	294	35	—	—	58,190	10
Kilmacolm: St Columba	100	16	—	—	44,340	4
Kilmaronock Gartocharn	290	—	—	—	8,471	—
Langbank	100	11	—	—	22,422	—
Linwood	120	14	17	—	25,830	1
Lomond	272	30	20	113,579	55,467	3
Milngavie: Cairns	261	25	—	175,404	76,635	11
Milngavie: St Luke's	300	8	—	61,315	43,898	12
Neilston	330	22	17	91,463	64,308	8
Old Kilpatrick Bowling	167	8	—	42,400	26,191	14
Paisley: Abbey	379	30	—	—	73,959	30
Paisley: North	318	38	—	—	34,766	7
Paisley: Oakshaw Trinity	380	47	—	136,495	50,063	67
Paisley: St George's	320	48	24	120,037	76,933	6
Paisley: St Mark's Oldhall	344	—	47	135,976	65,505	—
Paisley: Sherwood Greenlaw	263	47	—	118,414	62,183	40
Paisley: South	284	47	—	—	63,762	132
Paisley: West	214	35	—	55,035	30,222	52
Port Glasgow: Hamilton Bardrainney	176	17	13	34,373	21,461	33
Port Glasgow: New	419	49	21	—	50,869	168
Renfrew: North	491	49	30	—	62,077	102
Renfrew: Trinity	235	16	—	104,031	55,208	12

Congregation	Com	Eld	G	In23	GtoG	–18
Rhu and Shandon	133	17	—	—	29,419	6
Skelmorlie and Wemyss Bay	175	27	—	62,076	40,841	—
5. Glasgow						
Bishopbriggs: Kenmure	129	18	17	73,760	43,063	20
Bishopbriggs: Springfield Cambridge	498	26	60	135,495	69,721	21
Broom	371	36	—	151,050	68,043	166
Burnside Blairbeth	374	28	68	236,364	112,250	32
Busby	158	25	20	86,831	43,613	8
Cadder	362	54	43	—	82,322	100
Cambuslang	474	—	32	157,890	75,113	—
Cambuslang: Flemington Hallside	293	—	29	61,852	25,084	—
Campsie	119	19	22	—	25,802	17
Chryston	275	—	—	141,827	82,831	—
Cumbernauld: Abronhill	137	11	17	44,072	41,234	7
Cumbernauld: Condorrat	254	—	22	62,022	34,712	—
Cumbernauld: Kildrum and St Mungo's	348	—	—	67,092	55,950	—
Cumbernauld: Old	261	36	—	58,573	36,153	41
Eaglesham	400	44	36	171,107	71,054	270
Fernhill and Cathkin	201	—	—	—	16,883	—
Gartcosh	69	10	—	40,050	9,124	82
Glenboig	81	—	—	12,386	3,026	—
Giffnock: Orchardhill	261	38	—	208,512	85,129	197
Giffnock: South	500	47	31	193,877	88,813	26
Giffnock: The Park	217	15	—	67,775	29,575	15
Greenbank	621	59	52	191,320	99,204	182
Kilsyth: Anderson	207	20	39	—	50,362	80
Kilsyth: Burns and Old	326	27	30	78,606	45,227	—
Kirkintilloch: St Columba's Hillhead	198	30	30	114,522	72,266	36
Kirkintilloch: St David's Memorial Park	257	34	20	—	46,711	—
Kirkintilloch: St Mary's	596	35	—	141,260	72,902	10
Lenzie: Old	360	35	—	—	56,918	—
Lenzie: Union	487	42	48	218,651	103,623	156
Maxwell Mearns Castle	236	—	—	—	89,717	—
Mearns	470	32	—	—	86,734	31
Milton of Campsie	281	—	34	95,570	46,561	—
Moodiesburn	113	10	—	—	40,283	28
Netherlee and Stamperland	746	50	36	209,938	128,804	6
Newton Mearns	299	32	21	132,301	63,308	—
Rutherglen: Old	175	16	—	64,360	40,822	—
Rutherglen: Stonelaw	254	18	—	133,306	73,862	20
Rutherglen: West and Wardlawhill	237	40	—	80,891	35,363	45
Stepps	174	12	—	72,992	33,327	51
Thornliebank	98	10	23	—	25,717	4
Torrance	181	15	—	109,300	59,724	60
Williamwood	347	41	24	110,793	51,955	531
Glasgow: Baillieston Mure Memorial	268	26	44	—	46,937	101
Glasgow: Baillieston St Andrew's	231	13	13	—	30,569	12
Glasgow: Barlanark Greyfriars	47	10	12	—	7,636	161
Glasgow: Blawarthill	147	19	20	—	10,647	55

Congregation	Com	Eld	G	In23	GtoG	–18
Glasgow: St Columba	123	—	—	—	4,397	—
Glasgow: Bridgeton St Francis in the East	57	11	11	33,860	13,748	3
Glasgow: Broomhill Hyndland	418	62	20	183,547	74,550	80
Glasgow: Calton Parkhead	71	13	—	—	3,132	2
Glasgow: Cardonald	203	33	—	97,865	57,691	61
Glasgow: Carmunnock	155	20	—	43,454	19,850	—
Glasgow: Carmyle	57	3	—	16,767	8,314	48
Glasgow: Kenmuir Mount Vernon	112	9	—	82,821	41,691	18
Glasgow: Carntyne and Cranhill	233	—	—	63,092	39,016	—
Glasgow: Carnwadric	61	5	—	42,103	16,555	10
Glasgow: Castlemilk	88	14	10	—	8,533	10
Glasgow: Cathcart Old	184	31	21	—	49,942	4
Glasgow: Cathcart Trinity	242	40	—	—	83,045	22
Glasgow: Cathedral (High or St Mungo's)	292	27	—	95,523	60,521	—
Glasgow: Causeway (Tollcross)	141	24	18	41,309	24,080	37
Glasgow: Clincarthill	167	23	32	115,554	47,304	8
Glasgow: Colston Milton	40	6	—	29,188	5,340	12
Glasgow: Colston Wellpark	58	12	—	19,990	12,417	8
Glasgow: Croftfoot	221	32	23	—	47,824	127
Glasgow: Dennistoun New	142	21	—	75,494	40,305	39
Glasgow: Drumchapel St Andrew's	145	—	—	—	23,442	—
Glasgow: Drumchapel St Mark's	78	10	—	23,040	1,468	8
Glasgow: Easterhouse	51	7	—	—	4,345	78
Glasgow: Eastwood	146	—	—	116,618	57,963	—
Glasgow: Gairbraid	119	—	—	14,770	6,019	—
Glasgow: Gallowgate	31	7	—	—	8,138	5
Glasgow: Garthamlock and Craigend	53	—	—	—	1,890	—
Glasgow: Gorbals	104	12	—	—	15,051	9
Glasgow: Govan and Linthouse	90	19	20	—	37,980	7
Glasgow: Hillington Park	236	30	25	83,380	38,190	62
Glasgow: Ibrox	98	21	—	—	27,560	10
Glasgow: Jordanhill	333	36	37	194,571	91,219	17
Glasgow: Kelvinbridge	46	—	—	25,286	19,143	—
Glasgow: Kelvinside Hillhead	131	13	—	—	37,820	—
Glasgow: King's Park	383	45	—	137,809	75,663	10
Glasgow: Kinning Park	67	14	—	39,837	15,301	—
Glasgow: Knightswood Anniesland Trinity	287	28	—	—	63,528	125
Glasgow: Langside	174	35	—	89,106	53,075	8
Glasgow: Maryhill Ruchill	137	12	—	—	47,623	75
Glasgow: Merrylea	212	22	—	97,893	48,484	—
Glasgow: Newlands South	335	36	—	—	61,558	15
Glasgow: Partick Trinity	119	—	—	—	52,305	—
Glasgow: Partick Victoria Park	159	16	—	109,111	69,819	15
Glasgow: Pollokshaws	75	18	—	50,838	18,753	3
Glasgow: Pollokshields	100	17	—	—	33,364	8
Glasgow: Possilpark	78	16	—	—	9,310	11
Glasgow: Queen's Park Govanhill	119	—	—	98,486	62,442	
Glasgow: Robroyston	50	4	—	—	21,001	30
Glasgow: Ruchazie	30	—	—	—	5,418	—
Glasgow: St Andrew and St Nicholas	242	26	19	—	32,138	184

Congregation	Com	Eld	G	In23	GtoG	–18
Glasgow: St Andrew's East	31	11	18	—	10,352	—
Glasgow: St Andrew's West	118	13	15	—	31,277	1
Glasgow: St Christopher's Priesthill and Nitshill	55	7	—	—	12,000	10
Glasgow: St David's Knightswood	125	15	—	59,176	43,684	9
Glasgow: St Enoch's Hogganfield	90	10	—	—	17,504	—
Glasgow: St George's Tron	65	—	—	—	31,090	—
Glasgow: St James' (Pollok)	92	18	—	47,268	17,870	60
Glasgow: St John's Renfield	262	36	—	149,160	75,650	104
Glasgow: St Paul's	27	7	—	27,875	5,076	295
Glasgow: St Rollox	55	7	—	42,524	23,103	28
Glasgow: Sandyford Henderson Memorial	187	14	—	144,774	78,586	10
Glasgow: Sandyhills	178	16	32	—	40,471	43
Glasgow: Scotstoun	64	5	—	—	25,780	4
Glasgow: Shawlands Trinity	151	17	—	78,634	48,036	13
Glasgow: Sherbrooke Mosspark	268	38	21	—	87,290	23
Glasgow: Shettleston New	186	27	15	—	37,513	100
Glasgow: Springburn	180	17	14	—	32,825	61
Glasgow: Toryglen	35	3	—	14,994	6,661	3
Glasgow: Trinity Possil and Henry Drummond	41	4	—	53,908	36,308	8
Glasgow: Tron St Mary's	64	10	—	—	14,363	96
Glasgow: Wallacewell	35	—	—	20,961	50	—
Glasgow: Wellington	88	28	—	158,128	62,466	5
Glasgow: Whiteinch	51	7	—	—	30,958	7
Glasgow: Yoker	91	—	—	—	5,991	—
6. Forth Valley and Clydesdale						
Airdrie: Cairnlea	417	40	19	—	73,642	62
Calderbank	107	9	13	38,545	14,389	—
Airdrie: Clarkston	273	24	9	47,421	42,096	135
Airdrie: High	245	—	—	55,130	34,144	—
Caldercruix and Longriggend	128	9	—	43,272	30,608	4
Airdrie: Jackson	268	48	16	88,827	56,323	153
Airdrie: New Monkland	234	27	30	69,762	36,751	56
Greengairs	98	9	—	—	8,368	2
Airdrie: New Wellwynd	588	61	—	165,154	88,357	8
Airdrie: St Columba's	191	14	—	—	9,694	—
Airth	113	6	16	22,441	13,187	3
Bellshill: Central	116	24	26	55,485	33,824	4
Bellshill: West	313	26	—	68,001	39,762	5
Biggar	247	21	—	—	53,196	20
Black Mount	64	4	10	—	5,685	—
Blackbraes and Shieldhill	52	15	16	19,615	17,721	—
Muiravonside	74	13	—	—	14,635	—
Blantyre: Livingstone Memorial	155	19	—	74,281	28,454	21
Blantyre: St Andrew's	142	15	—	62,310	24,712	10
Blantyre: Old	198	14	—	57,937	27,656	19
Bo'ness: Old	263	25	9	56,054	32,426	3
Bo'ness: St Andrew's	303	12	—	—	27,031	5
Bonnybridge: St Helen's	165	—	—	—	24,149	—
Bothkennar and Carronshore	148	14	—	25,597	16,384	9

Congregation	Com	Eld	G	In23	GtoG	–18
Bothwell	424	34	26	217,918	75,510	16
Brightons	383	23	32	—	86,403	200
Cairngryffe	124	10	11	21,111	10,282	8
Libberton and Quothquan	69	6	—	10,401	8,890	—
Symington	122	—	19	10,521	16,026	—
Carluke: Kirkton	496	39	35	115,452	62,372	480
Carluke: St Andrew's	143	10	17	63,250	23,270	5
Carluke: St John's	442	32	25	85,867	45,505	21
Carnwath	78	9	15	—	7,598	5
Carstairs	136	8	11	52,980	25,619	2
Chapelhall	164	22	30	46,337	23,781	20
Kirk o' Shotts	118	9	—	—	14,601	14
Coalburn and Lesmahagow	144	18	12	58,443	39,300	—
Coatbridge: Blairhill Dundyvan	195	18	17	47,224	32,424	60
Coatbridge: Middle	206	30	20	—	15,739	98
Coatbridge: Calder	215	12	—	26,837	24,322	1
Coatbridge: Old Monkland	78	11	—	32,598	18,254	—
Coatbridge: New St Andrew's	242	39	28	—	57,610	167
Coatbridge: Townhead	99	15	—	18,153	14,492	46
Crossford	119	4	—	—	16,080	—
Kirkfieldbank	69	5	—	—	9,779	2
Dalserf	164	17	19	—	37,583	29
Denny: Old	236	32	19	56,595	29,817	60
Haggs	192	22	—	33,627	19,129	15
Denny: Westpark	315	28	19	81,155	49,179	28
Douglas Valley	209	17	31	—	22,184	—
Dunipace	145	16	—	60,061	36,564	20
East Kilbride: Claremont	310	31	—	—	81,047	28
East Kilbride: Greenhills	92	9	11	44,906	18,251	5
East Kilbride: Moncreiff	481	30	61	151,678	61,743	125
East Kilbride: Mossneuk	261	7	—	50,260	15,545	34
East Kilbride: Old	514	47	30	—	67,136	48
East Kilbride: South	112	20	—	56,414	33,779	145
East Kilbride: Stewartfield	24	3	—	5,100	5,159	—
East Kilbride: West	216	13	—	58,139	29,633	—
East Kilbride: Westwood	229	20	—	—	43,394	4
Falkirk: Bainsford	84	10	—	—	14,777	110
Falkirk: Camelon	133	11	—	—	32,132	38
Falkirk: Grahamston United	338	41	20	—	9,253	38
Falkirk: Laurieston	132	17	—	—	21,414	—
Redding and Westquarter	81	10	—	23,431	14,131	—
Falkirk: St Andrew's West	338	21	—	61,758	37,114	7
Falkirk: Trinity	360	29	—	—	80,806	38
Forth: St Paul's	265	19	28	—	29,925	132
Grangemouth: Abbotsgrange	254	33	—	55,328	31,334	127
Grangemouth: Kirk of the Holy Rood	218	22	—	46,932	25,551	3
Grangemouth: Zetland	416	43	28	86,741	50,077	30
Hamilton: Cadzow	304	36	28	97,286	63,013	31
Hamilton: Gilmour and Whitehill	93	19	—	65,730	26,409	4
Hamilton: West	142	27	—	60,841	30,752	2

Congregation	Com	Eld	G	In23	GtoG	–18
Hamilton: Hillhouse	306	27	—	74,207	35,647	80
Hamilton: Old	395	55	—	—	74,149	86
Hamilton: St John's	413	39	30	—	69,760	186
Hamilton: South	130	13	20	65,015	27,546	8
Quarter	85	11	—	25,129	14,083	—
Hamilton: Trinity	149	16	—	—	27,522	4
Holytown	112	20	19	43,705	24,745	42
New Stevenston: Wrangholm Kirk	58	6	—	—	14,529	3
Kirkmuirhill	130	6	37	83,210	51,313	6
Lanark: Greyfriars	437	—	—	—	51,939	—
Lanark: St Nicholas'	390	30	27	131,369	61,792	30
Larbert: East	498	46	34	135,237	73,243	38
Larbert: Old	208	15	15	95,970	36,860	39
Larbert: West	277	24	21	66,960	39,915	—
Larkhall: New	280	42	36	125,125	64,708	95
Larkhall: Trinity	126	13	21	36,875	24,743	63
Law	150	9	15	—	21,338	87
Motherwell: Crosshill	206	—	—	75,629	35,022	—
Motherwell: St Margaret's	333	10	—	29,805	16,828	1
Motherwell: Dalziel St Andrew's	369	48	46	—	79,869	130
Motherwell: North	118	20	25	54,032	37,844	54
Wishaw: Craigneuk and Belhaven	94	18	—	30,696	23,341	10
Motherwell: St Mary's	544	87	47	146,349	81,267	—
Motherwell: South	325	66	61	127,162	54,391	130
Newarthill and Carfin	154	14	—	57,616	31,506	42
Newmains: Bonkle	90	15	—	32,083	18,867	9
Newmains: Coltness Memorial	156	17	22	—	28,929	1
Overtown	231	27	30	77,317	33,547	102
Polmont: Old	254	19	—	84,732	50,015	8
Shotts: Calderhead Erskine	333	30	27	90,616	50,261	2
Slamannan	88	6	—	—	13,524	19
Stenhouse and Carron	264	19	—	—	27,962	—
Stonehouse: St Ninian's	325	39	40	—	1,187	143
Strathaven: Avendale Old and Drumclog	409	47	36	153,656	67,583	35
Strathaven: Trinity	757	106	30	—	81,508	230
Uddingston: Burnhead	240	24	8	70,189	32,627	36
Uddingston: Old	327	31	25	131,744	71,162	60
Uddingston: Viewpark	333	56	19	—	59,085	260
Upper Clyde	160	7	12	—	6,447	3
Wishaw: Cambusnethan North	349	32	—	65,965	46,493	39
Wishaw: Cambusnethan Old and Morningside	288	25	—	43,393	32,866	35
Wishaw: Old	151	16	—	37,576	19,098	25
Wishaw: St Mark's	213	21	31	57,661	35,042	124
Wishaw: South Wishaw	134	15	24	80,407	45,086	15

7. Fife

Congregation	Com	Eld	G	In23	GtoG	–18
Aberdour: St Fillan's	300	12	—	77,131	32,389	6
Anstruther and Cellardyke: St Ayle	317	31	32	81,191	29,923	—
Crail	251	20	22	47,804	27,232	10
Auchterderran Kinglassie	176	17	20	51,024	29,308	8

Congregation	Com	Eld	G	In23	GtoG	–18
Auchtertool	63	—	—	—	7,328	—
Balmerino	100	—	—	—	13,330	—
Beath and Cowdenbeath: North	106	11	—	46,895	27,781	4
Boarhills, Dunino and St Andrews: Holy Trinity	356	—	30	—	36,598	—
Buckhaven and Wemyss	147	19	12	—	16,480	—
Burntisland	192	27	18	—	40,475	2
Cairneyhill	77	16	—	33,017	11,972	—
Limekilns	204	21	—	—	37,355	4
Cameron	66	10	—	23,180	11,963	—
Carnbee	80	—	—	—	5,762	—
Pittenweem	204	—	—	18,781	7,090	—
Carnock and Oakley	129	13	16	36,742	25,095	5
Ceres, Kemback and Springfield	274	15	—	51,719	37,378	21
Cowdenbeath: Trinity	144	20	11	45,773	42,113	5
Creich, Flisk and Kilmany	64	9	—	23,752	10,884	1
Culross and Torryburn	41	5	—	27,593	23,067	—
Cupar: Old and St Michael of Tarvit	419	30	23	—	58,463	—
Monimail	68	—	—	—	8,325	—
Cupar: St John's and Dairsie United	456	36	—	—	52,994	8
Dalgety	430	—	23	—	62,718	—
Dunfermline: Abbey	429	33	—	141,598	68,650	10
Dunfermline: East	94	7	—	125,094	28,381	70
Dunfermline: Gillespie Memorial	100	11	15	—	27,147	9
Dunfermline: North	120	—	—	—	14,282	—
Dunfermline: St Andrew's Erskine	147	16	9	60,926	28,181	—
Dunfermline: St Leonard's	230	25	28	—	43,278	35
Dunfermline: St Margaret's	213	23	—	92,699	26,326	10
Dunfermline: St Ninian's	120	20	18	—	29,356	28
Dunfermline: Townhill and Kingseat	155	19	—	59,352	30,531	31
Dysart: St Clair	343	18	—	—	27,734	15
East Neuk Trinity	244	18	41	119,641	42,471	7
Edenshead	242	17	11	—	30,648	—
Falkland	91	8	—	22,704	15,444	—
Freuchie	87	14	18	37,933	14,605	19
Glenrothes: Christ's Kirk	150	—	17	41,439	19,024	—
Glenrothes: St Columba's	271	41	—	92,613	33,236	61
Glenrothes: St Margaret's	200	23	22	50,095	34,712	50
Glenrothes: St Ninian's	170	—	11	62,597	38,288	—
Howe of Fife	244	16	—	48,339	27,320	2
Inverkeithing	162	—	—	58,511	33,326	—
Kelty	162	15	16	91,447	34,541	6
Kennoway, Windygates and Balgonie: St Kenneth's	320	29	35	87,162	47,371	2
Leven	351	16	34	—	35,442	—
Kilrenny	81	10	—	30,986	11,553	4
Kinghorn	186	19	—	74,159	33,295	20
Kingsbarns	53	6	—	16,929	6,864	12
Kirkcaldy: Abbotshall	376	26	—	71,209	43,655	4
Kirkcaldy: Bennochy	269	24	—	—	44,843	5
Kirkcaldy: Hope	271	—	19	84,577	22,701	—

Congregation .... Com	Eld	G	In23	GtoG	–18
Kirkcaldy: Linktown 161	24	26	52,243	28,747	2
Kirkcaldy: Pathhead 261	20	24	76,295	35,686	50
Kirkcaldy: St Bryce Kirk 265	17	21	113,181	42,769	3
Largo 190	22	16	85,210	40,965	1
Largoward 44	—	—	—	5,407	—
Leslie: Trinity 106	—	—	18,018	8,436	—
Leuchars: St Athernase and Tayport 429	—	16	—	19,929	—
Lindores 239	22	—	44,609	15,633	40
Lochgelly and Benarty: St Serf's 156	23	—	60,000	30,875	4
Markinch and Thornton 360	—	—	76,974	44,096	—
Methil: Wellesley 234	22	18	99,993	32,725	105
Methilhill and Denbeath 156	17	22	33,447	14,935	7
Newport-on-Tay 301	—	—	81,426	42,600	—
North Queensferry 42	5	—	18,409	10,790	20
Rosyth 159	14	—	56,003	22,296	—
St Andrews: St Leonard's 364	35	27	144,779	64,220	3
St Andrews: St Mark's 432	36	15	128,626	79,964	
St Monans 175	7	25	51,730	13,521	—
Saline and Blairingone 116	14	—	41,440	19,989	—
Tulliallan and Kincardine 184	22	—	177,054	26,851	62
Wormit 148	11	27	—	21,124	—
8. Perth					
Aberdalgie and Forteviot 160	18	—	20,609	10,703	—
Dunbarney and Forgandenny 471	23	21	98,429	51,054	25
Aberfeldy 142	13	—	—	27,369	203
Dull and Weem 108	12	11	—	14,861	3
Grantully, Logierait and Strathtay 127	7	7	36,759	22,600	4
Aberfoyle 57	4	8	13,245	8,318	1
Aberlemno 174	10	—	24,390	16,642	—
Abernethy and Dron and Arngask 228	11	—	—	10,503	8
Abernyte 84	9	—	14,898	8,205	5
Inchture and Kinnaird 130	14		38,274	18,682	10
Longforgan 147	9	—	—	21,096	4
Aberuthven and Dunning 179	11	—	42,353	22,196	—
Alloa: Ludgate 261	—	10	69,729	38,537	—
Alloa: St Mungo's 277	21	16	—	39,294	12
Almondbank Tibbermore 166	—	18	—	24,470	—
Methven and Logiealmond 117	13	—	—	8,496	—
Alva 365	50	—	94,216	49,517	70
Alyth 559	20	—	69,442	33,655	4
Arbirlot 120	8	—	—	14,853	—
Arbroath: Old and Abbey 335	20	—	87,321	43,300	4
Arbroath: St Andrew's 456	33	32	146,555	77,433	40
Arbroath: St Vigeans 405	29	12	—	27,791	7
Arbroath: West Kirk 723	55	34	94,344	59,260	124
Ardler, Kettins and Meigle 324	14	17	33,600	12,079	—
Ardoch 135	13	24	41,297	23,616	21
Blackford 82	7	—	—	11,159	40
Auchterarder 458	28	40	140,563	51,330	121

Congregation	Com	Eld	G	In23	GtoG	–18
Auchtergaven and Moneydie	409	21	22	—	22,461	—
Redgorton and Stanley	278	10	25	25,782	10,952	32
Auchterhouse	116	10	16	30,541	14,527	4
Balfron	102	11	—	—	24,137	2
Fintry	80	8	—	—	9,748	—
Balquhidder	62	8	—	21,857	4,727	5
Killin and Ardeonaig	62	8	8	—	10,342	7
Bannockburn: Allan	202	26	—	41,426	27,195	11
Bannockburn: Ladywell	201	13	—	—	14,580	10
Barry	157	3	19	27,092	12,351	2
Bendochy	64	5	—	19,525	12,098	—
Coupar Angus: Abbey	229	14	—	—	21,754	1
Blair Atholl and Struan	77	10	—	15,393	5,976	—
Pitlochry	242	19	14	—	32,317	1
Blairgowrie	554	33	28	—	64,082	31
Braes of Rannoch	14	4	—	—	2,973	2
Foss and Rannoch	67	6	—	9,658	3,967	—
Brechin and Farnell	508	32	—	75,720	38,249	22
Bridge of Allan	598	32	40	126,183	52,315	20
Buchanan	91	6	—	15,452	9,311	2
Drymen	186	17	—	61,958	33,112	8
Buchlyvie	143	9	—	20,074	13,068	1
Callander	285	16	24	73,025	42,283	45
Cambusbarron: The Bruce Memorial	241	18	—	84,269	41,322	10
Caputh and Clunie	110	12	—	11,929	12,615	—
Kinclaven	84	10	15	—	11,894	5
Cargill Burrelton	72	8	14	—	9,343	—
Collace	96	7	—	10,718	6,211	—
Carmyllie	87	12	—	—	12,706	—
Carnoustie	240	12	18	69,462	45,488	2
Carnoustie: Panbride	576	—	—	—	45,326	—
Clackmannan	276	14	20	68,327	41,290	9
Sauchie and Coalsnaughton	325	14	18	48,411	30,240	5
Cleish	108	8	—	29,418	19,359	—
Fossoway: St Serf's and Devonside	179	15	—	50,287	29,064	20
Colliston	152	5	—	14,806	8,647	—
Comrie	309	25	10	101,583	52,775	50
Dundurn	47	6	—	16,151	8,774	—
Cowie and Plean	144	8	—	16,777	6,091	2
Fallin	214	13	—	—	11,724	60
Crieff	482	17	17	63,899	39,764	3
Dollar	191	15	52	93,049	47,349	15
Muckhart	72	7	—	25,506	16,484	10
Dunblane: Cathedral	697	55	21	220,593	100,421	197
Dunblane: St Blane's	239	22	34	69,508	44,565	—
Lecropt	120	12	—	63,203	22,211	1
Dundee: Balgay	133	13	—	—	29,621	—
Dundee: Barnhill St Margaret's	585	39	55	—	69,740	34
Dundee: Broughty Ferry New Kirk	523	32	40	104,500	54,583	5
Dundee: Broughty Ferry St James'	123	9	—	29,634	17,876	4

Congregation	Com	Eld	G	In23	GtoG	–18
Dundee: Broughty Ferry St Luke's and Queen Street	229	13	—	—	29,005	2
Dundee: Broughty Ferry St Stephen's and West	258	15	—	57,587	23,729	—
Dundee: Dundee (St Mary's)	396	39	—	67,255	31,427	2
Dundee: Camperdown	69	6	—	—	15,687	—
Dundee: Chalmers Ardler	139	19	—	64,351	39,450	12
Dundee: Coldside	150	14	—	—	21,446	40
Dundee: Craigiebank	44	3	—	—	8,150	—
Dundee: Douglas and Mid Craigie	71	4	—	—	7,291	2
Dundee: Downfield Mains	230	9	21	—	51,122	22
Dundee: Fintry	83	4	—	—	22,135	—
Dundee: Kingsgait	526	47	27	149,134	63,570	10
Dundee: Lochee	331	19	35	67,497	37,092	247
Dundee: Logie and St John's Cross	130	14	28	—	29,278	1
Dundee: Menzieshill	167	11	—	—	17,146	140
Dundee: St David's High Kirk	129	7	—	—	1,708	5
Dundee: Steeple	140	16	—	145,430	60,967	7
Dundee: Stobswell Trinity	643	46	—	—	56,395	9
Dundee: Strathmartine	196	21	18	38,119	24,670	—
Dundee: West	225	20	18	64,488	32,699	—
Dundee: Whitfield	32	4	—	—	7,935	—
Dunkeld	283	28	—	119,991	55,555	18
Dunnichen, Letham and Kirkden	202	11	12	29,889	17,131	—
Eassie, Nevay and Newtyle	176	13	16	21,812	8,323	20
Edzell	391	23	14	—	21,277	25
Errol	185	18	—	49,395	20,358	67
Forfar: East, Old and Inverarity	504	—	24	—	62,694	—
Forfar: Lowson Memorial	527	33	29	106,018	57,763	235
Forfar: St Margaret's	379	23	16	55,812	38,395	—
Fortingall, Glenlyon, Kenmore and Lawers	93	12	12	28,539	10,746	—
Fowlis and Liff	131	12	—	—	6,524	15
Friockheim Kinnell	107	7	22	17,147	7,707	—
Gargunnock	97	8	—	31,516	9,843	6
Kippen	132	11	11	31,555	21,721	4
Norrieston	73	8	5	23,421	10,094	5
Port of Menteith	49	9	—	17,404	7,023	—
Kilmadock	65	7	—	14,832	14,471	1
Kincardine—in—Menteith	60	3	—	7,588	6,949	—
Gartmore	53	8	—	13,454	10,176	2
Glamis	184	—	18	—	26,993	—
Glendevon	26	—	—	—	—	—
Guthrie and Rescobie	187	8	—	9,526	11,094	—
Invergowrie	199	38	25	56,811	31,839	6
Inverkeilor and Lunan	102	4	—	17,034	8,241	1
Isla Parishes	127	—	—	22,486	14,309	—
Killearn	286	13	42	—	50,066	11
Strathblane	131	14	33	67,034	40,509	16
Kinross	509	19	25	158,631	72,440	126
Kirkmichael, Straloch and Glenshee	53	4	—	13,009	9,317	—
Rattray	215	13	—	25,961	16,512	12

Congregation	Com	Eld	G	In23	GtoG	–18
Logie	421	24	—	85,033	48,460	3
Lundie and Muirhead	244	18	—	35,245	19,935	24
Menstrie	284	19	16	61,301	36,568	1
Mid Strathearn	287	21	—	64,467	28,057	35
Monifieth South Angus	801	56	44	—	74,037	112
Montrose: Trinity	1,059	—	22	—	88,272	—
Muthill	201	13	9	—	24,301	15
Oathlaw Tannadice	95	6	—	19,196	4,068	—
The Glens and Kirriemuir United	995	57	37	79,435	49,194	15
Orwell and Portmoak	343	24	—	70,704	32,265	30
Perth: Craigie and Moncrieffe	443	19	15	—	22,672	—
Perth: Kinnoull	328	37	18	—	30,812	162
Perth: Letham St Mark's	391	10	—	132,513	60,572	—
Perth: North	677	36	43	—	109,200	8
Perth: Riverside	61	6	—	—	21,607	65
Perth: St John's Kirk of Perth	319	23	—	79,967	36,136	—
Perth: St Leonard's—in—the—Fields	331	26	—	—	44,866	—
Perth: St Matthew's	327	33	20	169,721	55,094	—
St Madoes and Kinfauns	268	32	—	118,966	28,905	250
Scone and St Martins	718	28	39	117,526	52,758	40
Stirling: Holy Rude Viewfield	306	—	—	—	42,307	—
Stirling: North	325	24	22	90,914	35,843	20
Stirling: Park	412	42	—	174,958	75,908	60
Stirling: St Mark's	149	10	—	30,906	14,726	12
Stirling: St Ninians Old	422	44	—	—	61,058	45
Tenandry	31	8	—	28,216	11,654	—
Tillicoultry	342	51	27	95,199	46,525	60
Tullibody: St Serf's	263	21	25	—	30,522	20
9. North East and Northern Isles						
Aberdeen: Bridge of Don Oldmachar	158	9	—	57,070	17,641	87
Aberdeen: Devana	798	43	27	230,863	159,926	108
Aberdeen: Fountainhall	1,339	74	96	—	244,127	60
Aberdeen: Hillside	458	—	13	50,918	53,607	—
Aberdeen: Mannofield	724	53	19	184,343	88,703	70
Aberdeen: North	312	27	24	—	31,618	6
Aberdeen: St Columba's Bridge of Don	204	13	—	94,491	52,218	139
Aberdeen: St John's Church for Deaf People	82	—	—	—	—	—
Aberdeen: St Machar's Cathedral	413	31	—	216,413	75,163	—
Aberdeen: St Mary's	234	29	—	65,382	33,208	52
Aberdeen: St Nicholas Kincorth, South of	263	23	—	54,032	28,946	90
Aberdeen: St Stephen's	131	15	13	—	36,033	10
Aberdeen: Springfield	855	—	27	—	93,599	
Aberdeen: Stockethill	72	5	—	33,229	11,737	17
Aberdeen: Torry St Fittick's	237	17	11	—	29,275	14
Aberdour	88	7	—	8,371	4,507	—
Aberlour	194	14	28	48,484	19,497	5
Aberluthnott	57	—	—	15,233	3,397	—
Laurencekirk	203	—	—	22,696	8,021	—
Aboyne-Dinnet	231	8	11	43,886	22,962	17

Congregation	Com	Eld	G	In23	GtoG	–18
Cromar	176	—	—	29,390	17,823	—
Arbuthnott, Bervie and Kinneff	244	19	—	74,909	34,733	50
Auchterless and Auchaber	242	16	—	21,767	13,134	4
Banchory-Ternan: East	428	22	11	63,550	40,527	3
Banchory-Ternan: West	550	15	—	114,313	56,064	30
Banff	315	17	—	—	30,814	25
King Edward	121	—	—	16,404	10,476	—
Barthol Chapel	55	5	8	—	6,090	1
Belhelvie	284	23	15	—	43,650	33
Bellie and Speymouth	305	17	25	—	25,203	110
Bennachie	1,766	—	—	136,059	124,269	—
Birsay, Harray and Sandwick	258	—	51	38,787	18,122	—
Birse and Feughside	188	11	—	33,155	11,775	23
Braemar and Crathie	165	—	—	—	23,536	—
Brimmond	469	25	32	—	70,795	—
Buckie: North	219	22	27	57,554	23,478	14
Buckie: South and West	178	15	—	38,643	19,423	—
Crimond	129	—	—	19,749	13,932	—
Lonmay	85	8	9	10,236	7,115	25
Cruden	285	16	16	44,366	21,847	11
Cullen and Deskford	236	9	—	46,714	21,839	—
Culsalmond and Rayne	141	3	—	—	2,622	4
Daviot	131	6	—	9,321	5,712	3
Cults	588	42	34	192,383	80,184	49
Deer	487	15	17	—	10,535	2
Duffus, Spynie and Hopeman	185	26	—	46,696	25,671	9
Dyce	521	41	44	—	65,032	100
New Machar	332	—	—	—	17,754	—
East Mainland	213	15	12	25,371	4,392	—
Eday	2	—	—	—	852	—
Elgin	818	—	44	113,867	111,133	
Ellon	1,242	—	—	218,117	90,287	—
Enzie	44	4	—	2,602	788	2
Evie and Rendall	63	—	—	30,647	8,719	—
Firth	59	4	—	—	9,467	4
Findochty	38	8	9	23,510	11,369	18
Portknockie	46	7	14	24,221	11,833	43
Fintray Kinellar Keithhall	119	8	—	—	14,214	—
Flotta	19	4	—	—	381	—
Orphir and Stenness	112	10	—	15,528	11,308	—
Foveran	176	5	—	30,981	20,185	1
Fraserburgh: Old	394	—	44	—	55,903	—
Fraserburgh: South	227	16	—	—	21,437	—
Fraserburgh: West	349	31	—	46,573	36,900	96
Fyvie	134	12	14	37,886	20,125	12
Rothienorman	92	—	—	17,815	8,577	—
Glenmuick (Ballater)	203	15	—	31,877	13,191	—
Hoy and Walls	32	—	—	4,890	1,150	—
Huntly Cairnie Glass	551	—	—	—	24,619	—
Insch-Leslie-Premnay-Oyne	299	—	14	—	34,334	—

Congregation	Com	Eld	G	In23	GtoG	–18
Inverallochy and Rathen: East	63	6	—	—	9,230	13
Inverurie: St Andrew's	835	—	—	106,267	50,082	—
Inverurie: West	516	—	22	101,945	56,226	—
Keith: North, Newmill, Boharm and Rothiemay	404	—	16	45,767	55,157	—
Keith: St Rufus, Botriphnie and Grange	787	—	24	58,709	31,040	—
Kingshill	1,232	56	48	174,022	101,193	106
Kirkwall: East	275	—	—	—	33,999	—
Shapinsay	31	4	—	7,646	3,622	—
Kirkwall: St Magnus Cathedral	424	24	20	—	31,867	—
Rousay	10	—	—	601	—	—
Knockando, Elchies and Archiestown	198	—	—	40,728	20,446	—
Rothes	249	—	11	—	16,741	—
Longside	363	19	—	61,221	32,011	—
Lossiemouth: St Gerardine's High	168	7	13	—	26,130	5
Lossiemouth: St James'	167	12	33	46,467	24,340	9
Macduff	481	—	—	—	53,586	—
Marnoch	306	15	12	31,720	19,590	3
Maryculter: Trinity	123	13	7	51,624	21,733	2
Maud and Savoch	158	9	—	26,498	18,218	8
New Deer: St Kane's	232	—	17	39,299	25,286	—
Meldrum and Bourtie	351	19	31	83,099	34,638	42
Methlick	293	—	14	67,352	41,482	—
Mid Deeside	432	29	17	75,866	31,342	20
Monquhitter and New Byth	231	14	7	20,644	10,870	—
Turriff: St Andrew's	395	22	14	—	18,643	57
Mortlach and Cabrach	271	—	12	—	13,909	—
New Pitsligo	229	—	—	14,743	10,682	—
Newtonhill	198	10	14	—	11,406	32
North Ronaldsay	5	3	—	—	313	—
Ordiquhill and Cornhill	123	9	9	13,550	3,710	15
Whitehills	247	—	18	—	6,481	—
Papa Westray	7	4	—	12,886	3,330	6
Westray	78	17	21	—	16,599	45
Peterculter	810	42	—	—	87,798	—
Peterhead: New	427	19	24	44,683	24,300	16
Peterhead: St Andrew's	335	16	9	28,840	16,674	8
Pitsligo	74	—	—	—	8,910	—
Portlethen	236	9	—	—	19,175	2
Portsoy	232	10	25	—	24,973	—
Rathen: West	64	7	—	4,865	4,658	—
Rathven	53	—	11	—	7,011	—
St Andrew's-Lhanbryd and Urquhart	268	—	26	—	30,334	—
St Cyrus	197	—	—	27,799	15,523	—
St Fergus	88	—	9	—	796	—
Sanday	34	5	5	—	1,043	—
Sandhaven	63	—	—	—	2,382	—
Shetland	723	53	80	—	85,728	28
South Ronaldsay and Burray	102	7	12	27,676	8,012	—
Stonehaven: Carronside	685	22	—	—	28,470	4
Stonehaven: Fetteresso	495	—	26	—	90,401	—

Congregation	Com	Eld	G	In23	GtoG	–18
Strathbogie Drumblade	361	—	20	49,308	29,619	—
Strichen and Tyrie	311	16	20	60,814	29,818	5
Stromness	263	27	13	34,093	22,677	2
Stronsay: Moncur Memorial	44	9	—	15,743	3,626	1
Tarves	221	10	24	41,065	21,885	2
Turriff: St Ninian's and Forglen	471	16	15	—	42,330	10
Udny and Pitmedden	219	—	—	—	25,672	—
West Gordon (Alford, Strathdon, Rhynie)	1,103	—	32	91,537	82,631	—
West Mearns	395	—	14	—	28,287	—

10. Clèir Eilean Ì: Highlands and Islands

Congregation	Com	Eld	G	In23	GtoG	–18
Abernethy	125	10	—	57,244	32,820	30
Boat of Garten, Carrbridge and Kincardine	155	13	28	34,502	19,796	17
Acharacle and Ardnamurchan	37	9	—	30,783	13,207	3
Ardgour, Morven and Strontian	79	14	9	—	8,199	5
Alness	61	8	—	26,192	16,739	14
Altnaharra and Farr	20	—	—	—	4,644	—
Melness and Tongue	18	—	—	—	—	—
Alves and Burghead	95	13	23	—	17,204	8
Alvie and Insh	51	—	—	—	18,258	—
Rothiemurchus and Aviemore	56	7	—	21,095	6,838	6
Appin	78	12	16	—	11,435	10
Applecross, Lochcarron and Torridon	47	—	6	—	13,196	—
Ardchattan	69	9	—	—	17,902	6
Coll	16	3	—	2,964	2,953	—
Connel	92	—	—	47,618	11,390	—
Assynt and Stoer	13	2	—	22,572	3,655	7
Barra	31	—	—	—	7,850	—
South Uist	38	—	—	21,121	8,587	—
Benbecula	59	—	—	52,637	22,383	—
Carinish	60	7	—	—	28,697	5
Berneray and Lochmaddy	20	2	7	10,398	6,046	—
Kilmuir and Paible	21	4	—	37,573	13,043	4
Black Isle East	108	—	—	—	23,219	—
Bracadale, Duirinish and Snizort	68	—	6	—	26,835	—
Bute, United Church of	337	33	—	69,980	37,156	2
Campbeltown	917	—	—	95,066	61,708	—
Saddell and Carradale	127	13	16	—	11,976	—
Southend	198	12	13	30,244	14,853	—
Clyne	30	8	—	—	14,372	—
Kildonan and Loth Helmsdale	12	4	—	—	2,731	—
Colonsay and Oronsay	8	2	—	—	2,751	4
Netherlorn	186	—	—	22,291	10,085	—
Contin	38	8	—	—	2,858	3
Fodderty and Strathpeffer	79	16	—	31,817	14,261	15
Cowal Kirk	638	82	31	—	71,850	—
Creich	28	—	—	—	5,265	—
Cromdale and Advie	52	3	—	18,690	3,468	—
Grantown-on-Spey and Dulnain Bridge	170	14	—	58,588	26,273	12
Culloden and Ardersier	227	19	—	89,530	64,603	52

Congregation	Com	Eld	G	In23	GtoG	–18
Dallas	39	4	—	11,656	8,292	—
Dalriada Mid Argyll	331	38	21	—	66,830	5
Dingwall: Castle Street	104	10	—	—	29,353	11
Dingwall: St Clement's	184	22	15	68,158	32,569	—
Dores and Boleskine	46	5	—	11,056	5,817	2
Dornoch Cathedral	249	20	41	—	56,262	50
Durness and Kinlochbervie	25	3	—	18,536	9,046	30
Dyke and Edinkillie	135	10	11	36,542	5,710	27
Easter Ross Peninsula	136	—	19	—	40,863	—
Eddrachillis	6	—	—	—	8,820	—
Ferintosh	123	16	19	49,447	22,112	20
Forres: St Laurence	294	13	—	—	35,357	—
Forres: St Leonard's	97	10	24	—	29,739	10
Fort Augustus	53	7	—	—	7,771	2
Glengarry	25	5	10	—	5,073	4
Fort William Kilmallie	351	—	25	91,821	34,527	—
Kilmonivaig	46	13	10	19,743	8,664	8
Glenelg, Kintail and Lochalsh	53	8	8	38,265	14,134	—
Glenorchy and Strathfillan	60	10	—	11,750	3,142	—
Golspie	28	—	—	20,518	7,801	—
Halkirk Westerdale	32	6	—	13,377	3,735	—
Watten	11	—	—	—	710	—
Invergordon	90	—	—	45,722	28,260	24
Inverness: Crown	451	—	28	—	48,848	—
Inverness: Hilton	211	11	—	—	42,240	18
Inverness: Inshes East	389	18	—	311,027	165,788	85
Inverness: Kinmylies	68	8	—	—	24,624	55
Inverness: Ness Bank	457	29	23	175,857	89,286	100
Inverness: Old High St Stephen's	311	28	—	113,878	59,625	2
Inverness: St Columba	48	5	—	49,280	19,000	28
Inverness: Trinity Dalneigh	208	12	20	42,071	64,064	94
Iona and the Ross of Mull	34	—	—	—	4,926	—
North Mull	150	12	—	65,289	27,070	—
Jura	18	4	—	—	4,767	—
North and West Islay	91	23	7	27,354	11,588	—
South Islay	218	17	—	68,597	25,583	4
Kilchrenan and Dalavich	31	—	—	14,789	5,438	—
Muckairn	96	14	—	24,173	13,543	—
Killearnan	71	—	—	23,172	6,811	—
Kilmorack and Erchless	74	6	—	—	25,814	12
Kilmore and Oban	381	—	—	84,523	39,095	—
Tiree	47	5	—	—	5,289	1
Kilmuir and Logie Easter	56	9	14	42,580	16,462	8
Kilmuir and Stenscholl	25	4	—	34,924	14,029	3
Kilmun, Strone and Ardentinny: The Shore Kirk	135	—	—	17,997	9,777	—
West Cowal	143	17	—	—	29,084	3
Kiltarlity and Kirkhill	100	—	11	—	22,885	40
Kiltearn	52	5	—	31,860	19,652	1
Kincardine, Croick and Edderton	29	5	—	—	6,132	2
Kingussie	61	10	—	—	8,480	—

Congregation	Com	Eld	G	In23	GtoG	-18
Laggan and Newtonmore	84	13	—	—	24,814	2
Kinlochleven	41	4	9	22,791	11,629	—
Kinloss and Findhorn	56	11	—	—	15,873	—
Knockbain	22	—	—	—	122	—
Lairg	14	—	8	15,553	8,224	—
Rogart	11	4	—	—	5,038	—
Latheron	49	7	7	19,003	10,398	18
Lismore	34	—	—	—	5,534	—
Lochbroom and Ullapool	32	5	—	32,504	12,501	7
Lochgoilhead and Kilmorich	59	—	—	35,633	14,208	—
Strachur and Strachlachlan	88	7	10	20,357	7,921	—
Manish-Scarista	17	4	—	23,741	13,183	7
Mid Kintyre and Gigha	149	—	7	40,646	19,165	—
Tarbert, Loch Fyne and Kilberry	75	8	24	40,314	16,088	—
Nairn: Old	308	29	—	107,047	57,576	3
Nairn: St Ninian's and Auldearn and Dalmore	183	12	28	71,775	30,268	4
North Coast	29	—	17	—	8,667	—
North West Lochaber	74	8	—	—	15,614	16
Pentland	91	7	22	—	11,792	12
Portree	80	13	—	64,160	35,861	3
Rafford	41	5	—	—	6,409	—
Resolis and Urquhart	78	10	—	—	16,743	2
Rosehall	18	2	—	9,201	5,055	2
Rosskeen	99	11	12	53,091	22,879	45
Rothesay: Trinity	274	—	17	59,131	26,375	—
South Lochaber	95	12	15	29,791	12,800	—
Strath and Sleat	88	8	—	100,974	55,570	—
Strathnairn and Strathdearn	239	—	27	—	29,886	—
Tarbert	69	—	—	70,314	35,724	—
Thurso: St Peter's and St Andrew's	108	16	—	—	29,909	17
Thurso: West	128	21	17	49,211	28,632	4
Tomintoul, Glenlivet and Inveraven	106	11	—	—	7,869	—
Urquhart and Glenmoriston	83	6	—	39,940	24,487	—
Urray and Kilchrist	71	14	—	56,350	32,088	11
West Lochfyneside: Cumlodden, Inveraray and Lochgair	92	14	7	—	17,258	—
West Ross	68	3	—	68,668	32,644	3
Wick: Pulteneytown and Thrumster	166	11	16	—	30,172	30
Wick: St Fergus	130	—	—	34,732	12,953	—
11. Lewis						
Barvas	71	7	—	83,102	37,827	—
Carloway	45	5	—	33,486	14,238	—
Cross Ness	58	3	—	49,705	26,009	—
Kinloch	30	4	—	39,372	24,534	15
Knock	20	2	—	—	17,910	12
Lochs-Crossbost	8	3	—	12,225	9,033	—
Lochs-in-Bernera	28	4	—	—	8,905	—
Uig	18	4	—	—	10,515	—
Stornoway: High	89	9	—	85,464	37,872	24

Congregation	Com	Eld	G	In23	GtoG	–18
Stornoway: Martin's Memorial	344	13	—	189,043	92,726	71
Stornoway: St Columba	113	10	34	95,843	50,390	140
12. England and Channel Islands						
Corby	122	12	—	77,404	39,444	—
Guernsey: St Andrew's in the Grange	152	17	—	64,466	41,012	25
Jersey: St Columba's	101	9	—	62,162	34,917	5
London: Crown Court	187	28	3	90,481	46,708	12
London: St Columba's	728	56	—	—	162,706	10
Newcastle: St Andrew's	102	13	—	—	4,328	16
13. International Charges						
Amsterdam: English Reformed Church	337	12	—	—	—	10
Bermuda: Christ Church Warwick	463	42	—	—	—	25
Brussels: St Andrew's	284	16	—	—	—	33
Budapest: St Columba's	27	9	—	—	—	16
Colombo, Sri Lanka: St Andrew's Scots Kirk	103	—	—	—	—	—
Geneva	211	—	—	—	—	—
Lausanne: The Scots Kirk	101	14	—	—	—	7
Lisbon: St Andrew's	50	—	—	—	—	—
Malta: St Andrew's Scots Church	43	6	—	—	—	2
Paris: The Scots Kirk	87	7	—	—	—	10
Rome: St Andrew's	88	11	—	—	—	10
Rotterdam: Scots International Church	183	8	—	—	—	35
Trinidad: Greyfriars St Ann's, Port of Spain with Arouca and Sangre Grande	227	—	—	—	—	—

INDEX OF MINISTERS

Ministers who are members of a Presbytery are designated:
'A' if holding a parochial appointment in that Presbytery;
'A-1, A-2' etc. indicate the numerical order of congregations in that Presbytery;
'B' if in other appointments; or
'C' if 'Retaining'.
Ministers who have resigned their seat but are registered by Presbytery are designated:
'D' if in other appointments;
'E' if 'Retaining'; or
'F' if 'Inactive'.
Ministers serving overseas (List 6-E) are listed here under their Presbyteries.
Ordained Local Ministers and Auxiliary Ministers are listed here under their Presbyteries.
Ministers who have died since the compilation of the last *Year Book* are designated 'List 6-J'.
For reasons of spacing:
Edinburgh and West Lothian is given as 'Edinburgh/W.L.';
Forth Valley and Clydesdale is given as 'Forth V./C'dale';
Clèir Eilean Ì: Highlands and Hebrides is given as 'CEI:HH';
International Charges is given as 'Int. Charges'; and
England and Channel Islands is given as 'England/C.I.'

For a list of the Diaconate, see List 6-B.

Abeledo, B.J.A. Perth 8C
Ableitner, J.M. Glasgow 5A-14
Adam, G. D. Clyde 4A-65
Adams, D.G. Fife 7C
Adams, J.M. N. East/N. Isles 9B
Adamson, R.A. South West 3C
Addis, R. Edinburgh/W.L. 1A-25
Afrin, N.A. Glasgow 5A-105
Ahalıgan, A.K. Forth V./C'dale 6A-84
Aitchison, J.W. Edinburgh/W.L. 1C
Aitken, E.R. Edinburgh/W.L. 1D
Aitken, F.R. South West 3C
Aitken, I.M. N. East/N. Isles 9A-14
Aitken, J.D. Edinburgh/W.L. 1A-16
Albon, D.A. Forth V./C'dale 6C
Alexander, D.N. Clyde 4F
Alexander, H.J.R. Edinburgh/W.L. 1C
Alexander, I.W. Edinburgh/W.L. 1B
Allan, R.S.T. Forth V./C'dale 6A-58
Allardice, M. Fife 7B
Allen, V.L. Perth 8B
Allison, A. Lothian/Borders 2C
Allison, R.N. Lothian/Borders 2A-13
Alston, C.M. Fife 7C
Amed, P. Lewis 11C
Anderson, A.F. England/C.I. 12C
Anderson, D. N. East/N. Isles 9E
Anderson, D.M. CEI:HH 10C
Anderson, D.P. CEI:HH 10B
Anderson, D.U. Edinburgh/W.L. 1C
Anderson, F.R. Forth V./C'dale 6A-39
Anderson, R.A. South West 3C
Anderson, R.J.M. N. East/N. Isles 9C
Anderson, S.M. Glasgow 5E
Andrews, J.E. CEI:HH 10C
Archer, M. CEI:HH 10B
Archer, N.D.C. CEI:HH 10C
Arif, R. Forth V./C'dale 6A-40
Armitage, W.L. List 6-J
Armstrong, G.B. Clyde 4A-57
Armstrong, I.S. Perth 8A-16
Arnott, A.D.K. Lothian/Borders 2C
Ashley-Emery, S. Edinburgh/W.L. 1B
Astles, G.D. Lothian/Borders 2A-66
Atkins, Y.E.S. Lothian/Borders 2C
Atkinson, G.T. CEI:HH 10A-1
Attenburrow, A.A. CEI:HH 10C
Auld, A.G. Lothian/Borders 2F
Austin, G. Int. Charges 13A-13

Bain, B. N. East/N. Isles 9C
Baird, K.S. Edinburgh/W.L. 1C
Baker, C.M. South West 3C
Balaj, N.I. Edinburgh/W.L. 1A-71
Ballentine, A.M. Perth 8C
Barclay, I.C. Edinburgh/W.L. 1B
Barclay, N.W. Forth V./C'dale 6F
Barclay, S.G. Glasgow 5B
Bardgett, F.D. CEI:HH 10E
Barge, N.L. CEI:HH 10C
Barr, D.L.C. N. East/N. Isles 9A-56
Barr, G.R. Fife 7C
Barr, T.L. Perth 8C
Barrett, L.M. Fife 7C
Barrie, A.A. CEI:HH 10C
Barrie, A.P. Forth V./C'dale 6C
Barrie, D. Perth 8C
Barron, J.L. Fife 7A-13
Bartholomew, D.S. South West 3E
Batchelor, D.L. Edinburgh/W.L. 1A-25
Baxendale, G.M. List 6-J
Baxter, R. Glasgow 5A-115
Beattie, C.J. Glasgow 5A-18
Beattie, W.R. CEI:HH 10A-13
Beautyman, P.H. CEI:HH 10F
Becker, A.E. South West 3C
Beckett, D.M. Edinburgh/W.L. 1F
Beebee, G.W. Fife 7A-10
Begg, R. J. Perth 8B
Bell, G.K. CEI:HH 10C
Bell, I.W. Clyde 4C
Bell, J.L. Glasgow 5C
Bell, M. Clyde 4C
Bellis, P.A. South West 3A-19
Bender, A. C. N. East/N. Isles 9A-62
Bennett, A.G. Int. Charges 13A-2
Beresford, H. J. South West 3A-73
Berry, G.T. Lothian/Borders 2B
Bezuidenhout, L.C. N. East/N. Isles 9C
Bezuidenhout, W.J. CEI:HH 10A-7
Bicket, M.S. Edinburgh/W.L. 1C
Billes, R.H. Edinburgh/W.L. 1B
Binks, M. England/C.I. 12B
Birch, J. Glasgow 5C
Bircham, M.F. Perth 8A-108
Birnie, C. England/C.I. 12A-3
Bjarnason, S.S. Fife 7F
Black, A.R. South West 3C
Black, A.T. List 6-I
Black, D.R. Glasgow 5A-88
Black, D.W. Edinburgh/W.L. 1F
Black, G.W.G. Fife 7A-19

Black, I.W. Glasgow 5C
Black, J.M.K. Clyde 4F
Black, J.S. Lothian/Borders 2E
Black, S. Clyde 4A-62
Black, W.B. Glasgow 5C
Blackman, I.R. Forth V./C'dale 6A-68
Blackshaw, C.J. South West 3B
Blackwood, K.T. N. East/N. Isles 9A-5
Blair, F. N. East/N. Isles 9C
Blakesley, A.S. Clyde 4A-59
Blakey, R.S. Edinburgh/W.L. 1F
Blakey, S.A. Perth 8A-77
Blount, A.S. Glasgow 5C
Blount, G.K. Glasgow 5E
Bluett, P.B. Edinburgh/W.L. 1A-42
Blythe, S. Glasgow 5A-33
Boag, J.A.S. Glasgow 5A-3
Bogle, A.O. Perth 8C
Bogle, T.C. South West 3C
Bom, I.M.E. Int. Charges 13B
Bond, M.S. South West 3C
Boonzaaier, J. N. East/N. Isles 9A-31
Booth, F.M. Clyde 4F
Booth, J. Edinburgh/W.L. 1C
Borthwick, K.S. Edinburgh/W.L. 1C
Bosch, E. Forth V./C'dale 6A-59
Boshoff, M. Clyde 4A-20
Boswell, G.R. Fife 7C
Boyd, B.J. N. East/N. Isles 9C
Boyd, J.A. N. East/N. Isles 9C
Boyd, K.M. Edinburgh/W.L. 1E
Boyd, S. Edinburgh/W.L. 1A-78
Boyes, A.M. CEI:HH 10A-31
Boyle, E. South West 3A-75
Boyle, R.P. Fife 7C
Boyle, W.A. Clyde 4A-64
Bradley, A.W. Glasgow 5E
Bradley, I.C. Fife 7C
Bradwell, A.S. Lothian/Borders 2A-49
Brady, I.D. List 6-J
Brady, L. South West 3A-59
Brandon, W.C. South West 3A-22
Breingan, M.M. Clyde 4A-58
Bremner, J.S. Edinburgh/W.L. 5A-72
Brennan, A.J. Perth 8C
Brennan, L.J. South West 3A-50
Brewster, J. Fife 7C
Britchfield, A.E.P. Perth 8A-121
Broadley, L.J. N. East/N. Isles 9C
Brockie,C.G.F. South West 3C
Brodie, C.J. Perth 8A-59
Brook, S.A. Edinburgh/W.L. 1F
Brookes, R.E. CEI:HH 10A-97
Brough, C.M. Perth 8C
Brown, D.G. Lothian/Borders 2C
Brown, E. Perth 8C
Brown, H.T. South West 3C
Brown, J.M. South West 3C
Brown, J.M. Int. Charges 13C
Brown, K.I. Forth V./C'dale 6E
Brown, M.D. Perth 8C
Brown, R.F. N. East/N. Isles 9E
Brown, R.G. List 6-I
Brown, R.H. List 6-J
Brown, S.A. N. East/N. Isles 9A-9
Brown, S.J. Perth 8B
Brown, S.M. Lothian/Borders 2A-35
Brown, T.J. Forth V./C'dale 2E
Brown, W.D. Edinburgh/W.L. 1C
Browning, D. Edinburgh/W.L. 1A-38
Bruce, A.J. N. East/N. Isles 9A-46
Brunger, L.N. Forth V./C'dale 6C
Bryson, T.M. CEI:HH 10F
Buchan, A. List 6-J
Buchan, I.C. Perth 8C
Buchan, W. Forth V./C'dale 6E
Buchanan, F.C. Clyde 4C
Buchanan, N. Edinburgh/W.L. 1F
Buck, M. South West 3C
Buckley, R.G. Glasgow 5A-112
Buell, F.B. CEI:HH 10C
Bullock, F.C. Perth 8A-103
Burgess, P.C.J. South West 3C
Burns, J.H. South West 3C
Burns, T.T. CEI:HH 10A-86
Burnside, A.H. South West 3A-21
Burt, D.W.G. Clyde 4A-26
Burt, T.W. Lothian/Borders 2C
Burton, S.E. Fife 7C
Burton, S.W. Forth V./C'dale 6A-22
Butterfield, J.A. N. East/N. Isles 9C
Buwert, K.O.F. Perth 8C
Byun, B.D.W. N. East/N. Isles 9A-13

Cairns, A.B. South West 3C
Cairns, E. Perth 8C
Cairns, J.B. Lothian/Borders 2E
Cairns, W.A. England/C.I. 12C
Calder, B. Forth V./C'dale 6A-90
Calder, T.R. N. East/N. Isles 9A-58
Caldwell, G.J. Perth 8B
Calvert, R.A. Perth 8C
Cameron, A.J. Clyde 4C
Cameron, D.C. Fife 7C
Cameron, D.J. CEI:HH 10A-6
Cameron, D.S. South West 3A-68
Cameron, G.G. List 6-I
Cameron, R. Glasgow 5A-106
Cameron, R.N. England/C.I. 12C
Campbell, A.I. List 6-J
Campbell, C.F. Int. Charges 13A-2
Campbell, D. South West 3A-46
Campbell, D. South West 3B
Campbell, G.A. Perth 8B
Campbell, I.M. Lewis 11A-4
Campbell, J. Glasgow 5C
Campbell, J.E.R. List 6-J
Campbell, J.W. Forth V./C'dale 6C
Campbell, K.K. Edinburgh/W.L. 1A-35
Campbell, M.M. Lewis 11C
Campbell, N.G. South West 3B
Campbell, R.D.M. CEI:HH 10C
Campbell, R.F. Fife 7C
Campbell, R.S. Perth 8C
Campbell, S.L. N. East/N. Isles 9B
Campbell, T.R. Lothian/Borders 2C
Cant, T.M. South West 3C
Carmichael, D.J.M. Edinburgh/W.L. 1B
Carruthers, D. CEI:HH 10A-27
Carswell, W.J. Forth V./C'dale 6A-65
Cartlidge, G.R.G. Glasgow 5C
Cartwright, A.C.D. Lothian/Borders 2C
Casey, B.M. Glasgow 5A-110
Caskie, J.C. Perth 8C
Cathcart, I.A. Glasgow 5A-8
Cathcart, R.P. N. East/N. Isles 9A-61
Cato, J.A. Edinburgh/W.L. 1A-43
Cha, S.Y. Perth 8A-8
Chalmers, G.A. Forth V./C'dale 6F
Chalmers, J.P. Fife 7C
Chalmers, M. Edinburgh/W.L. 1F
Chambers, S.J. CEI:HH 10C
Charlton, I.A. N. East/N. Isles 9A-103
Cherry, A.J. Glasgow 5F
Chestnutt, D.A. Forth V./C'dale 6B
Chewachong, A.B. Fife 7A-56
Cheyne, R.U. N. East/N. Isles 9C
Chikanya, T.N. South West 3A-6
Childs, A. Edinburgh/W. L. 1A-13
Chisholm, A.F. CEI:HH 10F
Christie, A.A. Fife 7C
Christie, A.C. N. East/N. Isles 9C
Christie, H.F. Glasgow 5C
Christie, J.C. Clyde 4E
Christie, R.S. South West 3E
Clancy, P.J. South West 3B
Clark, C.M. England/C.I. 12C
Clark, D.M. Fife 7C
Clark, D.W. Clyde 4E
Clark, D.W. List 6-J
Clark, M.A. Perth 8C
Clarkson, D. Edinburgh/W.L. 1A-9
Cleland, R. CEI:HH 10C
Clinkenbeard, W.W. List 6-J
Clipston, J.A. N. East/N. Isles 9A-30
Clipston, S.F. South West 3A-9
Cloggie, J. Perth 8C
Cobain, A.R. Lothian/Borders 2B
Cochrane, J.P.N. Perth 8C
Cohen, H.L. Lothian/Borders 2A-55
Coleman, S.H. Perth 8C
Collard, J.K. Forth V./C'dale 6E
Collins, C.E.E. Fife 7C
Collins, D.A. Fife 7C
Collins, M. List 6-J
Coltart, I.O. Lothian/Borders 2C
Colvin, S.E.F. Forth V./C'dale 6C
Condeco, I.C. Forth V./C'dale 6A-58
Conkey, H. Fife 7C
Connolly, D. Fife 7C
Connolly, J. Perth 8A-61
Cook, A.W. Lothian/Borders 2A-39
Cook, F.M. Edinburgh/W.L. 1A-10
Cook, H.K.M. Perth 8C
Cook, J.A. N. East/N. Isles 9C
Cook, J.M. N. East/N. Isles 9C
Cook, J.S. Forth V./C'dale 6C
Corbett, R.T. Perth 8C
Cord, S. CEI:HH 10B
Corney, T.L. South West 3A-7
Coull, M.C. Clyde 4C
Coulter, D.G. England/C.I. 12C
Coutts, F. N. East/N. Isles 9C
Cowan, J.S.A. Forth V./C'dale 6C
Cowell, S.G. Forth V./C'dale 6F
Cowie, J.A. Edinburgh/W.L. 1C
Cowie, J.M. Lothian/Borders 2F
Cowie, M. Clyde 4C
Cowper, A.J. Perth 8C
Cox, L.P. South West 3E
Craggs, S.A. N. East/N. Isles 9C
Craig, A.J.D. N. East/N. Isles 9C
Craig, J.H. Perth 8C
Craig, R. Edinburgh/W.L. 1A-79
Cranfield, E.F. Fife 7A-54
Cranfield, M.M. N. East/N. Isles 9A-37
Crawford, F.M.E. Glasgow 5A-44
Crawford, G.W. Perth 8A-97
Crawford, S.J. Glasgow 5A-78
Creighton, D.R. Perth 8B
Crichton, J. South West 3C
Cringles, G.G. CEI:HH 10C
Crossan, M. South West 3A-25
Crossan, W. Edinburgh/W.L. 1E
Crosthwaite, M.D. Forth V./C'dale 6E
Crouch, S.A. N. East/N. Isles 9A-112
Cruickshank, N. South West 3C
Cubie, J.P. List 6-I
Cullen, William T. Glasgow 5F

Cumming, A. England/C.I. 12B
Cunningham, A. Glasgow 5C
Cunningham, I.D. Forth V./C'dale 6C
Cunningham, J.S.A. List 6-J
Curlewis, T. Int. Charges 12A-12
Currie, A.I. South West 3A-57
Currie, D.E.P. Forth V./C'dale 6C
Currie, M.F. Forth V./C'dale 6A-7
Cushman, B.W. CEI:HH 10C
Cuthbert, H.E. South West 3C
Cuthbertson, M. Glasgow 5C
Cuthell, T.C. Edinburgh/W.L. 1F
Cutler, J.S.H. Forth V./C'dale 7E
Cutler, S.J. Forth V./C'dale 6A-104

Dalton, M.F. Clyde 4B
Daramola, I.B. N. East/N. Isles 9C
Darroch, R.J.G. Edinburgh/W.L. 1F
Davidge, A.E.S. List 6-J
Davidge, P.L.V. Glasgow 5A-69
Davidson, A. South West 3E
Davidson, A.A.B. List 6-I
Davidson, D.H. Edinburgh/W.L. 1C
Davidson, E.M.L. Perth 8A-73
Davidson, I.M.P. Edinburgh/W.L. 1F
Davidson, M.R. Perth 8B
Davidson, S. Clyde 4A-56
Dawson, M.S. Perth 8E
de Beer, K.M. Forth V./C'dale 6A-9
de Jager, L. Edinburgh/W.L. 1A-47
de Villiers, J.J. Glasgow 5A-35
Deans, G.D.S. Fife 7C
Dee, O. South West 3C
Dempsey, B. CEI:HH 10A-29
Dempster, C.J. Perth 8C
Dempster, E.T. South West 3C
Denniston, D.W. Glasgow 5C
Denniston, J.M. Glasgow 5C
Devenney, D.J. Perth 8C
Dewar, J.S. Edinburgh/W.L. 1C
Dick, A.B. Lothian/Borders 2C
Dick, J.H.A. Fife 7C
Dick, J.R. Lothian/Borders 2F
Dickie, M.M. South West 3C
Dicks, S.M. N. East/N. Isles 9A-38
Dickson, G.T. Edinburgh/W.L. 1F
Digan, L. Glasgow 5A-116
Dillon, A.J. Glasgow 5A-108
Dingwall, B. Perth 8C
Dobby, D.B. South West 3C
Dobby, D.J. Fife 7A-5
Dobie, R.J.W. Lothian/Borders 2F
Dobney, C. Perth 8A-37
Dodd, M.E. Lothian/Borders 2C
Don, A. Lothian/Borders 2A-17
Donaghy, L.G. Forth V./C'dale 6E
Donald, A.C. Fife 7A-44
Donald, K.W. Fife 7C
Donald, P.H. Forth V./C'dale 6A-1
Donald, R.M. List 6-J
Donaldson, C.V. Fife 7F
Donaldson, D. Lothian/Borders 2C
Donaldson, G.M. Forth V./C'dale 6E
Dougall, N.J. Lothian/Borders 2A-61
Douglas, A.B. Edinburgh/W.L. 1C
Douglas, C.R. Edinburgh/W.L. 1E
Douglas, F.C. Perth 8B
Doyle, D.W. Forth V./C'dale 6C
Drake, W.F. Edinburgh/W.L. 1E
Drummond, A.J. CEI:HH 10A-60
Drummond, J.W. Glasgow 5C
Drummond, N.W. CEI:HH 10D
Dryden, I. List 6-J
du Toit, G.F. Edinburgh/W.L. 1A-32
Duff, S.M. N. East/N. Isles 9C
Duff, T.M.F. Glasgow 5C
Duff, V.J. Glasgow 5E
Duffin, G.L. Lothian/Borders 2A-52
Duncan, A.S. Glasgow 5A-99
Duncan, E. CEI:HH 10C
Duncan, J.C. Perth 8C
Duncan, M.M. Lothian/Borders 2C
Duncan, R.P. Lothian/Borders 2C
Duncanson, M.B. Edinburgh/W.L. 1E
Dunleavy, S. Edinburgh/W.L. 1C
Dunlop, A.J. CEI:HH 10F
Dunn, W.I.C. Edinburgh/W.L. 1C
Dunphy, R.B. Edinburgh/W.L. 1C
Dunsmore, B.W. Perth 8F
Dutch, M.M. Glasgow 5C
Dutton, D.W. Lothian/Borders 2F

Earl, J. CEI:HH 10C
Easton, D.J.C. Glasgow 5C
Easton-Berry, J.A. CEI:HH 10A-84
Eddie, D.C. N. East/N. Isles 9A-3
Edwards, D. Perth 8C
Edwards, F. Lothian/Borders 2A-44
Elliott, G.J. CEI:HH 10C
Elliott, K.C. South West 3C
Elston, I.J. Fife 7C
Elwell-Sutton, B.M.M. Perth 8A-59
Embleton, B.M. Edinburgh/W.L. 1C
Embleton, S.R. Edinburgh/W.L. 1C
Enslin, E. N. East/N. Isles 9A-83
Erskine, M.J. Perth 8A-11
Espie, H. Edinburgh/W.L. 1E
Evans-Boiten, J.H.G. Int. Charges 13B
Eve, J.C. Glasgow 5A-5
Ewart, W. Perth 8C
Ewart-Roberts, P. Perth 8C

Fair, W.M. Perth 8B
Fairlie, G. Fife 7C
Falconer, A.D. South West 3C
Falconer, J.B. N. East/N. Isles 9C
Faris, J.M. South West 3C
Farquhar, W.E. Fife 7C
Farquharson, G. Edinburgh/W.L. 1C
Farrington, A. Glasgow 5C
Fazakas, S. CEI:HH 10A-85
Fegan, C. Fife 7A-34
Fenwick, K.M. Perth 8A-68
Ferguson, J.A. Perth 8B
Ferguson, J.B. Glasgow 5C
Ferguson, R. N. East/N. Isles 9F
Fergusson, D.A.S. Edinburgh/W.L. 1B
Fiddes, G.R. South West 3C
Finch, G.S. South West 3C
Findlay, H.J.W. Forth V./C'dale 6E
Finlay, Q. Lothian/Borders 2F
Finlay, W.P. South West 3E
Finlayson, S.A. CEI:HH 10A-109
Finnie, B.H. Glasgow 5C
Finnie, C.J. CEI:HH 10A-5
Firth, J.S. List 6-J
Fisk, E.A. Fife 7C
Fleming, A.F. Glasgow 5F
Fleming, J.C. Clyde 4A-29
Fletcher, G.G. Clyde 4A-23
Fletcher, S.G. Lothian/Borders 2A-22
Foggie, J.P. Fife 7C
Foggitt, E.W. Int. Charges 13A-4
Foley, T.A. Lothian/Borders 2A-9
Forbes, F.A.M. CEI:HH 10C
Forbes, J.W.A. N. East/N. Isles 9F
Ford, A.A. List 6-J
Ford, C.H.M. N. East/N. Isles 9C
Forrest, M.R. Glasgow 5C
Forrester, I.L. Fife 7C
Forrester, M.R. Edinburgh/W.L. 1C
Forsyth, A.C. Edinburgh/W.L. 1A-36
Forsyth, A.R. Fife 7C
Forsythe, R. Glasgow 5A-80
Fortune, E.J. N. East/N. Isles 9C
Foster, J.G. Edinburgh/W.L. 1B
Foster, M.M. Edinburgh/W.L. 1A-45
Foster-Fulton, S. Glasgow 5B
Fothergill, A.P. CEI:HH 10C
Fowlie, R.A. N. East/N. Isles 9A-71
Frail, N.R. South West 3B
Francis, J. England/C.I. 12B
Fraser, A. Fife 7A-32
Fraser, A.G. Fife 7C
Fraser, A.M. Glasgow 5C
Fraser, D.W. Perth 8C
Fraser, I.C. Clyde 4F
Fraser, J. CEI:HH 10B
Fraser, J.W. Lothian/Borders 2F
Fraser, L.J. Edinburgh/W.L. 1A-69
Fraser, S.A. Edinburgh/W.L. 1C
Frater, A. Clyde 4A-50
Frazer, R.E. Edinburgh/W.L. 1C
Freeth, J. N. East/N. Isles 9A-68
Frew, M.W. Edinburgh/W.L. 1C
Frew, R. Lothian/Borders 2A-7
Froude, J.K. Fife 7C
Fucella, M.D. Forth V./C'dale 6A-11
Fulcher, C.P. CEI:HH 10C
Fulcher, S. CEI:HH 10C
Fuller, A.A. Forth V./C'dale 6F
Fulton, R.S.M. Glasgow 5C
Fyfe, L.K. Forth V./C'dale 6B

Galbraith, C.G. Edinburgh/W.L. 1B
Galbraith, D. N. East/N. Isles 9A-76
Galbraith, D.D. Fife 7C
Galbraith, N.W. Glasgow 5C
Gall, R. CEI:HH 10A-23
Gallacher, J.W. Forth V./C'dale 6A-43
Galloway, I.F. Glasgow 5C
Galloway, K.J. Glasgow 5F
Galloway, S.G. Edinburgh/W.L. 1A-44
Gardiner, K. Glasgow 5A-111, 114
Gardner, A. Perth 8A-16
Gardner, B.K. N. East/N. Isles 9E
Gardner, F.M.E. Glasgow 5A-80
Gardner, H.M. CEI:HH 10A-70
Gardner, J.V. Edinburgh/W.L. 1C
Gardner N.N. Edinburgh/W.L. 1A-12
Gardner, P.M. Glasgow 5B
Gargrave, M.R. Glasgow 5C
Garrett, M.V. Forth V./C'dale 6A-31
Garrity, T.A.W. South West 3C
Gaston, A.R.C. Perth 8C
Gatherer, J.F. South West 3A-76
Gatima, E. N. East/N. Isles 9A-12
Gauld, B.G.D.D. Forth V./C'dale 6E
Gauld, K.F. N. East/N. Isles 9C
Gay, D.C. Glasgow 5B
Gebbie, A. Forth V./C'dale 6A-70
Geddes, E. Clyde 4C
Gemmell, D.R. South West 3A-10
Gemmell, J. Glasgow 5A-53
Gemmell, J.R. Glasgow 5A-13
Gerbrandy-Baird, P.S. Fife 7C
Gibson, A.W. Forth V./C'dale 6A-91
Gibson, E.A. CEI:HH 10C
Gibson, J.M. Forth V./C'dale 6E

Gilchrist, E.J. Perth 8C
Gilchrist, K. Forth V./C'dale 6A-4
Gilchrist, M.M. Forth V./C'dale 6A-81
Gill, P.G. Perth 8C
Gillan, D.S. Jerusalem 14A
Gillies, J.E. Perth 8E
Gillon, C. B. Perth 8C
Gillon, D.R.M. South West 3F
Gilmour, I.Y. Edinburgh/W.L. 1C
Gilmour, W.M. Perth 8F
Glen, G.E.D. N. East/N. Isles 9A-26
Glencross, W.M. South West 3C
Glienecke, U. Edinburgh/W.L. 1B
Glover, G.M. Lothian/Borders 2A-30
Glover, N.M. Perth 8A-2
Glover, R.L. Lothian/Borders 2C
Godfrey, L. South West 3C
Gohar, A. Lothian/Borders 2A-26
Goldie, C.M. Clyde 4C
Goncalves, D.P. CEI:HH 10A-28
Goodison, M.J. Perth 8A-87
Gordon, A.M. Perth 8A-33
Gordon, E.J. Perth 8E
Gordon, I.D. Fife 7C
Gordon, P. Clyde 4A-3
Gordon, T.J. Lothian/Borders 2C
Goring, I.M. Perth 8C
Goss, M.S. Perth 8A-33
Goudie, S. CEI:HH 10C
Gough, I.G. Perth 8C
Gourlay, H. Perth 8A-68
Gow, J. N. East/N. Isles 9A-94
Graham, A.F. Fife 7C
Graham, A.G. Perth 8C
Graham, D.J. Lothian/Borders 2A-19
Graham, J.D. N. East/N. Isles 9C
Graham, K.E. Edinburgh/W.L. 1A-40
Graham, S.S. Perth 8C
Graham, W.P. Edinburgh/W.L. 1C
Grahame, R.J. Perth 8A-56
Grainger, A.J. Perth 8A-39
Grainger, H.L. N. East/N. Isles 9F
Granados, T.P. Glasgow 5A-74
Grant, N.M. Fife 7A-9
Grant, P.G.R. Forth V./C'dale 6B
Gray, D.T. Glasgow 5A-72
Gray, I. Perth 8A-91
Gray, K.N. Clyde 4A-11
Gray, W. CEI:HH 10F
Greenshields, I.M. Fife 7A-26
Greig, A. N. East/N. Isles 9C
Greig, C.H.M. N. East/N. Isles 9E
Greig, R.G. Edinburgh/W.L. 1C
Grier, J. Forth V./C'dale 6F
Grieve, L.E.T. Glasgow 5A-61
Griffiths, M.J. N. East/N. Isles 9C
Griffiths, R.I. CEI:HH 10C
Griggs, J.J. Edinburgh/W.L. 1A-15
Groenewald, A.J. Edinburgh/W.L. 1C
Groenewald, J. Edinburgh/W.L. 1A-73
Groves, I.B. N. East/N. Isles 9E
Gruer, K.R. N. East/N. Isles 9A-111
Gunn, A.M. Perth 8C
Gunn, F.D. Forth V./C'dale 6C
Gunn, P. CEI:HH 10A-3
Guthrie, J.A. South West 3C
Guy, S.C. Lothian/Borders 2C

Hacking, P.R. Perth 8A-41, 8B
Haddow, A.H. List 6-J
Haddow, A.N. Lothian/Borders 2A-15
Haddow, M.M. Perth 8C
Haggarty, K.O.N. Edinburgh/W.L. 1A-62
Haley, D. Glasgow 5C
Hall, K.F. Perth 8A-49
Hall, W.M. South West 3C
Halley, R. Edinburgh/W.L. 1C
Halliday, A.R. Perth 8C
Hamilton, A.J. Clyde 4A-6
Hamilton, D. Lothian/Borders 2A-76
Hamilton, D.G. Clyde 4C
Hamilton, D.S.M. Perth 8F
Hamilton, H.D. N. East/N. Isles 9E
Hamilton, I.W.F. Fife 7C
Hamilton, R.A. Clyde 4B
Hamilton, R.G. Clyde 4A-8
Hammond, R.J. South West 3C
Harbison, K.E. Clyde 4A-34
Hardman Moore, S. Edinburgh/W.L. 1E
Harkness, J. Edinburgh/W.L. 1C
Harley, E.S. Edinburgh/W.L. 1C
Harper, D.J. Perth 8A-26
Harper, D.L. South West 3C
Harris, J.W.F. Clyde 4F
Harris, S.M. South West 3F
Harrison, C. Fife 7C
Harrison, F. Lothian/Borders 2C
Harrison, S. Forth V./C'dale 6A-28
Harvey, P.R. South West 3B
Harvey, W.J. Glasgow 5F
Haslett, H.J. Lothian/Borders 2E
Hastie, G.I. Perth 8F
Hawthorn, D. N. East/N. Isles 9C
Hay, C. Perth 8A-12
Hay, J.W. Edinburgh/W.L. 1C
Hays, D.M. Perth 8A-111
Hearty, J. Glasgow 5A-27
Heenan, W.J. Lewis 11A-10
Henderson, D.R. Edinburgh/W.L. 1A-1
Henderson, E.M. Edinburgh/W.L. 1A-51
Henderson, F.M. South West 3A-87
Henderson, G.M. List 6-J
Henderson, J.M. Fife 7C
Henderson, R.J.M. Glasgow 5A-87
Henderson, S. Clyde 4A-17
Hendrie, B.R. South West 3A-16
Hendry, K.E. Glasgow 5A-64
Herbold Ross, K.M. Edinburgh/W.L. 1C
Hercus, H.J. CEI:HH 10A-72
Hetherington, R.M. List 6-J
Hewitt, W.C. South West 3C
Hill, R.E. Lothian/Borders 2A-32
Hilsley, B.C. Lothian/Borders 2C
Hine, K.I. South West 3C
Hobson, D.L. N. East/N. Isles 9E
Hogg, J. South West 3B
Hogg, T.M. Lothian/Borders 2C
Hogg, W.T. South West 3C
Holland, W. List 6-J
Holt, J. Edinburgh/W.L. 1C
Homewood, I.M. Int. Charges 13C
Hood, A.J.J. Lothian/Borders 2A-5
Hood, D.P. Clyde 4A-61
Hood, E.L. Clyde 4C
Hood, H.S.C. CEI:HH 10C
Hood, J.C. Forth V./C'dale 6A-69
Hope, E.P. Glasgow 5C
Hope, G.H. Lothian/Borders 2C
Horne, A.M. Forth V./C'dale 6A-57
Horne, D.A. CEI:HH 10C
Horsburgh, A.G. Lothian/Borders 2A-18
Horsburgh, G.E. South West 3C
Houston, E.W. Clyde 4C
Houston, W.R. Edinburgh/W.L. 1C
Howie, M.L.K. South West 3C
Howie, W. List 6-I
Howitt, J.M. Edinburgh/W.L. 1B
Hudson, H.R. Glasgow 5C
Huggett, J.A. South West 3C
Hughes, B. J. Perth 8A-115
Hughes, D.W. Glasgow 5A-66
Huie, D.F. List 6-I
Hume, D.A. South West 3A-1
Humphrey, J.W. Fife 7A-48
Hunt, M.J. Perth 8A-68
Hunt, R. Glasgow 5C
Hunt, T.G. CEI:HH 10C
Hunter, A.G. Glasgow 5C
Hunter, W.F. CEI:HH 10A-53
Hutcheson, N.M. South West 3C
Hutchison, A.M. N. East/N. Isles 9E
Hutchison, D.S. England/C.I. 12E

Inglis, A. Edinburgh/W.L. 1C
Irvin, S.D Glasgow 5A-40
Irvine, C.J. N. East/N. Isles 9A-60
Irving, D.R. South West 3C
Irving, W.D. Edinburgh/W.L. 1C
Izett, W.A.F. Perth 8C

Jack, A.M. Perth 8B
Jack, J.A.P. Edinburgh/W.L. 1A-23
Jackson, N.M. South West 3C
Jackson, W. South West 3E
Jaffrey, A. N. East/N. Isles 9A-55
Jalland, D.M. N.East/N. Isles 9A-1
Jamieson, A.J. Glasgow 5A-65
Jamieson, E.M.M. Lewis 11C
Jamieson, G.D. List 6-J
Jamieson, H.E. Forth V./C'dale 6C
Janse van Vuren, H.I. Edinburgh/W.L. 1A-74
Jefferson, M.S. Lothian/Borders 2A-54
Jeffrey, K.S. N. East/N. Isles 9B
Jenkins, G.F.C. Fife 7C
Jessamine, A.L. Forth V./C'dale 6E
Job, A.J. Forth V./C'dale 6F
Johnson, C.I.W. Glasgow 5C
Johnson Blythe, M.E. Glasgow 5A-92, 100
Johnston, C.D. Lothian/Borders 2A-12
Johnston, J.E. Lothian/Borders 2C
Johnston, J.P.N. N. East/N. Isles 9A-2
Johnston, M.H. Glasgow 5C
Johnston, R. Glasgow 5C
Johnston, R.W.M. Glasgow 5C
Johnston, T.N. Fife 7C
Johnston, W.A. N. East/N. Isles 9C
Johnstone, B. Lewis 11C
Johnstone, H.M.J. Glasgow 5C
Johnstone, M.E. Glasgow 5A-57
Johnstone, W. List 6-I
Jones, A.M. CEI:HH 10A-36
Jones, A.M. Lothian/Borders 2F
Jones, J.O. CEI:HH 10C
Jones, R. Forth V./C'dale 6C
Jones, W.G. South West 3A-80

Kavanagh, J.A. Glasgow 5C
Kay, D. Clyde 4F
Kay, E. Perth 8C
Keating, G.K. South West 3C
Keefe, J.A. Glasgow 5A-91
Keil, A.H. Edinburgh/W.L. 1C

Kellet, J.M. List 6-I
Kellock, C.N. Lothian/Borders 2B
Kelly, E.R. South West 3B
Kelly, T.C. Perth 8C
Kelly, W.W. South West 3C
Kemp, T. Clyde 4C
Kennedy, F. Edinburgh/W.L. 1B
Kennedy, G. Edinburgh/W.L. 1A-17
Kennedy, P. CEI:H&H 10A-26
Kennedy, R. Perth 8B
Kennon, S. Perth 8C
Kenny, C.G. Lothian/Borders 2F
Kenny, E.S.S. Fife 7C
Kent, R.M. List 6-J
Kenton, M.B. Edinburgh/W.L. 1A-72
Kerr, A. Forth V./C'dale 6E
Kerr, A.D.C. Perth 8A-54
Kerr, B. Forth V./C'dale 6A-77
Kerr, H.F. Glasgow 5F
Kesting, S.M. Fife 7C
Keyes, J.A. Glasgow 5C
Kimmitt, A.I.M. N. East/N. Isles 9A-16
Kimmitt, A.W.D. Fife 7A-34
Kingston, D.V.F. Lothian/Borders 2F
Kinnear, M. CEI:HH 10A-91
Kinnear, M.A. CEI:HH 10A-91
Kinsey, L. N. East/N. Isles 9C
Kirk, S.M. N. East/N. Isles 9A-40
Kirkland, N.J. Edinburgh/W.L. 1A-60
Kirkwood, G. Glasgow 5A-76
Kirkwood, J.A. Perth 8A-60
Kisitu, T.M. Edinburgh/W.L. 1A-60
Knox, A. Clyde 4A-38
Knox, J.W. Perth 8C
Kuzma, A.P. CEI:HH 10A-64
Kyle, C.A.E. South West 3C

la Grange, A. South West 3A-20
Lacy, D.W. South West 3C
Lafontaine, L.M. Edinburgh/W.L. 1A-11
Laidlaw, J.J. Perth 8C
Laidlaw, V.W.N. Fife 7C
Laing, D.A. Perth 8A-7
Lamarti, S.H. South West 3C
Lamb, A.D. N. East/N. Isles 9C
Lamont, S.J. Edinburgh/W.L. 1F
Lancaster, C. N. East/N. Isles 9B
Landale, W.S. Lothian/Borders 2C
Landman, A. South West 3A-32
Lane, M.R. Fife 7C
Langlands, C.H. List 6-J
Lawrie, B.B. Lothian/Borders 2F
Lawrie, D.R. Fife 7A-2
Lawrie, R.M. Clyde 4F
Lawson, D.G. Int. Charges 13C
Lawson, J.B. Perth 8C
Lawson, K.C. List 6-J
Ledgard, J.C. Lothian/Borders 2F
Lees, A.P. Clyde 4F
Legge, R. N. East/N. Isles 9C
Leitch, D.G. Fife 7C
Leitch, M. Clyde 4C
Lennox, L.I. South West 3C
Lennox-Trewren, N.D. N. East/N. Isles 9C
Levison, C.L. Lothian/Borders 2C
Liddiard, F.G.B. Perth 8F
Lillie, F.L. Perth 8C
Lincoln, J. CEI:HH 10C
Lind, G.K. South West 3C
Lind, M.J. CEI:HH 10C
Lindsay, W.D. List 6-J
Lines, C.M.D. South West 3C
Linford, T.N.C. Lothian/Borders 2A-34
Linford, V.J. Lothian/Borders 2B
Lister, F.A. N. East/N. Isles 9A-6
Lithgow, A.R. Edinburgh/W.L. 1F
Lochrie, J.S. South West 3C
Locke, D.I.W. N. East/N. Isles 9A-109
Lockerbie, C.R. Edinburgh/W.L. 1E
Logan, A.T. Edinburgh/W.L. 1C
Logan, T.M. South West 3F
London, D.K. Lothian/Borders 2A-77
Lough, A.J. Edinburgh/W.L. 1C
Louw, D. CEI:HH 10A-109
Louw, M. Int. Charges 13A-1
Love, S. Glasgow 5A-59
Lovett, M.F. England/C.I. 12B
Lowey, M. N. East/N. Isles 9A-106
Ludik, C.B. List 6-J
Lunan, D.W. Glasgow 5C
Lunn, D.I.M. England/C.I. 12C
Lusk, A.S. Forth V./C'dale 6E
Lyall, D. Lothian/Borders 2F
Lyall, M.G. Forth V./C'dale 6A-110
Lyon, M.M. Lothian/Borders 2A-58
Lyons, E.D. South West 3A-102

Macalister, E.E. N. East/N. Isles 9C
Macartney, D.J.B. CEI:HH 10C
Macaskill, D.M. Lewis 11A-2
Macaulay, G.D. Lothian/Borders 2E
MacCallum, A. CEI: HH 10A-59
Macdonald, A. Clyde 4C
Macdonald, C.D. Glasgow 5A-19
Macdonald, F.A.J. Lothian/Borders 2F
MacDonald, G. Forth V./C'dale 6E
Macdonald, I. CEI:HH 10A-11
MacDonald, I.A. Edinburgh/W.L. 1A-30
MacDonald, I.D. N. East/N. Isles 9A-89
MacDonald, I.M.M. CEI:HH 10A-98
MacDonald, J.W. Perth 8C
MacDonald, K.D. Glasgow 5C
Macdonald, M. Forth V./C'dale 6C
Macdonald, M.C. Forth V./C'dale 6A-14
Macdonald, M.J. CEI:HH 10B
MacDonald, M.J. Forth V./C'dale 6A-102
Macdonald, N.M. Forth V./C'dale 6A-111
MacDonald, R.I.T. South West 3C
Macdonald, S. CEI:HH 10A-34
Macdonald, W.J. Glasgow 5F
MacDougall, L.I. Forth V./C'dale 6A-97
MacDougall, M.I. Perth 8A-110
Macdougall, M.M. Lothian/Borders 2C
MacEwan, D.G. Fife 7B
MacEwan, J.A.I. CEI:HH 10C
MacFadyen, A.M. Glasgow 5C
Macfarlane, J. CEI:HH 10C
Macfarlane, P.T. England/C.I. 12C
Macgregor, A. N. East/N. Isles 9C
Macgregor, J. Perth 8C
MacGregor, J.B. Glasgow 5A-6
MacGregor, M.S. Edinburgh/W.L. 1E
MacGregor, N.I.M. CEI:HH 10C
Machado, K. Glasgow 5A-94
MacInnes, D.M. Glasgow 5A-68
Macintyre, T. South West 3C
MacIver, N. CEI:HH 10C
Mack, E.A. South West 3A-85
Mack, K.L. Lothian/Borders 2A-17
Mack, L. Perth 8C
MacKay, A.H. Glasgow 5F
Mackay, G.C. Glasgow 5A-47
Mackay, K.J. Edinburgh/W.L. 1C
Mackay, L.E. Forth V./C'dale 6A-78
Mackay, M.H. South West 3C
MacKay, S.A. England/C.I. 12B
MacKellar, J.K. CEI:HH 10A-63
Mackenzie, A.R.A Edinburgh/W.L. 1A-34
Mackenzie, C. Edinburgh/W.L.1A-62
Mackenzie, G.R. Glasgow 5C
MacKenzie, H.M. England/C.I. 12B
MacKenzie, I.C. Forth V./C'dale 6F
Mackenzie, J.G. Edinburgh/W.L. 1C
Mackenzie, K. Forth V./C'dale 6A-52
Mackenzie, K.I. N. East/N. Isles 9A-29
Mackenzie, R.K. CEI:HH 10A-72
Mackinnon, C. Glasgow 5C
MacKinnon, C.M. Glasgow 5C
MacLaughlan, G.R. Perth 8A-57
Maclean, A.G. Edinburgh/W.L. 1C
MacLean, E.D. Glasgow 5C
MacLean, E.J. N. East/N. Isles 9E
Maclean, E.J. CEI:HH 10A-2
MacLean, G.P. CEI:HH 10C
MacLean, M. Glasgow 5A-51
MacLean, M.A. N. East/N. Isles 9A-104
Macleod, B. CEI:HH 10A-43
MacLeod, C.A. England/C.I. 12A-5
MacLeod, C.I. Edinburgh/W.L. 1C
Macleod, D. Glasgow 5C
Macleod, G.M. Lewis 11A-8
MacLeod, I. South West 3C
MacLeod, I.A. CEI:HH 10A-9
MacLeod, K.D. CEI:HH 10C
MacLeod, R. CEI:HH 10F
MacLeod, R.A.R. CEI:HH 10B
MacLeod, R.N. CEI:HH 10A-37
Macleod, W. Lewis 11C
MacLeod-Mair, A.T. CEI:HH 10C
MacLeod Rivett, M.A. Edinburgh/W.L. 1A-26
MacMillan, A.R. Glasgow 5A-56
Macmillan, G.I. List 6-J
MacMillan, R.M. List 6-J
MacMurchie, F.L. Edinburgh/W.L. 1E
Macnaughton, G.F.H. N. East/N. Isles 9C
Macnee, I. N. East/N. Isles 9C
MacNeil, T. Lewis 11A-9
MacPherson, A.J. CEI:HH 10A-24
MacPherson, A.J. CEI:HH 10C
MacPherson, D. CEI:HH 10A-45
Macpherson, D.J. Forth V./C'dale 6B
MacPherson, G.C. South West 3C
MacPherson, J. CEI:HH 10C
MacQuarrie, A.J. Forth V./C'dale 6A-17
MacQuarrie, S.D. List 6-J
Macrae, E. South West 3A-122
MacRae, E.H. Glasgow 5C
MacRae, G. Glasgow 5C
MacRae, M.H. Perth 8C
MacSween, D.A. CEI:HH 10A-65
Magee, R. Lothian/Borders 2B
Mailer, C.M. Forth V./C'dale 6E
Main, A. List 6-J
Main, A.W.A. List 6-I
Main, D.M. List 6-J
Mair, M.J. N.East/N.Isles 9B

Mair, M.V.A. Perth 8C
Majcher, I.M.T. Forth V./C'dale 6A-21
Majcher, P.L. Perth 8C
Malcolm, A. Perth 8C
Malcolm, D.S.M. CEI:HH 10A-100
Malcolm, M. Glasgow 5A-10
Mallinson, R. Perth 8A-58
Malloch, P.R.M. Perth 8C
Malloch, R.J. Perth 8A-9
Manners, S. Edinburgh/W.L. 1C
Manson, E. Clyde 4C
Manson, I.A. CEI:HH 10A-58
Manson, J.A. List 6-J
Maromo, S. N. East/N. Isles 9A-18
Marshall, A.S. Edinburgh/W.L. 1C
Marshall, F. CEI:HH 10C
Marshall, H.A.S. Clyde 4A-12
Marshall, T.E. Clyde 4C
Marten, S. Edinburgh/W.L. 1A-29
Martin, G.M. CEI: HH 10C
Martin, J.A. Fife 7A-18
Masih, M. Forth V./C'dale 6A-51
Matandakufa, R. Forth V./C'dale 6A-61
Mateos, M.B. Fife 7A-25
Mather, J. England/C.I. 12B
Mathers, A. Forth V./C'dale 6E
Mathew, J.G. Perth 8C
Mathieson, A.R. Edinburgh/W.L. 1B
Mathieson, F.M. Edinburgh/W.L. 1A-55
Mathieson, J.S. Glasgow 5C
Matthews, J.C. South West 3C
Matthews, S.C. Glasgow 5A-82
Maxwell, D. Glasgow 5C
Maxwell, F.E. South West 3A-67
Maxwell, I.D. Edinburgh/W.L.1A-76
May, A.S. Forth V./C'dale 6A-87
May, J.S. Edinburgh/W.L. 1C
Mayes, R. South West 3C
McAdoo, M. N. East/N. Isles 9C
McAllister, A.C. South West 3C
McAlpine, J. Forth V./C'dale 6F
McAlpine, R.J. Fife 7C
McArthur, M. Clyde 4A-13
McAspurren, A.T. Edinburgh/W.L. 1A-18
McBrier, A.J.S. South West 3A-24
McCafferty, A. Fife 7B
McCallum, A.D. South West 3C
McCarthy, D.J. Perth 8C
McCarthy, I.S. England/C.I. 12A-1
McChlery, L.M. Perth 8A-14
McClements, L.J.E. Forth V./C'dale 6C
McConnell, N.S. Perth 8A-52
McCool, A.C. Clyde 4C
McCorkindale, D.G.B. CEI:HH 10A-2
McCormick, A.F. Perth 8C
McCormick, J.A. Perth 8A-29
McCracken, G.A. Forth V./C'dale 6E
McCree, I.W. CEI:HH 10C
McCrum, R. Perth 8C
McCrum, S. Clyde 4E
McCulloch, A.J.R. CEI:HH 10A-12
McCulloch, J.D. South West 3C
McCulloch, W.B. Fife 7C
McCutcheon, J. South West 3A-17
McDonald, A.D. N. East/N. Isles 9E
McDonald, A.L. N. East/N. Isles 9A-78
McDonald, A.P. Lothian/Borders 2A-36
McDonald, E. Perth 8B
McDonald, I.J.M. Perth 8C
McDonald, I.R.W. Forth V./C'dale 6A-3
McDonald, J.A. Forth V./C'dale 6F
McDonald, M. Edinburgh/W.L. 1A-14
McDonald, R.E. Glasgow 5A-52
McDonald, T. List 6-J
McDougall, H.N. Glasgow 5B
McDowall, R.J. List 6-J
McEnhill, P. England/C.I. 12C
McEwan, I.K. Clyde 4E
McFadyen, G. Fife 7C
McFadzean, I. Perth 8C
McFarlane, R.G. Clyde 4C
McFie, A.M. N. East/N. Isles 9A-77
McGeoch, G.G. Int. Charges 13B
McGillivray, A.G. Edinburgh/W.L. 1F
McGowan, A.T.B. CEI:HH 10C
McGregor, T.S. List 6-J
McGurk, A.F. South West 3C
McHaffie, R.D. Lothian/Borders 2C
McInnes, I.M.S. Glasgow 5A-63
McInnes, S. Perth 8A-113
McIntosh, C.G. Perth 8C
McIntosh, H.N.M. List 6-J
McIntyre, A.G. South West 3F
McIntyre, G. Clyde 4A-14
McIntyre, G.J. Perth 8A-116
McIntyre, J.A. Clyde 4F
McIntyre, J.A. Glasgow 5A-86
McIvor, A. CEI:HH 10C
McKay, D.M. South West 3C
McKay, E.M. N. East/N. Isles 9B
McKay, G.C. List 6-J
McKay, M.M. CEI:HH 10C
McKay, V.C.C. Fife 7C
McKean, A.T. CEI:HH 10E
McKee, G.D. N. East/N. Isles 9A-73
McKee, N.B. Forth V./C'dale 6C
McKellar-Young, C.S. Edinburgh/W.L. 1A-24
McKenna, E.C. N. East/N. Isles 9C
McKenna, S.S. South West 3A-14
McKenzie, A. Perth 8C
McKenzie, J.R. Edinburgh/W.L. 1A-62
McKenzie, M.O. Glasgow 5F
McKenzie, R.D. Forth V./C'dale 6F
McKenzie, W.M. South West 3C
McKeown, M.W.J. Glasgow 5A-32
McKeown, P. N. East/N. Isles 9A-24
McKibbin, F.L.J. Forth V./C'dale 6A-109
McKillop, A.G. Forth V./C'dale 6A-82
McKimmon, E.G. Fife 7C
McKinnon, E.W. Forth V./C'dale 6C
McKinnon, L.F.H. South West 3C
McLachlan, D.N. Glasgow 5C
McLachlan, E. Glasgow 5C
McLachlan, F.C. Glasgow 5F
McLachlan, T.A. Glasgow 5C
McLaren, D.M. Glasgow 5C
McLaren, W. England/C.I. 12A-5
McLarty, R.R. Lothian/Borders 2C
McLauchlan, M.C. South West 3C
McLay, N. England/C.I. 12B
McLean, G. CEI:HH 10E
McLean, I.A. Perth 8C
McLeish, R.S. N. East/N. Isles 9C
McLellan, A.R.C. Fife 7C
McLeod, A.G. Fife 7C
McLeod, D.C. South West 3C
McLeod, J. List 6-J
McLeod, T. South West 3A-33
McMahon, E.J. Clyde 4B
McMahon, J.K.S. England/C.I. 12B
McMillan, E.F. Perth 8C
McMillan, S. Perth 8C
McNab, D.G. Lothian/Borders 2C
McNaught, N.A. South West 3A-1
McNaught, S.M. Fife 7C
McNaughtan, J. South West 3A-70
McNaughton, D.J.H. Perth 8C
McNay, J.J. South West 3A-124
McNeil, J.N.R. Perth 8A-10
McNicol, B. Perth 8C
McNidder, R.H. South West 3C
McPake, J.L. Glasgow 5B
McPake, J.M. Edinburgh/W.L. 1C
McPhail, A.M. List 6-J
McPherson, M. Fife 7B
McPherson, S.M. Fife 7B
McPherson, W. Perth 8C
McRoberts, S.A. CEI:HH 10A-50
McRoberts, T.D. CEI:HH 10C
McWhirter, C. N. East/N. Isles 9A-41, 73
McWilliam, A. Glasgow 5C
McWilliam, T.M. CEI:HH 10E
McWilliams, G. South West 3A-36
Meager, P. Fife 7C
Meason, J.M. N. East/N. Isles 9A-67
Mehigan, A.C. CEI:HH 10A-77
Meikle, A.A. Forth V./C'dale 6A-62
Melville, D.D. Fife 7C
Merchant, M.C. N. East/N. Isles 9A-42
Meyer, N.W. N. East/N. Isles 9A-26
Michelin-Salomon, M. Glasgow 5A-58
Michie, M. Perth 8B
Middleton, P. England/C.I. 12B
Mill, D. CEI:HH 10C
Millar, A.M. Perth 8C
Millar, I.J. Clyde 4A-1
Millar, J.L. CEI:HH 10F
Millar, J.M. Perth 8C
Millar, M.R.M. CEI:HH 10C
Millar, P.W. Edinburgh/W.L. 1F
Miller, A.F. Perth 8A-112
Miller, E.A. Fife 7C
Miller, I.H. Clyde 4C
Miller, J.D. Glasgow 5C
Milliken, J.W. South West 3A-64
Milloy, A.M. Lothian/Borders 2E
Mills, P.W. England/C.I. 12C
Milne, R.B. Perth 8C
Milton, A.L. Lothian/Borders 2A-56
Milton, J.Z. Fife 7A-42
Mineard, T. Clyde 4A-4
Minto, J.E. CEI:HH 10F
Mitchell, A.B. Perth 8C
Mitchell, D. CEI:HH 10C
Mitchell, D.R. South West 3C
Mitchell, J. Lothian/Borders 2C
Mitchell, S.M. N. East/N. Isles 9A-26
Mitchell, V.A. N. East/N. Isles 9C
Moffat, R. Perth 8C
Moffat, R.G. CEI:HH 10A-32
Moffat, T. Glasgow 5C
Moir, I.A. Edinburgh/W.L. 1C
Moir, S.W. Lothian/Borders 2A-20
Monteith, W.G. Edinburgh/W.L. 1F
Montgomerie, J.B. N. East/N. Isles 9C
Moody, J.H.C. Glasgow 5A-31
Moore, A.J. Forth V./C'dale 6A-20
Moore, D.T. South West 3C
Moore, N. Clyde 4C
Moore, S. Edinburgh/W.L. 1A-39

Moran, T.C. Forth V./C'dale 6A-117
More, W.S. List 6-J
Morrice, A.A. Fife 7A-21
Morrice, A.M. Perth 8E
Morrison, A. Edinburgh/W.L. 1C
Morrison, A.H. South West 3C
Morrison, A.R N. East/N. Isles 9A-19
Morrison, C.M. Perth 8A-5, 76
Morrison, D. CEI:HH 10C
Morrison, D.J. CEI:HH 10C
Morrison, F.S. Glasgow 5A-42
Morrison, H. CEI:HH 10B
Morrison, I.C. Forth V./C'dale 6F
Morrison, J.A. CEI:HH 10A-109
Morrison, M.B. Edinburgh/W.L. 1E
Morrison, R.H.B. Glasgow 5A-26
Morton, A.J. N. East/N. Isles 9C
Morton, A.P. Fife 7A-37
Morton, G.M. CEI:HH 10C
Mowbray, H. Perth 8C
Muckart, G.W.M. CEI:HH 10E
Muir, A. South West 3A-116
Muir, E.D. CEI:HH 10F
Muirhead, M.Y. CEI:HH 10C
Munn, D.B. Edinburgh/W.L. 1A-20
Munro, A. List 6-J
Munro, A. Perth 8A-45
Munro, F.J. N. East/N. Isles 9E
Munro, G. Perth 8C
Munro, I. CEI:HH 10B
Munro, J.A. CEI:HH 10C
Munro, J.R. Edinburgh /W.L.1C
Munro, S. CEI:HH 10F
Munton, J.G. Forth V./C'dale 6F
Murdoch, C.M. Clyde 4A-18
Murdoch, I.C. Forth V./C'dale 6C
Murdoch, J.A.H. South West 3A-30
Murning, J. Clyde 4C
Murphy, F.E. Clyde 4A-28
Murphy, J. Forth V./C'dale 6A-15
Murray, A. N. East/N. Isles 9C
Murray, A.J.S. Perth 8C
Murray, B.I. N. East/N. Isles 9B
Murray, D.R. List 6-J
Murray, G.M. Glasgow 5E
Murray, J.W. Perth 8C
Musedza, E. CEI:HH 10A-24

Nash, G.P. Perth 8A-30
Neill, B.F. Lothian/Borders 2C
Neilson, P. Fife 7C
Nelson, G. Edinburgh/W.L.1C
Nelson, P. Edinburgh/W.L. 1A-56
Nelson, R.C. Perth 8C
Nelson, T. Glasgow 5C
Ness, D.T. South West 3C
Newell, A.M. Edinburgh/W.L. 1E
Newton, T. CEI:HH 10A-21
Nicholas, M.S. Lothian/Borders 2A-34
Nicholson, T.S. N. East/N. Isles 9E
Nicol, D.A.O. Edinburgh/W.L. 1C
Nicol, D.M. Glasgow 5C
Nicol, G.G. Fife 7C
Nicol, R.D. Perth 8B
Nicol, S.E.C. Fife 7C
Nicoll, A.N. Perth 8C
Nicolson, D. Clyde 4A-24
Nicolson, F.M. Forth V./C'dale 6A-35
Nicolson, J.M. Lewis 11A-3
Nimmo, P.W. Glasgow 5C
Ninian, E.J. Glasgow 5C
Nisbet, G.C. Fife 7C
Niven, G.A. South West 3A-112

Noble, A.B. N. East/N. Isles 9C
Norman, N.M. Lothian/Borders 2C
Norrie, G. Perth 8C
Notman, A. Perth 8C
Notman, J.R. N. East/N. Isles 9C
Nugent, J. CEI:HH 10C
Nutter, M.A.E. Clyde 4C

O'Brien, H. N. East/N. Isles 9C
O'Donnell, B.A. Clyde 4C
Obinna, E.O. Forth V./C'dale 6A-26
Oelofse, D.F. N. East/N. Isles 9A-45
Ogg, M.F. England/C.I. 12C
Ogilvie, C. Perth 8C
Ogston, E.J. South West 3C
Ogston, S. South West 3A-88
Okeke, S. South West 3A-13
Ormiston, H.C. Perth 8C
Orr, J.K. Perth 8A-94
Orr, S. Edinburgh/W.L.1B
Orr, S.I. N. East/N. Isles 9C
Ott, V.J. South West 3A-55
Ovens, S.B. Perth 8C
Owen, J.J.C. South West 3C
Oxburgh, B.H. Perth 8C

Pacitti, S.A. Glasgow 5C
Palmer, S. N. East/N. Isles 9A-45
Pandian, A.R. Perth 8B
Park, P.B. CEI:HH 10C
Paterson, A.E. Fife 7C
Paterson, D.S. Edinburgh/W.L. 1C
Paterson, G. Fife 7A-53
Paterson, J.L. South West 3C
Paterson, J.W. South West 3C
Paterson, M. Fife 7C
Paterson, S.J. Forth V./C'dale 6A-106
Paterson, W. Lothian/Borders 2E
Paton, A.S. Forth V./C'dale 6A-48
Paton, I.F. Perth 8C
Paton, M.J. Fife 7C
Patterson, P.W. Perth 8D
Peacock, G.J. South West 3A-62
Pearce, A.S.W. Perth 8A-64
Pearson, M.B. Jerusalem 14A
Pearson, W. Glasgow 5C
Peat, D.A. Glasgow 5C
Peden, L.M. CEI:HH 10A-75
Peel, J.L. Clyde 4B
Penman, I.D. Edinburgh/W.L. 1E
Penny, R.F. Perth 8A-63
Perkins, M. Perth 8A-13
Peterson, T.C. Clyde 4A-27
Petrie, I.D. Edinburgh/W.L. 1F
Petrie, J.G. CEI:HH 10C
Petrie, K.L. N. East/N. Isles 9C
Philip, A.J. Perth 8A-40
Phillippo, M. List 6-J
Phillips, P.A. Perth 8A-12
Pickles, J.G. South West 3A-3
Pickles, R.G.D.W. South West 3C
Pierce, A.C. N. East/N. Isles 9A-28
Pieterse, B. Fife 7E
Pitkeathly, D.G. England/C.I. 12C
Pitkeathly, T.C. Int. Charges 13E
Pizzuto-Pomaco, J. N. East/N. Isles 9A-91
Plate, M.A.G. Edinburgh/W.L. 1F
Pollock, R.E. N. East/N. Isles 9C
Pollock, T.L. Glasgow 5C
Polworth, S. CEI:HH 10A-47
Pope, D.H.N. Forth V./C'dale 6A-88
Porteous, B.W. Fife 7C

Porter, C.A. CEI:HH 10E
Potts, S.J. N. East/N. Isles 9A-20
Povey, J.M. Edinburgh/W.L. 1C
Prentice, D.K. CEI:HH 10C
Prentice, G. Clyde 4F
Prentice, M.W.M. List 6-J
Price, A.E. Edinburgh/W.L. 1A-59
Price, P.O. List 6-J
Provan, I.W. Edinburgh/W.L. 1E
Prowe, M.A. Perth 8A-5, 76
Purden, L.I. Lothian/Borders 2A-6
Purnell, D. Edinburgh/W.L. 1A-65
Purves, J.P.S. N. East/N. Isles 9C
Purves, J.S. Glasgow 5C

Quigley, B.D. Perth 8C
Quilter, A.I. Edinburgh/W.L. 1A-73

Raby, S. Edinburgh/W.L. 1C
Rae, P.C. List 6-J
Rae, R. List 6-J
Rae, S.M. South West 3C
Raeburn, A.C. Glasgow 5F
Ralph, M.R.H. South West 3A-4
Ramsay, A. CEI:HH 10F
Ramsay, A.M. Edinburgh/W.L. 1C
Ramsay, B. Perth 8C
Ramsay, R.J. Perth 8F
Randall, C. N. East/N. Isles 9A-90
Rankin, D.R. Perth 8A-100
Rankin, L-J. Lothian/Borders 2A-42
Rankine, C.A. Forth V./C'dale 6A-67
Rankine, H.I. Forth V./C'dale 6A-2
Rattenbury, C. CEI:HH 10A-86
Read, P.R. Clyde 4C
Reamonn, P. Int. Charges 13C
Reddick, W.L.T. Glasgow 5A-109
Redman, M.R.W. CEI:HH 10A-105
Redmayne, D.W. Fife 7C
Redmayne, G. Fife 7C
Redpath, A. Perth 8B
Redpath, J.G. Perth 8C
Reid, A.B. Perth 8F
Reid, A.D. Perth 8A-81
Reid, A.G. Clyde 4E
Reid, D.H. Edinburgh/W.L. 1A-25
Reid, I.M.A. Glasgow 5C
Reid, J. Fife 7A-8
Reid, R.G. Perth 8C
Reid, R.M.C. N. East/N. Isles 9C
Reid, S. Forth V./C'dale 6C
Rennick, J.M. Fife 7C
Rennie, L. CEI:HH 10C
Rennie, M.R. Fife 7A-20
Rennie, S.M. England/C.I. 12A-4
Rentoul, R.W. List 6-J
Renwick, C.C. Perth 8A-45
Reynolds, F.J. Edinburgh/W.L. 1C
Ribbons, F. Edinburgh/W.L. 1C
Richardson, T.C. N. East/N. Isles 9F
Richmond, G.S.M. South West 3A-120
Riddell, J.A. Lothian/Borders 2C
Riddell, T.S. Edinburgh/W.L. 1A-69
Ridland, A.K. Edinburgh/W.L. 1C
Ritchie, B. CEI:HH 10C
Ritchie, C.A.Y. CEI:HH 10C
Ritchie, E.S. Fife 7A-20
Ritchie, M.D. Clyde 4A-53
Ritchie, W.M. CEI:HH 10C
Robb, N.J. Fife 7C
Robertson, A.J. CEI:HH 10A-63
Robertson, B. N. East/N. Isles 9E
Robertson, C. Edinburgh/W.L. 1C

Robertson, C.J. Perth 8A-118
Robertson, D. Edinburgh/W.L. 1A-21
Robertson, D.R. CEI:HH 10A-44
Robertson, E.M.D. Perth 8A-19
Robertson, G.R. Perth 8C
Robertson, I.A.R. Clyde 4C
Robertson, J.H. Perth 8C
Robertson, J.M. Forth V./C'dale 6F
Robertson, M. Perth 8C
Robertson, M.A. CEI:HH 10B
Robertson, P. CEI:HH 10C
Robson, B. Edinburgh/W.L. 1E
Robson, G.K. Perth 8C
Roddick, J.N. Glasgow 5C
Roderick, M.R. Perth 8E
Rodger, M.A. List 6-J
Rodgers, D.M. N. East/N. Isles 9C
Rodwell, A.S. Lothian/Borders 2A-46
Roger, A.M. Edinburgh/W.L. 1C
Rollo, G.B. N. East/N. Isles 9C
Rooney, A.D. Glasgow 5C
Rooney, G. Glasgow 5A-17
Rooney, M.I.G. Perth 8C
Rose, D.S. Perth 8C
Rose, M.E.S. Forth V./C'dale 6C
Ross, D.M. Glasgow 5C
Ross, D.S. N. East/N. Isles 9C
Ross, E.J. Forth V./C'dale 6F
Ross, E.M. Forth V./C'dale 6E
Ross, F.C. South West 3A-66
Ross, J. Glasgow 5C
Ross, K.R. CEI:HH 10B
Ross, K.W. Forth V./C'dale 6C
Ross, M.Z. Edinburgh/W.L. 1B
Ross, S.L. Forth V./C'dale 6A-46
Ross, W.B. N. East/N. Isles 9C
Rowe, C.J. Glasgow 5A-60
Roy, A.D. Fife 7C
Roy, I.M. South West 3C
Russell, J. Perth 8C
Russell, K.G. Perth 8C
Russell, P.R. South West 3A-11
Ryrie, A.C. List 6-J

Sáfrány, Z. Fife 7A-52
Salmond, J.S. Forth V./C'dale 6C
Sanders, M.S. N. East/N. Isles 9C
Sanderson, A.M. South West 3C
Sandison, N.J. Perth 8A-47
Sarle, A. Forth V./C'dale 6A-53
Sass, S. CEI:HH 10A-17
Saunders, G.I.M. Perth 8C
Saunders, K. Glasgow 5E
Scott, D.D. Fife 7C
Scott, D.H. Lothian/Borders 2C
Scott, D.S. CEI:HH 10A-46
Scott, D.V. CEI:HH 10C
Scott, I.G. Lothian/Borders 2C
Scott, J. Perth 8C
Scott, J.E. Edinburgh/W.L. 1F
Scott, J.M.C. Edinburgh/W.L. 1C
Scott, R. CEI:HH 10C
Scouler, M.D. Lothian/Borders 2D
Searle, D.C. Perth 8C
Selemani, E. Forth V./C'dale 6A-37
Sewell, P.M.N. Perth 8C
Shackleton, S.J.S. England/C.I. 12B
Shadakshari, T.K. Lewis 11B
Shand, G.C. Lothian/Borders 2C
Shanks, N.J. Glasgow 5E
Shannon, W.G. List 6-J
Sharp, A. Fife 7C
Sharp, S.W. Perth 8A-78
Shaw, A.N. Clyde 4C
Shaw, C.A.M. South West 3C
Shaw, D. Edinburgh/W.L. 1C
Shaw, D. List 6-J
Shaw, H.M. Clyde 4A-58
Shayamunda, T. N. East/N. Isles 9A-26
Shearer, A.F. Perth 8A-10
Sheppard, M.J. South West 3C
Sheret, B.S. N. East/N. Isles 9C
Sherrard, H.D. List 6-J
Shewan, M.R.R. Perth 8C
Shields, J.M. Lothian/Borders 2F
Shields, R.B. Clyde 4A-51
Shuttleworth, A.J. Fife 7B
Shuttleworth, M. Perth 8B
Silver, R.M. Glasgow 5A-62
Sime, C.M. Perth 8C
Sim, D.R. CEI:HH 10A-37
Simpson, A-M. N. East/N. Isles 9A-41
Simpson, E.V. South West 3C
Simpson, J.A. List 6-J
Simpson, J.H. List 6-I
Simpson, R.R. Lothian/Borders 2C
Sinclair, B.H. Glasgow 5A-75
Sinclair, C.A.M. Lothian/Borders 2C
Sinclair, D.I. Fife 7C
Sinclair, T.D. Glasgow 5A-85
Singh, A.R. Glasgow 5A-15
Slater, D.G. Glasgow 5A-16
Sloan, R. Perth 8F
Sloan, R.P. Perth 8C
Smart, V.E. Edinburgh/W.L. 1E
Smith, A. Edinburgh/W.L. 1C
Smith, B.D. N. East/N. Isles 9A-113
Smith, D.J. Fife 7C
Smith, E. Forth V./C'dale 6F
Smith, F.E. Fife 7B
Smith, G.S. Forth V./C'dale 6C
Smith, G.W. List 6-J
Smith, H. N. East/N. Isles 9A-80
Smith, H.C. CEI:HH 10C
Smith, H.W. N. East/N. Isles 9D
Smith, M. N. East/N. Isles 9C
Smith, M. CEI:HH 10C
Smith, M.R.S. South West 3A-51
Smith, N.A. Lothian/Borders 2B
Smith, R. List 6-J
Smith, R. CEI:HH 10C
Smith, R.C.P. List 6-J
Smith, R.L. N. East/N. Isles 9B
Smith, R.W. Edinburgh/W.L. 1E
Smith, S. N. East/N. Isles 9A-105
Smith, S.J. Clyde 4A-43
Smith, S.J. CEI:HH 10A-48
Smith, W.A. N. East/N. Isles 9E
Smith, Y. Clyde 4A-9
Sneddon, G. Forth V./C'dale 6A-47
Somevi, J.K. N. East/N. Isles 9A-12
Sorensen, A.K. South West 3C
Souter, L.M. Lothian/Borders 2A-14
Speirs, A. Clyde 4E
Spence, E.G.B. Lothian/Borders 2C
Spence, S.M. Forth V./Clyde 6F
Spencer, D.H. Perth 8B
Spencer, J. Glasgow 5C
Spiers, J.M. Glasgow 5E
Spowart, M.G. Lothian/Borders 2F
Stanley, L. Perth 8A-26
Stark, C.M. Forth V./C'dale 6A-105
Stark, S.M. Edinburgh/W.L. 1C
Steel, G.H.B. N. East/N. Isles 9C
Steele, G.M.F. Perth 8B
Steele, H.D. South West 3C
Steele, L.M. Lothian/Borders 2C
Steele, M.D.J. Lothian/Borders 2C
Steell, S.C. Clyde 4A-66
Steenbergen, P. South West 3B
Stein, J. Lothian/Borders 2C
Stein, M.E. Lothian/Borders 2C
Stenhouse, E.M. Lothian/Borders 2A-1
Stenhouse, W.D. Perth 8C
Stephen, A.A. N. East/N. Isles 9A-22
Stephen, D.M. Edinburgh/W.L. 1F
Sterrett, J.B. CEI:HH 10A-40
Steven, H.A.M. Clyde 4F
Stevens, A.C. Int. Charges 13A-5
Stevens, L. Perth 8E
Stevenson, B. Perth 8B
Stevenson, D.F. N. East/N. Isles 9C
Stevenson, G. Lothian/Borders 2A-21
Stevenson, J. Edinburgh/W.L. 1C
Stevenson, J. Forth V./C'dale 6C
Stevenson, S. Clyde 4B
Stewart, A.E. Perth 8B
Stewart, A.T. Perth 8C
Stewart, C.E. Clyde 4E
Stewart, D. South West 3C
Stewart, D.J. N. East/N. Isles 9A-2
Stewart, F.M.C. CEI:HH 10E
Stewart, H. CEI:HH 10A-70
Stewart, H.M. Lewis 11A-7
Stewart, J. CEI:HH 10C
Stewart, J.C. List 6-J
Stewart, J.C. Perth 8A-98
Stewart, L. Perth 8A-83
Stewart, L.J. Edinburgh/W.L.1E
Stewart, N.D. Glasgow 5C
Stewart, R.J. Perth 8C
Stewart, U.B. Lothian/Borders 2E
Stewart, W. N. East/N. Isles 9B
Stewart, W.T. Forth V./C'dale 6C
Stirling, G.A.S. CEI:HH 10F
Stirling, I.R. South West 3C
Stobo, M.J. CEI:HH 10B
Stoddart, A.C. CEI:HH 10C
Stone, L.B. England/C.I. 12C
Storrar, W.F. Edinburgh/W.L. 1D
Storrie, J.C. Forth V./C'dale 6A-112
Stott, A.M. Perth 8B
Stott, K.D. Perth 8A-99
Strachan, D.G. N. East/N. Isles 9D
Strachan, I.M. N. East/N. Isles 9E
Strachan, P.D. Lothian/Borders 2C
Strachan, W.D. Perth 8B
Strang, G.I. Fife 7B
Strong, C.A. N. East/N. Isles 9A-82
Sturrock, R.D. Glasgow 5A-77, 115
Stutter, A. CEI:HH 10C
Suchanek-Seitz, B.V. South West 3A-15
Sutherland, C.A. South West 3C
Sutherland, D.A. Glasgow 5A-73
Sutherland, S.J. N. East/N. Isles 9C
Sutton, P.R.B. Edinburgh/W.L. 1A-54
Swan, D. Edinburgh/W.L. 1B
Sweetin, B.A. Clyde 4C
Swindells, A.I. N. East/N. Isles 9C
Swindells, S. N. East/N. Isles 9A-35
Swinton, J. N. East/N. Isles 9B
Symington, A.H. Fife 7C
Sztojka, S. Int. Charges 13A-5

Tait, A. N. East/N. Isles 9C
Tait, J.M. Edinburgh/W.L. 1C
Tallach, J.M. CEI:HH 10E

Taverner, D.J. Lothian/Borders 2C
Taylor, A.S. South West 3C
Taylor, C. Perth 8C
Taylor, C.G.D. Perth 8C
Taylor, G.J.A. Fife 7A-25
Taylor, I. Glasgow 5A-2
Taylor, J.C. Clyde 4F
Taylor, J.W. England/C.I. 12A-2
Taylor, K.A. Lothian/Borders 2A-75
Taylor, M.A. Lothian/Borders 2A-80
Taylor, T.A. Forth V./C'dale 6C
Taylor, W.R. Edinburgh/W.L. 1C
Taylor-Wintersgill, M N. East/N. Isles 9A-27, 108
Tchaikovsky, S.A. CEI:HH 10A-16
Teasdale, J.R. Glasgow 5A-67
Telfer, A.B. South West 3C
Telfer, I.J.M. N. East/N. Isles 9C
Telfer, T.W. CEI:HH 10A-54
Templeton, J.L. List 6-J
Thain, G.M. Glasgow 5A-97
Thane, B. Int. Charges 13A-10
Thom, D.J. England/C.I. 12B
Thom, I.G. Fife 7C
Thomas, M.R.H. Perth 8C
Thomson, A. Glasgow 5C
Thomson, A. CEI:HH 10E
Thomson, D.M. Edinburgh/W.L. 1E
Thomson, I.U. N. East/N. Isles 9C
Thomson, J.D. Fife 7C
Thomson, J.M.A. Forth V./C'dale 6C
Thomson, M. South West 3C
Thomson, M.E. CEI:HH 10B
Thomson, R. Perth 8C
Thomson, S. Perth 8C
Thorburn, R.J. N. East/N. Isles 9C
Thorburn, S. Perth 8B
Thorne, J.I. N. East/N. Isles 9A-42
Thornthwaite, A.P. Lothian/Borders 2E
Thorp, B. Glasgow 5A-104
Thrower, C.D. Fife 7E
Tippner, J. N. East/N. Isles 9A-100
Todd, J.F. Forth V./C'dale 6A-8
Tollick, F.C. List 6-I
Tomlinson, B.L. Fife 7C
Too, K. Forth V./C'dale 6A-41
Torrance, A.J. Fife 7C
Torrance, D.J. List 6-J
Torrance, D.W. Lothian/Borders 2F
Torrance, I.R. Edinburgh/W.L. 1E
Torrens, S.A.R. Edinburgh/W.L. 1A-63
Travers, R. South West 3E
Tunstall, L.H. Perth 8C
Turnbull, J.S. Lothian/Borders 2E
Turner, A. Glasgow 5F
Turner, F.K. CEI:HH 10C
Tuton, R.M. Glasgow 5C
Twaddle, L.H. Int. Charges 13A-7
Tweedie, F.J. Edinburgh/W.L. 1B

Unsworth, R. Fife 7C
Urquhart, J.A. South West 3A-71
Urquhart, J.C.C. Lothian/Borders 2A-67
Urquhart, N. South West 3A-64

van Sittert, P. N. East/N. Isles 9B
van Straaten, J.P.L. N. East/N. Isles 9A-63
van Tonder, A.J.J. Perth 8A-25
van Welie, D.L. Forth V./C'dale 6A-98
van Wyk, A. Perth 8A-114
Varwell, A.P.J. CEI:HH 10C
Verster, W.M. N. East/N. Isles 9C
Vidits, G. Edinburgh/W.L. 1A-61
Vincent, F.W. CEI:HH 10A-93
Vint, A.S. South West 3A-90
Vischer, J.D. Lothian/Borders 2A-31

Waddell, E.A. Forth V./C'dale 6C
Walker, D.K. CEI:HH 10C
Walker, J.B. Fife 7C
Walker, L.A.W. CEI:HH 10C
Walker, R.F. England/C.I. 12C
Wallace, C. N. East/N. Isles 9A-43
Wallace, D.M. CEI:HH 10A-108
Wallace, D.W. Forth V./C'dale 6F
Wallace, H.M. Fife 7C
Wallace, J.H. Lothian/Borders 2C
Wallace, J.K. Perth 8C
Wallace, M. South West 3A-81
Wallace, P.D. Clyde 4A-65
Wallace, W.F. N. East/N. Isles 9C
Wandrum, D.C. Forth V./C'dale 6B
Ward, A.H. South West 3C
Wark, A.C. South West 3C
Warwick, I.C. CEI:HH 10C
Watson, E.R.L. South West 3C
Watson, J.B. Lothian/Borders 2C
Watson, J.M. N. East/N. Isles 9C
Watson, M.D. Lothian/Borders 2A-57
Watson, N.G. Edinburgh/W.L. 1C
Watson, N.H. Glasgow 5A-36
Watson, T.D. South West 3A-36
Watson, V.G.C. Clyde 4F
Watt, A.G.N. Perth 8C
Watt, H.F. CEI:HH 10C
Watt, K. South West 3B
Watt, R.J. Fife 7C
Watt, W.D. Edinburgh/W.L. 1A-14
Waugh, J.L. CEI:HH 10F
Weaver, M.A. Fife 7A-22
Weaver, S.G. Edinburgh/W.L. 1A-47
Webster, A.F. Perth 8C
Webster, B.G. Clyde 4F
Webster, J.G. South West 3E
Webster, P. CEI:HH 10E
Webster, T.J. N. East/N. Isles 9A-3
Weir, J.J.C.M. N. East/N. Isles 9C
Wells, I.J. Edinburgh/W.L. 1C
Wells, J.R. Edinburgh/W.L. 1A-57
Welsh, A.M. South West 3C
Welsh, R.M. Edinburgh/W.L. 1A-30
Whillis, D. CEI:HH 10B
White, A.W. Forth V./C'dale 6B
White, C.P. Glasgow 5C
White, D.M. Glasgow 5C
Whitecross, J. South West 3C
Whiteman, D. South West 3A-2
Whitson, W.S. List 6-J
Whittaker, P.M. N. East/N. Isles 9A-8
Whittle, S.K. Fife 7A-39
Whyte, D.W. N. East/N. Isles 9C
Whyte, G.J. Edinburgh/W.L. 1C
Whyte, I.A. Fife 7F
Whyte, J. Glasgow 5C
Whyte, M. N. East/N. Isles 9A-11
Whyte, M.A. Clyde 4C
Whyte, N.R. South West 3C
Whyte, R.C. CEI:HH 10E
Whyte, W.B. Perth 8C
Wicks, A. Perth 8A-34
Wildner, J. South West 3A-44
Wiley, J.C. Edinburgh/W.L. 1A-2
Wilkie, G.D. List 6-J
Wilkie, J.L. List 6-J
Wilkie, R.F. Perth 8A-96
Wilkinson, W.B. CEI:HH 10C
Williams, J.M. Edinburgh/W.L. 1C
Williamson, J. List 6-J
Williamson, M.J.C N. East/N. Isles 9E
Willoughby, M.F. Lothian/Borders 2C
Wilson, A.G.N. N. East/N. Isles 9E
Wilson, A.J. Perth 8A-1
Wilson, F.A. South West 3A-38
Wilson, G.N. CEI:HH 10A-15
Wilson, G.R. Clyde 4A-7
Wilson, H. Perth 8C
Wilson, J. Clyde 4C
Wilson, J.L. Perth 8C
Wilson, J.M. Perth 8C
Wilson, J.M. Edinburgh/W.L. 1F
Wilson, M. List 6-I
Wilson, P.M. Glasgow 5C
Wilson R. Lothian/Borders 2A-43
Wilson, T. Fife 7C
Wilson, T.F. N. East/N. Isles 9F
Wilson, W.T.S. Glasgow 5A-4
Winning, A.A. CEI:HH 10C
Wintersgill, D.K. N. East/N. Isles 9A-27, 108
Wiseman, I. South West 3A-105
Wishart, E.M. Edinburgh/W.L. 1B
Wishart, J. N. East/N. Isles 9C
Wishart, W.M. Edinburgh/W.L. 1A-58
Wolf, D. Lewis 11C
Wood, D. N. East/N. Isles 9B
Wood, G.M. Glasgow 5A-45
Wood, J.L.K. N. East/N. Isles 9F
Wood, P.J. Lothian/Borders 2B
Wotherspoon, I.G. Fife 7C
Wotherspoon, R.C. List 6-J
Wright, A. England/C.I. 12B
Wright, P.A. Glasgow 5A-24
Wylie, J. Perth 8B
Wyllie, H.R. List 6-J
Wynne, A.T.E. Edinburgh/W.L. 1C

Yorke, K.B. South West 3C
Young, D.T. N. East/N. Isles 9B
Young, J.N. Edinburgh/W.L. 1A-62
Young, R.M. South West 3C
Younger, A. Glasgow 5C
Younger, A.S. CEI:HH 10C
Youngson, E.J.B. N. East/N. Isles 9C

Zambonini, J. Forth V./C'dale 6C

INDEX OF PARISHES AND PLACES

Numbers on the right of the column refer to the Presbytery in which the district lies. Names in brackets are given for ease of identification. They may refer to the name of the parish, which may be different from that of the district, or they distinguish places with the same name, or they indicate the first named place within a union. Where the place named in brackets includes more than one charge, any questions may be resolved by consulting the on-line section 9A: for example, that section will indicate which of the two Annan charges Dalton is now part of.

Abbey St Bathans (Duns) 2
Abdie (Lindores) 7
Aberchirder (Marnoch) 9
Abercorn, Pardovan, Kingscavil and Winchburgh 1
Aberdalgie and Forteviot 8
Aberdeen 9
Aberdour (Forthview) 7
Aberdour (Buchan) 9
Aberfeldy 8
Aberfoyle 8
Aberlady and Gullane 2
Aberlemno (Forfar) 8
Aberlour 9
Aberluthnott 9
Abernethy 10
Abernethy and Dron and Arngask 8
Abernyte 8
Aberuthven and Dunning 8
Abington (Upper Clyde) 6
Aboyne – Dinnet 9
Achahoish (Dalriada) 10
Acharacle and Ardnamurchan 10
Addiewell (Whitburn) 1
Advie (Cromdale) 10
Airdrie 6
Airlie (Isla Parishes) 8
Airth 6
Aith (Shetland) 9
Ale and Teviot United 2
Alexandria (Lomond) 4
Alford (West Gordon) 9
Alloa 8
Alloway and Fisherton 3
Almondbank Tibbermore 8
Alness 10
Altnaharra and Farr 10
Alva 8
Alves (West Moray) 10
Alvie and Insh 10
Alyth 8
Amsterdam 13
Amulree (Dunkeld) 8
Ancrum (Ale and Teviot) 2
Annan 3
Annbank 3
Anstruther and Cellardyke 7
Appin and Lismore 10
Applecross (South-West Ross) 10
Applegarth (Lockerbie) 3
Arbirlot (Arbroath) 8
Arbroath 8
Arbuthnott, Bervie and Kinneff 9
Archiestown (Knockando) 9
Ardchattan 10
Ardentinny (Kilmun) 10
Ardeonaig (Killin) 8
Ardersier (Culloden) 10
Ardgay (Dornoch Firth) 10
Ardgour, Morvern and Strontian 10
Ardler (Strathmore) 8
Ardnamurchan (Acharacle) 10
Ardoch 8
Ardrishaig (Dalriada) 10
Ardrossan 3
Ardwell (Stoneykirk) 3
Arisaig (North West Lochaber) 10
Armadale 1
Arngask (Abernethy) 8
Arnsheen Barrhill 3
Arouca and Sangre Grande (Trinidad) 13
Arran, Isle of 3
Arrochar 4
Ashkirk (Selkirk) 2
Assynt, Rosehall, and Scourie 10
Athelstaneford (Traprain) 2
Auchaber (Auchterless) 9
Auchenblae (West Mearns) 9
Auchencairn (Bengairn) 3
Auchinleck 3
Auchterarder 8
Auchterderran Kinglassie 7
Auchtergaven and Moneydie 8
Auchterhouse (Sidlaw) 8
Auchterless and Auchaber 9
Auchtermuchty (Edenshead) 7
Auchtertool 7
Auldearn (Nairn) 10
Aviemore (Rothiemurchus) 10
Avoch (Black Isle East) 10
Avonbridge 1
Ayr 3
Ayton 2

Baldernock 4
Balerno (Edinburgh) 1
Balfron 8
Balgonie (Kennoway) 7
Ballachulish (South Lochaber) 10
Ballantrae 3
Ballater (Glenmuick) 9
Ballingry (Lochgelly) 7
Balloch (Lomond) 4
Balmaclellan, Kells and Dalry 3
Balmaghie (Crossmichael) 3
Balmedie (Belhelvie) 9
Balmerino and Wormit 7
Balquhidder 8
Banchory-Devenick (Maryculter) 9
Banchory-Ternan 9
Banff 9
Bankfoot (Auchtergaven) 8
Bannockburn 8
Barr (Girvan Valley) 3
Barra 10
Barrhead 4
Barrhill (Arnsheen) 3
Barry (Carnoustie) 8
Barthol Chapel (Formartine) 9
Barvas 11
Bathgate 1
Bearsden 4
Beath 7
Beattock (Upper Annandale) 3
Beauly (Kilmorack) 10
Bedrule (Ruberslaw) 2
Beeswing (Lochend) 3
Beith 3
Belhaven and Spott 2
Belhelvie 9
Bellie and Speymouth 9
Bellshill 6
Benbecula 10
Bendochy 8
Bengairn Parishes 3
Bennachie 9
Bentpath (Westerkirk) 3
Bermuda 13
Berneray and Lochmaddy 10
Berriedale (Latheron) 10
Bervie (Arbuthnott) 9
Berwick-upon-Tweed and Lowick 2
Bettyhill (Farr) 10
Biggar 6
Bilston (Loanhead) 2
Birnie (Elgin) 9
Birsay, Harray and Sandwick 9
Birse and Feughside 9
Bishopbriggs 5
Bishopton 4
Blackbraes and Shieldhill 6
Blackburn (Whitburn) 1
Blackford 8
Black Isle East 10
Black Mount 6
Blackridge 1
Blair Atholl and Struan 8
Blairbeth (Burnside) 5
Blairdaff (Bennachie) 9
Blair Drummond (Dunblane) 8
Blairgowrie 8
Blairingone (Saline) 7
Blantyre 6
Boarhills, Dunino and St Andrews 7
Boat of Garten, Carrbridge and Kincardine 10
Bochum 13
Boharm (Keith) 9
Boleskine (Inverness) 10
Bolton (Lammermuir) 2
Bonar Bridge (Dornoch Firth) 10
Bo'ness 6
Bonhill 4
Bonkyl (Duns) 2
Bonnybridge 6
Bonnyrigg 2
Border Kirk 3
Boreland (Lockerbie) 3
Borgue (Gatehouse) 3
Borthwick (Tyne Valley) 2
Bothkennar and Carronshore 6
Bothwell 6
Botriphnie (Keith) 9
Bourtie (Meldrum) 9
Bowden and Melrose 2
Bowling (Old Kilpatrick) 4
Bowmore (South Islay) 10
Bracadale, Duirinish and Snizort 10
Braco (Ardoch) 8
Brae (Shetland) 9
Braemar and Crathie 9
Braes of Rannoch 8
Brechin and Farnell 8
Breich (Whitburn) 1
Bressay (Shetland) 9
Bridge of Allan 8
Bridge of Earn (Dunbarney) 8
Bridge of Weir 4
Brightons 6
Brimmond 9

Broadford (Strath) 10
Brodick (Arran, Isle of) 3
Broom 5
Brora (Clyne) 10
Broughton (Upper Tweeddale) 2
Broughty Ferry (Dundee) 8
Broxburn 1
Brussels 13
Brydekirk (Annan) 3
Buchanan 8
Buchlyvie and Gartmore 8
Buckhaven and Wemyss 7
Buckie 9
Bucksburn (Brimmond) 9
Budapest 13
Bunessan (Iona and the Ross of Mull) 10
Burghead (West Moray) 10
Burnmouth (Ayton) 2
Burnside Blairbeth 5
Burntisland and Kinghorn 7
Burra Isle (Shetland) 9
Burray (South Ronaldsay) 9
Burrelton (Cargill) 8
Busby 5
Bute, Isle of 10

Cabrach (Mortlach) 9
Cadder 5
Caddonfoot 2
Caerlaverock 3
Cairndow (Kilmorich) 10
Cairneyhill 7
Cairngryffe 6
Cairnie (Huntly) 9
Calder, Kirk of 1
Calder, West Kirk of 1
Calderbank 6
Caldercruix and Longriggend 6
Caldwell and Dunlop 3
Callander 8
Cambusbarron 8
Cambuslang 5
Cameron and St Andrews 7
Campbeltown 10
Campsie 5
Canisbay (Pentland) 10
Canonbie 3
Caputh and Clunie 8
Cardross 4
Carfin (Newarthill) 6
Cargill Burrelton 8
Carinish 10
Carlisle (Border Kirk) 3
Carlops 2
Carloway 11
Carluke 6
Carmichael (Cairngryffe) 6
Carmyllie (Arbroath) 8
Carnbee 7
Carnock and Oakley 7
Carnoustie 8
Carnwath 6
Carradale (Saddell) 10
Carrbridge (Boat of Garten) 10
Carrington (Cockpen) 2
Carron (Stenhouse) 6
Carronshore (Bothkennar) 6
Carsphairn 3
Carstairs 6
Castle Douglas 3
Castletown (Pentland) 10
Cathkin (Fernhill) 5
Catrine 3
Cavers and Kirkton 2
Cawdor (Strathnairn and Strathdearn) 10
Cellardyke (Anstruther) 7
Ceres, Kemback and Springfield 7
Channelkirk and Lauder 2
Chapelhall 6
Chapel of Garioch (Bennachie) 9
Chapelton (Strathaven) 6
Cheviot Churches 2
Chirnside (Whiteadder) 2
Chryston 5
Clachan (Mid Kintyre and Gigha) 10
Clackmannan 8
Cleish 8
Cleland (Wishaw) 6
Closeburn 3
Clova (The Glens) 8
Clunie (Caputh) 8
Cluny (Bennachie) 9
Clydebank 4
Clyne 10
Coalburn and Lesmahagow 6
Coalsnaughton (Sauchie) 8
Coatbridge 6
Cockburnspath (Dunglass) 2
Cockenzie and Port Seton 2
Cockpen and Carrington 2
Coldingham and St Abbs 2
Coldstream 2
Colinsburgh (East Neuk Trinity) 7
Colintraive (West Cowal) 10
Coll 10
Collace 8
Colliston (Arbroath) 8
Colmonell (Arnsheen) 3
Colombo, Sri Lanka 13
Colonsay and Oronsay 10
Colvend, Southwick and Kirkbean 3
Comrie 8
Connel 10
Conon Bridge (Ferintosh) 10
Contin 10
Cookney (Maryculter) 9
Corby 12
Corgarff (West Gordon) 9
Cornhill (Ordiquhill) 9
Corpach (Fort William) 10
Corrie (Arran, Isle of) 3
Corrie (Lockerbie) 3
Corsock and Kirkpatrick Durham 3
Cortachy (The Glens) 8
Coull (Cromar) 9
Coupar Angus 8
Cove (Craigrownie) 4
Cowdenbeath 7
Cowie and Plean 8
Coylton 3
Craigie Symington 3
Craignish (Netherlorn) 10
Craignure (North Mull) 10
Craigrownie 4
Crail 7
Crailing (Ale and Teviot) 2
Cranshaws (Duns) 2
Crathie (Braemar) 9
Crawford (Upper Clyde) 6
Crawfordjohn (Upper Clyde) 6
Creetown (Kirkmabreck) 3
Creich (Dornoch Firth) 10
Creich, Flisk and Kilmany 7
Crieff 8
Crimond 9
Croick (Dornoch Firth) 10
Cromar 9
Cromarty (Black Isle East) 10
Cromdale and Advie 10
Crook of Devon (Fossoway) 8
Crossbost (Lochs) 11
Crossford 6
Crosshill (North Carrick) 3
Crosshouse 3
Crossmichael, Parton and Balmaghie 3
Cross Ness 11
Croy (Strathnairn and Strathdearn) 10
Cruden 9
Cullen and Deskford 9
Culloden and Ardersier 10
Culross and Torryburn 7
Culsalmond and Rayne 9
Cults 9
Cumbernauld 5
Cumbrae, Fairlie and Largs 3
Cuminestown (Monquhitter) 9
Cumlodden (WestLochfyneside) 10
Cummertrees, Mouswald and Ruthwell 3
Cumnock 3
Cunningsburgh (Shetland) 9
Currie (Edinburgh) 1
Cushnie (West Gordon) 9
Cupar 7

Dailly (Girvan Valley) 3
Dairsie (Cupar) 7
Dalarossie (Strathnairn and Strathdearn) 10
Dalavich (Kilchrenan) 10
Dalbeattie and Kirkgunzeon 3
Dalgety (Forthview) 7
Dalkeith 2
Dallas (West Moray) 10
Dalmally (Glenorchy) 10
Dalmellington 3
Dalmeny (Edinburgh) 1
Dalmuir 4
Dalriada Mid Argyll 10
Dalry (Ayrshire) 3
Dalry (Balmaclellan) 3
Dalrymple 3
Dalserf 6
Dalton (Annan) 3
Darvel (Irvine Valley) 3
Daviot (Aberdeenshire) 9
Daviot (Strathnairn and Strathdearn) 10
Deer 9
Deerness (East Mainland) 9
Delting (Shetland) 9
Denbeath (Methilhill) 7
Denholm (Ruberslaw) 2
Denny 6
Dervaig (North Mull) 10
Deskford (Cullen) 9
Dingwall 10
Dinnet (Aboyne) 9
Dirleton 2
Dollar 8
Dolphinton (Black Mount) 6
Dores (Inverness) 10
Dornie (South-West Ross) 10
Dornoch (Dornoch Firth) 10
Dornoch Firth 10
Dornock (Annan) 3
Douglas Valley 6
Dounby (Birsay) 9
Doune (Dunblane) 8
Dreghorn (Irvine) 3
Dron (Abernethy) 8
Drongan 3
Drumblade (Strathbogie) 9
Drumclog (Strathaven) 6
Drumelzier (Stobo) 2
Drumlithie (West Mearns) 9
Drummore (Kirkmaiden) 3
Drumnadrochit (Urquhart) 10
Drumoak (Peterculter) 9
Dryburgh 2
Drymen 8
Dufftown (Mortlach) 9
Duffus, Spynie and Hopeman 9
Duirinish (Bracadale) 10
Dull and Weem 8
Dulnain Bridge (Grantown-on-Spey) 10
Dumbarton 4
Dumfries 3
Dun (Montrose) 8
Dunbar 2
Dunbarney and Forgandenny 8
Dunbeath (Latheron) 10
Dunblane 8
Dunbog (Lindores) 7
Dundee 8
Dundonald 3
Dundonnell (West Ross) 10
Dundrennan (Bengairn) 3
Dundurn 8
Dunfermline 7
Dunglass 2
Dunino (Boarhills) 7
Dunipace 6
Dunkeld 8
Dunlichity (Strathnairn and Strathdearn) 10
Dunlop (Caldwell) 3
Dunnet (Pentland) 10
Dunnichen (Forfar) 8
Dunning (Aberuthven) 8
Dunoon (Cowal) 10

Dunrossness (Shetland) 9
Duns 2
Dunscore 3
Dunsyre (Black Mount) 6
Duntocher (Clydebank) 4
Dunure (Alloway) 3
Durisdeer 3
Durness and Kinlochbervie 10
Duror (South Lochaber) 10
Durris (Peterculter) 9
Dyce 9
Dyke and Edinkillie 10
Dysart 7

Eaglesfield (Hoddom) 3
Eaglesham 5
Earlston 2
Eassie (Strathmore) 8
East Calder (Kirknewton) 1
Easter Ross Peninsula 10
East Kilbride 6
East Linton (Traprain) 2
East Mainland 9
East Neuk Trinity 7
Ecclefechan (Hoddom) 3
Eccles and Leitholm 2
Echt (Bennachie) 9
Eckford (Ale and Teviot) 2
Eday 9
Edderton (Dornoch Firth) 10
Eddleston 2
Edenshead 7
Edinburgh 1
Edinkillie (Dyke) 10
Ednam (Kelso) 2
Edrom (Duns) 2
Edzell 8
Elchies (Knockando) 9
Elderslie 4
Elgin 9
Elie (East Neuk Trinity) 7
Ellon 9
Elsrickle (Black Mount) 6
Enzie (Buckie) 9
Erchless (Kilmorack) 10
Errol 8
Erskine 4
Ervie Kirkcolm 3
Eskdalemuir (Langholm) 3
Ettrick and Yarrow 2
Evanton (Kiltearn) 10
Evie and Rendall 9
Ewes (Langholm) 3
Eyemouth 2

Fair Isle (Shetland) 9
Fairlie (Cumbrae) 3
Fala (Tyne Valley) 2
Falkirk 6
Falkland 7
Fallin 8
Farnell (Brechin) 8
Farr (Altnaharra) 10
Fauldhouse and Harthill 1
Fearn (Easter Ross Peninsula) 10
Fenwick 3
Ferintosh 10
Fernhill and Cathkin 5
Ferryden (Montrose) 8
Fetlar (Shetland) 9
Fettercairn (West Mearns) 9
Findhorn (West Moray) 10
Findochty 9
Finstown (Firth) 9
Fintray Kinellar Keithhall 9
Fintry 8
Finzean (Birse) 9
Firth 9
Fisherton (Alloway) 3
Flisk (Creich) 7
Flotta 9
Fochabers (Bellie) 9
Fodderty and Strathpeffer 10
Fogo 2
Ford (Dalriada) 10
Forfar 8
Forgandenny (Dunbarney) 8
Forglen (Turriff) 9
Forgue (Auchterless) 9
Formartine 9
Forres (West Moray) 10
Fort Augustus 10
Forteviot (Aberdalgie) 8
Forth 6
Forthview 7
Fortingall, Glenlyon, Kenmore and Lawers 8
Fortrose (Black Isle East) 10
Fort William 10
Foss and Rannoch 8
Fossoway and Devonside 8
Foulden (Ayton) 2
Foveran 9
Fowlis (Sidlaw) 8
Fowlis Wester (Mid Strathearn) 8
Fraserburgh 9
Freuchie 7
Friockheim (Arbroath) 8
Furnace (West Lochfyneside) 10
Fyvie 9

Gairloch (West Ross) 10
Galashiels 2
Galston (Irvine Valley) 3
Gardenstown (Macduff) 9
Garelochhead 4
Gargunnock 8
Gartcosh 5
Gartmore (Buchlyvie) 8
Gartocharn (Lomond) 4
Garvald and Morham 2
Gatehouse of Fleet 3
Gateside (Edenshead) 7
Gauldry (Balmerino) 7
Gavinton (Duns) 2
Geneva 13
Giffnock 5
Gifford (Lammermuir) 2
Gigha (Mid Kintyre) 10
Gilmerton (Mid Strathearn) 8
Girvan Valley 3
Gladsmuir 2
Glamis (Strathmore) 8
Glasgow 5
Glass (Huntly) 9
Glasserton, Isle of Whithorn and Whithorn 3
Glassford (Strathaven) 6
Glenbervie (West Mearns) 9
Glenboig 5
Glencairn and Moniaive 3
Glencaple (Caerlaverock) 3
Glencoe (South Lochaber) 10
Glendaruel (West Cowal) 10
Glenelg (South-West Ross) 10
Glenesk (Edzell) 8
Glenfarg (Arngask) 8
Glengarry 10
Glenisla (Isla Parishes) 8
Glenlivet (Tomintoul) 10
Glenluce (Luce Valley) 3
Glenlyon (Fortingall) 8
Glenmoriston (Urquhart) 10
Glenmuick (Ballater) 9
Glenorchy and Strathfillan 10
Glenrothes (Heart of Fife) 7
Glens, The and Kirriemuir United 8
Glenshee (Kirkmichael) 8
Golspie 10
Gordon 2
Gorebridge 2
Gourock 4
Grange (Keith) 9
Grangemouth 6
Grantown-on-Spey 10
Grantshouse (Ayton) 2
Grantully, Logierait and Strathtay 8
Greenbank 5
Greengairs 6
Greenlaw 2
Greenloaning (Ardoch) 8
Greenock 4
Gretna, Half Morton and Kirkpatrick Fleming 3
Guernsey 12
Gullane (Aberlady) 2
Guthrie (Forfar) 8

Haddington 2
Haggs 6
Half Morton (Gretna) 3
Halkirk Westerdale 10
Hamilton 6
Harray (Birsay) 9
Harthill (Fauldhouse) 1
Harwood (Polbeth) 1
Hawick 2
Heart of Fife 7
Helensburgh 4
Helmsdale (Kildonan) 10
Heriot (Stow) 2
Hightae (Annan) 3
Hillside (Montrose) 8
Hillswick (Shetland) 9
Hobkirk and Southdean 2
Hoddom, Kirtle-Eaglesfield and Middlebie 3
Holm (East Mainland) 9
Holytown 6
Hopeman (Duffus) 9
Houndwood (Ayton) 2
Houston and Killellan 4
Howe of Fife 7
Howgate (Penicuik) 2
Howwood 4
Hoy and Walls 9
Humbie (Lammermuir) 2
Huntly Cairnie Glass 9
Hurlford 3
Hutton (Whiteadder) 2

Inch (Luce Valley) 3
Inchinnan 4
Inchture and Kinnaird 8
Innellan (Cowal) 10
Innerleithen, Traquair and Walkerburn 2
Innerwick (Dunglass) 2
Innishael (Glenorchy) 10
Insch-Leslie-Premnay-Oyne 9
Insh (Alvie) 10
Inverallochy (Fraserburgh) 9
Inveraray (West Lochfyneside) 10
Inverarity (Forfar) 8
Inveraven (Tomintoul) 10
Inverbervie (Arbuthnott) 9
Invergordon 10
Invergowrie 8
Inverkeilor (Arbroath) 8
Inverkeithing (Forthview) 7
Inverkeithny (Auchterless) 9
Inverkip, Skelmorlie and Wemyss Bay 4
Inverness 10
Inverurie 9
Iona and the Ross of Mull 10
Irongray, Lochrutton and Terregles 3
Irvine 3
Isla Parishes 8
Isle of Arran 3
Isle of Bute 10
Isle of Whithorn (Glasserton) 3

Jamestown (Lomond) 4
Jedburgh 2
Jersey 12
Jerusalem 14
Johnshaven (St Cyrus) 9
Johnstone (Clyde) 4
Johnstone (Lockerbie) 3
Jura 10

Kames (West Cowal) 10
Keir (Penpont) 3
Keiss (Pentland) 10
Keith 9
Keithhall (Fintray) 9
Kells (Balmaclellan) 3
Kelso 2
Kelton (Bengairn) 3
Kelty 7
Kemback (Ceres) 7
Kemnay (Bennachie) 9
Kenmore (Fortingall) 8
Kennoway, Windygates and Balgonie 7
Kettins (Strathmore) 8
Kettle (Howe of Fife) 7
Kettleholm (Lochmaben) 3
Kilbarchan 4

Kilberry (Tarbert) 10
Kilbirnie 3
Kilbrandon (Netherlorn) 10
Kilcalmonell (Mid Kintyre and Gigha) 10
Kilchattan (Netherlorn) 10
Kilchenzie (Mid Kintyre and Gigha) 10
Kilchoman (North and West Islay) 10
Kilchrenan and Dalavich 10
Kilchrist (Urray) 10
Kilconquhar (East Neuk Trinity) 7
Kilcreggan (Craigrownie) 4
Kildonan (Arran, Isle of) 3
Kildonan and Loth Helmsdale 10
Kilfinan (West Cowal) 10
Killean (Mid Kintyre and Gigha) 10
Killearn 8
Killearnan 10
Killin and Ardeonaig 8
Kilmacolm 4
Kilmadock (Dunblane) 8
Kilmallie (Fort William) 10
Kilmany (Creich) 7
Kilmarnock 3
Kilmaronock (Lomond) 4
Kilmartin (Dalriada) 10
Kilmaurs 3
Kilmelford (Netherlorn) 10
Kilmeny (North and West Islay) 10
Kilmichael Glassary (Dalriada) 10
Kilmodan (West Cowal) 10
Kilmonivaig 10
Kilmorack and Erchless 10
Kilmore and Oban 10
Kilmorich (Lochgoilhead) 10
Kilmory (Arran, Isle of) 3
Kilmuir and Logie Easter 10
Kilmuir and Paible 10
Kilmuir and Stenscholl 10
Kilmun, Strone and Ardentinny 10
Kilninver (Netherlorn) 10
Kilrenny 7
Kilry (Isla Parishes) 8
Kilsyth 5
Kiltarlity 10
Kiltearn 10
Kilwinning 3
Kincardine (Boat of Garten) 10
Kincardine (Tulliallan) 7
Kincardine Coastal 9
Kincardine O'Neil (Mid Deeside) 9
Kinclaven 8
Kinellar (Fintray) 9
Kinfauns (St Madoes) 8
Kingairloch (Ardgour) 10
King Edward 9
Kinghorn (Burntisland) 7
Kinglassie (Auchterderran) 7
Kingoldrum (Isla Parishes) 9
Kingsbarns 7
Kingscavil (Abercorn) 1
Kingshill 9
Kingswells (Kingshill) 9
Kingussie 10
Kinloch 11
Kinlochbervie (Durness) 10
Kinlochewe (South-West Ross) 10
Kinlochleven (South Lochaber) 10
Kinlochrannoch (Foss) 8
Kinloss (West Moray) 10
Kinnaird (Inchture) 8
Kinneff (Arbuthnott) 9
Kinnell (Arbroath) 8
Kinnettles (Forfar) 8
Kinross 8
Kintail (South-West Ross) 10
Kintore (Bennachie) 9
Kippen and Norrieston 8
Kirkbean (Colvend) 3
Kirkcaldy 7
Kirkcolm (Ervie) 3
Kirkconnel 3
Kirkcowan 3
Kirkcudbright 3
Kirkden (Forfar) 8
Kirkfieldbank 6
Kirkgunzeon (Dalbeattie) 3
Kirkhill (Kiltarlity) 10
Kirkinner (Millisle) 3
Kirkintilloch 5
Kirkliston (Edinburgh) 1
Kirkmabreck 3
Kirkmahoe 3
Kirkmaiden 3
Kirkmichael (South West) 3
Kirkmichael (Tomintoul) 10
Kirkmichael, Straloch and Glenshee 8
Kirkmichael, Tinwald and Torthorwald 3
Kirkmuirhill 6
Kirknewton and East Calder 1
Kirk of Calder 1
Kirk o' Shotts 6
Kirkoswald (North Carrick) 3
Kirkpatrick Durham (Corsock) 3
Kirkpatrick Juxta 3
Kirkton (Cavers) 2
Kirkurd and Newlands 2
Kirkwall 9
Kirn (Cowal) 10
Kirriemuir (The Glens) 8
Kirtle-Eaglesfield (Hoddom) 3
Knock 11
Knockando, Elchies and Archiestown 9
Knockbain 10
Knoydart (North West Lochaber) 10
Kyle of Lochalsh (South-West Ross) 10

Ladybank (Howe of Fife) 7
Ladykirk (Coldstream) 2
Laggan and Newtonmore 10
Lairg 10
Lamington (Upper Clyde) 6
Lamlash (Arran, Isle of) 3
Lammermuir 2
Lanark 6
Langbank 4
Langholm, Eskdalemuir, Ewes and Westerkirk 3
Larbert 6
Largo 7
Largoward 7
Largs (Cumbrae) 3
Larkhall 6
Lasswade and Rosewell 2
Latheron 10
Lauder (Channelkirk) 2
Laurencekirk 9
Laurieston (Crossmichael) 3
Lausanne 13
Law 6
Lawers (Fortingall) 8
Leadhills (Upper Clyde) 6
Lecropt 8
Legerwood 2
Leith (Edinburgh) 1
Leitholm (Eccles) 2
Lenzie 5
Lerwick (Shetland) 9
Leslie (Heart of Fife) 7
Leslie (Insch) 9
Lesmahagow (Coalburn) 6
Leswalt 3
Letham (Forfar) 8
Leuchars 7
Leven 7
Lhanbryd (St Andrew's) 9
Libberton and Quothquan 6
Liddesdale 3
Liff (Sidlaw) 8
Lilliesleaf (Ale and Teviot) 2
Limekilns 7
Lindores 7
Linlithgow 1
Lintrathen (Isla Parishes) 8
Linwood 4
Lisbon 13
Lismore (Appin) 10
Livingston 1
Loanhead 2
Lochaline (Ardgour) 10
Lochbroom and Ullapool 10
Lochcarron (South-West Ross) 10
Lochend and New Abbey 3
Lochgair (West Lochfyneside) 10
Lochgelly and Benarty 7
Lochgilphead (Dalriada) 10
Lochgoilhead and Kilmorich 10
Lochinver (Assynt) 10
Lochmaben 3
Lochmaddy (Berneray) 10
Lochore (Lochgelly) 7
Lochranza (Arran, Isle of) 3
Lochrutton (Irongray) 3
Lochs-Crossbost 11
Lochs-in-Bernera 11
Lochwinnoch (Kilbarchan) 4
Lockerbie: Dryfesdale, Hutton, Corrie and Applegarth 3
Logie 8
Logiealmond (Methven) 8
Logie Coldstone (Cromar) 9
Logie Easter (Kilmuir) 10
Logierait (Grantully) 8
Lomond 4
London 12
Longforgan 8
Longformacus (Duns) 2
Longniddry 2
Longridge (Whitburn) 1
Longriggend (Caldercruix) 6
Longside 9
Longtown (Border Kirk) 3
Lonmay 9
Lossiemouth 9
Loth (Kildonan) 10
Lowick (Berwick) 2
Luce Valley and Inch 3
Lugar 3
Luing (Netherlorn) 10
Lumphanan (Mid Deeside) 9
Lumsden (West Gordon) 9
Lunan (Inverkeilor) 8
Lundie (Sidlaw) 8
Lunnasting (Shetland) 9
Luss 4
Lybster (Latheron) 10
Lyne and Manor 2

Macduff 9
Makerstoun (Kelso) 2
Mallaig (North West Lochaber) 10
Malta 13
Manish-Scarista 10
Manor (Lyne) 2
Markinch (Heart of Fife) 7
Marnoch 9
Maryburgh (Ferintosh) 10
Maryculter 9
Mauchline 3
Maud and Savoch 9
Maxton (Dryburgh) 2
Maxwell Mearns Castle 5
Maybole (North Carrick) 3
Mearns 5
Meigle (Strathmore) 8
Meldrum and Bourtie 9
Melness and Tongue 10
Melrose (Bowden) 2
Menmuir (Edzell) 8
Menstrie 8
Mertoun (Dryburgh) 2
Methil 7
Methilhill and Denbeath 7
Methlick 9
Methven and Logiealmond 8
Mid Calder (Kirk of Calder) 1
Mid Deeside 9
Middlebie (Hoddom) 3
Mid Kintyre and Gigha 10
Midmar (Bennachie) 9
Mid Strathearn 8
Millisle 3
Millport (Cumbrae) 3
Milnathort (Orwell) 8
Milngavie 4
Milton of Campsie 5
Minard (West Lochfyneside) 10

Minto (Ruberslaw) 2
Mochrum 3
Moffat (Upper Annandale) 3
Moneydie (Auchtergaven) 8
Moniaive (Glencairn) 3
Monifieth South Angus 8
Monigaff 3
Monikie (Monifieth) 8
Monimail 7
Monkton and Prestwick: North 3
Monquhitter and New Byth 9
Montrose 8
Monymusk (Bennachie) 9
Moodiesburn 5
Morar (North West Lochaber) 10
Morebattle (Cheviot Churches) 2
Morham (Garvald) 2
Mormond West 9
Mortlach and Cabrach 9
Morvern (Ardgour) 10
Motherwell 6
Mouswald (Cummertrees) 3
Moy (Strathnairn and Strathdearn) 10
Muckairn 10
Muckhart 8
Muiravonside 6
Muirhead (Sidlaw) 8
Muirkirk 3
Muir of Ord (Urray) 10
Munlochy (Knockbain) 10
Murroes (Monifieth) 8
Musselburgh 2
Muthill 8

Nairn 10
Neilston 4
Ness (Cross) 11
Nesting (Shetland) 9
Netherlee and Stamperland 5
Netherlorn 10
New Abbey (Lochend) 3
Newarthill and Carfin 6
Newbattle 2
Newbigging (Monifieth) 8
Newburgh (Foveran) 9
Newburgh (Lindores) 7
New Byth (Monquhitter) 9
Newcastle 12
Newcastleton (Liddesdale) 3
New Cumnock 3
New Deer 9
New Galloway (Balmaclellan) 3
Newhills (Brimmond) 9
Newlands (Kirkurd) 2
New Luce (Luce Valley and Inch) 3
New Machar 9
Newmains 6
Newmill (Keith) 9
Newmilns (Irvine Valley) 3
New Monkland (Airdrie) 6
New Pitsligo (Mormond West) 9
Newport-on-Tay 7
New Stevenston 6
Newton (Dalkeith) 2
Newtongrange (Newbattle) 2
Newtonhill (Kincardine Coastal) 9
Newton Mearns 5
Newtonmore (Laggan) 10
Newton Stewart (Penninghame) 3
Newtown (Dryburgh) 2
Newtyle (Strathmore) 8
Nigg (Easter Ross Peninsula) 10
Norrieston (Kippen) 8
North and West Islay 10
North Berwick 2
North Carrick 3
North Coast 10
Northmavine (Shetland) 9
North Mull 10
North Queensferry (Forthview) 7
North Ronaldsay 9
North West Lochaber 10

Oakley (Carnock) 7
Oathlaw Tannadice 8
Oban (Kilmore) 10
Ochiltree 3
Old Cumnock 3
Oldhamstocks (Dunglass) 2
Old Kilpatrick Bowling 4
Ollaberry (Shetland) 9
Onich (South Lochaber) 10
Ordiquhill and Cornhill 9
Ormiston 2
Oronsay (Colonsay) 10
Orphir and Stenness 9
Orwell and Portmoak 8
Overtown 6
Oxnam (Jedburgh) 2
Oxton (Channelkirk) 2
Oyne (Insch) 9

Paible (Kilmuir) 10
Paisley 4
Papa Westray 9
Pardovan (Abercorn) 1
Paris 13
Parton (Crossmichael) 3
Pathhead (Tyne Valley) 2
Patna Waterside 3
Paxton (Whiteadder) 2
Peebles 2
Pencaitland 2
Penicuik 2
Penninghame 3
Penpont, Keir and Tynron 3
Pentland 10
Perth 8
Peterculter 9
Peterhead 9
Pettinain (Cairngryffe) 6
Petty (Culloden) 10
Pirnmill (Arran, Isle of) 3
Pitlessie (Howe of Fife) 7
Pitlochry 8
Pitmedden (Formartine) 9
Pitsligo (Fraserburgh) 9
Pittenweem 7
Plean (Cowie) 8
Pluscarden (Elgin) 9
Polbeth Harwood 1
Polmont 6
Port Charlotte (North and West Islay) 10
Port Ellen (South Islay) 10
Port Glasgow 4
Portgordon (Buckie) 9
Portknockie 9
Portlethen (Kincardine Coastal) 9
Portmahomack (Easter Ross Peninsula) 10
Portmoak (Orwell) 8
Portnahaven (North and West Islay) 10
Port of Menteith 8
Port of Spain (Trinidad) 13
Portpatrick 3
Portree 10
Port Seton (Cockenzie) 2
Portsoy 9
Port William (Mochrum) 3
Premnay (Insch) 9
Prestonpans 2
Prestwick 3

Quarff (Shetland) 9
Quarter 6
Queensferry (Edinburgh: Dalmeny) 1
Quothquan (Libberton) 6

Rafford (West Moray) 10
Rannoch (Foss) 8
Rathen (Fraserburgh) 9
Ratho (Edinburgh) 1
Rathven (Buckie) 9
Rattray 8
Rayne (Culsalmond) 9
Reay (North Coast) 10
Redding and Westquarter 6
Redgorton and Stanley 8
Rendall (Evie) 9
Renfrew 4
Renton 4
Rescobie (Forfar) 8
Resolis and Urquhart 10
Reston (Ayton) 2
Rhu and Shandon 4
Rhynie (West Gordon) 9
Rigside (Douglas Valley) 6
Roberton (Hawick) 2
Roberton (Upper Clyde) 6
Rogart 10
Rome 13
Rosehall (Assynt) 10
Rosemarkie (Black Isle East) 10
Rosewell (Lasswade) 2
Roslin 2
Rosneath 4
Rosskeen (Alness) 10
Ross of Mull (Iona) 10
Rosyth (Forthview) 7
Rothes 9
Rothesay (Bute, Isle of) 10
Rothiemay (Keith) 9
Rothiemurchus and Aviemore 10
Rothienorman 9
Rotterdam 13
Rousay 9
Roxburgh (Kelso) 2
Ruberslaw 2
Rutherglen 5
Ruthven (Isla Parishes) 8
Ruthwell (Cummertrees) 3

Saddell and Carradale 10
St Abbs (Coldingham) 2
St Andrews 7
(see also Boarhills) 7
(see also Cameron) 7
St Andrew's (East Mainland) 9
St Andrew's-Lhanbryd and Urquhart 9
St Boswells (Dryburgh) 2
St Cyrus 9
St Fergus 9
St Fillans (Dundurn) 8
St Madoes and Kinfauns 8
St Martins (Scone) 8
St Monans 7
St Quivox (Ayr) 3
St Vigeans (Arbroath) 8
Salen (North Mull) 10
Saline and Blairingone 7
Saltcoats (Ardrossan) 3
Saltoun (Lammermuir) 2
Sanday 9
Sandbank (Cowal) 10
Sandhaven (Fraserburgh) 9
Sandhead (Stoneykirk) 3
Sandness (Shetland) 9
Sandsting (Shetland) 9
Sandwick (Birsay) 9
Sandwick (Shetland) 9
Sanquhar 3
Sauchie and Coalsnaughton 8
Savoch (Maud) 9
Scalloway (Shetland) 9
Scarista (Manish) 10
Scone and St Martins 8
Scourie (Assynt) 10
Seil (Netherlorn) 10
Selkirk and Ashkirk 2
Shandon (Rhu) 4
Shapinsay 9
Shetland 9
Shieldhill (Blackbraes) 6
Shiskine (Arran, Isle of) 3
Shotts 6
Sidlaw 8
Skelmorlie (Inverkip) 4
Skene (Kingshill) 9
Skerries (Shetland) 9
Skipness (Mid Kintyre and Gigha) 10
Skirling (Upper Tweeddale) 2
Slamannan 6
Sleat (Strath) 10
Smailholm (Kelso) 2
Small Isles (North West Lochaber) 10
Snizort (Bracadale) 10
Sorbie (Millisle) 3
Sorn 3
Southdean (Hobkirk) 2
Southend 10
South Islay 10
South Lochaber 10

South Ronaldsay and Burray 9
South Uist 10
South-West Ross 10
Southwick (Colvend) 3
Spean Bridge (Kilmonivaig) 10
Speymouth (Bellie) 9
Spott (Belhaven) 2
Springfield (Ceres) 7
Springside (Irvine) 3
Sprouston (Kelso) 2
Spynie (Duffus) 9
Sri Lanka (Colombo) 13
Stair 3
Stamperland (Netherlee) 5
Stanley (Redgorton) 8
Stenhouse and Carron 6
Stenness (Orphir) 9
Stenscholl (Kilmuir) 10
Stenton (Traprain) 2
Stepps 5
Stevenston 3
Stewarton 3
Stichill (Kelso) 2
Stirling 8
Stobo and Drumelzier 2
Stoer (Assynt) 10
Stonehaven 9
Stonehouse 6
Stoneyburn (Whitburn) 1
Stoneykirk 3
Stoneywood (Brimmond) 9
Stornoway 11
Stow and Heriot 2
Strachan (Birse) 9
Strachur and Strathlachlan 10
Straiton 3
Straloch (Kirkmichael) 8
Stranraer 3
Strath and Sleat 10
Strathaven 6
Strathblane 8
Strathbogie Drumblade 9
Strathbrock 1
Strathdon (West Gordon) 9
Strathfillan (Glenorchy) 10
Strathkinness (St Andrews) 7
Strathlachlan (Strachur) 10
Strathmiglo (Edenshead) 7
Strathmore 8
Strathnairn and Strathdearn 10
Strathpeffer (Fodderty) 10
Strathtay (Grantully) 8
Strathy (North Coast) 10
Strichen (Mormond West) 9
Stromness 9
Strone (Kilmun) 10
Stronsay 9
Strontian (Ardgour) 10
Struan (Blair Atholl) 8
Swinton (Coldstream) 2
Symington (Craigie) 3
Symington (Lanarkshire) 6

Tain (Easter Ross Peninsula) 10
Tannadice (Oathlaw) 8
Tarbat (Easter Ross Peninsula) 10
Tarbert, Loch Fyne and Kilberry 10
Tarbert (Uist) 10
Tarbolton 3
Tarff and Twynholm 3
Tarland (Cromar) 9
Tarves (Formartine) 9
Taynuilt (Muckairn) 10
Tayport (Leuchars) 7
Tayvallich (Dalriada) 10
Tealing (Monifieth) 8
Tenandry 8
Terregles (Irongray) 3
Teviothead 2
Thankerton (Cairngryffe) 6
The Glens and Kirriemuir United 8
Thornhill (Kippen) 8
Thornhill (South West) 3
Thornliebank 5
Thornton (Heart of Fife) 7
Thrumster (Wick) 10
Thurso 10
Tibbermore (Almondbank) 8
Tiberias (Jerusalem) 14
Tighnabruaich (West Cowal) 10
Tillicoultry 8
Tingwall (Shetland) 9
Tinwald (Kirkmichael) 3
Tiree 10
Tobermory (North Mull) 10
Tomatin (Strathnairn and Strathdearn) 10
Tomintoul, Glenlivet and Inveraven 10
Tongue (Melness) 10
Torphichen 1
Torphins (Mid Deeside) 9
Torrance 5
Torridon (South-West Ross) 10
Torryburn (Culross) 7
Torthorwald (Kirkmichael) 3
Tough (West Gordon) 9
Toward (Cowal) 10
Towie (West Gordon) 9
Tranent 2
Traprain 2
Traquair (Innerleithen) 2
Trinidad 13
Troon 3
Tulliallan and Kincardine 7
Tullibody 8
Tundergarth 3
Turriff 9
Tweedsmuir (Upper Tweeddale) 2
Twynholm (Tarff) 3
Tyne Valley 2
Tynron (Penpont) 3
Tyrie (Mormond West) 9

Uddingston 6
Udny (Formartine) 9
Uig 11
Ullapool (Lochbroom) 10
Unst (Shetland) 9
Uphall 1
Uplawmoor (Caldwell) 4
Upper Annandale 3
Upper Clyde 6
Upper Tweeddale 2
Urquhart (Resolis) 10
Urquhart (St Andrew's-Lhanbryd) 9
Urquhart and Glenmoriston 10
Urr 3
Urray and Kilchrist 10

Vidlin (Shetland) 9

Walkerburn (Innerleithen) 2
Walls (Hoy) 9
Walls (Shetland) 9
Walston (Black Mount) 6
Wamphray (Upper Annandale) 3
Wanlockhead (Upper Clyde) 6
Waterside (Patna) 3
Watten 10
Weem (Dull) 8
Wemyss (Buckhaven) 7
Wemyss Bay (Inverkip) 4
West Calder 1
West Cowal 10
Westerdale (Halkirk) 10
Westerkirk (Langholm) 3
West Gordon (Alford, Strathdon, Rhynie) 9
Westhill (Skene) 9
West Kilbride 3
West Linton 2
West Lochfyneside 10
West Mearns 9
West Moray 10
Westquarter (Redding) 6
Westray 9
West Ross 10
Whalsay (Shetland) 9
Whitburn 1
Whiteadder 2
Whitehills 9
Whithorn (Glasserton) 3
Whiting Bay (Arran, Isle of) 3
Whitsome (Coldstream) 2
Wick 10
Wigtown 3
Williamwood 5
Winchburgh (Abercorn) 1
Windygates (Kennoway) 7
Wishaw 6
Wiston (Upper Clyde) 6
Wormit (Balmerino) 7

Yarrow (Ettrick) 2
Yell (Shetland) 9
Yetholm (Cheviot Churches) 2
Ythan Wells (Auchterless) 9

INDEX OF SUBJECTS

Assembly Business Committee 11
Assembly Trustees 8
Associations (and Societies) 33
Audit Committee 12
Auxiliary Ministers 256

Baptism 50
Bible Society 36
Building Safety 14

Chaplains to HM Forces 265
Chaplains, Healthcare 261
Chaplains, Prison 270
Chaplains, University 272
Chaplains to the King 29
Charity Numbers 2, 279
Child protection 21
Christian Aid 34
Church buildings 279
Church locations 279
Church of Scotland Guild 15
Church of Scotland Housing and Loan Fund 15
Church of Scotland Insurance Services 14, 40
Church of Scotland Investors Trust 16
Church of Scotland Military Chaplains' Association 34
Church of Scotland Offices 2
Church of Scotland Pension Trustees 19
Church of Scotland Societies 33
Church of Scotland Trust 12
Church Offices 2
Church Service Society 34
Churches, Overseas 29
Churches Together in Britain and Ireland 13
Churches in the United Kingdom, other 28
Civil partnerships 50
Committee to Nominate the Moderator 12
Communications Department 13
Congregational readjustment and changes 281
Congregational Statistics 289
Council Education Committees: Church Representatives 273
Committees, List 7
Covenant Fellowship Scotland 34
CrossReach 2, 11

Deaf, congregations/missions for deaf people 66, 101, 137, 205
Deceased Ministers and Deacons 276
Departments, list 7
Diaconate, Membership of 259
Divinity Faculties/Schools, Scottish 32

Ecclesiastical buildings 14, 279
Eco-Congregation Scotland 34
Ecumenical Officer 13
Ecumenical Relations Committee 13
Editorial 6
Education 9, 273
Elder training 9
Energy conservation 14
Estates and Procurement Department 13
Ethical Oversight Committee 17

Faith Action Programme 9
Fasti Ecclesiae Scoticanae 47
Fellowship of St Andrew 34
Fire Safety 14
Forces Chaplains Committee 14
Funds (and Trusts) 39
Funeral services: conduct of and fees for 50

Gaelic in the Church 5, 26
General Assembly (2024) 53
Moderator of 5, 54
Officials of 53
General Assembly (2025), date of 2
General Assembly, Clerks 8
General Trustees 14
Giving to Grow contributions 290
Glebes 14
Grid references for churches 279
Guild, Church of Scotland 15
Guild membership 290

Health and safety 9
Healthcare Chaplaincies 261
Highland Theological College UHI 33
His Majesty's Household in Scotland: Ecclesiastical 29
Holidays for ministers 43, 44, 45, 46
Housing and Loan Fund 15
Human Resources Department 16
Hymns Ancient and Modern 21

Index of Ministers 315
Index of Parishes and Places 324
Information Technology Department 16
Insurance 40
Inter-Church Organisations 33
Investors Trust, Church of Scotland 16
Iona Community 17, 35

John Knox House 22

King's Chaplains 29

Law Department 17
Legal Names of Congregations 279

Legal Questions Committee 18
Life and Work 19
Long Service Certificates 47
Lord High Commissioners 30

Marriage 50
Marriage, same-sex 50
Marriage and Civil Partnership (Scotland) Act 2014 50
Marriage Services 50
Media Team: Press Office 13
Ministers deceased 276
Ministers not in Presbyteries (registered Employed/Retaining) 60
Ministers not in Presbyteries (registered Inactive) 60
Ministers ordained sixty years and upwards 274
Ministries Development Staff 60
Mission Partners serving internationally 268
Moderator of the General Assembly 5, 54
Moderators of the General Assembly (list) 31

Netherbow, The 22
Nomination Committee 19

Offices of the Church 2
Ordained Local Ministers 256
Ordnance Survey National Grid References 279
Organist training scheme 37
Overseas appointments/locations 250, 268
Overseas Churches 29

Parish and Congregational Names no longer in use 281
Parish boundaries 60
Parliamentary Office (Scottish Churches) 21
Pension Trustees 19
Personnel Department (Human Resources) 16
Place for Hope 36
Precedence 31
Presbytery lists 59
Presbytery Review Committee 20
Press Office: Media Team 13
Principal Clerk 8
Priority Areas 10
Prison Chaplains 270
Prison Fellowship Scotland 36
Pulpit Supply 51

Readers 60
Readjustment, recent 281
Records of the Church 47
Registration of Ministries Committee 20

Safeguarding Service 21
Saint Andrew Press 21
St Andrew's House Hotel, Jerusalem 35, 269
Sanctuary Development 14
Same-sex marriage 50
Schools of Divinity/Theology 32
Scotland's Churches Trust 45
Scots Hotel, Tiberias 269
Scottish Charity Numbers 2, 279
Scottish Church History Society 37
Scottish Church Society 37
Scottish Church Theology Society 37
Scottish Churches Parliamentary Office 21
Scottish Storytelling Centre 22
Seeds for Growth Funding 40
Small Grants Fund 40
Social Care Council (CrossReach) 11
Societies (and Associations) 33
Statistics, Congregational 289
Statistics, summary 290
Stewardship and Finance Department 22
Stewardship programmes 22
Student Christian Movement 38

Tabeetha School, Jaffa 35, 270
Theological Forum 23
Trustees, Assembly 8
Trusts (and Funds) 39

University Chaplains 272

Vacancy procedure 52
Vacancy schedules 52
Veterans Chaplaincy Scotland 268

World Council of Churches 13
World Day of Prayer 38

Year Book, contact editor 2